Stories of Ourselves

Volume 2

Cambridge Assessment International Education
Anthology of Stories in English

CAMBRIDGE
UNIVERSITY PRESS

Shaftesbury Road, Cambridge CB2 8EA, United Kingdom

One Liberty Plaza, 20th Floor, New York, NY 10006, USA

477 Williamstown Road, Port Melbourne, VIC 3207, Australia

314–321, 3rd Floor, Plot 3, Splendor Forum, Jasola District Centre, New Delhi – 110025, India

103 Penang Road, #05–06/07, Visioncrest Commercial, Singapore 238467

Cambridge University Press is part of the University of Cambridge.

It furthers the University's mission by disseminating knowledge in the pursuit of education, learning and research at the highest international levels of excellence.

www.cambridge.org
Information on this title: www.cambridge.org/9781108436199 (Paperback)

© Cambridge Assessment International Education 2018

First published 2018

20 19 18 17 16 15 14 13 12 11 10 9 8

Printed in the Netherlands by Wilco BV

A catalogue record for this publication is available from the British Library

ISBN 978-1-108-43619-9 Paperback

Contents

Contents

Contents

Introduction

This book is a sequel to *Stories of Ourselves,* 2008. Selections from this volume will be set for study for several Cambridge Assessment International Education Literature in English examinations. But this book is not simply a set text – it aims at being a stimulus to wider reading beyond the confines of the selections prescribed for study for the examinations, and it is also a resource for students of the language as well as literature.

While the stories in this book are drawn from and reflect many and diverse countries and cultures, what they have in common is their use of English – the language in which all the stories were written – to craft imaginative literature, and they demonstrate its endless range and depth.

It has been said the short story is 'a moment of truth'. If so, we might ask: whose truth? It is not always clear. Details of the setting, aspects of language, attitudes and ways of behaving described in a story may be quite alien, even uncomfortable to the reader. But reading short stories from different parts of our world helps us become aware of subjectivity: that there are many more points of view and ways of seeing than one's own. Many of the writers intend to make their readers see things sharply and differently. In all other ways, their intentions and effects vary greatly. Some aim to change the reader's mind, some to shock or frighten, some to amuse and entertain.

As the stories in this anthology collectively show, there is endless variety in the short story form in genre, length, scope, theme, style, tone and narrative technique. So there can be no one simple definition of what is required to make a successful short story. Each has a unique voice and shape – but there is no template for that shape.

For some readers, the best stories produce their effects of surprise, humour, fear or shock without being too obvious about it. Good stories may be very unusual, and they often seem to say that there is no pattern for a human life. Others, by contrast, show us the ordinary world in a vivid way. Sometimes stories seem to show the whole life by showing us just a part.

There are no rules: a successful story might be successful in all kinds of ways.

But we might say that stories need to be extraordinary enough to gain attention, but observe the ordinary – some kind of recognisable world – well enough to engage our belief, and often good stories make the ordinary, extraordinary and the extraordinary, ordinary.

It follows that there is no list of right answers in studying short stories, but there are many right questions. Here are a few to consider when reading the stories:

- When was the story written?

- When and where is the story set?

- Is it a fable, a fantasy, a kind of ghost or detective story, or is it in the form of 'realist' fiction? Perhaps it is a mixture, perhaps it fits no obvious category.

- Who is telling the story? Can we believe her or him? Are we committed to one point of view, or are there multiple perspectives?

- Is there a key event or incident, or a more complex plot – and in what ways is it shaped by the writer?

- How are our feelings played upon as the story develops?

- What use does the writer make of metaphor, images or symbols?

- How are characters created in a short space? Do they interact? Are they sketched in or more fully developed?

- How does the writing make me like this character so much?

- How has the author made this so funny?

It is endlessly enjoyable and instructive to make comparisons between stories. Readers are encouraged to explore their own links and contrasts between stories both within the anthology as a whole and outside it, including those featuring in *Stories of Ourselves* volume 1. Like that volume, the stories are listed chronological order.

It is expected that readers have access to a dictionary. The *Notes* aim to explain words or phrases whose meaning in the context of the story might be unclear to the general reader.

Editor's Acknowledgements

Special thanks are due to Tim Underhill, Jon Clewes, Helen Carr, Fay Head, Marica Lopez, Richard Feirn, Andrew Campbell, Noel Cassidy, Liz Whittome and Matthew Arcus for their advice, encouragement and practical help in making this anthology.

Mary Wilmer, Cambridge 2018

1

Death of the Laird's Jock

(1831)

Walter Scott

Scott was a Scottish novelist and poet, famous for novels such as Ivanhoe *and* Rob Roy *which established historical romance as a popular genre. This short story gives a good flavour of Scott's romantic fiction, with its interesting narrative technique, larger-than-life characters and Highland setting. In its discussion of the relationship between literature and painting, it also tries out what the new form of the short story can do.*

To the editor of 'The Keepsake'

You have asked me, sir, to point out a subject for the pencil, and I feel the difficulty of complying with your request; although I am not certainly unaccustomed to literary composition, or a total stranger to the stores of history and tradition, which afford the best copies for the painter's art. But although *Sicut pictura poesis* is an ancient and undisputed axiom—although poetry and painting both address themselves to the same object of exciting the human imagination, by presenting to it pleasing or sublime images of ideal scenes; yet the one conveying itself through the ears to the understanding, and the other applying itself only to the eyes, the subjects which are best suited to the bard or tale-teller are often totally unfit for painting, where the artist must present in a single glance all that his art has power to tell us. The artist can neither recapitulate the past nor intimate the future. The single *now* is all which he can present; and hence, unquestionably, many subjects which delight us in poetry, or in narrative, whether real or fictitious, cannot with advantage be transferred to the canvas.

Being in some degree aware of these difficulties, though doubtless unacquainted both with their extent and the means by which they may be modified or surmounted, I have, nevertheless, ventured to draw up the following traditional narrative as a story in which, when the general details are known, the interest is so much concentrated in one strong moment of agonizing passion, that it can be understood, and sympathized with, at a single glance. I therefore presume that it may be acceptable as a hint to some one among the numerous artists who have of late years distinguished themselves as rearing up and supporting the British school.

Enough has been said and sung about

The well-contested ground
The warlike Border-land—

to render the habits of the tribes who inhabited them before the union of England and Scotland familiar to most of your readers. The rougher and sterner features of their character were softened by their attachment to the fine arts, from which has arisen the saying that, on the frontiers, every dale had its battle, and every river its song. A rude species of chivalry was in constant use, and single combats were practised as the amusement of the few intervals of truce which suspended the exercise of war. The inveteracy of this custom may be inferred from the following incident:

Bernard Gilpin, the apostle of the north, the first who undertook to preach the Protestant doctrines to the Border dalesmen, was surprised on entering one of their churches, to see a gauntlet, or mail-glove, hanging above the altar. Upon inquiring the meaning of a symbol so indecorous being displayed in that sacred place, he was informed by the clerk that the glove was that of a famous swordsman who hung it there as an emblem of a general challenge and gage of battle, to any who should dare to take the fatal token down. 'Reach it to me,' said the reverend churchman. The clerk and sexton equally declined the perilous office; and the good Bernard Gilpin was obliged to remove the glove with his own hands, desiring those who were present to inform the champion that he, and no other, had possessed himself of the gage of defiance. But the champion was as much ashamed to face Bernard Gilpin as the officials of the church had been to displace his pledge of combat.

The date of the following story is about the latter years of Queen Elizabeth's reign; and the events took place in Liddesdale, a hilly and pastoral district of Roxburghshire, which, on a part of its boundary, is divided from England only by a small river.

During the good old times of *rugging and riving* (that is, tugging and tearing), under which term the disorderly doings of the warlike age are affectionately remembered, this valley was principally cultivated by the sept or clan of the Armstrongs. The chief of this warlike race was the Laird of Mangerton. At the period of which I speak, the estate of Mangerton, with the power and dignity of chief, was possessed by John Armstrong, a man of great size, strength, and courage. While his father was alive, he was distinguished from others of his clan who bore the same name by the epithet of the *Laird's Jock*, that is to say, the Laird's son Jock, or Jack. This name he distinguished by so many bold and desperate achievements, that he retained it even after his father's death, and is mentioned under it both in authentic records and in tradition. Some of his feats are recorded in the Minstrelsy of the Scottish Border, and others mentioned in contemporary chronicles.

At the species of singular combat which we have described, the Laird's Jock was unrivalled; and no champion of Cumberland, Westmoreland, or Northumberland, could endure the sway of the huge two-handed sword which he wielded, and which few others could even lift. This 'awful sword', as the common people term it, was as dear to him as Durindana or Fushberta to their respective masters, and was nearly as formidable to his enemies as those renowned falchions proved to the foes of Christendom. The weapon had been bequeathed to him by a celebrated English outlaw named Hobbie Noble, who, having committed some deed for which he was in danger from justice, fled to Liddesdale, and became a follower, or rather a brother-in-arms, to the renowned Laird's Jock; till, venturing into England with a small escort, a faithless guide, and with a light single-handed sword instead of his ponderous brand, Hobbie Noble, attacked by superior numbers, was made prisoner and executed.

With this weapon, and by means of his own strength and address, the Laird's Jock maintained the reputation of the best swordsman on the Border side, and defeated or slew many who ventured to dispute with him the formidable title.

But years pass on with the strong and the brave as with the feeble and the timid. In process of time, the Laird's Jock grew incapable of wielding his weapons, and finally of all active exertion, even of the most ordinary kind. The disabled champion became at length totally bed-ridden, and entirely dependent for his comfort on the pious duties of an only daughter, his perpetual attendant and companion.

Besides this dutiful child, the Laird's Jock had an only son, upon whom devolved the perilous task of leading the clan to battle, and maintaining the warlike renown of his native country, which was now disputed by the English upon many occasions. The young Armstrong was active, brave, and strong, and brought home from dangerous adventures many tokens of decided success. Still the ancient chief conceived, as it would seem, that his son was scarce yet entitled by age and experience to be entrusted with the two-handed sword, by the use of which he had himself been so dreadfully distinguished.

At length, an English champion, one of the name of Foster (if I rightly recollect) had the audacity to send a challenge to the best swordsman in Liddesdale; and young Armstrong, burning for chivalrous distinction, accepted the challenge.

The heart of the disabled old man swelled with joy when he heard that the challenge was passed and accepted, and the meeting fixed at a neutral spot, used as the place of rencontre upon such occasions, and which he himself had distinguished by numerous victories. He exulted so much in the conquest which he anticipated that, to nerve his son to still bolder exertions, he conferred upon him, as champion of his clan and province, the celebrated weapon which he had hitherto retained in his own custody.

This was not all. When the day of combat arrived, the Laird's Jock, in spite of his daughter's affectionate remonstrances, determined, though he had not left his bed for two years, to be a personal witness of the duel. His will was still a law to his people, who bore him on their shoulders, wrapped in plaids and blankets, to the spot where the combat was to take place, and seated him on a fragment of rock which is still called the Laird's Jock's stone. There he remained with eyes fixed on the lists or barrier, within which the champions were about to meet. His daughter, having done all she could for his accommodation, stood motionless beside him, divided between anxiety for his health, and for the event of the combat to her beloved brother. Ere yet the fight began, the old men gazed on their chief, now seen for the first time after several years, and sadly compared his altered features and wasted frame with the paragon of strength and manly beauty which they once remembered. The young men gazed on his large form and powerful make, as upon some antediluvian giant who had survived the destruction of the Flood.

But the sound of the trumpets on both sides recalled the attention of every one to the lists, surrounded as they were by numbers of both nations eager to witness the event of the day. The combatants met. It is needless to describe the struggle: the Scottish champion fell. Foster, placing his foot on his antagonist, seized on the redoubted sword, so precious in the eyes of its aged owner, and brandished it over his head as a trophy of his conquest. The English shouted in triumph. But the despairing cry of the aged champion, who saw his country dishonoured, and his sword, long the terror of their race, in possession of an Englishman, was heard high above the acclamations of victory. He seemed, for an instant, animated by all his wonted power; for he started from the rock on which he sat, and while the garments with which he had been invested fell from his wasted frame, and showed the ruins of his strength, he tossed his arms wildly to heaven, and uttered a cry of indignation, horror, and despair, which, tradition says, was heard to a preternatural distance, and resembled the cry of a dying lion more than a human sound.

His friends received him in their arms as he sank utterly exhausted by the effort, and bore him back to his castle in mute sorrow; while his daughter at once wept for her brother and endeavoured to mitigate and soothe the despair of her father. But this was impossible; the old man's only tie to life was rent rudely asunder, and his heart had broken with it. The death of his son had no part in his sorrow. If he thought of him at all, it was as the degenerate boy, through whom the honour of his country and clan had been lost; and he died in the course of three days, never even mentioning his name, but pouring out unintermitted lamentations for the loss of his noble sword.

I conceive that the moment when the disabled chief was roused into a last exertion by the agony of the moment is favourable to the object of a painter. He might obtain the full advantage of contrasting the form of the rugged old man, in the extremity of furious despair, with the softness and beauty of the female form. The fatal field might be thrown into perspective, so as to give full effect to these two principal figures, and with the single explanation that the piece represented a soldier beholding his son slain, and the honour of his country lost, the picture would be sufficiently intelligible at the first glance. If it was thought necessary to show more clearly the nature of the conflict, it might be indicated by the pennon of St. George being displayed at one end of the lists, and that of St. Andrew at the other.

I remain, Sir,
Your obedient servant,

The author of Waverley.

Notes

p. 1   *Laird's Jock* - A 'laird' is a Scottish word for 'chief'. The 'Laird's Jock' is the chief's son, who is named Jock.

p. 1   *The Keepsake* - a literary annual published every Christmas 1828–1857

p. 1   *Sicut pictura poesis* - poetry is like painting – i.e. it creates a picture

p. 1   *sublime* - the idea of the sublime was very important in painting and literature in the eighteenth and nineteenth centuries and goes beyond the idea of supreme beauty to mean a kind of moral greatness

p. 1   *the British school* - a 'school' or style of painting in the nineteenth century

p. 2   *The well-contested ground* - i.e. the lands on the border of England and Scotland, fought over for many years

p. 2   *The union of England and Scotland* - the Acts of Union in 1706 and 1707

p. 2   *rude species of chivalry* - a rough kind of chivalry, i.e. code of honour

p. 2   *gage* - a token such as a glove thrown down to challenge to a fight

p. 2   *Border dalesmen* - farmers in the Border lands

p. 2   *Minstrelsy* - ballads

p. 2   *Cumberland, Westmoreland, Northumberland* - counties of Northern England

p. 2   *Durindana, Fushberta* - swords (which were commonly given names) belonging to heroes of ancient epics – Durindana was Roland's sword in the medieval romance 'The Song of Roland'

p. 3   *ponderous brand* - heavy sword

p. 3   *rencontre* - place of meeting

p. 3   *plaids* - the tartan woollen cloth worn by Highlanders

p. 4   *pennon of St. George . . . St. Andrew* - flags of the patron saints of England and Scotland

Dr. Heidegger's Experiment

(1837)

Nathaniel Hawthorne

Hawthorne is regarded as one of the founders of American literature, and is now best known for his novel The Scarlet Letter. *In this story, an aged doctor appears to have discovered the secret of youth, which he tries out on some old friends with unexpected results.*

That very singular man, old Dr. Heidegger, once invited four venerable friends to meet him in his study. There were three white-bearded gentlemen, Mr. Medbourne, Colonel Killigrew, and Mr. Gascoigne, and a withered gentlewoman, whose name was the Widow Wycherly. They were all melancholy old creatures, who had been unfortunate in life, and whose greatest misfortune it was that they were not long ago in their graves. Mr. Medbourne, in the vigour of his age, had been a prosperous merchant, but had lost his all by a frantic speculation, and was now little better than a mendicant. Colonel Killigrew had wasted his best years, and his health and substance, in the pursuit of sinful pleasures, which had given birth to a brood of pains, such as the gout, and divers other torments of soul and body. Mr. Gascoigne was a ruined politician, a man of evil fame, or at least had been so, till time had buried him from the knowledge of the present generation, and made him obscure instead of infamous. As for the Widow Wycherly, tradition tells us that she was a great beauty in her day; but, for a long while past, she had lived in deep seclusion, on account of certain scandalous stories, which had prejudiced the gentry of the town against her. It is a circumstance worth mentioning, that each of these three old gentlemen, Mr. Medbourne, Colonel Killigrew, and Mr. Gascoigne, were early lovers of the Widow Wycherly, and had once been on the point of cutting each other's throats for her sake. And, before proceeding farther, I will merely hint, that Dr. Heidegger and all his four guests were sometimes thought to be a little beside themselves; as is not unfrequently the case with old people, when worried either by present troubles or woful recollections.

'My dear old friends,' said Dr. Heidegger, motioning them to be seated, 'I am desirous of your assistance in one of those little experiments with which I amuse myself here in my study.'

If all stories were true, Dr. Heidegger's study must have been a very curious place. It was a dim, old-fashioned chamber, festooned with cobwebs and besprinkled with antique dust. Around the walls stood several oaken bookcases, the lower shelves of which were filled with rows of gigantic folios and black-letter quartos, and the upper with little parchment-covered duodecimos. Over the central bookcase was a bronze bust of Hippocrates, with which, according to some authorities, Dr. Heidegger was accustomed to hold consultations, in all difficult cases of his practice. In the obscurest corner of the room stood a tall and narrow oaken closet, with its door ajar, within which doubtfully appeared a skeleton. Between two of the bookcases hung a looking-glass, presenting its high and dusty plate within a tarnished gilt frame. Among many wonderful stories related of this mirror, it was fabled that the spirits of all the doctor's deceased patients dwelt within its verge, and would stare him in the face whenever he looked thitherward. The opposite side of the chamber was ornamented with the full-length portrait of a young lady, arrayed in the faded magnificence of silk, satin, and brocade, and with a visage as faded as her dress. Above half a century ago, Dr. Heidegger had been on the point of marriage with his young lady; but, being affected with some slight disorder, she had swallowed one of her lover's prescriptions, and died on the bridal evening. The greatest curiosity of the study remains to be mentioned; it was a ponderous folio volume, bound in black leather, with massive silver clasps. There were no letters on the back, and nobody could tell the title of the book. But it was well known to be a book of magic; and once, when a chambermaid had lifted it, merely to brush away the dust, the skeleton had rattled in its closet, the picture of the young lady had stepped one foot upon the floor, and several ghastly faces had peeped forth from the mirror; while the brazen head of Hippocrates frowned, and said, 'Forbear!'

Such was Dr. Heidegger's study. On the summer afternoon of our tale, a small round table, as black as ebony, stood in the centre of the room, sustaining a cut-glass vase, of beautiful form and elaborate workmanship. The sunshine came through the window, between the heavy festoons of two faded damask curtains, and fell directly across this vase; so that a mild splendour was reflected from it on the ashen visages of the five old people who sat around. Four champagne-glasses were also on the table.

'My dear old friends,' repeated Dr. Heidegger, 'may I reckon on your aid in performing an exceedingly curious experiment?'

Now Dr. Heidegger was a very strange old gentleman, whose eccentricity had become the nucleus for a thousand fantastic stories. Some of these fables, to my shame be it spoken, might possibly be traced back to mine own veracious self; and if any passages of the present tale should startle the reader's faith, I must be content to bear the stigma of a fiction-monger.

When the doctor's four guests heard him talk of his proposed experiment, they anticipated nothing more wonderful than the murder of a mouse in an air pump, or the examination of a cobweb by the microscope, or some similar nonsense, with which he was constantly in the habit of pestering his intimates. But without waiting for a reply, Dr. Heidegger hobbled across the chamber, and returned with the same ponderous folio, bound in black leather, which common report affirmed to be a book of magic. Undoing the silver clasps, he opened the volume, and took from among its black-letter pages a rose, or what was once a rose, though now the green leaves and crimson petals had assumed one brownish hue, and the ancient flower seemed ready to crumble to dust in the doctor's hands.

'This rose,' said Dr. Heidegger, with a sigh, 'this same withered and crumbling flower, blossomed five-and-fifty years ago. It was given me by Sylvia Ward, whose portrait hangs yonder; and I meant to wear it in my bosom at our wedding. Five-and-fifty years it has been treasured between the leaves of this old volume. Now, would you deem it possible that this rose of half a century could ever bloom again?'

'Nonsense!' said the Widow Wycherly, with a peevish toss of her head. 'You might as well ask whether an old woman's wrinkled face could ever bloom again.'

'See!' answered Dr. Heidegger.

He uncovered the vase, and threw the faded rose into the water which it contained. At first, it lay lightly on the surface of the fluid, appearing to imbibe none of its moisture. Soon, however, a singular change began to be visible. The crushed and dried petals stirred, and assumed a deepening tinge of crimson, as if the flower were reviving from a deathlike slumber; the slender stalk and twigs of foliage became green; and there was the rose of half a century, looking as fresh as when Sylvia Ward had first given it to her lover. It was scarcely full-blown; for some of its delicate red leaves curled modestly around its moist bosom, within which two or three dewdrops were sparkling.

'That is certainly a very pretty deception,' said the doctor's friends; carelessly, however, for they had witnessed greater miracles at a conjurer's show; 'pray how was it effected?'

'Did you never hear of the "Fountain of Youth",' asked Dr. Heidegger, 'which Ponce de Leon, the Spanish adventurer, went in search of, two or three centuries ago?'

'But did Ponce de Leon ever find it?' said the Widow Wycherly.

'No,' answered Dr. Heidegger, 'for he never sought it in the right place. The famous Fountain of Youth, if I am rightly informed, is situated in the southern part of the Floridan peninsula, not far from Lake Macaco. Its source is overshadowed by several gigantic magnolias, which, though numberless centuries old, have been kept as fresh as violets, by the virtues of this wonderful water. An acquaintance of mine, knowing my curiosity in such matters, has sent me what you see in the vase.'

'Ahem!' said Colonel Killigrew, who believed not a word of the doctor's story; 'and what may be the effect of this fluid on the human frame?'

'You shall judge for yourself, my dear Colonel,' replied Dr. Heidegger; 'and all of you, my respected friends, are welcome to so much of this admirable fluid as may restore to you the bloom of youth. For my own part, having had much trouble in growing old, I am in no hurry to grow young again. With your permission, therefore, I will merely watch the progress of the experiment.'

While he spoke, Dr. Heidegger had been filling the four champagne-glasses with the water of the Fountain of Youth. It was apparently impregnated with an effervescent gas, for little bubbles were continually ascending from the depths of the glasses, and bursting in silvery spray at the surface. As the liquor diffused a pleasant perfume, the old people doubted not that it possessed cordial and comfortable properties; and, though utter sceptics as to its rejuvenescent power, they were inclined to swallow it at once. But Dr. Heidegger besought them to stay a moment.

'Before you drink, my respectable old friends,' said he, 'it would be well that, with the experience of a lifetime to direct you, you should draw up a few general rules for your guidance, in passing a second time through the perils of youth. Think what a sin and shame it would be, if, with your peculiar advantages, you should not become patterns of virtue and wisdom to all the young people of the age.'

The doctor's four venerable friends made him no answer, except by a feeble and tremulous laugh; so very ridiculous was the idea, that, knowing how closely repentance treads behind the steps of error, they should ever go astray again.

'Drink, then,' said the doctor, bowing. 'I rejoice that I have so well selected the subjects of my experiment.'

With palsied hands, they raised the glasses to their lips. The liquor, if it really possessed such virtues as Dr. Heidegger imputed to it, could not have been bestowed on four human beings who needed it more wofully. They looked as if they had never known what youth or pleasure was, but had been the offspring of Nature's dotage, and always the grey, decrepit, sapless, miserable creatures who now sat stooping round the doctor's table, without life enough in their souls or bodies to be animated even by the prospect of growing young again. They drank off the water, and replaced their glasses on the table.

Assuredly there was an almost immediate improvement in the aspect of the party, not unlike what might have been produced by a glass of generous wine, together with a sudden glow of cheerful sunshine, brightening over all their visages at once. There was a healthful suffusion on their cheeks, instead of the ashen hue that had made them look so corpse-like. They gazed at one another, and fancied that some magic power had really begun to smooth away the deep and sad inscription which Father Time had been so long engraving on their brows. The Widow Wycherly adjusted her cap, for she felt almost like a woman again.

'Give us more of this wondrous water!' cried they, eagerly. 'We are younger,—but we are still too old! Quick,—give us more!'

'Patience, patience!' quoth Dr. Heidegger, who sat watching the experiment, with philosophic coolness. 'You have been a long time growing old. Surely, you might be content to grow young in half-an-hour! But the water is at your service.'

Again he filled their glasses with the liquor of youth, enough of which still remained in the vase to turn half the old people in the city to the age of their own grandchildren. While the bubbles were yet sparkling on the brim, the doctor's four guests snatched their glasses from the table, and swallowed the contents at a single gulp. Was it delusion? even while the draught was passing down their throats, it seemed to have wrought a change on their whole systems. Their eyes grew clear and bright; a dark shade deepened among their silvery locks; they sat around the table, three gentlemen of middle age, and a woman, hardly beyond her buxom prime.

'My dear widow, you are charming!' cried Colonel Killigrew, whose eyes had been fixed upon her face, while the shadows of age were flitting from it like darkness from the crimson daybreak.

The fair widow knew, of old, that Colonel Killigrew's compliments were not always measured by sober truth; so she started up and ran to the mirror, still dreading that the ugly visage of an old woman would meet her gaze. Meanwhile, the three gentlemen behaved in such a manner, as proved that the water of the Fountain of Youth possessed some intoxicating qualities; unless, indeed, their exhilaration of spirits were merely a lightsome dizziness, caused by the sudden removal of the weight of years. Mr. Gascoigne's mind seemed to run on political topics, but whether relating to the past, present, or future, could not easily be determined, since the same ideas and phrases have been in vogue these fifty years. Now he rattled forth full-throated sentences about patriotism, national glory, and the people's right; now he muttered some perilous stuff or other, in a sly and doubtful whisper, so cautiously that even his own conscience could scarely catch the secret; and now, again, he spoke in measured accents, and a deeply deferential tone, as if a royal ear were listening to his well-turned periods. Colonel Killigrew all this time had been trolling forth a jolly bottle-song, and ringing his glass in symphony with the chorus, while his eyes wandered toward the buxom figure of the Widow Wycherly. On the other side of the table, Mr. Medbourne was involved in a calculation of dollars and cents, with which was strangely intermingled a project for supplying the East Indies with ice, by harnessing a team of whales to the polar icebergs.

As for the Widow Wycherly, she stood before the mirror curtsying and simpering to her own image, and greeting it as the friend whom she loved better than all the world beside. She thrust her face close to the glass, to see whether some long-remembered wrinkle or crow's-foot had indeed vanished. She examined whether the snow had so entirely melted from her hair, that the venerable cap could be safely thrown aside. At last, turning briskly away, she came with a sort of dancing step to the table.

'My dear old doctor,' cried she, 'pray favour me with another glass!'

'Certainly, my dear madam, certainly!' replied the complaisant doctor; 'see! I have already filled the glasses.'

There, in fact, stood the four glasses, brimful of this wonderful water, the delicate spray of which, as it effervesced from the surface, resembled the tremulous glitter of diamonds. It was now so nearly sunset, that the chamber had grown duskier than ever; but a mild and moonlike splendour gleamed from within the vase, and rested alike on the four guests, and on the doctor's venerable figure. He sat in a high-backed, elaborately carved oaken armchair, with a grey dignity of aspect that might have well befitted that very Father Time, whose power had never been disputed, save by this fortunate company. Even while quaffing the third draught of the Fountain of Youth, they were almost awed by the expression of his mysterious visage.

But, the next moment, the exhilarating gush of young life shot through their veins. They were now in the happy prime of youth. Age, with its miserable train of cares, and sorrows, and diseases, was remembered only as the trouble of a dream, from which they had joyously awoke. The fresh gloss of the soul, so early lost, and without which the world's successive scenes had been but a gallery of faded pictures, again threw its enchantment over all their prospects. They felt like new-created beings, in a new-created universe.

'We are young! We are young!' they cried exultingly.

Youth, like the extremity of age, had effaced the strongly marked characteristics of middle life, and mutually assimilated them all. They were a group of merry youngsters, almost maddened with the exuberant frolicsomeness of their years. The most singular effect of their gaiety was an impulse to mock the infirmity and decrepitude of which they had so lately been the victims. They laughed loudly at their old-fashioned attire, the wide-skirted coats and flapped waistcoats of the young men, and the ancient cap and gown of the blooming girl. One limped across the floor, like a gouty grandfather; one set a pair of spectacles astride of his nose, and pretended to pore over the black-letter pages of the book of magic; a third seated himself in an armchair, and strove to imitate the venerable dignity of Dr. Heidegger. Then all shouted mirthfully, and leaped about the room. The Widow Wycherly—if so fresh a damsel could be called a widow—tripped up to the doctor's chair, with a mischievous merriment in her rosy face.

'Doctor, you dear old soul,' cried she, 'get up and dance with me!' And then the four young people laughed louder than ever, to think what a queer figure the poor old doctor would cut.

'Pray excuse me,' answered the doctor, quietly. 'I am old and rheumatic, and my dancing days were over long ago. But either of these gay young gentlemen will be glad of so pretty a partner.'

'Dance with me, Clara!' cried Colonel Killigrew.

'No, no, I will be her partner!' shouted Mr. Gascoigne.

'She promised me her hand, fifty years ago!' exclaimed Mr. Medbourne.

They all gathered round her. One caught both her hands in his passionate grasp,—another threw his arm about her waist,—the third buried his hand among the glossy curls that clustered beneath the widow's cap. Blushing, panting, struggling, chiding, laughing, her warm breath fanning each of their faces by turns, she strove to disengage herself, yet still remained in their triple embrace. Never was there a livelier picture of youthful rivalship, with bewitching beauty for the prize. Yet, by a strange deception, owing to the duskiness of the chamber, and the antique dresses which they still wore, the tall mirror is said to have reflected the figures of three old, grey, withered grandsires, ridiculously contending for the skinny ugliness of a shrivelled grandam.

But they were young: their burning passions proved them so. Inflamed to madness by the coquetry of the girl-widow, who neither granted nor quite withheld her favours, the three rivals began to interchange threatening glances. Still keeping hold of the fair prize, they grappled fiercely at one another's throats. As they struggled to and fro, the table was overturned, and the vase dashed into a thousand fragments. The precious Water of Youth flowed in a bright stream across the floor, moistening the wings of a butterfly, which, grown old in the decline of summer, had alighted there to die. The insect fluttered lightly through the chamber, and settled on the snowy head of Dr. Heidegger.

'Come, come, gentlemen!—come, Madam Wycherly,' exclaimed the doctor, 'I really must protest against this riot.'

They stood still and shivered; for it seemed as if grey Time were calling them back from their sunny youth, far down into the chill and darksome vale of years. They looked at old Dr. Heidegger, who sat in his carved armchair, holding the rose of half a century, which he had rescued from among the fragments of the shattered vase. At the motion of his hand, the four rioters resumed their seats; the more readily, because their violent exertions had wearied them, youthful though they were.

'My poor Sylvia's rose!' ejaculated Dr. Heidegger, holding it in the light of the sunset clouds; 'it appears to be fading again.'

And so it was. Even while the party were looking at it, the flower continued to shrivel up, till it became as dry and fragile as when the doctor had first thrown it into the vase. He shook off the few drops of moisture which clung to its petals.

'I love it as well thus, as in its dewy freshness,' observed he, pressing the withered rose to his withered lips. While he spoke, the butterfly fluttered down from the doctor's snowy head, and fell upon the floor.

His guests shivered again. A strange chilliness, whether of the body or spirit they could not tell, was creeping gradually over them all. They gazed at one another, and fancied that each fleeting moment snatched away a charm, and left a deepening furrow where none had been before. Was it an illusion? Had the changes of a lifetime been crowded into so brief a space, and were they now four aged people, sitting with their old friend, Dr. Heidegger?

'Are we grown old again, so soon?' cried they, dolefully.

In truth, they had. The Water of Youth possessed merely a virtue more transient than that of wine. The delirium which it created had effervesced away. Yes! they were old again. With a shuddering impulse, that showed her a woman still, the widow clasped her skinny hands before her face, and wished that the coffin-lid were over it, since it could be no longer beautiful.

'Yes, friends, ye are old again,' said Dr. Heidegger; 'and lo! the Water of Youth is all lavished on the ground. Well, I bemoan it not; for if the fountain gushed at my very doorstep, I would not stoop to bathe my lips in it; no, though its delirium were for years instead of moments. Such is the lesson ye have taught me!'

But the doctor's four friends had taught no such lesson to themselves. They resolved forthwith to make a pilgrimage to Florida, and quaff at morning, noon, and night from the Fountain of Youth.

Notes

p. 6	*singular* - remarkable	
p. 6	*frantic speculation* - mad money-making scheme	
p 6	*mendicant* - beggar	
p. 6	*of evil fame* - of bad reputation	

p. 6   *beside themselves* - not quite in their right minds

pp. 6–7   *folios . . .quartos . . . duodecimos* - books of different sizes

p. 7   *Hippocrates* - classical Greek doctor – the founder of Western medicine

p. 7   *thitherward* - at it or towards it

p. 7   *visage* - face

p. 7   *ponderous* - heavy

p. 7   *forbear!* - do not (touch it)

p. 8   *Fountain of Youth . . . Ponce de Leon* - a real Spanish explorer; according to
               some myths found a 'fountain of youth' in Florida in 1513

p. 8   *Floridan peninsular . . . Lake Macaco* - large lake in Florida now called Lake
               Okeechobee

p. 9   *palsied* - afflicted by palsy; shaking

p. 10   *trolling* - singing

p. 10   *a calculation . . . icebergs . . .* - Another one of his 'frantic speculations' -
               ludicrous project that will never work and will lose money

3

Nick

(1850)

Christina Rossetti

One of the great English poets, Rossetti, also wrote some poetic stories. This story is in the form of a fable in which a man given to vain wishes finds his wishes come true and lives to regret it. This story has similar qualities to poems such as 'Goblin Market' in its strong structure, universal theme and sometimes grotesque imagination.

There dwelt in a small village, not a thousand miles from Fairyland, a poor man, who had no family to labour for or friend to assist. When I call him poor, you must not suppose he was a homeless wanderer, trusting to charity for a night's lodging; on the contrary, his stone house, with its green verandah and flower-garden, was the prettiest and snuggest in all the place, the doctor's only excepted. Neither was his store of provisions running low: his farm supplied him with milk, eggs, mutton, butter, poultry, and cheese in abundance; his fields with hops and barley for beer, and wheat for bread; his orchard with fruit and cider; and his kitchen-garden with vegetables and wholesome herbs. He had, moreover, health, an appetite to enjoy all these good things, and strength to walk about his possessions. No, I call him poor because, with all these, he was discontented and envious. It was in vain that his apples were the largest for miles around, if his neighbour's vines were the most productive by a single bunch; it was in vain that his lambs were fat and thriving, if some one else's sheep bore twins: so, instead of enjoying his own prosperity, and being glad when his neighbours prospered too, he would sit grumbling and bemoaning himself as if every other man's riches were his poverty. And thus it was that one day our friend Nick leaned over Giles Hodge's gate, counting his cherries.

'Yes,' he muttered, 'I wish I were sparrows to eat them up, or a blight to kill your fine trees altogether.'

The words were scarcely uttered when he felt a tap on his shoulder, and looking round, perceived a little rosy woman, no bigger than a butterfly, who held her tiny fist clenched in a menacing attitude. She looked scornfully at him, and said: 'Now listen, you churl, you! henceforward you shall straightway become everything you wish; only mind, you must remain under one form for at least an hour.' Then she gave him a slap in the face, which made his cheek tingle as if a bee had stung him, and disappeared with just so much sound as a dewdrop makes in falling.

Nick rubbed his cheek in a pet, pulling wry faces and showing his teeth. He was boiling over with vexation, but dared not vent it in words lest some unlucky wish should escape him. Just then the sun seemed to shine brighter than ever, the wind blew spicy from the south; all Giles's roses looked redder and larger than before, while his cherries seemed to multiply, swell, ripen. He could refrain no longer, but, heedless of the fairy-gift he had just received, exclaimed, 'I wish I were sparrows eating—' No sooner said than done: in a moment he found himself a whole flight of hungry birds, pecking, devouring, and bidding fair to devastate the envied cherry-trees. But honest Giles was on the watch hard by; for that very morning it had struck him he must make nets for the protection of his fine fruit. Forthwith he ran home, and speedily returned with a revolver furnished with quite a marvellous array of barrels. Pop, bang – pop, bang! he made short work of the sparrows, and soon reduced the enemy to one crestfallen biped with broken leg and wing, who limped to hide himself under a holly-bush. But though the fun was over, the hour was not; so Nick must needs sit out his allotted time. Next a pelting shower came down, which soaked him through his torn, ruffled feathers; and then, exactly as the last drops fell and the sun came out with a beautiful rainbow, a tabby cat pounced upon him. Giving himself up for lost, he chirped in desperation, 'O, I wish I were a dog to worry you!' Instantly – for the hour was just passed – in the grip of his horrified adversary, he turned at bay, a savage bull-dog. A shake, a deep bite, and poor puss was out of her pain. Nick, with immense satisfaction, tore her fur to bits, wishing he could in like manner exterminate all her progeny. At last, glutted with vengence, he lay down beside his victim, relaxed his ears and tail, and fell asleep.

Now that tabby-cat was the property and special pet of no less a personage than the doctor's lady; so when dinner-time came, and not the cat, a general consternation pervaded the household. The kitchens were searched, the cellars, the attics; every apartment was ransacked; even the watch-dog's kennel was visited. Next the stable was rummaged, then the hay-loft; lastly, the bereaved lady wandered disconsolately through her own private garden into the shrubbery, calling 'Puss, puss,' and looking so intently up the trees as not to perceive what lay close before her feet. Thus it was that, unawares, she stumbled over Nick, and trod upon his tail.

Up jumped our hero, snarling, biting, and rushing at her with such blind fury as to miss his aim. She ran, he ran. Gathering up his strength, he took a flying-leap after his victim; her foot caught in the spreading root of an oaktree, she fell, and he went over her head, clear over, into a bed of stinging-nettles. Then she found breath to raise that fatal cry, 'Mad dog!' Nick's blood curdled in his veins; he would have slunk away if he could; but already a stout labouring-man, to whom he had done many an ill turn in the time of his humanity, had spied him, and, bludgeon in hand, was preparing to give chase. However, Nick had the start of him, and used it too; while the lady, far behind, went on vociferating, 'Mad dog, mad dog!' inciting doctor, servants, and vagabonds to the pursuit. Finally, the whole village came pouring out to swell the hue and cry.

The dog kept ahead gallantly, distancing more and more the asthmatic doctor, fat Giles, and, in fact, all his pursuers except the bludgeon-bearing labourer, who was just near enough to persecute his tail. Nick knew the magic hour must be almost over, and so kept forming wish after wish as he ran, – that he were a viper only to get trodden on, a thorn to run into some one's foot, a man-trap in the path, even the detested bludgeon to miss its aim and break. This wish crossed his mind at the propitious moment; the bull-dog vanished, and the labourer, overreaching himself, fell flat on his face, while his weapon struck deep into the earth, and snapped.

A strict search was instituted after the missing dog, but without success. During two whole days the village children were exhorted to keep indoors and beware of dogs; on the third an inoffensive bull pup was hanged, and the panic subsided.

Meanwhile the labourer, with his shattered stick, walked home in silent wonder, pondering on the mysterious disappearance. But the puzzle was beyond his solution; so he only made up his mind not to tell his wife the whole story till after tea. He found her preparing for that meal, the bread and cheese set out, and the kettle singing softly on the fire. 'Here's something to make the kettle boil, mother,' said he, thrusting our hero between the bars and seating himself; 'for I'm mortal tired and thirsty.'

Nick crackled and blazed away cheerfully, throwing out bright sparks, and lighting up every corner of the little room. He toasted the cheese to a nicety, made the kettle boil without spilling a drop, set the cat purring with comfort, and illuminated the pots and pans into splendour. It was provocation enough to be burned; but to contribute by his misfortune to the well-being of his tormentors was still more aggravating. He heard, too, all their remarks and wonderment about the supposed mad-dog, and saw the doctor's lady's own maid bring the labourer five shillings as a reward for his exertions. Then followed a discussion as to what should be purchased with the gift, till at last it was resolved to have their best window glazed with real glass. The prospect of their grandeur put the finishing-stroke to Nick's indignation. Sending up a sudden flare, he wished with all his might that he were fire to burn the cottage.

Forthwith the flame leaped higher than ever flame leaped before. It played for a moment about a ham, and smoked it to a nicety; then, fastening on the woodwork above the chimney-corner, flashed full into a blaze. The labourer ran for help, while his wife, a timid woman, with three small children, overturned two pails of water on the floor, and set the beer-tap running. This done, she hurried, wringing her hands, to the door, and threw it wide open. The sudden draught of air did more mischief than all Nick's malice, and fanned him into quite a conflagration. He danced upon the rafters, melted a pewter-pot and a pat of butter, licked up the beer, and was just making his way towards the bedroom, when through the thatch and down the chimney came a rush of water. This arrested his progress for the moment; and before he could recover himself, a second and a third discharge from the enemy completed his discomfiture. Reduced ere long to one blue flame, and entirely surrounded by a wall of wet ashes, Nick sat and smouldered; while the good-natured neighbours did their best to remedy the mishap, – saved a small remnant of beer, assured the labourer that his landlord was certain to do the repairs, and observed that the ham would eat 'beautiful'.

Our hero now had leisure for reflection. His situation precluded all hope of doing further mischief; and the disagreeable conviction kept forcing itself upon his mind that, after all, he had caused more injury to himself than to any of his neighbours. Remembering, too, how contemptuously the fairy woman had looked and spoken, he began to wonder how he could ever have expected to enjoy her gift. Then it occurred to him, that if he merely studied his own advantage without trying to annoy other people, perhaps his persecutor might be propitiated; so he fell to thinking over all his acquaintance, their fortunes and misfortunes; and, having weighed well their several claims on his preference, ended by wishing himself the rich old man who lived in a handsome house just beyond the turnpike. In this wish he burned out.

The last glimmer had scarcely died away, when Nick found himself in a bed hung round with faded curtains, and occupying the centre of a large room. A night-lamp, burning on the chimney-piece, just enabled him to discern a few shabby old articles of furniture, a scanty carpet, and some writing materials on a table. These objects looked somewhat dreary; but for his comfort he felt an inward consciousness of a goodly money-chest stowed away under his bed, and of sundry precious documents hidden in a secret cupboard in the wall.

So he lay very cosily, and listened to the clock ticking, the mice squeaking, and the house-dog barking down below. This was, however, but a drowsy occupation; and he soon bore witness to its somniferous influence by sinking into a fantastic dream about his money-chest. First, it was broken open, then shipwrecked, then burned; lastly, some men in masks, whom he knew instinctively to be his own servants, began dragging it away. Nick started up, clutched hold of something in the dark, found his last dream true, and the next moment was stretched on the floor – lifeless, yet not insensible – by a heavy blow from a crowbar.

The men now proceeded to secure their booty, leaving our hero where he fell. They carried off the chest, broke open and ransacked the secret closet, overturned the furniture, to make sure that no hiding-place of treasure escaped them, and at length, whispering together, left the room. Nick felt quite discouraged by his ill success, and now entertained only one wish – that he was himself again. Yet even this wish gave him some anxiety; for he feared that if the servants returned and found him in his original shape they might take him for a spy, and murder him in downright earnest. While he lay thus cogitating two of the men reappeared, bearing a shutter and some tools.. They lifted him up, laid him on the shutter, and carried him out of the room, down the backstairs, through a long vaulted passage, into the open air. No word was spoken; but Nick knew they were going to bury him.

An utter horror seized him, while, at the same time, he felt a strange consciousness that his hair would not stand on end because he was dead. The men set him down, and began in silence to dig his grave. It was soon ready to receive him; they threw the body roughly in, and cast upon it the first shovelful of earth.

But the moment of deliverance had arrived. His wish suddenly found vent in a prolonged unearthly yell. Damp with night dew, pale as death, and shivering from head to foot, he sat bolt upright, with starting, staring eyes and chattering teeth. The murderers, in mortal fear, cast down their tools, plunged deep into a wood hard by, and were never heard of more.

Under cover of night Nick made the best of his way home, silent and pondering. Next morning he gave Giles Hodge a rare tulip-root, with full directions for rearing it; he sent the doctor's wife a Persian cat twice the size of her lost pet; the labourer's cottage was repaired, his window glazed, and his beer-barrel replaced by unknown agency; and when a vague rumour reached the village that the miser was dead, that his ghost had been heard bemoaning itself, and that all his treasures had been carried off, our hero was one of the few persons who did not say, 'And served him right, too.'

Finally, Nick was never again heard to utter a wish.

Notes

p. 14   *churl* - a rude, surly person
p. 14   *pet* - childish bad temper
p. 15   *bidding fair to* - looking likely to
p. 16   *bludgeon* - short stick with one heavy end, used as a weapon
p. 17   *turnpike* - toll gate
p. 17   *crowbar* - heavy iron bar

4

George Silverman's Explanation

(1868)

Charles Dickens

The great novelist, Charles Dickens, was a Londoner who depicted the squalor of London like no other writer, both in his novels – for example, David Copperfield, Oliver Twist *and* Hard Times, Bleak House *– and in his journalism and short stories, for he was not only a novelist but a journalist and editor. This powerful first-person narrative of a poor boy given a chance in life is almost a Dickens novel in miniature. An innocent abroad discovers human wickedness.*

FIRST CHAPTER

It happened in this wise:

– But, sitting with my pen in my hand looking at those words again, without descrying any hint in them of the words that should follow, it comes into my mind that they have an abrupt appearance. They may serve, however, if I let them remain, to suggest how very difficult I find it to begin to explain my Explanation. An uncouth phrase: and yet I do not see my way to a better.

SECOND CHAPTER

It happened in *this* wise:

– But, looking at those words, and comparing them with my former opening, I find they are the selfsame words repeated. This is the more surprising to me, because I employ them in quite a new connection. For indeed I declare that my intention was to discard the commencement I first had in my thoughts, and to give the preference to another of an entirely different nature, dating my explanation from an anterior period of my life. I will make a third trial, without erasing this second failure, protesting that it is not my design to conceal any of my infirmities, whether they be of head or heart.

THIRD CHAPTER

Not as yet directly aiming at how it came to pass, I will come upon it by degrees. The natural manner, after all, for God knows that is how it came upon me!

My parents were in a miserable condition of life, and my infant home was a cellar in Preston. I recollect the sound of Father's Lancashire clogs on the street pavement above, as being different in my young hearing from the sound of all other clogs; and I recollect that, when Mother came down the cellar-steps, I used tremblingly to speculate on her feet having a good or an ill-tempered look, – on her knees – on her waist, – until finally her face came into view and settled the question. From this it will be seen that I was timid, and that the cellar-steps were steep, and that the doorway was very low.

Mother had the gripe and clutch of Poverty upon her face, upon her figure, and not least of all upon her voice. Her sharp and high-pitched words were squeezed out of her, as by the compression of bony fingers on a leathern-bag; and she had a way of rolling her eyes about and about the cellar, as she scolded, that was gaunt and hungry. Father, with his shoulders rounded, would sit quiet on a three-legged stool, looking at the empty grate, until she would pluck the stool from under him, and bid him go bring some money home. Then he would dismally ascend the steps, and I, holding my ragged shirt and trousers together with a hand (my only braces), would feint and dodge from Mother's pursuing grasp at my hair.

A worldly little devil was Mother's usual name for me. Whether I cried for that I was in the dark, or for that it was cold, or for that I was hungry, or whether I squeezed myself into a warm corner when there was a fire, or ate voraciously when there was food, she would still say, 'O you worldly little devil!' And the sting of it was, that I quite well knew myself to be a worldly little devil. Worldly as to wanting to be housed and warmed, worldly as to wanting to be fed, worldly as to the greed with which I inwardly compared how much I got of those good things with how much Father and Mother got, when, rarely, those good things were going.

Sometimes they both went away seeking work, and then I would be locked up in the cellar for a day or two at a time. I was at my worldliest then. Left alone, I yielded myself up to a worldly yearning for enough of anything (except misery), and for the death of Mother's father, who was a machine-maker at Birmingham, and on whose decease, I had heard Mother say, she would come into a whole courtful of houses 'if she had her rights'. Worldly little devil, I would stand about, musingly fitting my cold bare feet into cracked bricks and crevices of the damp cellar floor, – walking over my grandfather's body, so to speak, into the courtful of houses, and selling them for meat and drink, and clothes to wear.

At last a change came down into our cellar. The universal change came down even as low as that, – so will it mount to any height on which a human creature can perch, – and brought other changes with it.

We had a heap of I don't know what foul litter in the darkest corner, which we called 'the bed.' For three days Mother lay upon it without getting up, and then began at times to laugh. If I had ever heard her laugh before, it had been so seldom that the strange sound frightened me. It frightened Father, too, and we took it by turns to give her water. Then she began to move her head from side to side, and sing. After that, she getting no better, Father fell a laughing and a singing, and then there was only I to give them both water, and they both died.

FOURTH CHAPTER

When I was lifted out of the cellar by two men, of whom one came peeping down alone first, and ran away and brought the other, I could hardly bear the light of the street. I was sitting in the roadway, blinking at it, and at a ring of people collected around me, but not close to me, when, true to my character of worldly little devil, I broke silence by saying, 'I am hungry and thirsty!'

'Does he know they are dead?' asked one of another.

'Do you know your father and mother are both dead of fever?' asked a third of me, severely.

'I don't know what it is to be dead. I supposed it meant that, when the cup rattled against their teeth and the water spilt over them. I am hungry and thirsty.' That was all I had to say about it.

The ring of people widened outward from the inner side as I looked around me; and I smelt vinegar, and what I now know to be camphor, thrown in towards where I sat. Presently some one put a great vessel of smoking vinegar on the ground near me, and then they all looked at me in silent horror as I ate and drank of what was brought for me. I knew at the time they had a horror of me, but I couldn't help it.

I was still eating and drinking, and a murmur of discussion had begun to arise respecting what was to be done with me next, when I heard a cracked voice somewhere in the ring say, 'My name is Hawkyard, Mr Verity Hawkyard, of West Bromwich.' Then the ring split in one place, and a yellow-faced, peak-nosed gentleman, clad all in iron-gray to his gaiters, pressed forward with a policeman and another official of some sort. He came forward close to the vessel of smoking vinegar; from which he sprinkled himself carefully, and me copiously.

'He had a grandfather at Birmingham, this young boy, who is just dead too,' said Mr Hawkyard.

I turned my eyes upon the speaker, and said in a ravening manner, 'Where's his houses?'

'Hah! Horrible worldliness on the edge of the grave,' said Mr Hawkyard, casting more of the vinegar over me, as if to get my devil out of me. 'I have undertaken a slight – a very slight – trust in behalf of this boy; quite a voluntary trust; a matter of mere honor, if not of mere sentiment; still I have taken it upon myself, and it shall be (O yes, it shall be!) discharged.'

The by-standers seemed to form an opinion of this gentleman much more favourable than their opinion of me.

'He shall be taught,' said Mr Hawkyard, '(O yes, he shall be taught!) but what is to be done with him for the present? He may be infected. He may disseminate infection.' The ring widened considerably. 'What is to be done with him?'

He held some talk with the two officials. I could distinguish no word save 'Farm-house.' There was another sound several times repeated, which was wholly meaningless in my ears then, but which I knew soon afterwards to be 'Hoghton Towers.'

'Yes,' said Mr Hawkyard, 'I think that sound promising. I think that sounds hopeful. And he can be put by himself in a Ward, for a night or two, you say?'

It seemed to be the police-officer who had said so, for it was he who replied, Yes. It was he, too, who finally took me by the arm and walked me before him through the streets, into a whitewashed room in a bare building, where I had a chair to sit in, a table to sit at, an iron bedstead and good mattress to lie upon, and a rug and blanket to cover me. Where I had enough to eat too, and was shown how to clean the tin porringer in which it was conveyed to me, until it was as good as a looking-glass. Here, likewise, I was put in a bath, and had new clothes brought to me, and my old rags were burnt, and I was camphored and vinegared, and disinfected in a variety of ways.

When all this was done, – I don't know in how many days or how few, but it matters not, – Mr Hawkyard stepped in at the door, remaining close to it, and said: 'Go and stand against the opposite wall, George Silverman. As far off as you can. That'll do. How do you feel?'

I told him that I didn't feel cold, and didn't feel hungry, and didn't feel thirsty. That was the whole round of human feelings, as far as I knew, except the pain of being beaten.

'Well,' said he, 'you are going, George, to a healthy farm-house to be purified. Keep in the air there, as much as you can. Live an out-of-door life there, until you are fetched away. You had better not say much – in fact, you had better be very careful not to say anything – about what your parents died of, or they might not like to take you in. Behave well, and I'll put you to school, (O yes, I'll put you to school!) though I am not obligated to do it. I am a servant of the Lord, George, and I have been a good servant to him (I have!) these five-and-thirty years. The Lord has had a good servant in me, and he knows it.'

What I then supposed him to mean by this, I cannot imagine. As little do I know when I began to comprehend that he was a prominent member of some obscure denomination or congregation, every member of which held forth to the rest when so inclined, and among whom he was called Brother Hawkyard. It was enough for me to know, on that day in the Ward, that the farmer's cart was waiting for me at the street corner. I was not slow to get into it, for it was the first ride I ever had in my life.

It made me sleepy, and I slept. First, I stared at Preston streets as long as they lasted, and meanwhile I may have had some small dumb wondering within me whereabouts our cellar was. But I doubt it. Such a worldly little devil was I, that I took no thought who would bury Father and Mother, or where they would be buried, or when. The question whether the eating and drinking by day, and the covering by night, would be as good at the farm-house as at the Ward superseded those questions.

The jolting of the cart on a loose stony road awoke me, and I found that we were mounting a steep hill, where the road was a rutty by-road through a field. And so, by fragments of an ancient terrace, and by some rugged out-buildings that had once been fortified, and passing under a ruined gateway, we came to the old farm-house in the thick stone wall outside the old quadrangle of Hoghton Towers. Which I looked at, like a stupid savage; seeing no specialty in; seeing no antiquity in; assuming all farm-houses to resemble it; assigning the decay I noticed to the one potent cause of all ruin that I knew, – Poverty; eyeing the pigeons in their flights, the cattle in their stalls, the ducks in the pond, and the fowls pecking about the yard, with a hungry hope that plenty of them might be killed for dinner while I stayed there; wondering whether the scrubbed dairy vessels drying in the sunlight could be the goodly porringers out of which the master ate his belly-filling food, and which he polished when he had done, according to my Ward experience; shrinkingly doubtful whether the shadows passing over that airy height on the bright spring day were not something in the nature of frowns; sordid, afraid, unadmiring, a small Brute to shudder at.

To that time I had never had the faintest impression of beauty. I had had no knowledge whatever that there was anything lovely in this life. When I had occasionally slunk up the cellar steps into the street, and glared in at shop-windows, I had done so with no higher feelings than we may suppose to animate a mangy young dog or wolf-cub. It is equally the fact that I had never been alone, in the sense of holding unselfish converse with myself. I had been solitary often enough, but nothing better.

Such was my condition when I sat down to my dinner that day, in the kitchen of the old farm-house. Such was my condition when I lay on my bed in the old farm-house that night, stretched out opposite the narrow mullioned window, in the cold light of the moon, like a young Vampire.

FIFTH CHAPTER

What do I know now of Hoghton Towers? Very little, for I have been gratefully unwilling to disturb my first impressions. A house, centuries old, on high ground a mile or so removed from the road between Preston and Blackburn, where the first James of England, in his hurry to make money by making Baronets, perhaps made some of those remunerative dignitaries. A house, centuries old, deserted and falling to pieces, its woods and gardens long since grass-land or ploughed up, the rivers Ribble and Darwen glancing below it, and a vague haze of smoke, against which not even the supernatural prescience of the first Stuart could foresee a Counterblast, hinting at Steam Power, powerful in two distances.

What did I know then of Hoghton Towers? When I first peeped in at the gate of the lifeless quadrangle, and started from the mouldering statue becoming visible to me like its Guardian Ghost; when I stole round by the back of the farm-house, and got in among the ancient rooms, many of them with their floors and ceilings falling, the beams and rafters hanging dangerously down, the plaster dropping as I trod, the oaken panels stripped away, the windows half walled up, half broken; when I discovered a gallery commanding the old kitchen, and looked down between balustrades upon a massive old table and benches, fearing to see I know not what dead-alive creatures come in and seat themselves, and look up with I know not what dreadful eyes, or lack of eyes, at me; when all over the house I was awed by gaps and chinks where the sky stared sorrowfully at me, where the birds passed, and the ivy rustled, and the stains of winter-weather blotched the rotten floors; when down at the bottom of dark pits of staircase, into which the stairs had sunk, green leaves trembled, butterflies fluttered, and bees hummed in and out through the broken doorways; when encircling the whole ruin were sweet scents and sights of fresh green growth and ever-renewing life, that I had never dreamed of, – I say, when I passed into such clouded perception of these things as my dark soul could compass, what did I know then of Hoghton Towers?

I have written that the sky stared sorrowfully at me. Therein have I anticipated the answer. I knew that all these things looked sorrowfully at me. That they seemed to sigh or whisper, not without pity for me: 'Alas! Poor worldly little devil!'

There were two or three rats at the bottom of one of the smaller pits of broken staircase when I craned over and looked in. They were scuffling for some prey that was there. And when they started and hid themselves, close together in the dark, I thought of the old life (it had grown old already) in the cellar.

How not to be this worldly little devil? How not to have a repugnance towards myself as I had towards the rats? I hid in a corner of one of the smaller chambers, frightened at myself, and crying (it was the first time I had ever cried for any cause not purely physical), and I tried to think about it. One of the farm-ploughs came into my range of view just then, and it seemed to help me as it went on with its two horses up and down the field so peacefully and quietly.

There was a girl of about my own age in the farm-house family, and she sat opposite to me at the narrow table at meal-times. It had come into my mind at our first dinner that she might take the fever from me. The thought had not disquieted me then; I had only speculated how she would look under the altered circumstances, and whether she would die. But it came into my mind now, that I might try to prevent her taking the fever, by keeping away from her. I knew I should have but scrambling board if I did; so much the less worldly and less devilish the deed would be, I thought.

From that hour I withdrew myself at early morning into secret corners of the ruined house, and remained hidden there until she went to bed. At first, when meals were ready, I used to hear them calling me; and then my resolution weakened. But I strengthened it again, by going further off into the ruin, and getting out of hearing. I often watched for her at the dim windows; and, when I saw that she was fresh and rosy, felt much happier.

Out of this holding her in my thoughts, to the humanizing of myself, I suppose some childish love arose within me. I felt in some sort dignified by the pride of protecting her, by the pride of making the sacrifice for her. As my heart swelled with that new feeling, it insensibly softened about Mother and Father. It seemed to have been frozen before and now to be thawed. The old ruin and all the lovely things that haunted it were not sorrowful for me only, but sorrowful for Mother and Father as well. Therefore did I cry again, and often too.

The farm-house family conceived me to be of a morose temper, and were very short with me; though they never stinted me in such broken fare as was to be got out of regular hours. One night when I lifted the kitchen latch at my usual time, Sylvia (that was her pretty name) had but just gone out of the room. Seeing her ascending the opposite stairs, I stood still at the door. She had heard the clink of the latch, and looked round.

'George,' she called to me, in a pleased voice, 'tomorrow is my birthday, and we are to have a fiddler, and there's a party of boys and girls coming in a cart, and we shall dance. I invite you. Be sociable for once, George.'

'I am very sorry, miss,' I answered,' but I – but no; I can't come.'

'You are a disagreeable, ill-humoured lad,' she returned, disdainfully, 'and I ought not to have asked you. I shall never speak to you again.'

As I stood with my eyes fixed on the fire after she was gone, I felt that the farmer bent his brows upon me.

'Eh, lad,' said he, 'Sylvy's right. You're as moody and broody a lad as never I set eyes on yet!'

I tried to assure him that I meant no harm; but he only said coldly: 'Maybe not, maybe not. There! Get thy supper, get thy supper, and then thou canst sulk to thy heart's content again.'

Ah! If they could have seen me next day in the ruin, watching for the arrival of the cart full of merry young guests; if they could have seen me at night, gliding out from behind the ghostly statue, listening to the music and the fall of dancing feet, and watching the lighted farm-house windows from the quadrangle when all the ruin was dark; if they could have read my heart as I crept up to bed by the back way, comforting myself with the reflection, 'They will take no hurt from me,' – they would not have thought mine a morose or an unsocial nature!

It was in these ways that I began to form a shy disposition; to be of a timidly silent character under misconstruction; to have an inexpressible, perhaps a morbid, dread of ever being sordid or worldly. It was in these ways that my nature came to shape itself to such a mould, even before it was affected by the influences of the studious and retired life of a poor scholar.

SIXTH CHAPTER

Brother Hawkyard (as he insisted on my calling him) put me to school, and told me to work my way. 'You are all right, George,' he said. 'I have been the best servant the Lord has had in his service for this five-and-thirty years, (O, I have!) and he knows the value of such a servant as I have been to him, (O yes, he does!) and he'll prosper your schooling as a part of my reward. That's what *he*'ll do, George. He'll do it for me.'

From the first I could not like this familiar knowledge of the ways of the sublime inscrutable Almighty, on Brother Hawkyard's part. As I grew a little wiser and still a little wiser, I liked it less and less. His manner, too, of confirming himself in a parenthesis, – as if, knowing himself, he doubted his own word, – I found distasteful. I cannot tell how much these dislikes cost me, for I had a dread that they were worldly.

As time went on, I became a Foundation-Boy on a good Foundation, and I cost Brother Hawkyard nothing. When I had worked my way so far, I worked yet harder, in the hope of ultimately getting a presentation to College and a Fellowship. My health has never been strong (some vapour from the Preston cellar cleaves to me I think), and what with much work and some weakness, I came again to be regarded – that is, by my fellow-students – as unsocial.

All through my time as a Foundation-Boy I was within a few miles of Brother Hawkyard's congregation, and whenever I was what we called a Leave-Boy on a Sunday, I went over there, at his desire. Before the knowledge became forced upon me that outside their place of meeting these Brothers and Sisters were no better than the rest of the human family, but on the whole were, to put the case mildly, as bad as most, in respect of giving short weight in their shops, and not speaking the truth, – I say, before this knowledge became forced upon me, their prolix addresses, their inordinate conceit, their daring ignorance, their investment of the Supreme Ruler of Heaven and Earth with their own miserable meannesses and littlenesses greatly shocked me. Still, as their term for the frame of mind that could not perceive them to be in an exalted state of Grace was the 'worldly' state, I did for a time suffer tortures under my inquiries of myself whether that young worldly-devilish spirit of mine could secretly be lingering at the bottom of my non-appreciation.

Brother Hawkyard was the popular expounder in this assembly, and generally occupied the platform (there was a little platform with a table on it, in lieu of a pulpit) first, on a Sunday afternoon. He was by trade a drysalter. Brother Gimblet, an elderly man with a crabbed face, a large dog's-eared shirt-collar, and a spotted blue neckerchief reaching up behind to the crown of his head, was also a drysalter, and an expounder. Brother Gimblet professed the greatest admiration for Brother Hawkyard, but (I had thought more than once) bore him a jealous grudge.

Let whosoever may peruse these lines kindly take the pains here to read twice my solemn pledge, that what I write of the language and customs of the congregation in question I write scrupulously, literally, exactly from the life and the truth.

On the first Sunday after I had won what I had so long tried for, and when it was certain that I was going up to college, Brother Hawkyard concluded a long exhortation thus:

'Well, my friends and fellow-sinners, now I told you, when I began, that I didn't know a word of what I was going to say to you, (and no, I did not!) but that it was all one to me, because I knew the Lord would put into my mouth the words I wanted.'

('That's it!' From Brother Gimblet.)

'And he did put into my mouth the words I wanted.'

('So he did!' From Brother Gimblet.)

'And why?'

('Ah! Let's have that!' From Brother Gimblet.)

'Because I have been his faithful servant for five-and-thirty years, and because he knows it. For five-and-thirty years! And he knows it, mind you! I got those words that I wanted, on account of my wages. I got 'em from the Lord, my fellow-sinners. Down. I said, "Here's a heap of wages due; let us have something down on account." And I got it down, and I paid it over to you, and you won't wrap it up in a napkin, nor yet in a towel, nor yet pocket hankercher, but you'll put it out at good interest. Very well. Now, my brothers and sisters and fellow-sinners, I am going to conclude with a question, and I'll make it so plain (with the help of the Lord, after five-and-thirty years, I should rather hope!) as that the Devil shall not be able to confuse it in your heads. Which he would be overjoyed to do.'

('Just his way. Crafty old blackguard!' From Brother Gimblet.)

'And the question is this. Are the Angels learned?'

('Not they. Not a bit on it.' From Brother Gimbiet, with the greatest confidence.)

'Not they. And where's the proof? Sent ready-made by the hand of the Lord. Why, there's one among us here now, that has got all the Learning that can be crammed into him. *I* got him all the Learning that could be crammed into him. His grandfather' (this I had never heard before) 'was a Brother of ours. He was Brother Parksop. That's what he was. Parksop. Brother Parksop. His worldly name was Parksop, and he was a Brother of this Brotherhood. Then wasn't he Brother Parksop?'

('Must be. Couldn't help hisself.' From Brother Gimblet.)

'Well. He left that one now here present among us to the care of a Brother-Sinner of his, (and that Brother-Sinner, mind you, was a sinner of a bigger size in his time than any of you, Praise the Lord!) Brother Hawkyard. Me *I* got him, without fee or reward, – without a morsel of myrrh, or frankincense, nor yet Amber, letting alone the honeycomb, – all the Learning that could be crammed into him. Has it brought him into our Temple, in the spirit? No. Have we had any ignorant Brothers and Sisters that didn't know round O from crooked S, come in among us meanwhile? Many. Then the Angels are *not* learned. Then they don't so much as know their alphabet. And now, my friends and fellow-sinners, having brought it to that, perhaps some Brother present – perhaps you, Brother Gimblet – will pray a bit for us?'

Brother Gimblet undertook the sacred function, after having drawn his sleeve across his mouth, and muttered: 'Well! I don't know as I see my way to hitting any of you quite in the right place neither.' He said this with a dark smile, and then began to bellow. What we were specially to be preserved from, according to his solicitations, was despoilment of the orphan, suppression of testamentary intentions on the part of a Father or (say) Grandfather, appropriation of the orphan's house-property, feigning to give in charity to the wronged one from whom we withheld his due; and that class of sins. He ended with the petition, 'Give us peace!' Which, speaking for myself, was very much needed after twenty minutes of his bellowing.

27

Even though I had not seen him when he rose from his knees, steaming with perspiration, glance at Brother Hawkyard, and even though I had not heard Brother Hawkyard's tone of congratulating him on the vigor with which he had roared, I should have detected a malicious application in this prayer. Unformed suspicions to a similar effect had sometimes passed through my mind in my earlier schooldays, and had always caused me great distress; for they were worldly in their nature, and wide, very wide, of the spirit that had drawn me from Sylvia. They were sordid suspicions, without a shadow of proof. They were worthy to have originated in the unwholesome cellar. They were not only without proof, but against proof. For was I not myself a living proof of what Brother Hawkyard had done? And without him, how should I ever have seen the sky look sorrowfully down upon that wretched boy at Hoghton Towers?

Although the dread of a relapse into a state of savage selfishness was less strong upon me as I approached manhood, and could act in an increased degree for myself, yet I was always on my guard against any tendency to such relapse. After getting these suspicions under my feet, I had been troubled by not being able to like Brother Hawkyard's manner, or his professed religion. So it came about, that, as I walked back that Sunday evening, I thought it would be an act of reparation for any such injury my struggling thoughts had unwillingly done him, if I wrote, and placed in his hands, before going to College, a full acknowledgment of his goodness to me, and an ample tribute of thanks. It might serve as an implied vindication of him against any dark scandal from a rival Brother and Expounder, or from any other quarter.

Accordingly I wrote the document with much care. I may add with much feeling, too, for it affected me as I went on. Having no set studies to pursue, in the brief interval between leaving the Foundation and going to Cambridge, I determined to walk out to his place of business and give it into his own hands.

It was a winter afternoon when I tapped at the door of his little counting-house, which was at the farther end of his long, low shop. As I did so (having entered by the back yard, where casks and boxes were taken in, and where there was the inscription, 'Private Way to the Counting-house'), a shopman called to me from the counter that he was engaged.

'Brother Gimblet,' said the shopman (who was one of the Brotherhood), 'is with him.'

I thought this all the better for my purpose, and made bold to tap again. They were talking in a low tone, and money was passing, for I heard it being counted out.

'Who is it?' asked Brother Hawkyard, sharply.

'George Silverman,' I answered, holding the door open. 'May I come in?'

Both Brothers seemed so astounded to see me that I felt shier than usual. But they looked quite cadaverous in the early gaslight, and perhaps that accidental circumstance exaggerated the expression of their faces.

'What is the matter?' asked Brother Hawkyard.

'Ay! What is the matter?' asked Brother Gimblet.

'Nothing at all,' I said, diffidently producing my document. 'I am only the bearer of a letter from myself.'

'From yourself, George?' cried Brother Hawkyard.

'And to you,' said I.

'And to me, George?'

He turned paler, and opened it hurriedly; but looking over it, and seeing generally what it was, became less hurried, recovered his colour, and said, 'Praise the Lord!'

'That's it!' cried Brother Gimblet. 'Well put! Amen.'

Brother Hawkyard then said, in a livelier strain: 'You must know, George, that Brother Gimblet and I are going to make our two businesses one. We are going into partnership. We are settling it now. Brother Gimblet is to take one clear half of the profits. (O yes! And he shall have it, he shall have it to the last farthing!)'

'D. V.!' said Brother Gimblet, with his right fist firmly clenched on his right leg.

'There is no objection,' pursued Brother Hawkyard, 'to my reading this aloud. George?'

As it was what I expressly desired should be done, after yesterday's prayer, I more than readily begged him to read it aloud. He did so, and Brother Gimblet listened with a crabbed smile.

'It was in a good hour that I came here,' he said, wrinkling up his eyes. 'It was in a good hour, likewise, that I was moved yesterday to depict for the terror of evil-doers a character the direct opposite of Brother Hawkyard's. But it was the Lord that done it. I felt him at it, while I was perspiring.'

After that, it was proposed by both of them that I should attend the congregation once more, before my final departure. What my shy reserve would undergo, from being expressly preached at and prayed at, I knew beforehand. But I reflected that it would be for the last time, and that it might add to the weight of my letter. It was well known to the Brothers and Sisters that there was no place taken for me in *their* Paradise; and if I showed this last token of deference to Brother Hawkyard, notoriously in despite of my own sinful inclinations, it might go some little way in aid of my statement that he had been good to me, and that I was grateful to him. Merely stipulating, therefore, that no express endeavor should be made for my conversion, – which would involve the rolling of several Brothers and Sisters on the floor, declaring that they felt all their sins in a heap on their left side, weighing so many pounds avoirdupois, as I knew from what I had seen of those repulsive mysteries, – I promised.

Since the reading of my letter, Brother Gimblet had been at intervals wiping one eye with an end of his spotted blue neckerchief, and grinning to himself. It was, however, a habit that Brother had, to grin in an ugly manner even while expounding. I call to mind a delighted snarl with which he used to detail from the platform the torments reserved for the wicked (meaning all human creation except the Brotherhood), as being remarkably hideous.

I left the two to settle their articles of partnership, and count money; and I never saw them again but on the following Sunday. Brother Hawkyard died within two or three years, leaving all he possessed to Brother Gimblet, in virtue of a will dated (as I have been told) that very day.

Now, I was so far at rest with myself when Sunday came, knowing that I had conquered my own mistrust, and righted Brother Hawkyard in the jaundiced vision of a rival, that I went, even to that coarse chapel, in a less sensitive state than usual. How could I foresee that the delicate, perhaps the diseased, corner of my mind, where I winced and shrunk when it was touched, or was even approached, would be handled as the theme of the whole proceedings?

On this occasion it was assigned to Brother Hawkyard to pray, and to Brother Gimblet to preach. The prayer was to open the ceremonies; the discourse was to come next. Brothers Hawkyard and Gimblet were both on the platform; Brother Hawkyard on his knees at the table, unmusically ready to pray; Brother Gimblet sitting against the wall, grinningly ready to preach.

'Let us offer up the sacrifice of prayer, my brothers and sisters and fellow-sinners.' Yes. But it was I who was the sacrifice. It was our poor sinful worldly-minded Brother here present who was wrestled for. The now-opening career of this our unawakened Brother might lead to his becoming a minister of what was called The Church. That was what *he* looked to. The Church. Not the chapel, Lord. The Church. No rectors, no vicars, no archdeacons, no bishops, no archbishops in the chapel, but, O Lord, many such in the Church! Protect our sinful Brother from his love of lucre. Cleanse from our unawakened Brother's breast his sin of worldly-mindedness. The prayer said infinitely more in words, but nothing more to any intelligible effect.

Then Brother Gimblet came forward, and took (as I knew he would) the text, My kingdom is not of this world. Ah! But whose was, my fellow-sinners? Whose? Why, our Brother's here present was. The only kingdom he had an idea of was of this world ('That's it!' from several of the congregation). What did the woman do when she lost the piece of money? Went and looked for it. What should our Brother do when he lost his way? ('Go and look for it,' from a Sister.) Go and look for it. True. But must he look for it in the right direction or in the wrong? ('In the right,' from a Brother.) There spake the prophets! He must look for it in the right direction, or he couldn't find it. But he had turned his back upon the right direction, and he wouldn't find it. Now, my fellow-sinners, to show you the difference betwixt worldly-mindedness and unworldly-mindedness, betwixt kingdoms not of this world and kingdoms *of* this world, here was a letter wrote by even our worldly-minded Brother unto Brother Hawkyard. Judge, from hearing of it read, whether Brother Hawkyard was the faithful steward that the Lord had in his mind only t' other day, when, in this very place, he drew you the picter of the unfaithful one. For it was him that done it, not me. Don't doubt that!

Brother Gimblet then grinned and bellowed his way through my composition, and subsequently through an hour. The service closed with a hymn, in which the Brothers unanimously roared, and the Sisters unanimously shrieked, at me, that I by wiles of worldly gain was mocked, and they on waters of sweet love were rocked; that I with Mammon struggled in the dark, while they were floating in a second Ark.

I went out from all this with an aching heart and a weary spirit; not because I was quite so weak as to consider these narrow creatures interpreters of the Divine majesty and wisdom; but because I was weak enough to feel as though it were my hard fortune to be misrepresented and misunderstood, when I most tried to subdue any risings of mere worldliness within me, and when I most hoped, that, by dint of trying earnestly, I had succeeded.

SEVENTH CHAPTER

My timidity and my obscurity occasioned me to live a secluded life at College, and to be little known. No relative ever came to visit me, for I had no relative. No intimate friends broke in upon my studies, for I made no intimate friends. I supported myself on my scholarship, and read much. My College time was otherwise not so very different from my time at Hoghton Towers.

Knowing myself to be unfit for the noisier stir of social existence, but believing myself qualified to do my duty in a moderate though earnest way if I could obtain some small preferment in the Church, I applied my mind to the clerical profession. In due sequence I took orders, was ordained, and began to look about me for employment. I must observe that I had taken a good degree, that I had succeeded in winning a good fellowship, and that my means were ample for my retired way of life. By this time I had read with several young men, and the occupation increased my income, while it was highly interesting to me. I once accidentally overheard our greatest Don say, to my boundless joy, 'That he heard it reported of Silverman that his gift of quiet explanation, his patience, his amiable temper, and his conscientiousness, made him the best of Coaches.' May my 'gift of quiet explanation' come more seasonably and powerfully to my aid in this present explanation than I think it will!

It may be, in a certain degree, owing to the situation of my College rooms (in a corner where the daylight was sobered), but it is in a much larger degree referable to the state of my own mind, that I seem to myself, on looking back to this time of my life, to have been always in the peaceful shade. I can see others in the sunlight; I can see our boats' crews and our athletic young men on the glistening water, or speckled with the moving lights of sunlit leaves; but I myself am always in the shadow looking on. Not unsympathetically, – God forbid! – but looking on, alone, much as I looked at Sylvia from the shadows of the ruined house, or looked at the red gleam shining through the farmer's windows, and listened to the fall of dancing feet, when all the ruin was dark that night in the quadrangle.

I now come to the reason of my quoting that laudation of myself above given. Without such reason, to repeat it would have been mere boastfulness.

Among those who had read with me was Mr Fareway, second son of Lady Fareway, widow of Sir Gaston Fareway, Baronet. This young gentleman's abilities were much above the average, but he came of a rich family, and was idle and luxurious. He presented himself to me too late, and afterwards came to me too irregularly, to admit of my being of much service to him. In the end I considered it my duty to dissuade him from going up for an examination which he could never pass, and he left College without taking a degree. After his departure, Lady Fareway wrote to me representing the justice of my returning half my fee, as I had been of so little use to her son. Within my knowledge a similar demand had not been made in any other case, and I most freely admit that the justice of it had not occurred to me until it was pointed out. But I at once perceived it, yielded to it, and returned the money.

Mr Fareway had been gone two years or more and I had forgotten him, when he one day walked into my rooms as I was sitting at my books.

Said he, after the usual salutations had passed: 'Mr Silverman, my mother is in town here, at the hotel, and wishes me to present you to her.'

I was not comfortable with strangers, and I dare say I betrayed that I was a little nervous or unwilling. For, said he, without my having spoken, 'I think the interview may tend to the advancement of your prospects.'

It put me to the blush to think that I should be tempted by a worldly reason, and I rose immediately.

Said Mr Fareway, as we went along, 'Are you a good hand at business?'

'I think not,' said I.

Said Mr Fareway then, 'My mother is.'

'Truly?' said I.

'Yes. My mother is what is usually called a managing woman. Doesn't make a bad thing, for instance, even out of the spendthrift habits of my eldest brother abroad. In short, a managing woman. This is in confidence.'

He had never spoken to me in confidence, and I was surprised by his doing so. I said I should respect his confidence, of course, and said no more on the delicate subject. We had but a little way to walk, and I was soon in his mother's company. He presented me, shook hands with me, and left us two (as he said) to business.

I saw in my Lady Fareway a handsome, well-preserved lady of somewhat large stature, with a steady glare in her great round dark eyes that embarrassed me.

Said my Lady: 'I have heard from my son, Mr Silverman, that you would be glad of some preferment in the Church?'

I gave my Lady to understand that was so.

'I don't know whether you are aware,' my Lady proceeded, 'that we have a presentation to a living? I say *we* have, but in point of fact *I* have.'

I gave my Lady to understand that I had not been aware of this.

Said my Lady: 'So it is. Indeed, I have two presentations: one, to two hundred a year; one, to six. Both livings are in our county, – North Devonshire, as you probably know. The first is vacant. Would you like it?'

What with my Lady's eyes, and what with the suddenness of this proposed gift, I was much confused.

'I am sorry it is not the larger presentation,' said my Lady, rather coldly, 'though I will not, Mr Silverman, pay you the bad compliment of supposing that *you* are, because that would be mercenary, – and mercenary I am persuaded you are not.'

Said I, with my utmost earnestness: 'Thank you, Lady Fareway, thank you, thank you! I should be deeply hurt if I thought I bore the character.'

'Naturally,' said my Lady. 'Always detestable, but particularly in a clergyman. You have not said whether you will like the Living?'

With apologies for my remissness or indistinctness, I assured my Lady that I accepted it most readily and gratefully. I added that I hoped she would not estimate my appreciation of the generosity of her choice by my flow of words, for I was not a ready man in that respect when taken by surprise or touched at heart.

'The affair is concluded,' said my Lady. 'Concluded. You will find the duties very light, Mr Silverman. Charming house; charming little garden, orchard, and all that. You will be able to take pupils. By the by! No. I will return to the word afterwards. What was I going to mention, when it put me out?'

My Lady stared at me, as if I knew. And I didn't know. And that perplexed me afresh.

Said my Lady, after some consideration: 'Oh! Of course. How very dull of me! The last incumbent, – least mercenary man I ever saw, – in consideration of the duties being so light and the house so delicious, couldn't rest, he said, unless I permitted him to help me with my correspondence, accounts, and various little things of that kind; nothing in themselves, but which it worries a lady to cope with. Would Mr Silverman also like to – ? Or shall I – ?'

I hastened to say that my poor help would be always at her ladyship's service.

'I am absolutely blessed,' said my Lady, casting up her eyes (and so taking them off of me for one moment), 'in having to do with gentlemen who cannot endure an approach to the idea of being mercenary!' She shivered at the word. 'And now as to the pupil.'

'The —?' I was quite at a loss.

'Mr Silverman, you have no idea what she is. She is,' said my Lady, laying her touch upon my coat-sleeve, 'I do verily believe, the most extraordinary girl in this world. Already knows more Greek and Latin than Lady Jane Grey. And taught herself! Has not yet, remember, derived a moment's advantage from Mr Silverman's classical acquirements. To say nothing of mathematics, which she is bent upon becoming versed in, and in which (as I hear from my son and others) Mr Silverman's reputation is so deservedly high!'

Under my Lady's eyes, I must have lost the clew, I felt persuaded; and yet I did not know where I could have dropped it.

'Adelina,' said my Lady, 'is my only daughter. If I did not feel quite convinced that I am not blinded by a mother's partiality; unless I was absolutely sure that when you know her, Mr Silverman, you will esteem it a high and unusual privilege to direct her studies, – I should introduce a mercenary element into this conversation, and ask you on what terms –'

I entreated my Lady to go no further. My Lady saw that I was troubled, and did me the honour to comply with my request.

EIGHTH CHAPTER

Everything in mental acquisition that her brother might have been, if he would, and everything in all gracious charms and admirable qualities that no one but herself could be, – this was Adelina.

I will not expatiate upon her beauty. I will not expatiate upon her intelligence, her quickness of perception, her powers of memory, her sweet consideration from the first moment for the slow-paced tutor who ministered to her wonderful gifts. I was thirty then; I am over sixty now; she is ever present to me in these hours as she was in those, bright and beautiful and young, wise and fanciful and good.

When I discovered that I loved her, how can I say? In the first day? In the first week? In the first month? Impossible to trace. If I be (as I am) unable to represent to myself any previous period of my life as quite separable from her attracting power, how can I answer for this one detail?

Whensoever I made the discovery, it laid a heavy burden on me. And yet, comparing it with the far heavier burden that I afterwards took up, it does not seem to me now to have been very hard to bear. In the knowledge that I did love her, and that I should love her while my life lasted, and that I was ever to hide my secret deep in my own breast, and she was never to find it, there was a kind of sustaining joy or pride or comfort mingled with my pain.

But later on – say a year later on – when I made another discovery, then indeed my suffering and my struggle were strong. That other discovery was – ?

These words will never see the light, if ever, until my heart is dust; until her bright spirit has returned to the regions of which, when imprisoned here, it surely retained some unusual glimpse of remembrance; until all the pulses that ever beat around us shall have long been quiet; until all the fruits of all the tiny victories and defeats achieved in our little breasts shall have withered away. That discovery was, that she loved me.

She may have enhanced my knowledge, and loved me for that; she may have overvalued my discharge of duty to her, and loved me for that; she may have refined upon a playful compassion which she would sometimes show for what she called my want of wisdom according to the light of the world's dark lanterns, and loved me for that; she may – she must – have confused the borrowed light of what I had only learned, with its brightness in its pure original rays; but she loved me at that time, and she made me know it.

Pride of family and pride of wealth put me as far off from her in my Lady's eyes as if I had been some domesticated creature of another kind. But they could not put me farther from her than I put myself when I set my merits against hers. More than that. They could not put me, by millions of fathoms, half so low beneath her as I put myself when in imagination I took advantage of her noble trustfulness, took the fortune that I knew she must possess in her own right, and left her to find herself, in the zenith of her beauty and genius, bound to poor rusty plodding Me.

No. Worldliness should not enter here, at any cost. If I had tried to keep it out of other ground, how much harder was I bound to try to keep it from this sacred place.

But there was something daring in her broad generous character that demanded at so delicate a crisis to be delicately and patiently addressed. After many and many a bitter night (O, I found I could cry for reasons not purely physical, at this pass of my life!) I took my course.

My Lady had in our first interview unconsciously overstated the accommodation of my pretty house. There was room in it for only one pupil. He was a young gentleman near coming of age, very well connected, but what is called a poor relation. His parents were dead. The charges of his living and reading with me were defrayed by an uncle, and he and I were to do our utmost together for three years towards qualifying him to make his way. At this time he had entered into his second year with me. He was well-looking, clever, energetic, enthusiastic, bold; in the best sense of the term, a thorough young Anglo-Saxon.

I resolved to bring these two together.

NINTH CHAPTER

Said I, one night when I had conquered myself: 'Mr Granville,' – Mr Granville Wharton his name was, – 'I doubt if you have ever yet so much as seen Miss Fareway.'

'Well, sir,' returned he, laughing, 'you see her so much yourself, that you hardly leave another fellow a chance of seeing her.'

'I am her tutor, you know,' said I.

And there the subject dropped for that time. But I so contrived as that they should come together shortly afterwards. I had previously so contrived as to keep them asunder, for while I loved her – I mean before I had determined on my sacrifice – a lurking jealousy of Mr Granville lay within my unworthy breast.

It was quite an ordinary interview in the Fareway Park; but they talked easily together for some time; like takes to like, and they had many points of resemblance. Said Mr Granville to me, when he and I sat at our supper that night: 'Miss Fareway is remarkably beautiful, sir, and remarkably engaging. Don't you think so?' 'I think so,' said I. And I stole a glance at him, and saw that he had reddened and was thoughtful. I remember it most vividly, because the mixed feeling of grave pleasure and acute pain that the slight circumstance caused me was the first of a long, long series of such mixed impressions under which my hair turned slowly gray.

I had not much need to feign to be subdued, but I counterfeited to be older than I was in all respects, (Heaven knows, my heart being all too young the while!) and feigned to be more of a recluse and bookworm than I had really become, and gradually set up more and more of a fatherly manner towards Adelina. Likewise, I made my tuition less imaginative than before; separated myself from my poets and philosophers; was, careful to present them in their own light, and me, their lowly servant, in my own shade.

Moreover, in the matter of apparel I was equally mindful. Not that I had ever been dapper that way, but that I was slovenly now.

As I depressed myself with one hand, so did I labor to raise Mr Granville with the other; directing his attention to such subjects as I too well knew most interested her, and fashioning him (do not deride or misconstrue the expression, unknown reader of this writing, for I have suffered!) into a greater resemblance to myself in my solitary one strong aspect. And gradually, gradually, as I saw him take more and more to these thrown-out lures of mine, then did I come to know better and better that love was drawing him on, and was drawing Her from me.

So passed more than another year; every day a year in its number of my mixed impressions of grave pleasure and acute pain; and then, these two being of age and free to act legally for themselves, came before me, hand in hand (my hair being now quite white), and entreated me that I would unite them together. 'And indeed, dear Tutor,' said Adelina, 'it is but consistent in you that you should do this thing for us, seeing that we should never have spoken together that first time but for you, and that but for you we could never have met so often afterwards.' The whole of which was literally true, for I had availed myself on my many business attendances on, and conferences with, my Lady, to take Mr Granville to the house, and leave him in the outer room with Adelina.

I knew that my Lady would object to such a marriage for her daughter, or to any marriage that was other than an exchange of her for stipulated lands, goods, and moneys. But, looking on the two, and seeing with full eyes that they were both young and beautiful; and knowing that they were alike in the tastes and acquirements that will outlive youth and beauty; and considering that Adelina had a fortune now, in her own keeping; and considering further that Mr Granville, though for the present poor, was of a good family that had never lived in a cellar in Preston; and believing that their love would endure, neither having any great discrepancy to find out in the other, – I told them of my readiness to do this thing which Adelina asked of her dear Tutor, and to send them forth, Husband and Wife, into the shining world with golden gates that awaited them.

It was on a summer morning that I rose before the sun, to compose myself for the crowning of my work with this end. And my dwelling being near to the sea, I walked down to the rocks on the shore, in order that I might behold the sun rise in his majesty.

The tranquillity upon the Deep and on the firmament, the orderly withdrawal of the stars, the calm promise of coming day, the rosy suffusion of the sky and waters, the ineffable splendor that then burst forth, attuned my mind afresh after the discords of the night. Methought that all I looked on said to me, and that all I heard in the sea and in the air said to me, 'Be comforted, mortal, that thy life is so short. Our preparation for what is to follow has endured, and shall endure, for unimaginable ages.'

I married them. I knew that my hand was cold when I placed it on their hands clasped together; but the words with which I had to accompany the action I could say without faltering, and I was at peace.

They being well away from my house and from the place, after our simple breakfast, the time was come when I must do what I had pledged myself to them that I would do, – break the intelligence to my Lady.

I went up to the house, and found my Lady in her ordinary business-room. She happened to have an unusual amount of commissions to intrust to me that day, and she had filled my hands with papers before I could originate a word.

'My Lady,' – I then began, as I stood beside her table.

'Why, what's the matter?' she said, quickly, looking up.

'Not much, I would fain hope, after you shall have prepared yourself, and considered a little.'

'Prepared myself! And considered a little! You appear to have prepared *your*self but indifferently, anyhow, Mr Silverman.' This, mighty scornfully, as I experienced my usual embarrassment under her stare.

Said I, in self-extenuation, once for all: 'Lady Fareway, I have but to say for myself that I have tried to do my duty.'

'For yourself?' repeated my Lady. 'Then there are others concerned, I see. Who are they?'

I was about to answer, when she made towards the bell with a dart that stopped me, and said, 'Why, where is Adelina?'

'Forbear. Be calm, my Lady. I married her this morning to Mr Granville Wharton.'

She set her lips, looked more intently at me than ever, raised her right hand and smote me hard upon the cheek.

'Give me back those papers, give me back those papers!' She tore them out of my hands and tossed them on her table. Then seating herself defiantly in her great chair, and folding her arms, she stabbed me to the heart with the unlooked-for reproach: 'You worldly wretch!'

'Worldly?' I cried. 'Worldly!'

'This, if you please,' she went on with supreme scorn, pointing me out as if there were some one there to see, – 'this, if you please, is the disinterested scholar, with not a design beyond his books! This, if you please, is the simple creature whom any one could overreach in a bargain! This, if you please, is Mr Silverman! Not of this world, not he! He has too much simplicity for this world's cunning. He has too much singleness of purpose to be a match for this world's double-dealing. What did he give you for it?'

'For what? And who?'

'How much,' she asked, bending forward in her great chair, and insultingly tapping the fingers of her right hand on the palm of her left, – 'how much does Mr Granville Wharton pay you for getting him Adelina's money? What is the amount of your percentage upon Adelina's fortune? What were the terms of the agreement that you proposed to this boy when you, the Reverend George Silverman, licensed to marry, engaged to put him in possession of this girl? You made good terms for yourself, whatever they were. He would stand a poor chance against your keenness.'

Bewildered, horrified, stunned by this cruel perversion, I could not speak. But I trust that I looked innocent, being so.

'Listen to me, shrewd hypocrite,' said my Lady, whose anger increased as she gave it utterance. 'Attend to my words, you cunning schemer who have carried this plot through with such a practised double face that I have never suspected you. I had my projects for my daughter; projects for family connection; projects for fortune. You have thwarted them, and overreached me; but I am not one to be thwarted and overreached without retaliation. Do you mean to hold this Living another month?'

'Do you deem it possible, Lady Fareway, that I can hold it another hour, under your injurious words?'

'Is it resigned, then?'

'It was mentally resigned, my Lady, some minutes ago.'

'Don't equivocate, sir. *Is* it resigned?'

'Unconditionally and entirely. And I would that I had never, never come near it!'

'A cordial response from me to *that* wish, Mr Silverman! But take this with you, sir. If you had not resigned it, I would have had you deprived of it. And though you have resigned it, you will not get quit of me as easily as you think for. I will pursue you with this story. I will make this nefarious conspiracy of yours, for money, known. You have made money by it, but you have at the same time made an enemy by it. *You* will take good care that the money sticks to you; *I* will take good care that the enemy sticks to you.'

Then said I, finally: 'Lady Fareway, I think my heart is broken. Until I came into this room just now, the possibility of such mean wickedness as you have imputed to me never dawned upon my thoughts. Your suspicions –'

'Suspicions! Pah!' said she, indignantly. 'Certainties.'

'Your certainties, my Lady, as you call them, your suspicions, as I call them, are cruel, unjust, wholly devoid of foundation in fact. I can declare no more, except that I have not acted for my own profit or my own pleasure. I have not in this proceeding considered myself. Once again, I think my heart is broken. If I have unwittingly done any wrong with a righteous motive, that is some penalty to pay.'

She received this with another and a more indignant 'Pah!' and I made my way out of her room (I think I felt my way out with my hands, although my eyes were open), almost suspecting that my voice had a repulsive sound, and that I was a repulsive object.

There was a great stir made, the Bishop was appealed to, I received a severe reprimand, and narrowly escaped suspension. For years a cloud hung over me, and my name was tarnished. But my heart did not break, if a broken heart involves death; for I lived through it.

They stood by me, Adelina and her husband, through it all. Those who had known me at College, and even most of those who had only known me there by reputation, stood by me too. Little by little, the belief widened that I was not capable of what was laid to my charge. At length I was presented to a College-Living in a sequestered place, and there I now pen my Explanation. I pen it at my open window in the summer-time; before me, lying the churchyard, equal resting-place for sound hearts, wounded hearts, and broken hearts. I pen it for the relief of my own mind, not foreseeing whether or no it will ever have a reader.

Notes

p. 20   *Preston* - a town in the North of England

p. 20   *feint* - dodge

p. 20   *courtful* - London housing, including some of the worst slums in the nineteenth century, was often arranged in squares or courts, so a courtful is a number of houses

p. 21   *camphor . . . vinegar* - the transmission of disease by bacteria was not understood and it was thought that camphor and vinegar could ward off sickness by purifying the air; it was understood that diseases such as typhoid were infectious in some way, however, and so the infected were much feared and shunned, as in this story

p. 21   *gaiters* - covering for lower legs

p. 22   *Ward* - the 'casual ward' of a workhouse, a rough emergency lodging, a doss house

p. 22   *porringer* - small bowl

p. 22   *denomination or congregation* - sect or group within the Protestant Church

p. 23   *mullioned* - a window divided into sections with stone or wooden bars

p. 23   *First James of England* - first Stuart king reigned 1603–1625

p. 23   *Steam Power* - i.e. the people of that era could not have foreseen that the area would become dominated by coal mines – producing the coal needed for the steam that ran the industrial revolution

p. 24   *scrambling board* - struggling to be fed, so a meagre diet

p. 26   *Foundation . . . College . . . Fellowship* - an educational charity providing scholarships for poor boys to school and then a college at Oxford or Cambridge University

p. 26   *drysalter* - a dealer in dried food, preserves and medicines

p. 27   *hisself* - himself

p. 27   *myrrh . . . frankincense . . . Amber* - (quoting from the Bible in a confused way) – precious gifts

p. 27   *Temple* - i.e. a pretentious reference to his church

p. 27   *didn't know round O from crooked S* - i.e. were ignorant, unlearned – Brother Hawkyard is criticising educated people such as the hero

p. 29   *D. V.* - *Deo Volente*: God willing

p. 30   *lucre* - money

p. 30   *Mammon . . . Ark* - more confused Biblical quoting in Hawkyard's sermon –
          Ark referring to Noah's ark, suggesting he and his chosen followers are
          saved, while George is still wrestling with the devil
p. 31   *Don* - teaching fellow at the University
p. 31   *preferment . . . presentation to a living* - landowning families and the
          aristocracy had the power to prefer – appoint clergymen to a paid post or
          'living' as vicars/rectors of churches on their estates

The Nightingale and the Rose

(1888)

Oscar Wilde

Wilde was an Irish playwright, poet and author of essays and stories, who is famous for his witty comedies such as The Importance of Being Earnest. *His stories have a different quality but are still dramatic, in that they are very good to read aloud. From* The Happy Prince, *a book of tales for children and adults, this story about love and beauty is a perfect example of Wilde's poetic style.*

'She said that she would dance with me if I brought her red roses,' cried the young Student; 'but in all my garden there is no red rose.'

From her nest in the holm-oak tree the Nightingale heard him, and she looked out through the leaves, and wondered.

'No red rose in all my garden!' he cried, and his beautiful eyes filled with tears. 'Ah, on what little things does happiness depend! I have read all that the wise men have written, and all the secrets of philosophy are mine, yet for want of a red rose is my life made wretched.'

'Here at last is a true lover,' said the Nightingale. 'Night after night have I sung of him, though I knew him not: night after night have I told his story to the stars, and now I see him. His hair is dark as the hyacinth-blossom, and his lips are red as the rose of his desire; but passion has made his face like pale ivory, and sorrow has set her seal upon his brow.'

'The Prince gives a ball to-morrow night,' murmured the young Student, 'and my love will be of the company. If I bring her a red rose she will dance with me till dawn. If I bring her a red rose, I shall hold her in my arms, and she will lean her head upon my shoulder, and her hand will be clasped in mine. But there is no red rose in my garden, so I shall sit lonely, and she will pass me by. She will have no heed of me, and my heart will break.'

'Here indeed is the true lover,' said the Nightingale. 'What I sing of, he suffers: what is joy to me, to him is pain. Surely Love is a wonderful thing. It is more precious than emeralds, and dearer than fine opals. Pearls and pomegranates cannot buy it, nor is it set forth in the market-place. It may not be purchased of the merchants, nor can it be weighed out in the balance for gold.'

'The musicians will sit in their gallery,' said the young Student, 'and play upon their stringed instruments, and my love will dance to the sound of the harp and the violin. She will dance so lightly that her feet will not touch the floor, and the courtiers in their gay dresses will throng round her. But with me she will not dance, for I have no red rose to give her;' and he flung himself down on the grass, and buried his face in his hands, and wept.

'Why is he weeping?' asked a little Green Lizard, as he ran past him with his tail in the air.

'Why, indeed?' said a Butterfly, who was fluttering about after a sunbeam.

'Why, indeed?' whispered a Daisy to his neighbour, in a soft, low voice.

'He is weeping for a red rose,' said the Nightingale.

'For a red rose!' they cried; 'how very ridiculous!' and the little Lizard, who was something of a cynic, laughed outright.

But the Nightingale understood the secret of the Student's sorrow, and she sat silent in the oak-tree, and thought about the mystery of Love.

Suddenly she spread her brown wings for flight, and soared into the air. She passed through the grove like a shadow, and like a shadow she sailed across the garden.

In the centre of the grass-plot was standing a beautiful Rose-tree, and when she saw it, she flew over to it, and lit upon a spray.

'Give me a red rose,' she cried, 'and I will sing you my sweetest song.'

But the Tree shook its head.

'My roses are white,' it answered; 'as white as the foam of the sea, and whiter than the snow upon the mountain. But go to my brother who grows round the old sun-dial, and perhaps he will give you what you want.'

So the Nightingale flew over to the Rose-tree that was growing round the old sun-dial.

'Give me a red rose,' she cried, 'and I will sing you my sweetest song.'

But the Tree shook its head.

'My roses are yellow,' it answered; 'as yellow as the hair of the mermaiden who sits upon an amber throne, and yellower than the daffodil that blooms in the meadow before the mower comes with his scythe. But go to my brother who grows beneath the Student's window, and perhaps he will give you what you want.'

So the Nightingale flew over to the Rose-tree that was growing beneath the Student's window.

'Give me a red rose,' she cried, 'and I will sing you my sweetest song.'

But the Tree shook its head.

'My roses are red,' it answered, 'as red as the feet of the dove, and redder than the great fans of coral that wave and wave in the ocean-cavern. But the winter has chilled my veins, and the frost has nipped my buds, and the storm has broken my branches, and I shall have no roses at all this year.'

'One red rose is all I want,' cried the Nightingale, 'only one red rose! Is there no way by which I can get it?'

'There is a way,' answered the Tree; 'but it is so terrible that I dare not tell it to you.'

'Tell it to me,' said the Nightingale, 'I am not afraid.'

'If you want a red rose,' said the Tree, 'you must build it out of music by moonlight, and stain it with your own heart's-blood. You must sing to me with your breast against a thorn. All night long you must sing to me, and the thorn must pierce your heart, and your life-blood must flow into my veins, and become mine.'

'Death is a great price to pay for a red rose,' cried the Nightingale, 'and Life is very dear to all. It is pleasant to sit in the green wood, and to watch the Sun in his chariot of gold, and the Moon in her chariot of pearl. Sweet is the scent of the hawthorn, and sweet are the bluebells that hide in the valley, and the heather that blows on the hill. Yet Love is better than Life, and what is the heart of a bird compared to the heart of a man?'

So she spread her brown wings for flight, and soared into the air. She swept over the garden like a shadow, and like a shadow she sailed through the grove.

The young Student was still lying on the grass, where she had left him, and the tears were not yet dry in his beautiful eyes.

'Be happy,' cried the Nightingale, 'be happy; you shall have your red rose. I will build it out of music by moonlight, and stain it with my own heart's-blood. All that I ask of you in return is that you will be a true lover, for Love is wiser than Philosophy, though she is wise, and mightier than Power, though he is mighty. Flame-coloured are his wings, and coloured like flame is his body. His lips are sweet as honey, and his breath is like frankincense.'

The Student looked up from the grass, and listened, but he could not understand what the Nightingale was saying to him, for he only knew the things that are written down in books.

But the Oak-tree understood, and felt sad, for he was very fond of the little Nightingale who had built her nest in his branches.

'Sing me one last song,' he whispered; 'I shall feel very lonely when you are gone.'

So the Nightingale sang to the Oak-tree, and her voice was like water bubbling from a silver jar.

When she had finished her song the Student got up, and pulled a note-book and a lead-pencil out of his pocket.

'She has form,' he said to himself, as he walked away through the grove – 'that cannot be denied to her; but has she got feeling? I am afraid not. In fact, she is like most artists; she is all style, without any sincerity. She would not sacrifice herself for others. She thinks merely of music, and everybody knows that the arts are selfish. Still, it must be admitted that she has some beautiful notes in her voice. What a pity it is that they do not mean anything, or do any practical good.' And he went into his room, and lay down on his little pallet-bed, and began to think of his love; and, after a time, he fell asleep.

And when the Moon shone in the heavens the Nightingale flew to the Rose-tree, and set her breast against the thorn. All night long she sang with her breast against the thorn, and the cold crystal Moon leaned down and listened. All night long she sang, and the thorn went deeper and deeper into her breast, and her life-blood ebbed away from her.

She sang first of the birth of love in the heart of a boy and a girl. And on the topmost spray of the Rose-tree there blossomed a marvellous rose, petal following petal, as song followed song. Pale was it, at first, as the mist that hangs over the river – pale as the feet of the morning, and silver as the wings of the dawn. As the shadow of a rose in a mirror of silver, as the shadow of a rose in a water-pool, so was the rose that blossomed on the topmost spray of the Tree.

But the Tree cried to the Nightingale to press closer against the thorn. 'Press closer, little Nightingale,' cried the Tree, 'or the Day will come before the rose is finished.'

So the Nightingale pressed closer against the thorn, and louder and louder grew her song, for she sang of the birth of passion in the soul of a man and a maid.

And a delicate flush of pink came into the leaves of the rose, like the flush in the face of the bridegroom when he kisses the lips of the bride. But the thorn had not yet reached her heart, so the rose's heart remained white, for only a Nightingale's heart's-blood can crimson the heart of a rose.

And the Tree cried to the Nightingale to press closer against the thorn. 'Press closer, little Nightingale,' cried the Tree, 'or the Day will come before the rose is finished.'

So the Nightingale pressed closer against the thorn, and the thorn touched her heart, and a fierce pang of pain shot through her. Bitter, bitter was the pain, and wilder and wilder grew her song, for she sang of the Love that is perfected by Death, of the Love that dies not in the tomb.

And the marvellous rose became crimson, like the rose of the eastern sky. Crimson was the girdle of petals, and crimson as a ruby was the heart.

But the Nightingale's voice grew fainter, and her little wings began to beat, and a film came over her eyes. Fainter and fainter grew her song, and she felt something choking her in her throat.

Then she gave one last burst of music. The white Moon heard it, and she forgot the dawn, and lingered on in the sky. The red rose heard it, and it trembled all over with ecstasy, and opened its petals to the cold morning air. Echo bore it to her purple cavern in the hills, and woke the sleeping shepherds from their dreams. It floated through the reeds of the river, and they carried its message to the sea.

'Look, look!' cried the Tree, 'the rose is finished now;' but the Nightingale made no answer, for she was lying dead in the long grass, with the thorn in her heart.

And at noon the Student opened his window and looked out.

'Why, what a wonderful piece of luck!' he cried; 'here is a red rose! I have never seen any rose like it in all my life. It is so beautiful that I am sure it has a long Latin name;' and he leaned down and plucked it.

Then he put on his hat, and ran up to the Professor's house with the rose in his hand.

The daughter of the Professor was sitting in the doorway winding blue silk on a reel, and her little dog was lying at her feet.

'You said that you would dance with me if I brought you a red rose,' cried the Student. 'Here is the reddest rose in all the world. You will wear it to-night next your heart, and as we dance together it will tell you how I love you.'

But the girl frowned.

'I am afraid it will not go with my dress,' she answered; 'and, besides, the Chamberlain's nephew has sent me some real jewels, and everybody knows that jewels cost far more than flowers.'

'Well, upon my word, you are very ungrateful,' said the Student angrily; and he threw the rose into the street, where it fell into the gutter, and a cart-wheel went over it.

'Ungrateful!' said the girl. 'I tell you what, you are very rude; and, after all, who are you? Only a Student. Why, I don't believe you have even got silver buckles to your shoes as the Chamberlain's nephew has;' and she got up from her chair and went into the house.

'What a silly thing Love is,' said the Student as he walked away. 'It is not half as useful as Logic, for it does not prove anything, and it is always telling one of things that are not going to happen, and making one believe things that are not true. In fact, it is quite unpractical, and, as in this age to be practical is everything, I shall go back to Philosophy and study Metaphysics.'

So he returned to his room and pulled out a great dusty book, and began to read.

Notes

p. 41   *Nightingale* - a small brown bird with a famously beautiful, musical song

p. 41   *holm-oak tree* - an evergreen tree

p. 42   *mermaiden* - mythical sea creature, a woman with a tail like a fish

p. 43   *frankincense* - a scented oil from the East

p. 43   *pallet-bed* - a hard, narrow bed

p. 44   *Echo* - in Greek mythology, Echo was a nymph who was only able to speak the last words of others, and could not tell her love for Narcissus, who then saw his reflection in a pool and fell in love with himself

p. 45   *Chamberlain* - a court official in charge of the royal household

p. 45   *Metaphysics* - type of philosophy dealing with abstract ideas

6

An Occurrence at Owl Creek Bridge

(1888)

Ambrose Bierce

Bierce was an American writer of short stories and a journalist, best known for his bitterly satirical stories told with deadly precision and great tension. In this story, set during the Civil War, the Federal army have captured a Southerner who has been sabotaging their advance and he is about to be executed.

I

A man stood upon a railroad bridge in northern Alabama, looking down into the swift water twenty feet below. The man's hands were behind his back, the wrists bound with a cord. A rope closely encircled his neck. It was attached to a stout cross-timber above his head and the slack fell to the level of his knees. Some loose boards laid upon the sleepers supporting the metals of the railway supplied a footing for him and his executioners—two private soldiers of the Federal army, directed by a sergeant who in civil life may have been a deputy sheriff. At a short remove upon the same temporary platform was an officer in the uniform of his rank, armed. He was a captain. A sentinel at each end of the bridge stood with his rifle in the position known as "support," that is to say, vertical in front of the left shoulder, the hammer resting on the forearm thrown straight across the chest—a formal and unnatural position, enforcing an erect carriage of the body. It did not appear to be the duty of these two men to know what was occurring at the centre of the bridge; they merely blockaded the two ends of the foot planking that traversed it.

Beyond one of the sentinels nobody was in sight; the railroad ran straight away into a forest for a hundred yards, then, curving, was lost to view. Doubtless there was an outpost farther along. The other bank of the stream was open ground—a gentle acclivity topped with a stockade of vertical tree trunks, loopholed for rifles, with a single embrasure through which protruded the muzzle of a brass cannon commanding the bridge. Midway of the slope between bridge and fort were the spectators—a single company of infantry in line, at "parade rest," the butts of the rifles on the ground, the barrels inclining slightly backward against the right shoulder, the hands crossed upon the stock. A lieutenant stood at the right of the line, the point of his sword upon the ground, his left hand resting upon his right. Excepting the group of four at the centre of the bridge, not a man moved. The company faced the bridge, staring stonily, motionless. The sentinels, facing the banks of the stream, might have been statues to adorn the bridge. The captain stood with folded arms, silent, observing the work of his subordinates, but making no sign. Death is a dignitary who when he comes announced is to be received with formal manifestations of respect, even by those most familiar with him. In the code of military etiquette silence and fixity are forms of deference.

The man who was engaged in being hanged was apparently about thirty-five years of age. He was a civilian, if one might judge from his habit, which was that of a planter. His features were good—a straight nose, firm mouth, broad forehead, from which his long, dark hair was combed straight back, falling behind his ears to the collar of his well-fitting frock-coat. He wore a mustache and pointed beard, but no whiskers; his eyes were large and dark gray, and had a kindly expression which one would hardly have expected in one whose neck was in the hemp. Evidently this was no vulgar assassin. The liberal military code makes provision for hanging many kinds of persons, and gentlemen are not excluded.

The preparations being complete, the two private soldiers stepped aside and each drew away the plank upon which he had been standing. The sergeant turned to the captain, saluted and placed himself immediately behind that officer, who in turn moved apart one pace. These movements left the condemned man and the sergeant standing on the two ends of the same plank, which spanned three of the cross-ties of the bridge. The end upon which the civilian stood almost, but not quite, reached a fourth. This plank had been held in place by the weight of the captain; it was now held by that of the sergeant. At a signal from the former the latter would step aside, the plank would tilt and the condemned man go down between two ties. The arrangement commended itself to his judgment as simple and effective. His face had not been covered nor his eyes bandaged. He looked a moment at his "unsteadfast footing," then let his gaze wander to the swirling water of the stream racing madly beneath his feet. A piece of dancing driftwood caught his attention and his eyes followed it down the current. How slowly it appeared to move! What a sluggish stream!

He closed his eyes in order to fix his last thoughts upon his wife and children. The water, touched to gold by the early sun, the brooding mists under the banks at some distance down the stream, the fort, the soldiers, the piece of drift—all had distracted him. And now he became conscious of a new disturbance. Striking through the thought of his dear ones was a sound which he could neither ignore nor understand, a sharp, distinct, metallic percussion like the stroke of a blacksmith's hammer upon the anvil; it had the same ringing quality. He wondered what it was, and whether immeasurably distant or near by—it seemed both. Its recurrence was regular, but as slow as the tolling of a death knell. He awaited each stroke with impatience and—he knew not why—apprehension. The intervals of silence grew progressively longer; the delays became maddening. With their greater infrequency the sounds increased in strength and sharpness. They hurt his ear like the thrust of a knife; he feared he would shriek. What he heard was the ticking of his watch.

He unclosed his eyes and saw again the water below him. "If I could free my hands," he thought, "I might throw off the noose and spring into the stream. By diving I could evade the bullets and, swimming vigorously, reach the bank, take to the woods and get away home. My home, thank God, is as yet outside their lines; my wife and little ones are still beyond the invader's farthest advance."

As these thoughts, which have here to be set down in words, were flashed into the doomed man's brain rather than evolved from it the captain nodded to the sergeant. The sergeant stepped aside.

II

Peyton Farquhar was a well-to-do planter, of an old and highly respected Alabama family. Being a slave owner and like other slave owners a politician he was naturally an original secessionist and ardently devoted to the Southern cause. Circumstances of an imperious nature, which it is unnecessary to relate here, had prevented him from taking service with the gallant army that had fought the disastrous campaigns ending with the fall of Corinth, and he chafed under the inglorious restraint, longing for the release of his energies, the larger life of the soldier, the opportunity for distinction. That opportunity, he felt, would come, as it comes to all in war time. Meanwhile he did what he could. No service was too humble for him to perform in aid of the South, no adventure too perilous for him to undertake if consistent with the character of a civilian who was at heart a soldier, and who in good faith and without too much qualification assented to at least a part of the frankly villainous dictum that all is fair in love and war.

One evening while Farquhar and his wife were sitting on a rustic bench near the entrance to his grounds, a gray-clad soldier rode up to the gate and asked for a drink of water. Mrs. Farquhar was only too happy to serve him with her own white hands. While she was fetching the water her husband approached the dusty horseman and inquired eagerly for news from the front.

"The Yanks are repairing the railroads," said the man, "and are getting ready for another advance. They have reached the Owl Creek bridge, put it in order and built a stockade on the north bank. The commandant has issued an order, which is posted everywhere, declaring that any civilian caught interfering with the railroad, its bridges, tunnels or trains will be summarily hanged. I saw the order."

"How far is it to the Owl Creek bridge?" Farquhar asked.

"About thirty miles."

"Is there no force on this side the creek?"

"Only a picket post half a mile out, on the railroad, and a single sentinel at this end of the bridge."

"Suppose a man—a civilian and student of hanging—should elude the picket post and perhaps get the better of the sentinel," said Farquhar, smiling, "what could he accomplish?"

The soldier reflected. "I was there a month ago," he replied. "I observed that the flood of last winter had lodged a great quantity of driftwood against the wooden pier at this end of the bridge. It is now dry and would burn like tow."

The lady had now brought the water, which the soldier drank. He thanked her ceremoniously, bowed to her husband and rode away. An hour later, after nightfall, he repassed the plantation, going northward in the direction from which he had come. He was a Federal scout.

III

As Peyton Farquhar fell straight downward through the bridge he lost consciousness and was as one already dead. From this state he was awakened—ages later, it seemed to him—by the pain of a sharp pressure upon his throat, followed by a sense of suffocation. Keen, poignant agonies seemed to shoot from his neck downward through every fibre of his body and limbs. These pains appeared to flash along well-defined lines of ramification and to beat with an inconceivably rapid periodicity. They seemed like streams of pulsating fire heating him to an intolerable temperature. As to his head, he was conscious of nothing but a feeling of fulness—of congestion. These sensations were unaccompanied by thought. The intellectual part of his nature was already effaced; he had power only to feel, and feeling was torment. He was conscious of motion. Encompassed in a luminous cloud, of which he was now merely the fiery heart, without material substance, he swung through unthinkable arcs of oscillation, like a vast pendulum. Then all at once, with terrible suddenness, the light about him shot upward with the noise of a loud plash; a frightful roaring was in his ears, and all was cold and dark. The power of thought was restored; he knew that the rope had broken and he had fallen into the stream. There was no additional strangulation; the noose about his neck was already suffocating him and kept the water from his lungs. To die of hanging at the bottom of a river!—the idea seemed to him ludicrous. He opened his eyes in the darkness and saw above him a gleam of light, but how distant, how inaccessible! He was still sinking, for the light became fainter and fainter until it was a mere glimmer. Then it began to grow and brighten, and he knew that he was rising toward the surface—knew it with reluctance, for he was now very comfortable. "To be hanged and drowned," he thought, "that is not so bad; but I do not wish to be shot. No; I will not be shot; that is not fair."

He was not conscious of an effort, but a sharp pain in his wrist apprised him that he was trying to free his hands. He gave the struggle his attention, as an idler might observe the feat of a juggler, without interest in the outcome. What splendid effort!—what magnificent, what superhuman strength! Ah, that was a fine endeavor! Bravo! The cord fell away; his arms parted and floated upward, the hands dimly seen on each side in the growing light. He watched them with a new interest as first one and then the other pounced upon the noose at his neck. They tore it away and thrust it fiercely aside, its undulations resembling those of a water-snake. "Put it back, put it back!" He thought he shouted these words to his hands, for the undoing of the noose had been succeeded by the direst pang that he had yet experienced. His neck ached horribly; his brain was on fire; his heart, which had been fluttering faintly, gave a great leap, trying to force itself out at his mouth. His whole body was racked and wrenched with an insupportable anguish! But his disobedient hands gave no heed to the command. They beat the water vigorously with quick, downward strokes, forcing him to the surface. He felt his head emerge; his eyes were blinded by the sunlight; his chest expanded convulsively, and with a supreme and crowning agony his lungs engulfed a great draught of air, which instantly he expelled in a shriek!

He was now in full possession of his physical senses. They were, indeed, preternaturally keen and alert. Something in the awful disturbance of his organic system had so exalted and refined them that they made record of things never before perceived. He felt the ripples upon his face and heard their separate sounds as they struck.

He looked at the forest on the bank of the stream, saw the individual trees, the leaves and the veining of each leaf—saw the very insects upon them: the locusts, the brilliant-bodied flies, the gray spiders stretching their webs from twig to twig. He noted the prismatic colors in all the dewdrops upon a million blades of grass. The humming of the gnats that danced above the eddies of the stream, the beating of the dragon-flies' wings, the strokes of the water-spiders' legs, like oars which had lifted their boat—all these made audible music. A fish slid along beneath his eyes and he heard the rush of its body parting the water.

He had come to the surface facing down the stream; in a moment the visible world seemed to wheel slowly round, himself the pivotal point, and he saw the bridge, the fort, the soldiers upon the bridge, the captain, the sergeant, the two privates, his executioners. They were in silhouette against the blue sky. They shouted and gesticulated, pointing at him. The captain had drawn his pistol, but did not fire; the others were unarmed. Their movements were grotesque and horrible, their forms gigantic.

Suddenly he heard a sharp report and something struck the water smartly within a few inches of his head, spattering his face with spray. He heard a second report, and saw one of the sentinels with his rifle at his shoulder, a light cloud of blue smoke rising from the muzzle. The man in the water saw the eye of the man on the bridge gazing into his own through the sights of the rifle. He observed that it was a gray eye and remembered having read that gray eyes were keenest, and that all famous marksmen had them. Nevertheless, this one had missed.

A counter-swirl had caught Farquhar and turned him half round; he was again looking into the forest on the bank opposite the fort. The sound of a clear, high voice in a monotonous singsong now rang out behind him and came across the water with a distinctness that pierced and subdued all other sounds, even the beating of the ripples in his ears. Although no soldier, he had frequented camps enough to know the dread significance of that deliberate, drawling, aspirated chant; the lieutenant on shore was taking a part in the morning's work. How coldly and pitilessly—with what an even, calm intonation, presaging, and enforcing tranquillity in the men—with what accurately measured intervals fell those cruel words:

"Attention, company! . . . Shoulder arms! . . . Ready! . . . Aim! . . . Fire!"

Farquhar dived—dived as deeply as he could. The water roared in his ears like the voice of Niagara, yet he heard the dulled thunder of the volley and, rising again toward the surface, met shining bits of metal, singularly flattened, oscillating slowly downward.

Some of them touched him on the face and hands, then fell away, continuing their descent. One lodged between his collar and neck; it was uncomfortably warm and he snatched it out.

As he rose to the surface, gasping for breath, he saw that he had been a long time under water; he was perceptibly farther down stream—nearer to safety. The soldiers had almost finished reloading; the metal ramrods flashed all at once in the sunshine as they were drawn from the barrels, turned in the air, and thrust into their sockets. The two sentinels fired again, independently and ineffectually.

The hunted man saw all this over his shoulder; he was now swimming vigorously with the current. His brain was as energetic as his arms and legs; he thought with the rapidity of lightning.

"The officer," he reasoned, "will not make that martinet's error a second time. It is as easy to dodge a volley as a single shot. He has probably already given the command to fire at will. God help me, I cannot dodge them all!"

An appalling plash within two yards of him was followed by a loud, rushing sound, *diminuendo*, which seemed to travel back through the air to the fort and died in an explosion which stirred the very river to its deeps! A rising sheet of water curved over him, fell down upon him, blinded him, strangled him! The cannon had taken a hand in the game. As he shook his head free from the commotion of the smitten water he heard the deflected shot humming through the air ahead, and in an instant it was cracking and smashing the branches in the forest beyond.

"They will not do that again," he thought; "the next time they will use a charge of grape. I must keep my eye upon the gun; the smoke will apprise me—the report arrives too late; it lags behind the missile. That is a good gun."

Suddenly he felt himself whirled round and round—spinning like a top. The water, the banks, the forests, the now distant bridge, fort and men—all were commingled and blurred. Objects were represented by their colors only; circular horizontal streaks of color—that was all he saw. He had been caught in a vortex and was being whirled on with a velocity of advance and gyration that made him giddy and sick. In a few moments he was flung upon the gravel at the foot of the left bank of the stream—the southern bank—and behind a projecting point which concealed him from his enemies. The sudden arrest of his motion, the abrasion of one of his hands on the gravel, restored him, and he wept with delight. He dug his fingers into the sand, threw it over himself in handfuls and audibly blessed it. It looked like diamonds, rubies, emeralds; he could think of nothing beautiful which it did not resemble. The trees upon the bank were giant garden plants; he noted a definite order in their arrangement, inhaled the fragrance of their blooms. A strange, roseate light shone through the spaces among their trunks and the wind made in their branches the music of æolian harps. He had no wish to perfect his escape—was content to remain in that enchanting spot until retaken.

A whiz and rattle of grapeshot among the branches high above his head roused him from his dream. The baffled cannoneer had fired him a random farewell. He sprang to his feet, rushed up the sloping bank, and plunged into the forest.

All that day he traveled, laying his course by the rounding sun. The forest seemed interminable; nowhere did he discover a bre ak in it, not even a woodman's road. He had not known that he lived in so wild a region. There was something uncanny in the revelation.

By night fall he was fatigued, footsore, famishing. The thought of his wife and children urged him on. At last he found a road which led him in what he knew to be the right direction. It was as wide and straight as a city street, yet it seemed untraveled. No fields bordered it, no dwelling anywhere. Not so much as the barking of a dog suggested human habitation. The black bodies of the trees formed a straight wall on both sides, terminating on the horizon in a point, like a diagram in a lesson in perspective. Overhead, as he looked up through this rift in the wood, shone great golden stars looking unfamiliar and grouped in strange constellations. He was sure they were arranged in some order which had a secret and malign significance. The wood on either side was full of singular noises, among which—once, twice, and again, he distinctly heard whispers in an unknown tongue.

His neck was in pain and lifting his hand to it he found it horribly swollen. He knew that it had a circle of black where the rope had bruised it. His eyes felt congested; he could no longer close them. His tongue was swollen with thirst; he relieved its fever by thrusting it forward from between his teeth into the cold air. How softly the turf had carpeted the untraveled avenue—he could no longer feel the roadway beneath his feet!

Doubtless, despite his suffering, he had fallen asleep while walking, for now he sees another scene—perhaps he has merely recovered from a delirium. He stands at the gate of his own home. All is as he left it, and all bright and beautiful in the morning sunshine. He must have traveled the entire night. As he pushes open the gate and passes up the wide white walk, he sees a flutter of female garments; his wife, looking fresh and cool and sweet, steps down from the veranda to meet him. At the bottom of the steps she stands waiting, with a smile of ineffable joy, an attitude of matchless grace and dignity. Ah, how beautiful she is! He springs forward with extended arms. As he is about to clasp her he feels a stunning blow upon the back of the neck; a blinding white light blazes all about him with a sound like the shock of a cannon—then all is darkness and silence!

Peyton Farquhar was dead; his body, with a broken neck, swung gently from side to side beneath the timbers of the Owl Creek bridge.

Notes

pp. 46, 48	*Federal Army . . . secessionist* - The story takes place during the American Civil War of 1861–1865. Southern states withdrew from the United States in 1860–1861– the 'secessionists' became a Confederation. The Federal army of the Northern states –'the Union' – fought the Confederate army of the Southern states
p. 46	*sentinel* - soldier placed on guard
p. 46	*acclivity* - upward slope
p. 46	*stockade* - fence of upright posts, a barrier against attack
p. 46	*embrasure* - an opening in the stockade

p. 47   *habit* - clothes
p. 47   *planter* - a Southern farmer, and slave-owner
p. 47   *hemp* - rope-noose
p. 47   *unsteadfast footing* - quoting Shakespeare *Henry IV Part 1*:

> 'As full of peril and adventurous spirit
> As to o'erwalk a current roaring loud
> On the unsteadfast footing of a spear.'

p. 48   *Southern cause* - see opening note
p. 48   *Circumstances of an imperious nature* - i.e. circumstances beyond his control
p. 48   *fall of Corinth* - battle in which the Confederate army were defeated in 1862
p. 48   *Yanks* - men from the North, Union soldiers
p. 49   *tow* - dry hemp – material used to make rope
p. 51   *martinet* - drill master – officer in charge of company firing rifles
p. 51   *diminuendo* - decrease in loudness
p. 51   *grape* - cluster of small iron balls fired by cannon and falling over a wide area
p. 51   *æolian harp* - musical instrument, a box with strings hung in a tree to be played by the wind

7

The Melancholy Hussar of the German Legion

(1889)

Thomas Hardy

Hardy, the famous English poet and novelist, best known for novels such as Tess of the D'Urbervilles, The Mayor of Casterbridge *and* Far from the Madding Crowd, *wrote mainly about a rural England which was already vanishing in his lifetime; he also wrote many short stories. In this story, set in England during the Napoleonic Wars, a young woman is dazzled by the romance of the German soldiers billeted in her small rural village and falls in love with one of them; but family, nationality and the military divide the lovers. This is a story which encompasses Hardy's characteristic rural romance of sympathetic characters set against the harsh laws of Fate and social custom.*

I

Here stretch the downs, high and breezy and green, absolutely unchanged since those eventful days. A plough has never disturbed the turf, and the sod that was uppermost then is uppermost now. Here stood the camp; here are distinct traces of the banks thrown up for the horses of the cavalry, and spots where the midden-heaps lay are still to be observed. At night when I walk across the lonely place it is impossible to avoid hearing, amid the scourings of the wind over the grass-bents and thistles, the old trumpet and bugle calls, the rattle of the halters; to help seeing rows of spectral tents and the *impedimenta* of the soldiery; from within the canvases come guttural syllables of foreign tongues, and broken songs of the fatherland; for they were mainly regiments of the King's German legion that slept round the tent-poles hereabout at that time.

It was nearly ninety years ago. The British uniform of the period, with its immense epaulettes, queer cocked hat, breeches, gaiters, ponderous cartridge-box, buckled shoes, and what not, would look strange and barbarous now. Ideas have changed; invention has followed invention. Soldiers were monumental objects then. A divinity still hedged kings here and there; and war was considered a glorious thing.

Secluded old manor-houses and hamlets lie in the ravines and hollows among these hills, where a stranger had hardly ever been seen till the King chose to take the baths yearly at the sea-side watering-place a few miles to the south; as a consequence of which battalions descended in a cloud upon the open country around. Is it necessary to add that the echoes of many characteristic tales, dating from that picturesque time, still linger about here, in more or less fragmentary form to be caught by the attentive ear? Some of them I have repeated; most of them I have forgotten; one I have never repeated, and assuredly can never forget.

Phyllis told me the story with her own lips. She was then an old lady of seventy-five, and her auditor a lad of fifteen. She enjoined silence as to her share in the incident till she should be "dead, buried, and forgotten." Her life was prolonged twelve years after the day of her narration, and she has now been dead nearly twenty. The oblivion which, in her modesty and humility, she courted for herself, has only partially fallen on her, with the unfortunate result of inflicting an injustice upon her memory; since such fragments of her story as got abroad at the time, and have been kept alive ever since, are precisely those which are most unfavourable to her character.

It all began with the arrival of the York Hussars, one of the foreign regiments above alluded to. Before that day scarcely a soul had been seen near her father's house for weeks. When a noise like the brushing skirt of a visitor was heard on the doorstep it proved to be a scudding leaf; when a carriage seemed to be nearing the door it was her father grinding his sickle on the stone in the garden for his favourite relaxation of trimming the box-tree borders to the plots. A sound like luggage thrown down from the coach was a gun far away at sea; and what looked like a tall man by the gate at dusk was a yew bush cut into a quaint and attenuated shape. There is no such solitude in country places now as there was in those old days.

Yet all the while King George and his court were at his favourite sea-side resort, not more than five miles off.

The daughter's seclusion was great, but beyond the seclusion of the girl lay the seclusion of the father. If her social condition was twilight his was darkness. Yet he enjoyed his darkness while her twilight oppressed her. Dr Grove had been a professional man whose taste for lonely meditation over metaphysical questions had diminished his practice till it no longer paid him to keep it going; after which he had relinquished it and hired at a nominal rent the small, dilapidated, half farm half manor-house of this obscure inland nook, to make a sufficiency of an income which in a town would have been inadequate for their maintenance. He stayed in his garden the greater part of the day, growing more and more irritable with the lapse of time, and the increasing perception that he had wasted his life in the pursuit of illusions. He saw his friends less and less frequently. Phyllis became so shy that if she met a stranger anywhere in her short rambles she felt ashamed at his gaze, walked awkwardly, and blushed to her shoulders.

Yet Phyllis was discovered even here by an admirer, and her hand most unexpectedly asked in marriage.

The king as aforesaid was at the neighbouring town, where he had taken up his abode at Gloucester Lodge; and his presence in the town naturally brought many county people thither. Among these idlers, many of whom professed to have connections and interests with the Court, was one Humphrey Gould, a bachelor; a personage neither young nor old; neither good-looking nor positively plain. Too steady going to be "a buck" (as fast and unmarried men were then called) he was an approximately fashionable man of a mild type. This bachelor of thirty found his way to the village on the down; beheld Phyllis, made her father's acquaintance in order to make hers; and by some means or other she sufficiently inflamed his heart to lead him in that direction almost daily: till he became engaged to marry her.

As he was of an old local family, some of whose members were held in respect in the county, Phyllis, in bringing him to her feet, had accomplished what was considered a brilliant move for one in her constrained position. How she had done it was not quite known to Phyllis herself. In those days unequal marriages were regarded rather as a violation of the laws of nature than as a mere infringement of convention, the more modern view; and hence when Phyllis of the watering-place *bourgeoisie* was chosen by such a gentlemanly fellow it was as if she were going to be taken to Heaven; though perhaps the uninformed would have seen no great difference in the respective positions of the pair, the said Gould being as poor as a crow.

This pecuniary condition was his excuse—probably a true one—for postponing their union; and as the winter drew nearer, and the king departed for the season, Mr Humphrey Gould set out for Bath, promising to return to Phyllis in a few weeks. The winter arrived, the date of his promise passed; yet Gould postponed his coming, on the ground that he could not very easily leave his father in the city of their sojourn, the elder having no other relative near him. Phyllis, though lonely in the extreme, was content. The man who had asked her in marriage was a desirable husband for her in many ways; her father highly approved of his suit: but this neglect of her was awkward if not painful for Phyllis. Love him in the true sense of the word she assured me she never did; but she had a genuine regard for him; admired a certain methodical and dogged way in which he sometimes took his pleasure; valued his knowledge of what the Court was doing, had done, or was about to do; and she was not without a feeling of pride that he had chosen her when he might have exercised a more ambitious choice.

But he did not come; and the spring developed. His letters were regular though formal; and it is not to be wondered that the uncertainty of her position, linked with the fact that there was not much passion in her thoughts of Humphrey, bred an indescribable dreariness in the heart of Phyllis Grove. The spring was soon summer, and the summer brought the king; but still no Humphrey Gould. All this while the engagement by letter was maintained intact.

At this point of time a golden radiance flashed in upon the lives of people here, and charged all youthful thought with emotional interest. This radiance was the aforesaid York Hussars.

II

The present generation has probably but a very dim notion of the celebrated York Hussars of ninety years ago. They were one of the regiments of the King's German Legion and (though they somewhat degenerated later on) their brilliant uniform, their splendid horses, and above all, their foreign air, and mustachios (rare appendages then) drew crowds of admirers of both sexes wherever they went. These, with other regiments had come to encamp on the downs and pastures, because of the presence of the king in the neighbouring town.

The spot was high and airy, and the view extensive, commanding Portland—the Isle of Slingers—in front, and reaching to St. Aldhelm's Head eastward, and almost to the Start on the west.

Phyllis, though not precisely a girl of the village, was as interested as any of them in this military investment. Her father's home stood somewhat apart, and on the highest point of ground, to which the lane ascended, so that it was almost level with the top of the church tower in the lower part of the parish. Immediately from the outside of the garden wall the grass spread away to a great distance, and it was crossed by a path which came close to the wall. Ever since her childhood it had been Phyllis's pleasure to clamber up this fence, and sit on the top, a feat not so difficult as it may seem, the walls in this district being built of rubble, without mortar so that there were plenty of crevices for small toes.

She was sitting up here one day, listlessly surveying the pasture without, when her attention was arrested by a solitary figure walking along the path. It was one of the renowned German Hussars, and he moved onward with his eyes on the ground, and with the manner of one who wished to escape company. His head would probably have been bent like his eyes but for his stiff neck-gear. On nearer view she perceived that his face was marked with deep sadness. Without observing her he advanced by the footpath till it brought him almost immediately under the wall.

Phyllis was much surprised to see a fine tall soldier in such a mood as this. Her theory of the military, and of the York Hussars in particular (derived entirely from hearsay, for she had never talked to a soldier in her life) was that their hearts were as gay as their accoutrements.

At this moment the Hussar lifted his eyes and noticed her on her perch, the white muslin neckerchief which covered her shoulders and neck where left bare by her low gown, and her white raiment in general, showing conspicuously in the bright sunlight of this summer day. He blushed a little at the suddenness of the encounter, and without halting a moment from his pace passed on.

All that day the foreigner's face haunted Phyllis; its aspect was so striking, so handsome, and his eyes were so blue, and sad, and abstracted. It was perhaps only natural that on some following day at the same hour she should look over that wall again, and wait till he had passed a second time. On this occasion he was reading a letter, and at the sight of her his manner was that of one who had half expected or hoped to discover her. He almost stopped, smiled, and made a courteous salute. The end of the meeting was that they exchanged a few words. She asked him what he was reading, and he readily informed her that he was reperusing letters from his mother in Germany; he did not get them often, he said, and was forced to read the old ones a great many times. This was all that passed at the present interview; but others of the same kind followed.

Phyllis used to say that his English, though not good, was quite intelligible to her, so that their acquaintance was never hindered by difficulties of speech. Whenever the subject became too delicate, subtle, or tender, for such words of English as were at his command, the eyes no doubt helped out the tongue, and—though this was later on—the lips helped out the eyes. In short this acquaintance, unguardedly made, and rash enough on her part, developed, and ripened. Like Desdemona, she pitied him, and learnt his history.

His name was Matthäus Tina, and Saarbruck his native town, where his mother was still living. His age was twenty-two, and he had already risen to the grade of corporal, though he had not long been in the army. Phyllis used to assert that no such refined or well-educated young man could have been found in the ranks of the purely English regiments, some of these foreign soldiers having rather the graceful manner and presence of our native officers than of our rank and file.

She by degrees learnt from her foreign friend a circumstance about himself and his comrades which Phyllis would least have expected of the York Hussars. So far from being as gay as its uniform the regiment was pervaded by a dreadful melancholy, a chronic home-sickness, which depressed many of the men to such an extent that they could hardly attend to their drill. The worst sufferers were the younger soldiers who had not been over here long. They hated England and English life; they took no interest whatever in King George and his island kingdom, and they only wished to be out of it and never to see it any more. Their bodies were here, but their hearts and minds were always far away in their dear fatherland, of which—brave men and stoical as they were in many ways—they would speak with tears in their eyes. One of the worst of the sufferers from this home-woe, as he called it in his own tongue, was Matthäus Tina, whose dreamy musing nature felt the gloom of exile still more intensely from the fact that he had left a lonely mother at home with nobody to cheer her.

Though Phyllis, touched by all this, and interested in his history, did not disdain her soldier's acquaintance, she declined (according to her own account at least) to permit the young man to over-step the line of mere friendship for a long while—as long, indeed, as she considered herself likely to become the possession of another; though it is probable that she had lost her heart to Matthäus before she was herself aware, The stone wall of necessity made anything like intimacy difficult; and he had never ventured to come, or to ask to come, inside the garden, so that all their conversation had been overtly conducted across this boundary.

III

But news reached the village from a friend of Phyllis's father, concerning Mr Humphrey Gould, her remarkably cool and patient betrothed. This gentleman had been heard to say in Bath that he considered his overtures to Miss Phyllis Grove to have reached only the stage of a half-understanding; and in view of his enforced absence on his father's account, who was too great an invalid now to attend to his affairs, he thought it best that there should be no definite promise as yet on either side. He was not sure, indeed, that he might not cast his eyes elsewhere.

This account—though only a piece of hearsay and as such entitled to no absolute credit—tallied so well with the infrequency of his letters, and their lack of warmth, that Phyllis did not doubt its truth for one moment; and from that hour she felt herself free to bestow her heart as she should choose. Not so her father; he declared the whole story to be a fabrication. He had known Mr Gould's family from his boyhood; and if there was one proverb which expressed the matrimonial aspect of that family well it was "Love me little love me long." Humphrey was an honourable man who would not think of treating his engagement so lightly. "Do you wait in patience," he said. "All will be right enough in time."

From these words Phyllis at first imagined that her father was in correspondence with Mr Gould; and her heart sank within her; for in spite of her original intentions she had been relieved to hear that her engagement had come to nothing. But she presently learnt that her father had heard no more of Humphrey Gould than she herself had done: while he would not write and address her affianced directly on the subject lest it should be deemed an imputation on that bachelor's honour.

"You want an excuse for encouraging one or other of those foreign fellows to flatter you with his unmeaning attentions," her father exclaimed, his mood having of late been a very unkind one towards her. "I see more than I say. Don't you ever set foot outside that garden-fence without my permission. If you want to see the camp I'll take you myself some Sunday afternoon."

Phyllis had not the smallest intention of disobeying him in her actions, but she assumed herself to be independent with respect to her feelings. She no longer checked her fancy for the Hussar, though she was far from regarding him as her lover in the serious sense in which an Englishman might have been regarded as such. The young foreign soldier was almost an ideal being to her, with none of the appurtenances of an ordinary house-dweller; one who had descended she knew not whence, and would disappear she knew not whither; the subject of a fascinating dream, no more.

They met continually now—mostly at dusk—during the brief interval between the going down of the sun and the minute at which the last trumpet-call summoned him to his tent. Perhaps her manner had become less restrained latterly: at any rate that of the Hussar was so; he had grown more tender every day, and at parting after these hurried interviews she reached down her hand from the top of the wall that he might press it. One evening he held it such a while that she exclaimed, "The wall is white, and somebody in the field may see your shape against it."

He lingered so long that night that it was with the greatest difficulty that he could run across the intervening stretch of ground and enter the camp in time. On the next occasion of his awaiting her she did not appear in her usual place at the usual hour. His disappointment was unspeakably keen: he remained staring blankly at the spot, like a man in a trance. The trumpets and tattoo sounded, and still he did not go.

She had been delayed purely by an accident. When she arrived she was anxious because of the lateness of the hour, having heard as well as he the sounds denoting the closing of the camp. She implored him to leave immediately.

"No," he said, gloomily. "I shall not go in yet—the moment you come—I have thought of your coming all day."

"But you may be disgraced at being after time?"

"I don't mind that. I should have disappeared from the world some time ago if it had not been for two persons—my beloved, here; and my mother in Saarbruck. I hate the army. I care more for a minute of your company than for all the promotion in the world."

Thus he stayed and talked to her, and told her interesting details of his native place, and incidents of his childhood, till she was in a simmer of distress at his recklessness in remaining. It was only because she insisted on bidding him good night and leaving the wall that he returned to his quarters.

The next time that she saw him he was without the stripes that had adorned his sleeve. He had been broken to the level of private for his lateness that night: and as Phyllis considered herself to be the cause of his disgrace her sorrow was great. But the position was now reversed: it was his turn to cheer her.

"Don't grieve meine Liebliche!" he said. "I have got a remedy for whatever comes. First, even supposing I regain my stripes, would your father allow you to marry a non-commissioned officer in the York Hussars?"

She flushed. This practical step had not been in her mind in relation to such an unrealistic person as he was; and a moment's reflection was enough for it. "My father would not— certainly would not," she answered unflinchingly. "It cannot be thought of! My dear friend, please do forget me: I fear I am ruining you and your prospects!"

"Not at all!" said he. "You are giving this country of yours just sufficient interest to me to make me care to keep alive in it. If my dear land were here also, and my old parent, with you, I could be happy as I am, and would do my best as a soldier. But it is not so. And now listen. This is my plan. That you go with me to my own country, and be my wife there, and live there with my mother and me. I am not a Hanoverian, as you know, though I entered the army as such, my country is by the Saar, and is at peace with France, and if I were once in it I should be free."

"But how get there?" she asked. Phyllis had been rather amazed than shocked at his proposition. Her position in her father's house was growing irksome and painful in the extreme; his parental affection seemed to be quite dried up. She was not a native of the village, like all the joyous girls around her, and in some way Matthäus Tina had infected her with his own passionate longing for his country and mother and home.

"But how?" she repeated, finding that he did not answer. "Will you buy your discharge?"

"Ah, no," he said. "That's impossible in these times. No. I came here against my will: why should I not escape? Now is the time, as we shall soon be striking camp, and I might see you no more. This is my scheme. I will ask you to meet me on the highway two miles off on some calm night next week that may be appointed. There will be nothing unbecoming in it, or to cause you shame; you will not fly alone with me, for I will bring with me my devoted young friend Christoph, an Alsatian, who has lately joined the regiment, and who has agreed to assist in this enterprise. We shall have come from yonder harbour, where we shall have examined the boats, and found one suited to our purpose. Christoph has already a chart of the channel, and we will then go to the harbour, and at midnight cut the boat from her moorings, and row away round the point out of sight; and by the next morning we are on the coast of France, near Cherbourg. The rest is easy, for I have saved money for the land journey, and can get a change of clothes. I will write to my mother; who will meet us on the way."

He added details in reply to her inquiries which left no doubt in Phyllis's mind of the feasibility of the undertaking. But its magnitude almost appalled her; and it is questionable if she would ever have gone further in the wild adventure if, on entering the house that night, her father had not accosted her in the most significant terms.

"How about the York Hussars?" he said.

"They are still at the Camp; but they are soon going away, I believe."

"It is useless for you to attempt to cloak your actions in that way. You have been meeting one of those fellows: you have been seen walking with him—foreign barbarians not much better than the French themselves. I have made up my mind— don't speak a word till I have done please!—I have made up my mind that you shall stay here no longer while they are on the spot. You shall go to your Aunt's."

It was useless for her to protest that she had never taken a walk with any soldier or man under the sun except himself. Her protestations were feeble too, for though he was not literally correct in his assertion he was virtually only half in error.

The house of her father's sister was a prison to Phyllis. She had quite recently undergone experience of its gloom; and when her father went on to direct her to pack what would be necessary for her to take her heart died within her. In after years she never attempted to excuse her conduct during this week of agitation; but the result of her self-communing was that she decided to join in the scheme of her lover and his friend, and fly to the country which he had coloured with such lovely hues in her imagination. She always said that the one feature in his proposal which overcame her hesitation was the obvious purity and straightforwardness of his intentions. He showed himself to be so virtuous and kind: he treated her with a respect to which she had never before been accustomed; and she was braced to the obvious risks of the voyage by her confidence in him.

IV

It was on a soft, dark evening of the following week that they engaged in the adventure. Tina was to meet her at a point in the highway at which the lane to the village branched off. Christoph was to go ahead of them to the harbour where the boat lay, row it round the Nothe—or Look-out as it was called in those days—and pick them up on the other side of the promontory, which they were to reach by crossing the harbour bridge on foot, and climbing over the Look-out hill.

As soon as her father had ascended to his room she left the house, and, bundle in hand, proceeded at a trot along the lane. At such an hour not a soul was afoot anywhere in the village, and she reached the junction of the lane with the highway unobserved. Here she took up her position in the obscurity formed by the angle of a fence, whence she could discern every one who approached along the turnpike road, without being herself seen.

She had not remained thus waiting for her lover longer than a minute—though from the tension of her nerves the lapse of even that short time was trying—when, instead of the expected footsteps the stage-coach could be heard descending the hill. She knew that Tina would not show himself till the road was dear, and waited impatiently for the coach to pass. Nearing the corner where she was it slackened speed, and, instead of going by as usual, drew up within a few yards of her. A passenger alighted, and she heard his voice. It was Humphrey Gould's.

He had brought a friend with him, and luggage. The luggage was deposited on the grass, and the coach went on its route to the royal watering-place.

"I wonder where that young man is with the horse and trap?" said her former admirer to his companion. "I hope we shan't have to wait here long. I told him half-past nine o'clock precisely."

"Have you got her present safe?"

"Phyllis's? O yes. It is in this trunk. I hope it will please her."

"Of course it will. What woman would not be pleased with such a handsome peace-offering."

"Well—she deserves it. I've treated her rather badly. But she has been in my mind these last two days much more than I should care to confess to everybody. Ah well; I'll say no more about that. It cannot be that she is so bad as they make out, I am quite sure that a girl of her good wit would know better than to get entangled with any of those Hanoverian soldiers. I won't believe it of her. and there's an end on't."

More words in the same strain were casually dropped as the two men waited; words which revealed to her, as by a sudden illumination, the enormity of her conduct. The conversation was at length cut off by the arrival of the man with the vehicle. The luggage was placed in it, and they mounted, and were driven on in the direction from which she had just come.

Phyllis was so conscience-stricken that she was at first inclined to follow them; but a moment's reflection led her to feel that it would only be bare justice to Matthäus to wait till he arrived, and explain candidly that she had changed her mind—difficult as the struggle would be when she stood face to face with him. She bitterly reproached herself for having believed reports which represented Humphrey Gould as false to his engagement, when, from what she now heard from his own lips she gathered that he had been living full of trust in her; but she knew well enough who had won her love. Without him her life seemed a dreary prospect; yet the more she looked at his proposal the more she feared to accept it—so wild as it was, so vague, so venturesome. She had promised Humphrey Gould, and it was only his assumed faithlessness which had led her to treat that promise as nought. His solicitude in bringing her these gifts touched her; her promise must be kept, and esteem must take the place of love. She would preserve her self-respect. She would stay at home, and marry him, and suffer.

Phyllis had thus braced herself to an exceptional fortitude when, a few minutes later, the outline of Matthäus Tina appeared behind a field-gate; over which he lightly leapt as she stepped forward. There was no evading it: he pressed her to his breast.

"It is the first and last time!" she wildly thought as she stood encircled by his arms.

How Phyllis got through the terrible ordeal of that night she could never clearly recollect. She always attributed her success in carrying out her resolve to her lover's honour, for as soon as she declared to him in feeble words that she had changed her mind, and felt that she could not, dared not, fly with him; he forbore to urge her, grieved as he was at her decision. Unscrupulous pressure on his part, seeing how romantically she had become attached to him, would no doubt have turned the balance in his favour. But he did nothing to tempt her unduly or unfairly.

On her side, fearing for his safety, she begged him to remain. This, he declared, could not be. "I cannot break faith with my friend," said he. Had he stood alone he would have abandoned his plan. But Christoph, with the boat and compass and chart, was waiting on the shore; the tide would soon turn; his mother had been warned of his coming; go he must.

Many precious minutes were lost while he tarried, unable to tear himself away. Phyllis held to her resolve, though it cost her many a bitter pang. At last they parted, and he went down the hill. Before his footsteps had quite died away she felt a desire to behold at least his outline once more, and running noiselessly after him regained view of his diminishing figure. For one moment she was sufficiently excited to be on the point of rushing forward and linking her fate with his. But she could not. The courage which at the critical instant failed Cleopatra of Egypt could scarcely be expected of Phyllis Grove.

A dark shape similar to his own joined him in the highway: it was Christoph his friend. She could see no more; they had hastened on in the direction of the town and harbour, four miles ahead. With a feeling akin to despair she turned and slowly pursued her way homeward. Tattoo sounded in the camp; but there was no camp for her now. It was as dead as the camp of the Assyrians after the passage of the destroying angel.

She noiselessly entered the house, seeing nobody; and went to bed. Grief, which kept her awake at first, ultimately wrapt her in a heavy sleep. The next morning her father met her at the foot of the stairs.

"Mr. Gould is come!" he said triumphantly.

Humphrey was staying at the inn, and had already called to inquire for her. He had brought her a present of a very handsome looking-glass in a frame of *repoussé* silver-work, which her father held in his hand. He had promised to call again in the course of an hour, to ask Phyllis to walk with him.

Pretty mirrors were rarer in country-houses at that day than they are now, and the one before her won Phyllis's admiration. She looked into it, saw how heavy her eyes were, and endeavoured to brighten them. She was in that wretched state of mind which leads a woman to move mechanically onward in what she conceives to be her allotted path. Mr Humphrey had, in his undemonstrative way, been adhering all along to the old understanding: it was for her to do the same; and to say not a word of her own lapse. She put on her bonnet and tippet, and when he arrived at the hour named she was at the door awaiting him.

V

Phyllis thanked him for his beautiful gift; but the talking was soon entirely on Humphrey's side as they walked along. He told her of the latest movements of the world of fashion—a subject which she willingly discussed to the exclusion of anything more personal—and his measured language helped to still her disquieted heart and brain. Had not her own sadness been what it was she must have observed his embarrassment. At last he abruptly changed the subject.

"I am glad you are pleased with my little present," he said. "The truth is that I brought it to propitiate 'ee, and to get you to help me out of a mighty difficulty."

It was inconceivable to Phyllis that this independent bachelor—whom she admired in some respects—could have a difficulty.

"Phyllis—I'll tell you my secret at once; for I have a monstrous secret to confide before I can ask your counsel. The case is, then, that I am married: yes, I have privately married a dear young *belle*; and if you knew her, and I hope you will, you would say everything in her praise. But she is not quite the one that my father would have chose for me—you know the paternal idea as well as I—and I have kept it secret. There will be a terrible noise, no doubt; but I think that with your help I may get over it. If you would only do me this good turn—when I have told my father I mean—say that you never could have married me, you know, or something of that sort—'pon my life it will help to smooth the way vastly. I am so anxious to win him round to my point of view, and not to cause any estrangement."

What Phyllis replied she scarcely knew, or how she counselled him as to his unexpected situation. Yet the relief that his announcement brought her was perceptible. To have confided her trouble in return was what her aching heart longed to do; and had Humphrey been a woman she would instantly have poured out her tale. But to him she feared to confess; and there was a real reason for silence till a sufficient time had elapsed to allow her lover and his comrade to get out of harm's way.

As soon as she reached home again she sought a solitary place, and spent the time in half regretting that she had not gone away, and in dreaming over the meetings with Matthäus Tina from their beginning to their end. In his own country, amongst his own countrywomen, he would possibly soon forget her, even to her very name.

Her listlessness was such that she did not go out of the house for several days. There came a morning which broke in fog and mist, behind which the down could be discerned in greenish gray; and the outlines of the tents, and the rows of horses at the ropes. The smoke from the canteen fires drooped heavily.

The spot at the bottom of the garden where she had been accustomed to climb the wall to meet Matthäus was the only inch of English ground in which she took any interest; and in spite of the disagreeable haze prevailing she walked out there till she reached the well-known corner. Every blade of grass was weighted with little liquid globes, and slugs and snails had crept out upon the plots. She could hear the usual faint noises from the camp, and in the other direction the trot of farmers on the road to the town, for it was market-day. She observed that her frequent visits to this corner had quite trodden down the grass in the angle of the wall and left marks of garden-soil on the stepping-stones by which she had mounted to look over the top: seldom having gone there till dusk she had not considered that her traces might be visible by day. Perhaps it was these which had revealed her trysts to her father.

While she paused in melancholy regard she fancied that the customary sounds from the tents were changing their character. Indifferent as Phyllis was to camp doings now, she mounted by the steps to the old place. What she beheld at first awed and perplexed her: then she stood rigid, her fingers hooked to the wall, her eyes starting out of her head, and her face as if hardened to stone.

On the open green stretching before her all the regiments in the camp were drawn up in line, in the mid-front of which two empty coffins lay on the ground. The unwonted sounds which she had noticed came from an advancing procession; it consisted of the band of the York Hussars playing a dead march; next two soldiers of that regiment in a mourning coach, guarded on each side, and accompanied by two priests. Behind came a crowd of rustics who had been attracted by the event. The melancholy procession marched along the front of the line, returned to the centre, and halted beside the coffins, where the two condemned men were blind-folded, and each placed kneeling on his coffin; a few minutes pause was now given, while they prayed.

A firing-party of twenty-four men stood ready with levelled carbines. The commanding officer, who had his sword drawn, waved it through some cuts of the sword-exercise till he reached the downward stroke, whereat the firing party discharged their volley. The two victims fell, one upon his face across his coffin, the other backwards.

As the volley resounded there arose a shriek from the wall of Dr Grove's garden, and some one fell down inside; but nobody among the spectators without noticed it at the time.

The two executed hussars were Matthäus Tina and his friend Christoph. The soldiers on guard placed the bodies in the coffins almost instantly; but the Colonel of the regiment—an Englishman—rode up and exclaimed in a stern voice: "Turn them out—as an example to the men!"

The coffins were lifted endwise, and the dead Germans flung out upon their faces on the grass. Then all the regiments wheeled in sections, and marched past the spot in slow time. When the survey was over the corpses were again coffined, and borne away.

Meanwhile Dr Grove, attracted by the noise of the volley, had rushed out into his garden, where he saw his wretched daughter lying motionless against the wall. She was taken indoors, but it was long before she recovered consciousness; and for weeks they despaired of her reason.

It transpired that the luckless deserters from the York Hussars had cut the boat from her moorings in the adjacent harbour, according to their plan, and, with two other comrades who were smarting under ill-treatment from their Colonel, had sailed in safety across the Channel. But mistaking their bearings they steered into Jersey, thinking that island the French coast. Here they were perceived to be deserters, and delivered up to the authorities. Matthäus and Christoph interceded for the other two at the court-martial, saying that it was entirely by the formers' representations that these were induced to go. Their sentence was accordingly commuted to flogging, the death punishment being reserved for their leaders.

The visitor to the well-known old Georgian watering-place, who may care to ramble to the neighbouring village under the hills, and examine the register of burials, will there find two entries in these words:—"*Matth: Tina (Corpl.) in His Majesty's Regmt. of York Hussars and Shot for Desertion was Buried June 30th 1801, aged 22 Years. Born in the town of Sarrbruk Germany.*

"*Christopher Bless belonging to His Majesty's Regmt. of York Hussars who was Shot for Desertion was Buried June 30th 1801, aged 22 Years. Born at Lothaargen Alsassia.*"

Their graves were dug at the back of the little church, near the wall. There is no memorial to mark the spot, but Phyllis pointed it out to me. While she lived she used to keep their mounds neat; but now they are over-grown with nettles, and sunk nearly flat. The older villagers, however, who know of the episode from their parents, still recollect the place where the soldiers lie. Phyllis lies near.

Notes

p. 54   *Hussar* - hussars were lightly armed troops, who went into battle on horses. The story takes place in England during the Napoleonic wars (1793–1815) when it was thought France would invade the South of England at any time, and soldiers were stationed at various strategic points: Germany was England's ally and some German soldiers were posted to England at this time.

p. 54   *the downs* - the story takes place in Hardy's Dorset; the land is mainly moorland, grazing for sheep, and has never been cultivated for growing crops, so its surface is undisturbed over the centuries

p. 54   *midden-heaps* - rubbish heaps

p. 54   *impedimenta* - equipment

p. 54   *canvases* - i.e. of their tents

p. 54   *epaulettes* - ornamental shoulder pieces for a uniform

p. 54   *gaiters* - protective coverings for lower legs

p. 54   *ponderous cartridge box* - heavy box for cartridges containing bullets/shot for rifles

p. 54   *A divinity . . . hedged kings* - referring to Shakespeare: 'There's such divinity doth hedge a king' *Hamlet*, Act 4 Scene 5 i.e. a king is appointed by God and shielded by divine protection

p. 54   *The King* - King George III, reigned 1760–1820

p. 55   *auditor* - the one listening, i.e. the author as a boy

p. 56   *bourgeoisie* - middle class

p. 56   *mustachios* - moustaches

p. 57   *Portland. . .west* - the cliffs of the Dorset coast

p. 57   *accoutrements* - clothing, outfit

p. 57   *raiment* - clothing

p. 57   *Desdemona* - referring to Desdemona, listening to Othello's tales in Shakespeare's *Othello*:

> 'She loved me for the dangers I had passed
> And I loved her that she did pity them'
> *Othello* Act 1 Scene 3

p. 59   *appurtenances* - accessories

p. 59   *trumpets and tattoo* - a tattoo is a particular drum beat; together with the trumpets a military rallying call to gather at the camp

p. 60   *The stripes . . . private* - as a punishment he has been demoted from an officer to a private – the stripes on his shoulder signalled his rank

p. 60   *meine Liebliche* - German, 'my love'

p. 60   *non-commissioned officer* - a lowly form of officer

p. 60   *Hanoverian . . . Saar* - Hanover in the North of Germany, linked to Great Britain by royal ties – the royal family were from the House of Hanover from King George I in 1714; Matthäus is saying that he is from the South of Germany, and does not feel any loyalty to Hanover, Great Britain, or the campaign

p. 60   *buy your discharge* - in peace-time soldiers enlisted for set periods but could buy their way out of the army, but not in time of war, as Matthäus says

p. 60   *striking camp* - breaking up the camp and moving on

p. 61   *Alsatian* - man from Alsace, a region between France and Germany

p. 61   *Nothe* - a white chalk headland on the coast, a well-known landmark in Dorset

p. 62   *trap* - cart

p. 63   *Cleopatra* - reference to the occasion in ancient history when Cleopatra went into a sea battle with Antony against Julius Caesar but, at the sight of the enemy, fled with all her ships, causing Antony to follow her, thus losing the battle and his honour

p. 63   *Assyrians. . .destroying angel* - a biblical reference to an episode when God sent an angel to destroy a whole army in the night

p. 63   *repoussé* - decorative metalwork

p. 64   *tippet* - scarf

p. 64   *belle* - beauty

8

The Copper Beeches

(1892)

Arthur Conan Doyle

Conan Doyle is famous for his detective, Sherlock Holmes, who featured in 56 stories and 4 novels. One of his mottos occurs in this story: 'Crime is common. Logic is rare.' Conan Doyle also wrote many other stories, historical novels and plays. In this story, Sherlock Holmes is visited by a young woman who is about to take up a lucrative but odd appointment deep in the countryside. She asks for his advice.

'To the man who loves art for its own sake,' remarked Sherlock Holmes, tossing aside the advertisement sheet of the *Daily Telegraph*, 'it is frequently in its least important and lowliest manifestations that the keenest pleasure is to be derived. It is pleasant to me to observe, Watson, that you have so far grasped this truth that in these little records of our cases which you have been good enough to draw up, and, I am bound to say, occasionally to embellish, you have given prominence not so much to the many *causes célèbres* and sensational trials in which I have figured, but rather to those incidents which may have been trivial in themselves, but which have given room for those faculties of deduction and of logical synthesis which I have made my special province.'

'And yet,' said I, smiling, 'I cannot quite hold myself absolved from the charge of sensationalism which has been urged against my records.'

'You have erred, perhaps,' he observed, taking up a glowing cinder with the tongs and lighting with it the long cherry-wood pipe which was wont to replace his clay when he was in a disputatious rather than a meditative mood – 'you have erred perhaps in attempting to put colour and life into each of your statements instead of confining yourself to the task of placing upon record that severe reasoning from cause to effect which is really the only notable feature about the thing.'

'It seems to me that I have done you full justice in the matter,' I remarked with some coldness, for I was repelled by the egotism which I had more than once observed to be a strong factor in my friend's singular character.

'No, it is not selfishness or conceit,' said he, answering, as was his wont, my thoughts rather than my words. 'If I claim full justice for my art, it is because it is an impersonal thing – a thing beyond myself. Crime is common. Logic is rare. Therefore it is upon the logic rather than upon the crime that you should dwell. You have degraded what should have been a course of lectures into a series of tales.'

It was a cold morning of the early spring, and we sat after breakfast on either side of a cheery fire in the old room at Baker Street. A thick fog rolled down between the lines of dun-coloured houses, and the opposing windows loomed like dark, shapeless blurs through the heavy yellow wreaths. Our gas was lit and shone on the white cloth and glimmer of china and metal, for the table had not been cleared yet. Sherlock Holmes had been silent all the morning, dipping continuously into the advertisement columns of a succession of papers until at last, having apparently given up his search, he had emerged in no very sweet temper to lecture me upon my literary shortcomings.

'At the same time,' he remarked after a pause, during which he had sat puffing at his long pipe and gazing down into the fire, 'you can hardly be open to a charge of sensationalism, for out of these cases which you have been so kind as to interest yourself in, a fair proportion do not treat of crime, in its legal sense, at all. The small matter in which I endeavoured to help the King of Bohemia, the singular experience of Miss Mary Sutherland, the problem connected with the man with the twisted lip and the incident of the noble bachelor were all matters which are outside the pale of the law. But in avoiding the sensational, I fear that you may have bordered on the trivial.'

'The end may have been so,' I answered, 'but the methods I hold to have been novel and of interest.'

'Pshaw, my dear fellow, what do the public, the great unobservant public, who could hardly tell a weaver by his tooth or a compositor by his left thumb, care about the finer shades of analysis and deduction! But, indeed, if you are trivial, I cannot blame you, for the days of the great cases are past. Man, or at least criminal man, has lost all enterprise and originality. As to my own little practice, it seems to be degenerating into an agency for recovering lost lead pencils and giving advice to young ladies from boarding-schools. I think that I have touched bottom at last, however. This note I had this morning marks my zero-point, I fancy. Read it!' He tossed a crumpled letter across to me.

It was dated from Montague Place upon the preceding evening, and ran thus:

Dear Mr Holmes – I am very anxious to consult you as to whether I should or should not accept a situation which has been offered to me as governess. I shall call at half-past ten tomorrow if I do not inconvenience you.

Yours faithfully,

Violet Hunter

'Do you know the young lady?' I asked.

'Not I.'

'It is half-past ten now.'

'Yes, and I have no doubt that is her ring.'

'It may turn out to be of more interest than you think. You remember that the affair of the blue carbuncle, which appeared to be a mere whim at first, developed into a serious investigation. It may be so in this case, also.'

'Well, let us hope so. But our doubts will very soon be solved, for here, unless I am much mistaken, is the person in question.'

As he spoke the door opened and a young lady entered the room. She was plainly but neatly dressed, with a bright, quick face, freckled like a plover's egg, and with the brisk manner of a woman who has had her own way to make in the world.

'You will excuse my troubling you, I am sure,' said she, as my companion rose to greet her, 'but I have had a very strange experience, and as I have no parents or relations of any sort from whom I could ask advice, I thought that perhaps you would be kind enough to tell me what I should do.'

'Pray take a seat, Miss Hunter. I shall be happy to do anything that I can to serve you.'

I could see that Holmes was favourably impressed by the manner and speech of his new client. He looked her over in his searching fashion, and then composed himself, with his lids drooping and his fingertips together, to listen to her story.

'I have been a governess for five years,' said she, 'in the family of Colonel Spence Munro, but two months ago the colonel received an appointment at Halifax, in Nova Scotia, and took his children over to America with him, so that I found myself without a situation. I advertised, and I answered advertisements, but without success. At last the little money which I had saved began to run short, and I was at my wit's end as to what I should do.

'There is a well-known agency for governesses in the West End called Westaway's, and there I used to call about once a week in order to see whether anything had turned up which might suit me. Westaway was the name of the founder of the business, but it is really managed by Miss Stoper. She sits in her own little office, and the ladies who are seeking employment wait in an ante-room, and are then shown in one by one, when she consults her ledgers and sees whether she has anything which would suit them.

'Well, when I called last week I was shown into the little office as usual, but I found that Miss Stoper was not alone. A prodigiously stout man, with a very smiling face and a great heavy chin which rolled down in fold upon fold over his throat, sat at her elbow with a pair of glasses on his nose, looking very earnestly at the ladies who entered. As I came in he gave quite a jump in his chair and turned quickly to Miss Stoper. "That will do," said he; "I could not ask for anything better. Capital! Capital!" He seemed quite enthusiastic and rubbed his hands together in the most genial fashion. He was such a comfortable-looking man that it was quite a pleasure to look at him.

'"You are looking for a situation, miss?" he asked.

'"Yes, sir."

'"As governess?"

'"Yes, sir."

'"And what salary do you ask?"

'"I had four pounds a month in my last place with Colonel Spence Munro."

"'Oh, tut, tut! Sweating – rank sweating!" he cried, throwing his fat hands out into the air like a man who is in a boiling passion. "How could anyone offer so pitiful a sum to a lady with such attractions and accomplishments?"

"'My accomplishments, sir, may be less than you imagine," said I. "A little French, a little German, music and drawing –"

"'Tut, tut!" he cried. "This is all quite beside the question. The point is, have you or have you not the bearing and deportment of a lady? There it is in a nutshell. If you have not, you are not fitted for the rearing of a child who may someday play a considerable part in the history of the country. But if you have – why, then, how could any gentleman ask you to condescend to accept anything under the three figures? Your salary with me, madam, would commence at a hundred pounds a year."

'You may imagine, Mr Holmes, that to me, destitute as I was, such an offer seemed almost too good to be true. The gentleman, however, seeing perhaps the look of incredulity upon my face, opened a pocket-book and took out a note.

"'It is also my custom," said he, smiling in the most pleasant fashion until his eyes were just two little shining slits amid the white creases of his face, "to advance to my young ladies half their salary beforehand, so that they may meet any little expenses of their journey and their wardrobe."

'It seemed to me that I had never met so fascinating and so thoughtful a man. As I was already in debt to my tradesmen, the advance was a great convenience, and yet there was something unnatural about the whole transaction which made me wish to know a little more before I quite committed myself.

"'May I ask where you live, sir?" said I.

"'Hampshire. Charming rural place. The Copper Beeches, five miles on the far side of Winchester. It is the most lovely country, my dear young lady, and the dearest old country-house."

"'And my duties, sir? I should be glad to know what they would be."

"'One child – one dear little romper just six years old. Oh, if you could see him killing cockroaches with a slipper! Smack! smack! smack! Three gone before you could wink!" He leaned back in his chair and laughed his eyes into his head again.

'I was a little startled at the nature of the child's amusement, but the father's laughter made me think that perhaps he was joking.

"'My sole duties, then," I asked, "are to take charge of a single child?"

"'No, no, not the sole, not the sole, my dear young lady," he cried. "Your duty would be, as I am sure your good sense would suggest, to obey any little commands my wife might give, provided always that they were such commands as a lady might with propriety obey. You see no difficulty, heh?"

"'I should be happy to make myself useful."

"'Quite so. In dress now, for example. We are faddy people, you know – faddy but kind-hearted. If you were asked to wear any dress which we might give you, you would not object to our little whim. Heh?"

'"No," said I, considerably astonished at his words.

'"Or to sit here, or sit there, that would not be offensive to you?"

'"Oh, no."

'"Or to cut your hair quite short before you come to us?"

'I could hardly believe my ears. As you may observe, Mr Holmes, my hair is somewhat luxuriant, and of a rather peculiar tint of chestnut. It has been considered artistic. I could not dream of sacrificing it in this offhand fashion.

'"I am afraid that that is quite impossible," said I. He had been watching me eagerly out of his small eyes, and I could see a shadow pass over his face as I spoke.

'"I am afraid that it is quite essential," said he. "It is a little fancy of my wife's, and ladies' fancies, you know, madam, ladies' fancies must be consulted. And so you won't cut your hair?"

'"No, sir, I really could not," I answered firmly.

'"Ah, very well; then that quite settles the matter. It is a pity, because in other respects you would really have done very nicely. In that case, Miss Stoper, I had best inspect a few more of your young ladies."

'The manageress had sat all this while busy with her papers without a word to either of us, but she glanced at me now with so much annoyance upon her face that I could not help suspecting that she had lost a handsome commission through my refusal.

'"Do you desire your name to be kept upon the books?" she asked.

'"If you please, Miss Stoper."

'"Well, really, it seems rather useless, since you refuse the most excellent offers in this fashion," said she sharply. "You can hardly expect us to exert ourselves to find another such opening for you. Good-day to you, Miss Hunter." She struck a gong upon the table, and I was shown out by the page.

'Well, Mr Holmes, when I got back to my lodgings and found little enough in the cupboard, and two or three bills upon the table. I began to ask myself whether I had not done a very foolish thing. After all, if these people had strange fads and expected obedience on the most extraordinary matters, they were at least ready to pay for their eccentricity. Very few governesses in England are getting a hundred pounds a year. Besides, what use was my hair to me? Many people are improved by wearing it short and perhaps I should be among the number. Next day I was inclined to think that I had made a mistake, and by the day after I was sure of it. I had almost overcome my pride so far as to go back to the agency and enquire whether the place was still open, when I received this letter from the gentleman himself.

'I have it here and I will read it to you:

The Copper Beeches, near Winchester

Dear Miss Hunter – Miss Stoper has very kindly given me your address, and I write from here to ask you whether you have reconsidered your decision.

My wife is very anxious that you should come, for she has been much attracted by my description of you. We are willing to give thirty pounds a quarter, or a hundred and twenty a year, so as to recompense you for any little inconvenience which our fads may cause you. They are not very exacting, after all. My wife is fond of a particular shade of electric blue and would like you to wear such a dress indoors in the morning. You need not, however, go to the expense of purchasing one, as we have one belonging to my dear daughter Alice (now in Philadelphia), which would, I should think, fit you very well. Then, as to sitting here or there, or amusing yourself in any manner indicated, that need cause you no inconvenience. As regards your hair, it is no doubt a pity, especially as I could not help remarking its beauty during our short interview, but I am afraid that I must remain firm upon this point, and I only hope that the increased salary may recompense you for the loss. Your duties, as far as the child is concerned, are very light. Now do try to come, and I shall meet you with the dogcart at Winchester. Let me know your train.

Yours faithfully,

Jephro Rucastle

'That is the letter which I have just received, Mr Holmes, and my mind is made up that I will accept it. I thought, however, that before taking the final step I should like to submit the whole matter to your consideration.'

'Well, Miss Hunter, if your mind is made up, that settles the question,' said Holmes, smiling.

'But you would not advise me to refuse?'

'I confess that it is not the situation which I should like to see a sister of mine apply for.'

'What is the meaning of it all, Mr Holmes?'

'Ah, I have no data. I cannot tell. Perhaps you have yourself formed some opinion?'

'Well, there seems to me to be only one possible solution. Mr Rucastle seemed to be a very kind, good-natured man. Is it not possible that his wife is a lunatic, that he desires to keep the matter quiet for fear she should be taken to an asylum, and that he humours her fancies in every way in order to prevent an outbreak?'

'That is a possible solution – in fact, as matters stand, it is the most probable one. But in any case it does not seem to be a nice household for a young lady.'

'But the money, Mr Holmes, the money!'

'Well, yes, of course the pay is good – too good. That is what makes me uneasy. Why should they give you a hundred and twenty a year, when they could have their pick for forty? There must be some strong reason behind it.'

'I thought that if I told you the circumstances you would understand afterwards if I wanted your help. I should feel so much stronger if I felt that you were at the back of me.'

'Oh, you may carry that feeling away with you. I assure you that your little problem promises to be the most interesting which has come my way for some months. There is something distinctly novel about some of the features. If you should find yourself in doubt or in danger –'

'Danger! What danger do you foresee?'

Holmes shook his head gravely. 'It would cease to be a danger if we could define it,' said he. 'But at any time, day or night, a telegram would bring me down to your help.'

'That is enough.' She rose briskly from her chair with the anxiety all swept from her face. 'I shall go down to Hampshire quite easy in my mind now. I shall write to Mr Rucastle at once, sacrifice my poor hair tonight, and start for Winchester tomorrow.' With a few grateful words to Holmes, she bade us both good-night and bustled off upon her way.

'At least,' said I, as we heard her quick firm steps descending the stairs, 'she seems to be a young lady who is very well able to take care of herself.'

'And she would need to be,' said Holmes gravely. 'I am much mistaken if we do not hear from her before many days are past.'

It was not very long before my friend's prediction was fulfilled. A fortnight went by, during which I frequently found my thoughts turning in her direction and wondering what strange side-alley of human experience this lonely woman had strayed into. The unusual salary, the curious conditions, the light duties, all pointed to something abnormal, though whether a fad or a plot, or whether the man were a philanthropist or a villain, it was quite beyond my powers to determine. As to Holmes, I observed that he sat frequently for half an hour on end, with knitted brows and an abstracted air, but he swept the matter away with a wave of his hand when I mentioned it. 'Data! data! data!' he cried impatiently. 'I can't make bricks without clay.' And yet he would always wind up by muttering that no sister of his should ever have accepted such a situation.

The telegram which we eventually received came late one night just as I was thinking of turning in and Holmes was settling down to one of those all-night chemical researches which he frequently indulged in, when I would leave him stooping over a retort and a test-tube at night and find him in the same position when I came down to breakfast in the morning. He opened the yellow envelope, and then, glancing at the message, threw it across to me.

'Just look up the trains in Bradshaw,' said he, and turned back to his chemical studies.

The summons was a brief and urgent one. 'Please be at the Black Swan Hotel at Winchester at midday tomorrow [it said]. Do come! I am at my wit's end. Hunter.'

'Will you come with me?' asked Holmes, glancing up.

'I should wish to.'

'Just look it up, then.'

'There is a train at half-past nine,' said I, glancing over my Bradshaw. 'It is due at Winchester at 11:30.'

'That will do very nicely. Then perhaps I had better postpone my analysis of the acetones, as we may need to be at our best in the morning.'

By eleven o'clock the next day we were well upon our way to the old English capital. Holmes had been buried in the morning papers all the way down, but after we had passed the Hampshire border he threw them down and began to admire the scenery. It was an ideal spring day, a light blue sky, flecked with little fleecy white clouds drifting across from west to east. The sun was shining very brightly, and yet there was an exhilarating nip in the air, which set an edge to a man's energy. All over the countryside, away to the rolling hills around Aldershot, the little red and grey roofs of the farm steadings peeped out from amid the light green of the new foliage.

'Are they not fresh and beautiful?' I cried with all the enthusiasm of a man fresh from the fogs of Baker Street.

But Holmes shook his head gravely.

'Do you know, Watson,' said he, 'that it is one of the curses of a mind with a turn like mine that I must look at everything with reference to my own special subject. You look at these scattered houses, and you are impressed by their beauty. I look at them, and the only thought which comes to me is a feeling of their isolation and of the impunity with which crime may be committed there.'

'Good heavens!' I cried. 'Who would associate crime with these dear old homesteads?'

'They always fill me with a certain horror. It is my belief, Watson, founded upon my experience, that the lowest and vilest alleys in London do not present a more dreadful record of sin than does the smiling and beautiful countryside.'

'You horrify me!'

'But the reason is very obvious. The pressure of public opinion can do in the town what the law cannot accomplish. There is no lane so vile that the scream of a tortured child or the thud of a drunkard's blow does not beget sympathy and indignation among the neighbours, and then the whole machinery of justice is ever so close that a word of complaint can set it going and there is but a step between the crime and the dock. But look at these lonely houses, each in its own fields, filled for the most part with poor ignorant folk who know little of the law. Think of the deeds of hellish cruelty, the hidden wickedness which may go on, year in, year out, in such places, and none the wiser. Had this lady who appeals to us for help gone to live in Winchester, I should never have had a fear for her. It is the five miles of country which makes the danger. Still, it is clear that she is not personally threatened.'

'No. If she can come to Winchester to meet us she can get away.'

'Quite so. She has her freedom.'

'What *can* be the matter, then? Can you suggest no explanation?'

'I have devised seven separate explanations, each of which would cover the facts as far as we know them. But which of these is correct can only be determined by the fresh information which we shall no doubt find waiting for us. Well, there is the tower of the cathedral, and we shall soon learn all that Miss Hunter has to tell.'

The Black Swan is an inn of repute in the High Street, at no distance from the station, and there we found the young lady waiting for us. She had engaged a sitting-room, and our lunch awaited us upon the table.

'I am so delighted that you have come,' she said earnestly. 'It is so very kind of you both; but indeed I do not know what I should do. Your advice will be altogether invaluable to me.'

'Pray tell us what has happened to you.'

'I will do so, and I must be quick, for I have promised Mr Rucastle to be back before three. I got his leave to come into town this morning, though he little knew for what purpose.'

'Let us have everything in its due order.' Holmes thrust his long thin legs out towards the fire and composed himself to listen.

'In the first place, I may say that I have met, on the whole, with no actual ill-treatment from Mr and Mrs Rucastle. It is only fair to them to say that. But I cannot understand them, and I am not easy in my mind about them.'

'What can you not understand?'

'Their reasons for their conduct. But you shall have it all just as it occurred. When I came down, Mr Rucastle met me here and drove me in his dogcart to the Copper Beeches. It is, as he said, beautifully situated, but it is not beautiful in itself, for it is a large square block of a house, whitewashed, but all stained and streaked with damp and bad weather. There are grounds round it, woods on three sides, and on the fourth a field which slopes down to the Southampton high road, which curves past about a hundred yards from the front door. This ground in front belongs to the house, but the woods all round are part of Lord Southerton's preserves. A clump of copper beeches immediately in front of the hall door has given the place its name.

'I was driven over by my employer, who was as amiable as ever, and was introduced by him that evening to his wife and the child. There was no truth, Mr Holmes, in the conjecture which seemed to us to be probable in your rooms at Baker Street. Mrs Rucastle is not mad. I found her to be a silent, pale-faced woman, much younger than her husband, not more than thirty, I should think, while he can hardly be less than forty-five. From their conversation I have gathered that they have been married about seven years, that he was a widower, and that his only child by the first wife was the daughter who has gone to Philadelphia. Mr Rucastle told me in private that the reason why she had left them was that she had an unreasoning aversion to her stepmother. As the daughter could not have been less than twenty, I can quite imagine that her position must have been uncomfortable with her father's young wife.

'Mrs Rucastle seemed to me to be colourless in mind as well as in feature. She impressed me neither favourably nor the reverse. She was a nonentity. It was easy to see that she was passionately devoted both to her husband and to her little son. Her light grey eyes wandered continually from one to the other, noting every little want and forestalling it if possible. He was kind to her also in his bluff, boisterous fashion, and on the whole they seemed to be a happy couple. And yet she had some secret sorrow, this woman. She would often be lost in deep thought, with the saddest look upon her face. More than once I have surprised her in tears. I have thought sometimes that it was the disposition of her child which weighed upon her mind, for I have never met so utterly spoiled and so ill-natured a little creature. He is small for his age, with a head which is quite disproportionately large. His whole life appears to be spent in an alternation between savage fits of passion and gloomy intervals of sulking. Giving pain to any creature weaker than himself seems to be his one idea of amusement, and he shows quite remarkable talent in planning the capture of mice, little birds and insects. But I would rather not talk about the creature, Mr Holmes, and, indeed, he has little to do with my story.'

'I am glad of all details,' remarked my friend, 'whether they seem to you to be relevant or not.'

'I shall try not to miss anything of importance. The one unpleasant thing about the house, which struck me at once, was the appearance and conduct of the servants. There are only two, a man and his wife. Toller, for that is his name, is a rough, uncouth man, with grizzled hair and whiskers and a perpetual smell of drink. Twice since I have been with them he has been quite drunk, and yet Mr Rucastle seemed to take no notice of it. His wife is a very tall and strong woman with a sour face, as silent as Mrs Rucastle and much less amiable. They are a most unpleasant couple, but fortunately I spend most of my time in the nursery and my own room, which are next to each other in one corner of the building.

'For two days after my arrival at the Copper Beeches my life was very quiet; on the third, Mrs Rucastle came down just after breakfast and whispered something to her husband.

'"Oh, yes," said he, turning to me, "we are very much obliged to you, Miss Hunter, for falling in with our whims so far as to cut your hair. I assure you that it has not detracted in the tiniest iota from your appearance. We shall now see how the electric-blue dress will become you. You will find it laid out upon the bed in your room, and if you would be so good as to put it on we should both be extremely obliged."

'The dress which I found waiting for me was of a peculiar shade of blue. It was of excellent material, a sort of beige, but it bore unmistakable signs of having been worn before. It could not have been a better fit if I had been measured for it. Both Mr and Mrs Rucastle expressed a delight at the look of it, which seemed quite exaggerated in its vehemence. They were waiting for me in the drawing-room, which is a very large room, stretching along the entire front of the house, with three long windows reaching down to the floor. A chair had been placed close to the central window, with its back turned towards it. In this I was asked to sit, and then Mr Rucastle, walking up and down on the other side of the room, began to tell me a series of the funniest stories that I have ever listened to. You cannot imagine how comical he was, and I laughed until I was quite weary. Mrs Rucastle, however, who has evidently no sense of humour, never so much as smiled, but sat with her hands in her lap, and a sad, anxious look upon her face. After an hour or so, Mr Rucastle suddenly remarked that it was time to commence the duties of the day, and that I might change my dress and go to little Edward in the nursery.

'Two days later this same performance was gone through under exactly similar circumstances. Again I changed my dress, again I sat in the window, and again I laughed very heartily at the funny stories of which my employer had an immense repertoire, and which he told inimitably. Then he handed me a yellow-backed novel, and moving my chair a little sideways, that my own shadow might not fall upon the page, he begged me to read aloud to him. I read for about ten minutes, beginning in the heart of a chapter, and then suddenly, in the middle of a sentence, he ordered me to cease and to change my dress.

'You can easily imagine, Mr Holmes, how curious I became as to what the meaning of this extraordinary performance could possibly be. They were always very careful, I observed, to turn my face away from the window, so that I became consumed with the desire to see what was going on behind my back. At first it seemed to be impossible, but I soon devised a means. My hand-mirror had been broken, so a happy thought seized me, and I concealed a piece of the glass in my handkerchief. On the next occasion, in the midst of my laughter, I put my handkerchief up to my eyes, and was able with a little management to see all that there was behind me. I confess that I was disappointed There was nothing. At least that was my first impression. At the second glance, however, I perceived that there was a man standing in the Southampton Road, a small bearded man in a grey suit, who seemed to be looking in my direction. The road is an important highway, and there are usually people there. This man, however, was leaning against the railings which bordered our field and was looking earnestly up. I lowered my handkerchief and glanced at Mrs Rucastle to find her eyes fixed upon me with a most searching gaze. She said nothing, but I am convinced that she had divined that I had a mirror in my hand and had seen what was behind me. She rose at once.

'"Jephro," said she, "there is an impertinent fellow upon the road there who stares up at Miss Hunter."

'"No friend of yours, Miss Hunter?" he asked.

'"No, I know no one in these parts."

'"Dear me! How very impertinent! Kindly turn round and motion to him to go away."

'"Surely it would be better to take no notice."

'"No, no, we should have him loitering here always. Kindly turn round and wave him away like that."

'I did as I was told, and at the same instant Mrs Rucastle drew down the blind. That was a week ago, and from that time I have not sat again in the window, nor have I worn the blue dress, nor seen the man in the road.'

'Pray continue,' said Holmes. 'Your narrative promises to be a most interesting one.'

'You will find it rather disconnected, I fear, and there may prove to be little relation between the different incidents of which I speak. On the very first day that I was at the Copper Beeches, Mr Rucastle took me to a small outhouse which stands near the kitchen door. As we approached it, I heard the sharp rattling of a chain and the sound as of a large animal moving about.

'"Look in here!" said Mr Rucastle, showing me a slit between two planks. "Is he not a beauty?"

'I looked through and was conscious of two glowing eyes, and of a vague figure huddled up in the darkness.

'Don't be frightened," said my employer, laughing at the start which I had given. "It's only Carlo, my mastiff. I call him mine, but really old Toller, my groom, is the only man who can do anything with him. We feed him once a day, and not too much then, so that he is always as keen as mustard. Toller lets him loose every night, and God help the trespasser whom he lays his fangs upon. For goodness' sake don't you ever on any pretext set your foot over the threshold at night, for it's as much as your life is worth."

'The warning was no idle one, for two nights later I happened to look out of my bedroom window about two o'clock in the morning. It was a beautiful moonlight night, and the lawn in front of the house was silvered over and almost as bright as day. I was standing, rapt in the peaceful beauty of the scene, when I was aware that something was moving under the shadow of the copper beeches. As it emerged into the moonshine I saw what it was. It was a giant dog, as large as a calf, tawny tinted, with hanging jowl, black muzzle and huge projecting bones. It walked slowly across the lawn and vanished into the shadow upon the other side. That dreadful sentinel sent a chill to my heart which I do not think any burglar could have done.

'And now I have a very strange experience to tell you. I had, as you know, cut off my hair in London, and I had placed it in a great coil at the bottom of my trunk. One evening, after the child was in bed, I began to amuse myself by examining the furniture of my room and by rearranging my own little things. There was an old chest of drawers in the room, the two upper ones empty and open, the lower one locked. I had filled the first two with my linen, and as I had still much to pack away I was naturally annoyed at not having the use of the third drawer. It struck me that it might have been fastened by a mere oversight, so I took out my bunch of keys and tried to open it. The very first key fitted to perfection, and I drew the drawer open. There was only one thing in it, but I am sure that you would never guess what it was. It was my coil of hair.

'I took it up and examined it. It was of the same peculiar tint, and the same thickness. But then the impossibility of the thing obtruded itself upon me. How could my hair have been locked in the drawer? With trembling hands I undid my trunk, turned out the contents, and drew from the bottom my own hair. I laid the two tresses together, and I assure you that they were identical. Was it not extraordinary? Puzzle as I would, I could make nothing at all of what it meant. I returned the strange hair to the drawer, and I said nothing of the matter to the Rucastles as I felt that I had put myself in the wrong by opening a drawer which they had locked.

'I am naturally observant, as you may have remarked, Mr Holmes, and I soon had a pretty good plan of the whole house in my head. There was one wing, however, which appeared not to be inhabited at all. A door which faced that which led into the quarters of the Tollers opened into this suite, but it was invariably locked. One day, however, as I ascended the stair, I met Mr Rucastle coming out through this door, his keys in his hand and a look on his face which made him a very different person to the round, jovial man to whom I was accustomed. His cheeks were red, his brow was all crinkled with anger and the veins stood out at his temples with passion. He locked the door and hurried past me without a word or a look.

'This aroused my curiosity, so when I went out for a walk in the grounds with my charge, I strolled round to the side from which I could see the windows of this part of the house. There were four of them in a row, three of which were simply dirty, while the fourth was shuttered up. They were evidently all deserted. As I strolled up and down, glancing at them occasionally, Mr Rucastle came out to me, looking as merry and jovial as ever.

'"Ah!" said he, "you must not think me rude if I passed you without a word, my dear young lady. I was preoccupied with business matters."

'I assured him that I was not offended. "By the way," said I, "you seem to have quite a suite of spare rooms up there, and one of them has the shutters up."

'He looked surprised and, as it seemed to me, a little startled at my remark.

'"Photography is one of my hobbies," said he. "I have made my dark room up there. But, dear me! what an observant young lady we have come upon. Who would have believed it? Who would have ever believed it?" He spoke in a jesting tone, but there was no jest in his eyes as he looked at me. I read suspicion there and annoyance, but no jest.

'Well, Mr Holmes, from the moment I understood there was something about that suite of rooms which I was not to know, I was all on fire to go over them. It was not mere curiosity, though I have my share of that. It was more a feeling of duty – a feeling that some good might come from my penetrating to this place. They talk of woman's instinct; perhaps it was woman's instinct which gave me that feeling. At any rate, it was there, and I was keenly on the lookout for any chance to pass the forbidden door.

'It was only yesterday that the chance came. I may tell you that, besides Mr Rucastle, both Toller and his wife find something to do in these deserted rooms, and I once saw him carrying a large black linen bag with him through the door. Recently he has been drinking hard, and yesterday evening he was very drunk; and when I came upstairs there was the key in the door. I have no doubt at all that he had left it there. Mr and Mrs Rucastle were both downstairs, and the child was with them, so that I had an admirable opportunity. I turned the key gently in the lock, opened the door, and slipped through.

'There was a little passage in front of me, unpapered and uncarpeted, which turned at a right angle at the farther end. Round this corner were three doors in a line, the first and third of which were open. They each led into an empty room, dusty and cheerless, with two windows in the one and one in the other, so thick with dirt that the evening light glimmered only dimly through them. The centre door was closed, and across the outside of it had been fastened one of the broad bars of an iron bed, padlocked at one end to a ring in the wall, and fastened at the other with stout cord. The door itself was locked as well, and the key was not there. This barricaded door corresponded clearly with the shuttered window outside, and yet I could see by the glimmer from beneath it that the room was not in darkness. Evidently there was a skylight which let in light from above. As I stood in the passage gazing at the sinister door and wondering what secret it might veil, I suddenly heard the sound of steps within the room and saw a shadow pass backwards and forwards against the little slit of dim light which shone out from under the door. A mad, unreasoning terror rose up in me at the sight, Mr Holmes. My overstrung nerves failed me suddenly and I turned and ran – ran as though some dreadful hand were behind me, clutching at the skirt of my dress. I rushed down the passage, through the door, and straight into the arms of Mr Rucastle, who was waiting outside.

'"So," said he, smiling, "it was you, then. I thought that it must be when I saw the door open."

'"Oh, I am so frightened!" I panted.

'"My dear young lady! my dear young lady!" – you can't think how caressing and soothing his manner was – "and what has frightened you, my dear young lady?"

'But his voice was just a little too coaxing. He overdid it. I was keenly on my guard against him.

'"I was foolish enough to go into the empty wing," I answered. "But it is so lonely and eerie in this dim light that I was frightened and ran out again. Oh, it is so dreadfully still in there!"

'"Only that?" said he, looking at me keenly.

'"Why, what did you think?" I asked.

'"Why do you think that I lock this door?"

'"I am sure that I do not know."

'"It is to keep people out who have no business there. Do you see?" He was still smiling in the most amiable manner.

'"I am sure if I had known –"

'"Well, then, you know now. And if you ever put your foot over that threshold again" – here in an instant the smile hardened into a grin of rage, and he glared down at me with the face of a demon – "I'll throw you to the mastiff."

'I was so terrified that I do not know what I did. I suppose that I must have rushed past him into my room. I remember nothing until I found myself lying on my bed trembling all over. Then I thought of you, Mr Holmes. I could not live there longer without some advice. I was frightened of the house, of the man, of the woman, of the servants, even of the child. They were all horrible to me. If I could only bring you down, all would be well. Of course I might have fled from the house, but my curiosity was almost as strong as my fears. My mind was soon made up. I would send you a wire. I put on my hat and cloak, went down to the office, which is about half a mile from the house, and then returned, feeling very much easier. A horrible doubt came into my mind as I approached the door lest the dog might be loose, but I remembered that Toller had drunk himself into a state of insensibility that evening, and I knew that he was the only one in the household who had any influence with the savage creature, or who would venture to set him free. I slipped in in safety and lay awake half the night in my joy at the thought of seeing you. I had no difficulty in getting leave to come into Winchester this morning, but I must be back before three o'clock, for Mr and Mrs Rucastle are going on a visit and will be away all the evening, so that I must look after the child. Now I have told you all my adventures, Mr Holmes, and I should be very glad if you could tell me what it all means, and above all, what I should do.'

Holmes and I had listened spellbound to this extraordinary story. My friend rose now and paced up and down the room, his hands in his pockets and an expression of the most profound gravity upon his face.

'Is Toller still drunk?' he asked.

'Yes. I heard his wife tell Mrs Rucastle that she could do nothing with him.'

'That is well. And the Rucastles go out tonight?'

'Yes.'

'Is there a cellar with a good strong lock?'

'Yes, the wine-cellar.'

'You seem to me to have acted all through this matter like a very brave and sensible girl, Miss Hunter. Do you think that you could perform one more feat? I should not ask it of you if I did not think you a quite exceptional woman.'

'I will try. What is it?'

'We shall be at the Copper Beeches by seven o'clock, my friend and I. The Rucastles will be gone by that time, and Toller will, we hope, be incapable. There only remains Mrs Toller, who might give the alarm. If you could send her into the cellar on some errand, and then turn the key upon her, you would facilitate matters immensely.'

'I will do it.'

'Excellent! We shall then look thoroughly into the affair. Of course there is only one feasible explanation. You have been brought there to personate someone, and the real person is imprisoned in this chamber. That is obvious. As to who this prisoner is, I have no doubt that it is the daughter, Miss Alice Rucastle, if I remember right, who was said to have gone to America. You were chosen, doubtless, as resembling her in height, figure and the colour of your hair. Hers had been cut off, very possibly in some illness through which she has passed, and so, of course, yours had to be sacrificed also. By a curious chance you came upon her tresses. The man in the road was undoubtedly some friend of hers – possibly her fiancé – and no doubt, as you wore the girl's dress and were so like her, he was convinced from your laughter, whenever he saw you, and afterwards from your gesture, that Miss Rucastle was perfectly happy, and that she no longer desired his attentions. The dog is let loose at night to prevent him from endeavouring to communicate with her. So much is fairly clear. The most serious point in the case is the disposition of the child.'

'What on earth has that to do with it?' I ejaculated.

'My dear Watson, you as a medical man are continually gaining light as to the tendencies of a child by the study of the parents. Don't you see that the converse is equally valid. I have frequently gained my first real insight into the character of parents by studying their children. This child's disposition is abnormally cruel, merely for cruelty's sake, and whether he derives this from his smiling father, as I should suspect, or from his mother, it bodes evil for the poor girl who is in their power.'

'I am sure that you are right, Mr Holmes,' cried our client. 'A thousand things come back to me which make me certain that you have hit it. Oh, let us lose not an instant in bringing help to this poor creature.'

'We must be circumspect, for we are dealing with a very cunning man. We can do nothing until seven o'clock. At that hour we shall be with you, and it will not be long before we solve the mystery.'

We were as good as our word, for it was just seven when we reached the Copper Beeches, having put up our trap at a wayside public-house. The group of trees, with their dark leaves shining like burnished metal in the light of the setting sun, were sufficient to mark the house even had Miss Hunter not been standing smiling on the doorstep.

'Have you managed it?' asked Holmes.

A loud thudding noise came from somewhere downstairs. 'That is Mrs Toller in the cellar,' said she. 'Her husband lies snoring on the kitchen rug. Here are his keys, which are the duplicates of Mr Rucastle's.'

'You have done well indeed!' cried Holmes with enthusiasm. 'Now lead the way, and we shall soon see the end of this black business.'

We passed up the stair, unlocked the door, followed on down a passage, and found ourselves in front of the barricade which Miss Hunter had described. Holmes cut the cord and removed the transverse bar. Then he tried the various keys in the lock, but without success. No sound came from within, and at the silence Holmes's face clouded over.

'I trust that we are not too late,' said he. 'I think, Miss Hunter, that we had better go in without you. Now, Watson, put your shoulder to it, and we shall see whether we cannot make our way in.'

It was an old rickety door and gave at once before our united strength. Together we rushed into the room. It was empty. There was no furniture save a little pallet bed, a small table and a basketful of linen. The skylight above was open, and the prisoner gone.

'There has been some villainy here,' said Holmes; 'this beauty has guessed Miss Hunter's intentions and has carried his victim off.'

'But how?'

'Through the skylight. We shall soon see how he managed it.' He swung himself up on to the roof. 'Ah, yes,' he cried, 'here's the end of a long light ladder against the eaves. That is how he did it.'

'But it is impossible,' said Miss Hunter; 'the ladder was not there when the Rucastles went away.'

'He has come back and done it. I tell you that he is a clever and dangerous man. I should not be very much surprised if this were he whose step I hear now upon the stair. I think, Watson, that it would be as well for you to have your pistol ready.'

The words were hardly out of his mouth before a man appeared at the door of the room, a very fat and burly man, with a heavy stick in his hand. Miss Hunter screamed and shrank against the wall at the sight of him, but Sherlock Holmes sprang forward and confronted him.

'You villain!' said he, 'where's your daughter?'

The fat man cast his eyes round, and then up at the open skylight.

'It is for me to ask you that,' he shrieked, 'you thieves! Spies and thieves! I have caught you, have I? You are in my power. I'll serve you!' He turned and clattered down the stairs as hard as he could go.

'He's gone for the dog!' cried Miss Hunter.

'I have my revolver,' said I.

'Better close the front door,' cried Holmes, and we all rushed down the stairs together. We had hardly reached the hall when we heard the baying of a hound, and then a scream of agony, with a horrible worrying sound which it was dreadful to listen to. An elderly man with a red face and shaking limbs came staggering out of a side door.

'My God!' he cried. 'Someone has loosed the dog. It's not been fed for two days. Quick, quick, or it'll be too late!'

Holmes and I rushed out and round the angle of the house, with Toller hurrying behind us. There was the huge famished brute, its black muzzle buried in Rucastle's throat, while he writhed and screamed upon the ground. Running up, I blew its brains out, and it fell over with its keen white teeth still meeting in the great creases of his neck. With much labour we separated them and carried him, living but horribly mangled, into the house. We laid him upon the drawing-room sofa, and having dispatched the sobered Toller to bear the news to his wife, I did what I could to relieve his pain. We were all assembled round him when the door opened, and a tall, gaunt woman entered the room.

'Mrs Toller!' cried Miss Hunter.

'Yes, miss. Mr Rucastle let me out when he came back before he went up to you. Ah, miss, it is a pity you didn't let me know what you were planning, for I would have told you that your pains were wasted.'

'Ha!' said Holmes, looking keenly at her. 'It is clear that Mrs Toller knows more about this matter than anyone else.'

'Yes, sir, I do, and I am ready enough to tell what I know.'

'Then, pray, sit down, and let us hear it, for there are several points on which I must confess that I am still in the dark.'

'I will soon make it clear to you,' said she; 'and I'd have done so before now if I could ha' got out from the cellar. If there's police-court business over this, you'll remember that I was the one that stood your friend, and that I was Miss Alice's friend too.

'She was never happy at home, Miss Alice wasn't, from the time that her father married again. She was slighted like and had no say in anything, but it never really became bad for her until after she met Mr Fowler at a friend's house. As well as I could learn, Miss Alice had rights of her own by will, but she was so quiet and patient, she was, that she never said a word about them but just left everything in Mr Rucastle's hands. He knew he was safe with her; but when there was a chance of a husband coming forward, who would ask for all that the law would give him, then her father thought it time to put a stop on it. He wanted her to sign a paper, so that whether she married or not, he could use her money. When she wouldn't do it, he kept on worrying her until she got brain-fever, and for six weeks was at death's door. Then she got better at last, all worn to a shadow, and with her beautiful hair cut off; but that didn't make no change in her young man, and he stuck to her as true as man could be.'

'Ah,' said Holmes, 'I think that what you have been good enough to tell us makes the matter fairly clear, and that I can deduce all that remains. Mr Rucastle then, I presume, took to this system of imprisonment?'

'Yes, sir.'

'And brought Miss Hunter down from London in order to get rid of the disagreeable persistence of Mr Fowler.'

'That was it, sir.'

'But Mr Fowler, being a persevering man, as a good seaman should be, blockaded the house, and having met you, succeeded by certain arguments, metallic or otherwise, in convincing you that your interests were the same as his.'

'Mr Fowler was a very kind-spoken, free-handed gentleman,' said Mrs Toller serenely.

'And in this way he managed that your good man should have no want of drink, and that a ladder should be ready at the moment when your master had gone out.'

'You have it, sir, just as it happened.'

'I am sure we owe you an apology, Mrs Toller,' said Holmes, 'for you have certainly cleared up everything which puzzled us. And here comes the country surgeon and Mrs Rucastle, so I think, Watson, that we had best escort Miss Hunter back to Winchester, as it seems to me that our *locus standi* now is rather a questionable one.'

And thus was solved the mystery of the sinister house with the copper beeches in front of the door. Mr Rucastle survived, but was always a broken man, kept alive solely through the care of his devoted wife. They still live with their old servants, who probably know so much of Rucastle's past life that he finds it difficult to part from them. Mr Fowler and Miss Rucastle were married, by special licence, in Southampton the day after their flight, and he is now the holder of a government appointment on the island of Mauritius. As to Miss Violet Hunter, my friend Holmes, rather to my disappointment, manifested no further interest in her when once she had ceased to be the centre of one of his problems, and she is now the head of a private school in Walsall, where I believe that she has met with considerable success.

Notes

p. 68	*causes célèbres* - famous cases
p. 68	*cherry-wood pipe . . . his clay* - different kinds of pipes for smoking tobacco
p. 68	*singular* - remarkable, and here with the sense of unique
p. 69	*gas* - before electricity, Victorian homes were lit by gas
p. 69	*compositor* - one who sets up the type for a printing press
p. 70	*plover's egg* - the eggs of the plover, a small water bird, are cream coloured with light brown speckles
p. 71	*rank sweating* - to sweat: to employ for very long hours for very low pay; rank: extremely nasty
p. 71	*faddy* - subject to fads / having odd ideas
p. 74	*Bradshaw* - the Victorian standard book of train timetables
p. 75	*farm steadings* - farm buildings
p. 75	*homesteads* - small farms
p. 75	*inn of repute* - an inn with a good reputation
p. 76	*dogcart* - small horse-drawn cart

p. 76   *preserves* - woods full of pheasants kept (preserved) – specially for shooting for sport

p. 77   *beige* - undyed woollen fabric

p. 77   *yellow-backed novels* - cheap novels, the popular paperback of the nineteenth century

p. 78   *mastiff* - a breed of large dog

p. 79   *sentinel* - guard (the dog)

p. 82   *put up our trap* - parked our horse and cart

p. 83   *skylight* - window in the ceiling/roof

p. 85   *locus standi* - right to be here

9

A Story of a Wedding Tour

(1894)

Margaret Oliphant

Oliphant was a British writer who was very popular in her day. She wrote almost 100 novels, as well as short stories, biographies and historical works. Her work was admired by M.R. James and has been compared to Trollope, but Oliphant has a much better understanding of women characters. One critic has called her 'a gentle subversive' – which fits this story, in which an innocent young woman finds herself married to a boorish older man. When she realises that he does not love her, she plans to escape.

CHAPTER I

They had been married exactly a week when this incident occurred.

It was not a love marriage. The man, indeed, had been universally described as being "very much in love," but the girl was not by any one supposed to be in that desirable condition. She was a very lonely little girl, without parents, almost without relations. Her guardian was a man who had been engaged in business relations with her father, and who had accepted the charge of the little orphan as his duty. But neither he nor his wife had any love to expend on her, and they did not feel that such visionary sentiments came within the line of duty. He was a very honourable man, and took charge of her small – very small – property with unimpeachable care.

If anything, he wronged himself rather than Janey, charging her nothing for the transfers which he made of her farthing's worth of stock from time to time, to get a scarcely appreciable rise of interest and income for her. The whole thing was scarcely appreciable, and to a large-handed man like Mr Midhurst, dealing with hundreds of thousands, it was almost ridiculous to give a moment's attention to what a few hundreds might produce. But he did so; and if there is any angel who has to do with trade affairs, I hope it was carefully put to his account to balance some of the occasions on which he was not perhaps so particular. Nor did Mrs Midhurst shrink from her duty in all substantial and real good offices to the girl. She, who spent hundreds at the dressmaker's every year on account of her many daughters, did not disdain to get Janey's serge frocks at a cheaper shop, and to have them made by an inexpensive workwoman, so that the girl should have the very utmost she could get for her poor little money.

Was not this real goodness, real honesty, and devotion to their duty? But to love a little thing like that with no real claim upon them, and nothing that could be called specially attractive about her, who could be expected to do it? They had plenty – almost more than enough – of children of their own. These children were big boys and girls, gradually growing, in relays, into manhood and womanhood, when this child came upon their hands. There was no room for her in the full and noisy house. When she was grown up most of the Midhurst children were married, but there was one son at home, who, in the well-known contradictiousness of young people – it being a very wrong and, indeed, impossible thing – was quite capable of falling in love with Janey – and one daughter, with whom it was also possible that Janey might come into competition.

The young Midhursts were nice-looking young people enough; but Janey was very pretty. If Providence did but fully consider all the circumstances, it cannot but be felt that Providence would not carry out, as often is done, such ridiculous arrangements. Janey was very pretty. Could anything more inconvenient, more inappropriate, be conceived?

The poor little girl had, accordingly, spent most of her life at school, where she had, let it not be doubted, made many friendships and little loves; but these were broken up by holidays, by the returning home of the other pupils, while she stayed for ever at school: and not at one school, but several – for in his extreme conscientiousness her guardian desired to do her "every justice," as he said, and prepare her fully for the life – probably that of a governess – which lay before her. Therefore, when she had become proficient in one part of her education she was carried on to another, with the highest devotion to her commercial value no doubt, but a sublime indifference to her little feelings. Thus, she had been in France for two years, and in Germany for two years, so as to be able to state that French and German acquired in these countries were among the list of her accomplishments. English, of course, was the foundation of all; and Janey had spent some time at a famous academy of music, – her guardian adding something out of his own pocket to her scanty means, that she might be fully equipped for her profession. And then she was brought, I will not say home: Janey fondly said home, but she knew very well it did not mean home. And it was while Mrs Midhurst was actually writing out the advertisement for 'The Times,' and the 'Morning Post,' and 'The Guardian,' which was to announce to all the world that a young lady desired an engagement as governess, that her husband burst in with the extraordinary news that Mr Rosendale, who had chanced to travel with Janey from Flushing, on her return, and who afterwards, by a still greater chance, met her when asked to lunch at the Midhursts', and stared very much at her, as they all remarked – had fallen in love with, and wanted to marry, this humble little girl.

"Fallen in love with Janey!" Mrs Midhurst cried. "Fallen in love with you, Janey!" said Agnes Midhurst, with a little emphasis on the pronoun. He was not, indeed, quite good enough to have permitted himself the luxury of falling in love with Mr Midhurst's daughter, but he was an astonishing match for Janey. He was a man who was very well off: he could afford himself such a caprice as that. He was not handsome. He was a thick-set little man, and did not dress or talk in perfect taste; but – in love! These two words had made all the difference. Nobody had ever loved her, much less been "in love" with her. Janey consented willingly enough for the magic of these two words. She felt that she was going to be like the best of women at last – to have some one who loved her, some one who was in love with her. He might not be "joli, joli," as they say in France. She might not feel any very strong impulse on her own part towards him; but if he were in love with her – in love! Romeo was no more than that with Juliet. The thought went to Janey's head. She married him quire willingly for the sake of this.

I am afraid that Janey, being young, and shy, and strange, was a good deal frightened, horrified, and even revolted, by her first discoveries of what it meant to be in love. She had made tremendous discoveries in the course of a week. She had found out that Mr Rosendale, her husband, was in love with her beauty, but as indifferent to herself as any of the persons she had quitted to give herself to him. He did not care at all what she thought, how she felt, what she liked or disliked. He did not care even for her comfort, or that she should be pleased and happy, which, in the first moment even of such a union, and out of pure self-regard to make a woman more agreeable to himself, a man – even the most brutal – generally regards more or less. He was, perhaps, not aware that he did not regard it. He took it for granted that, being his wife, she would naturally be pleased with what pleased him, and his mind went no further than this.

Therefore, as far as Janey liked the things he liked, all went well enough. She had these, but no other. Her wishes were not consulted further, nor did he know that he failed in any way towards her. He had little to say to her, except expressions of admiration. When he was not telling her that she was a little beauty, or admiring her pretty hair, her pretty eyes, the softness of her skin, and the smallness of her waist, he had nothing to say. He read his paper, disappearing behind it in the morning; he went to sleep after his midday meal (for the weather was warm;) he played billiards in the evening in the hotels to which he took her on their wedding journey; or he overwhelmed her with caresses from which she shrank in disgust, almost in terror. That was all that being in love meant, she found; and to say that she was disappointed cruelly was to express in the very mildest way the dreadful downfall of all her expectations and hopes which happened to Janey before she had been seven days a wife. It is not disagreeable to be told that you are a little beauty, prettier than any one else. Janey would have been very well pleased to put up with that; but to be petted like a little lapdog and then left as a lapdog is – to be quiet and not to trouble in the intervals of petting – was to the poor little girl, unaccustomed to love and athirst for it, who had hoped to be loved, and to find a companion to whom she would be truly dear, a disenchantment and disappointment which was almost more than flesh and blood could bear.

She was in the full bitterness of these discoveries when the strange incident occurred which was of so much importance in her life. They were travelling through France in one of those long night journeys to which we are all accustomed nowadays; and Janey, pale and tired, had been contemplating for some time the figure of her husband thrown back in the corner opposite, snoring complacently with his mouth open, and looking the worst that a middle-aged man can look in the utter abandonment of self-indulgence and rude comfort, when the train began to slacken its speed, and to prepare to enter one of those large stations which look so ghastly in the desertion of the night.

Rosendale jumped up instinctively, only half awake, as the train stopped. The other people in the carriage were leaving it, having attained the end of their journey, but he pushed through them and their baggage to get out, with the impatience which some men show at any pause of the kind, and determination to stretch their legs, or get something to drink, which mark the breaks in their journey. He did not even say anything to Janey as he forced his way out, but she was so familiar with his ways by this time that she took no notice. She did take notice, however, when, her fellow-passengers and their packages having all been cleared away, she suddenly became sensible that the train was getting slowly into motion again without any sign of her husband.

She thought she caught a glimpse of him strolling about on the opposite platform before she was quite sure of what was happening. And then there was a scurry of hurrying feet, a slamming of doors, and as she rose and ran to the window bewildered, she saw him, along with some other men, running at full speed, but quite hopelessly, to catch the train. The last she saw was his face, fully revealed by the light of the lamp, convulsed with rage and astonishment, evidently with a yell of denunciation on the lips. Janey trembled at the sight. There was that in him, too, though as yet in her submissiveness she had never called it forth, a temper as unrestrained as his love-making, and as little touched by any thought save that of his own gratification. Her first sensation was fright, a terror that she was in fault and was about to be crushed to pieces in his rage: and then Janey sank back in her corner, and a flood of feeling of quite another kind took possession of her breast.

Was it possible that she was alone? Was it possible that for the first time since that terrible moment of her marriage she was more safely by herself than any locked door or even watchful guardian could keep her, quite unapproachable in the isolation of the train? Alone!

"Safe!" Janey ventured to say to herself, clasping her hands together with a mingled sensation of excitement and terror and tremulous delight which words could not tell.

She did not know what to think at first. The sound of the train plunging along through the darkness, through the unknown country, filled her mind as if some one was talking to her. And she was fluttered by the strangeness of the incident and disturbed by alarms. There was a fearful joy in thus being alone, in having a few hours, perhaps a whole long tranquil night, to herself: whatever came of it, that was always so much gained. But then she seemed to see him in the morning coming in upon her heated and angry. She had always felt that the moment would come when he would be angry, and more terrible to confront than any governess, or even principal of a ladies' college. He would come in furious, accusing her of being the cause of the accident, or doing something to set the train in motion; or else he would come in fatigued and dusty, claiming her services as if she were his valet – a thing which had, more or less, happened already, and against which Janey's pride and her sense of what was fit had risen in arms. She thought of this for a little time with trouble, and of the difficulties she would have in arriving, and where she would go to, and what she would say. It was an absurd story to tell, not to his advantage, "I lost my husband at Montbard." How could she say it? The hotel people would think she was a deceiver. Perhaps they would not take her in. And how would he know where to find her when he arrived? He would feel that he had lost her, as much as she had lost him.

Just as this idea rose in her mind, like a new thing full of strange suggestions, the train began to shorten speed again, and presently stopped once more. She felt it to do so with a pang of horror. No doubt he had climbed up somewhere, at the end or upon the engine, and was now to be restored to his legitimate place, to fall upon her either in fondness or in rage, delighted to get back to her, or angry with her for leaving him behind: she did not know which would be the worst. Her heart began to beat with fright and anticipation. But to her great relief it was only the guard who came to the door. He wanted to know if madame was the lady whose husband had been left behind; and to offer a hundred apologies and explanations. One of those fools at Montbard had proclaimed twenty minutes' pause when there were but five. If he had but heard he would have put it right, but he was at the other end of the train. But madame must not be too much distressed; a few hours would put it all right.

"Then there is another train?" said Janey, her poor little head buzzing between excitement and relief.

"Not for some hours," said the guard. "Madame will understand that there is not more than one *rapide* in the middle of the night; but in the morning quite early there is the train omnibus. Oh, very early, at five o'clock. Before madame is ready for her dinner monsieur will be at her side."

"Not till evening, then?" said Janey, with again a sudden acceleration of the movement of her heart.

The guard was desolated. "Not before evening. But if madame will remain quietly in the carriage when the train arrives at the station, I will find the omnibus of the hotel for her – I will see to everything! Madame, no doubt, knows which hotel to go to?"

Janey, as a matter of fact, did not know. Her husband had told her none of the details of the journey; but she said with a quick breath of excitement –

"I will go to the one that is nearest, the one at the Gare. There will be no need for any omnibus."

"And the baggage? Madame has her ticket?"

"I have nothing," cried Janey, "except my travelling-bag. You must explain that for me. But otherwise – otherwise, I think I can manage."

"Madame speaks French so well," the man said, with admiration. It was, indeed, a piece of good fortune that she had been made to acquire the language in the country: that she was not frightened to find herself in a foreign place, and surrounded by people speaking a strange tongue, as many a young English bride would have been. There was a moment of tremendous excitement and noise at the station while all was explained to a serious *chef de Gare*, and a gesticulating band of porters and attendants, whose loud voices, as they all spoke together, would have frightened an ordinary English girl out of her wits. But Janey, in the strange excitement which had taken possession of her, and in her fortunate acquaintance with the language, stood still as a little rock amid all the confusion. "I will wait at the hotel till my husband comes," she said, taking out the travelling-bag and her wraps, and maintaining a composure worthy of all admiration. Not a tear, not an outcry. How astonishing are these English, cried the little crowd, with that swift classification which the Frenchman loves.

Janey walked into the hotel with her little belongings, not knowing whether she was indeed walking upon her feet or floating upon wings. She was quite composed. But if any one could only have seen the commotion within that youthful bosom! She locked the door of the little delightful solitary room in which she was placed. It was not delightful at all. But to Janey it was a haven of peace, as sweet, as secluded from everything alarming and terrible, as any bower. Not till evening could he by any possibility arrive – the man who had caused such a revolution in her life. She had some ten hours of divine quiet before her, of blessed solitude, of thought. She did not refuse to take the little meal that was brought to her, the breakfast of which she stood in need; and she was glad to be able to bathe her face, to take off her dusty dress, and put on the soft and fresh one, which, happily, had folded into a very small space, and therefore could be put into her bag. Her head still buzzed with the strangeness of the position, yet began to settle a little. When she had made all these little arrangements she sat down to consider. Perhaps you will think there was very little to consider, nothing but how to wait till the next train brought him, which, after all, was not a very great thing to do. Appalling, perhaps, to a little inexperienced bride; but not to Janey, who had travelled alone so often, and knew the language, and all that.

But whoever had been able to look into Janey's mind would have seen that something more was there, – a very, very different thing from the question of how best to await his coming back. Oh, if he had loved her, Janey would have put up with many things! She would have schooled herself out of all her private repugnances; she would have been so grateful to him, so touched by the affection which nobody had ever bestowed upon her before! But he did not love her. He cared nothing about herself, Janey; did not even know her, or want to know her, or take into consideration her ways or her wishes. He was in love with her pretty face, her fresh little beauty, her power of pleasing him. If ever that power ceased, which it was sure to do, sooner or later, she would be to him less than nothing, the dreary little wife whom everybody has seen attached to a careless man: Janey felt that this was what was in store for her. She felt the horror of him, and his kind of loving, which had been such a miserable revelation to her. She felt the relief, the happiness, ah, the bliss, of having lost him for a moment, of being alone.

She took out her purse from her pocket, which was full of the change she had got in Paris of one of the ten-pound notes which her guardian had given her when she left his house on her wedding morning. She took out the clumsy pocket-book, an old one, in which there were still nine ten-pound notes. It was all her fortune, except a very, very small investment which brought her in some seven pounds a year. This was the remainder of another small investment which had been withdrawn in order to provide her with her simple trousseau, leaving this sum of a hundred pounds which her guardian had given her, advising her to place it at once for security in her husband's hands. Janey had not done this, she scarcely could tell why. She spread them on the table – the nine notes, the twelve napoleons of shining French money. A hundred pounds; she had still the twelve francs which made up the sum. She had spent nothing. There were even the few coppers over for the *agio*. She spread them all out, and counted them from right to left, and again from left to right. Nine ten-pound notes, twelve and a-half French napoleons – or louis, as people call them nowadays – making a hundred pounds. A hundred pounds is a big sum in the eyes of a girl. It may not be much to you and me, who know that it means only ten times ten pounds, and that ten pounds goes like the wind as soon as you begin to spend it. But to Janey! Why, she could live upon a hundred pounds for – certainly for two years; for two long delightful years, with nobody to trouble her, nobody to scold, nobody to interfere. Something mounted to her head like the fumes of wine. Everything began to buzz again, to turn round, to sweep her away as on a rapidly mounting current. She put back all the money in the pocket-book – her fortune, the great sum that made her independent; and she put back her things into the bag. A sudden energy of resolution seized her. She put on her hat again, and as she looked at herself in the glass encountered the vision of a little face which was new to her. It was not that of Janey, the little governess-pupil; it was not young Mrs. Rosendale. It was full of life, and meaning, and energy, and strength. Who was it? Janey? Janey herself, the real woman, whom nobody had ever seen before.

CHAPTER II

It is astonishing how many things can be done in sudden excitement and passion which could not be possible under any other circumstances. Janey was by nature a shy girl and easily frightened, accustomed indeed to do many things for herself, and to move quietly without attracting observation through the midst of a crowd; but she had never taken any initiative, and since her marriage had been reduced to such a state of complete dependence on her husband's wishes and plans that she had not attempted the smallest step on her own impulse.

Now, however, she moved about with a quiet assurance and decision which astonished herself. She carried her few possessions back again to the railway station, leaving the small gold piece of ten francs to pay, and much overpay, her hour's shelter and entertainment at the hotel.

Nobody noticed her as she went through the bustle of the place and back to the crowded station, where a little leisurely local train was about starting – a slow train occupied by peasants and country folk, and which stopped at every station along the line. English people abound in that place at all hours, except at this particular moment, when the *rapide* going towards Italy had but newly left and the little country train was preparing in peace. Nobody seemed to notice Janey as she moved about with her bag on her arm. She took her ticket in her irreproachable French "acquired in the country," which attracted no attention. She got into a second-class carriage in which there were already various country people, and especially a young mother with a baby, and its nurse in a white round cap with long streaming ribbons. Janey's heart went out to these people. She wondered if the young woman was happy, if her husband loved her, if it was not very sweet to have a child – a child must love you; it would not mind whether your cheeks were rosy or pale, whether you were pretty or not, whether you had accomplishments or languages acquired in the country.

Looking at this baby, Janey almost forgot that she was going out upon the world alone, and did not know where. It is a tremendous thing to do this, to separate from all the world you are acquainted with, to plunge into the unknown. Men do it often enough, though seldom without some clue, some link of connection with the past and way of return. Janey was about to cut herself off as by the Fury's shears from everything. She would never join her husband again. She would never fear her guardian again. She must drop out of sight like a stone into the sea. There was no longing love to search for her, no pardon to be offered, no one who would be heart-struck at the thought of the little girl lost and unhappy. Only anger would be excited by her running away, and a desire to punish, to shake her little fragile person to pieces, to make her suffer. She knew that if she did it at all, it must be final. But this did not overwhelm her. What troubled Janey a great deal more than the act of severance which she was about to accomplish, was the inevitable fib or fibs she must tell in order to account for her appearance in the unknown. She did not like to tell a fib, even a justifiable one. It was against all her traditions, against her nature. She felt that she could never do it anything but badly, never without exciting suspicions; and she must needs have some story, some way of accounting for herself.

This occupied her mind while the slow train crawled from station to station. It was the most friendly, idle, gossiping little train. It seemed to stop at the merest signal-box to have a talk, to drink as it were a social glass administered through that black hose, with a friend; it stopped wherever there were a few houses, it carried little parcels, it took up a leisurely passenger going next door, and the little electric bell went on tingling, and the guard cried "En voiture!" and the little bugle sounded. Janey was amused by all these little sounds and sights, and the country all flooded with sunshine, and the flowers everywhere, though it was only March, and dark black weather when she had left home.

Left home! and she had no home now, anywhere, no place to take refuge in, nobody to write to, to appeal to, to tell if she was happy or unhappy. But Janey did not care! She felt a strange elation of ease and relief. All alone, but everybody smiling upon her, the young mother opposite beginning to chatter, the baby to crow to her, the nurse to smile and approve of the *bonne petite* dame who took so much notice of the child. Her head was swimming, but with pleasure, and the blessed sensation of freedom – pleasure tinctured with the exhilaration of escape, and the thrill of fright which added to the excitement. Yet at that moment she was certainly in no danger. He was toiling along no doubt, fuming and perhaps swearing, on another slow train on the other side of Marseilles. Janey laughed to herself a little guiltily at the thought.

And she had escaped! It was not her doing primarily. She might have gone on all her life till she had died, but for that accident which was none of her doing. It was destiny that had done it, fate. The cage door had been opened and the bird had flown away. And how nice it would be to settle down, with this little mother, just about her own age, for a neighbour, and to help to bring the baby up! The kind, sweet faces they all had, mother and baby and *bonne* all smiling upon her! When Janey looked out on the other side she saw the sea flashing in the sunshine, the red porphyry rocks reflecting themselves in the brilliant blue, and village after village perched upon a promontory or in the hollow of a bay. She had never in all her life before felt that sensation of blessedness, of being able to do what she liked, of having no one to call to her account. She did not know where she was going, but that was part of the pleasure. She did not want to know where she was going.

Then suddenly this sentiment changed, and she saw in a moment a place that smiled at her like the smiling of the mother and baby. It was one of those villages in a bay: a range of blue mountains threw forth a protecting arm into the sea to shield it: the roofs were red, the houses were white, they were all blazing in the sun. Soft olives and palms fringed the deep green of the pines that rolled back in waves of verdure over the country behind, and strayed down in groups and scattered files to the shore below. Oh, what a cheerful, delightsome place! and this was where the little group with the baby were preparing to get out. "I will go too," said Janey to herself; and her heart gave a little bound of pleasure. She was delighted to reach the place where she was going to stay – just as she had been delighted to go on in the little pottering train, not knowing where she was going; and not wishing to know.

This was how Janey settled herself on the day of her flight from the world. She scarcely knew what story it was she told to the young woman whose face had so charmed her, and whom she asked whether she would be likely to find lodgings anywhere, lodgings that would not be too expensive.

"My husband is – at sea," Janey heard herself saying. She could scarcely tell what it was that put those words into her head.

"Oh, but yes," the other young woman cried with rapture. Nothing was more easy to get than a lodging in St Honorat, which was beginning to try to be a winter resort, and was eager to attract strangers. Janey had dreamed of a cottage and a garden, but she was not dissatisfied when she found herself in a sunbright room on the second floor of a tall white house facing the sea. It had a little balcony all to itself. The water rippled on the shore just over the road, the curve of the blue mountains was before her eyes.

I do not say that when she had settled down, when the thrill of movement was no longer in her brain, Janey was not without a shiver at the thought of what she had done. When the sun set, and that little chill which comes into the air of the south at the moment of its setting breathed a momentary cold about her, and when the woman of the house carefully closed the shutters and shut out the shining of the bay, and she was left alone with her candle, something sank in Janey's heart – something of the unreasonable elation, the fantastic happiness, of the day. She thought of "Mr. Rosendale" (she had never got so near her husband as to call him by any other name) arriving, of the fuss there would be about her and the inquiries.

Was it rash to have come to a place so near as this – within an hour or two of where he was? Was there a danger that some one might have seen her? that it might be found out that she had taken her ticket? But then she had taken her ticket for a place much farther along the coast. She thought she could see him arrive all flaming with anger and eagerness, and the group that would gather round him, and how he would be betrayed by his bad French, and the rage he would get into! Again she laughed guiltily; but then got very grave again trying to count up all the chances – how some porter might have noticed and might betray her, how he might yet come down upon her furiously, to wreak upon her all the fury of his discomfiture. Janey knew by instinct that though it was in no way her fault, her husband would wreak his vengeance upon her even for being left behind by the train. She became desperate as she sat and thought it all over. It would be better for her to leap from the window, to throw herself into the sea, than to fall into his hands. There would be no forgiveness for her if he once laid hands upon her. Now that she had taken this desperate step, she must stand by it to the death.

CHAPTER III

Ten years had passed away since the time of that wedding tour.

Ten years! It is a very long time in a life. It makes a young man middle-aged, and a middle-aged man old. It takes away the bloom of youth, and the ignorance of the most inexperienced; and yet what a little while it is! – no more than a day when you look back upon it. The train from Marseilles to Nice, which is called the *rapide*, goes every day, and most people one time or another have travelled by it.

One day last winter one of the passengers in this train established very comfortably in the best corner of a sleeping carriage in which he had passed the night luxuriously, and from which he was now looking out upon the shining sea, the red rocks, the many bays and headlands of the coast, suddenly received such a shock and sensation as seldom occurs to any one. He was a man of middle-age and not of engaging aspect. His face was red, and his eyes were dull yet fiery. He had the air of a man who had indulged himself much and all his inclinations, had loved good living and all the joys of the flesh, had denied himself nothing – and was now paying the penalties. Such men, to tell the truth, are not at all unusual apparitions on that beautiful coast or in the train *rapide*. No doubt appearances are deceitful, and it is not always a bad man who bears that aspect or who pays those penalties: but in this case few people would have doubted.

His eyes were bloodshot, he had a scowl upon his brow, his foot was supported upon a cushion. He had a servant with him to whom he rarely spoke but with an insult. Not an agreeable man – and the life he was now leading, whatever it had been, was not an agreeable life. He was staring out at the window upon the curves of the coast, sometimes putting up the collar of his fur coat over his ears, though it was a warm morning, and the sun had all the force of April. What he was thinking of it would be difficult to divine – perhaps of the good dinner that awaited him at Monte Carlo when he got there, perhaps of his good luck in being out of England when the east winds began to blow, perhaps of something quite different – some recollection of his past. The *rapide* does not stop at St Honorat, which indeed had not succeeded in making itself a winter resort. It was still a very small place. There were a few people on the platform when the train rushed through. It seemed to pass like a whirlwind, yet notwithstanding, in that moment two things happened. The gentleman in the corner of the carriage started in his seat, and flung himself half out of the window, with a sudden roar which lost itself in the tunnel into which the train plunged. There was an awful minute in that tunnel: for the servant thought his master had taken a fit, and there was no light to see what convulsions he might have fallen into, while at the same time he fought furiously against the man's efforts to loose his wrappings and place him in a recumbent position, exclaiming furiously all the time. He had not taken a fit, but when the train emerged into the light he was as near to it as possible – purple-red in his face, and shouting with rage and pain.

"Stop the train! stop the train!" he shouted. "Do you hear, you fool? stop the train! Ring the bell or whatever it is! break the – thing! Stop the train!"

"Sir, sir! if you will only be quiet, I will get your medicine in a moment!"

"Medicine, indeed!" cried the master, indignantly, and every furious name that he could think of mounted to his lips – fool, idiot, ass, swine – there was no end to his epithets. "I tell you I saw her, I saw her!" he shouted. "Stop the train! Stop the train!"

On the other hand, among the few insignificant persons, peasants and others, who had been standing on the platform at St Honorat when the *rapide* dashed past, there had been a woman and a child. The woman was not a peasant: she was very simply dressed in black, with one of the small bonnets which were a few years ago so distinctively English, and with an air which corresponded to that simple coiffure. She was young, and yet had the air of responsibility and motherhood which marks a woman who is no longer in the first chapter of life. The child, a boy of nine or ten, standing close by her side, had seized her hand just as the train appeared impatiently to call her attention to something else; but, by some strange spell of attraction or coincidence, her eyes fixed upon that window out of which the gouty traveller was looking. She saw him as he saw her, and fell back dragging the boy with her as if she would have sunk into the ground. It was only a moment and the *rapide* was gone, screaming and roaring into the tunnel, making too much noise with the rush and sweep of its going to permit the shout of the passenger to be heard.

Ten years, ten long years, during which life had undergone so many changes! They all seemed to fly away in a moment, and the girl who had arrived at the little station of St Honorat alone, a fugitive, elated and intoxicated with her freedom, suddenly felt herself again the little Janey who had emancipated herself so strangely, – though she had for a long time been frightened by every train that passed and every stranger who came near.

In the course of these long years all this had changed. Her baby had been born, her forlorn state had called forth great pity, great remark and criticism, in the village where she had found refuge, – great censure also, for the fact of her marriage was not believed by everybody. Bur she was so lonely, so modest, and so friendly, that the poor little English stranger was soon forgiven. Perhaps her simple neighbours were glad to find that a prim English-woman, supposed to stand so fierce on her virtue, was in reality so fallible – or perhaps pity put all other sentiments out of court. She told her real story to the priest when the boy was baptised, and though he tried to persuade her to return to her husband, he only half believed in that husband, since the story was not told under any seal of confession. Janey never became absolutely one of his flock. She was a prim little Protestant in her heart, standing strong against the saints, but devoutly attending church, believing with simple religiousness that to go to church was better than not to go to church, whatever the rites might be, and reading her little English service steadily through all the prayers of the Mass, which she never learned to follow. But her boy was like the other children of St Honorat, and learned his catechism and said his lessons with the rest.

There were various things which she did to get a living, and got it very innocently and sufficiently, though in the humblest way. She taught English to the children of some of the richer people in the village: she taught them music. She had so much credit in this latter branch, that she often held the organ in church on a holiday and pleased everybody. Then she worked very well with her needle, and would help on an emergency at first for pure kindness, and then, as her faculties and her powers of service became known, for pay, with diligence and readiness. She found a niche in the little place which she filled perfectly, though only accident seemed to have made it for her. She had fifty pounds of her little fortune laid by for the boy. She had a share of a cottage in a garden – not an English cottage indeed, but the upper floor of a two-storeyed French house; and she and her boy did much in the garden, cultivating prettinesses which do not commend themselves much to the villagers of St Honorat. Whether she ever regretted the step she had taken nobody ever knew. She might have been a lady with a larger house than any in St Honorat, and servants at her call. Perhaps she sometimes thought of that; perhaps she felt herself happier as she was; sometimes, I think, she felt that if she had known the boy was coming she might have possessed her soul in patience, and borne even with Mr Rosendale. But then at the time the decisive step was taken she did not know.

She hurried home in a great fright, not knowing what to do; then calmed herself with the thought that even if he had recognised her, there were many chances against his following her, or at least finding her, with no clue, and after so many years. And then a dreadful panic seized her at the thought that he might take her boy from her. He had known nothing about the boy: but if he discovered that fact it would make a great difference. He could not compel Janey to return to him, but he could take the boy. When this occurred to her she started up again, having just sat down, and put on her bonnet and called the child.

"Are you going out again, mother?" he cried.

"Yes, directly, directly: come, John, come, come!" she said, putting his cap upon his head and seizing him by the hand. She led him straight to the presbytery, and asked for the *curé*, and went in to the good priest in great agitation, leaving the boy with his housekeeper.

"M. l'Abbé," she said, with what the village called her English directness, "I have just seen my husband go past in the train!"

"Not possible!" said M. l'Abbé, who only half believed there was a husband at all.

"And he saw me. He will come back, and I am afraid he will find me. I want you to do something for me."

"With pleasure," said the priest; "I will come and meet Monsieur your husband, and I will explain –"

"That is not what I want you to do. I want you to let John stay with you to keep him here till – till – He will want to take him away from me!" she cried.

"He will want to take you both away, *chère petite dame*. He has a right to do so."

"No, no! but I do not ask you what is his right. I ask you to keep John safe; to keep him here – till the danger has passed away!"

The priest tried to reason, to entreat, to persuade her that a father, not to say a husband, had his rights. But Janey would hear no reason: had she heard reason either from herself or another, she would not have been at St Honorat now. And he gave at last a reluctant consent. There was perhaps no harm in it after all. If a man came to claim his rights, he would not certainly go away again without some appeal to the authorities – which was a thing it must come to sooner or later, – if there was indeed a husband at all, and the story was true.

Janey then went back to her home. She thought she could await him there and defy him. "I will not go with you," she would say. "I may be your wife, but I am not your slave. You have left me alone for ten years. I will not go with you now!" She repeated this to herself many times, but it did not subdue the commotion in her being. She went out again when it became too much for her, locking her door with a strange sense that she might never come back again. She walked along the sea shore, repeating these words to herself, and then she walked up and down the streets, and went into the church and made the round of it, passing all the altars and wondering if the saints did pay attention to the poor women who were there, as always, telling St. Joseph or the Blessed Mary all about it. She sunk down in a dark corner, and said –

"Oh, my God! oh, my God!"

She could not tell Him about it in her agitation, with her heart beating so, but only call His attention, as the woman in the Bible touched the Redeemer's robe. And then she went out and walked up and down again. I cannot tell what drew her back to the station – what fascination, what dreadful spell. Before she knew what she was doing she found herself there, walking up and down, up and down.

As if she were waiting for some one! "You have come to meet a friend?" some one said to her, with an air of suspicion. And she first nodded and then shook her head; but still continued in spite of herself to walk up and down. Then she said to herself that it was best so – that to get it over would be a great thing, now John was out of the way; he would be sure to find her sooner or later – far better to get it over! When the train came in, the slow local train, coming in from the side of Italy, she drew herself back a little to watch. There was a great commotion when it drew up at the platform. A man got out and called all the loungers about to help to lift out a gentleman who was ill, – who had had a bad attack in the train.

"Is there anywhere here we can take him to? Is there any decent hotel? Is there a room fit to put my master in?" he cried.

He was English with not much French at his command, and in great distress. Janey, forgetting herself and her terrors, and strong in the relief of the moment that he whom she feared had not come, went up to offer her help. She answered the man's questions; she called the right people to help him; she summoned the *chef de Gare* to make some provision for carrying the stricken man to the hotel.

"I will go with you," she said to the servant, who felt as if an angel speaking English had suddenly come to his help. She stood by full of pity, as they lifted that great inert mass out of the carriage. Then she gave a great cry and fell back against the wall.

It was a dreadful sight the men said afterwards, enough to overcome the tender heart of any lady, especially of one so kind as Madame Jeanne. A huge man, helpless, unconscious, with a purple countenance, staring eyes, breathing so that you could hear him a mile off. No wonder that she covered her eyes with her hands not to see him: but finally she hurried away to the hotel to prepare for him, and to call the doctor, that no time should be lost. Janey felt as if she was restored for the moment to life when there was something she could do. The questions were all postponed. She did not think of flight or concealment, or even of John at the presbytery. "He is my husband," she said, with awe in her heart.

This was how the train brought back to Janey the man whom the train had separated from her ten years before. The whole tragedy was one of the railway, the noisy carriages, the snorting locomotives. He was taken to the hotel, but he never came to himself again, and died there the next day, without being able to say what his object was, or why he had got out of the *rapide*, though unable to walk, and insisted on returning to St Honorat. It cost him his life; but then his life was not worth a day's purchase, all the doctors said, in the condition in which he was.

Friends had to be summoned, and men of business, and it was impossible but that Janey's secret should be made known. When she found herself and her son recognised, and that there could be no doubt that the boy was his father's heir, she was struck with a great honor which she never quite got over all her life. She had not blamed herself before; but now seemed to herself no less than the murderer of her husband: and could not forgive herself, nor get out of her eyes the face she had seen, nor out of her ears the dreadful sound of that labouring breath.

Notes

p. 87   *farthing* - smallest of coins – a quarter of an old penny
p. 87   *serge* - woven fabric
p. 88   *joli joli* - attractive
p. 90   *valet* - a man's personal servant who dresses him and looks after his clothes
p. 91   *rapide* - express train
p. 91   *Gare* - station
p. 91   *chef de Gare* - station master
p. 92   *trousseau* - clothes and linen collected by a woman for her marriage
p. 92   *napoleons* - French coins
p. 92   *agio* - percentage payable for currency exchange
p. 94   *the Fury's shears* - this confuses the Furies – in Greek mythology, goddesses of
          vengeance – with the Fates – goddesses of destiny, who spun the thread of
          mortal lives and whose shears were used to cut the thread at death
p. 94   *bonne* - nursemaid
p. 94   *train . . . drink . . . hose* - steam trains had to take on water
p. 94   *en voiture* - all aboard!
p. 94   *bonne petite* - pretty little (woman)
p. 94   *porphyry* - rock that is full of crystals
p. 95   *verdure* - greenery
p. 96   *Marseille . . . Nice* - ports in the South of France

p. 96   *Monte Carlo* - town in the South of France – becoming well known as a
            seaside resort for the rich
p. 100   *presbytery* - priest's house
p. 98   *curé* - priest
p. 98   *M. l'Abbé* - formal address for the priest, English equivalent of 'Father'
p. 98   *chére petite dame* - my dear little woman
p. 99   *woman . . . touched the Redeemer's robe* - in the Bible a sick woman is cured
            miraculously merely by touching Christ's robe.

10

The Shrinking Shoe

(1895)

Walter Besant

Besant was a British Victorian writer, who wrote many novels, stories and works of history. Like Dickens, he campaigned through his writing on behalf of the poor of London. The Victorians loved fairy-tales and there were many brilliant examples of the genre, as well as re-tellings of traditional tales, in this period. Here Besant makes interesting use of the Cinderella story.

I

'Oh you poor dear!' said the two Elder Sisters in duet, 'you've got to stay at home while we go to the ball. Good night, then. We *are* so sorry for you! We did hope that you were going too!'

'Good night, Elder Sisters,' said the youngest, with a tear just showing in either eye, but not rolling down her cheek. 'Go and be happy. If you *should* see the Prince you may tell him that I am waiting for the Fairy and the Pumpkin and the Mice.'

The Elder Sisters fastened the last button—the sixth, was it? or the tenth perhaps—took one last critical, and reassuring, look at the glass, and departed.

When the door shut the Youngest Sister sat down by the fire; and one, two, three tears rolled down her cheeks.

Mind you, she had very good cause to cry. Many girls cry for much less. She was seventeen: she had understood that she would come out at this visit to London. Coming out, to this country girl, meant just this one dance and nothing more. But no—her sisters were invited and she was not. She was left alone in the house. And she sat down by the fire and allowed herself to be filled with gloom and sadness, and with such thoughts as, in certain antiquated histories, used to be called rebellious. In short, she was in a very bad temper indeed. Never before had she been in such a bad temper. As a general rule she was sweet-tempered as the day is long. But—which is a terrible thing to remember—there are always the possibilities of bad temper in every one: even in Katharine—Katie—Kitty, who generally looked as if she could never, never, never show by any outward sign that she was vexed, or cross, or put out, or rebellious. And now, alas! she was in a bad temper. No hope, no sunshine, no future prospects; her life was blasted—her young spring life. Disaster irretrievable had fallen upon her. She could not go to the ball. What made things worse was, that the more angry she grew the louder she heard the dance music, though the band was distant more than a mile. Quite plainly she heard the musicians. They were playing a valse which she knew—a delicious, delirious, dreamy, swinging valse. She saw her sisters among a crowd of the most lovely girls in the world, whirling in the cadence that she loved upon a floor as smooth as ice, with cavaliers gallant and gay. The room was filled with maidens beautifully dressed, like her sisters, and with young men come to meet and greet them on their way. Oh, happy young men! Oh, happy girls! Katie had been brought up with such simplicity that she envied no other girl, whether for her riches or for her dresses; and was always ready to acknowledge the loveliness and the sweetness and the grace of any number of girls— even of her own age. As regards her own sex, indeed, this child of seventeen had but one fault; she considered twenty as already a serious age, and wondered how anybody could possibly laugh after five-and-twenty. And, as many, or most, girls believe, she thought that beauty was entirely a matter of dress; and that, except on state occasions, no one should think of beauty—*i.e.*, of fine dress.

She sat there for half an hour. She began to think that it would be best to go to bed and sleep off her chagrin, when a Rat-tat-tat at the door roused her. Who was that? Could it—could it—could it be the Fairy with the Pumpkin and the Mice?

'My dear Katie'—it was not the Fairy, but it was the Godmother—'how sorry I am! Quick—lay out the things, Ladbrooke.' Ladbrooke was a maid, and she bore a parcel. 'It's not my fault. The stupid people only brought the things just now. It was my little surprise, dear. We will dress her here, Ladbrooke. I was going to bring the things in good time, to surprise you at the last moment. Never mind: you will only be a little late. I hope and trust the things will fit. I got one of your frocks, and Ladbrooke here can, if necessary—— There, Katie! What do you think of that for your first ball dress?'

Katie was so astonished that she could say nothing, not even to thank her godmother. Her heart beat and her hands trembled; the maid dressed her and did her hair; her godmother gave her a necklace of pearls and a little bunch of flowers: she put on the most charming pair of white satin shoes: she found in the parcel a pair of white gloves with ever so many buttons, and a white fan with painted flowers. When she looked at the glass she could not understand it at all; for she was transformed. But never was any girl dressed so quickly.

'Oh!' she cried. 'You *are* a Fairy. And you've got a Pumpkin as well?'

'The Pumpkin is at the door with the Mice. Come, dear. I shall be proud of my *débutante.*'

The odd thing was that all the time she was dressing, and all the time she sat in the carriage, Katie heard that valse tune ringing in her ears, and when they entered the ball-room that very same identical valse was being played, and the smooth floor was covered with dancers, gallant young men and lovely maidens—all as she had seen and heard in her vision. Oh! there is something in the world more than coincidence. There must be; else, why did Katie . . .

'Oh, my dear,' said the Elder Sisters, stopping in their dance, 'you have come at last! We knew you were coming, but we couldn't tell. Shall we tell the Prince you are here?'

Then a young gentleman was presented to her. But Katie was too nervous to look up when he bowed and begged. After a little, Katie found that his step went very well with hers. She was then able to consider things a little. Her first partner in her first ball was quite a young man—she had not caught his name, Mr Geoffrey something— a handsome young man, she thought, but rather shy. He began to talk about the usual things.

'I live in the country,' she said, to explain her ignorance. 'And this is my first ball. So, you see, I do not know any people or anything.'

He danced with her again: she was a wonderfully light dancer; she was strangely graceful; he found her, also, sweet to look at; she had soft eyes and a curiously soft voice, which was as if all the sympathy in all the world had been collected together and deposited in that little brain. He had the good fortune to take her in to supper; and, being a young man at that time singularly open to the charms of maidens, he lavished upon her all the attentions possible. Presently he was so far subdued by her winning manner that he committed the foolishness of Samson with his charmer. He told his secret. Just because she showed a little interest in him, and regarded him with eyes of wonder, he told her the great secret of his life—his ambition, the dream of his youth, his purpose. Next morning he felt he had been a fool. The girl would tell other girls, and they would all laugh together. He felt hot and ashamed for a moment. Then he thought of her eyes, and how they lightened when he whispered; and of her voice, and how it sank when she murmured sympathy and hope and faith. No—with such a girl his secret was safe.

So it was. But for her, if you think of it, was promotion indeed! For a girl who a few days before had been at school, under rules and laws, hardly daring to speak—certainly not daring to have an opinion of her own—now receiving deferential homage from a young man at least four years her senior, and actually being entrusted with his secret ambitions! More; there were other young men waiting about, asking for a dance; all treating her as if—well, modern manners do not treat young ladies with the old reverential courtesy—as if she were a person of considerable importance. But she liked the first young man the best. He had such an honest face, this young man. It was a charming supper, and, with her charming companion, Katie talked quite freely and at her ease. How nice to begin with a partner with whom one could be quite at one's ease! But everything at this ball was delightful.

After the young man had told his secret, blushing profoundly, Katie told hers—how she had as nearly as possible missed her first ball; and how her sisters had gone without her and left her in the cinders, crying.

'Fairy Godmother turned up at the last moment, and when I was dressed and we went out,' she laughed merrily, 'we found the Pumpkin and the Mice turned into a lovely carriage and pair.'

'It is a new version of the old story,' said the young man.

'Yes,' she replied thoughtfully, 'and now all I want is to find the Prince.'

The young man raised his eyes quickly. Then said, with great humility, 'If I could only be the Prince!' She read those words, and she blushed and became confused, and they talked no more that night.

'It was all lovely,' she said in the carriage going home. 'All but one thing—one thing that I said—oh, such a stupid thing!'

'What was it you said, Katie?'

'No: I could never tell anybody. It was *too* stupid. Oh! To think of it makes me turn red. It almost spoiled the evening. And he saw it too.'

'What was it, Katie?'

But she would not tell the Elder Sisters.

'Who was it,' asked one of them, 'that took Katie in to supper?'

'A young man named Armiger, I believe. Horace told me,' said the other Elder. Horace was a cousin. 'Horace says he is a cousin of a Sir Roland Armiger, about whom I know nothing. Horace says he is a good fellow—very young yet—an undergraduate somewhat. He is a nice-looking boy.'

Then the Elder Sisters began to talk about matters really serious—namely, themselves and their own engagements—and Katie was forgotten.

Two days after the ball there arrived a parcel addressed to the three sisters collectively—'The Misses De Lisle'. The three sisters opened it together, with Evelike curiosity.

It contained a white satin shoe; a silver buckle set with pearls adorned it, and a row of pearls ran round the open part. A most dainty shoe; a most attractive shoe; a most bewildering shoe.

'This,' said the Elder Sisters, solemnly, 'must be tried on by all of us in succession.'

The Elder Sisters began: it was too small for either, though they squeezed and made faces and an effort and a fuss, and everything that could be made except making the foot go into the shoe. Then Katie tried it on. Wonderful to relate, the foot slipped in quite easily. Yet they say that there is nothing but coincidence in the world.

Katie blushed and laughed and blushed again. Then she folded up the shoe in its silver paper and carried it away; and nobody ever heard her mention that shoe again. But everybody knew that she kept it, and the Elder Sisters marvelled because the young prince did not come to see that shoe tried on. He did not appear. Why not? Well—because he was too shy to call.

There are six thousand five hundred and sixty-three variants of this story, as has been discovered through the invaluable researches of the Folk-Lore Society, and it would be strange if they all ended in the same way.

II

The young man told his secret; he revealed what he had never before whispered to any living person; he told his ambition—the most sacred thing that a young man possesses or can reveal.

There are many kinds of ambition; many of them are laudable; we are mostly ambitious of those things which seem to the lowest imagination to be within our reach—such, for instance, as the saving of money. Those who aspire to things which seem out of reach suffer the pain and the penalty of the common snub. This young man aspired to things which seemed to other people quite beyond his reach; for he had no money, and his otherwise highly respectable family had no political influence, and such a thing had never before been heard of among his people that one of themselves should aspire to greater greatness than the succession to the family title with the family property. As a part of the new Revolution, which is already upon us, there will be few things indeed which an ambitious young man will consider beyond his reach. At the present moment, if I were to declare my ambition to become, when I grow up, Her Britannic Majesty's Ambassador at Paris, the thing would be actually received with derision. My young life would be blasted with contempt. Wait, however, for fifty years: you shall then see to what heights I will reach out my climbing hands.

Geoffrey Armiger would have soared. He saw before him the cases of Canning, of Burke, of Disraeli, of Robert Lowe, and of many others who started without any political influence and with no money, and he said to himself, 'I, too, will become a Statesman.'

That was the secret which he confided into Katie's ear; it was in answer to a question of hers, put quite as he could have wished, as to his future career. 'I have told no one,' he replied in a low voice, and with conscious flush. 'I have never ventured to tell any one, because my people would not understand; they are not easily moved out of the ordinary groove. There is a family living, and I am to have it: that is the fate to which I am condemned. But——' his lips snapped; resolution flamed in his eyes.

'Oh!' cried Katie. 'It is splendid! You must succeed. Oh! To be a great Statesman. Oh! There is only one thing better—to be a great Poet. You might be both.'

Geoffrey replied modestly that, although he had written verse, he hardly expected to accomplish both greatness in poetry and greatness as a legislator. The latter, he declared, would be good enough for him.

That was the secret which this young man confided to the girl. You must own that, for such a young man to reveal such a secret to this girl, on the very first evening that he met her, argues for the maiden the possession of sympathetic qualities quite above the common.

III

Five years change a boy of twenty into a mature man of twenty-five, and a *débutante* of seventeen into an old woman of twenty-two. The acknowledgment of such a fact may save the historian a vast quantity of trouble.

It was five years after the great event of the ball. The family cousin, Horace, of whom mention has been already made, was sitting in his chambers at ten or eleven in the evening. With him sat his friend Sir Geoffrey Armiger, a young man whom you have already met. The death of his cousin had transformed him from a penniless youth into a baronet with a great estate (which might have been in Spain or Ireland for all the good it was), and with a great fortune in stocks. There was now no occasion for him to take the family living: that had gone to a deserving stranger; a clear field lay open for his wildest ambitions. This bad fortune to the cousin, who was still quite young, happened the year after the ball. Of course, therefore, the young man of vast ambition had already both feet on the ladder? You shall see.

'What are you going to do all the summer?' asked the family cousin, Horace.

'I don't know,' Geoffrey replied languidly. 'Take the yacht somewhere, I suppose. Into the Baltic, perhaps. Will you come too?'

'Can't. I've got work to do. I shall run over to Switzerland for three weeks perhaps. Better come with me and do some climbing.'

Geoffrey shook his head.

'Man!' cried the other impatiently, 'you want something to do. Doesn't it bore you—just going on day after day, day after day, with nothing to think of but your own amusement?'

Geoffrey yawned. 'The Profession of Amusement,' he said, 'is, in fact, deadly dull.'

'Then why follow it?'

'Because I am so rich. You fellows who've got nothing *must* work. When a man is not obliged to work, there are a thousand excuses. I don't believe that I *could* work now if I wanted to. Yet I used to have ambitions.'

'You did. When it was difficult to find a way to live while you worked, you had enormous ambitions. "If only I was not obliged to provide for the daily bread"; that was what you used to say. Well, now the daily bread is provided, what excuse have you?'

'I tell you a thousand excuses present themselves the moment I think of doing any work. Besides, the ambitions are dead!'

'Dead! And at five-and-twenty! They can't be dead.'

'They are. Dead and buried. Killed by five years' racket. Profession of Pleasure—Pleasure, I believe they call it. No man can follow more than one profession.'

'Well, old man, if the world's pleasures are already rather dry in the mouth, what will they be when you've been running after them for fifty years?'

'There are cards, I believe. Cards are always left. No,'—he got up and leaned over the mantelshelf,——'I can't say that the fortune has brought much happiness with it. That's the worst of being rich. You see very well that you are not half so happy as the fellows who are making their own way, and yet you can't give up your money and start fair with the rest. I always think of that story of the young man who was told to give up all he had to the poor. He couldn't, you see. He saw very clearly that it would be best for him; but he couldn't. I am that young man. If I was like you, with all the world to conquer, I should be ten times as strong and a hundred times as clever. I know it—yet I cannot give up the money.'

'Nobody wants you to give it up. But surely you could go on like other fellows—as if you hadn't got it, I mean.'

'No—you don't understand. It's like a millstone tied round your neck. It drags you down and keeps you down.'

'Why don't you marry?'

'Why don't I? Well, when I meet the girl I fancy I will marry if she will have me. I suppose I'm constitutionally cold, because as yet—— Who is this girl?' He took up a cabinet photograph which stood on the mantelshelf. 'I seem to know the face. It's a winning kind of face—what they call a beseeching face. Where have I seen it?'

'That? It is the portrait of a cousin of mine. I don't think you can have met her anywhere, because she lives entirely in the country.'

'I have certainly seen her somewhere. Perhaps in a picture. Beatrice, perhaps. It is the face of an angel. Faces sometimes deceive, though: I know a girl in quite the smartest set who can assume the most saintly face when she pleases. She puts it on when she converses with the curate; when she goes to church she becomes simply angelic. At other times—— Your cousin does not, however, I should say, follow the Profession of Amusement.'

'Not exactly. She lives in a quiet little seaside place where they've got a convalescent home, and she slaves for the patients.'

'It is a beautiful face,' Geoffrey repeated. 'But I seem to know it.' He looked at the back of the photograph. 'What are these lines written at the back?'

'They are some nonsense rhymes written by herself. There is a little family tradition that Katie is waiting for her Prince—she says so herself—she has refused a good many men. I think she will never marry, because she certainly will not find the man she dreams of.'

'May I read the lines?' He read them aloud:—

> Oh! tell me, Willow-wren and White-throat, beating
> The sluggish breeze with eager homeward wing,
> Bear you no message for me—not a greeting
> From him you left behind—my Prince and King?
>
> You come from far—from south and east and west;
> Somewhere you left him, daring some great thing,
> I know not what, save that it is the best:
> Somewhere you saw him—saw my Prince and King.
>
> You cannot choose but know him: by the crown
> They place upon his head—the crown and ring;
> And by the loud and many-voiced renown
> After the footsteps of my Prince and King.
>
> He speaks, and lo! the listening world obeys;
> He leads, and all men follow; and they cling,

And hang around the words and works and ways,
As of a Prophet—of my Prince and King.

What matter if he comes not, though I wait?
Bear you no greeting for me, birds of spring?
Again—what matter, since his work is great,
And greater grows his name—my Prince and King.

'You see,' said the cousin, 'she has set up an ideal man.'

'Yes. Why does she call him her Prince?'

The cousin laughed. 'There is a story about a ball—her first ball—her last too, poor child, because—well, there were losses, you know. Like the landlady, Katie has known better days; and friends died, and so she lives by herself in this little village, and looks after her patient convalescents.'

'What about her first ball?'

'Well, she nearly missed it, because her godmother, who meant to give her a surprise, lost a train or got late somehow. So her Elder Sisters went without her, and she arrived late; and they said that, to complete the story, nothing was wanted but the Prince.'

Geoffrey started and changed colour.

'That's all. She imagined a Prince, and goes on with her dream. She enacts a novel which never comes to an end, and has no situations, and has an invisible hero.'

Geoffrey laid down the photograph. He now remembered everything, including the sending of the slipper. But the cousin had quite forgotten his own part in the story.

'I must go,' he said. 'I think I shall take the yacht somewhere round the coast. You say your cousin lives at——'

'Oh! Yes, she lives at Shellacomb Bay, near Torquay. Sit down again.'

'No. Dull place, Shellacomb Bay: I've been there, I think.' He was rather irresolute, but that was his way. 'I must go. I rather think there are some men coming into my place about this time. There will be nap. All professionals, you know—Professors of Amusement. It's dull work. I say, if your cousin found her Prince, what an awful, awful disappointment it would be!'

IV

At five in the morning Geoffrey was left alone. The night's play was over. He turned back the curtains and opened the windows, letting in the fresh morning air of April. He leaned out and took a deep breath.Then he returned to the room. The table was littered with packs of cards. There was a smell of a thousand cigarettes. It is an acrid smell, not like the honest downright smell of pipes and cigars; the board was covered with empty soda-water and champagne bottles.

'The Professional Pursuer of Pleasure', he murmured. 'It's a learned profession, I suppose. Quite a close profession. Very costly to get into, and beastly stupid and dull when you are in it. A learned profession, certainly.'

He sat down, and his thoughts returned to the girl who had made for herself a Prince. 'Her Prince!' he said bitterly. And then the words came back to him—

> Daring some great thing,
> I know not what, save that it is the best:
> Somewhere you saw him—saw my Prince and King.

'For one short night I was her Prince and King,' he murmured. 'And I sent her the slipper—was stone-broke a whole term after through buying that slipper. And after all I was afraid to call at the house. Her Prince and King. I wonder——' He looked about him again—looked at the empty bottles. '*What* a Prince and King!' he laughed bitterly.

Then he sprang to his feet; he opened a drawer and took from it a bundle of letters, photographs, cards of invitation which were lying there piled up in confusion. He threw these on the fire in a heap; he opened another drawer and pulled out another bundle of notes and papers. These also he threw on the fire. 'There!' he said resolutely. What he meant I know not, for he did not wait to see them burned, but went into his bedroom and so to bed.

V

Geoffrey spoke no more than the simple truth when he said that Katie De Lisle had a saintly face—the face of an angel. It was a lovely face when he first saw it—the face of a girl passing into womanhood. Five years of tranquil life, undisturbed by strong emotions, devoted to unselfish labours and to meditation, had now made that face saintly indeed. It was true that she had created for herself a Prince, one who was at once a Galahad of romance and a leader of the present day, chivalrous knight and Paladin of Parliament. What she did with her Prince I do not know. Whether she thought of him continually or only seldom, whether she believed in him or only hoped for him, no one can tell. When a man proposed to her—which happened whenever a man was presented to her—she refused him graciously, and told her sisters, who were now matrons, that another person had come representing himself to be the Prince, but that she had detected an impostor, for he was not the Prince. And it really seemed as if she never would find this impossible Prince, which was a great pity, if only because she had a very little income, and the Elder Sisters, who lived in great houses, desired her also to have a great house. Of course, every Prince who regards his own dignity must have a big house of his own.

Now, one afternoon in April, when the sun sets about a quarter-past seven and it is light until eight, Katie was sitting on one of the benches placed on the shore for the convenience of the convalescents, two or three of whom were strolling along the shore. The sun was getting low; a warmth and glow lay upon the bay like an illuminated mist.

Katie had a book in her hand, but she let it drop into her lap, and sat watching the beauty and the splendour and the colour of the scene before her. Then there came, rounding the southern headland, a steam yacht, which slowly crept into the bay, and dropped anchor and let off steam: a graceful little craft, with her slender spars and her dainty curves. The girl watched with a little interest. Not often did craft of any kind put into that bay. There were bays to the east and bays to the west, where ships, boats, fishing smacks, and all kind of craft put in; but not in that bay, where there was no quay, or port, or anything but the convalescents, and Katie the volunteer nurse. So she watched, sitting on the bench, with the western sun falling upon her face.

After a little a boat was lowered, and a man and a boy got into it. The boy took the sculls and rowed the man ashore. The man jumped out, stood irresolutely looking about him, observed Katie on the bench, looked at her rather rudely it seemed, and walked quickly towards her. What made her face turn pale? What made her cheek turn red and pale? Nothing less than the appearance of her Prince—her Prince. She knew him at once. Her Prince! It was her Prince come to her at last.

But the Prince did not hold out both hands and cry, 'I have come.' Not at all. He gravely and politely took off his hat. 'Miss De Lisle,' he said. 'I cannot hope that you remember me. I only met you once. But I—I heard that you were here, and I remembered your face at once.'

'I seldom forget people,' she replied, rising and giving him her hand. 'You are Mr Geoffrey Armiger. We danced together one night. I remember it especially, because it was my first ball.'

'Which you nearly missed, and were left at home like Cinderella, till the fairy godmother came. I—I am cruising about here. I learned that you were living here from your cousin in the Temple, and—and I thought that, if we put in here, I might, perhaps, venture to call.'

'Certainly. I shall be very glad to see you, Mr Armiger. It is seven o'clock now. Will you come to tea to-morrow afternoon?'

'With the greatest pleasure. May I walk with you—in your direction?'

The situation was delicate. What Geoffrey wanted to convey was this: 'You once received the confidences of a young man who hoped to do great things in the world. You have gone on believing that he would do great things. You have built up an ideal man, before whom all other men are small creatures. Well, that ideal must be totally disconnected with the young fellow who started it, because he has gone to the bad. He is only a Professor of Amusement, an idle killer of time, a man who wastes all his gifts and powers.' A difficult thing to say, because it involved charging the girl with, or telling her he knew that she had been, actually thinking of him for five years.

That evening he got very little way. He reminded her again of the ball. He said that she had altered very little, which was true; for at twenty-two Katie preserved much the same ethereal beauty that she had at seventeen. That done, his jaws stuck, to use a classical phrase. He could say no more. He left her at the door of her cottage,—she lived in a cottage in the midst of tree fuchsias and covered with roses,—and went back to his yacht, where he had a solitary dinner and passed a morose evening.

111

At five o'clock in the afternoon next day he called again. Miss De Lisle was at the Home, but would come back immediately. The books on the girl's table betrayed the character of her mind. Katie's books showed the level of her thoughts and the standard of her ideals. They were the books of a girl who meditates. There are such people, even in this busy and noisy age. Geoffrey took them up with a sinking heart. Professors of Amusement never read such books.

Then she came in, quiet, serene; and they sat down, and the tea was brought in.

'Now, tell me,' she said abruptly. 'I see by your card that you have a title. What did you do to get it?'

'Nothing. I succeeded.'

'Oh!' Her face fell a little. 'When I saw you—the only time that I saw you—I remember that you had great ambitions. What have you done?'

'Nothing. Nothing at all. I have wasted my time. I have lived a life of what they call pleasure. I don't know that I ought to have called upon you at all.'

'Is it possible? Oh! Can it be possible? Only a life of pleasure? And you—you with your noble dreams? Oh! Is it possible?'

'It is possible. It is quite true. I am the prodigal son, who has so much money that he cannot get through it. But do you remember the silly things I said? Why, you see, what happened was, that when the temptation came all the noble dream vanished?'

'Is it possible?' she repeated. 'Oh! I am so very, very sorry!'—in fact, the tears came into her eyes. 'You have destroyed the one illusion that I nourished.' Every one thinks that he has only one illusion and a clear eye for everything else. That is the Great, the Merciful, Illusion. 'I thought that there was one true man at least in the world, fighting for the right. I had been honoured as a girl with the noble ambitions of that man when he was quite young. I thought I should hear of him from time to time winning recognition, power, and authority. It was a beautiful dream. It made me feel almost as if I were myself taking part in that great career, even from this obscure corner in the country. No one knows the pleasure that a woman has in watching the career of a brave and wise man. And now it is gone. I am sorry you called,'—her voice became stony and her eyes hard: even an angel or a saint has moments of righteous indignation,—'I am very sorry, Sir Geoffrey Armiger, that you took the trouble to call.'

Her visitor rose. 'I am also very sorry,' he said, 'that I have said or done anything to pain you. Forgive me: I will go.'

But he lingered. He took up a paper-knife, and considered it as if it were something rare and curious. He laid it down. Then he laughed a little short laugh, and turned to Katie with smiling lips and solemn eyes.

'Did that slipper fit?' he asked, abruptly.

She blushed. But she answered him.

'It was too small for my Elder Sisters, but it fitted me.'

'Will you try it on again?'

She went out of the room and presently returned with the pretty, jewelled, little slipper. She took off her shoe, sat down, and tried it on.

'You see,' she said, 'it is now too small for my foot. Oh! my foot has not changed in the least. It has grown too small.'

'Try again.' The Prince looked on anxiously. 'Perhaps, with a little effort, a little goodwill——'

'No; it is quite hopeless. The slipper has shrunk; you can see for yourself, if you remember what it was like when you bought it. See, it is ever so much smaller than it was, Sir Geoffrey.' She looked up, gravely. 'See for yourself. And the silver buckle is black, and even the pearls are tarnished. See!' There was a world of meaning in her words. 'Think what it was five years ago.'

He took it from her hand and turned it round and round disconsolately.

'You remember it—five years ago—when it was new?' the girl asked again.

'I remember. Oh! yes, I remember. A pretty thing it was then, wasn't it? A world of promise in it, I remember. Hope, and courage, and—and all kinds of possibilities. Pity—silver gone black, pearls tarnished, colour faded, the thing itself shrunken. Yes.' He gave it back to her. 'I'm glad you've kept it.'

'Of course I kept it.'

'Yes, of course. Will you go on keeping it?'

'I think so. One likes to remember a time of promise, and of hope, and courage, and, as you say, all kinds of possibilities.'

He sighed.

'Slippers are so. There are untold sympathies in slippers. I call this the Oracle of the slipper. Not that I am in the least surprised. I came here, in fact, on purpose to ascertain, if I could, the amount of shrinkage. It would be interesting to return every five years or so, just to see how much it shrinks every year. Next time it would be a doll's shoe, for instance. Well, now'—again he fell back upon the paper-knife—'there was something else I had to say; something else——' He dropped his eyes and examined the paper-knife closely. 'The other day in your cousin's rooms I saw your photograph; and I remembered the kind of young fellow I was when we talked about ambitions and you sympathised with me. I think I should like to take up those ambitions again, if it is not too late. I am sick and weary of the Profession of Pleasure. I have wasted five good years, but perhaps they can be retrieved. Let me, if possible, burnish up that silver, expand the shrinking shoe, renew those dreams.'

'Do you mean it? Are you strong enough? Oh! You have fallen so low. Are you strong enough to rise?'

'I don't know. If the event should prove—if that slipper should enlarge again—if it should once more fit your foot——'

'If! Oh! how can a man say *if,* when he ought to say *shall*?'

'The slipper *shall* enlarge,' he said quietly, but with as much determination as one can expect from an Emeritus Professor of Pleasure.

'When it does, then come again. Till then, do not, if you please, seek me out in my obscurity. It would only be the final destruction of a renewed hope. Farewell, Sir Geoffrey.'

'*Au revoir*. Not farewell.'

He stooped and kissed her hand and left her.

Notes

p. 102   *glass* - looking-glass, mirror

p. 102   *come out* - start to take part in adult social life; stop being a child

p. 103   *cadence* - rhythm

p. 103   *cavaliers* - young men who are dancing partners

p. 103   *valse* - waltz

p. 106   *débutante* - one who is coming out, as in note above

p. 104   *Samson with his charmer* - reference to the Biblical story in which Samson's strength is retained in his hair, cut off by the cunning Delilah as he sleeps

p. 106   *Canning . . . Burke . . . Disraeli . . . Robert Lowe* - nineteenth-century politicians, who rose very high from relatively lowly origins

p. 106   *family living* - post as a clergyman

p. 107   *stocks* - investments on the stock exchange, shares

p. 107   *racket* - riotous living

p. 108   *Beatrice* - the beloved of Dante in the medieval poem, often referred to in the Victorian period as an ideal of womanhood and often featuring in paintings

p. 108   *Willow-wren and White-throat* - small birds

p. 109   *Shellacomb Bay, Torquay* - seaside resorts on the Devon coast of England

p. 109   *nap* - short for Napoleon, a card game

p. 110   *stone-broke* - penniless, having run out of money

p. 110   *Galahad* - a Knight of King Arthur's round table, famously pure and good, and a favourite Victorian role model for young men

p. 110   *Paladin of Parliament* - Paladin, the most important rank of knight in French medieval romances; so, a kind of modern-day chivalrous knight, pursuing justice through politics – in Parliament – rather than in battle

p. 111   *spars* - masts

p. 111   *smacks* - small fishing boats with a sail

p. 111   *sculls* - oars of the boat

p. 111   *Temple* - the Temple Inn in London, home of barristers and their pupils

p. 111   *his jaws stuck* - he could think of nothing to say, could not speak

p. 112   *prodigal son* - from the Bible, the son who has run away and wasted his father's money is welcomed home in a parable of God's forgiveness of sinners

p. 113   *Emeritus* - an emeritus title is one retained by the holder when retired

p. 114   *Au revoir* - until we meet again

11

The Middle Years

(1895)

Henry James

Henry James – an American who became a British citizen – was not just a great novelist (Portrait of a Lady, The Wings of a Dove) *he wrote hundreds of stories, novellas such as* Washington Square, *and some long stories that might be called novellas, such as* The Turn of the Screw *and* The Aspern Papers. *He revised all his work, including this story where only small revisions were made, first published in 1895 – for the complete New York edition of his works in 1909. The story focuses on an author who is also a great reviser of his work, coming to the end of his life, he fears, after a long illness. He is slightly cheered by the arrival of the first copy of his latest novel.*

I

The April day was soft and bright, and poor Dencombe, happy in the conceit of reasserted strength, stood in the garden of the hotel, comparing, with a deliberation in which however there was still something of languor, the attractions of easy strolls. He liked the feeling of the south so far as you could have it in the north, he liked the sandy cliffs and the clustered pines, he liked even the colourless sea. 'Bournemouth as a health-resort' had sounded like a mere advertisement, but he was thankful now for the commonest conveniences. The sociable country postman, passing through the garden, had just given him a small parcel which he took out with him, leaving the hotel to the right and creeping to a bench he had already haunted, a safe recess in the cliff. It looked to the south, to the tinted walls of the Island, and was protected behind by the sloping shoulder of the down. He was tired enough when he reached it, and for a moment was disappointed; he was better of course, but better, after all, than what? He should never again, as at one or two great moments of the past, be better than himself. The infinite of life was gone, and what remained of the dose a small glass scored like a thermometer by the apothecary. He sat and stared at the sea, which appeared all surface and twinkle, far shallower than the spirit of man. It was the abyss of human illusion that was the real, the tideless deep. He held his packet, which had come by book-post, unopened on his knee, liking, in the lapse of so many joys – his illness had made him feel his age – to know it was there, but taking for granted there could be no complete renewal of the pleasure, dear to young experience, of seeing one's self 'just out'. Dencombe, who had a reputation, had come out too often and knew too well in advance how he should look.

His postponement associated itself vaguely, after a little, with a group of three persons, two ladies and a young man, whom, beneath him, straggling and seemingly silent, he could see move slowly together along the sands. The gentleman had his head bent over a book and was occasionally brought to a stop by the charm of this volume, which, as Dencombe could perceive even at a distance, had a cover alluringly red. Then his companions, going a little further, waited for him to come up, poking their parasols into the beach, looking around them at the sea and sky and clearly sensible of the beauty of the day. To these things the young man with the book was still more clearly indifferent; lingering, credulous, absorbed, he was an object of envy to an observer from whose connexion with literature all such artlessness had faded. One of the ladies was large and mature; the other had the spareness of comparative youth and of a social situation possibly inferior. The large lady carried back Dencombe's imagination to the age of crinoline; she wore a hat of the shape of a mushroom, decorated with a blue veil, and had the air, in her aggressive amplitude, of clinging to a vanished fashion or even a lost cause. Presently her companion produced from under the folds of a mantle a limp portable chair which she stiffened out and of which the large lady took possession. This act, and something in the movement of either party, at once characterised the performers – they performed for Dencombe's recreation – as opulent matron and humble dependent. Where moreover was the virtue of an approved novelist if one couldn't establish a relation between such figures? the clever theory for instance that the young man was the son of the opulent matron and that the humble dependent, the daughter of a clergyman or an officer, nourished a secret passion for him. Was that not visible from the way she stole behind her protectress to look back at him? – back to where he had let himself come to a full stop when his mother sat down to rest. His book was a novel, it had the catchpenny binding; so that while the romance of life stood neglected at his side he lost himself in that of the circulating library. He moved mechanically to where the sand was softer and ended by plumping down in it to finish his chapter at his ease. The humble dependent, discouraged by his remoteness, wandered with a martyred droop of the head in another direction, and the exorbitant lady, watching the waves, offered a confused resemblance to a flying-machine that had broken down.

When his drama began to fail Dencombe remembered that he had after all another pastime. Though such promptitude on the part of the publisher was rare he was already able to draw from its wrapper his 'latest', perhaps his last. The cover of 'The Middle Years' was duly meretricious, the smell of the fresh pages the very odour of sanctity; but for the moment he went no further – he had become conscious of a strange alienation. He had forgotten what his book was about. Had the assault of his old ailment, which he had so fallaciously come to Bournemouth to ward off, interposed utter blankness as to what had preceded it? He had finished the revision of proof before quitting London, but his subsequent fortnight in bed had passed the sponge over colour. He couldn't have chanted to himself a single sentence, couldn't have turned with curiosity or confidence to any particular page. His subject had already gone from him, leaving scarce a superstition behind. He uttered a low moan as he breathed the chill of this dark void, so desperately it seemed to represent the completion of a sinister process. The tears filled his mild eyes; something precious had passed away. This was the pang that had been sharpest during the last few years – the sense of ebbing time, of shrinking opportunity; and now he felt not so much that his last chance was going as that it was gone indeed. He had done all he should ever do, and yet hadn't done what he wanted. This was the laceration – that practically his career was over: it was as violent as a grip at his throat. He rose from his seat nervously – a creature hunted by a dread; then he fell back in his weakness and nervously opened his book. It was a single volume; he preferred single volumes and aimed at a rare compression. He began to read and, little by little, in this occupation, was pacified and reassured. Everything came back to him, but came back with a wonder, came back above all with a high and magnificent beauty. He read his own prose, he turned his own leaves, and had as he sat there with the spring sunshine on the page an emotion peculiar and intense. His career was over, no doubt, but it was over, when all was said, with *that*.

He had forgotten during his illness the work of the previous year; but what he had chiefly forgotten was that it was extraordinarily good. He dived once more into his story and was drawn down, as by a siren's hand, to where, in the dim underworld of fiction, the great glazed tank of art, strange silent subjects float. He recognised his motive and surrendered to his talent. Never probably had that talent, such as it was, been so fine. His difficulties were still there, but what was also there, to his perception, though probably, alas! to nobody's else, was the art that in most cases had surmounted them. In his surprised enjoyment of this ability he had a glimpse of a possible reprieve. Surely its force wasn't spent – there was life and service in it yet. It hadn't come to him easily, it had been backward and roundabout. It was the child of time, the nursling of delay; he had struggled and suffered for it, making sacrifices not to be counted, and now that it was really mature was it to cease to yield, to confess itself brutally beaten? There was an infinite charm for Dencombe in feeling as he had never felt before that diligence *vincit omnia*. The result produced in his little book was somehow a result beyond his conscious intention: it was as if he had planted his genius, had trusted his method, and they had grown up and flowered with this sweetness. If the achievement had been real, however, the process had been painful enough. What he saw so intensely today, what he felt as a nail driven in, was that only now, at the very last, had he come into possession. His development had been abnormally slow, almost grotesquely gradual. He had been hindered and retarded by experience, he had for long periods only groped his way. It had taken too much of his life to produce too little of his art. The art had come, but it had come after everything else. At such a rate a first existence was too short – long enough only to collect material; so that to fructify, to use the material, one should have a second age, an extension. This extension was what poor Dencombe sighed for. As he turned the last leaves of his volume he murmured 'Ah for another go, ah for a better chance!'

The three persons drawing his attention to the sands had vanished and then reappeared; they had now wandered up a path, an artificial and easy ascent, which led to the top of the cliff. Dencombe's bench was halfway down, on a sheltered ledge, and the large lady, a massive heterogeneous person with bold black eyes and kind red cheeks, now took a few moments to rest. She wore dirty gauntlets and immense diamond ear-rings; at first she looked vulgar, but she contradicted this announcement in an agreeable off-hand tone. While her companions stood waiting for her she spread her skirts on the end of Dencombe's seat. The young man had gold spectacles, through which, with his finger still in his red-covered book, he glanced at the volume, bound in the same shade of the same colour, lying on the lap of the original occupant of the bench. After an instant Dencombe felt him struck with a resemblance; he had recognised the gilt stamp on the crimson cloth, was reading 'The Middle Years' and now noted that somebody else had kept pace with him. The stranger was startled, possibly even a little ruffled, to find himself not the only person favoured with an early copy. The eyes of the two proprietors met a moment, and Dencombe borrowed amusement from the expression of those of his competitor, those, it might even be inferred, of his admirer. They confessed to some resentment – they seemed to say: 'Hang it, has he got it *already*? Of course he's a brute of a reviewer!' Dencombe shuffled his copy out of sight while the opulent matron, rising from her repose, broke out: 'I feel already the good of this air!'

'I can't say I do,' said the angular lady. 'I find myself quite let down.'

'I find myself horribly hungry. At what time did you order luncheon?' her protectress pursued.

The young person put the question by. 'Doctor Hugh always orders it.'

'I ordered nothing to-day – I'm going to make you diet,' said their comrade.

'Then I shall go home and sleep. *Qui dort dîne!*'

'Can I trust you to Miss Vernham?' asked Doctor Hugh of his elder companion.

'Don't I trust you?' she archly enquired.

'Not too much!' Miss Vernham, with her eyes on the ground, permitted herself to declare. 'You must come with us at least to the house,' she went on while the personage on whom they appeared to be in attendance began to mount higher. She had got a little out of ear-shot; nevertheless Miss Vernham became, so far as Dencombe was concerned, less distinctly audible to murmur to the young man: 'I don't think you realise all you owe the Countess!'

Absently, a moment, Doctor Hugh caused his gold-rimmed spectacles to shine at her. 'Is that the way I strike you? I see – I see!'

'She's awfully good to us,' continued Miss Vernham, compelled by the lapse of the other's motion to stand there in spite of his discussion of private matters. Of what use would it have been that Dencombe should be sensitive to shades hadn't he detected in that arrest a strange influence from the quiet old convalescent in the great tweed cape? Miss Vernham appeared suddenly to become aware of some such connexion, for she added in a moment: 'If you want to sun yourself here you can come back after you've seen us home.'

Doctor Hugh, at this, hesitated, and Dencombe, in spite of a desire to pass for unconscious, risked a covert glance at him. What his eyes met this time, as happened, was, on the part of the young lady, a queer stare, naturally vitreous, which made her remind him of some figure – he couldn't name it – in a play or a novel, some sinister governess or tragic old maid. She seemed to scan him, to challenge him, to say out of general spite: 'What have you got to do with us?' At the same instant the rich humour of the Countess reached them from above: 'Come, come, my little lambs; you should follow your old *bergère*!' Miss Vernham turned away for it, pursuing the ascent, and Doctor Hugh, after another mute appeal to Dencombe and a minute's evident demur, deposited his book on the bench as if to keep his place, or even as a gage of earnest return, and bounded without difficulty up the rougher part of the cliff.

Equally innocent and infinite are the pleasures of observation and the resources engendered by the trick of analysing life. It amused poor Dencombe, as he dawdled in his tepid air-bath, to believe himself awaiting a revelation of something at the back of a fine young mind. He looked hard at the book on the end of the bench, but wouldn't have touched it for the world. It served his purpose to have a theory that shouldn't be exposed to refutation. He already felt better of his melancholy; he had, according to his old formula, put his head at the window. A passing Countess could draw off the fancy when, like the elder of the ladies who had just retreated, she was as obvious as the giantess of a caravan. It was indeed general views that were terrible; short ones, contrary to an opinion sometimes expressed, were the refuge, were the remedy. Doctor Hugh couldn't possibly be anything but a reviewer who had understandings for early copies with publishers or with newspapers. He reappeared in a quarter of an hour with visible relief at finding Dencombe on the spot and the gleam of white teeth in an embarrassed but generous smile. He was perceptibly disappointed at the eclipse of the other copy of the book; it made a pretext the less for speaking to the quiet gentleman. But he spoke notwithstanding; he held up his own copy and broke out pleadingly: '*Do* say, if you have occasion to speak of it, that it's the best thing he has done yet!'

Dencombe responded with a laugh: 'Done yet' was so amusing to him, made such a grand avenue of the future. Better still, the young man took *him* for a reviewer. He pulled out 'The Middle Years' from under his cape, but instinctively concealed any telltale look of fatherhood. This was partly because a person was always a fool for insisting to others on his work. 'Is that what you're going to say yourself?' he put to his visitor.

'I'm not quite sure I shall write anything. I don't, as a regular thing – I enjoy in peace. But it's awfully fine.'

Dencombe just debated. If the young man had begun to abuse him he would have confessed on the spot to his identity, but there was no harm in drawing out any impulse to praise. He drew it out with such success that in a few moments his new acquaintance, seated by his side, was confessing candidly that the works of the author of the volume before them were the only ones he could read a second time. He had come the day before from London, where a friend of his, a journalist, had lent him his copy of the last, the copy sent to the office of the journal and already the subject of a 'notice' which, as was pretended there – but one had to allow for 'swagger' – it had taken a full quarter of an hour to prepare. He intimated that he was ashamed for his friend, and in the case of a work demanding and repaying study, of such inferior manners; and, with his fresh appreciation and his so irregular wish to express it, he speedily became for poor Dencombe a remarkable, a delightful apparition. Chance had brought the weary man of letters face to face with the greatest admirer in the new generation of whom it was supposable he might boast. The admirer in truth was mystifying, so rare a case was it to find a bristling young doctor – he looked like a German physiologist – enamoured of literary form. It was an accident, but happier than most accidents, so that Dencombe, exhilarated as well as confounded, spent half an hour in making his visitor talk while he kept himself quiet. He explained his premature possession of 'The Middle Years' by an allusion to the friendship of the publisher, who, knowing he was at Bournemouth for his health, had paid him this graceful attention. He allowed he had been ill, for Doctor Hugh would infallibly have guessed it; he even went so far as to wonder if he mightn't look for some hygienic 'tip' from a personage combining so bright an enthusiasm with a presumable knowledge of the remedies now in vogue. It would shake his faith a little perhaps to have to take a doctor seriously who could take *him* so seriously, but he enjoyed this gushing modern youth and felt with an acute pang that there would still be work to do in a world in which such odd combinations were presented. It wasn't true, what he had tried for renunciation's sake to believe, that all the combinations were exhausted. They weren't by any means – they were infinite: the exhaustion was in the miserable artist.

Doctor Hugh, an ardent physiologist, was saturated with the spirit of the age – in other words he had just taken his degree; but he was independent and various, he talked like a man who would have preferred to love literature best. He would fain have made fine phrases, but nature had denied him the trick. Some of the finest in 'The Middle Years' had struck him inordinately, and he took the liberty of reading them to Dencombe in support of his plea. He grew vivid, in the balmy air, to his companion, for whose deep refreshment he seemed to have been sent; and was particularly ingenuous in describing how recently he had become acquainted, and how instantly infatuated, with the only man who had put flesh between the ribs of an art that was starving on superstitions. He hadn't yet written to him – he was deterred by a strain of respect. Dencombe at this moment rejoiced more inwardly than ever that he had never answered the photographers. His visitor's attitude promised him a luxury of intercourse, though he was sure a due freedom for Doctor Hugh would depend not a little on the Countess. He learned without delay what type of Countess was involved, mastering as well the nature of the tie that united the curious trio. The large lady, an Englishwoman by birth and the daughter of a celebrated baritone, whose taste *minus* his talent she had inherited, was the widow of a French nobleman and mistress of all that remained of the handsome fortune, the fruit of her father's earnings, that had constituted her dower. Miss Vernham, an odd creature but an accomplished pianist, was attached to her person at a salary. The Countess was generous, independent, eccentric; she travelled with her minstrel and her medical man. Ignorant and passionate she had nevertheless moments in which she was almost irresistible. Dencombe saw her sit for her portrait in Doctor Hugh's free sketch, and felt the picture of his young friend's relation to her frame itself in his mind. This young friend, for a representative of the new psychology, was himself easily hypnotised, and if he became abnormally communicative it was only a sign of his real subjection. Dencombe did accordingly what he wanted with him, even without being known as Dencombe.

Taken ill on a journey in Switzerland the Countess had picked him up at an hotel, and the accident of his happening to please her had made her offer him, with her imperious liberality, terms that couldn't fail to dazzle a practitioner without patients and whose resources had been drained dry by his studies. It wasn't the way he would have proposed to spend his time, but it was time that would pass quickly, and meanwhile she was wonderfully kind. She exacted perpetual attention, but it was impossible not to like her. He gave details about his queer patient, a 'type' if there ever was one, who had in connexion with her flushed obesity, and in addition to the morbid strain of a violent and aimless will, a grave organic disorder; but he came back to his loved novelist, whom he was so good as to pronounce more essentially a poet than many of those who went in for verse, with a zeal excited, as all his indiscretion had been excited, by the happy chance of Dencombe's sympathy and the coincidence of their occupation. Dencombe had confessed to a slight personal acquaintance with the author of 'The Middle Years,' but had not felt himself as ready as he could have wished when his companion, who had never yet encountered a being so privileged, began to be eager for particulars. He even divined in Doctor Hugh's eye at that moment a glimmer of suspicion. But the young man was too inflamed to be shrewd and repeatedly caught up the book to exclaim: 'Did you notice this?' or 'Weren't you immensely struck with that?' 'There's a beautiful passage toward the end,' he broke out; and again he laid his hand on the volume. As he turned the pages he came upon something else, while Dencombe saw him suddenly change colour. He had taken up as it lay on the bench Dencombe's copy instead of his own, and his neighbour at once guessed the reason of his start. Doctor Hugh looked grave an instant; then he said: 'I see you've been altering the text!' Dencombe was a passionate corrector, a fingerer of style; the last thing he ever arrived at was a form final for himself. His ideal would have been to publish secretly, and then, on the published text, treat himself to the terrified revise, sacrificing always a first edition and beginning for posterity and even for the collectors, poor dears, with a second. This morning, in "The Middle Years', his pencil had pricked a dozen lights. He was amused at the effect of the young man's reproach; for an instant it made him change colour. He stammered at any rate ambiguously, then through a blur of ebbing consciousness saw Doctor Hugh's mystified eyes. He only had time to feel he was about to be ill again – that emotion, excitement, fatigue, the heat of the sun, the solicitation of the air, had combined to play him a trick, before, stretching out a hand to his visitor with a plaintive cry, he lost his senses altogether.

Later he knew he had fainted and that Doctor Hugh had got him home in a Bath-chair, the conductor of which, prowling within hail for custom, had happened to remember seeing him in the garden of the hotel. He had recovered his perception on the way, and had, in bed that afternoon, a vague recollection of Doctor Hugh's young face, as they went together, bent over him in a comforting laugh and expressive of something more than a suspicion of his identity. That identity was ineffaceable now, and all the more that he was rueful and sore. He had been rash, been stupid, had gone out too soon, stayed out too long. He oughtn't to have exposed himself to strangers, he ought to have taken his servant. He felt as if he had fallen into a hole too deep to descry any little patch of heaven. He was confused about the time that had passed – he pieced the fragments together. He had seen his doctor, the real one, the one who had treated him from the first and who had again been very kind. His servant was in and out on tiptoe, looking very wise after the fact. He said more than once something about the sharp young gentleman.

The rest was vagueness in so far as it wasn't despair. The vagueness, however, justified itself by dreams, dozing anxieties from which he finally emerged to the consciousness of a dark room and a shaded candle.

'You'll be all right again – I know all about you now,' said a voice near him that he felt to be young. Then his meeting with Doctor Hugh came back. He was too discouraged to joke about it yet, but made out after a little that the interest was intense for his visitor. 'Of course I can't attend you professionally – you've got your own man, with whom I've talked and who's excellent,' Doctor Hugh went on. 'But you must let me come to see you as a good friend. I've just looked in before going to bed. You're doing beautifully, but it's a good job I was with you on the cliff. I shall come in early to-morrow. I want to do something for you. I want to do everything. You've done a tremendous lot for me.' The young man held his hand, hanging over him, and poor Dencombe, weakly aware of this living pressure, simply lay there and accepted his devotion. He couldn't do anything less – he needed help too much.

The idea of the help he needed was very present to him that night, which he spent in a lucid stillness, an intensity of thought that constituted a reaction from his hours of stupor. He was lost, he was lost – he was lost if he couldn't be saved. He wasn't afraid of suffering, of death, wasn't even in love with life; but he had had a deep demonstration of desire. It came over him in the long quiet hours that only with 'The Middle Years' had he taken his flight; only on that day, visited by soundless processions, had he recognised his kingdom. He had had a revelation of his range. What he dreaded was the idea that his reputation should stand on the unfinished. It wasn't with his past but with his future that it should properly be concerned. Illness and age rose before him like spectres with pitiless eyes: how was he to bribe such fates to give him the second chance? He had had the one chance that all men have – he had had the chance of life. He went to sleep again very late, and when he awoke Doctor Hugh was sitting at hand. There was already by this time something beautifully familiar in him.

'Don't think I've turned out your physician,' he said; 'I'm acting with his consent. He has been here and seen you. Somehow he seems to trust me. I told him how we happened to come together yesterday, and he recognises that I've a peculiar right.'

Dencombe felt his own face pressing. 'How have you squared the Countess?'

The young man blushed a little, but turned it off. 'Oh never mind the Countess!'

'You told me she was very exacting.'

Doctor Hugh had a wait. 'So she is.'

'And Miss Vernham's an *intrigante*.'

'How do you know that?'

'I know everything. One has to, to write decently!'

'I think she's mad,' said limpid Doctor Hugh.

'Well, don't quarrel with the Countess – she's a present help to you.'

'I don't quarrel,' Doctor Hugh returned. 'But I don't get on with silly women.' Presently he added: 'You seem very much alone.'

'That often happens at my age. I've outlived, I've lost by the way.'

Doctor Hugh faltered; then surmounting a soft scruple: 'Whom have you lost?'

'Everyone.'

'Ah no,' the young man breathed, laying a hand on his arm.

'I once had a wife – I once had a son. My wife died when my child was born, and my boy, at school, was carried off by typhoid.'

'I wish I'd been there!' cried Doctor Hugh.

'Well – if you're here!' Dencombe answered with a smile that, in spite of dimness, showed how he valued being sure of his companion's whereabouts.

'You talk strangely of your age. You're not old.'

'Hypocrite – so early!'

'I speak physiologically.'

'That's the way I've been speaking for the last five years, and it's exactly what I've been saying to myself. It isn't till we *are* old that we begin to tell ourselves we're not.'

'Yet I know I myself am young,' Doctor Hugh returned.

'Not so well as I!' laughed his patient, whose visitor indeed would have established the truth in question by the honesty with which he changed the point of view, remarking that it must be one of the charms of age – at any rate in the case of high distinction – to feel that one has laboured and achieved. Doctor Hugh employed the common phrase about earning one's rest, and it made poor Dencombe for an instant almost angry. He recovered himself, however, to explain, lucidly enough, that if, ungraciously, he knew nothing of such a balm, it was doubtless because he had wasted inestimable years. He had followed literature from the first, but he had taken a lifetime to get abreast of her. Only to-day at last had he begun to *see*, so that all he had hitherto shown was a movement without a direction. He had ripened too late and was so clumsily constituted that he had had to teach himself by mistakes.

'I prefer your flowers then to other people's fruit, and your mistakes to other people's successes,' said gallant Doctor Hugh. 'It's for your mistakes I admire you.'

'You're happy – you don't know,' Dencombe answered.

Looking at his watch the young man had got up; he named the hour of the afternoon at which he would return. Dencombe warned him against committing himself too deeply, and expressed again all his dread of making him neglect the Countess – perhaps incur her displeasure.

'I want to be, like you – I want to learn by mistakes!' Doctor Hugh laughed.

'Take care you don't make too grave a one! But do come back,' Dencombe added with the glimmer of a new idea.

'You should have had more vanity!' His friend spoke as if he knew the exact amount required to make a man of letters normal.

'No, no – I only should have had more time. I want another go.'

'Another go?'

'I want an extension.'

'An extension?' Again Doctor Hugh repeated Dencombe's words, with which he seemed to have been struck.

'Don't you know? – I want to what they call "live".'

The young man, for good-bye, had taken his hand, which closed with a certain force. They looked at each other hard. 'You *will* live,' said Doctor Hugh.

'Don't be superficial. It's too serious!'

'You *shall* live!' Dencombe's visitor declared, turning pale.

'Ah that's better!' And as he retired the invalid, with a troubled laugh, sank gratefully back.

All that day and all the following night he wondered if it mightn't be arranged. His doctor came again, his servant was attentive, but it was to his confident young friend that he felt himself mentally appeal. His collapse on the cliff was plausibly explained and his liberation, on a better basis, promised for the morrow; meanwhile, however, the intensity of his meditations kept him tranquil and made him indifferent. The idea that occupied him was none the less absorbing because it was a morbid fancy. Here was a clever son of the age, ingenious and ardent, who happened to have set him up for connoisseurs to worship. This servant of his altar had all the new learning in science and all the old reverence in faith; wouldn't he therefore put his knowledge at the disposal of his sympathy, his craft at the disposal of his love? Couldn't he be trusted to invent a remedy for a poor artist to whose art he had paid a tribute? If he couldn't the alternative was hard: Dencombe would have to surrender to silence unvindicated and undivined. The rest of the day and all the next he toyed in secret with this sweet futility. Who would work the miracle for him but the young man who could combine such lucidity with such passion? He thought of the fairy-tales of science and charmed himself into forgetting that he looked for a magic that was not of this world. Doctor Hugh was an apparition, and that placed him above the law. He came and went while his patient, who now sat up, followed him with supplicating eyes. The interest of knowing the great author had made the young man begin 'The Middle Years' afresh and would help him to find a richer sense between its covers. Dencombe had told him what he 'tried for'; with all his intelligence, on a first perusal, Doctor Hugh had failed to guess it. The baffled celebrity wondered then who in the world *would* guess it: he was amused once more at the diffused massive weight that could be thrown into the missing of an intention. Yet he wouldn't rail at the general mind to-day – consoling as that ever had been: the revelation of his own slowness had seemed to make all stupidity sacred.

Doctor Hugh, after a little, was visibly worried, confessing, on enquiry, to a source of embarrassment at home. 'Stick to the Countess – don't mind me,' Dencombe said repeatedly; for his companion was frank enough about the large lady's attitude. She was so jealous that she had fallen ill – she resented such a breach of allegiance. She paid so much for his fidelity that she must have it all: she refused him the right to other sympathies, charged him with scheming to make her die alone, for it was needless to point out how little Miss Vernham was a resource in trouble. When Doctor Hugh mentioned that the Countess would already have left Bournemouth if he hadn't kept her in bed, poor Dencombe held his arm tighter and said with decision: 'Take her straight away.' They had gone out together, walking back to the sheltered nook in which, the other day, they had met: The young man, who had given his companion a personal support, declared with emphasis that his conscience was clear – he could ride two horses at once. Didn't he dream for his future of a time when he should have to ride five hundred? Longing equally for virtue, Dencombe replied that in that golden age no patient would pretend to have contracted with him for his whole attention. On the part of the Countess wasn't such an avidity lawful? Doctor Hugh denied it, said there was no contract, but only a free understanding, and that a sordid servitude was impossible to a generous spirit; he liked moreover to talk about art, and that was the subject on which, this time, as they sat together on the sunny bench, he tried most to engage the author of 'The Middle Years'. Dencombe, soaring again a little on the weak wings of convalescence and still haunted by that happy notion of an organised rescue, found another strain of eloquence to plead the cause of a certain splendid 'last manner', the very citadel, as it would prove, of his reputation, the stronghold into which his real treasure would be gathered. While his listener gave up the morning and the great still sea ostensibly waited he had a wondrous explanatory hour. Even for himself he was inspired as he told what his treasure would consist of; the precious metals he would dig from the mine, the jewels rare, strings of pearls, he would hang between the columns of his temple. He was wondrous for himself, so thick his convictions crowded, but still more wondrous for Doctor Hugh, who assured him none the less that the very pages he had just published were already encrusted with gems. This admirer, however, panted for the combinations to come and, before the face of the beautiful day, renewed to Dencombe his guarantee that his profession would hold itself responsible for such a life. Then he suddenly clapped his hand upon his watch-pocket and asked leave to absent himself for half an hour. Dencombe waited there for his return, but was at last recalled to the actual by the fall of a shadow across the ground. The shadow darkened into that of Miss Vernham, the young lady in attendance on the Countess; whom Dencombe, recognising her, perceived so clearly to have come to speak to him that he rose from his bench to acknowledge the civility. Miss Vernham indeed proved not particularly civil; she looked strangely agitated, and her type was now unmistakeable.

'Excuse me if I do ask,' she said, 'whether it's too much to hope that you may be induced to leave Doctor Hugh alone.' Then before our poor friend, greatly disconcerted, could protest: 'You ought to be informed that you stand in his light – that you may do him a terrible injury.'

'Do you mean by causing the Countess to dispense with his services?'

'By causing her to disinherit him.' Dencombe stared at this, and Miss Vernham pursued, in the gratification of seeing she could produce an impression: 'It has depended on himself to come into something very handsome. He has had a grand prospect, but I think you've succeeded in spoiling it.'

'Not intentionally, I assure you. Is there no hope the accident may be repaired?' Dencombe asked.

'She was ready to do anything for him. She takes great fancies, she lets herself go – it's her way. She has no relations, she's free to dispose of her money, and she's very ill,' said Miss Vernham for a climax.

'I'm very sorry to hear it,' Dencombe stammered.

'Wouldn't it be possible for you to leave Bournemouth? That's what I've come to see about'

He sank to his bench. 'I'm very ill myself, but I'll try!'

Miss Vernham still stood there with her colourless eyes and the brutality of her good conscience. 'Before it's too late, please!' she said; and with this she turned her back, in order, quickly, as if it had been a business to which she could spare but a precious moment, to pass out of his sight.

Oh yes, after this Dencombe was certainly very ill. Miss Vernham had upset him with her rough fierce news; it was the sharpest shock to him to discover what was at stake for a penniless young man of fine parts. He sat trembling on his bench, staring at the waste of waters, feeling sick with the directness of the blow. He was indeed too weak, too unsteady, too alarmed; but he would make the effort to get away, for he couldn't accept the guilt of interference and his honour was really involved. He would hobble home, at any rate, and then think what was to be done. He made his way back to the hotel and, as he went, had a characteristic vision of Miss Vernham's great motive. The Countess hated women of course – Dencombe was lucid about that; so the hungry pianist had no personal hopes and could only console herself with the bold conception of helping Doctor Hugh in order to marry him after he should get his money or else induce him to recognise her claim for compensation and buy her off. If she had befriended him at a fruitful crisis he would really, as a man of delicacy – and she knew what to think of that point – have to reckon with her.

At the hotel Dencombe's servant insisted on his going back to bed. The invalid had talked about catching a train and had begun with orders to pack; after which his racked nerves had yielded to a sense of sickness. He consented to see his physician, who immediately was sent for, but he wished it to be understood that his door was irrevocably closed to Doctor Hugh. He had his plan, which was so fine that he rejoiced in it after getting back to bed. Doctor Hugh, suddenly finding himself snubbed without mercy, would, in natural disgust and to the joy of Miss Vernham, renew his allegiance to the Countess. When his physician arrived Dencombe learned that he was feverish and that this was very wrong: he was to cultivate calmness and try, if possible, not to think. For the rest of the day he wooed stupidity; but there was an ache that kept him sentient, the probable sacrifice of his 'extension,' the limit of his course. His medical adviser was anything but pleased; his successive relapses were ominous. He charged this personage to put out a strong hand and take Doctor Hugh off his mind – it would contribute so much to his being quiet. The agitating name, in his room, was not mentioned again, but his security was a smothered fear, and it was not confirmed by the receipt, at ten o'clock that evening, of a telegram which his servant opened and read him and to which, with an address in London, the signature of Miss Vernham was attached. 'Beseech you to use all influence to make our friend join us here in the morning. Countess much the worse for dreadful journey, but everything may still be saved.' The two ladies had gathered themselves up and had been capable in the afternoon of a spiteful revolution. They had started for the capital, and if the elder one, as Miss Vernham had announced, was very ill, she had wished to make it clear that she was proportionately reckless. Poor Dencombe, who was not reckless and who only desired that everything should indeed be 'saved', sent this missive straight off to the young man's lodging and had on the morrow the pleasure of knowing that he had quitted Bournemouth by an early train.

Two days later he pressed in with a copy of a literary journal in his hand. He had returned because he was anxious and for the pleasure of flourishing the great review of 'The Middle Years'. Here at least was something adequate – it rose to the occasion; it was an acclamation, a reparation, a critical attempt to place the author in the niche he had fairly won. Dencombe accepted and submitted; he made neither objection nor enquiry, for old complications had returned and he had had two dismal days. He was convinced not only that he should never again leave his bed, so that his young friend might pardonably remain, but that the demand he should make on the patience of beholders would be of the most moderate. Doctor Hugh had been to town, and he tried to find in his eyes some confession that the Countess was pacified and his legacy clinched; but all he could see there was the light of his juvenile joy in two or three of the phrases of the newspaper. Dencombe couldn't read them, but when his visitor had insisted on repeating them more than once he was able to shake an unintoxicated head. 'Ah no – but they would have been true of what I *could* have done!'

'What people "could have done" is mainly what they've in fact done,' Doctor Hugh contended.

'Mainly, yes; but I've been an idiot!' Dencombe said.

Doctor Hugh did remain; the end was coming fast. Two days later his patient observed to him, by way of the feeblest of jokes, that there would now be no question whatever of a second chance. At this the young man stared; then he exclaimed: 'Why it has come to pass – it has come to pass! The second chance has been the public's – the chance to find the point of view, to pick up the pearl!'

'Oh the pearl!' poor Dencombe uneasily sighed. A smile as cold as a winter sunset flickered on his drawn lips as he added: 'The pearl is the unwritten – the pearl is the unalloyed, the *rest*, the lost!'

From that hour he was less and less present, heedless to all appearance of what went on round him. His disease was definitely mortal, of an action as relentless, after the short arrest that had enabled him to fall in with Doctor Hugh, as a leak in a great ship. Sinking steadily, though this visitor, a man of rare resources, now cordially approved by his physician, showed endless art in guarding him from pain, poor Dencombe kept no reckoning of favour or neglect, betrayed no symptom of regret or speculation. Yet toward the last he gave a sign of having noticed how for two days Doctor Hugh hadn't been in his room, a sign that consisted of his suddenly opening his eyes to put a question. Had he spent those days with the Countess?

'The Countess is dead,' said Doctor Hugh. 'I knew that in a particular contingency she wouldn't resist. I went to her grave.'

Dencombe's eyes opened wider. 'She left you "something handsome"?'

The young man gave a laugh almost too light for a chamber of woe. 'Never a penny. She roundly cursed me.'

'Cursed you?' Dencombe wailed.

'For giving her up. I gave her up for *you*. I had to choose,' his companion explained.

'You chose to let a fortune go?'

'I chose to accept, whatever they might be, the consequences of my infatuation,' smiled Doctor Hugh. Then as a larger pleasantry: 'The fortune be hanged! It's your own fault if I can't get your things out of my head.'

The immediate tribute to his humour was a long bewildered moan; after which, for many hours, many days, Dencombe lay motionless and absent. A response so absolute, such a glimpse of a definite result and such a sense of credit, worked together in his mind and, producing a strange commotion, slowly altered and transfigured his despair. The sense of cold submersion left him – he seemed to float without an effort. The incident was extraordinary as evidence, and it shed an intenser light. At the last he signed to Doctor Hugh to listen and, when he was down on his knees by the pillow, brought him very near. 'You've made me think it all a delusion.'

'Not your glory, my dear friend,' stammered the young man.

'Not my glory – what there is of it! It *is* glory – to have been tested, to have had our little quality and cast our little spell. The thing is to have made somebody care. You happen to be crazy of course, but that doesn't affect the law.'

'You're a great success!' said Doctor Hugh, putting into his young voice the ring of a marriage-bell.

Dencombe lay taking this in: then he gathered strength to speak once more. 'A second chance – *that's* the delusion. There never was to be but one. We work in the dark – we do what we can – we give what we have. Our doubt is our passion and our passion is our task. The rest is the madness of art.'

'If you've doubted, if you've despaired, you've always "done" it,' his visitor subtly argued.

'We've done something or other,' Dencombe conceded.

'Something or other is everything. It's the feasible. It's *you*!'

'Comforter!' poor Dencombe ironically sighed.

'But it's true,' insisted his friend.

'It's true. It's frustration that doesn't count.'

'Frustration's only life,' said Doctor Hugh.

'Yes, it's what passes.' Poor Dencombe was barely audible, but he had marked with the words the virtual end of his first and only chance.

Notes

p. 115   *Bournemouth* - in Dorset on the south coast of England

p. 115   *the Island* - the Isle of Wight

p. 116   *seeing oneself 'just out'* - seeing one's latest book in print

p. 116   *crinoline* - stiffened, very wide underskirt most popular in the 1850s and 1860s

p. 116   *catchpenny* - cheaply attractive, a bright, lurid design meant to lure readers

p. 116   *odour of sanctity* - scent alleged to come from the body of dead saint

p. 116   *passed the sponge over colour* - the metaphor is of a painter's palette – a sponge wiping away the colours used for a painting

p. 117   *single volume* - novels appearing in three volumes were normal in the nineteenth century, up until the 1890s

p. 117   *siren's hand* - in Greek mythology, sirens were women living by the sea and luring sailors to their doom with their beauty

p. 117   *vincit omnia* - conquers all

p. 118   *Qui dort dine* - he who sleeps forgets his hunger

p. 118   *vitreous* - glassy

p. 119   *bergère* - shepherdess

p. 119   *air-bath* - i.e. he is 'taking the air'

p. 119   *notice* - review

p. 119   *swagger* - showing off

p. 120   *the only man* - i.e. he is talking about Dencombe himself but Dencombe conceals his identity

p. 121   *pricked a dozen lights* - made small amendments to the text: the metaphor is from a decorative technique of pricking holes in paper, literally letting light through to create pattern

p. 122   *intrigante* - a female intriguer

p. 127   *complications* - i.e. of his illness

12

Going Blind

(1896)

Henry Lawson

The most celebrated Australian writer of his time, Lawson had worked on the land and on building sites and knew the harsh realities of such work in the Australian bush. He became a journalist and wrote novels and poems, developing a distinctive style which reflected the reality of the world around him, and rejected romantic idealism and elaborate style. In this story, a 'bushman' in the outback, short of money at a cheap men's boarding house, observes a fellow boarder who may be going blind and reflects on his struggles.

I met him in the Full and Plenty Dining Rooms. It was a cheap place in the city, with good beds upstairs let at one shilling per night – 'Board and residence for respectable single men, fifteen shillings per week'. I was a respectable single man then. I boarded and resided there. I boarded at a greasy little table in the greasy little corner under the fluffy little staircase in the hot and greasy little dining-room or restaurant downstairs. They called it dining-rooms, but it was only one room, and there wasn't half enough room in it to work your elbows when the seven little tables and forty-nine chairs were occupied. There was not room for an ordinary-sized steward to pass up and down between the tables; but our waiter was not an ordinary-sized man – he was a living skeleton in miniature. We handed the soup, and the 'roast beef one' and 'roast lamb one', 'corn beef and cabbage one', 'veal and pickled pork one' – or two, or three, as the case may be – and the tea and coffee, and the various kinds of pudding – we handed over each other, and dodged the drops as well as we could. The very hot and very greasy little kitchen was adjacent, and it contained the bath-room and other conveniences, behind screens of whitewashed boards.

I resided upstairs in a room where there were five beds and one wash-stand; one candle-stick, with a very short bit of soft yellow candle in it; the back of a hair-brush, with about a dozen bristles in it; and half a comb – the big tooth end – with nine and a half teeth at irregular distances apart.

He was a typical bushman, not one of those tall, straight, wiry, brown men of the West, but from the old Selection Districts, where many drovers came from, and of the old bush school; one of those slight, active little fellows whom we used to see in cabbage-tree hats, Crimean shirts, strapped trousers, and elastic-side boots – 'larstins', they called

130

them. They could dance well, sing indifferently, and mostly through their noses, the old bush songs; play the concertina horribly; and ride like – like – well, they *could* ride.

He seemed as if he had forgotten to grow old and die out with this old colonial school to which he belonged. They *had* careless and forgetful ways about them. His name was Jack Gunther, he said, and he'd come to Sydney to try to get something done to his eyes. He had a portmanteau, a carpet bag, some things in a three-bushel bag, and a tin box. I sat beside him on his bed, and struck up an acquaintance, and he told me all about it. First he asked me would I mind shifting round to the other side, as he was rather deaf in that ear. He'd been kicked on the side of the head by a horse, he said, and had been a little dull o' hearing on that side ever since.

He was as good as blind. 'I can see the people near me,' he said, 'but I can't make out their faces. I can just make out the pavement and the houses close at hand, and all the rest is a sort of white blur.' He looked up: 'That ceiling is kind of white, ain't it? And this,' tapping the wall and putting his nose close to it, 'is a sort of green, ain't it:' The ceiling might have been whiter. The prevalent tints of the wall-paper had originally been blue and red, but it was mostly green enough now – a damp, rotten green; but I was ready to swear that the ceiling was snow and that the walls were as green as grass if it would have made him feel more comfortable. His sight began to get bad about six years before, he said; he didn't take much notice of it at first, and then he saw a quack, who made his eyes worse. He had already the manner of the blind – the touch in every finger, and even the gentleness in his speech. He had a boy down with him – a 'sorter cousin of his' – and the boy saw him round. 'I'll have to be sending that youngster back,' he said. 'I think I'll send him home next week. He'll be picking up and learning too much down here.'

I happened to know the district he came from, and we would sit by the hour and talk about the country, and chaps by the name of this and chaps by the name of that – drovers mostly, whom we had met or had heard of. He asked me if I'd ever heard of a chap by the name of Joe Scott – a big, sandy-complexioned chap, who might be droving; he was his brother, or, at least, his half-brother, but he hadn't heard of him for years; he'd last heard of him at Blackall, in Queensland; he might have gone overland to Western Australia with Tyson's cattle to the new country.

We talked about grubbing and fencing and digging and droving and shearing – all about the bush – and it all came back to me as we talked. 'I can see it all now,' he said once, in an abstracted tone, seeming to fix his helpless eyes on the wall opposite. But he didn't see the dirty blind wall, nor the dingy window, nor the skimpy little bed, nor the greasy wash-stand: he saw the dark blue ridges in the sunlight, the grassy sidings and flats, the creek with clumps of she-oak here and there, the course of the willow-fringed river below, the distant peaks and ranges fading away into a lighter azure; the granite ridge in the middle distance, and the rocky rises, the stringy-bark and the apple-tree flats, the shrubs, and the sunlit plains – and all. I could see it too – plainer than I ever did.

He had done a bit of fencing in his time, and we got talking about timber. He didn't believe in having fencing-posts with big butts; he reckoned it was a mistake. 'You see,' he said, 'the top of the butt catches the rain water and make the post rot quicker. I'd back posts without any butt at all to last as long or longer than posts with 'em – that's if the post is well put up and well rammed.' He had supplied fencing stuff, and fenced by contract, and – well, you can get more posts without butts out of a tree than posts with them. He also objected to charring the butts. He said it only made work, and wasted time – the butts lasted longer without being charred.

I asked him if he'd ever got stringy-bark palings or shingles out of mountain ash, and he smiled a smile that did my heart good to see, and said he had. He had also got them out of various other kinds of trees.

We talked about soil and grass, and gold-digging, and many other things which came back to one like a revelation as we yarned.

He had been to the hospital several times. 'The doctors don't say they can cure me,' he said; 'they say they might be able to improve my sight and hearing, but it would take a long time – anyway, the treatment would improve my general health. They know what's the matter with my eyes,' and he explained it as well as he could. 'I wish I'd seen a good doctor when my eyes first began to get weak; but young chaps are always careless over things. It's harder to get cured of anything when you're done growing.'

He was always hopeful and cheerful. 'If the worst comes to the worst,' he said, 'there's things I can do where I come from. I might do a bit o' wool-sorting, for instance. I'm a pretty fair expert. Or else when they're weeding out I could help. I'd just have to sit down and they'd bring the sheep to me, and I'd feel the wool and tell them what it was – being blind improves the feeling, you know.'

He had a packet of portraits, but he couldn't make them out very well now. They were sort of blurred to him, but I described them, and he told me who they were. 'That's a girl o' mine,' he said, with reference to one – a jolly, good-looking bush girl. 'I got a letter from her yesterday. I managed to scribble something, but I'll get you, if you don't mind, to write something more I want to put in on another piece of paper, and address an envelope for me.'

Darkness fell quickly upon him now – or, rather, the 'sort of white blur' increased and closed in. But his hearing was better, he said, and he was glad of that and still cheerful. I thought it natural that his hearing should improve as he went blind.

One day he said that he did not think he would bother going to the hospital any more. He reckoned he'd get back to where he was known. He'd stayed down too long already, and the 'stuff' wouldn't stand it. He was expecting a letter that didn't come. I was away for a couple of days, and when I came back he had been shifted out of the room, and had a bed in an angle of the landing on top of the staircase, with people brushing against him and stumbling over his things all day on their way up and down. I felt indignant, thinking that – the house being full – the boss had taken advantage of the bushman's helplessness and good nature to put him there. But he said that he was quite comfortable. 'I can get a whiff of air here,' he said.

Going in next day I thought for a moment that I had dropped suddenly back into the past and into a bush dance, for there was a concertina going upstairs. He was sitting on the bed, with his legs crossed, and a new cheap concertina on his knee, and his eyes turned to the patch of ceiling as if it were a piece of music and he could read it. 'I'm trying to knock a few tunes into my head,' he said, with a brave smile, 'in case the worst comes to the worst.' He tried to be cheerful, but seemed worried and anxious. The letter hadn't come. I thought of the many blind musicians in Sydney, and I thought of the bushman's chance, standing at a corner swanking a cheap concertina, and I felt very sorry for him.

I went out with a vague idea of seeing someone about the matter, and getting something done for the bushman – of bringing a little influence to his assistance; but I suddenly remembered that my clothes were worn out, my hat in a shocking state, my boots burst, and that I owed for a week's board and lodging, and was likely to be thrown out at any moment myself; and so I was not in a position to go where there was influence.

When I went back to the restaurant there was a long, gaunt, sandy-complexioned bushman sitting by Jack's side. Jack introduced him as his brother, who had returned unexpectedly to his native district, and had followed him to Sydney. The brother was rather short with me at first, and seemed to regard the restaurant people – all of us, in fact – in the light of spielers, who wouldn't hesitate to take advantage of Jack's blindness if he left him a moment; and he looked ready to knock down the first man who stumbled across Jack, or over his luggage – but that soon wore off. Jack was going to stay with Joe at the Coffee Palace for a few weeks, and then go up country, he told me. He was excited and happy. His brother's manner towards him was as if Jack had just lost his wife, or boy, or someone very dear to him. He would not allow him to do anything for himself, nor try to – not even lace up his boots. He seemed to think that he was thoroughly helpless, and when I saw him pack up Jack's things, and help him at the table, and fix his tie and collar with his great muscular hands, which trembled all the time with grief and gentleness, and make Jack sit down on the bed whilst he got a cab and carried the traps down to it, and take him downstairs as if he were made of thin glass, and settle the landlord – then I knew Jack was all right.

We had a drink together – Joe, Jack, the cabman and I. Joe was very careful to hand Jack the glass, and Jack made a joke about it for Joe's benefit. He swore he could see a glass yet, and Joe laughed, but looked extra troubled the next moment.

I felt their grips on my hand for five minutes after we parted.

Notes

p. 130   *steward* - waiter
p. 130   *drover* - horseman who moves herds of sheep or cattle over long distances
p. 130   *the old bush school* - an old-fashioned country worker
p. 130   *cabbage-tree hat* - sun hat made from the leaves of a kind of Australian palm tree
p. 130   *Crimean shirt* - a flannel shirt
p. 131   *portmanteau* - large travelling bag
p. 131   *tin box* - a sort of mug for tea
p. 131   *Tyson's cattle* - biggest Australian cattle farm business

p. 132   *butts* - a support fixed to the base of a fence
p. 132   *charring the butts* - some thought that burning the bottom end of the fence
post before it was driven into the ground preserved the wood for longer,
but the bushman disputes this
p. 132   *stringy-bark palings . . . shingles* - thin pieces of wood used to cover roofs –
planks used in a fence
p. 132   *stuff* - money
p. 133   *swanking* - playing
p. 133   *spielers* - tricksters/conmen

13

The Little Regiment

(1896)

Stephen Crane

Crane, an American writer, had a sadly short life, but developed his mature literary voice very early. His famous novel The Red Badge of Courage *and his story* The Open Boat, *which appears in Stories of Ourselves volume 1, are examples of his unique and gripping descriptive style. Like* Occurrence at Owl Creek Bridge, *this story is about the American Civil War (see Introductory note to that story) but it has a timeless quality that makes the precise historical setting less important. Two brothers go through a terrible battle.*

I

The fog made the clothes of the men of the column in the roadway seem of a luminous quality. It imparted to the heavy infantry overcoats a new colour, a kind of blue which was so pale that a regiment might have been merely a long, low shadow in the mist. However, a muttering, one part grumble, three parts joke, hovered in the air above the thick ranks, and blended in an undertoned roar, which was the voice of the column.

The town on the southern shore of the little river loomed spectrally, a faint etching upon the gray cloud-masses which were shifting with oily languor. A long row of guns upon the northern bank had been pitiless in their hatred, but a little battered belfry could be dimly seen still pointing with invincible resolution toward the heavens.

The enclouded air vibrated with noises made by hidden colossal things. The infantry tramplings, the heavy rumbling of the artillery, made the earth speak of gigantic preparation. Guns on distant heights thundered from time to time with sudden, nervous roar, as if unable to endure in silence a knowledge of hostile troops massing, other guns going to position. These sounds, near and remote, defined an immense battleground, described the tremendous width of the stage of the prospective drama. The voices of the guns, slightly casual, unexcited in their challenges and warnings, could not destroy the unutterable eloquence of the word in the air, a meaning of impending struggle which made the breath halt at the lips.

The column in the roadway was ankle-deep in mud. The men swore piously at the rain which drizzled upon them, compelling them to stand always very erect in fear of the drops that would sweep in under their coat-collars. The fog was as cold as wet cloths. The men stuffed their hands deep in their pockets, and huddled their muskets in their arms. The machinery of orders had rooted these soldiers deeply into the mud precisely as almighty nature roots mullein stalks.

They listened and speculated when a tumult of fighting came from the dim town across the river. When the noise lulled for a time they resumed their descriptions of the mud and graphically exaggerated the number of hours they had been kept waiting. The general commanding their division rode along the ranks, and they cheered admiringly, affectionately, crying out to him gleeful prophecies of the coming battle. Each man scanned him with a peculiarly keen personal interest, and afterward spoke of him with unquestioning devotion and confidence, narrating anecdotes which were mainly untrue.

When the jokers lifted the shrill voices which invariably belonged to them, flinging witticisms at their comrades, a loud laugh would sweep from rank to rank, and soldiers who had not heard would lean forward and demand repetition. When were borne past them some wounded men with gray and blood-smeared faces, and eyes that rolled in that helpless beseeching for assistance from the sky which comes with supreme pain, the soldiers in the mud watched intently, and from time to time asked of the bearers an account of the affair. Frequently they bragged of their corps, their division, their brigade, their regiment. Anon they referred to the mud and the cold drizzle. Upon this threshold of a wild scene of death they, in short, defied the proportion of events with that splendour of heedlessness which belongs only to veterans.

"Like a lot of wooden soldiers," swore Billie Dempster, moving his feet in the thick mass, and casting a vindictive glance indefinitely; "standing in the mud for a hundred years."

"Oh, shut up!" murmured his brother Dan. The manner of his words implied that this fraternal voice near him was an indescribable bore.

"Why should I shut up?" demanded Billie.

"Because you're a fool," cried Dan, taking no time to debate it; "the biggest fool in the regiment."

There was but one man between them, and he was habituated. These insults from brother to brother had swept across his chest, flown past his face, many times during two long campaigns. Upon this occasion he simply grinned first at one, then at the other.

The way of these brothers was not an unknown topic in regimental gossip. They had enlisted simultaneously, with each sneering loudly at the other for doing it. They left their little town, and went forward with the flag, exchanging protestations of undying suspicion. In the camp life they so openly despised each other that, when entertaining quarrels were lacking, their companions often contrived situations calculated to bring forth display of this fraternal dislike.

Both were large-limbed, strong young men, and often fought with friends in camp unless one was near to interfere with the other. This latter happened rather frequently, because Dan, preposterously willing for any manner of combat, had a very great horror of seeing Billie in a fight; and Billie, almost odiously ready himself, simply refused to see

Dan stripped to his shirt and with his fists aloft. This sat queerly upon them, and made them the objects of plots.

When Dan jumped through a ring of eager soldiers and dragged forth his raving brother by the arm, a thing often predicted would almost come to pass. When Billie performed the same office for Dan, the prediction would again miss fulfilment by an inch. But indeed they never fought together, although they were perpetually upon the verge.

They expressed longing for such conflict. As a matter of truth, they had at one time made full arrangement for it, but even with the encouragement and interest of half of the regiment they somehow failed to achieve collision.

If Dan became a victim of police duty, no jeering was so destructive to the feelings as Billie's comment. If Billie got a call to appear at the headquarters, none would so genially prophesy his complete undoing as Dan. Small misfortunes to one were, in truth, invariably greeted with hilarity by the other, who seemed to see in them great re-enforcement of his opinion.

As soldiers, they expressed each for each a scorn intense and blasting. After a certain battle, Billie was promoted to corporal. When Dan was told of it, he seemed smitten dumb with astonishment and patriotic indignation. He stared in silence, while the dark blood rushed to Billie's forehead, and he shifted his weight from foot to foot, Dan at last found his tongue, and said: "Well, I'm durned!" If he had heard that an army mule had been appointed to the post of corps commander, his tone could not have had more derision in it. Afterward, he adopted a fervid insubordination, an almost religious reluctance to obey the new corporal's orders, which came near to developing the desired strife.

It is here finally to be recorded also that Dan, most ferociously profane in speech, very rarely swore in the presence of his brother; and that Billie, whose oaths came from his lips with the grace of falling pebbles, was seldom known to express himself in this manner when near his brother Dan.

At last the afternoon contained a suggestion of evening. Metallic cries rang suddenly from end to end of the column. They inspired at once a quick, business-like adjustment. The long thing stirred in the mud. The men had hushed, and were looking across the river. A moment later the shadowy mass of pale blue figures was moving steadily toward the stream. There could be heard from the town a clash of swift fighting and cheering. The noise of the shooting coming through the heavy air had its sharpness taken from it, and sounded in thuds.

There was a halt upon the bank above the pontoons. When the column went winding down the incline, and streamed out upon the bridge, the fog had faded to a great degree, and in the clearer dusk the guns on a distant ridge were enabled to perceive the crossing. The long whirling outcries of the shells came into the air above the men. An occasional solid shot struck the surface of the river, and dashed into view a sudden vertical jet. The distance was subtly illuminated by the lightning from the deep-booming guns. One by one the batteries on the northern shore aroused, the innumerable guns bellowing in angry oration at the distant ridge. The rolling thunder crashed and reverberated as a wild surf sounds on a still night, and to this music the column marched across the pontoons.

The waters of the grim river curled away in a smile from the ends of the great boats, and slid swiftly beneath the planking. The dark, riddled walls of the town upreared before the troops, and from a region hidden by these hammered and tumbled houses came incessantly the yells and firings of a prolonged and close skirmish.

When Dan had called his brother a fool, his voice had been so decisive, so brightly assured, that many men had laughed, considering it to be great humour under the circumstances. The incident happened to rankle deep in Billie. It was not any strange thing that his brother had called him a fool. In fact, he often called him a fool with exactly the same amount of cheerful and prompt conviction, and before large audiences, too. Billie wondered in his own mind why he took such profound offence in this case; but, at any rate, as he slid down the bank and on to the bridge with his regiment, he was searching his knowledge for something that would pierce Dan's blithesome spirit. But he could contrive nothing at this time, and his impotency made the glance which he was once able to give his brother still more malignant.

The guns far and near were roaring a fearful and grand introduction for this column which was marching upon the stage of death. Billie felt it, but only in a numb way. His heart was cased in that curious dissonant metal which covers a man's emotions at such times. The terrible voices from the hills told him that in this wide conflict his life was an insignificant fact, and that his death would be an insignificant fact. They portended the whirlwind to which he would be as necessary as a butterfly's waved wing. The solemnity, the sadness of it came near enough to make him wonder why he was neither solemn nor sad. When his mind vaguely adjusted events according to their importance to him, it appeared that the uppermost thing was the fact that upon the eve of battle, and before many comrades, his brother had called him a fool.

Dan was in a particularly happy mood. "Hurray! Look at 'em shoot," he said, when the long witches' croon of the shells came into the air. It enraged Billie when he felt the little thorn in him, and saw at the same time that his brother had completely forgotten it.

The column went from the bridge into more mud. At this southern end there was a chaos of hoarse directions and commands. Darkness was coming upon the earth, and regiments were being hurried up the slippery bank. As Billie floundered in the black mud, amid the swearing, sliding crowd, he suddenly resolved that, in the absence of other means of hurting Dan, he would avoid looking at him, refrain from speaking to him, pay absolutely no heed to his existence; and this done skilfully would, he imagined, soon reduce his brother to a poignant sensitiveness.

At the top of the bank the column again halted and rearranged itself, as a man after a climb rearranges his clothing. Presently the great steel-backed brigade, an infinitely graceful thing in the rhythm and ease of its veteran movement, swung up a little narrow, slanting street.

Evening had come so swiftly that the fighting on the remote borders of the town was indicated by thin flashes of flame. Some building was on fire, and its reflection upon the clouds was an oval of delicate pink.

II

All demeanour of rural serenity had been wrenched violently from the little town by the guns and by the waves of men which had surged through it. The hand of war laid upon this village had in an instant changed it to a thing of remnants. It resembled the place of a monstrous shaking of the earth itself. The windows, now mere unsightly holes, made the tumbled and blackened dwellings seem skeletons. Doors lay splintered to fragments. Chimneys had flung their bricks everywhere. The artillery fire had not neglected the rows of gentle shade-trees which had lined the streets. Branches and heavy trunks cluttered the mud in driftwood tangles, while a few shattered forms had contrived to remain dejectedly, mournfully upright. They expressed an innocence, a helplessness, which perforce created a pity for their happening into this cauldron of battle. Furthermore, there was under foot a vast collection of odd things reminiscent of the charge, the fight, the retreat. There were boxes and barrels filled with earth, behind which riflemen had lain snugly, and in these little trenches were the dead in blue with the dead in gray, the poses eloquent of the struggles for possession of the town until the history of the whole conflict was written plainly in the streets.

And yet the spirit of this little city, its quaint individuality, poised in the air above the ruins, defying the guns, the sweeping volleys; holding in contempt those avaricious blazes which had attacked many dwellings. The hard earthen sidewalks proclaimed the games that had been played there during long lazy days, in the careful shadows of the trees. "General Merchandise," in faint letters upon a long board, had to be read with a slanted glance, for the sign dangled by one end; but the porch of the old store was a palpable legend of wide-hatted men, smoking.

This subtle essence, this soul of the life that had been, brushed like invisible wings the thoughts of the men in the swift columns that came up from the river.

In the darkness a loud and endless humming arose from the great blue crowds bivouacked in the streets. From time to time a sharp spatter of firing from far picket lines entered this bass chorus. The smell from the smouldering ruins floated on the cold night breeze.

Dan, seated ruefully upon the doorstep of a shot-pierced house, was proclaiming the campaign badly managed. Orders had been issued forbidding camp-fires.

Suddenly he ceased his oration, and scanning the group of his comrades, said: "Where's Billie? Do you know?"

"Gone on picket."

"Get out! Has he?" said Dan. "No business to go on picket. Why don't some of them other corporals take their turn?"

A bearded private was smoking his pipe of confiscated tobacco, seated comfortably upon a horse-hair trunk which he had dragged from the house. He observed: "*Was* his turn."

"No such thing," cried Dan. He and the man on the horse-hair trunk held discussion in which Dan stoutly maintained that if his brother had been sent on picket it was an injustice. He ceased his argument when another soldier, upon whose arms could faintly be seen the two stripes of a corporal, entered the circle. "Humph," said Dan, "where you been?"

The corporal made no answer. Presently Dan said: "Billie, where you been?"

His brother did not seem to hear these inquiries. He glanced at the house which towered above them, and remarked casually to the man on the horse-hair trunk: "Funny, ain't it? After the pelting this town got, you'd think there wouldn't be one brick left on another."

"Oh," said Dan, glowering at his brother's back. "Getting mighty smart, ain't you?"

The absence of camp-fires allowed the evening to make apparent its quality of faint silver light in which the blue clothes of the throng became black, and the faces became white expanses, void of expression. There was considerable excitement a short distance from the group around the doorstep. A soldier had chanced upon a hoop-skirt, and arrayed in it he was performing a dance amid the applause of his companions. Billie and a greater part of the men immediately poured over there to witness the exhibition.

"What's the matter with Billie?" demanded Dan of the man upon the horse-hair trunk.

"How do I know?" rejoined the other in mild resentment. He arose and walked away. When he returned he said briefly, in a weather-wise tone, that it would rain during the night.

Dan took a seat upon one end of the horse-hair trunk. He was facing the crowd around the dancer, which in its hilarity swung this way and that way. At times he imagined that he could recognise his brother's face.

He and the man on the other end of the trunk thoughtfully talked of the army's position. To their minds, infantry and artillery were in a most precarious jumble in the streets of the town; but they did not grow nervous over it, for they were used to having the army appear in a precarious jumble to their minds. They had learned to accept such puzzling situations as a consequence of their position in the ranks, and were now usually in possession of a simple but perfectly immovable faith that somebody understood the jumble. Even if they had been convinced that the army was a headless monster, they would merely have nodded with the veteran's singular cynicism. It was none of their business as soldiers. Their duty was to grab sleep and food when occasion permitted, and cheerfully fight wherever their feet were planted until more orders came. This was a task sufficiently absorbing.

They spoke of other corps, and this talk being confidential, their voices dropped to tones of awe. "The Ninth"—"The First"—"The Fifth"—"The Sixth"—"The Third"— the simple numerals rang with eloquence, each having a meaning which was to float through many years as no intangible arithmetical mist, but as pregnant with individuality as the names of cities.

Of their own corps they spoke with a deep veneration, an idolatry, a supreme confidence which apparently would not blanch to see it match against everything.

It was as if their respect for other corps was due partly to a wonder that organizations not blessed with their own famous numeral could take such an interest in war. They could prove that their division was the best in the corps, and that their brigade was the best in the division. And their regiment—it was plain that no fortune of life was equal to the chance which caused a man to be born, so to speak, into this command, the keystone of the defending arch.

At times Dan covered with insults the character of a vague, unnamed general to whose petulance and busy-body spirit he ascribed the order which made hot coffee impossible.

Dan said that victory was certain in the coming battle. The other man seemed rather dubious. He remarked upon the fortified line of hills, which had impressed him even from the other side of the river. "Shucks," said Dan. "Why, we—" He pictured a splendid overflowing of these hills by the sea of men in blue. During the period of this conversation Dan's glance searched the merry throng about the dancer. Above the babble of voices in the street a faraway thunder could sometimes be heard—evidently from the very edge of the horizon—the boom-boom of restless guns.

III

Ultimately the night deepened to the tone of black velvet. The outlines of the fireless camp were like the faint drawings upon ancient tapestry. The glint of a rifle, the shine of a button, might have been of threads of silver and gold sewn upon the fabric of the night. There was little presented to the vision, but to a sense more subtle there was discernible in the atmosphere something like a pulse; a mystic beating which would have told a stranger of the presence of a giant thing—the slumbering mass of regiments and batteries.

With fires forbidden, the floor of a dry old kitchen was thought to be a good exchange for the cold earth of December, even if a shell had exploded in it and knocked it so out of shape that when a man lay curled in his blanket his last waking thought was likely to be of the wall that bellied out above him as if strongly anxious to topple upon the score of soldiers.

Billie looked at the bricks ever about to descend in a shower upon his face, listened to the industrious pickets plying their rifles on the border of the town, imagined some measure of the din of the coming battle, thought of Dan and Dan's chagrin, and rolling over in his blanket went to sleep with satisfaction.

At an unknown hour he was aroused by the creaking of boards. Lifting himself upon his elbow, he saw a sergeant prowling among the sleeping forms. The sergeant carried a candle in an old brass candle-stick. He would have resembled some old farmer on an unusual midnight tour if it were not for the significance of his gleaming buttons and striped sleeves.

Billie blinked stupidly at the light until his mind returned from the journeys of slumber. The sergeant stooped among the unconscious soldiers, holding the candle close, and peering into each face.

"Hello, Haines," said Billie. "Relief?"

"Hello, Billie," said the sergeant. "Special duty."

"Dan got to go?"

"Jameson, Huntcr, McCormack, D. Dempster. Yes. Where is he?"

"Over there by the winder," said Billie, gesturing. "What is it for, Haines?"

"You don't think I know, do you?" demanded the sergeant. He began to pipe sharply but cheerily at men upon the floor. "Come, Mac, get up here. Here's a special for you. Wake up, Jameson. Come along, Dannie, me boy."

Each man at once took this call to duty as a personal affront. They pulled themselves out of their blankets, rubbed their eyes, and swore at whoever was responsible. "Them's orders," cried the sergeant. "Come! Get out of here." An undetailed head with dishevelled hair thrust out from a blanket, and a sleepy voice said: "Shut up, Haines, and go home."

When the detail clanked out of the kitchen, all but one of the remaining men seemed to be again asleep. Billie, leaning on his elbow, was gazing into darkness. When the footsteps died to silence, he curled himself into his blanket.

At the first cool lavender lights of daybreak he aroused again, and scanned his recumbent companions. Seeing a wakeful one he asked: "Is Dan back yet?"

The man said: "Hain't seem 'im."

Billie put both hands behind his head, and scowled into the air. "Can't see the use of these cussed details in the night-time," he muttered in his most unreasonable tones. "Darn nuisances. Why can't they—" He grumbled at length and graphically.

When Dan entered with the squad, however, Billie was convincingly asleep.

IV

The regiment trotted in double time along the street, and the colonel seemed to quarrel over the right of way with many artillery officers. Batteries were waiting in the mud, and the men of them, exasperated by the bustle of this ambitious infantry, shook their fists from saddle and caisson, exchanging all manner of taunts and jests. The slanted guns continued to look reflectively at the ground.

On the outskirts of the crumbled town a fringe of blue figures were firing into the fog. The regiment swung out into skirmish lines, and the fringe of blue figures departed, turning their backs and going joyfully around the flank.

The bullets began a low moan off toward a ridge which loomed faintly in the heavy mist. When the swift crescendo had reached its climax, the missiles zipped just overhead, as if piercing an invisible curtain. A battery on the hill was crashing with such tumult that it was as if the guns had quarrelled and had fallen pell-mell and snarling upon each other. The shells howled on their journey toward the town. From short range distance there came a spatter of musketry, sweeping along an invisible line and making faint sheets of orange light.

Some in the new skirmish lines were beginning to fire at various shadows discerned in the vapour, forms of men suddenly revealed by some humour of the laggard masses of clouds. The crackle of musketry began to dominate the purring of the hostile bullets. Dan, in the front rank, held his rifle poised, and looked into the fog keenly, coldly, with the air of a sportsman. His nerves were so steady that it was as if they had been drawn from his body, leaving him merely a muscular machine; but his numb heart was somehow beating to the pealing march of the fight.

The waving skirmish line went backward and forward, ran this way and that way. Men got lost in the fog, and men were found again. Once they got too close to the formidable ridge, and the thing burst out as if repulsing a general attack. Once another blue regiment was apprehended on the very edge of firing into them. Once a friendly battery began an elaborate and scientific process of extermination. Always as busy as brokers, the men slid here and there over the plain, fighting their foes, escaping from their friends, leaving a history of many movements in the wet yellow turf, cursing the atmosphere, blazing away every time they could identify the enemy.

In one mystic changing of the fog, as if the fingers of spirits were drawing aside these draperies, a small group of the gray skirmishers, silent, statuesque, were suddenly disclosed to Dan and those about him. So vivid and near were they that there was something uncanny in the revelation.

There might have been a second of mutual staring. Then each rifle in each group was at the shoulder. As Dan's glance flashed along the barrel of his weapon, the figure of a man suddenly loomed as if the musket had been a telescope. The short black beard, the slouch hat, the pose of the man as he sighted to shoot, made a quick picture in Dan's mind. The same moment, it would seem, he pulled his own trigger, and the man, smitten, lurched forward, while his exploding rifle made a slanting crimson streak in the air, and the slouch hat fell before the body. The billows of the fog, governed by singular impulses, rolled between.

"You got that feller such enough," said a comrade to Dan. Dan looked at him absent-mindedly.

V

When the next morning calmly displayed another fog, the men of the regiment exchanged eloquent comments; but they did not abuse it at length, because the streets of the town now contained enough galloping aides to make three troops of cavalry, and they knew that they had come to the verge of the great fight.

Dan conversed with the man who had once possessed a horse-hair trunk; but they did not mention the line of hills which had furnished them in more careless moments with an agreeable topic. They avoided it now as condemned men do the subject of death, and yet the thought of it stayed in their eyes as they looked at each other and talked gravely of other things.

The expectant regiment heaved a long sigh of relief when the sharp call: "Fall in," repeated indefinitely, arose in the streets. It was inevitable that a bloody battle was to be fought, and they wanted to get it off their minds. They were, however, doomed again to spend a long period planted firmly in the mud. They craned their necks, and wondered where some of the other regiments were going.

At last the mists rolled carelessly away. Nature made at this time all provisions to enable foes to see each other, and immediately the roar of guns resounded from every hill. The endless cracking of the skirmish had swelled to rolling crashes of musketry. Shells screamed with panther-like noises at the houses. Dan looked at the man of the horse-hair trunk, and the man said; "Well, here she comes!"

The tenor voices of younger officers and the deep and hoarse voices of the older ones rang in the streets. These cries pricked like spurs. The masses of men vibrated from the suddenness with which they were plunged into the situation of troops about to fight. That the orders were long-expected did not concern the emotion.

Simultaneous movement was imparted to all these thick bodies of men and horses that lay in the town. Regiment after regiment swung rapidly into the streets that faced the sinister ridge.

This exodus was theatrical. The little sober-hued village had been like the cloak which disguises the king of drama. It was now put aside, and an army, splendid thing of steel and blue, stood forth in the sunlight.

Even the soldiers in the heavy columns drew deep breaths at the sight, more majestic than they had dreamed. The heights of the enemy's position were crowded with men who resembled people come to witness some mighty pageant. But as the column moved steadily to their positions, the guns, matter-of-fact warriors, doubled their number, and shells burst with red thrilling tumult on the crowded plain. One came into the ranks of the regiment, and after the smoke and the wrath of it had faded, leaving motionless figures, everyone stormed according to the limits of his vocabulary, for veterans detest being killed when they are not busy.

The regiment sometimes looked sideways at its brigade companions composed of men who had never been in battle; but no frozen blood could withstand the heat of the splendour of this army before the eyes on the plain, these lines so long that the flanks were little streaks, this mass of men of one intention. The recruits carried themselves heedlessly. At the rear was an idle battery, and three artillery men in a foolish row on a caisson nudged each other and grinned at the recruits. "You'll catch it pretty soon," they called out. They were impersonally gleeful, as if they themselves were not also likely to catch it pretty soon. But with this picture of an army in their hearts, the new men perhaps felt the devotion which the drops may feel for the wave; they were of its power and glory; they smiled jauntily at the foolish row of gunners, and told them to go to blazes.

The column trotted across some little bridges, and spread quickly into lines of battle. Before them was a bit of plain, and back of the plain was the ridge. There was no time left for considerations. The men were staring at the plain, mightily wondering how it would feel to be out there, when a brigade in advance yelled and charged. The hill was all gray smoke and fire-points.

That fierce elation in the terrors of war, catching a man's heart and making it burn with such ardour that he becomes capable of dying, flashed in the faces of the men like coloured lights, and made them resemble leashed animals, eager, ferocious, daunting at nothing. The line was really in its first leap before the wild, hoarse crying of the orders.

The greed for close quarters which is the emotion of a bayonet charge, came then into the minds of the men and developed until it was a madness. The field, with its faded grass of a Southern winter, seemed to this fury miles in width.

High, slow-moving masses of smoke, with an odour of burning cotton, engulfed the line until the men might have been swimmers. Before them the ridge, the shore of this gray sea, was outlined, crossed, and recrossed by sheets of flame. The howl of the battle arose to the noise of innumerable wind demons.

The line, galloping, scrambling, plunging like a herd of wounded horses, went over a field that was sown with corpses, the records of other charges.

Directly in front of the black-faced, whooping Dan, carousing in this onward sweep like a new kind of fiend, a wounded man appeared, raising his shattered body, and staring at this rush of men down upon him. It seemed to occur to him that he was to be trampled; he made a desperate, piteous effort to escape; then finally huddled in a waiting heap. Dan and the soldier near him widened the interval between them without looking down, without appearing to heed the wounded man. This little clump of blue seemed to reel past them as boulders reel past a train.

Bursting through a smoke-wave, the scampering, unformed bunches came upon the wreck of the brigade that had preceded them, a floundering mass stopped afar from the hill by the swirling volleys.

It was as if a necromancer had suddenly shown them a picture of the fate which awaited them; but the line with muscular spasm hurled itself over this wreckage and onward, until men were stumbling amid the relics of other assaults, the point where the fire from the ridge consumed.

The men, panting, perspiring, with crazed faces, tried to push against it; but it was as if they had come to a wall. The wave halted, shuddered in an agony from the quick struggle of its two desires, then toppled, and broke into a fragmentary thing which has no name.

Veterans could now at last be distinguished from recruits. The new regiments were instantly gone, lost, scattered, as if they never had been. But the sweeping failure of the charge, the battle, could not make the veterans forget their business. With a last throe, the band of maniacs drew itself up and blazed a volley at the hill, insignificant to those iron intrenchments, but nevertheless expressing that singular final despair which enables men coolly to defy the walls of a city of death.

After this episode the men renamed their command. They called it the Little Regiment.

VI

"I seen Dan shoot a feller yesterday. Yes sir. I'm sure it was him that done it. And maybe he thinks about that feller now, and wonders if *he* tumbled down just about the same way. Them things come up in a man's mind."

Bivouac fires upon the sidewalks, in the streets, in the yards, threw high their wavering reflections, which examined, like slim, red fingers, the dingy, scarred walls and the piles of tumbled brick. The droning of voices again arose from great blue crowds.

The odour of frying bacon, the fragrance from countless little coffee-pails floated among the ruins. The rifles, stacked in the shadows, emitted flashes of steely light. Wherever a flag lay horizontally from one stack to another was the bed of an eagle which had led men into the mystic smoke.

The men about a particular fire were engaged in holding in check their jovial spirits. They moved whispering around the blaze, although they looked at it with a certain fine contentment, like labourers after a day's hard work.

There was one who sat apart. They did not address him save in tones suddenly changed. They did not regard him directly, but always in little sidelong glances.

At last a soldier from a distant fire came into this circle of light. He studied for a time the man who sat apart. Then he hesitatingly stepped closer, and said: "Got any news, Dan?"

"No," said Dan.

The new-comer shifted his feet. He looked at the fire, at the sky, at the other men, at Dan. His face expressed a curious despair; his tongue was plainly in rebellion. Finally, however, he contrived to say: "Well, there's some chance yet, Dan. Lots of the wounded are still lying out there, you know. There's some chance yet."

"Yes," said Dan.

The soldier shifted his feet again, and looked miserably into the air. After another struggle he said: "Well, there's some chance yet, Dan." He moved hastily away.

One of the men of the squad, perhaps encouraged by this example, now approached the still figure. "No news yet, hey?" he said, after coughing behind his hand.

"No," said Dan.

"Well," said the man, "I've been thinking of how he was fretting about you the night you went on special duty. You recollect? Well, sir, I was surprised. He couldn't say enough about it. I swear, I don't believe he slep' a wink after you left, but just lay awake cussing special duty and worrying. I was surprised. But there he lay cussing. He—"

Dan made a curious sound, as if a stone had wedged in his throat. He said: "Shut up, will you?"

Afterward the men would not allow this moody contemplation of the fire to be interrupted.

"Oh, let him alone, can't you?"

"Come away from there, Casey!"

"Say, can't you leave him be?"

They moved with reverence about the immovable figure, with its countenance of mask-like invulnerability.

VII

After the red round eye of the sun had stared long at the little plain and its burden, darkness, a sable mercy, came heavily upon it, and the wan hands of the dead were no longer seen in strange frozen gestures.

The heights in front of the plain shone with tiny camp-fires, and from the town in the rear, small shimmerings ascended from the blazes of the bivouac. The plain was a black expanse upon which, from time to time, dots of light, lanterns, floated slowly here and there. These fields were long steeped in grim mystery.

Suddenly, upon one dark spot, there was a resurrection. A strange thing had been groaning there, prostrate. Then it suddenly dragged itself to a sitting posture, and became a man.

The man stared stupidly for a moment at the lights on the hill, then turned and contemplated the faint colouring over the town. For some moments he remained thus, staring with dull eyes, his face unemotional, wooden.

Finally he looked around him at the corpses dimly to be seen. No change flashed into his face upon viewing these men. They seemed to suggest merely that his information concerning himself was not too complete. He ran his fingers over his arms and chest, bearing always the air of an idiot upon a bench at an almshouse door.

Finding no wound in his arms nor in his chest, he raised his hand to his head, and the fingers came away with some dark liquid upon them. Holding these fingers close to his eyes, he scanned them in the same stupid fashion, while his body gently swayed.

The soldier rolled his eyes again toward the town. When he arose, his clothing peeled from the frozen ground like wet paper. Hearing the sound of it, he seemed to see reason for deliberation. He paused and looked at the ground, then at his trousers, then at the ground.

Finally he went slowly off toward the faint reflection, holding his hands palm outward before him, and walking in the manner of a blind man.

VIII

The immovable Dan again sat unaddressed in the midst of comrades, who did not joke aloud. The dampness of the usual morning fog seemed to make the little camp-fires furious.

Suddenly a cry arose in the streets, a shout of amazement and delight. The men making breakfast at the fire looked up quickly. They broke forth in clamorous exclamation: "Well! Of all things! Dan! Dan! Look who's coming! Oh, Dan!"

Dan the silent raised his eyes and saw a man, with a bandage of the size of a helmet about his head, receiving a furious demonstration from the company. He was shaking hands, and explaining, and haranguing to a high degree.

Dan started. His face of bronze flushed to his temples. He seemed about to leap from the ground, but then suddenly he sank back, and resumed his impassive gazing.

The men were in a flurry. They looked from one to the other. "Dan! Look! See who's coming!" some cried again. "Dan! Look!"

He scowled at last, and moved his shoulders sullenly. "Well, don't I know it?"

But they could not be convinced that his eyes were in service. "Dan! Why can't you look? See who's coming!"

He made a gesture then of irritation and rage. "Curse it! Don't I know it?"

The man with a bandage of the size of a helmet moved forward, always shaking hands and explaining. At times his glance wandered to Dan, who saw with his eyes riveted.

After a series of shiftings, it occurred naturally that the man with the bandage was very near to the man who saw the flames. He paused, and there was a little silence. Finally he said:

"Hello, Dan."

"Hello, Billie."

Notes

p. 136   *mullein* - tall flowering plant

p. 136   *musket* - a light, long-barrelled gun used by infantry (foot soldiers)

p. 137   *pontoon* - a temporary bridge across a river

p. 137   *batteries* - fortified gun towers

p. 138   *blithesome* - cheerful

p. 139   *dead in blue . . . gray* - the Federal blue uniforms and the Confederate gray

p. 139   *picket* - on guard (watching for the enemy while the regiment sleeps)

p. 139   *horse-hair trunk* - a sort of chest used as both a storage box and a stool; horse-hair was often used for upholstery in the nineteenth century

p. 141   *Shucks* - American slang meaning 'Oh it was nothing'

p. 142   *undetailed . . . detail* - the detail is one assigned a military task or duty

p. 142   *caisson* - a large box of ammunition

p. 143   *aides* - seconds-in-command to senior officers

p. 143   *fall in* - take their places in military ranks

p. 144   *stormed* - swore, spoke angrily

p. 144   *veterans . . . recruits* - soldiers who have been in battle before, as opposed to new recruits

p. 145   *necromancer* - a magician who communicates with or raises the dead

p. 145   *Bivouac fires* - camp fires

p. 145   *bed of an eagle* - the eagle, a symbol of the regiment, on a flag or device, now lying in the mud

14

The Woman's Rose

(1899)

Olive Schreiner

Schreiner was a South African writer best known for her outstandingly original and gripping novel The Story of an African Farm. *In this story, a woman looks back to her youth and remembers an occasion when cynicism was overcome and female solidarity triumphed over petty competition. This is a symbolic affirmative tale.*

I have an old, brown carved box; the lid is broken and tied with a string. In it I keep little squares of paper, with hair inside, and a little picture which hung over my brother's bed when we were children, and other things as small. I have in it a rose. Other women also have such boxes where they keep such trifles, but no one has my rose.

When my eye is dim, and my heart grows faint, and my faith in woman flickers, and her present is an agony to me, and her future a despair, the scent of that dead rose, withered for twelve years, comes back to me. I know there will be spring; as surely as the birds know it when they see above the snow two tiny, quivering green leaves. Spring cannot fail us.

There were other flowers in the box once; a bunch of white acacia flowers, gathered by the strong hand of a man, as we passed down a village street on a sultry afternoon, when it had rained, and the drops fell on us from the leaves of the acacia trees. The flowers were damp; they made mildew marks on the paper I folded them in. After many years I threw them away. There is nothing of them left in the box now, but a faint, strong smell of dried acacia, that recalls that sultry summer afternoon; but the rose is in the box still.

It is many years ago now; I was a girl of fifteen, and I went to visit in a small up-country town. It was young in those days, and two days' journey from the nearest village; the population consisted mainly of men. A few were married, and had their wives and children, but most were single. There was only one young girl there when I came. She was about seventeen, fair, and rather fully-fleshed; she had large dreamy blue eyes, and wavy light hair; full, rather heavy lips, until she smiled; then her face broke into dimples, and all her white teeth shone. The hotel-keeper may have had a daughter, and the farmer in the outskirts had two, but we never saw them. She reigned alone. All the men worshipped her. She was the only woman they had to think of. They talked of her on the stoep, at

149

the market, at the hotel; they watched for her at street corners; they hated the man she bowed to or walked with down the street. They brought flowers to the front door; they offered her their horses; they begged her to marry them when they dared. Partly, there was something noble and heroic in this devotion of men to the best woman they knew; partly there was something natural in it, that these men, shut off from the world, should pour at the feet of one woman the worship that otherwise would have been given to twenty; and partly there was something mean in their envy of one another. If she had raised her little finger, I suppose, she might have married any one out of twenty of them.

Then I came. I do not think I was prettier; I do not think I was so pretty as she was. I was certainly not as handsome. But I was vital, and I was new, and she was old—they all forsook her and followed me. They worshipped me. It was to my door that the flowers came; it was I had twenty horses offered me when I could only ride one; it was for me they waited at street corners; it was what I said and did that they talked of. Partly I liked it. I had lived alone all my life; no one ever had told me I was beautiful and a woman. I believed them. I did not know it was simply a fashion, which one man had set and the rest followed unreasoningly. I liked them to ask me to marry them, and to say, No. I despised them. The mother heart had not swelled in me yet; I did not know all men were my children, as the large woman knows when her heart is grown. I was too small to be tender. I liked my power. I was like a child with a new whip, which it goes about cracking everywhere, not caring against what. I could not wind it up and put it away. Men were curious creatures, who liked me, I could never tell why. Only one thing took from my pleasure; I could not bear that they had deserted her for me. I liked her great dreamy blue eyes, I liked her slow walk and drawl; when I saw her sitting among men, she seemed to me much too good to be among them; I would have given all their compliments if she would once have smiled at me as she smiled at them, with all her face breaking into radiance, with her dimples and flashing teeth. But I knew it never could be; I felt sure she hated me; that she wished I was dead; that she wished I had never come to the village. She did not know, when we went out riding, and a man who had always ridden beside her came to ride beside me, that I sent him away; that once when a man thought to win my favour by ridiculing her slow drawl before me I turned on him so fiercely that he never dared come before me again. I knew she knew that at the hotel men had made a bet as to which was the prettier, she or I, and had asked each man who came in, and that the one who had staked on me won. I hated them for it, but I would not let her see that I cared about what she felt towards me.

She and I never spoke to each other.

If we met in the village street we bowed and passed on; when we shook hands we did so silently, and did not look at each other. But I thought she felt my presence in a room just as I felt hers.

At last the time for my going came. I was to leave the next day. Some one I knew gave a party in my honour, to which all the village was invited.

It was midwinter. There was nothing in the gardens but a few dahlias and chrysanthemums, and I suppose that for two hundred miles round there was not a rose to be bought for love or money. Only in the garden of a friend of mine, in a sunny corner between the oven and the brick wall, there was a rose tree growing which had on it one bud. It was white, and it had been promised to the fair haired girl to wear at the party.

The evening came; when I arrived and went to the waiting-room, to take off my mantle, I found the girl there already. She was dressed in pure white, with her great white arms and shoulders showing, and her bright hair glittering in the candle-light, and the white rose fastened at her breast. She looked like a queen. I said "Good-evening," and turned away quickly to the glass to arrange my old black scarf across my old black dress.

Then I felt a hand touch my hair.

"Stand still," she said.

I looked in the glass. She had taken the white rose from her breast, and was fastening it in my hair.

"How nice dark hair is; it sets off flowers so." She stepped back and looked at me. "It looks much better there!"

I turned round.

"You are so beautiful to me," I said.

"Y-e-s," she said, with her slow Colonial drawl; "I'm so glad."

We stood looking at each other.

Then they came in and swept us away to dance. All the evening we did not come near to each other. Only once, as she passed, she smiled at me.

The next morning I left the town.

I never saw her again.

Years afterwards I heard she had married and gone to America; it may or may not be so—but the rose—the rose is in the box still! When my faith in woman grows dim, and it seems that for want of love and magnanimity she can play no part in any future heaven; then the scent of that small withered thing comes back:—spring cannot fail us.

Matjesfontein, South Africa.

Note

p. 149   *stoep* - verandah in front of house

15

The Lady's Maid's Bell

(1902)

Edith Wharton

Wharton wrote many novels, most notably The Age of Innocence *and* The House of Mirth, *but also many short stories. She was American by birth but in some ways also European as she travelled and lived in Europe for much of her life. This is a ghost story but, as with all good examples of the genre, it is more than that.*

It was the autumn after I had the typhoid. I'd been three months in hospital, and when I came out I looked so weak and tottery that the two or three ladies I applied to were afraid to engage me. Most of my money was gone, and after I'd boarded for two months, hanging about the employment-agencies, and answering any advertisement that looked any way respectable, I pretty nearly lost heart, for fretting hadn't made me fatter, and I didn't see why my luck should ever turn. It did though—or I thought so at the time. A Mrs. Railton, a friend of the lady that first brought me out to the States, met me one day and stopped to speak to me: she was one that had always a friendly way with her. She asked me what ailed me to look so white, and when I told her, "Why, Hartley," says she, "I believe I've got the very place for you. Come in to-morrow and we'll talk about it."

The next day, when I called, she told me the lady she'd in mind was a niece of hers, a Mrs. Brympton, a youngish lady, but something of an invalid, who lived all the year round at her country-place on the Hudson, owing to not being able to stand the fatigue of town life.

"Now, Hartley," Mrs. Railton said, in that cheery way that always made me feel things must be going to take a turn for the better—"now understand me; it's not a cheerful place I'm sending you to. The house is big and gloomy; my niece is nervous, vapourish; her husband—well, he's generally away; and the two children are dead. A year ago I would as soon have thought of shutting a rosy active girl like you into a vault; but you're not particularly brisk yourself just now, are you? and a quiet place, with country air and wholesome food and early hours, ought to be the very thing for you. Don't mistake me," she added, for I suppose I looked a trifle downcast; "you may find it dull but you won't be unhappy. My niece is an angel. Her former maid, who died last spring, had been with her twenty years and worshipped the ground she walked on. She's a kind mistress to all, and where the mistress is kind, as you know, the servants are generally good-humoured, so you'll probably get on well enough with the rest of the household. And you're the very woman I want for my niece: quiet, well-mannered, and educated above your station. You read aloud well, I think? That's a good thing; my niece likes to be read to. She wants a maid that can be something of a companion: her last was, and I can't say how she misses her. It's a lonely life . . . Well, have you decided?"

"Why, ma'am," I said, "I'm not afraid of solitude."

"Well, then, go; my niece will take you on my recommendation. I'll telegraph her at once and you can take the afternoon train. She has no one to wait on her at present, and I don't want you to lose any time."

I was ready enough to start, yet something in me hung back; and to gain time I asked, "And the gentleman, ma'am?"

"The gentleman's almost always away, I tell you," said Mrs. Railton, quick-like—"and when he's there," says she suddenly, "you've only to keep out of his way."

I took the afternoon train and got out at D——station at about four o'clock. A groom in a dog-cart was waiting, and we drove off at a smart pace. It was a dull October day, with rain hanging close overhead, and by the time we turned into Brympton Place woods the daylight was almost gone. The drive wound through the woods for a mile or two, and came out on a gravel court shut in with thickets of tall black-looking shrubs. There were no lights in the windows, and the house *did* look a bit gloomy.

I had asked no questions of the groom, for I never was one to get my notion of new masters from their other servants: I prefer to wait and see for myself. But I could tell by the look of everything that I had got into the right kind of house, and that things were done handsomely. A pleasant-faced cook met me at the back door and called the house-maid to show me up to my room. "You'll see madam later," she said. "Mrs. Brympton has a visitor."

I hadn't fancied Mrs. Brympton was a lady to have many visitors, and somehow the words cheered me. I followed the house-maid upstairs, and saw, through a door on the upper landing, that the main part of the house seemed well furnished, with dark panelling and a number of old portraits. Another flight of stairs led us up to the servants' wing. It was almost dark now, and the house-maid excused herself for not having brought a light. "But there's matches in your room," she said, "and if you go careful you'll be all right. Mind the step at the end of the passage. Your room is just beyond."

I looked ahead as she spoke, and half-way down the passage I saw a woman standing. She drew back into a doorway as we passed and the house-maid didn't appear to notice her. She was a thin woman with a white face, and a darkish stuff gown and apron. I took her for the housekeeper and thought it odd that she didn't speak, but just gave me a long look as she went by. My room opened into a square hall at the end of the passage. Facing my door was another which stood open: the house-maid exclaimed when she saw it:

"There—Mrs. Blinder's left that door open again!" said she, closing it.

"Is Mrs. Blinder the housekeeper?"

"There's no housekeeper: Mrs. Blinder's the cook."

"And is that her room?"

"Laws, no," said the house-maid, cross-like. "That's nobody's room. It's empty, I mean, and the door hadn't ought to be open. Mrs. Brympton wants it kept locked."

She opened my door and led me into a neat room, nicely furnished, with a picture or two on the walls; and having lit a candle she took leave, telling me that the servants'-hall tea was at six, and that Mrs. Brympton would see me afterward.

I found them a pleasant-spoken set in the servants' hall, and by what they let fall I gathered that, as Mrs. Railton had said, Mrs. Brympton was the kindest of ladies; but I didn't take much notice of their talk, for I was watching to see the pale woman in the dark gown come in. She didn't show herself, however, and I wondered if she ate apart; but if she wasn't the housekeeper, why should she? Suddenly it struck me that she might be a trained nurse, and in that case her meals would of course be served in her room. If Mrs. Brympton was an invalid it was likely enough she had a nurse. The idea annoyed me, I own, for they're not always the easiest to get on with, and if I'd known I shouldn't have taken the place. But there I was and there was no use pulling a long face over it; and not being one to ask questions I waited to see what would turn up.

When tea was over the house-maid said to the footman: "Has Mr. Ranford gone?" and when he said yes, she told me to come up with her to Mrs. Brympton.

Mrs. Brympton was lying down in her bedroom. Her lounge stood near the fire and beside it was a shaded lamp. She was a delicate-looking lady, but when she smiled I felt there was nothing I wouldn't do for her. She spoke very pleasantly, in a low voice, asking me my name and age and so on, and if I had everything I wanted, and if I wasn't afraid of feeling lonely in the country.

"Not with you I wouldn't be, madam," I said, and the words surprised me when I'd spoken them, for I'm not an impulsive person; but it was just as if I'd thought aloud.

She seemed pleased at that, and said she hoped I'd continue in the same mind; then she gave me a few directions about her toilet, and said Agnes the house-maid would show me next morning where things were kept.

"I am tired to-night, and shall dine upstairs," she said. "Agnes will bring me my tray, that you may have time to unpack and settle yourself; and later you may come and undress me."

"Very well, ma'am," I said. "You'll ring, I suppose?"

I thought she looked odd.

"No—Agnes will fetch you," says she quickly, and took up her book again.

Well—that was certainly strange: a lady's-maid having to be fetched by the house-maid whenever her lady wanted her! I wondered if there were no bells in the house; but the next day I satisfied myself that there was one in every room, and a special one ringing from my mistress's room to mine; and after that it did strike me as queer that, whenever Mrs. Brympton wanted anything, she rang for Agnes, who had to walk the whole length of the servants' wing to call me.

But that wasn't the only queer thing in the house. The very next day I found out that Mrs. Brympton had no nurse; and then I asked Agnes about the woman I had seen in the passage the afternoon before. Agnes said she had seen no one, and I saw that she thought I was dreaming. To be sure, it was dusk when we went down the passage, and she had excused herself for not bringing a light; but I had seen the woman plain enough to know her again if we should meet. I decided that she must have been a friend of the cook's, or of one of the other women-servants; perhaps she had come down from town for a night's visit, and the servants wanted it kept secret. Some ladies are very stiff about having their servants' friends in the house overnight. At any rate, I made up my mind to ask no more questions.

In a day or two another odd thing happened. I was chatting one afternoon with Mrs. Blinder, who was a friendly disposed woman, and had been longer in the house than the other servants, and she asked me if I was quite comfortable and had everything I needed. I said I had no fault to find with my place or with my mistress, but I thought it odd that in so large a house there was no sewing-room for the lady's maid.

"Why," says she, "there *is* one: the room you're in is the old sewing-room."

"Oh," said I; "and where did the other lady's maid sleep?"

At that she grew confused, and said hurriedly that the servants' rooms had all been changed about last year, and she didn't rightly remember.

That struck me as peculiar, but I went on as if I hadn't noticed: "Well, there's a vacant room opposite mine, and I mean to ask Mrs. Brympton if I mayn't use that as a sewing-room."

To my astonishment, Mrs. Blinder went white, and gave my hand a kind of squeeze. "Don't do that, my dear," said she, trembling-like. "To tell you the truth, that was Emma Saxon's room, and my mistress has kept it closed ever since her death."

"And who was Emma Saxon?"

"Mrs. Brympton's former maid."

"The one that was with her so many years?" said I, remembering what Mrs. Railton had told me.

Mrs. Blinder nodded.

"What sort of woman was she?"

"No better walked the earth," said Mrs. Blinder. "My mistress loved her like a sister."

"But I mean—what did she look like?"

Mrs. Blinder got up and gave me a kind of angry stare. "I'm no great hand at describing," she said; "and I believe my pastry's rising." And she walked off into the kitchen and shut the door after her.

II

I had been near a week at Brympton before I saw my master. Word came that he was arriving one afternoon, and a change passed over the whole household. It was plain that nobody loved him below stairs. Mrs. Blinder took uncommon care with the dinner that night, but she snapped at the kitchen-maid in a way quite unusual with her; and

Mr. Wace, the butler, a serious, slow-spoken man, went about his duties as if he'd been getting ready for a funeral. He was a great Bible-reader, Mr. Wace was, and had a beautiful assortment of texts at his command; but that day he used such dreadful language, that I was about to leave the table, when he assured me it was all out of Isaiah; and I noticed that whenever the master came Mr. Wace took to the prophets.

About seven, Agnes called me to my mistress's room; and there I found Mr. Brympton. He was standing on the hearth; a big fair bull-necked man, with a red face and little bad-tempered blue eyes: the kind of man a young simpleton might have thought handsome, and would have been like to pay dear for thinking it.

He swung about when I came in, and looked me over in a trice. I knew what the look meant, from having experienced it once or twice in my former places. Then he turned his back on me, and went on talking to his wife; and I knew what *that* meant, too. I was not the kind of morsel he was after. The typhoid had served me well enough in one way: it kept that kind of gentleman at arm's-length.

"This is my new maid, Hartley," says Mrs. Brympton in her kind voice; and he nodded and went on with what he was saying.

In a minute or two he went off, and left my mistress to dress for dinner, and I noticed as I waited on her that she was white, and chill to the touch.

Mr. Brympton took himself off the next morning, and the whole house drew a long breath when he drove away. As for my mistress, she put on her hat and furs (for it was a fine winter morning) and went out for a walk in the gardens, coming back quite fresh and rosy, so that for a minute, before her colour faded, I could guess what a pretty young lady she must have been, and not so long ago, either.

She had met Mr. Ranford in the grounds, and the two came back together, I remember, smiling and talking as they walked along the terrace under my window. That was the first time I saw Mr. Ranford, though I had often heard his name mentioned in the hall. He was a neighbour, it appeared, living a mile or two beyond Brympton, at the end of the village; and as he was in the habit of spending his winters in the country he was almost the only company my mistress had at that season. He was a slight tall gentleman of about thirty, and I thought him rather melancholy-looking till I saw his smile, which had a kind of surprise in it, like the first warm day in spring. He was a great reader, I heard, like my mistress, and the two were for ever borrowing books of one another, and sometimes (Mr. Wace told me) he would read aloud to Mrs. Brympton by the hour, in the big dark library where she sat in the winter afternoons. The servants all liked him, and perhaps that's more of a compliment than the masters suspect. He had a friendly word for every one of us, and we were all glad to think that Mrs. Brympton had a pleasant companionable gentleman like that to keep her company when the master was away. Mr. Ranford seemed on excellent terms with Mr. Brympton too; though I couldn't but wonder that two gentlemen so unlike each other should be so friendly. But then I knew how the real quality can keep their feelings to themselves.

As for Mr. Brympton, he came and went, never staying more than a day or two, cursing the dulness and the solitude, grumbling at everything, and (as I soon found out) drinking a deal more than was good for him. After Mrs. Brympton left the table he would sit half the night over the old Brympton port and madeira, and once, as I was leaving my mistress's room rather later than usual, I met him coming up the stairs in such a state that I turned sick to think of what some ladies have to endure and hold their tongues about.

The servants said very little about their master; but from what they let drop I could see it had been an unhappy match from the beginning. Mr. Brympton was coarse, loud and pleasure-loving; my mistress quiet, retiring, and perhaps a trifle cold. Not that she was not always pleasant-spoken to him: I thought her wonderfully forbearing; but to a gentleman as free as Mr. Brympton I daresay she seemed a little offish.

Well, things went on quietly for several weeks. My mistress was kind, my duties were light, and I got on well with the other servants. In short, I had nothing to complain of; yet there was always a weight on me. I can't say why it was so, but I know it was not the loneliness that I felt. I soon got used to that; and being still languid from the fever, I was thankful for the quiet and the good country air. Nevertheless, I was never quite easy in my mind. My mistress, knowing I had been ill, insisted that I should take my walk regular, and often invented errands for me:—a yard of ribbon to be fetched from the village, a letter posted, or a book returned to Mr. Ranford. As soon as I was out of doors my spirits rose, and I looked forward to my walks through the bare moist-smelling woods; but the moment I caught sight of the house again my heart dropped down like a stone in a well. It was not a gloomy house exactly, yet I never entered it but a feeling of gloom came over me.

Mrs. Brympton seldom went out in winter; only on the finest days did she walk an hour at noon on the south terrace. Excepting Mr. Ranford, we had no visitors but the doctor, who drove over from D—— about once a week. He sent for me once or twice to give me some trifling direction about my mistress, and though he never told me what her illness was, I thought, from a waxy look she had now and then of a morning, that it might be the heart that ailed her. The season was soft and unwholesome, and in January we had a long spell of rain. That was a sore trial to me, I own, for I couldn't go out, and sitting over my sewing all day, listening to the drip, drip of the eaves, I grew so nervous that the least sound made me jump. Somehow, the thought of that locked room across the passage began to weigh on me. Once or twice, in the long rainy nights, I fancied I heard noises there; but that was nonsense, of course, and the daylight drove such notions out of my head. Well, one morning Mrs. Brympton gave me quite a start of pleasure by telling me she wished me to go to town for some shopping. I hadn't known till then how low my spirits had fallen. I set off in high glee, and my first sight of the crowded streets and the cheerful-looking shops quite took me out of myself. Toward afternoon, however, the noise and confusion began to tire me, and I was actually looking forward to the quiet of Brympton, and thinking how I should enjoy the drive home through the dark woods, when I ran across an old acquaintance, a maid I had once been in service with. We had lost sight of each other for a number of years, and I had to stop and tell her what had happened to me in the interval. When I mentioned where I was living she rolled up her eyes and pulled a long face.

"What! The Mrs. Brympton that lives all the year at her place on the Hudson? My dear, you won't stay there three months."

"Oh, but I don't mind the country," says I, offended somehow at her tone. "Since the fever I'm glad to be quiet."

She shook her head. "It's not the country I'm thinking of. All I know is she's had four maids in the last six months, and the last one, who was a friend of mine, told me nobody could stay in the house."

"Did she say why?" I asked.

"No—she wouldn't give me her reason. But she says to me, *Mrs. Ansey*, she says, *if ever a young woman as you know of thinks of going there, you tell her it's not worth while to unpack her boxes.*"

"Is she young and handsome?" said I, thinking of Mr. Brympton.

"Not her! She's the kind that mothers engage when they've gay young gentlemen at college."

Well, though I knew the woman was an idle gossip, the words stuck in my head, and my heart sank lower than ever as I drove up to Brympton in the dusk. There *was* something about the house—I was sure of it now . . .

When I went in to tea I heard that Mr. Brympton had arrived, and I saw at a glance that there had been a disturbance of some kind. Mrs. Blinder's hand shook so that she could hardly pour the tea, and Mr. Wace quoted the most dreadful texts full of brimstone. Nobody said a word to me then, but when I went up to my room Mrs. Blinder followed me.

"Oh, my dear," says she, taking my hand, "I'm so glad and thankful you've come back to us!"

That struck me, as you may imagine. "Why," said I, "did you think I was leaving for good?"

"No, no, to be sure," said she, a little confused, "but I can't a-bear to have madam left alone for a day even." She pressed my hand hard, and, "Oh, Miss Hartley," says she, "be good to your mistress, as you're a Christian woman." And with that she hurried away, and left me staring.

A moment later Agnes called me to Mrs. Brympton. Hearing Mr. Brympton's voice in her room, I went round by the dressing-room, thinking I would lay out her dinner-gown before going in. The dressing-room is a large room with a window over the portico that looks toward the gardens. Mr. Brympton's apartments are beyond. When I went in, the door into the bedroom was ajar, and I heard Mr. Brympton saying angrily:—"One would suppose he was the only person fit for you to talk to."

"I don't have many visitors in winter," Mrs. Brympton answered quietly.

"You have *me!*" he flung at her, sneeringly.

"You are here so seldom," said she.

"Well—whose fault is that? You make the place about as lively as the family vault—"

With that I rattled the toilet-things, to give my mistress warning, and she rose and called me in.

The two dined alone, as usual, and I knew by Mr. Wace's manner at supper that things must be going badly. He quoted the prophets something terrible, and worked on the kitchen-maid so that she declared she wouldn't go down alone to put the cold meat in the ice-box. I felt nervous myself, and after I had put my mistress to bed I was half-tempted to go down again and persuade Mrs. Blinder to sit up awhile over a game of cards. But I heard her door closing for the night and so I went on to my own room. The rain had begun again, and the drip, drip, drip seemed to be dropping into my brain. I lay awake listening to it, and turning over what my friend in town had said. What puzzled me was that it was always the maids who left . . .

After a while I slept; but suddenly a loud noise wakened me. My bell had rung. I sat up, terrified by the unusual sound, which seemed to go on jangling through the darkness. My hands shook so that I couldn't find the matches. At length I struck a light and jumped out of bed. I began to think I must have been dreaming; but I looked at the bell against the wall, and there was the little hammer still quivering.

I was just beginning to huddle on my clothes when I heard another sound. This time it was the door of the locked room opposite mine softly opening and closing. I heard the sound distinctly, and it frightened me so that I stood stock still. Then I heard a footstep hurrying down the passage toward the main house. The floor being carpeted, the sound was very faint, but I was quite sure it was a woman's step. I turned cold with the thought of it, and for a minute to two I dursn't breathe or move. Then I came to my senses.

"Alice Hartley," says I to myself, "someone left that room just now and ran down the passage ahead of you. The idea isn't pleasant, but you may as well face it. Your mistress has rung for you, and to answer her bell you've got to go the way that other woman has gone."

Well—I did it. I never walked faster in my life, yet I thought I should never get to the end of the passage or reach Mrs. Brympton's room. On the way I heard nothing and saw nothing: all was dark and quiet as the grave. When I reached my mistress's door the silence was so deep that I began to think I must be dreaming, and was half-minded to turn back. Then a panic seized me, and I knocked.

There was no answer, and I knocked again, loudly. To my astonishment the door was opened by Mr. Brympton. He started back when he saw me, and in the light of my candle his face looked red and savage.

"*You?*" he said, in a queer voice. "*How many of you are there, in God's name?*"

At that I felt the ground give under me; but I said to myself that he had been drinking, and answered as steadily as I could: "May I go in, sir? Mrs. Brympton has rung for me."

"You may all go in, for what I care," says he, and, pushing by me, walked down the hall to his own bedroom. I looked after him as he went, and to my surprise I saw that he walked as straight as a sober man.

I found my mistress lying very weak and still, but she forced a smile when she saw me, and signed to me to pour out some drops for her. After that she lay without speaking, her breath coming quick, and her eyes closed. Suddenly she groped out with her hand, and "*Emma*," says she, faintly.

"It's Hartley, madam," I said. "Do you want anything?"

She opened her eyes wide and gave me a startled look.

"I was dreaming," she said. "You may go, now, Hartley, and thank you kindly. I'm quite well again, you see." And she turned her face away from me.

III

There was no more sleep for me that night, and I was thankful when daylight came.

Soon afterward, Agnes called me to Mrs. Brympton. I was afraid she was ill again, for she seldom sent for me before nine, but I found her sitting up in bed, pale and drawn-looking, but quite herself.

"Hartley," says she quickly, "will you put on your things at once and go down to the village for me? I want this prescription made up—" here she hesitated a minute and blushed— "and I should like you to be back again before Mr. Brympton is up."

"Certainly, madam," I said.

"And—stay a moment—" she called me back as if an idea had just struck her—"while you're waiting for the mixture, you'll have time to go on to Mr. Ranford's with this note."

It was a two-mile walk to the village, and on my way I had time to turn things over in my mind. It struck me as peculiar that my mistress should wish the prescription made up without Mr. Brympton's knowledge; and, putting this together with the scene of the night before, and with much else that I had noticed and suspected, I began to wonder if the poor lady was weary of her life, and had come to the mad resolve of ending it. The idea took such hold on me that I reached the village on a run, and dropped breathless into a chair before the chemist's counter. The good man, who was just taking down his shutters, stared at me so hard that it brought me to myself.

"Mr. Limmel," I says, trying to speak indifferent, "will you run your eye over this, and tell me if it's quite right?"

He put on his spectacles and studied the prescription.

"Why, it's one of Dr. Walton's," says he. "What should be wrong with it?"

"Well—is it dangerous to take?"

"Dangerous—how do you mean?"

I could have shaken the man for his stupidity.

"I mean—if a person was to take too much of it—by mistake of course—" says I, my heart in my throat.

"Lord bless you, no. It's only lime-water. You might feed it to a baby by the bottleful."

I gave a great sigh of relief and hurried on to Mr. Ranford's. But on the way another thought struck me. If there was nothing to conceal about my visit to the chemist's, was it my other errand that Mrs. Brympton wished me to keep private? Somehow, that thought frightened me worse than the other. Yet the two gentlemen seemed fast friends, and I would have staked my head on my mistress's goodness. I felt ashamed of my suspicions, and concluded that I was still disturbed by the strange events of the night. I left the note at Mr. Ranford's, and hurrying back to Brympton, slipped in by a side door without being seen, as I thought.

An hour later, however, as I was carrying in my mistress's breakfast, I was stopped in the hall by Mr. Brympton.

"What were you doing out so early?" he says, looking hard at me.

"Early—me, sir?" I said, in a tremble.

"Come, come," he says, an angry red spot coming out on his forehead, "didn't I see you scuttling home through the shrubbery an hour or more ago?"

I'm a truthful woman by nature, but at that a lie popped out ready-made. "No, sir, you didn't," said I and looked straight back at him.

He shrugged his shoulders and gave a sullen laugh. "I suppose you think I was drunk last night?" he asked suddenly.

"No, sir, I don't," I answered, this time truthfully enough.

He turned away with another shrug. "A pretty notion my servants have of me!" I heard him mutter as he walked off.

Not till I had settled down to my afternoon's sewing did I realise how the events of the night had shaken me. I couldn't pass that locked door without a shiver. I knew I had heard someone come out of it, and walk down the passage ahead of me. I thought of speaking to Mrs. Blinder or to Mr. Wace, the only two in the house who appeared to have an inkling of what was going on, but I had a feeling that if I questioned them they would deny everything, and that I might learn more by holding my tongue and keeping my eyes open. The idea of spending another night opposite the locked room sickened me, and once I was seized with the notion of packing my trunk and taking the first train to town; but it wasn't in me to throw over a kind mistress in that manner, and I tried to go on with my sewing as if nothing had happened. I hadn't worked ten minutes before the sewing machine broke down. It was one I had found in the house, a good machine but a trifle out of order: Mrs. Blinder said it had never been used since Emma Saxon's death. I stopped to see what was wrong, and as I was working at the machine a drawer which I had never been able to open slid forward and a photograph fell out. I picked it up and sat looking at it in a maze. It was a woman's likeness, and I knew I had seen the face somewhere—the eyes had an asking look that I had felt on me before. And suddenly I remembered the pale woman in the passage.

I stood up, cold all over, and ran out of the room. My heart seemed to be thumping in the top of my head, and I felt as if I should never get away from the look in those eyes. I went straight to Mrs. Blinder. She was taking her afternoon nap, and sat up with a jump when I came in.

"Mrs. Blinder," said I, "who is that?" And I held out the photograph.

She rubbed her eyes and stared.

"Why, Emma Saxon," says she. "Where did you find it?"

I looked hard at her for a minute. "Mrs. Blinder," I said, "I've seen that face before."

Mrs. Blinder got up and walked over to the looking-glass. "Dear me! I must have been asleep," she says. "My front is all over one ear. And now do run along, Miss Hartley, dear, for I hear the clock striking four, and I must go down this very minute and put on the Virginia ham for Mr. Brympton's dinner."

IV

To all appearances, things went on as usual for a week or two. The only difference was that Mr. Brympton stayed on, instead of going off as he usually did, and that Mr. Ranford never showed himself. I heard Mr. Brympton remark on this one afternoon when he was sitting in my mistress's room before dinner:

"Where's Ranford?" says he. "He hasn't been near the house for a week. Does he keep away because I'm here?"

Mrs. Brympton spoke so low that I couldn't catch her answer.

"Well," he went on, "two's company and three's trumpery; I'm sorry to be in Ranford's way, and I suppose I shall have to take myself off again in a day or two and give him a show." And he laughed at his own joke.

The very next day, as it happened, Mr. Ranford called. The footman said the three were very merry over their tea in the library, and Mr. Brympton strolled down to the gate with Mr. Ranford when he left.

I have said that things went on as usual; and so they did with the rest of the household; but as for myself, I had never been the same since the night my bell had rung. Night after night I used to lie awake, listening for it to ring again, and for the door of the locked room to open stealthily. But the bell never rang, and I heard no sound across the passage. At last the silence began to be more dreadful to me than the most mysterious sounds. I felt that *someone* was cowering there, behind the locked door, watching and listening as I watched and listened, and I could almost have cried out, "Whoever you are, come out and let me see you face to face, but don't lurk there and spy on me in the darkness!"

Feeling as I did, you may wonder I didn't give warning. Once I very nearly did so; but at the last moment something held me back. Whether it was compassion for my mistress, who had grown more and more dependent on me, or unwillingness to try a new place, or some other feeling that I couldn't put a name to, I lingered on as if spell-bound, though every night was dreadful to me, and the days but little better.

For one thing, I didn't like Mrs. Brympton's looks. She had never been the same since that night, no more than I had. I thought she would brighten up after Mr. Brympton left, but though she seemed easier in her mind, her spirits didn't revive, nor her strength either. She had grown attached to me, and seemed to like to have me about; and Agnes told me one day that, since Emma Saxon's death, I was the only maid her mistress had taken to. This gave me a warm feeling for the poor lady, though after all there was little I could do to help her.

After Mr. Brympton's departure, Mr. Ranford took to coming again, though less often than formerly. I met him once or twice in the grounds, or in the village, and I couldn't but think there was a change in him too; but I set it down to my disordered fancy.

The weeks passed, and Mr. Brympton had now been a month absent. We heard he was cruising with a friend in the West Indies, and Mr. Wace said that was a long way off, but though you had the wings of a dove and went to the uttermost parts of the earth, you couldn't get away from the Almighty. Agnes said that as long as he stayed away from Brympton the Almighty might have him and welcome; and this raised a laugh, though Mrs. Blinder tried to look shocked, and Mr. Wace said the bears would eat us.

We were all glad to hear that the West Indies were a long way off, and I remember that, in spite of Mr. Wace's solemn looks, we had a very merry dinner that day in the hall. I don't know if it was because of my being in better spirits, but I fancied Mrs. Brympton looked better too, and seemed more cheerful in her manner. She had been for a walk in the morning, and after luncheon she lay down in her room, and I read aloud to her. When she dismissed me I went to my own room feeling quite bright and happy, and for the first time in weeks walked past the locked door without thinking of it. As I sat down to my work I looked out and saw a few snow-flakes falling. The sight was pleasanter than the eternal rain, and I pictured to myself how pretty the bare gardens would look in their white mantle. It seemed to me as if the snow would cover up all the dreariness, indoors as well as out.

The fancy had hardly crossed my mind when I heard a step at my side. I looked up, thinking it was Agnes.

"Well, Agnes—" said I, and the words froze on my tongue; for there, in the door, stood Emma Saxon.

I don't know how long she stood there. I only know I couldn't stir or take my eyes from her. Afterward I was terribly frightened, but at the time it wasn't fear I felt, but something deeper and quieter. She looked at me long and long, and her face was just one dumb prayer to me—but how in the world was I to help her? Suddenly she turned, and I heard her walk down the passage. This time I wasn't afraid to follow— I felt that I must know what she wanted. I sprang up and ran out. She was at the other end of the passage, and I expected her to take the turn toward my mistress's room; but instead of that she pushed open the door that led to the backstairs. I followed her down the stairs, and across the passageway to the back door. The kitchen and hall were empty at that hour, the servants being off duty, except for the footman, who was in the pantry. At the door she stood still a moment, with another look at me, then she turned the handle, and stepped out. For a minute I hesitated. Where was she leading me to? The door had closed softly after her, and I opened it and looked out, half-expecting to find that she had disappeared. But I saw her a few yards off hurrying across the court-yard to the path through the woods. Her figure looked black and lonely in the snow, and for a second my heart failed me and I thought of turning back. But all the while she was drawing me after her; and catching up an old shawl of Mrs. Blinder's I ran out into the open.

Emma Saxon was in the wood-path now. She walked on steadily, and I followed at the same pace, till we passed out of the gates and reached the high-road. Then she struck across the open fields to the village. By this time the ground was white, and as she climbed the slope of a bare hill ahead of me I noticed that she left no foot-prints behind her. At sight of that my heart shrivelled up within me, and my knees were water. Somehow, it was worse here than indoors. She made the whole countryside seem lonely as the grave, with none but us two in it, and no help in the wide world.

Once I tried to go back; but she turned and looked at me, and it was as if she had dragged me with ropes. After that I followed her like a dog. We came to the village and she led me through it, past the church and the blacksmith's shop, and down the lane to Mr. Ranford's. Mr. Ranford's house stands close to the road: a plain old-fashioned building, with a flagged path leading to the door between box-borders. The lane was deserted, and as I turned into it I saw Emma Saxon pause under the old elm by the gate. And now another fear came over me. I saw that we had reached the end of our journey, and that it was my turn to act. All the way from Brympton I had been asking myself what she wanted of me, but I had followed in a trance, as it were, and not till I saw her stop at Mr. Ranford's gate did my brain begin to clear itself. I stood a little way off in the snow, my heart beating fit to strangle me, and my feet frozen to the ground; and she stood under the elm and watched me.

I knew well enough that she hadn't led me there for nothing. I felt there was something I ought to say or do—but how was I to guess what it was? I had never thought harm of my mistress and Mr. Ranford, but I was sure now that, from one cause or another, some dreadful thing hung over them. *She* knew what it was; she would tell me if she could; perhaps she would answer if I questioned her.

It turned me faint to think of speaking to her; but I plucked up heart and dragged myself across the few yards between us. As I did so, I heard the house-door open and saw Mr. Ranford approaching. He looked handsome and cheerful, as my mistress had looked that morning, and at sight of him the blood began to flow again in my veins.

"Why, Hartley," said he, "what's the matter? I saw you coming down the lane just now, and came out to see if you had taken root in the snow." He stopped and stared at me, "What are you looking at?" he says.

I turned toward the elm as he spoke, and his eyes followed me; but there was no one there. The lane was empty as far as the eye could reach.

A sense of helplessness came over me. She was gone, and I had not been able to guess what she wanted. Her last look had pierced me to the marrow; and yet it had not told me! All at once, I felt more desolate than when she had stood there watching me. It seemed as if she had left me all alone to carry the weight of the secret I couldn't guess. The snow went round me in great circles, and the ground fell away from me . . .

A drop of brandy and the warmth of Mr. Ranford's fire soon brought me to, and I insisted on being driven back at once to Brympton. It was nearly dark, and I was afraid my mistress might be wanting me. I explained to Mr. Ranford that I had been out for a walk and had been taken with a fit of giddiness as I passed his gate. This was true enough; yet I never felt more like a liar than when I said it.

When I dressed Mrs. Brympton for dinner she remarked on my pale looks and asked what ailed me. I told her I had a headache, and she said she would not require me again that evening, and advised me to go to bed.

It was a fact that I could scarcely keep on my feet; yet I had no fancy to spend a solitary evening in my room. I sat downstairs in the hall as long as I could hold my head up; but by nine I crept upstairs, too weary to care what happened if I could but get my head on a pillow. The rest of the household went to bed soon afterward; they kept early hours when the master was away, and before ten I heard Mrs. Blinder's door close, and Mr. Wace's soon after.

It was a very still night, earth and air all muffled in snow. Once in bed I felt easier, and lay quiet, listening to the strange noises that come out in a house after dark. Once I thought I heard a door open and close again below: it might have been the glass door that led to the gardens. I got up and peered out of the window; but it was in the dark of the moon, and nothing visible outside but the streaking of snow against the panes.

I went back to bed and must have dozed, for I jumped awake to the furious ringing of my bell. Before my head was clear I had sprung out of bed, and was dragging on my clothes. *It is going to happen now*, I heard myself saying; but what I meant I had no notion. My hands seemed to be covered with glue—I thought I should never get into my clothes. At last I opened my door and peered down the passage. As far as my candle-flame carried, I could see nothing unusual ahead of me. I hurried on, breathless; but as I pushed open the baize door leading to the main hall my heart stood still, for there at the head of the stairs was Emma Saxon, peering dreadfully down into the darkness.

For a second I couldn't stir; but my hand slipped from the door, and as it swung shut the figure vanished. At the same instant there came another sound from below stairs—a stealthy mysterious sound, as of a latch-key turning in the house-door. I ran to Mrs. Brympton's room and knocked.

There was no answer, and I knocked again. This time I heard someone moving in the room; the bolt slipped back and my mistress stood before me. To my surprise I saw that she had not undressed for the night. She gave me a startled look.

"What is this, Hartley?" she says in a whisper. "Are you ill? What are you doing here at this hour?"

"I am not ill, madam; but my bell rang."

At that she turned pale, and seemed about to fall.

"You are mistaken," she said harshly; "I didn't ring. You must have been dreaming." I had never heard her speak in such a tone. "Go back to bed," she said, closing the door on me.

But as she spoke I heard sounds again in the hall below: a man's step this time; and the truth leaped out on me.

"Madam," I said, pushing past her, "there is someone in the house—"

"Someone—?"

"Mr. Brympton, I think—I hear his step below—"

A dreadful look came over her, and without a word, she dropped flat at my feet. I fell on my knees and tried to lift her: by the way she breathed I saw it was no common faint. But as I raised her head there came quick steps on the stairs and across the hall: the door was flung open, and there stood Mr. Brympton, in his travelling-clothes, the snow dripping from him. He drew back with a start as he saw me kneeling by my mistress.

"What the devil is this?" he shouted. He was less high-coloured than usual, and the red spot came out on his forehead.

"Mrs. Brympton has fainted, sir," said I.

He laughed unsteadily and pushed by me. "It's a pity she didn't choose a more convenient moment. I'm sorry to disturb her, but—"

I raised myself up aghast at the man's action.

"Sir," said I, "are you mad? What are you doing?"

"Going to meet a friend," said he, and seemed to make for the dressing-room.

At that my heart turned over. I don't know what I thought or feared; but I sprang up and caught him by the sleeve.

"Sir, sir," said I, "for pity's sake look at your wife!"

He shook me off furiously.

"It seems that's done for me," says he, and caught hold of the dressing-room door.

At that moment I heard a slight noise inside. Slight as it was, he heard it too, and tore the door open; but as he did so he dropped back. On the threshold stood Emma Saxon. All was dark behind her, but I saw her plainly, and so did he. He threw up his hands as if to hide his face from her; and when I looked again she was gone.

He stood motionless, as if the strength had run out of him; and in the stillness my mistress suddenly raised herself, and opening her eyes fixed a look on him. Then she fell back, and I saw the death-flutter pass over her . . .

We buried her on the third day, in a driving snow-storm. There were few people in the church, for it was bad weather to come from town, and I've a notion my mistress was one that hadn't many near friends. Mr. Ranford was among the last to come, just before they carried her up the aisle. He was in black, of course, being such a friend of the family, and I never saw a gentleman so pale. As he passed me, I noticed that he leaned a trifle on a stick he carried; and I fancy Mr. Brympton noticed it too, for the red spot came out sharp on his forehead, and all through the service he kept staring across the church at Mr. Ranford, instead of following the prayers as a mourner should.

When it was over and we went out to the graveyard, Mr. Ranford had disappeared, and as soon as my poor mistress's body was underground, Mr. Brympton jumped into the carriage nearest the gate and drove off without a word to any of us. I heard him call out, "To the station," and we servants went back alone to the house.

Notes

p. 152   *typhoid* - a fever which can be fatal
p. 152   *vault* - burial chamber
p. 152   *the Hudson* - river in New York
p. 153   *dog-cart* - small cart pulled by a horse
p. 153   *stuff* - fabric
p. 154   *Laws* - 'good Lord!' a mild exclamation

16

The Furnished Room

(1902)

O. Henry

An American writer of hundreds of short stories for magazines, O. Henry's most characteristic work was inspired by New York City, which is the setting for this story. Here a man searching for his lost love takes a seedy room and becomes convinced that she has been a previous occupant; but is he deluded?

Restless, shifting, fugacious as time itself, is a certain vast bulk of the population of the redbrick district of the lower West Side. Homeless, they have a hundred homes. They flit from furnished room to furnished room, transients for ever – transients in abode, transients in heart and mind. They sing 'Home Sweet Home' in ragtime; they carry their *lares et penates* in a bandbox; their vine is entwined about a picture hat; a rubber plant is their fig tree.

Hence the houses of this district, having had a thousand dwellers, should have a thousand tales to tell, mostly dull ones, no doubt; but it would be strange if there could not be found a ghost or two in the wake of all these vagrant ghosts.

One evening after dark a young man prowled among these crumbling red mansions, ringing their bells. At the twelfth he rested his lean hand-baggage upon the step and wiped the dust from his hat-band and forehead. The bell sounded faint and far away in some remote, hollow depths.

To the door of this, the twelfth house whose bell he had rung, came a housekeeper who made him think of an unwholesome, surfeited worm that had eaten its nut to a hollow shell and now sought to fill the vacancy with edible lodgers.

He asked if there was a room to let.

'Come in,' said the housekeeper. Her voice came from her throat; her throat seemed lined with fur. 'I have the third floor back, vacant since a week back. Should you wish to look at it?'

The young man followed her up the stairs. A faint light from no particular source mitigated the shadows of the halls. They trod noiselessly upon a stair carpet that its own loom would have forsworn. It seemed to have become vegetable; to have degenerated in that rank, sunless air to lush lichen or spreading moss that grew in patches to the staircase and was viscid under the foot like organic matter. At each turn of the stairs were vacant niches in the wall. Perhaps plants had once been set within them. If so they had died in that foul and tainted air. It may be that statues of the saints had stood there, but it was not difficult to conceive that imps and devils had dragged them forth in the darkness and down to the unholy depths of some furnished pit below.

'This is the room,' said the housekeeper, from her furry throat. 'It's a nice room. It ain't often vacant. I had some most elegant people in it last summer – no trouble at all, and paid in advance to the minute. The water's at the end of the hall. Sprowls and Mooney kept it three months. They done a vaudeville sketch. Miss B'retta Sprowls – you may have heard of her – Oh, that was just the stage names – right there over the dresser is where the marriage certificate hung, framed. The gas is here, and you see there is plenty of closet room. It's a room everybody likes. It never stays idle long.'

'Do you have many theatrical people rooming here?' asked the young man.

'They comes and goes. A good proportion of my lodgers is connected with the theatres. Yes, sir, this is the theatrical district. Actor people never stays long anywhere. I get my share. Yes, they comes and they goes.'

He engaged the room, paying for a week in advance. He was tired, he said, and would take possession at once. He counted out the money. The room had been made ready, she said, even to towels and water. As the housekeeper moved away he put, for the thousandth time, the question that he carried at the end of his tongue.

'A young girl – Miss Vashner – Miss Eloise Vashner – do you remember such a one among your lodgers? She would be singing on the stage, most likely. A fair girl, of medium height and slender, with reddish gold hair and a dark mole near her left eyebrow.'

'No, I don't remember the name. Them stage people has names they change as often as their rooms. They comes and they goes. No, I don't call that one to mind.'

No. Always no. Five months of ceaseless interrogation and the inevitable negative. So much time spent by day in questioning managers, agents, schools and choruses; by night among the audiences of theatres from all-star casts down to music-halls so low that he dreaded to find what he most hoped for. He who had loved her best had tried to find her. He was sure that since her disappearance from home this great water-girt city held her somewhere, but it was like a monstrous quicksand, shifting its particles constantly, with no foundation, its upper granules of to-day buried to-morrow in ooze and slime.

The furnished room received its latest guest with a first glow of pseudo-hospitality, a hectic, haggard, perfunctory welcome like the specious smile of a demirep. The sophistical comfort came in reflected gleams from the decayed furniture, the ragged brocade upholstery of a couch and two chairs, a footwide cheap pier glass between the two windows, from one or two gilt picture frames and a brass bedstead in a corner.

The guest reclined, inert, upon a chair, while the room, confused in speech as though it were an apartment in Babel, tried to discourse to him of its divers tenantry.

A polychromatic rug like some brilliant-flowered, rectangular, tropical islet lay surrounded by a billowy sea of soiled matting. Upon the gay-papered wall were those pictures that pursue the homeless one from house to house – The Huguenot Lovers, The First Quarrel, The Wedding Breakfast, Psyche at the Fountain. The mantel's chastely severe outline was ingloriously veiled behind some pert drapery drawn rakishly askew like the sashes of the Amazonian ballet. Upon it was some desolate flotsam cast aside by the room's marooned when a lucky sail had borne them to a fresh port – a trifling vase or two, pictures of actresses, a medicine bottle, some stray cards out of a deck.

One by one, as the characters of a cryptograph become explicit, the little signs left by the furnished room's procession of guests developed a significance. The threadbare space in the rug in front of the dresser told that lovely woman had marched in the throng. Tiny finger-prints on the wall spoke of little prisoners trying to feel their way to sun and air. A splattered stain, raying like the shadow of a bursting bomb, witnessed where a hurled glass or bottle had splintered with its contents against the wall. Across the pier glass had been scrawled with a diamond in staggering letters the name 'Marie.' It seemed that the succession of dwellers in the furnished room had turned in fury – perhaps tempted beyond forbearance by its garish coldness – and wreaked upon it their passions. The furniture was chipped and bruised; the couch, distorted by bursting springs, seemed a horrible monster that had been slain during the stress of some grotesque convulsion. Some more potent upheaval had cloven a great slice from the marble mantel. Each plank in the floor owned its particular cant and shriek as from a separate and individual agony. It seemed incredible that all this malice and injury had been wrought upon the room by those who had called it for a time their home; and yet it may have been the cheated home instinct surviving blindly, the resentful rage at false household gods that had kindled their wrath. A hut that is our own we can sweep and adorn and cherish.

The young tenant in the chair allowed these thoughts to file, soft-shod, through his mind, while there drifted into the room furnished sounds and furnished scents. He heard in one room a tittering and incontinent, slack laughter; in others the monologue of a scold, the rattling of dice, a lullaby, and one crying dully; above him a banjo tinkled with spirit. Doors banged somewhere; the elevated trains roared intermittently; a cat yowled miserably upon a back fence. And he breathed the breath of the house – a dank savour rather than a smell – a cold, musty effluvium as from underground vaults mingled with the reeking exhalations of linoleum and mildewed and rotten woodwork.

Then, suddenly, as he rested there, the room was filled with the strong, sweet odour of mignonette. It came as upon a single buffet of wind with such sureness and fragrance and emphasis that it almost seemed a living visitant. And the man cried aloud, 'What, dear?' as if he had been called, and sprang up and faced about. The rich odour clung to him and wrapped him about. He reached out his arms for it, all his senses for the time confused and commingled. How could one be peremptorily called by an odour? Surely it must have been a sound. But, was it not the sound that had touched, that had caressed him?

'She has been in this room,' he cried, and he sprang to wrest from it a token, for he knew he would recognize the smallest thing that had belonged to her or that she had touched. This enveloping scent of mignonette, the odour that she had loved and made her own – whence came it?

The room had been but carelessly set in order. Scattered upon the flimsy dresser scarf were half a dozen hairpins – those discreet, indistinguishable friends of womankind, feminine of gender, infinite of mood and uncommunicative of tense. These he ignored, conscious of their triumphant lack of identity. Ransacking the drawers of the dresser he came upon a discarded, tiny, ragged handkerchief. He pressed it to his face. It was racy and insolent with heliotrope; he hurled it to the floor. In another drawer he found odd buttons, a theatre programme, a pawnbroker's card, two lost marshmallows, a book on the divination of dreams. In the last was a woman's black satin hair-bow, which halted him, poised between ice and fire. But the black satin hair-bow also is femininity's demure, impersonal, common ornament, and tells no tales.

And then he traversed the room like a hound on the scent, skimming the walls, considering the corners of the bulging matting on his hands and knees, rummaging mantel and tables, the curtains and hangings, the drunken cabinet in the corner, for a visible sign, unable to perceive that she was there beside, around, against, within, above him, clinging to him, wooing him, calling him so poignantly through the finer senses that even his grosser ones became cognizant of the call. Once again he answered loudly, 'Yes, dear!' and turned, wild-eyed, to gaze on vacancy, for he could not yet discern form and colour and love and outstretched arms in the odour of mignonette. Oh, God! whence that odour, and since when have odours had a voice to call? Thus he groped.

He burrowed in crevices and corners, and found corks and cigarettes. These he passed in passive contempt. But once he found in a fold of the matting a half-smoked cigar, and this he ground beneath his heel with a green and trenchant oath. He sifted the room from end to end. He found dreary and ignoble small records of many a peripatetic tenant; but of her whom he sought, and who may have lodged there, and whose spirit seemed to hover there, he found no trace.

And then he thought of the housekeeper.

He ran from the haunted room downstairs and to a door that showed a crack of light. She came out to his knock. He smothered his excitement as best he could.

'Will you tell me, madam,' he besought her, 'who occupied the room I have before I came?'

'Yes, sir. I can tell you again. 'Twas Sprowls and Mooney, as I said. Miss B'retta Sprowls it was in the theatres, but Missis Mooney she was. My house is well known for respectability. The marriage certificate hung, framed, on a nail over –'

'What kind of a lady was Miss Sprowls – in looks, I mean?'

'Why, black-haired, sir, short and stout, with a comical face. They left a week ago Tuesday.'

'And before they occupied it?'

'Why, there was a single gentleman connected with the draying business. He left owing me a week. Before him was Missis Crowder and her two children, that stayed four months; and back of them was old Mr. Doyle, whose sons paid for him. He kept the room six months. That goes back a year, sir, and further I do not remember.'

He thanked her and crept back to his room. The room was dead. The essence that had vivified it was gone. The perfume of mignonette had departed. In its place was the old, stale odour of mouldy house furniture, of atmosphere in storage.

The ebbing of his hope drained his faith. He sat staring at the yellow, singing gaslight. Soon he walked to the bed and began to tear the sheets into strips. With the blade of his knife he drove them tightly into every crevice around windows and door. When all was snug and taut he turned out the light, turned the gas full on again and laid himself gratefully upon the bed.

✳✳✳✳✳

It was Mrs. McCool's night to go with the can for beer. So she fetched it and sat with Mrs. Purdy in one of those subterranean retreats where housekeepers foregather and the worm dieth seldom.

'I rented out my third floor back, this evening,' said Mrs. Purdy, across a fine circle of foam. 'A young man took it. He went up to bed two hours ago.'

'Now, did ye, Mrs. Purdy, ma'am?' said Mrs. McCool, with intense admiration. 'You do be a wonder for rentin' rooms of that kind. And did ye tell him, then?' she concluded in a husky whisper, laden with mystery.

'Rooms,' said Mrs. Purdy, in her furriest tones, 'are furnished for to rent. I did not tell him, Mrs. McCool.'

''Tis right ye are, ma'am; 'tis by renting rooms we kape alive. Ye have the rale sense for business, ma'am. There be many people will rayjict the rentin' of a room if they be tould a suicide has been after dyin' in the bed of it.'

'As you say, we has our living to be making,' remarked Mrs. Purdy.

'Yis, ma'am; 'tis true. 'Tis just one wake ago this day I helped ye lay out the third floor back. A pretty slip of a colleen she was to be killin' herself wid the gas; a swate little face she had, Mrs. Purdy, ma'am.'

'She'd a-been called handsome, as you say,' said Mrs. Purdy, assenting but critical, 'but for that mole she had a-growin' by her left eyebrow. Do fill up your glass again, Mrs. McCool.'

Notes

p. 168	*fugacious* - fleeting	
p. 168	*lower West Side* - at the time, a humble area of New York City	
p. 168	*ragtime* - a type of early jazz	
p. 168	*lares et penates* - gods of the house	
p. 168	*bandbox* - a light box for clothes or hats	
p. 168	*vine . . . fig tree* - referring to the Biblical phrase 'sitting under their own vine and fig tree', i.e. being at home	
p. 169	*water* - some kind of basic bathroom	
p. 169	*vaudeville* - variety act in a music hall theatre	
p. 169	*stage names* - not their real names – she hastens to reassure him they were married	

p. 169	*marriage certificate on the wall* - to show it is a respectable house
p. 169	*water-girt* - surrounded by water
p. 169	*demirep* - a condemnatory term for a woman who may not be 'chaste'
p. 170	*pier glass* - large mirror
p. 169	*Babel* - according to Jewish and Christian tradition, the tower of Babel in Jewish and Christian myth was built after the Great Flood to be tall enough to reach heaven: God, wanting to humble human beings, confused them so that they could no longer understand one another – and so a variety of languages came into being: this is a story which explains the development of different languages and cultures
p. 170	*pictures* - cheap reproductions of well-known sentimental paintings
p. 170	*Amazonian ballet* - probably a reference to a mildly risqué entertainment by scantily clad women
p. 170	*cryptograph* - piece of writing in code
p. 170	*incontinent* - here meaning unable to stop (laughing)
p. 170	*effluvium* - bad smell
p. 170	*mignonette* - sweet smelling herb used in scent
p. 171	*racy and insolent with heliotrope* - describing a type of brash perfume – heliotrope is a strongly scented flower
p. 171	*peripatetic* - constantly moving
p. 172	*tear the sheets* - i.e. to insulate the room so that the gas (then of a poisonous kind) can't escape – he is committing suicide
p. 172	*circle of foam* - on a mug of beer
p. 172	*kape* - keep
p. 172	*rale* - real
p. 172	*rayjict* - reject
p. 172	*tould* - told
p. 172	*colleen* - young girl (Irish word)
p. 172	*swate* - sweet

Gabriel-Ernest

(1909)

Saki (Hector Hugh Munro)

Saki was the famous pen name of Hector Hugh Munro, a British author who wrote satirical, sometimes very dark stories in a most original style. In this story, a man comes across a strange wild boy in a wood. He recognises something threatening and frightening and tries to avoid him. But others more innocent take him in, with terrible consequences.

"There is a wild beast in your woods," said the artist Cunningham, as he was being driven to the station. It was the only remark he had made during the drive, but as Van Cheele had talked incessantly his companion's silence had not been noticeable.

"A stray fox or two and some resident weasels. Nothing more formidable," said Van Cheele. The artist said nothing.

"What did you mean about a wild beast?" said Van Cheele later, when they were on the platform.

"Nothing. My imagination. Here is the train," said Cunningham.

That afternoon Van Cheele went for one of his frequent rambles through his woodland property. He had a stuffed bittern in his study, and knew the names of quite a number of wild flowers, so his aunt had possibly some justification in describing him as a great naturalist. At any rate, he was a great walker. It was his custom to take mental notes of everything he saw during his walks, not so much for the purpose of assisting contemporary science as to provide topics for conversation afterwards. When the bluebells began to show themselves in flower he made a point of informing every one of the fact; the season of the year might have warned his hearers of the likelihood of such an occurrence, but at least they felt that he was being absolutely frank with them.

What Van Cheele saw on this particular afternoon was, however, something far removed from his ordinary range of experience. On a shelf of smooth stone overhanging a deep pool in the hollow of an oak coppice a boy of about sixteen lay asprawl, drying his wet brown limbs luxuriously in the sun. His wet hair, parted by a recent dive, lay close to his head, and his light-brown eyes, so light that there was an almost tigerish gleam in them, were turned towards Van Cheele with a certain lazy watchfulness. It was an unexpected apparition, and Van Cheele found himself engaged in the novel process of thinking before he spoke. Where on earth could this wild-looking boy hail from? The miller's wife had lost a child some two months ago, supposed to have been swept away by the mill-race, but that had been a mere baby, not a half-grown lad.

"What are you doing there?" he demanded.

"Obviously, sunning myself," replied the boy.

"Where do you live?"

"Here, in these woods."

"You can't live in the woods," said Van Cheele.

"They are very nice woods," said the boy, with a touch of patronage in his voice.

"But where do you sleep at night?"

"I don't sleep at night; that's my busiest time."

Van Cheele began to have an irritated feeling that he was grappling with a problem that was eluding him.

"What do you feed on?" he asked.

"Flesh" said the boy, and he pronounced the word with slow relish, as though he were tasting it.

"Flesh! What flesh?"

"Since it interests you, rabbits, wild-fowl, hares, poultry, lambs in their season, children when I can get any; they're usually too well locked in at night, when I do most of my hunting. It's quite two months since I tasted child-flesh."

Ignoring the chaffing nature of the last remark Van Cheele tried to draw the boy on the subject of possible poaching operations.

"You're talking rather through your hat when you speak of feeding on hares." (Considering the nature of the boy's toilet the simile was hardly an apt one.) "Our hillside hares aren't easily caught."

"At night I hunt on four feet," was the somewhat cryptic response.

"I suppose you mean that you hunt with a dog?" hazarded Van Cheele.

The boy rolled slowly over on to his back, and laughed a weird low laugh, that was pleasantly like a chuckle and disagreeably like a snarl.

"I don't fancy any dog would be very anxious for my company, especially at night."

Van Cheele began to feel that there was something positively uncanny about the strange-eyed, strange-tongued youngster.

"I can't have you staying in these woods," he declared authoritatively.

"I fancy you'd rather have me here than in your house," said the boy.

The prospect of this wild, nude animal in Van Cheele's primly ordered house was certainly an alarming one.

"If you don't go I shall have to make you," said Van Cheele.

The boy turned like a flash, plunged into the pool, and in a moment had flung his wet and glistening body half-way up the bank where Van Cheele was standing. In an otter the movement would not have been remarkable; in a boy Van Cheele found it sufficiently startling. His foot slipped as he made an involuntary backward movement, and he found himself almost prostrate on the slippery weed-grown bank, with those tigerish yellow eyes not very far from his own. Almost instinctively he half raised his hand to his throat. The boy laughed again, a laugh in which the snarl had nearly driven out the chuckle, and then, with another of his astonishing lightning movements, plunged out of view into a yielding tangle of weed and fern.

"What an extraordinary wild animal!" said Van Cheele as he picked himself up. And then he recalled Cunningham's remark, "There is a wild beast in your woods."

Walking slowly homeward, Van Cheele began to turn over in his mind various local occurrences which might be traceable to the existence of this astonishing young savage.

Something had been thinning the game in the woods lately, poultry had been missing from the farms, hares were growing unaccountably scarcer, and complaints had reached him of lambs being carried off bodily from the hills. Was it possible that this wild boy was really hunting the countryside in company with some clever poacher dog? He had spoken of hunting "four-footed" by night, but then, again, he had hinted strangely at no dog caring to come near him, "especially at night." It was certainly puzzling. And then, as Van Cheele ran his mind over the various depredations that had been committed during the last month or two, he came suddenly to a dead stop, alike in his walk and his speculations. The child missing from the mill two months ago—the accepted theory was that it had tumbled into the mill-race and been swept away; but the mother had always declared she had heard a shriek on the hill side of the house, in the opposite direction from the water. It was unthinkable, of course, but he wished that the boy had not made that uncanny remark about childflesh eaten two months ago. Such dreadful things should not be said even in fun.

Van Cheele, contrary to his usual wont, did not feel disposed to be communicative about his discovery in the wood. His position as a parish councillor and justice of the peace seemed somehow compromised by the fact that he was harbouring a personality of such doubtful repute on his property; there was even a possibility that a heavy bill of damages for raided lambs and poultry might be laid at his door. At dinner that night he was quite unusually silent.

"Where's your voice gone to?" said his aunt. "One would think you had seen a wolf."

Van Cheele, who was not familiar with the old saying, thought the remark rather foolish; if he *had* seen a wolf on his property his tongue would have been extraordinarily busy with the subject.

At breakfast next morning Van Cheele was conscious that his feeling of uneasiness regarding yesterday's episode had not wholly disappeared, and he resolved to go by train to the neighbouring cathedral town, hunt up Cunningham, and learn from him what he had really seen that had prompted the remark about a wild beast in the woods. With this resolution taken, his usual cheerfulness partially returned, and he hummed a bright little melody as he sauntered to the morning-room for his customary cigarette. As he entered the room the melody made way abruptly for a pious invocation. Gracefully asprawl on the ottoman, in an attitude of almost exaggerated repose, was the boy of the woods. He was drier than when Van Cheele had last seen him, but no other alteration was noticeable in his toilet.

"How dare you come here?" asked Van Cheele furiously.

"You told me I was not to stay in the woods," said the boy calmly.

"But not to come here. Supposing my aunt should see you!"

And with a view to minimizing that catastrophe Van Cheele hastily obscured as much of his unwelcome guest as possible under the folds of a *Morning Post*. At that moment his aunt entered the room.

"This is a poor boy who has lost his way – and lost his memory. He doesn't know who he is or where he comes from," explained Van Cheele desperately, glancing apprehensively at the waif's face to see whether he was going to add inconvenient candour to his other savage propensities.

Miss Van Cheele was enormously interested.

"Perhaps his underlinen is marked," she suggested.

"He seems to have lost most of that, too," said Van Cheele, making frantic little grabs at the *Morning Post* to keep it in its place.

A naked homeless child appealed to Miss Van Cheele as warmly as a stray kitten or derelict puppy would have done.

"We must do all we can for him," she decided, and in a very short time a messenger, dispatched to the rectory, where a page-boy was kept, had returned with a suit of pantry clothes, and the necessary accessories of shirt, shoes, collar, etc. Clothed, clean, and groomed, the boy lost none of his uncanniness in Van Cheele's eyes, but his aunt found him sweet.

"We must call him something till we know who he really is, she said. "Gabriel-Ernest, I think; those are nice suitable names."

Van Cheele agreed, but he privately doubted whether they were being grafted on to a nice suitable child. His misgivings were not diminished by the fact that his staid and elderly spaniel had bolted out of the house at the first incoming of the boy, and now obstinately remained shivering and yapping at the farther end of the orchard, while the canary, usually as vocally industrious as Van Cheele himself, had put itself on an allowance of frightened cheeps.

More than ever he was resolved to consult Cunningham without loss of time.

As he drove off to the station his aunt was arranging that Gabriel-Ernest should help her to entertain the infant members of her Sunday-school class at tea that afternoon.

Cunningham was not at first disposed to be communicative.

"My mother died of some brain trouble," he explained, "so you will understand why I am averse to dwelling on anything of an impossibly fantastic nature that I may see or think that I have seen."

"But what *did* you see?" persisted Van Cheele.

"What I thought I saw was something so extraordinary that no really sane man could dignify it with the credit of having actually happened. I was standing, the last evening I was with you, half-hidden in the hedge growth by the orchard gate, watching the dying glow of the sunset. Suddenly I became aware of a naked boy, a bather from some neighbouring pool, I took him to be, who was standing out on the bare hillside also watching the sunset. His pose was so suggestive of some wild faun of Pagan myth that I instantly wanted to engage him as a model, and in another moment I think I should have hailed him. But just then the sun dipped out of view, and all the orange and pink slid out of the landscape, leaving it cold and grey. And at the same moment an astounding thing happened—the boy vanished too!"

"What! vanished away into nothing?" asked Van Cheele excitedly.

"No; that is the dreadful part of it," answered the artist; "on the open hillside where the boy had been standing a second ago, stood a large wolf, blackish in colour, with gleaming fangs and cruel yellow eyes. You may think—"

But Van Cheele did not stop for anything as futile as thought. Already he was tearing at top speed towards the station. He dismissed the idea of a telegram. "Gabriel-Ernest is a werewolf" was a hopelessly inadequate effort at conveying the situation, and his aunt would think it was a code message to which he had omitted to give her the key. His one hope was that he might reach home before sundown. The cab which he chartered at the other end of the railway journey bore him with what seemed exasperating slowness along the country roads, which were pink and mauve with the flush of the sinking sun. His aunt was putting away some unfinished jams and cake when he arrived.

"Where is Gabriel-Ernest?" he almost screamed.

"He is taking the little Toop child home," said his aunt. "It was getting so late, I thought it wasn't safe to let it go back alone. What a lovely sunset, isn't it?"

But Van Cheele, although not oblivious of the glow in the western sky, did not stay to discuss its beauties. At a speed for which he was scarcely geared he raced along the narrow lane that led to the home of the Toops. On one side ran the swift current of the mill-stream, on the other rose the stretch of bare hillside. A dwindling rim of red sun showed still on the skyline, and the next turning must bring him in view of the ill-assorted couple he was pursuing. Then the colour went suddenly out of things, and a grey light settled itself with a quick shiver over the landscape. Van Cheele heard a shrill wail of fear, and stopped running.

Nothing was ever seen again of the Toop child or Gabriel-Ernest, but the latter's discarded garments were found lying in the road, so it was assumed that the child had fallen into the water, and that the boy had stripped and jumped in, in a vain endeavour to save it. Van Cheele and some workmen who were near by at the time testified to having heard a child scream loudly just near the spot where the clothes were found. Mrs. Toop, who had eleven other children, was decently resigned to her bereavement, but Miss Van Cheele sincerely mourned her lost foundling. It was on her initiative that a memorial brass was put up in the parish church to "Gabriel-Ernest, an unknown boy, who bravely sacrificed his life for another."

Van Cheele gave way to his aunt in most things, but he flatly refused to subscribe to the Gabriel-Ernest memorial.

Notes

p. 174   *bittern* - large bird, of interest to a naturalist because of its rarity

p. 174   *oak coppice* - a type of woodland that is managed to produce firewood

p. 175   *hares* - hares are very fast animals

p. 175   *toilet* - i.e. clothing, or the lack of it

p. 177   *ottoman* - a large low stool

p. 177   *page-boy* - a junior servant boy – so his clothes will fit

p. 177   *pantry clothes* - junior servant's clothes

p. 178   *werewolf* - mythical creature, supposed to be human by day, wolf by night

18

The Widow's Might

(1911)

Charlotte Perkins Gilman

Gilman, an American writer, is famous for her story The Yellow Wallpaper, *but also wrote nearly 200 stories for periodicals, and the feminist utopian novel* Herland. *Here, Gilman satirises a family assembling after their father's death, expecting to have to take care of their aged mother.*

James had come on to the funeral, but his wife had not; she could not leave the children—that is what he said. She said, privately, to him, that she would not go. She never was willing to leave New York except for Europe or for Summer vacations; and a trip to Denver in November—to attend a funeral—was not a possibility to her mind.

Ellen and Adelaide were both there: they felt it a duty—but neither of their husbands had come. Mr Jennings could not leave his classes in Cambridge, and Mr Oswald could not leave his business in Pittsburg—that is what they said.

The last services were over. They had had a cold, melancholy lunch and were all to take the night train home again. Meanwhile the lawyer was coming at four to read the will.

'It is only a formality. There can't be much left,' said James.

'No,' agreed Adelaide, 'I suppose not.'

'A long illness eats up everything,' said Ellen, and sighed. Her husband had come to Colorado for his lungs years before and was still delicate.

'Well,' said James rather abruptly, 'What are we going to do with Mother?'

'Why, of course—' Ellen began, 'We *could* take her. It would depend a good deal on how much property there is—I mean, on where she'd want to go. Edward's salary is more than needed now,' Ellen's mental processes seemed a little mixed.

'She can come to me if she prefers, of course,' said Adelaide. 'But I don't think it would be very pleasant for her. Mother never did like Pittsburg.'

James looked from one to the other.

'Let me see—how old is Mother?'

'Oh she's all of fifty,' answered Ellen, 'and much broken, I think. It's been a long strain, you know.' She turned plaintively to her brother. 'I should think you could make her more comfortable than either of us, James—with your big house.'

'I think a woman is always happier living with a son than with a daughter's husband,' said Adelaide. 'I've always thought so.'

'That is often true,' her brother admitted. 'But it depends.' He stopped, and the sisters exchanged glances. They knew upon what it depended.

'Perhaps if she stayed with me, you could—help some,' suggested Ellen.

'Of course, of course, I could do that,' he agreed with evident relief. 'She might visit between you—take turns—and I could pay her board. About how much ought it to amount to? We might as well arrange everything now.'

'Things cost awfully in these days,' Ellen said with a criss-cross of fine wrinkles on her pale forehead. 'But of course it would be only just *what* it costs. I shouldn't want to *make* anything.'

'It's work and care, Ellen, and you may as well admit it. You need all your strength—with those sickly children and Edward on your hands. When she comes to me, there need be no expense, James, except for clothes. I have room enough and Mr Oswald will never notice the difference in the house bills—but he does hate to pay out money for clothes.'

'Mother must be provided for properly,' her son declared. 'How much ought it to cost—a year—for clothes.'

'You know what your wife's cost?' suggested Adelaide, with a flicker of a smile about her lips.

'Oh, *no*,' said Ellen. 'That's no criterion! Maude is in society, you see. Mother wouldn't *dream* of having so much.'

James looked at her gratefully. 'Board—and clothes—all told; what should you say, Ellen?'

Ellen scrabbled in her small black hand bag for a piece of paper, and found none. James handed her an envelope and a fountain pen.

'Food—just plain food materials—costs all of four dollars a week now—for one person,' said she. 'And heat—and light—and extra service. I should think six a week would be the *least*, James. And for clothes and carfare and small expenses—I should say—well, three hundred dollars!'

'That would make over six hundred a year,' said James slowly. 'How about Oswald sharing that, Adelaide?'

Adelaide flushed. 'I do not think he would be willing, James. Of course if it were absolutely necessary—'

'He has money enough,' said her brother.

'Yes, but he never seems to have any outside of his business—and he has his own parents to carry now. No—I can give her a home, but that's all.'

'You see, you'd have none of the care and trouble, James,' said Ellen. 'We—the girls—are each willing to have her with us, while perhaps Maude wouldn't care to, but if you could just pay the money—'

'Maybe there's some left after all,' suggested Adelaide. 'And this place ought to sell for something.'

'This place' was a piece of rolling land within ten miles of Denver. It had a bit of river bottom, and ran up towards the foothills. From the house the view ran north and south along the precipitous ranks of the 'Big Rockies' to westward. To the east lay the vast stretches of sloping plain.

'There ought to be at least six or eight thousand dollars from it, I should say,' he concluded.

'Speaking of clothes,' Adelaide rather irrelevantly suggested, 'I see Mother didn't get any new black. She's always worn it as long as I can remember.'

'Mother's a long time,' said Ellen. 'I wonder if she wants anything, I'll go up and see.'

'No,' said Adelaide, 'She said she wanted to be let alone—and rest. She said she'd be down by the time Mr Frankland got here.'

'She's bearing it pretty well,' Ellen suggested, after a little silence.

'It's not like a broken heart,' Adelaide explained. 'Of course Father meant well—'

'He was a man who always did his duty,' admitted Ellen. 'But we none of us—loved him—very much.'

'He is dead and buried,' said James. 'We can at least respect his memory.'

'We've hardly seen Mother—under that black veil.' Ellen went on. 'It must have aged her. This long nursing.'

'She had help toward the last—a man nurse,' said Adelaide.

'Yes, but a long illness is an awful strain—and Mother never was good at nursing. She has surely done her duty,' pursued Ellen.

'And now she's entitled to a rest,' said James, rising and walking about the room. 'I wonder how soon we can close up affairs here—and get rid of this place. There might be enough in it to give her almost a living—properly invested.'

Ellen looked out across the dusty stretches of land.

'How I did hate to live here!' she said.

'So did I,' said Adelaide.

'So did I,' said James.

And they all smiled rather grimly.

'We don't any of us seem to be very—affectionate, about Mother,' Adelaide presently admitted, 'I don't know why it is— we never were an affectionate family, I guess.'

'Nobody could be affectionate with Father,' Ellen suggested timidly.

'And Mother—poor Mother! She's had an awful life.'

'Mother has always done her duty,' said James in a determined voice, 'and so did Father, as he saw it. Now we'll do ours.'

'Ah,' exclaimed Ellen, jumping to her feet. 'Here comes the lawyer, I'll call Mother.'

She ran quickly upstairs and tapped at her mother's door.

'Mother, oh Mother,' she cried. 'Mr Frankland's come.'

'I know it,' came back a voice from within. 'Tell him to go ahead and read the will. I know what's in it. I'll be down in a few minutes.'

Ellen went slowly back downstairs with the fine criss-cross of wrinkles showing on her pale forehead again, and delivered her mother's message.

The other two glanced at each other hesitatingly, but Mr Frankland spoke up briskly.

'Quite natural, of course, under the circumstances. Sorry I couldn't get to the funeral. A case on this morning.'

The will was short. The estate was left to be divided among the children in four equal parts, two to the son and one each to the daughters after the mother's legal share had been deducted, if she were still living. In such case they were furthermore directed to provide for their mother while she lived. The estate, as described, consisted of the ranch, the large, rambling house on it, with all the furniture, stock and implements, and some $5,000 in mining stocks.

'That is less than I had supposed,' said James.

'This will was made ten years ago,' Mr Frankland explained. 'I have done business for your father since that time. He kept his faculties to the end, and I think that you will find that the property has appreciated. Mrs McPherson has taken excellent care of the ranch, I understand—and has had some boarders.'

Both the sisters exchanged pained glances.

'There's an end to all that now,' said James.

At this moment, the door opened and a tall black figure, cloaked and veiled, came into the room.

'I'm glad to hear you say that Mr McPherson kept his faculties to the last, Mr Frankland,' said the widow. 'It's true. I didn't come down to hear that old will. It's no good now.'

They all turned in their chairs.

'Is there a later will, madam?' inquired the lawyer.

'Not that I know of. Mr McPherson had no property when he died.'

'No property! My dear lady—four years ago he certainly had some.'

'Yes, but three years and a-half ago he gave it all to me. Here are the deeds.'

There they were, in very truth—formal and correct, and quite simple and clear—for deeds, James R. McPherson, Sr, had assuredly given to his wife the whole estate.

'You remember that was the panic year,' she continued. 'There was pressure from some of Mr McPherson's creditors; he thought it would be safer so.'

'Why—yes,' remarked Mr Frankland, 'I do remember now his advising with me about it. But I thought the step unnecessary.'

James cleared his throat.

'Well, Mother, this does complicate matters a little. We were hoping that we could settle up all the business this afternoon—with Mr Frankland's help—and take you back with us.'

'We can't be spared any longer, you see, Mother,' said Ellen.

'Can't you deed it back again, Mother,' Adelaide suggested, 'to James, or to—all of us, so we can get away?'

'Why should I?'

'Now, Mother,' Ellen put in persuasively, 'we know how badly you feel, and you are nervous and tired, but I told you this morning when we came, that we expected to take you back with us. You know you've been packing—'

'Yes, I've been packing,' replied the voice behind the veil.

'I dare say it was safer—to have the property in your name—technically,' James admitted, 'but now I think it would be the simplest way for you to make it over to me in a lump, and I will see that Father's wishes are carried out to the letter.'

'Your father is dead,' remarked the voice.

'Yes, Mother, we know—we know how you feel,' Ellen ventured.

'I am alive,' said Mrs McPherson.

'Dear Mother, it's very trying to talk business to you at such a time. We all realize it,' Adelaide explained with a touch of asperity, 'But we told you we couldn't stay as soon as we got here.'

'And the business has to be settled,' James added conclusively.

'It is settled.'

'Perhaps Mr Frankland can make it clear to you,' went on James with forced patience.

'I do not doubt that your mother understands perfectly,' murmured the lawyer. 'I have always found her a woman of remarkable intelligence.'

'Thank you, Mr Frankland. Possibly you may be able to make my children understand that this property—such as it is—is mine now.'

'Why assuredly, assuredly, Mrs McPherson. We all see that. But we assume, as a matter of course, that you will consider Mr McPherson's wishes in regard to the disposition of the estate.'

'I have considered Mr McPherson's wishes for thirty years,' she replied. 'Now, I'll consider mine. I have done my duty since the day I married him. It it eleven hundred days—to-day.' The last with sudden intensity.

'But madam, your children—'

'I have no children, Mr Frankland. I have two daughters and a son. These two grown persons here, grown up, married, having children of their own—or ought to have—were my children. I did my duty by them, and they did their duty by me—and would yet, no doubt.' The tone changed suddenly. 'But they don't have to. I'm tired of duty.'

The little group of listeners looked up, startled.

'You don't know how things have been going on here,' the voice went on. 'I didn't trouble you with my affairs. But I'll tell you now. When your father saw fit to make over the property to me—to save it—and when he knew that he hadn't many years to live, I took hold of things. I had to have a nurse for your father—and a doctor coming: the house was a sort of hospital, so I made it a little more so. I had a half a dozen patients and nurses here—and made money by it. I ran the garden—kept cows—raised my own chickens—worked out doors—slept out of doors. I'm a stronger woman to-day than I ever was in my life!'

She stood up, tall, strong and straight, and drew a deep breath.

'Your father's property amounted to about $8,000 when he died,' she continued. 'That would be $4,000 to James and $2,000 to each of the girls. That I'm willing to give you now—each of you—in your own name. But if my daughters will take my advice, they'd better let me send them the yearly income—in cash—to spend as they like. It is good for a woman to have some money of her own.'

'I think you are right, Mother,' said Adelaide.

'Yes indeed,' murmured Ellen.

'Don't you need it yourself, Mother?' asked James, with a sudden feeling of tenderness for the stiff figure in black.

'No, James, I shall keep the ranch, you see. I have good reliable help. I've made $2,000 a year—clear—off it so far, and now I've rented it for that to a doctor friend of mine—woman doctor.'

'I think you have done remarkably well, Mrs McPherson—wonderfully well,' said Mr Frankland.

'And you'll have an income of $2,000 a year,' said Adelaide incredulously.

'You'll come and live with me, won't you,' ventured Ellen.

'Thank you, my dear, I will not.'

'You're more than welcome in my big house,' said Adelaide.

'No thank you, my dear.'

'I don't doubt Maude will be glad to have you,' James rather hesitatingly offered.

'I do. I doubt it very much. No thank you, my dear.'

'But what *are* you going to do?'

Ellen seemed genuinely concerned.

'I'm going to do what I never did before. I'm going to *live*!'

With a firm swift step, the tall figure moved to the windows and pulled up the lowered shades. The brilliant Colorado sunshine poured into the room. She threw off the long black veil.

'That's borrowed,' she said. 'I didn't want to hurt your feelings at the funeral.'

She unbuttoned the long black cloak and dropped it at her feet, standing there in the full sunlight, a little flushed and smiling, dressed in a well-made traveling suit of dull mixed colors.

'If you want to know my plans, I'll tell you. I've got $6,000 of my own. I earned it in three years—off my little rancho-sanitarium. One thousand I have put in the savings bank—to bring me back from anywhere on earth, and to put me in an old lady's home if it is necessary. Here is an agreement with a cremation company. They'll import me, if necessary, and have me duly—expurgated—or they don't get the money. But I've got $5,000 to play with, and I'm going to play.'

Her daughters looked shocked.

'Why Mother—'

'At your age—'

James drew down his upper lip and looked like his father.

'I knew you wouldn't any of you understand,' she continued more quietly. 'But it doesn't matter any more. Thirty years I've given you—and your father. Now I'll have thirty years of my own.'

'Are you—are you sure you're—well, Mother,' Ellen urged with real anxiety.

Her mother laughed outright.

'Well, really well, never was better, have been doing business up to to-day—good medical testimony that. No question of my sanity, my dears! I want you to grasp the fact that your mother is a Real Person with some interests of her own and half a lifetime yet. The first twenty didn't count for much—I was growing up and couldn't help myself. The last thirty have been—hard. James perhaps realizes that more than you girls, but you all know it. Now, I'm free.'

'Where *do* you mean to go, Mother?' James asked.

She looked around the little circle with a serene air of decision and replied.

'To New Zealand. I've always wanted to go there,' she pursued. 'Now I'm going. And to Australia—and Tasmania—and Madagascar—and Terra del Fuego. I shall be gone some time.'

They separated that night—three going East, one West.

Notes

p. 180   *Denver* - city in Colorado
p. 180   *Cambridge* - city in Massachusetts
p. 182   *Big Rockies* - Rocky Mountains
p. 183   *boarders* - lodgers
p. 185   *rancho-sanatorium* - her ranch – a large cattle farm, is up in the mountains
        where the air is thought healthy for the sick who therefore come and stay
        as if it was a sanatorium, nursing home

19

Eveline

(1914)

James Joyce

The great Irish novelist and modernist began his career with short stories. This is from Dubliners, *his early masterpiece. A woman is torn between staying in Ireland to care for her mother and emigrating with her lover. The story is a haunting evocation of her situation.*

She sat at the window watching the evening invade the avenue. Her head was leaned against the window curtains and in her nostrils was the odour of dusty cretonne. She was tired.

Few people passed. The man out of the last house passed on his way home; she heard his footsteps clacking along the concrete pavement and afterwards crunching on the cinder path before the new red houses. One time there used to be a field there in which they used to play every evening with other people's children. Then a man from Belfast bought the field and built houses in it – not like their little brown houses but bright brick houses with shining roofs. The children of the avenue used to play together in that field – the Devines, the Waters, the Dunns, little Keogh the cripple, she and her brothers and sisters. Ernest, however, never played: he was too grown up. Her father used often to hunt them in out of the field with his blackthorn stick; but usually little Keogh used to keep *nix* and call out when he saw her father coming. Still they seemed to have been rather happy then. Her father was not so bad then; and besides, her mother was alive. That was a long time ago; she and her brothers and sisters were all grown up; her mother was dead. Tizzie Dunn was dead, too, and the Waters had gone back to England. Everything changes. Now she was going to go away like the others, to leave her home.

Home! She looked round the room, reviewing all its familiar objects which she had dusted once a week for so many years, wondering where on earth all the dust came from. Perhaps she would never see again those familiar objects from which she had never dreamed of being divided. And yet during all those years she had never found out the name of the priest whose yellowing photograph hung on the wall above the broken harmonium beside the coloured print of the promises made to Blessed

Margaret Mary Alacoque. He had been a school friend of her father. Whenever he showed the photograph to a visitor her father used to pass it with a casual word:

—He is in Melbourne now.

She had consented to go away, to leave her home. Was that wise? She tried to weigh each side of the question. In her home anyway she had shelter and food; she had those whom she had known all her life about her. Of course she had to work hard both in the house and at business. What would they say of her in the Stores when they found out that she had run away with a fellow? Say she was a fool, perhaps; and her place would be filled up by advertisement. Miss Gavan would be glad. She had always had an edge on her, especially whenever there were people listening.

—Miss Hill, don't you see these ladies are waiting?

—Look lively, Miss Hill, please.

She would not cry many tears at leaving the Stores.

But in her new home, in a distant unknown country, it would not be like that. Then she would be married – she, Eveline. People would treat her with respect then. She would not be treated as her mother had been. Even now, though she was over nineteen, she sometimes felt herself in danger of her father's violence. She knew it was that that had given her the palpitations. When they were growing up he had never gone for her, like he used to go for Harry and Ernest, because she was a girl; but latterly he had begun to threaten her and say what he would do to her only for her dead mother's sake. And now she had nobody to protect her. Ernest was dead and Harry, who was in the church decorating business, was nearly always down somewhere in the country. Besides, the invariable squabble for money on Saturday nights had begun to weary her unspeakably. She always gave her entire wages – seven shillings – and Harry always sent up what he could but the trouble was to get any money from her father. He said she used to squander the money, that she had no head, that he wasn't going to give her his hard-earned money to throw about the streets, and much more, for he was usually fairly bad of a Saturday night. In the end he would give her the money and ask her had she any intention of buying Sunday's dinner. Then she had to rush out as quickly as she could and do her marketing, holding her black leather purse tightly in her hand as she elbowed her way through the crowds and returning home late under her load of provisions. She had hard work to keep the house together and to see that the two young children who had been left to her charge went to school regularly and got their meals regularly. It was hard work – a hard life – but now that she was about to leave it she did not find it a wholly undesirable life.

She was about to explore another life with Frank. Frank was very kind, manly, open-hearted. She was to go away with him by the night-boat to be his wife and to live with him in Buenos Ayres where he had a home waiting for her. How well she remembered the first time she had seen him; he was lodging in a house on the main road where she used to visit. It seemed a few weeks ago. He was standing at the gate, his peaked cap pushed back on his head and his hair tumbled forward over a face of bronze. Then they had come to know each other. He used to meet her outside the Stores every evening and see her home. He took her to see *The Bohemian Girl* and she felt elated as she sat in an unaccustomed part of the theatre with him. He was awfully fond of music and sang a little. People knew that they were courting and, when he sang about the lass that loves a sailor, she always felt pleasantly confused. He used to call her Poppens out of fun. First of all it had been an excitement for her to have a fellow and then she had begun to like him. He had tales of distant countries. He had started as a deck boy at a pound a month on a ship of the Allan Line going out to Canada. He told her the names of the ships he had been on and the names of the different services. He had sailed through the Straits of Magellan and he told her stories of the terrible Patagonians. He had fallen on his feet in Buenos Ayres, he said, and had come over to the old country just for a holiday. Of course, her father had found out the affair and had forbidden her to have anything to say to him.

—I know these sailor chaps, he said.

One day he had quarrelled with Frank and after that she had to meet her lover secretly.

The evening deepened in the avenue. The white of two letters in her lap grew indistinct. One was to Harry; the other was to her father. Ernest had been her favourite but she liked Harry too. Her father was becoming old lately, she noticed; he would miss her. Sometimes he could be very nice. Not long before, when she had been laid up for a day, he had read her out a ghost story and made toast for her at the fire. Another day, when their mother was alive, they had all gone for a picnic to the Hill of Howth. She remembered her father putting on her mother's bonnet to make the children laugh.

Her time was running out but she continued to sit by the window, leaning her head against the window curtain, inhaling the odour of dusty cretonne. Down far in the avenue she could hear a street organ playing. She knew the air. Strange that it should come that very night to remind her of the promise to her mother, her promise to keep the home together as long as she could. She remembered the last night of her mother's illness; she was again in the close dark room at the other side of the hall and outside she heard a melancholy air of Italy. The organ-player had been ordered to go away and given sixpence. She remembered her father strutting back into the sickroom saying:

—Damned Italians! coming over here!

As she mused the pitiful vision of her mother's life laid its spell on the very quick of her being – that life of commonplace sacrifices closing in final craziness. She trembled as she heard again her mother's voice saying constantly with foolish insistence:

—Derevaun Seraun! Derevaun Seraun!

She stood up in a sudden impulse of terror. Escape! She must escape! Frank would save her. He would give her life, perhaps love, too. But she wanted to live. Why should she be unhappy? She had a right to happiness. Frank would take her in his arms, fold her in his arms. He would save her.

She stood among the swaying crowd in the station at the North Wall. He held her hand and she knew that he was speaking to her, saying something about the passage over and over again. The station was full of soldiers with brown baggages. Through the wide doors of the sheds she caught a glimpse of the black mass of the boat, lying in beside the quay wall, with illumined portholes. She answered nothing. She felt her cheek pale and cold and, out of a maze of distress, she prayed to God to direct her, to show her what was her duty. The boat blew a long mournful whistle into the mist. If she went, to-morrow she would be on the sea with Frank, steaming towards Buenos Ayres. Their passage had been booked. Could she still draw back after all he had done for her? Her distress awoke a nausea in her body and she kept moving her lips in silent fervent prayer.

A bell clanged upon her heart. She felt him seize her hand:

—Come!

All the seas of the world tumbled about her heart. He was drawing her into them: he would drown her. She gripped with both hands at the iron railing.

—Come!

No! No! No! It was impossible. Her hands clutched the iron in frenzy. Amid the seas she sent a cry of anguish!

—Eveline! Evvy!

He rushed beyond the barrier and called to her to follow. He was shouted at to go on but he still called to her. She set her white face to him, passive, like a helpless animal. Her eyes gave him no sign of love or farewell or recognition.

Notes

p. 187   *cretonne* - printed cotton fabric

p. 187   *Belfast* - Northern Irish, industrial city

p. 187   *keep nix* - keep watch

p. 187   *harmonium* - small organ

pp. 187–88   *Blessed Margaret Mary Alacoque* - a popular Roman Catholic saint in Ireland at the time

p. 188   *Melbourne* - in Australia, where many Irish people emigrated

p. 188   *Stores* - the large department store where she works as a shop assistant

p. 188   *Buenos Ayres* - capital of Argentina, another emigrant destination

p. 188   *The Bohemian Girl* - a musical theatre show

p. 189   *Allan Line* - large shipping firm which ran passenger liners between England, Ireland and America and carried many emigrants

p. 189   *Straits of Magellan* - a sea route in South America

p. 189   *Patagonians* - people of Argentina

p. 189   *Hill of Howth* - seaside near Dublin

p. 189   *Damned Italians* - there was a small community of Italian immigrants in Ireland

p. 189   *Derevaun Seraun!* - this could be a nonsense phrase, uttered in delirium, or it could be a confused Gaelic phrase meaning something like 'The end of everything is pain'

p. 189   *North Wall* - the Dublin dock where ferries sailed from Dublin to Liverpool in England, from where the liner sailed to South America

20

Them Others

(1923)

Stacy Aumonier

Aumonier was a British writer specialising in short stories of great variety and originality. In this story set during the First World War, the author observes a family and their reaction as their only son goes to war and is then missing in action. The point of view is framed in an interesting way and the widespread horror of the situation is explored from an original viewpoint, with very idiosyncratic characters.

It is always disturbing to me when things fall into pattern form, when, in fact, incidents of real life dovetail with each other in such a manner as to suggest the shape of a story. A story is a nice neat little thing with what is called a 'working-up' and a climax, and life is a clumsy, ungraspable thing, very incomplete in its periods, and with a poor sense of climax. In fact, death – which is a very uncertain quantity – is the only definite note it strikes, and even death has an uncomfortable way of setting other things in motion. If, therefore, in telling you about my friend Mrs Ward, I am driven to the usual shifts of the story-teller, you must believe me that it is because this narrative concerns visions: Mrs Ward's visions, my visions, and your visions. Consequently I am dependent upon my own poor powers of transcription to mould these visions into some sort of shape, and am driven into the position of a story-teller against my will.

The first vision, then, concerns the back view of the Sheldrake Road, which, as you know, butts on to the railway embankment near Dalston Junction station. If you are of an adventurous turn of mind you shall accompany me, and we will creep up on to the embankment together and look down into these back yards. (We shall be liable to a fine of £2, according to a bye-law of the Railway Company, for doing so, but the experience will justify us.)

There are twenty-two of these small buff-brick houses huddled together in this road, and there is surely no more certain way of judging not only the character of the individual inhabitants but of their mode of life than by a survey of these somewhat pathetic yards. Is it not, for instance, easy to determine the timid, well-ordered mind of little Miss Porson, the dressmaker at number nine, by its garden of neat mud paths, with its thin patch of meagre grass, and the small bed of skimpy geraniums? Cannot one read the tragedy of those dreadful Alleson people at number four? The garden is a wilderness of filth and broken bottles, where even the weeds seem chary of establishing themselves. In fact, if we listen carefully – and the trains are not making too much noise – we can hear the shrill crescendo of Mrs Alleson's voice cursing at her husband in the kitchen, the half-empty gin bottle between them.

The methodical pushfulness and practicability of young Mr and Mrs Andrew MacFarlane is evident at number fourteen. They have actually grown a patch of potatoes, and some scarlet-runners, and there is a chicken-run near the house.

Those irresponsible people, the O'Neals, have grown a bed of hollyhocks, but for the rest the garden is untidy and unkempt. One could almost swear they were connected in some obscure way with the theatrical profession.

Mrs Abbot's garden is a sort of playground. It has asphalt paths, always swarming with small and not too clean children, and there are five lines of washing suspended above the mud. Every day seems to be Mrs Abbot's washing day. Perhaps she 'does' for others. Sam Abbot is certainly a lazy, insolent old rascal, and such always seem destined to be richly fertile. Mrs Abbot is a pleasant 'body', though.

The Greens are the swells of the road. George Green is in the grocery line, and both his sons are earning good money, and one daughter has piano lessons. The narrow strip of yard is actually divided into two sections, a flower-garden and a kitchen-garden. And they are the only people who have flower-boxes in the front.

Number eight is a curious place. Old Mr Bilge lives there. He spends most of his time in the garden, but nothing ever seems to come up. He stands about in his shirt-sleeves, and with a circular paper hat on his head, like a printer. They say he was formerly a corn merchant, but has lost all his money. He keeps the garden very neat and tidy, but nothing seems to grow. He stands there staring at the beds, as though he found their barrenness quite unaccountable.

Number eleven is unoccupied, and number twelve is Mrs Ward's.

We come now to an important vision, and I want you to come down with me from the embankment and to view Mrs Ward's garden from inside, and also Mrs Ward as I saw her on that evening when I had occasion to pay my first visit.

It had been raining, but the sun had come out. We wandered round the paths together, and I can see her old face now, lined and seamed with years of anxious toil and struggle; her long bony arms, slightly withered, but moving restlessly in the direction of snails and slugs.

'Oh dear! Oh dear!' she was saying. 'What with the dogs, and the cats, and the snails, and the trains, it's wonderful anything comes up at all!'

Mrs Ward's garden has a character of its own, and I cannot account for it. There is nothing very special growing – a few pansies and a narrow border of London Pride, several clumps of unrecognizable things that haven't flowered, the grass patch in only fair order, and at the bottom of the garden an unfinished rabbit-hutch. But there is about Mrs Ward's garden an atmosphere. There is something about it that reflects in her placid eye the calm, somewhat contemplative way she has of looking right through things, as though they didn't concern her too closely. As though, in fact, she were too occupied with her own inner visions.

'No,' she says in answer to my query. 'We don't mind the trains at all. In fact, me and my Tom we often come out here and sit after supper. And Tom smokes his pipe. We like to hear the trains go by.'

She gazes abstractedly at the embankment.

'I like to hear things . . . going on and that. It's Dalston Junction a little further on. The trains go from there to all parts, right out into the country they do . . . ever so far . . . My Ernie went from Dalston.'

She adds the last in a changed tone of voice. And now perhaps we come to the most important vision of all – Mrs Ward's vision of 'my Ernie'.

I ought perhaps to mention that I had never met 'my Ernie'. I can only see him through Mrs Ward's eyes. At the time when I met her, he had been away at the War for nearly a year. I need hardly say that 'my Ernie' was a paragon of sons. He was brilliant, handsome, and incredibly clever. Everything that 'my Ernie' said was treasured. Every opinion that he expressed stood. If 'my Ernie' liked anyone, that person was always a welcome guest. If 'my Ernie' disliked anyone they were not to be tolerated, however plausible they might appear.

I had seen Ernie's photograph, and I must confess that he appeared a rather weak, extremely ordinary-looking young man, but then I would rather trust to Mrs Ward's visions than the art of any photographer.

Tom Ward was a mild, ineffectual-looking old man, with something of Mrs Ward's placidity but with nothing of her strong individual poise. He had some job in a gasworks. There was also a daughter named Lily, a brilliant person who served in a tea-shop, and sometimes went to theatres with young men. To both husband and daughter Mrs Ward adopted an affectionate, mothering, almost pitying attitude. But with 'my Ernie', it was quite a different thing. I can see her stooping figure, and her silver-white hair gleaming in the sun as we come to the unfinished rabbit-hutch, and the curious wistful tones of her voice as she touches it and says:

'When my Ernie comes home . . .'

The War to her was some unimaginable but disconcerting affair centred round Ernie. People seemed to have got into some desperate trouble, and Ernie was the only one capable of getting them out of it. I could not at that time gauge how much Mrs Ward realized the dangers the boy was experiencing. She always spoke with conviction that he would return safely. Nearly every other sentence contained some reference to things that were to happen 'when my Ernie comes home'. What doubts and fears she had were only recognizable by the subtlest shades in her voice.

When we looked over the wall into the deserted garden next door, she said:

'Oh dear! I'm afraid they'll never let that place. It's been empty since the Stellings went away. Oh, years ago, before this old war.'

It was on the occasion of my second visit that Mrs Ward told me more about the Stellings. It appeared that they were a German family, of all things! There was a Mr Stelling, and a Mrs Frow Stelling, and two boys.

Mr Stelling was a watchmaker, and he came from a place called Bremen. It was a very sad story, Mrs Ward told me. They had only been over here for ten months when Mr Stelling died, and Mrs Frow Stelling and the boys went back to Germany.

During the time of the Stellings' sojourn in the Sheldrake Road it appeared that the Wards had seen quite a good deal of them, and though it would be an exaggeration to say that they ever became great friends, they certainly got through that period without any unpleasantness, and even developed a certain degree of intimacy.

'Allowing for their being foreigners,' Mrs Ward explained, 'they were quite pleasant people.'

On one or two occasions they invited each other to supper, and I wish my visions were sufficiently clear to envisage those two families indulging this social habit.

According to Mrs Ward, Mr Stelling was a kind little man with a round fat face. He spoke English fluently, but Mrs Ward objected to his table manners.

'When my Tom eats,' she said, 'you don't hear a sound – I look after that! But that Mr Stelling . . . Oh dear!'

The trouble with Mrs Stelling was that she could only speak a few words of English, but Mrs Ward said 'she was a pleasant enough little body', and she established herself quite definitely in Mrs Ward's affections for the reason that she was so obviously and so passionately devoted to her two sons.

'Oh, my word, though, they do have funny ways – these foreigners,' she continued. 'The things they used to eat! Most peculiar! I've known them eat stewed prunes with hot meat!'

Mrs Ward repeated, 'Stewed prunes with hot meat!' several times, and shook her head, as though this exotic mixture was a thing to be sternly discouraged. But she acknowledged that Mrs Frow Stelling was in some ways a very good cook; in fact, her cakes were really wonderful, 'the sort of thing you can't ever buy in a shop'.

About the boys there seemed to be a little divergence of opinion. They were both also fat-faced, and their heads were 'almost shaved like convicts'. The elder one wore spectacles and was rather noisy, but 'My Ernie liked the younger one. Oh yes, my Ernie said that young Hans was quite a nice boy. It was funny the way they spoke, funny and difficult to understand.'

It was very patent that between the elder boy and Ernie, who were of about the same age, there was an element of rivalry which was perhaps more accentuated in the attitude of the mothers than in the boys themselves. Mrs Ward could find little virtue in this elder boy. Most of her criticism of the family was levelled against him. The rest she found only a little peculiar. She said she had never heard such a funny Christian name as Frow. Florrie she had heard of, and even Flora, but not *Frow*. I suggested that perhaps Frow might be some sort of title, but she shook her head and said that that was what she was always known as in the Sheldrake Road, 'Mrs Frow Stelling'.

In spite of Mrs Ward's lack of opportunity for greater intimacy on account of the language problem, her own fine imaginative qualities helped her a great deal. And in one particular she seemed curiously vivid. She gathered an account from one of them – I'm not sure whether it was Mr or Mrs Frow Stelling or one of the boys – of a place they described near their home in Bremen. There was a narrow street of high buildings by a canal, and a little bridge that led over into a gentleman's park. At a point where the canal turned sharply eastwards there was a clump of linden-trees, where one could go in the summer-time, and under their shade one might sit and drink light beer, and listen to a band that played in the early part of the evening.

Mrs Ward was curiously clear about that. She said she often thought about Mr Stelling sitting there after his day's work. It must have been very pleasant for him, and he seemed to miss this luxury in Dalston more than anything. Once Ernie, in a friendly mood, had taken him into the four-ale bar of the Unicorn at the corner of the Sheldrake Road, but Mr Stelling did not seem happy. Ernie acknowledged afterwards that it had been an unfortunate evening. The bar had been rather crowded, and there was a man and two women who had all been drinking too much. In any case, Mr Stelling had been obviously restless there, and he had said afterwards:

'It is not that one wishes to drink only . . .'

And he had shaken his fat little head, and had never been known to visit the Unicorn again.

Mr Stelling died quite suddenly of some heart trouble, and Mrs Ward could not get it out of her head that his last illness was brought about by his disappointment and grief in not being able to go and sit quietly under the linden-trees after his day's work and listen to a band.

'You know, my dear,' she said, 'when you get accustomed to a thing it's *bad* for you to leave it off.'

When poor Mr Stelling died, Mrs Frow Stelling was heartbroken, and I have reason to believe that Mrs Ward went in and wept with her, and in their dumb way they forged the chains of some desperate understanding. When Mrs Frow Stelling went back to Germany they promised to write to each other. But they never did, and for a very good reason. As Mrs Ward said, she was 'no scholard', and as for Mrs Frow Stelling, her English was such a doubtful quantity, she probably never got beyond addressing the envelope.

'That was three years ago,' said Mrs Ward. 'Them boys must be eighteen and nineteen now.'

If I had intruded too greatly into the intimacy of Mrs Ward's life, one of my excuses must be, not that I am 'a scholard', but that I am in any case able to read a simple English letter. I was, in fact, on several occasions 'requisitioned'. When Lily was not at home, someone had to read Ernie's letters out loud. The arrival of Ernie's letters was always an inspiring experience. I should perhaps be in the garden with Mrs Ward when Tom would come hurrying out to the back, and call out:

'Mother! a letter from Ernie!'

And then there would be such excitement and commotion. The first thing was always to hunt for Mrs Ward's spectacles. They were never where she had put them. Tom would keep on turning the letter over in his hands, and examining the postmark, and he would reiterate:

'Well, what did you do with them, Mother?'

At length they would be found in some unlikely place, and she would take the letter tremblingly to the light. I never knew quite how much Mrs Ward could read. She could certainly read a certain amount. I saw her old eyes sparkling and her tongue moving jerkily between her parted lips, as though she were formulating the words she read, and she would keep on repeating:

'T'ch! T'ch! Oh dear, oh dear, the *things* he says!'

And Tom impatiently by the door would say:

'Well, what *does* he say?'

She never attempted to read the letter out loud, but at last she would wipe her spectacles and say:

'Oh, you read it, sir. The *things* he says!'

They were indeed very good letters of Ernie's, written apparently in the highest spirits. There was never a grumble, not a word. One might gather that he was away with a lot of young bloods on some sporting expedition, in which football, rags, sing-songs, and strange feeds played a conspicuous part. I read a good many of Ernie's letters, and I do not remember that he ever made a single reference to the horrors of war, or said anything about his own personal discomforts. The boy must have had something of his mother in him in spite of the photograph.

And between the kitchen and the yard Mrs Ward would spend her day placidly content, for Ernie never failed to write. There was sometimes a lapse of a few days, but the letter seldom failed to come every fortnight.

It would be difficult to know what Mrs Ward's actual conception of the War was. She never read the newspapers, for the reason, as she explained, that 'There was nothing in them these days except about this old war.' She occasionally dived into *Reynolds' Newspaper* on Sundays to see if there were any interesting law cases or any news of a romantic character. There was nothing romantic in the war news. It was all preposterous. She did indeed read the papers for the first few weeks, but this was for the reason that she had some vague idea that they might contain some account of Ernie's doings. But as they did not, she dismissed them with contempt.

But I found her one night in a peculiarly preoccupied mood. She was out in the garden, and she kept staring abstractedly over the fence into the unoccupied ground next door. It appeared that it had dawned upon her that the War was to do with 'these Germans', that in fact we were fighting the Germans, and then she thought of the Stellings. Those boys would now be about eighteen and nineteen. They would be fighting too. They would be fighting against Ernie. This seemed very peculiar.

'Of course,' she said, 'I never took to that elder boy – a greedy, rough sort of a boy he was. But I'm sure my Ernie wouldn't hurt young Hans.'

She meditated for a moment as though she were contemplating what particular action Ernie would take in the matter. She knew he didn't like the elder boy, but she doubted whether he would want to do anything very violent to him.

'They went out to a music-hall one night together,' she explained, as though a friendship cemented in this luxurious fashion could hardly be broken by an unreasonable display of passion.

It was a few weeks later that the terror suddenly crept into Mrs Ward's life. Ernie's letters ceased abruptly. The fortnight passed, then three weeks, four weeks, five weeks, and not a word. I don't think that Mrs Ward's character at any time stood out so vividly as during those weeks of stress. It is true she appeared a little feebler, and she trembled in her movements, whilst her eyes seemed abstracted as though all the power in them were concentrated in her ears, alert for the bell or the knock. She started visibly at odd moments, and her imagination was always carrying her tempestuously to the front door, only to answer – a milkman or a casual hawker. But she never expressed her fear in words. When Tom came home – he seemed to have aged rapidly – he would come bustling into the garden, and cry out tremblingly:

'There ain't been no letter to-day, Mother?'

And she would say quite placidly:

'No, not to-day, Tom. It'll come to-morrow, I expect.'

And she would rally him and talk of little things, and get busy with his supper. And in the garden I would try and talk to her about her clumps of pansies, and the latest yarn about the neighbours, and I tried to get between her and the rabbit-hutch with its dumb appeal of incompletion. And I would notice her staring curiously over into the empty garden next door, as though she were being assailed by some disturbing apprehensions. Ernie would not hurt that eldest boy . . . but suppose . . . if things were reversed . . . There was something inexplicable and terrible lurking in this passive silence.

During this period the old man was suddenly taken very ill. He came home one night with a high temperature and developed pneumonia. He was laid up for many weeks, and she kept back the telegram that came while he was almost unconscious, and she tended him night and day, nursing her own anguish with a calm face.

For the telegram told her that her Ernie was 'missing and believed wounded'.

I do not know at what period she told the father this news, but it was certainly not till he was convalescent. And the old man seemed to sink into a kind of apathy. He sat feebly in front of the kitchen fire, coughing and making no effort to control his grief.

Outside the great trains went rushing by, night and day. Things were 'going on', but they were all meaningless, cruel.

We made inquiries at the War Office, but they could not amplify the laconic telegram.

And then the winter came on, and the gardens were bleak in the Sheldrake Road. And Lily ran away and married a young tobacconist, who was earning twenty-five shillings a week. And old Tom was dismissed from the gasworks. His work was not proving satisfactory. And he sat about at home and moped. And in the meantime the price of foodstuffs was going up, and coals were a luxury. And so in the early morning Mrs Ward would go off and work for Mrs Abbot at the wash-tub, and she would earn eight or twelve shillings a week.

It is difficult to know how they managed during those days, but one could see that Mrs Ward was buoyed up by some poignant hope. She would not give way. Eventually old Tom did get some work to do at a stationer's. The work was comparatively light, and the pay equally so, so Mrs Ward still continued to work for Mrs Abbot.

My next vision of Mrs Ward concerns a certain winter evening. I could not see inside the kitchen, but the old man could be heard complaining. His querulous voice was rambling on, and Mrs Ward was standing by the door leading into the garden. She had returned from her day's work and was scraping a pan out into a bin near the door. A train shrieked by, and the wind was blowing a fine rain against the house. Suddenly she stood up and looked at the sky; then she pushed back her hair from her brow and frowned at the dark house next door. Then she turned and said:

'Oh, I don't know, Tom; if we've got to do it, we *must* do it. If them others can stand it, we can stand it. Whatever them others do, we can do.'

And then my visions jump rather wildly. And the War becomes to me epitomized in two women. One in this dim doorway in our obscure suburb of Dalston, scraping out a pan, and the other perhaps in some dark high house near a canal on the outskirts of Bremen. Them others! These two women silently enduring. And the trains rushing by, and all the dark, mysterious forces of the night operating on them equivocally.

Poor Mrs Frow Stelling! Perhaps those boys of hers are 'missing, believed killed'. Perhaps they are killed for certain. She is as much outside 'the things going on' as Mrs Ward. Perhaps she is equally as patient, as brave.

And Mrs Ward enters the kitchen, and her eyes are blazing with a strange light as she says:

'We'll hear to-morrow, Tom. And if we don't hear tomorrow, we'll hear the next day. And if we don't hear the next day, we'll hear the day after. And if we don't . . . if we don't never hear . . . again . . . if them others can stand it, we can stand it, I say.'

And then her voice breaks, and she cries a little, for endurance has its limitations, and – the work is hard at Mrs Abbot's.

And the months go by, and she stoops a little more as she walks, and – someone has thrown a cloth over the rabbit-hutch with its unfinished roof. And Mrs Ward is curiously introspective. It is useless to tell her of the things of the active world. She listens politely but she does not hear. She is full of reminiscences of Ernie's and Lily's childhood. She recounts again and again the story of how Ernie when he was a little boy ordered five tons of coal from a coal merchant to be sent to a girls' school in Dalston High Road. She describes the coal carts arriving in the morning, and the consternation of the head-mistress.

'Oh dear, oh dear,' she says; 'the things he did!'

She does not talk much of the Stellings, but one day she says meditatively:

'Mrs Frow Stelling thought a lot of that boy Hans. So she did of the other, as far as that goes. It's only natural like, I suppose.'

As time went on Tom Ward lost all hope. He said he was convinced that the boy was killed. Having arrived at this conclusion he seemed to become more composed. He gradually began to accustom himself to the new point of view. But with Mrs Ward the exact opposite was the case.

She was convinced that the boy was alive, but she suffered terribly.

There came a time – it was in early April – when one felt that the strain could not last. She seemed to lose all interest in the passing world and lived entirely within herself. Even the arrival of Lily's baby did not rouse her. She looked at the child queerly, as though she doubted whether any useful or happy purpose was served by its appearance.

It was a boy.

In spite of her averred optimism she lost her tremulous sense of apprehension when the bell went or the front door was tapped. She let the milkman – and even the postman – wait.

When she spoke it was invariably of things that happened years ago.

Sometimes she talked about the Stellings, and one Sunday she made a strange pilgrimage out to Finchley and visited Mr Stelling's grave. I don't know what she did there, but she returned looking very exhausted and unwell. As a matter of fact she was unwell for some days after this visit, and she suffered violent twinges of rheumatism in her legs.

I now come to my most unforgettable vision of Mrs Ward.

It was a day at the end of April, and warm for the time of the year. I was standing in the garden with her and it was nearly dark. A goods train had been shunting, and making a great deal of noise in front of the house, and at last had disappeared. I had not been able to help noticing that Mrs Ward's garden was curiously neglected for her for the time of year. The grass was growing on the paths, and the snails had left their silver trail over all the fences.

I was telling her a rumour I had heard about the railway porter and his wife at number twenty-three, and she seemed fairly interested, for she had known John Hemsley, the porter, fifteen years ago, when Ernie was a baby. There were two old broken Windsor chairs in the garden, and on one was a zinc basin in which were some potatoes. She was peeling them, as Lily and her husband were coming to supper. By the kitchen door was a small sink. When she had finished the potatoes, she stood up and began to pour the water down the sink, taking care not to let the skins go too. I was noticing her old bent back, and her long bony hands gripping the sides of the basin, when suddenly a figure came limping round the bend of the house from the side passage, and two arms were thrown around her waist, and a voice said:

'Mind them skins don't go down the sink, Mother. They'll stop it up!'

As I explained to Ernie afterwards, it was an extremely foolish thing to do. If his mother had had anything wrong with her heart, it might have been very serious. There have been many cases of people dying from the shock of such an experience.

As it was, she merely dropped the basin and stood there trembling like a leaf, and Ernie laughed loud and uproariously. It must have been three or four minutes before she could regain her speech, and then all she could manage to say was:

'Ernie! . . . My Ernie!'

And the boy laughed and ragged his mother, and pulled her into the house, and Tom appeared and stared at his son, and said feebly:

'Well, I never!'

I don't know how it was that I found myself intruding upon the sanctity of the inner life of the Ward family that evening. I had never had a meal there before, but I felt I was holding a sort of watching brief over the soul and body of Mrs Ward. I had had a little medical training in my early youth, and this may have been one of the reasons which prompted me to stay.

When Lily and her husband appeared we sat down to a meal of mashed potatoes and onions stewed in milk, with bread and cheese, and very excellent it was.

Lily and her husband took the whole thing in a boisterous, high comedy manner that fitted in with the mood of Ernie. Old Tom sat there staring at his son, and repeating at intervals:

'Well, I never!'

And Mrs Ward hovered round the boy's plate. Her eyes divided their time between his plate and his face, and she hardly spoke all the evening.

Ernie's story was remarkable enough. He told it disconnectedly and rather incoherently. There were moments when he rambled in a rather peculiar way, and sometimes he stammered, and seemed unable to frame a sentence. Lily's husband went out to fetch some beer to celebrate the joyful occasion, and Ernie drank his in little sips, and spluttered. The boy must have suffered considerably, and he had a wound in the abdomen, and another in the right forearm which for a time had paralysed him.

As far as I could gather, his story was this:

He and a platoon of men had been ambushed and had had to surrender. When being sent back to a base, three of them tried to escape from the train, which had been held up at night. He did not know what had happened to the other two men, but it was on this occasion that he received his abdominal wound at the hands of a guard.

He had then been sent to some infirmary, where he was fairly well treated; but as soon as his wound had healed a little, he had been suddenly sent to some fortress prison, presumably as a punishment. He hadn't the faintest idea how long he had been confined there. He said it seemed like fifteen years. It was probably nine months. He had solitary confinement in a cell, which was like a small lavatory. He had fifteen minutes' exercise every day in a yard with some other prisoners, who were Russians, he thought. He spoke to no one. He used to sing and recite in his cell, and there were times when he was quite convinced that he was 'off his chump'. He said he had lost 'all sense of everything' when he was suddenly transferred to another prison. Here the conditions were somewhat better and he was made to work. He said he wrote six or seven letters home from there, but received no reply. The letters certainly never reached Dalston. The food was execrable, but a big improvement on the dungeon. He was only there a few weeks when he and some thirty prisoners were sent suddenly to work on the land at a kind of settlement. He said that the life there would have been tolerable if it hadn't been for the fact that the Commandant was an absolute brute. The food was worse than in the prison, and they were punished severely for the most trivial offences.

It was here, however, that he met a sailor named Martin, a Royal Naval Reservist, an elderly, thick-set man with a black beard and only one eye. Ernie said that this Martin 'was an artist. He wangled everything. He had a genius for getting what he wanted. He would get a beef-steak out of a stone.' In fact, it was obvious that the whole of Ernie's narrative was coloured by his vision of Martin. He said he'd never met such a chap in his life. He admired him enormously, and he was also a little afraid of him.

By some miraculous means peculiar to sailors, Martin acquired a compass. Ernie hardly knew what a compass was, but the sailor explained to him that it was all that was necessary to take you straight to England. Ernie said he 'had had enough of escaping. It didn't agree with his health,' but so strong was his faith and belief in Martin that he ultimately agreed to try with him.

He said Martin's method of escape was the coolest thing he'd ever seen. He planned it all beforehand. It was the fag-end of the day, and the whistle had gone, and the prisoners were trooping back across a potato field. Martin and Ernie were very slow. They lingered apparently to discuss some matter connected with the soil. There were two sentries in sight, one near them and the other perhaps a hundred yards away. The potato field was on a slope; at the bottom of the field were two lines of barbed-wire entanglements. The other prisoners passed out of sight, and the sentry near them called out something, probably telling them to hurry up. They started to go up the field when suddenly Martin staggered and clutched his throat. Then he fell over backwards and commenced to have an epileptic fit. Ernie said it was the realest thing he'd ever seen. The sentry ran up, at the same time whistling to his comrade. Ernie released Martin's collar-band and tried to help him. Both the sentries approached, and Ernie stood back. He saw them bending over the prostrate man, when suddenly a most extraordinary thing happened. Both their heads were brought together with fearful violence. One fell completely senseless, but the other staggered forward and groped for his rifle.

When Ernie told this part of the story he kept dabbing his forehead with his handkerchief.

'I never seen such a man as Martin, I don't think,' he said. 'Lord! he had a fist like a leg of mutton. He laid 'em out neatly on the grass, took off their coats and most of their other clothes, and flung 'em over the barbed wire, and then swarmed over like a cat. I had more difficulty, but he got me across too, somehow. Then we carted the clothes away to the next line.

'We got up into a wood that night, and Martin draws out his compass and he says: "We've got a hundred and seven miles to do in night shifts, cully. And if we make a slip we're shot as safe as a knife." It sounded the maddest scheme in the world, but somehow I felt that Martin would get through it. The only thing that saved me was that – that I didn't have to think. I simply left everything to him. If I'd started thinking I should have gone mad. I had it fixed in my mind, "Either he does it or he doesn't do it. I can't help it." I reely don't remember much about that journey. It was all a dream like. We did all our travellin' at night by compass, and hid by day. Neither of us had a word of German. But Gawd's truth! that man Martin was a marvel! He turned our trousers inside out, and made 'em look like ordinary labourers' trousers. He disappeared the first night and came back with some other old clothes. We lived mostly on raw potatoes we dug out of the ground with our hands, but not always. I believe Martin could have stole an egg from under a hen without her noticing it. He was the coolest card there ever was. Of course there was a lot of trouble one way and another. It wasn't always easy to find wooded country or protection of any sort. We often ran into people and they stared at us, and we shifted our course. But I think we were only addressed three or four times by men, and then Martin's methods were the simplest in the world. He just looked sort of blank for a moment, and then knocked them clean out and bolted. Of course they were after us all the time, and it was this constant tacking and shifting ground that took so long. Fancy! he had never a map, you know, nothing but the compass. We didn't know what sort of country we were coming to, nothing. We just crept through the night like cats. I believe Martin could see in the dark . . . He killed a dog one night with his hands . . . It was necessary.'

It was impossible to discover from Ernie how long this amazing journey lasted – the best part of two months, I believe. He was himself a little uncertain with regard to many incidents, whether they were true or whether they were hallucinations. He suffered greatly from his wound and had periods of feverishness. But one morning, he said, Martin began 'prancing'. He seemed to develop some curious sense that they were near the Dutch frontier. And then, according to Ernie, 'a cat wasn't in it with Martin'.

He was very mysterious about the actual crossing. I gather that there had been some 'clumsy' work with sentries. It was at that time that Ernie got a bullet through his arm. When he got to Holland he was very ill. It was not that the wound was, a serious one, but, as he explained:

'Me blood was in a bad state. I was nearly down and out.'

He was very kindly treated by some Dutch Sisters in a convent hospital. But he was delirious for a long time, and when he became more normal they wanted to communicate with his people in England, but this didn't appeal to the dramatic sense of Ernie.

'I thought I'd spring a surprise packet on you,' he said, grinning.

We asked about Martin, but Ernie said he never saw him again. He went away while Ernie was delirious, and they said he had gone to Rotterdam to take ship somewhere. He thought Holland was a dull place.

During the relation of this narrative my attention was divided between watching the face of Ernie and the face of Ernie's mother.

I am quite convinced that she did not listen to the story at all. She never took her eyes from his face, and although her tongue was following the flow of his remarks, her mind was occupied with the vision of Ernie when he was a little boy, and when he ordered five tons of coal to be sent to the girls' school.

When he had finished, she said:

'Did you meet either of them young Stellings?'

And Ernie laughed rather uproariously and said no, he didn't have the pleasure of renewing their acquaintance.

On his way home, it appeared, he had reported himself at Headquarters, and his discharge was inevitable.

'So now you'll be able to finish the rabbit-hutch,' said Lily's husband, and we all laughed again, with the exception of Mrs Ward.

I found her later standing alone in the garden. It was a warm spring night. There was no moon, but the sky appeared restless with its burden of trembling stars. She had an old shawl drawn round her shoulders, and she stood there very silently with her arms crossed.

'Well, this is splendid news, Mrs Ward,' I said.

She started a little, and coughed, and pulled the shawl closer round her.

She said, 'Yes, sir,' very faintly.

I don't think she was very conscious of me. She still appeared immersed in the contemplation of her inner visions. Her eyes settled upon the empty house next door, and I thought I detected the trail of a tear glistening on her cheeks. I lighted my pipe. We could hear Ernie, and Lily, and Lily's husband still laughing and talking inside.

'She used to make a very good puddin',' Mrs Ward said suddenly, at random. 'Dried fruit inside, and that. My Ernie liked it very much . . .'

Somewhere away in the distance – probably outside the Unicorn – someone was playing a cornet. A train crashed by and disappeared, leaving a trail of foul smoke which obscured the sky. The smoke cleared slowly away. I struck another match to light my pipe.

It was quite true. On either side of her cheek a tear had trickled. She was trembling a little, worn out by the emotions of the evening.

There was a moment of silence, unusual for Dalston.

'It's all very . . . perplexin' and that,' she said quietly.

And then I knew for certain that in that great hour of her happiness her mind was assailed by strange and tremulous doubts. She was thinking of 'them others' a little wistfully. She was doubting whether one could rejoice – when the thing became clear and actual to one – without sending out one's thoughts into the dark garden to 'them others' who were suffering too. And she had come out into this little meagre yard at Dalston, and had gazed through the mist and smoke upwards to the stars, because she wanted peace intensely, and so she sought it within herself, because she knew that real peace is a thing which concerns the heart alone.

And so I left her standing there, and I went my way, for I knew that she was wiser than I.

Notes

p. 191   *dovetail* - fit together
p. 191   *Dalston Junction* - a major railway junction in North London
p. 191   *buff-brick* - pale coloured brick
p. 192   *scarlet-runners* - runner beans which have scarlet flowers

p. 192   *hollyhocks* - tall flowers –'irresponsible' because they do not grow vegetables to help the war effort

p. 192   *'body'* - used of an old person, not unkindly, 'old thing'

p. 192   *swells* - smart people

p. 192   *paper hat . . . printer* - a hat made of folded paper, to keep ink and dust out of the hair, it was disposable, as it would get very dirty

p. 192   *London Pride* - pink flowers which flourish on poor soil

p. 193   *Frow* - Mrs Ward's version of Frau, German: 'Mrs'

p. 195   *four-ale bar of the Unicorn* - public house; rather a seedy place where drunkenness is common, unlike the German café

p. 195   *scholard* - scholar

p. 196   *young bloods* - boisterous young men

p. 196   *rags* - jokes, tricks

p. 196   *strange feeds* - unusual meals

p. 196   *Reynolds' Newspaper* - a popular, entertaining Sunday newspaper

p. 197   *hawker* - door-to-door salesman

p. 197   *dumb appeal* - because Ernie was building the rabbit hutch and has left it unfinished

p. 200   *off his chump* - mad

p. 201   *cully* - an easily tricked, gullible person

p. 202   *card* - an eccentric person

p. 202   *'a cat wasn't in it'* - a cat was not in the race, i.e. he was even more agile than a cat

21

The Doll's House

(1923)

Katherine Mansfield

Mansfield, a New Zealander, lived in the UK and Europe most of her life and is one of the very best short story writers of any time. In this story, a well-to-do family receives a marvellous present for their daughters of a large and magnificent doll's house. It is the talk of their school, but there are two children in the class who are social outcasts and will not be allowed to come and view the doll's house.

When dear old Mrs. Hay went back to town after staying with the Burnells she sent the children a doll's house. It was so big that the carter and Pat carried it into the courtyard, and there it stayed, propped up on two wooden boxes beside the feed-room door. No harm could come to it; it was summer. And perhaps the smell of paint would have gone off by the time it had to be taken in. For, really, the smell of paint coming from that doll's house ("Sweet of old Mrs. Hay, of course; most sweet and generous!")—but the smell of paint was quite enough to make anyone seriously ill, in Aunt Beryl's opinion. Even before the sacking was taken off. And when it was . . .

There stood the doll's house, a dark, oily, spinach green, picked out with bright yellow. Its two solid little chimneys, glued on to the roof, were painted red and white, and the door, gleaming with yellow varnish, was like a little slab of toffee. Four windows, real windows, were divided into panes by a broad streak of green. There was actually a tiny porch, too, painted yellow, with big lumps of congealed paint hanging along the edge.

But perfect, perfect little house! Who could possibly mind the smell. It was part of the joy, part of the newness.

"Open it quickly, someone!"

The hook at the side was stuck fast. Pat prised it open with his penknife, and the whole house front swung back, and—there you were, gazing at one and the same moment into the drawing-room and dining-room, the kitchen and two bedrooms. That is the way for a house to open! Why don't all houses open like that? How much more exciting than peering through the slit of a door into a mean little hall with a hat-stand and two umbrellas! That is—isn't it?—what you long to know about a house when you put your hand on the knocker. Perhaps it is the way God opens houses at the dead of night when He is taking a quiet turn with an angel. . . .

"Oh-oh!" The Burnell children sounded as though they were in despair. It was too marvellous; it was too much for them. They had never seen anything like it in their lives. All the rooms were papered. There were pictures on the walls, painted on the paper, with gold frames complete. Red carpet covered all the floors except the kitchen; red plush chairs in the drawing-room, green in the dining-room; tables, beds with real bedclothes, a cradle, a stove, a dresser with tiny plates and one big jug. But what Kezia liked more than anything, what she liked frightfully, was the lamp. It stood in the middle of the dining-room table, an exquisite little amber lamp with a white globe. It was even filled all ready for lighting, though, of course, you couldn't light it. But there was something inside that looked like oil and moved when you shook it.

The father and mother dolls, who sprawled very stiff as though they had fainted in the drawing-room, and their two little children asleep upstairs, were really too big for the doll's house. They didn't look as though they belonged. But the lamp was perfect. It seemed to smile at Kezia, to say, "I live here." The lamp was real.

The Burnell children could hardly walk to school fast enough the next morning.

They burned to tell everybody, to describe, to—well—to boast about their doll's house before the school-bell rang.

"I'm to tell," said Isabel, "because I'm the eldest. And you two can join in after. But I'm to tell first."

There was nothing to answer. Isabel was bossy, but she was always right, and Lottie and Kezia knew too well the powers that went with being eldest. They brushed through the thick buttercups at the road edge and said nothing.

"And I'm to choose who's to come and see it first. Mother said I might."

For it had been arranged that while the doll's house stood in the courtyard they might ask the girls at school, two at a time, to come and look. Not to stay to tea, of course, or to come traipsing through the house. But just to stand quietly in the courtyard while Isabel pointed out the beauties, and Lottie and Kezia looked pleased. . . .

But hurry as they might, by the time they had reached the tarred palings of the boys' playground the bell had begun to jangle. They only just had time to whip off their hats and fall into line before the roll was called. Never mind. Isabel tried to make up for it by looking very important and mysterious and by whispering behind her hand to the girls near her, "Got something to tell you at playtime."

Playtime came and Isabel was surrounded. The girls of her class nearly fought to put their arms round her, to walk away with her, to beam flatteringly, to be her special friend. She held quite a court under the huge pine trees at the side of the playground. Nudging, giggling together, the little girls pressed up close. And the only two who stayed outside the ring were the two who were always outside, the little Kelveys. They knew better than to come anywhere near the Burnells.

For the fact was, the school the Burnell children went to was not at all the kind of place their parents would have chosen if there had been any choice. But there was none. It was the only school for miles. And the consequence was all the children of the neighbourhood, the Judge's little girls, the doctor's daughters, the store-keeper's children, the milkman's, were forced to mix together. Not to speak of there being an equal number of rude, rough little boys as well. But the line had to be drawn somewhere. It was drawn at the Kelveys. Many of the children, including the Burnells, were not allowed even to speak to them. They walked past the Kelveys with their heads in the air, and as they set the fashion in all matters of behaviour, the Kelveys were shunned by everybody. Even the teacher had a special voice for them, and a special smile for the other children when Lil Kelvey came up to her desk with a bunch of dreadfully common-looking flowers.

They were the daughters of a spry, hard-working little washerwoman, who went about from house to house by the day. This was awful enough. But where was Mr. Kelvey? Nobody knew for certain. But everybody said he was in prison. So they were the daughters of a washerwoman and a gaolbird. Very nice company for other people's children! And they looked it. Why Mrs. Kelvey made them so conspicuous was hard to understand. The truth was they were dressed in "bits" given to her by the people for whom she worked. Lil, for instance, who was a stout, plain child, with big freckles, came to school in a dress made from a green art-serge tablecloth of the Burnells', with red plush sleeves from the Logans' curtains. Her hat, perched on top of her high forehead, was a grown-up woman's hat, once the property of Miss Lecky, the postmistress. It was turned up at the back and trimmed with a large scarlet quill. What a little guy she looked! It was impossible not to laugh. And her little sister, our Else, wore a long white dress, rather like a nightgown, and a pair of little boy's boots. But whatever our Else wore she would have looked strange. She was a tiny wishbone of a child, with cropped hair and enormous solemn eyes—a little white owl. Nobody had ever seen her smile; she scarcely ever spoke. She went through life holding on to Lil, with a piece of Lil's skirt screwed up in her hand. Where Lil went, our Else followed. In the playground, on the road going to and from school, there was Lil marching in front and our Else holding on behind. Only when she wanted anything, or when she was out of breath, our Else gave Lil a tug, a twitch, and Lil stopped and turned round. The Kelveys never failed to understand each other.

Now they hovered at the edge; you couldn't stop them listening. When the little girls turned round and sneered, Lil, as usual, gave her silly, shamefaced smile, but our Else only looked.

And Isabel's voice, so very proud, went on telling. The carpet made a great sensation, but so did the beds with real bedclothes, and the stove with an oven door.

When she finished Kezia broke in. "You've forgotten the lamp, Isabel."

"Oh yes," said Isabel, "and there's a teeny little lamp, all made of yellow glass, with a white globe that stands on the dining-room table. You couldn't tell it from a real one."

"The lamp's best of all," cried Kezia. She thought Isabel wasn't making half enough of the little lamp. But nobody paid any attention. Isabel was choosing the two who were to come back with them that afternoon and see it. She chose Emmie Cole and Lena Logan. But when the others knew they were all to have a chance, they couldn't be nice enough to Isabel. One by one they put their arms round Isabel's waist and walked her off. They had something to whisper to her, a secret. "Isabel's *my* friend."

Only the little Kelveys moved away forgotten; there was nothing more for them to hear.

Days passed, and as more children saw the doll's house, the fame of it spread. It became the one subject, the rage. The one question was, "Have you seen Burnells' doll's house? Oh, ain't it lovely!" "Haven't you seen it? Oh, I say!"

Even the dinner hour was given up to talking about it. The little girls sat under the pines eating their thick mutton sandwiches and big slabs of johnny cake spread with butter. While always, as near as they could get, sat the Kelveys, our Else holding on to Lil, listening too, while they chewed their jam sandwiches out of a newspaper soaked with large red blobs.

"Mother," said Kezia, "can't I ask the Kelveys just once?"

"Certainly not, Kezia."

"But why not?"

"Run away, Kezia; you know quite well why not."

At last everybody had seen it except them. On that day the subject rather flagged. It was the dinner hour. The children stood together under the pine trees, and suddenly, as they looked at the Kelveys eating out of their paper, always by themselves, always listening, they wanted to be horrid to them. Emmie Cole started the whisper.

"Lil Kelvey's going to be a servant when she grows up."

"O-oh, how awful!" said Isabel Burnell, and she made eyes at Emmie.

Emmie swallowed in a very meaning way and nodded to Isabel as she'd seen her mother do on those occasions.

"It's true—it's true—it's true," she said.

Then Lena Logan's little eyes snapped. "Shall I ask her?" she whispered.

"Bet you don't," said Jessie May.

"Pooh, I'm not frightened," said Lena. Suddenly she gave a little squeal and danced in front of the other girls. "Watch! Watch me! Watch me now!" said Lena. And sliding, gliding, digging one foot, giggling behind her hand, Lena went over to the Kelveys.

Lil looked up from her dinner. She wrapped the rest quickly away. Our Else stopped chewing. What was coming now?

"Is it true you're going to be a servant when you grow up, Lil Kelvey?" shrilled Lena.

Dead silence. But instead of answering, Lil only gave her silly, shamefaced smile. She didn't seem to mind the question at all. What a sell for Lena! The girls began to titter.

Lena couldn't stand that. She put her hands on her hips; she shot forward. "Yah, yer father's in prison!" she hissed spitefully.

This was such a marvellous thing to have said that the little girls rushed away in a body, deeply, deeply excited, wild with joy. Someone found a long rope, and they began skipping. And never did they skip so high, run in and out so fast, or do such daring things as on that morning.

In the afternoon Pat called for the Burnell children with the buggy and they drove home. There were visitors. Isabel and Lottie, who liked visitors, went upstairs to change their pinafores. But Kezia thieved out at the back. Nobody was about; she began to swing on the big white gates of the courtyard. Presently, looking along the road, she saw two little dots. They grew bigger, they were coming towards her. Now she could see that one was in front and one close behind. Now she could see that they were the Kelveys. Kezia stopped swinging. She slipped off the gate as if she was going to run away. Then she hesitated. The Kelveys came nearer, and beside them walked their shadows, very long, stretching right across the road with their heads in the buttercups. Kezia clambered back on the gate; she had made up her mind; she swung out.

"Hullo," she said to the passing Kelveys.

They were so astounded that they stopped. Lil gave her silly smile. Our Else stared.

"You can come and see our doll's house if you want to," said Kezia, and she dragged one toe on the ground. But at that Lil turned red and shook her head quickly.

"Why not?" asked Kezia.

Lil gasped, then she said, "Your ma told our ma you wasn't to speak to us."

"Oh, well," said Kezia. She didn't know what to reply. "It doesn't matter. You can come and see our doll's house all the same. Come on. Nobody's looking."

But Lil shook her head still harder.

"Don't you want to?" asked Kezia.

Suddenly there was a twitch, a tug at Lil's skirt. She turned round. Our Else was looking at her with big, imploring eyes; she was frowning; she wanted to go. For a moment Lil looked at our Else very doubtfully. But then our Else twitched her skirt again. She started forward. Kezia led the way. Like two little stray cats they followed across the courtyard to where the doll's house stood.

"There it is," said Kezia.

There was a pause. Lil breathed loudly, almost snorted; our Else was still as stone.

"I'll open it for you," said Kezia kindly. She undid the hook and they looked inside.

"There's the drawing-room and the dining-room, and that's the—"

"Kezia!"

Oh, what a start they gave!

"Kezia!"

It was Aunt Beryl's voice. They turned round. At the back door stood Aunt Beryl, staring as if she couldn't believe what she saw.

"How dare you ask the little Kelveys into the courtyard!" said her cold, furious voice. "You know as well as I do, you're not allowed to talk to them. Run away, children, run away at once. And don't come back again," said Aunt Beryl. And she stepped into the yard and shooed them out as if they were chickens.

"Off you go immediately!" she called, cold and proud.

They did not need telling twice. Burning with shame, shrinking together, Lil huddling along like her mother, our Else dazed, somehow they crossed the big courtyard and squeezed through the white gate.

"Wicked, disobedient little girl!" said Aunt Beryl bitterly to Kezia, and she slammed the doll's house to.

The afternoon had been awful. A letter had come from Willie Brent, a terrifying, threatening letter, saying if she did not meet him that evening in Pulman's Bush, he'd come to the front door and ask the reason why! But now that she had frightened those little rats of Kelveys and given Kezia a good scolding, her heart felt lighter. That ghastly pressure was gone. She went back to the house humming.

When the Kelveys were well out of sight of Burnells', they sat down to rest on a big red drainpipe by the side of the road. Lil's cheeks were still burning; she took off the hat with the quill and held it on her knee. Dreamily they looked over the hay paddocks, past the creek, to the group of wattles where Logan's cows stood waiting to be milked. What were their thoughts?

Presently our Else nudged up close to her sister. But now she had forgotten the cross lady. She put out a finger and stroked her sister's quill; she smiled her rare smile.

"I seen the little lamp," she said softly.

Then both were silent once more.

Notes

p. 205   *carter* - one who transports goods with a horse and cart
p. 205   *feed-room* - where the horse or cattle feed is kept on a farm
p. 206   *buttercups* - wild flowers that are a rich golden yellow
p. 206   *tarred palings* - fence
p. 207   *art-serge* - heavy fabric
p. 207   *quill* - feather
p. 208   *johnny cake* - a kind of flat bread
p. 209   *buggy* - small open cart
p. 210   *wattle* - sticks and twigs woven to make a fence or wall

A Warning to the Curious

(1925)

M.R. James

An English academic, James was a specialist in medieval history, which is reflected in this story. In his fiction writing, he reinvented the ghost story, moving away from the gothic horror style to more 'ordinary settings', often leaving much unsaid. In this story, two gentlemen are on a mild golfing holiday in East Anglia, when they meet a young man, an archaeologist and amateur historian, who seems strangely jumpy; they then find out why.

The place on the east coast which the reader is asked to consider is Seaburgh. It is not very different now from what I remember it to have been when I was a child. Marshes intersected by dykes to the south, recalling the early chapters of *Great Expectations*; flat fields to the north, merging into heath; heath, fir woods, and, above all, gorse, inland. A long sea-front and a street: behind that a spacious church of flint, with a broad, solid western tower and a peal of six bells. How well I remember their sound on a hot Sunday in August, as our party went slowly up the white, dusty slope of road towards them, for the church stands at the top of a short, steep incline. They rang with a flat clacking sort of sound on those hot days, but when the air was softer they were mellower too. The railway ran down to its little terminus farther along the same road. There was a gay white windmill just before you came to the station, and another down near the shingle at the south end of the town, and yet others on higher ground to the north. There were cottages of bright red brick with slate roofs . . . but why do I encumber you with these commonplace details? The fact is that they come crowding to the point of the pencil when it begins to write of Seaburgh. I should like to be sure that I had allowed the right ones to get on to the paper. But I forgot. I have not quite done with the word-painting business yet.

Walk away from the sea and the town, pass the station, and turn up the road on the right. It is a sandy road, parallel with the railway, and if you follow it, it climbs to somewhat higher ground. On your left (you are now going northward) is heath, on your right (the side towards the sea) is a belt of old firs, wind-beaten, thick at the top, with the slope that old seaside trees have; seen on the skyline from the train they would tell you in an instant, if you did not know it, that you were approaching a windy coast. Well, at the top of my little hill, a line of these firs strikes out and runs towards the sea, for there is a ridge that goes that way; and the ridge ends in a rather well-defined mound commanding the level fields of rough grass, and a little knot of fir trees crowns it. And here you may sit on a hot spring day, very well content to look at blue sea, white windmills, red cottages, bright green grass, church tower, and distant martello tower on the south.

As I have said, I began to know Seaburgh as a child; but a gap of a good many years separates my early knowledge from that which is more recent. Still it keeps its place in my affections, and any tales of it that I pick up have an interest for me. One such tale is this: it came to me in a place very remote from Seaburgh, and quite accidentally, from a man whom I had been able to oblige—enough in his opinion to justify his making me his confidant to this extent.

I know all that country more or less (he said). I used to go to Seaburgh pretty regularly for golf in the spring. I generally put up at the 'Bear', with a friend—Henry Long it was, you knew him perhaps—('Slightly,' I said) and we used to take a sitting-room and be very happy there. Since he died I haven't cared to go there. And I don't know that I should anyhow after the particular thing that happened on our last visit.

It was in April 19— we were there, and by some chance we were almost the only people in the hotel. So the ordinary public rooms were practically empty, and we were the more surprised when, after dinner, our sitting-room door opened, and a young man put his head in. We were aware of this young man. He was rather a rabbity anaemic subject—light hair and light eyes—but not unpleasing. So when he said: 'I beg your pardon, is this a private room?' we did not growl and say: 'Yes, it is,' but Long said, or I did—no matter which: 'Please come in.' 'Oh, may I?' he said, and seemed relieved. Of course it was obvious that he wanted company; and as he was a reasonable kind of person—not the sort to bestow his whole family history on you—we urged him to make himself at home. 'I dare say you find the other rooms rather bleak,' I said. Yes, he did: but it was really too good of us, and so on. That being got over, he made some pretence of reading a book. Long was playing Patience, I was writing. It became plain to me after a few minutes that this visitor of ours was in rather a state of fidgets or nerves, which communicated itself to me, and so I put away my writing and turned to at engaging him in talk.

After some remarks, which I forget, he became rather confidential. 'You'll think it very odd of me' (this was the sort of way he began), 'but the fact is I've had something of a shock.' Well, I recommended a drink of some cheering kind, and we had it. The waiter coming in made an interruption (and I thought our young man seemed very jumpy when the door opened), but after a while he got back to his woes again. There was nobody he knew in the place, and he did happen to know who we both were (it turned out there was some common acquaintance in town), and really he did want a word of advice, if we didn't mind. Of course we both said: 'By all means,' or 'Not at all,' and Long put away his cards. And we settled down to hear what his difficulty was.

'It began,' he said, 'more than a week ago, when I bicycled over to Froston, only about five or six miles, to see the church; I'm very much interested in architecture, and it's got one of those pretty porches with niches and shields. I took a photograph of it, and then an old man who was tidying up in the churchyard came and asked if I'd care to look into the church. I said yes, and he produced a key and let me in. There wasn't much inside, but I told him it was a nice little church, and he kept it very clean, "but," I said, "the porch is the best part of it." We were just outside the porch then, and he said, "Ah, yes, that is a nice porch; and do you know, sir, what's the meanin' of that coat of arms there?"

'It was the one with the three crowns, and though I'm not much of a herald, I was able to say yes, I thought it was the old arms of the kingdom of East Anglia.

"'That's right, sir," he said, "and do you know the meanin' of them three crowns that's on it?"

'I said I'd no doubt it was known, but I couldn't recollect to have heard it myself.

"'Well, then," he said, "for all you're a scholard, I can tell you something you don't know. Them's the three 'oly crowns what was buried in the ground near by the coast to keep the Germans from landing—ah, I can see you don't believe that. But I tell you, if it hadn't have been for one of them 'oly crowns bein' there still, them Germans would a landed here time and again, they would. Landed with their ships, and killed man, woman and child in their beds. Now then, that's the truth what I'm telling you, that is; and if you don't believe me, you ast the rector. There he comes: you ast him, I says."

'I looked round, and there was the rector, a nice-looking old man, coming up the path; and before I could begin assuring my old man, who was getting quite excited, that I didn't disbelieve him, the rector struck in, and said: "What's all this about, John? Good day to you, sir. Have you been looking at our little church?"

'So then there was a little talk which allowed the old man to calm down, and then the rector asked him again what was the matter.

"'Oh," he said, "it warn't nothink, only I was telling this gentleman he'd ought to ast you about them 'oly crowns."

"'Ah, yes, to be sure," said the rector, "that's a very curious matter, isn't it? But I don't know whether the gentleman is interested in our old stories, eh?"

"'Oh, he'll be interested fast enough," says the old man, "he'll put his confidence in what you tells him, sir; why, you known William Ager yourself, father and son too."

'Then I put in a word to say how much I should like to hear all about it, and before many minutes I was walking up the village street with the rector, who had one or two words to say to parishioners, and then to the rectory, where he took me into his study. He had made out, on the way, that I really was capable of taking an intelligent interest in a piece of folk-lore, and not quite the ordinary tripper. So he was very willing to talk, and it is rather surprising to me that the particular legend he told me has not made its way into print before. His account of it was this: "There has always been a belief in these parts in the three holy crowns. The old people say they were buried in different places near the coast to keep off the Danes or the French or the Germans. And they say that onc of the three was dug up a long time ago, and another has disappeared by the encroaching of the sea, and one's still left doing its work, keeping off invaders. Well, now, if you have read the ordinary guides and histories of this county, you will remember perhaps that in 1687 a crown, which was said to be the crown of Redwald, King of the East Angles, was dug up at Rendlesham, and alas! alas! melted down before it was even properly described or drawn. Well, Rendlesham isn't on the coast, but it isn't so very far inland, and it's on a very important line of access. And I believe that is the crown which the people mean when they say that one has been dug up. Then on the south you don't want me to tell you where there was a Saxon royal palace which is now under the sea, eh? Well, there was the second crown, I take it. And up beyond these two, they say, lies the third."

'"Do they say where it is?" of course I asked.

'He said, "Yes, indeed, they do, but they don't tell," and his manner did not encourage me to put the obvious question. Instead of that I waited a moment, and said: "What did the old man mean when he said you knew William Ager, as if that had something to do with the crowns?"

'"To be sure," he said, "now that's another curious story. These Agers—it's a very old name in these parts, but I can't find that they were ever people of quality or big owners— these Agers say, or said, that their branch of the family were the guardians of the last crown. A certain old Nathaniel Ager was the first one I knew—I was born and brought up quite near here—and he, I believe, camped out at the place during the whole of the war of 1870. William, his son, did the same, I know, during the South African War. And young William, *his* son, who has only died fairly recently, took lodgings at the cottage nearest the spot, and I've no doubt hastened his end, for he was a consumptive, by exposure and night watching. And he was the last of that branch. It was a dreadful grief to him to think that he was the last, but he could do nothing, the only relations at all near to him were in the colonies. I wrote letters for him to them imploring them to come over on business very important to the family, but there has been no answer. So the last of the holy crowns, if it's there, has no guardian now."

'That was what the rector told me, and you can fancy how interesting I found it. The only thing I could think of when I left him was how to hit upon the spot where the crown was supposed to be. I wish I'd left it alone.

'But there was a sort of fate in it, for as I bicycled back past the churchyard wall my eye caught a fairly new gravestone, and on it was the name of William Ager. Of course I got off and read it. It said "of this parish, died at Seaburgh 19—, aged 28." There it was, you see. A little judicious questioning in the right place, and I should at least find the cottage nearest the spot. Only I didn't quite know what was the right place to begin my questioning at. Again there was fate: it took me to the curiosity-shop down that way— you know—and I turned over some old books, and, if you please, one was a prayer-book of 1740 odd, in a rather handsome binding—I'll just go and get it, it's in my room.'

He left us in a state of some surprise, but we had hardly time to exchange any remarks when he was back, panting, and handed us the book opened at the fly-leaf, on which was, in a straggly hand:

> Nathaniel Ager is my name and England is my nation,
> Seaburgh is my dwelling-place and Christ is my Salvation,
> When I am dead and in my Grave, and all my bones are rotton,
> I hope the Lord will think on me when I am quite forgotton.

This poem was dated 1754, and there were many more entries of Agers, Nathaniel, Frederick, William, and so on, ending with William, 19—.

'You see,' he said, 'anybody would call it the greatest bit of luck. *I* did, but I don't now. Of course I asked the shopman about William Ager, and of course he happened to remember that he lodged in a cottage in the North Field and died there. This was just chalking the road for me. I knew which the cottage must be: there is only one sizable one about there. The next thing was to scrape some sort of acquaintance with the people, and I took a walk that way at once. A dog did the business for me: he made at me so fiercely that they had to run out and beat him off, and then naturally begged my pardon, and we got into talk. I had only to bring up Ager's name, and pretend I knew, or thought I knew something of him, and then the woman said how sad it was him dying so young, and she was sure it came of him spending the night out of doors in the cold weather. Then I had to say: "Did he go out on the sea at night?" and she said: "Oh, no, it was on the hillock yonder with the trees on it." And there I was.

'I know something about digging in these barrows: I've opened many of them in the down country. But that was with owner's leave, and in broad daylight and with men to help. I had to prospect very carefully here before I put a spade in: I couldn't trench across the mound, and with those old firs growing there I knew there would be awkward tree roots. Still the soil was very light and sandy and easy, and there was a rabbit hole or so that might be developed into a sort of tunnel. The going out and coming back at odd hours to the hotel was going to be the awkward part. When I made up my mind about the way to excavate I told the people that I was called away for a night, and I spent it out there. I made my tunnel: I won't bore you with the details of how I supported it and filled it in when I'd done, but the main thing is that I got the crown.'

Naturally we both broke out into exclamations of surprise and interest. I for one had long known about the finding of the crown at Rendlesham and had often lamented its fate. No one has ever seen an Anglo-Saxon crown—at least no one had. But our man gazed at us with a rueful eye. 'Yes,' he said, 'and the worst of it is I don't know how to put it back.'

'Put it back?' we cried out. 'Why, my dear sir, you've made one of the most exciting finds ever heard of in this country. Of course it ought to go to the Jewel House at the Tower. What's your difficulty? If you're thinking about the owner of the land, and treasure-trove, and all that, we can certainly help you through. Nobody's going to make a fuss about technicalities in a case of this kind.'

Probably more was said, but all he did was to put his face in his hands, and mutter: 'I don't know how to put it back.'

At last Long said: 'You'll forgive me, I hope, if I seem impertinent, but are you *quite* sure you've got it?' I was wanting to ask much the same question myself, for of course the story did seem a lunatic's dream when one thought over it. But I hadn't quite dared to say what might hurt the poor young man's feelings. However, he took it quite calmly— really, with the calm of despair, you might say. He sat up and said: 'Oh yes, there's no doubt of that: I have it here, in my room, locked up in my bag. You can come and look at it if you like: I won't offer to bring it here.'

We were not likely to let the chance slip. We went with him; his room was only a few doors off. The boots was just collecting shoes in the passage: or so we thought: afterwards we were not sure. Our visitor—his name was Paxton—was in a worse state of shivers than before, and went hurriedly into the room, and beckoned us after him, turned on the light, and shut the door carefully. Then he unlocked his kit-bag, and produced a bundle of clean pocket-handkerchiefs in which something was wrapped, laid it on the bed, and undid it. I can now say I *have* seen an actual Anglo-Saxon crown. It was of silver—as the Rendlesham one is always said to have been—it was set with some gems, mostly antique intaglios and cameos, and was of rather plain, almost rough workmanship. In fact, it was like those you see on the coins and in the manuscripts. I found no reason to think it was later than the ninth century. I was intensely interested, of course, and I wanted to turn it over in my hands, but Paxton prevented me. 'Don't *you* touch it,' he said, 'I'll do that.' And with a sigh that was, I declare to you, dreadful to hear, he took it up and turned it about so that we could see every part of it. 'Seen enough?' he said at last, and we nodded. He wrapped it up and locked it in his bag, and stood looking at us dumbly. 'Come back to our room,' Long said, 'and tell us what the trouble is.' He thanked us, and said: 'Will you go first and see if—if the coast is clear?' That wasn't very intelligible, for our proceedings hadn't been, after all, very suspicious, and the hotel, as I said, was practically empty. However, we were beginning to have inklings of—we didn't know what, and anyhow nerves are infectious. So we did go, first peering out as we opened the door, and fancying (I found we both had the fancy) that a shadow, or more than a shadow—but it made no sound—passed from before us to one side as we came out into the passage. 'It's all right,' we whispered to Paxton—whispering seemed the proper tone— and we went, with him between us, back to our sitting-room. I was preparing, when we got there, to be ecstatic about the unique interest of what we had seen, but when I looked at Paxton I saw that would be terribly out of place, and I left it to him to begin.

'What is to be done?' was his opening. Long thought it right (as he explained to me afterwards) to be obtuse, and said: 'Why not find out who the owner of the land is, and inform—' 'Oh, no, no!' Paxton broke in impatiently, 'I beg your pardon: you've been very kind, but don't you see it's *got* to go back, and I daren't be there at night, and daytime's impossible. Perhaps, though, you don't see: well, then, the truth is that I've never been alone since I touched it.' I was beginning some fairly stupid comment, but Long caught my eye, and I stopped. Long said: 'I think I do see, perhaps: but wouldn't it be—a relief— to tell us a little more clearly what the situation is?'

Then it all came out: Paxton looked over his shoulder and beckoned to us to come nearer to him, and began speaking in a low voice: we listened most intently, of course, and compared notes afterwards, and I wrote down our version, so I am confident I have what he told us almost word for word. He said: 'It began when I was first prospecting, and put me off again and again. There was always somebody—a man— standing by one of the firs. This was in daylight, you know. He was never in front of me. I always saw him with the tail of my eye on the left or the right, and he was never there when I looked straight for him. I would lie down for quite a long time and take careful observations, and make sure there was no one, and then when I got up and began prospecting again, there he was. And he began to give me hints, besides; for wherever I put that prayer-book—short of locking it up, which I did at last—when I came back to my room it was always out on my table open at the fly-leaf where the names are, and one of my razors across it to keep it open. I'm sure he just can't open my bag, or something more would have happened. You see, he's light and weak, but all the same I daren't face him. Well, then, when I was making the tunnel, of course it was worse, and if I hadn't been so keen I should have dropped the whole thing and run. It was like someone scraping at my back all the time: I thought for a long time it was only soil dropping on me, but as I got nearer the—the crown, it was unmistakable. And when I actually laid it bare and got my fingers into the ring of it and pulled it out, there came a sort of cry behind me—oh, I can't tell you how desolate it was! And horribly threatening too. It spoilt all my pleasure in my find—cut it off that moment. And if I hadn't been the wretched fool I am, I should have put the thing back and left it. But I didn't. The rest of the time was just awful. I had hours to get through before I could decently come back to the hotel. First I spent time filling up my tunnel and covering my tracks, and all the while he was there trying to thwart me. Sometimes, you know, you see him, and sometimes you don't, just as he pleases, I think: he's there, but he has some power over your eyes. Well, I wasn't off the spot very long before sunrise, and then I had to get to the junction for Seaburgh, and take a train back. And though it was daylight fairly soon, I don't know if that made it much better. There were always hedges, or gorse-bushes, or park fences along the road—some sort of cover, I mean—and I was never easy for a second. And then when I began to meet people going to work, they always looked behind me very strangely: it might have been that they were surprised at seeing anyone so early; but I didn't think it was only that, and I don't now: they didn't look exactly at *me*. And the porter at the train was like that too. And the guard held open the door after I'd got into the carriage—just as he would if there was somebody else coming, you know. Oh, you may be very sure it isn't my fancy,' he said with a dull sort of laugh. Then he went on: 'And even if I do get it put back, he won't forgive me: I can tell that. And I was so happy a fortnight ago.' He dropped into a chair, and I believe he began to cry.

We didn't know what to say, but we felt we must come to the rescue somehow, and so—it really seemed the only thing—we said if he was so set on putting the crown back in its place, we would help him. And I must say that after what we had heard it did seem the right thing. If these horrid consequences had come on this poor man, might there not really be something in the original idea of the crown having some curious power bound up with it, to guard the coast? At least, that was my feeling, and I think it was Long's too. Our offer was very welcome to Paxton, anyhow. When could we do it? It was nearing half-past ten. Could we contrive to make a late walk plausible to the hotel people that very night? We looked out of the window: there was a brilliant full moon—the Paschal moon. Long undertook to tackle the boots and propitiate him. He was to say that we should not be much over the hour, and if we did find it so pleasant that we stopped out a bit longer we would see that he didn't lose by sitting up. Well, we were pretty regular customers of the hotel, and did not give much trouble, and were considered by the servants to be not under the mark in the way of tips; and so the boots *was* propitiated, and let us out on to the sea-front, and remained, as we heard later, looking after us. Paxton had a large coat over his arm, under which was the wrapped-up crown.

217

So we were off on this strange errand before we had time to think how very much out of the way it was. I have told this part quite shortly on purpose, for it really does represent the haste with which we settled our plan and took action. 'The shortest way is up the hill and through the churchyard,' Paxton said, as we stood a moment before the hotel looking up and down the front. There was nobody about—nobody at all. Seaburgh out of the season is an early, quiet place. 'We can't go along the dyke by the cottage, because of the dog,' Paxton also said, when I pointed to what I thought a shorter way along the front and across two fields. The reason he gave was good enough. We went up the road to the church, and turned in at the churchyard gate. I confess to having thought that there might be some lying there who might be conscious of our business: but if it was so, they were also conscious that one who was on their side, so to say, had us under surveillance, and we saw no sign of them. But under observation we felt we were, as I have never felt it at another time. Specially was it so when we passed out of the churchyard into a narrow path with close high hedges, through which we hurried as Christian did through that Valley; and so got out into open fields. Then along hedges, though I would sooner have been in the open, where I could see if anyone was visible behind me; over a gate or two, and then a swerve to the left, taking us up on to the ridge which ended in that mound.

As we neared it, Henry Long felt, and I felt too, that there were what I can only call dim presences waiting for us, as well as a far more actual one attending us. Of Paxton's agitation all this time I can give you no adequate picture: he breathed like a hunted beast, and we could not either of us look at his face. How he would manage when we got to the very place we had not troubled to think: he had seemed so sure that that would not be difficult. Nor was it. I never saw anything like the dash with which he flung himself at a particular spot in the side of the mound, and tore at it, so that in a very few minutes the greater part of his body was out of sight. We stood holding the coat and that bundle of handkerchiefs, and looking, very fearfully, I must admit, about us. There was nothing to be seen: a line of dark firs behind us made one skyline, more trees and the church tower half a mile off on the right, cottages and a windmill on the horizon on the left, calm sea dead in front, faint barking of a dog at a cottage on a gleaming dyke between us and it: full moon making that path we know across the sea: the eternal whisper of the Scotch firs just above us, and of the sea in front. Yet, in all this quiet, an acute, an acrid consciousness of a restrained hostility very near us, like a dog on a leash that might be let go at any moment.

Paxton pulled himself out of the hole, and stretched a hand back to us. 'Give it to me,' he whispered, 'unwrapped.' We pulled off the handkerchiefs, and he took the crown. The moonlight just fell on it as he snatched it. We had not ourselves touched that bit of metal, and I have thought since that it was just as well. In another moment Paxton was out of the hole again and busy shovelling back the soil with hands that were already bleeding. He would have none of our help, though. It was much the longest part of the job to get the place to look undisturbed: yet—I don't know how—he made a wonderful success of it. At last he was satisfied, and we turned back.

We were a couple of hundred yards from the hill when Long suddenly said to him: 'I say, you've left your coat there. That won't do. See?' And I certainly did see it—the long dark overcoat lying where the tunnel had been. Paxton had not stopped, however: he only shook his head, and held up the coat on his arm. And when we joined him, he said, without any excitement, but as if nothing mattered any more: 'That wasn't my coat.' And, indeed, when we looked back again, that dark thing was not to be seen.

Well, we got out on to the road, and came rapidly back that way. It was well before twelve when we got in, trying to put a good face on it, and saying—Long and I—what a lovely night it was for a walk. The boots was on the look-out for us, and we made remarks like that for his edification as we entered the hotel. He gave another look up and down the sea-front before he locked the front door, and said: 'You didn't meet many people about, I s'pose, sir?' 'No, indeed, not a soul,' I said; at which I remember Paxton looked oddly at me. 'Only I thought I see someone turn up the station road after you gentlemen,' said the boots. 'Still, you was three together, and I don't suppose he meant mischief.' I didn't know what to say; Long merely said 'Good night,' and we went off upstairs, promising to turn out all lights, and to go to bed in a few minutes.

Back in our room, we did our very best to make Paxton take a cheerful view. 'There's the crown safe back,' we said; 'very likely you'd have done better not to touch it (and he heavily assented to that), 'but no real harm has been done, and we shall never give this away to anyone who would be so mad as to go near it. Besides, don't you feel better yourself? I don't mind confessing,' I said, 'that on the way there I was very much inclined to take your view about—well, about being followed; but going back, it wasn't at all the same thing, was it?' No, it wouldn't do: '*You've* nothing to trouble yourselves about,' he said, 'but I'm not forgiven. I've got to pay for that miserable sacrilege still. I know what you are going to say. The Church might help. Yes, but it's the body that has to suffer. It's true I'm not feeling that he's waiting outside for me just now. But—' Then he stopped. Then he turned to thanking us, and we put him off as soon as we could. And naturally we pressed him to use our sitting-room next day, and said we should be glad to go out with him. Or did he play golf, perhaps? Yes, he did, but he didn't think he should care about that tomorrow. Well, we recommended him to get up late and sit in our room in the morning while we were playing, and we would have a walk later in the day. He was very submissive and *piano* about it all: ready to do just what we thought best, but clearly quite certain in his own mind that what was coming could not be averted or palliated. You'll wonder why we didn't insist on accompanying him to his home and seeing him safe into the care of brothers or someone. The fact was he had nobody. He had had a flat in town, but lately he had made up his mind to settle for a time in Sweden, and he had dismantled his flat and shipped off his belongings, and was whiling away a fortnight or three weeks before he made a start. Anyhow, we didn't see what we could do better than sleep on it—or not sleep very much, as was my case—and see what we felt like tomorrow morning.

We felt very different, Long and I, on as beautiful an April morning as you could desire; and Paxton also looked very different when we saw him at breakfast. 'The first approach to a decent night I seem ever to have had,' was what he said. But he was going to do as we had settled: stay in probably all the morning, and come out with us later. We went to the links; we met some other men and played with them in the morning, and had lunch there rather early, so as not to be late back. All the same, the snares of death overtook him.

Whether it could have been prevented, I don't know. I think he would have been got at somehow, do what we might. Anyhow, this is what happened.

We went straight up to our room. Paxton was there, reading quite peaceably. 'Ready to come out shortly?' said Long, 'say in half an hour's time?' 'Certainly,' he said: and I said we would change first, and perhaps have baths, and call for him in half an hour. I had my bath first, and went and lay down on my bed, and slept for about ten minutes. We came out of our rooms at the same time, and went together to the sitting-room. Paxton wasn't there—only his book. Nor was he in his room, nor in the downstair rooms. We shouted for him. A servant came out and said: 'Why, I thought you gentlemen was gone out already, and so did the other gentleman. He heard you a-calling from the path there, and run out in a hurry, and I looked out of the coffee-room window, but I didn't see you. 'Owever, he run off down the beach that way.'

Without a word we ran that way too—it was the opposite direction to that of last night's expedition. It wasn't quite four o'clock, and the day was fair, though not so fair as it had been, so there was really no reason, you'd say, for anxiety: with people about, surely a man couldn't come to much harm.

But something in our look as we ran out must have struck the servant, for she came out on the steps, and pointed, and said, 'Yes, that's the way he went.' We ran on as far as the top of the shingle bank, and there pulled up. There was a choice of ways: past the houses on the sea-front, or along the sand at the bottom of the beach, which, the tide being now out, was fairly broad. Or of course we might keep along the shingle between these two tracks and have some view of both of them; only that was heavy going. We chose the sand, for that was the loneliest, and someone *might* come to harm there without being seen from the public path.

Long said he saw Paxton some distance ahead, running and waving his stick, as if he wanted to signal to people who were on ahead of him. I couldn't be sure: one of these sea-mists was coming up very quickly from the south. There was someone, that's all I could say. And there were tracks on the sand as of someone running who wore shoes; and there were other tracks made before those—for the shoes sometimes trod in them and interfered with them—of someone not in shoes. Oh, of course, it's only my word you've got to take for all this: Long's dead, we'd no time or means to make sketches or take casts, and the next tide washed everything away. All we could do was to notice these marks as we hurried on. But there they were over and over again, and we had no doubt whatever that what we saw was the track of a bare foot, and one that showed more bones than flesh.

The notion of Paxton running after—after anything like this, and supposing it to be the friends he was looking for, was very dreadful to us. You can guess what we fancied: how the thing he was following might stop suddenly and turn round on him, and what sort of face it would show, half-seen at first in the mist—which all the while was getting thicker and thicker. And as I ran on wondering how the poor wretch could have been lured into mistaking that other thing for us, I remembered his saying, 'He has some power over your eyes.' And then I wondered what the end would be, for I had no hope now that the end could be averted, and— well, there is no need to tell all the dismal and horrid thoughts that flitted through my head as we ran on into the mist. It was uncanny, too, that the sun should still be bright in the sky and we could see nothing. We could only tell that we were now past the houses and had reached that gap there is between them and the old martello tower. When you are past the tower, you know, there is nothing but shingle for a long way—not a house, not a human creature, just that spit of land, or rather shingle, with the river on your right and the sea on your left.

But just before that, just by the martello tower, you remember there is the old battery, close to the sea. I believe there are only a few blocks of concrete left now the rest has all been washed away, but at this time there was a lot more, though the place was a ruin. Well, when we got there, we clambered to the top as quick as we could to take breath and look over the shingle in front if by chance the mist would let us see anything. But a moment's rest we must have. We had run a mile at least. Nothing whatever was visible ahead of us, and we were just turning by common consent to get down and run hopelessly on, when we heard what I can only call a laugh: and if you can understand what I mean by a breathless, a lungless laugh, you have it: but I don't suppose you can. It came from below, and swerved away into the mist. That was enough. We bent over the wall. Paxton was there at the bottom.

You don't need to be told that he was dead. His tracks showed that he had run along the side of the battery, had turned sharp round the corner of it, and, small doubt of it, must have dashed straight into the open arms of someone who was waiting there. His mouth was full of sand and stones, and his teeth and jaws were broken to bits. I only glanced once at his face.

At the same moment, just as we were scrambling down from the battery to get to the body, we heard a shout, and saw a man running down the bank of the martello tower. He was the caretaker stationed there, and his keen old eyes had managed to descry through the mist that something was wrong. He had seen Paxton fall, and had seen us a moment after, running up—fortunate this, for otherwise we could hardly have escaped suspicion of being concerned in the dreadful business. Had he, we asked, caught sight of anybody attacking our friend? He could not be sure.

We sent him off for help, and stayed by the dead man till they came with the stretcher. It was then that we traced out how he had come, on the narrow fringe of sand under the battery wall. The rest was shingle, and it was hopelessly impossible to tell whither the other had gone.

What were we to say at the inquest? It was a duty, we felt, not to give up, there and then, the secret of the crown, to be published in every paper. I don't know how much you would have told; but what we did agree upon was this: to say that we had only made acquaintance with Paxton the day before, and that he had told us he was under some apprehension of danger at the hands of a man called William Ager. Also that we had seen some other tracks besides Paxton's when we followed him along the beach. But of course by that time everything was gone from the sands.

No one had any knowledge, fortunately, of any William Ager living in the district. The evidence of the man at the martello tower freed us from all suspicion. All that could be done was to return a verdict of wilful murder by some person or persons unknown.

Paxton was so totally without connections that all the inquiries that were subsequently made ended in a No Thoroughfare. And I have not been at Seaburgh, or even near it, since.

Notes

p. 211   *dykes* - mounds of earth that stop rivers, canals and drainage ditches flooding

p. 211   *Great Expectations* - the novel by Dickens

p. 211   *fir* - large evergreen tree

p. 212   *Bear* - an inn

p. 212   *Patience* - a card game for one

p. 213   *old arms of the kingdom of East Anglia* - arms – an emblem or crest as on a flag or badge; East Anglia was an ancient kingdom long before it became part of England

p. 213   *scholard* - scholar

p. 213   *warn't nothink* - it was nothing

p. 213   *ast* - ask

p. 213   *'oly* - holy

p. 213   *made out* - realised

p. 213   *tripper* - tourist

p. 214   *war of 1870* - war between France and Prussia, which resulted in Prussian victory, and the unification of Germany – a strong and possibly aggressive new power: for a time there were fears of invasion

p. 214   *South African War* - the 'Boer' wars which began in 1879

p. 215   *hillock* - small hill

p. 215   *yonder* - over there

p. 215   *barrows* - grave mounds

p. 229   *Jewel House* - very secure building at the heart of the Tower of London where the crown jewels are kept

p. 215   *treasure trove* - a 'find' of treasure might become the property of the owner of the land where it is found, or if over a certain value might become the property of the state – the one who digs it up has no natural right to it

p. 216   *intaglios and cameos* - decoratively carved gemstones

p. 216   *boots* - junior servant who cleans the boots at the Inn – who is also in charge of opening the door at night

p. 217   *looking after us* - watching from a distance

p. 218   *Christian . . . Valley* - a reference to the hero of John Bunyan's *The Pilgrim's Progress*, which is a parable of the soul's journey through life

p. 219   *links* - golf course

p. 221   *battery* - a fortified tower for heavy guns or cannon

23

Death in the Woods

(1926)

Sherwood Anderson

Anderson was an American writer who developed a spare stripped-down style that influenced Hemingway and many other American writers. In this story, a poor old woman struggles to keep her farm going, and one night carries a heavy load home from the nearby town, in a grim tale of hardship, poverty and endurance.

She was an old woman and lived on a farm near the town in which I lived. All country and small-town people have seen such old women, but no one knows much about them. Such an old woman comes into town driving an old worn-out horse or she comes afoot carrying a basket. She may own a few hens and have eggs to sell. She brings them in a basket and takes them to a grocer. There she trades them in. She gets some salt pork and some beans. Then she gets a pound or two of sugar and some flour.

Afterwards she goes to the butcher's and asks for some dog-meat. She may spend ten or fifteen cents, but when she does she asks for something. Formerly the butchers gave liver to any one who wanted to carry it away. In our family we were always having it. Once one of my brothers got a whole cow's liver at the slaughter-house near the fairgrounds in our town. We had it until we were sick of it. It never cost a cent. I have hated the thought of it ever since.

The old farm woman got some liver and a soup-bone. She never visited with any one, and as soon as she got what she wanted she lit out for home. It made quite a load for such an old body. No one gave her a lift. People drive right down a road and never notice an old woman like that.

There was such an old woman who used to come into town past our house one Summer and Fall when I was a young boy and was sick with what was called inflammatory rheumatism. She went home later carrying a heavy pack on her back. Two or three large gaunt-looking dogs followed at her heels.

The old woman was nothing special. She was one of the nameless ones that hardly any one knows, but she got into my thoughts. I have just suddenly now, after all these years, remembered her and what happened. It is a story. Her name was Grimes, and she lived with her husband and son in a small unpainted house on the bank of a small creek four miles from town.

The husband and son were a tough lot. Although the son was but twenty-one, he had already served a term in jail. It was whispered about that the woman's husband stole horses and ran them off to some other county. Now and then, when a horse turned up missing, the man had also disappeared. No one ever caught him. Once, when I was loafing at Tom Whitehead's livery-barn, the man came there and sat on the bench in front. Two or three other men were there, but no one spoke to him. He sat for a few minutes and then got up and went away. When he was leaving he turned around and stared at the men. There was a look of defiance in his eyes. "Well, I have tried to be friendly. You don't want to talk to me. It has been so wherever I have gone in this town. If, some day, one of your fine horses turns up missing, well, then what?" He did not say anything actually. "I'd like to bust one of you on the jaw," was about what his eyes said. I remember how the look in his eyes made me shiver.

The old man belonged to a family that had had money once. His name was Jake Grimes. It all comes back clearly now. His father, John Grimes, had owned a sawmill when the country was new, and had made money. Then he got to drinking and running after women. When he died there wasn't much left.

Jake blew in the rest. Pretty soon there wasn't any more lumber to cut and his land was nearly all gone.

He got his wife off a German farmer, for whom he went to work one June day in the wheat harvest. She was a young thing then and scared to death. You see, the farmer was up to something with the girl—she was, I think, a bound girl and his wife had her suspicions. She took it out on the girl when the man wasn't around. Then, when the wife had to go off to town for supplies, the farmer got after her. She told young Jake that nothing really ever happened, but he didn't know whether to believe it or not.

He got her pretty easy himself, the first time he was out with her. He wouldn't have married her if the German farmer hadn't tried to tell him where to get off. He got her to go riding with him in his buggy one night when he was threshing on the place, and then he came for her the next Sunday night.

She managed to get out of the house without her employer's seeing, but when she was getting into the buggy he showed up. It was almost dark, and he just popped up suddenly at the horse's head. He grabbed the horse by the bridle and Jake got out his buggy-whip.

They had it out all right! The German was a tough, one. Maybe he didn't care whether his wife knew or not. Jake hit him over the face and shoulders with the buggy-whip, but the horse got to acting up and he had to get out.

Then the two men went for it. The girl didn't see it. The horse started to run away and went nearly a mile down the road before the girl got him stopped. Then she managed tie him to a tree beside the road. (I wonder how I know all this. It must have stuck in my mind from small-town tales when I was a boy.) Jake found her there after he got through with the German. She was huddled up in the buggy seat, crying, scared to death. She told Jake a lot of stuff, how the German had tried to get her, how he chased her once, into the barn, how another time, when they happened to be alone in the house together, he tore her dress open clear down the front. The German, she said, might have got her that time if he hadn't heard his old woman drive in at the gate. She had been off to town for supplies. Well, she would be putting the horse in the barn. The German managed to sneak off to the fields without his wife seeing. He told the girl he would kill her if she told. What could she do? She told a lie about ripping her dress in the barn when she was feeding the stock. I remember now that she was a bound girl and did not know where her father and mother were. Maybe she did not have any father. You know what I mean.

Such bound children were often enough cruelly treated. They were children who had no parents, slaves really. There were very few orphan homes then. They were legally bound into some home. It was a matter of pure luck how it came out.

II

She married Jake and had a son and daughter, but the daughter died.

Then she settled down to feed stock. That was her job. At the German's place she had cooked the food for the German and his wife. The wife was a strong woman, with big hips and worked most of the time in the fields with her husband. She fed them and fed the cows in the barn, fed the pigs, the horses and the chickens. Every moment of every day, as a young girl, was spent feeding something.

Then she married Jake Grimes and he had to be fed. She was a slight thing, and when she had been married for three or four years, and after the two children were born, her slender shoulders became stooped.

Jake always had a lot of big dogs around the house, that stood near the unused sawmill near the creek. He was always trading horses when he wasn't stealing something and had a lot of poor bony ones about. Also he kept three or four pigs and a cow. They were all pastured in the few acres left of the Grimes place and Jake did little enough work.

He went into debt for a threshing outfit and ran it for several years, but it did not pay. People did not trust him. They were afraid he would steal the grain at night. He had to go a long way off to get work and it cost too much to get there. In the Winter he hunted and cut a little firewood, to be sold in some nearby town. When the son grew up he was just like the father. They got drunk together. If there wasn't anything to eat in the house when they came home the old man gave his old woman a cut over the head. She had a few chickens of her own and had to kill one of them in a hurry. When they were all killed she wouldn't have any eggs to sell when she went to town, and then what would she do?

She had to scheme all her life about getting things fed, getting the pigs fed so they would grow fat and could be butchered in the Fall. When they were butchered her husband took most of the meat off to town and sold it. If he did not do it first the boy did. They fought sometimes and when they fought the old woman stood aside trembling.

She had got the habit of silence anyway—that was fixed. Sometimes, when she began to look old—she wasn't forty yet —and when the husband and son were both off, trading horses or drinking or hunting or stealing, she went around the house and the barnyard muttering to herself.

How was she going to get everything fed?—that was her problem. The dogs had to be fed. There wasn't enough hay in the barn for the horses and the cow. If she didn't feed the chickens how could they lay eggs? Without eggs to sell how could she get things in town, things she had to have to keep the life of the farm going? Thank heaven, she did not have to feed her husband—in a certain way. That hadn't lasted long after their marriage and after the babies came. Where he went on his long trips she did not know. Sometimes he was gone from home for weeks, and after the boy grew up they went off together.

They left everything at home for her to manage and she had no money. She knew no one. No one ever talked to her in town. When it was Winter she had to gather sticks of wood for her fire, had to try to keep the stock fed with very little grain.

The stock in the barn cried to her hungrily, the dogs followed her about. In the Winter the hens laid few enough eggs. They huddled in the corners of the barn and she kept watching them. If a hen lays an egg in the barn in the Winter and you do not find it, it freezes and breaks.

One day in Winter the old woman went off to town with a few eggs and the dogs followed her. She did not get started until nearly three o'clock and the snow was heavy. She hadn't been feeling very well for several days and so she went muttering along, scantily clad, her shoulders stooped. She had an old grain bag in which she carried her eggs, tucked away down in the bottom. There weren't many of them, but in Winter the price of eggs is up. She would get a little meat in exchange for the eggs, some salt pork, a little sugar, and some coffee perhaps. It might be the butcher would give her a piece of liver.

When she had got to town and was trading in her eggs the dogs lay by the door outside. She did pretty well, got the things she needed, more than she had hoped. Then she went to the butcher and he gave her some liver and some dog-meat.

It was the first time any one had spoken to her in a friendly way for a long time. The butcher was alone in his shop when she came in and was annoyed by the thought of such a sick-looking old woman out on such a day. It was bitter cold and the snow, that had let up during the afternoon, was falling again. The butcher said something about her husband and her son, swore at them, and the old woman stared at him, a, look of mild surprise in her eyes as he talked. He said that if either the husband or the son were going to get any of the liver or the heavy bones with scraps of meat hanging to them that he had put into the grain bag, he'd see him starve first.

Starve, eh? Well, things had to be fed. Men had to be fed, and the horses that weren't any good but maybe could be traded off, and the poor thin cow that hadn't given any milk for three months.

Horses, cows, pigs, dogs, men.

III

The old woman had to get back before darkness came if she could. The dogs followed at her heels, sniffing at the heavy grain bag she had fastened on her back. When she got to the edge of town she stopped by a fence and tied the bag on her back with a piece of rope she had carried in her dress-pocket for just that purpose. That was an easier way to carry it. Her arms ached. It was hard when she had to crawl over fences and once she fell over and landed in the snow. The dogs went frisking about. She had to struggle to get to her feet again, but she made it. The point of climbing over the fences was that there was a short cut over a hill and through a woods. She might have gone around by the road, but it was a mile farther that way. She was afraid she couldn't make it. And then, besides, the stock had to be fed. There was a little hay left and a little corn. Perhaps her husband and son would bring some home when they came. They had driven off in the only buggy the Grimes family had, a rickety thing, a rickety horse hitched to the buggy, two other rickety horses led by halters. They were going to trade horses, get a little money if they could. They might come home drunk. It would be well to have something in the house when they came back.

The son had an affair on with a woman at the county seat, fifteen miles away. She was a rough enough woman, a tough one. Once, in the Summer, the son had brought her to the house. Both she and the son had been drinking. Jake Grimes was away and the son and his woman ordered the old woman about like a servant. She didn't mind much; she was used to it. Whatever happened she never said anything. That was her way of getting along. She had managed that way when she was a young girl at the German's and ever since she had married Jake. That time her son brought his woman to the house they stayed all night, sleeping together just as though they were married. It hadn't shocked the old woman, not much. She had got past being shocked early in life.

With the pack on her back she went painfully along across an open field, wading in the deep snow, and got into the woods.

There was a path, but it was hard to follow. Just beyond the top of the hill, where the woods was thickest, there was a small clearing. Had some one once thought of building a house there? The clearing was as large as a building lot in town, large enough for a house and a garden. The path ran along the side of the clearing, and when she got there the old woman sat down to rest at the foot of a tree.

It was a foolish thing to do. When she got herself placed, the pack against the tree's trunk, it was nice, but what about getting up again? She worried about that for a moment and then quietly closed her eyes.

She must have slept for a time. When you are about so cold you can't get any colder. The afternoon grew a little warmer and the snow came thicker than ever. Then after a time the weather cleared. The moon even came out.

There were four Grimes dogs that had followed Mrs. Grimes into town, all tall gaunt fellows. Such men as Jake Grimes and his son always keep just such dogs. They kick and abuse them, but they stay. The Grimes dogs, in order to keep from starving, had to do a lot of foraging for themselves, and they had been at it while the old woman slept with her back to the tree at the side of the clearing. They had been chasing rabbits in the woods, and in adjoining fields and in their ranging had picked up three other farm dogs.

After a time all the dogs came back to the clearing. They were excited about something. Such nights, cold and clear and with a moon, do things to dogs. It may be that some old instinct, come down from the time when they were wolves and ranged the woods in packs on Winter nights, comes back into them.

The dogs in the clearing, before the old woman, had caught two or three rabbits and their immediate hunger had been satisfied. They began to play, running in circles in the clearing. Round and round they ran, each dog's nose at the tail of the next dog. In the clearing, under the snow-laden trees and under the wintry moon they made a strange picture, running thus silently, in a circle their running had beaten in the soft snow. The dogs made no sound. They ran around and around in the circle.

It may have been that the old woman saw them doing that before she died. She may have awakened once or twice and looked at the strange sight with dim old eyes.

She wouldn't be very cold now, just drowsy. Life hangs on a long time. Perhaps the old woman was out of her head. She may have dreamed of her girlhood, at the German's, and before that, when she was a child and before her mother lit out and left her.

Her dreams couldn't have been very pleasant. Not many pleasant things had happened to her. Now and then one of the Grimes dogs left the running circle and came to stand before her. The dog thrust his face close to her face. His red tongue was hanging out .

The running of the dogs may have been a kind of death ceremony. It may have been that the primitive instinct of the wolf, having been aroused in the dogs by the night and the running, made them somehow afraid.

"Now we are no longer wolves. We are dogs, the servants of men. Keep alive, man! When man dies we becomes wolves again."

When one of the dogs came to where the old woman sat with her back against the tree and thrust his nose close to her face he seemed satisfied and went back to run with the pack. All the Grimes dogs did it at some time during: the evening, before she died. I knew all about it afterward, when I grew to be a man, because once in a woods in Illinois, on another winter night, I saw a pack of dogs act just like that. The dogs were waiting for me to die as they had waited for the old woman that night when I was a child, but when it happened to me I was a young man and had no intention whatever of dying.

The old woman died softly and quietly. When she was dead and when one of the Grimes dogs had come to her and had found her dead all the dogs stopped running.

They gathered about her.

Well, she was dead now. She had fed the Grimes dogs when she was alive, what about now?

There was the pack on her back, the grain bag containing the piece of salt pork, the liver the butcher had given her, the dog-meat, the soup bones. The butcher in town, having been suddenly overcome with a feeling of pity, had loaded her grain bag heavily. It had been a big haul for the old woman.

It was a big haul for the dogs now.

IV

One of the Grimes dogs sprang suddenly out from among the others and began worrying the pack on the old woman's back. Had the dogs really been wolves that one would have been the leader of the pack. What he did, all the others did.

All of them sank their teeth into the grain bag the old woman had fastened with ropes to her back.

They dragged the old woman's body out into the open clearing. The worn-out dress was quickly torn from her shoulders. When she was found, a day or two later, the dress had been torn from her body clear to the hips, but the dogs had not touched her body. They had got the meat out of the grain bag, that was all. Her body was frozen stiff when it was found, and the shoulders were so narrow and the body so slight that in death it looked like the body of some charming young girl.

Such things happened in towns of the Middle West, on farms near town, when I was a boy. A hunter out after rabbits found the old woman's body and did not touch it. Something, the beaten round path in the little snow-covered clearing, the silence of the place, the place where the dogs had worried the body trying to pull the grain bag away or tear it open—something startled the man and he hurried off to town.

I was in Main street with one of my brothers who was town newsboy and who was taking the afternoon papers to the stores. It was almost night.

The hunter came into a grocery and told his story. Then he went to a hardware-shop and into a drugstore. Men began to gather on the sidewalks. Then they started out along the road to the place in the woods.

My brother should have gone on about his business of distributing papers but he didn't. Every one was going to the woods. The undertaker went and the town marshal. Several men got on a dray and rode out to where the path left the road and went into the woods, but the horses weren't very sharply shod and slid about on the slippery roads. They made no better time than those of us who walked.

The town marshal was a large man whose leg had been injured in the Civil War. He carried a heavy cane and limped rapidly along the road. My brother and I followed at his heels, and as we went other men and boys joined the crowd.

It had grown dark by the time we got to where the old woman had left the road but the moon had come out. The marshal was thinking there might have been a murder. He kept asking the hunter questions. The hunter went along with his gun across his shoulders, a dog following at his heels. It isn't often a rabbit hunter has a chance to be so conspicuous. He was taking full advantage of it, leading the procession with the town marshal. "I didn't see any wounds. She was a beautiful young girl. Her face was buried in the snow. No, I didn't know her." As a matter of fact, the hunter had not looked closely at the body. He had been frightened. She might have been murdered and some one might spring out from behind a tree and murder him. In a woods, in the late afternoon, when the trees are all bare and there is white snow on the ground, when all is silent, something creepy steals over the mind and body. If something strange or uncanny has happened in the neighborhood all you think about is getting away from there as fast as you can.

The crowd of men and boys had got to where the old woman had crossed thc field and went, following the marshal and the hunter, up the slight incline and into the woods.

My brother and I were silent. He had his bundle of papers in a bag slung across his shoulder. When he got back to town he would have to go on distributing his papers before he went home to supper. If I went along, as he had no doubt already determined I should, we would both be late. Either mother or our older sister would have to warm our supper.

Well, we would have something to tell. A boy did not get such a chance very often. It was lucky we just happened to go into the grocery when the hunter came in. The hunter was a country fellow. Neither of us had ever seen him before.

Now the crowd of men and boys had got to the clearing. Darkness comes quickly on such Winter nights, but the full moon made everything clear. My brother and I stood near the tree, beneath which the old woman had died.

She did not look old, lying there in that light, frozen and still. One of the men turned her over in the snow and I saw everything. My body trembled with some strange mystical feeling and so did my brother's. It might have been the cold.

Neither of us had ever seen a woman's body before. It may have been the snow, clinging to the frozen flesh; that made it look so white and lovely, so like marble. No woman had come with the party from town; but one of the men, he was the town blacksmith, took off his overcoat and spread it over her. Then he gathered her into his arms and started off to town, all the others following silently. At that time no one knew who she was.

V

I had seen everything, had seen the oval in the snow, like a miniature race-track, where the dogs had run, had seen how the men were mystified, had seen the white bare young looking shoulders, had heard the whispered comments of the men.

The men were simply mystified. They took the body to the undertaker's, and when the blacksmith, the hunter, the marshal and several others had got inside they closed the door. If father had been there perhaps he could have got in, but we boys couldn't.

I went with my brother to distribute the rest of his papers and when we got home it was my brother who told the story.

I kept silent and went to bed early. It may have been I was not satisfied with the way he told it.

Later, in the town, I must have heard other fragments of the old woman's story. She was recognized the next day and there was an investigation.

The husband and son were found somewhere and brought to town and there was an attempt to connect them with the woman's death, but it did not work. They had perfect enough alibis.

However, the town was against them. They had to get out. Where they went I never heard.

I remember only the picture there in the forest, the men standing about, the naked girlish-looking figure, face down in the snow, the tracks made by the running dogs and the clear cold Winter sky above. White fragments of clouds were drifting across the sky. They went racing across the little open space among the trees.

The scene in the forest had become for me, without my knowing it, the foundation for the real story I am now trying to tell. The fragments, you see, had to be picked up slowly, long afterwards.

Things happened. When I was a young man I worked on the farm of a German. The hired-girl was afraid of her employer. The farmer's wife hated her.

I saw things at that place. Once later, I had a half-uncanny, mystical adventure with dogs in an Illinois forest on a clear, moon-lit Winter night. When I was a schoolboy, and on a Summer day, I went with a boy friend out along a creek some miles from town and came to the house where the old woman had lived. No one had lived in the house since her death. The doors were broken from, the hinges; the window lights were all broken. As the boy and I stood in the road outside, two dogs, just roving farm dogs no doubt, came running around the corner of the house. The dogs were tall, gaunt fellows and came down to the fence and glared through at us, standing in the road.

The whole thing, the story of the old woman's death, was to me as I grew older like music heard from far off. The notes had to be picked up slowly one at a time. Something had to be understood.

The woman who died was one destined to feed animal life. Anyway, that is all she ever did. She was feeding animal life before she was born, as a child, as a young woman working on the farm of the German, after she married, when she grew old and when she died. She fed animal life in cows, in chickens, in pigs, in horses, in dogs, in men. Her daughter had died in childhood and with her one son she had no articulate relations. On the night when she died she was hurrying homeward, bearing on her body food for animal life.

She died in the clearing in the woods and even after her death continued feeding animal life.

You see it is likely that, when my brother told the story, that night when we got home and my mother and sister sat listening, I did not think he got the point. He was too young and so was I. A thing so complete has its own beauty.

I shall not try to emphasize the point. I am only explaining why I was dissatisfied then and have been ever since. I speak of that only that you may understand why I have been impelled to try to tell the simple story over again.

Notes

p. 224   *livery barn* - stables
p. 224   *sawmill* - for producing wood
p. 224   *blew in* - wasted
p. 224   *bound girl* - type of servant bound by law to an employer and little better than a slave
p. 224   *threshing* - separating the grain of wheat from the chaff – the inedible husk
p. 229   *drugstore* - small shop
p. 229   *dray* - a small horse-drawn cart for delivering goods

24

Indian Summer of an Uncle

(1930)

P.G. Wodehouse

P.G. Wodehouse was a great British comic writer and master of style. His Jeeves and Wooster stories, mostly set in and around the smart part of London in the early twentieth century, are his most celebrated work. They feature the rather idle and apparently dim-witted, but jovial, wealthy 'man-about-town' Wooster, and his 'gentleman's gentleman'– a personal servant or valet, Jeeves, who is staggeringly clever. Here, Wooster's uncle contemplates an 'unsuitable' marriage and Wooster is deputed to extricate him, but, of course, has to rely on Jeeves's brilliant planning to bring happy resolutions all round.

Ask anyone at the Drones, and they will tell you that Bertram Wooster is a fellow whom it is dashed difficult to deceive. Old Lynx-Eye is about what it amounts to. I observe and deduce. I weigh the evidence and draw my conclusions. And that is why Uncle George had not been in my midst more than about two minutes before I, so to speak, saw all. To my trained eye the thing stuck out a mile.

And yet it seemed so dashed absurd. Consider the facts, if you know what I mean.

I mean to say, for years, right back to the time when I first went to school, this bulging relative had been one of the recognized eyesores of London. He was fat then, and day by day in every way has been getting fatter ever since, till now tailors measure him just for the sake of the exercise. He is what they call a prominent London clubman – one of those birds in tight morning-coats and grey toppers whom you see toddling along St James's Street on fine afternoons, puffing a bit as they make the grade. Slip a ferret into any good club between Piccadilly and Pall Mall, and you would start half a dozen Uncle Georges.

He spends his time lunching and dining at the Buffers and, between meals, sucking down spots in the smoking-room and talking to anyone who will listen about the lining of his stomach. About twice a year his liver lodges a formal protest and he goes off to Harrogate or Carlsbad to get planed down. Then back again and on with the programme. The last bloke in the world, in short, who you would think would ever fall a victim to the divine pash. And yet, if you will believe me, that was absolutely the strength of it.

This old pestilence blew in on me one morning at about the hour of the after-breakfast cigarette.

'Oh, Bertie,' he said.

'Hullo?'

'You know those ties you've been wearing. Where did you get them?'

'Blucher's, in the Burlington Arcade.'

'Thanks.'

He walked across to the mirror and stood in front of it, gazing at himself in an earnest manner.

'Smut on your nose?' I asked courteously.

Then I suddenly perceived that he was wearing a sort of horrible simper, and I confess it chilled the blood to no little extent. Uncle George, with face in repose, is hard enough on the eye. Simpering, he goes right above the odds.

'Ha!' he said.

He heaved a long sigh, and turned away. Not too soon, for the mirror was on the point of cracking.

'I'm not so old,' he said, in a musing sort of voice.

'So old as what?'

'Properly considered, I'm in my prime. Besides, what a young and inexperienced girl needs is a man of weight and years to lean on. The sturdy oak, not the sapling.'

It was at this point that, as I said above, I saw all.

'Great Scott, Uncle George!' I said. 'You aren't thinking of getting married?'

'Who isn't?' he said.

'You aren't,' I said.

'Yes, I am. Why not?'

'Oh, well –'

'Marriage is an honourable state.'

'Oh, absolutely.'

'It might make you a better man, Bertie.'

'Who says so?'

'I say so. Marriage might turn you from a frivolous young scallywag into – er – a non-scallywag. Yes, confound you, I *am* thinking of getting married, and if Agatha comes sticking her oar in I'll – I'll – well, I shall know what to do about it.'

He exited on the big line, and I rang the bell for Jeeves. The situation seemed to me one that called for a cosy talk.

'Jeeves,' I said.

'Sir?'

'You know my Uncle George?'

'Yes, sir. His lordship has been familiar to me for some years.'

'I don't mean do you know my Uncle George. I mean do you know what my Uncle George is thinking of doing?'

'Contracting a matrimonial alliance, sir.'

'Good Lord! Did he tell you?'

'No, sir. Oddly enough, I chance to be acquainted with the other party in the matter.'

'The girl?'

'The young person, yes, sir. It was from her aunt, with whom she resides, that I received the information that his lordship was contemplating matrimony.'

'Who is she?'

'A Miss Platt, sir. Miss Rhoda Platt. Of Wistaria Lodge, Kitchener Road, East Dulwich.'

'Young?'

'Yes, sir.'

'The old fathead!'

'Yes, sir. The expression is one which I would, of course, not have ventured to employ myself, but I confess to thinking his lordship somewhat ill-advised. One must remember, however, that it is not unusual to find gentlemen of a certain age yielding to what might be described as a sentimental urge. They appear to experience what I may term a sort of Indian summer, a kind of temporarily renewed youth. The phenomenon is particularly noticeable, I am given to understand, in the United States of America among the wealthier inhabitants of the city of Pittsburgh. It is notorious, I am told, that sooner or later, unless restrained, they always endeavour to marry chorus-girls. Why this should be so, I am at a loss to say, but –'

I saw that this was going to take some time. I tuned out.

'From something in Uncle George's manner, Jeeves, as he referred to my Aunt Agatha's probable reception of the news, I gather that this Miss Platt is not of the *noblesse*.'

'No, sir. She is a waitress at his lordship's club.'

'My God! The proletariat!'

'The lower middle classes, sir.'

'Well, yes, by stretching it a bit, perhaps. Still, you know what I mean.'

'Yes, sir.'

'Rummy thing, Jeeves,' I said thoughtfully, 'this modern tendency to marry waitresses. If you remember, before he settled down, young Bingo Little was repeatedly trying to do it.'

'Yes, sir.'

'Odd!'

'Yes, sir.'

'Still, there it is, of course. The point to be considered now is, what will Aunt Agatha do about this? You know her, Jeeves. She is not like me. I'm broad-minded. If Uncle George wants to marry waitresses, let him, say I. I hold that the rank is but the penny stamp –'

'Guinea stamp, sir.'

'All right, guinea stamp. Though I don't believe there is such a thing. I shouldn't have thought they came higher than five bob. Well, as I was saying, I maintain that the rank is but the guinea stamp and a girl's a girl for all that.'

'"For *a'* that," sir. The poet Burns wrote in the North British dialect.'

'Well, "a' that," then, if you prefer it.'

'I have no preference in the matter, sir. It is simply that the poet Burns –'

'Never mind about the poet Burns.'

'No, sir.'

'Forget the poet Burns.'

'Very good, sir.'

'Expunge the poet Burns from your mind.'

'I will do so immediately, sir.'

'What we have to consider is not the poet Burns but the Aunt Agatha. She will kick, Jeeves.'

'Very probably, sir.'

'And, what's worse, she will lug me into the mess. There is only one thing to be done. Pack the toothbrush and let us escape while we may, leaving no address.'

'Very good, sir.'

At this moment the bell rang.

'Ha!' I said. 'Someone at the door.'

'Yes, sir.'

'Probably Uncle George back again. I'll answer it. You go and get ahead with the packing.'

'Very good, sir.'

I sauntered along the passage, whistling carelessly, and there on the mat was Aunt Agatha. Herself. Not a picture.

A nasty jar.

'Oh, hullo!' I said, it seeming but little good to tell her I was out of town and not expected back for some weeks.

'I wish to speak to you, Bertie,' said the Family Curse. 'I am greatly upset.'

She legged it into the sitting-room and volplaned into a chair. I followed, thinking wistfully of Jeeves packing in the bedroom. That suitcase would not be needed now. I knew what she must have come about.

'I've just seen Uncle George,' I said, giving her a lead.

'So have I,' said Aunt Agatha, shivering in a marked manner. 'He called on me while I was still in bed to inform me of his intention of marrying some impossible girl from South Norwood.'

'East Dulwich, the *cognoscente* informed me.'

'Well, East Dulwich, then. It is the same thing. But who told you?'

'Jeeves.'

'And how, pray, does Jeeves come to know all about it?'

'There are very few things in this world, Aunt Agatha,' I said gravely, 'that Jeeves doesn't know all about. He's met the girl.'

'Who is she?'

'One of the waitresses at the Buffers.'

I had expected this to register and it did. The relative let out a screech rather like the Cornish Express going through a junction.

'I take it from your manner, Aunt Agatha,' I said, 'that you want this thing stopped.'

'Of course it must be stopped.'

'Then there is but one policy to pursue. Let me ring for Jeeves and ask his advice.'

Aunt Agatha stiffened visibly. Very much the *grande dame* of the old *régime*.

'Are you seriously suggesting that we should discuss this intimate family matter with your man-servant?'

'Absolutely. Jeeves will find the way.'

'I have always known that you were an imbecile, Bertie,' said the flesh-and-blood, now down at about three degrees Fahrenheit, 'but I did suppose that you had some proper feeling, some pride, some respect for your position.'

'Well, you know what the poet Burns says.'

She squelched me with a glance.

'Obviously the only thing to do,' she said, 'is to offer this girl money.'

'Money?'

'Certainly. It will not be the first time your uncle has made such a course necessary.'

We sat for a bit, brooding. The family always sits brooding when the subject of Uncle George's early romance comes up. I was too young to be actually in on it at the time, but I've had the details frequently from many sources, including Uncle George. Let him get even the slightest bit pickled, and he will tell you the whole story, sometimes twice in an evening. It was a barmaid at the Criterion, just before he came into the title. Her name was Maudie and he loved her dearly, but the family would have none of it. They dug down into the sock and paid her off. Just one of those human-interest stories, if you know what I mean.

I wasn't so sold on this money-offering scheme.

'Well, just as you like, of course,' I said, 'but you're taking an awful chance. I mean, whenever people do it in novels and plays, they always get the dickens of a welt. The girl gets the sympathy of the audience every time. She just draws herself up and looks at them with clear, steady eyes, causing them to feel not a little cheesy. If I were you, I would sit tight and let Nature take its course.'

'I don't understand you.'

'Well, consider for a moment what Uncle George looks like. No Greta Garbo, believe me. I should simply let the girl go on looking at him. Take it from me, Aunt Agatha, I've studied human nature and I don't believe there's a female in the world who could see Uncle George fairly often in those waistcoats he wears without feeling that it was due to her better self to give him the gate. Besides, this girl sees him at meal-times, and Uncle George with his head down among the food-stuffs is a spectacle which –'

'If it is not troubling you too much, Bertie, I should be greatly obliged if you would stop drivelling.'

'Just as you say. All the same, I think you're going to find it dashed embarrassing, offering this girl money.'

'I am not proposing to do so. *You* will undertake the negotiations.'

'Me?'

'Certainly. I should think a hundred pounds would be ample. But I will give you a blank cheque, and you are at liberty to fill it in for a higher sum if it becomes necessary. The essential point is that, cost what it may, your uncle must be released from this entanglement.'

'So you're going to shove this off on me?'

'It is quite time you did something for the family.'

'And when she draws herself up and looks at me with clear, steady eyes, what do I do for an encore?'

'There is no need to discuss the matter any further. You can get down to East Dulwich in half an hour. There is a frequent service of trains, I will remain here to await your report.'

'But, listen!'

'Bertie, you will go and see this woman immediately.'

'Yes, but dash it!'

'Bertie!'

I threw in the towel.

'Oh, right ho, if you say so.'

'I do say so.'

'Oh, well, in that case, right ho.'

I don't know if you have ever tooled off to East Dulwich to offer a strange female a hundred smackers to release your Uncle George. In case you haven't, I may tell you that there are plenty of things that are lots better fun. I didn't feel any too good driving to the station. I didn't feel any too good in the train. And I didn't feel any too good as I walked to Kitchener Road. But the moment when I felt least good was when I had actually pressed the front-door bell and a rather grubby-looking maid had let me in and shown me down a passage and into a room with pink paper on the walls, a piano in the corner and a lot of photographs on the mantelpiece.

Barring a dentist's waiting-room, which it rather resembles, there isn't anything that quells the spirit much more than one of these suburban parlours. They are extremely apt to have stuffed birds in glass cases standing about on small tables, and if there is one thing which gives the man of sensibility that sinking feeling it is the cold, accusing eye of a ptarmigan or whatever it may be that has had its interior organs removed and sawdust substituted.

There were three of these cases in the parlour of Wistaria Lodge, so that, wherever you looked, you were sure to connect. Two were singletons, the third a family group, consisting of a father bullfinch, a mother bullfinch, and little Master Bullfinch, the last-named of whom wore an expression that was definitely that of a thug, and did more to damp my *joie de vivre* than all the rest of them put together.

I had moved to the window and was examining the aspidistra in order to avoid this creature's gaze, when I heard the door open and, turning, found myself confronted by something which, since it could hardly be the girl, I took to be the aunt.

'Oh, what ho,' I said. 'Good morning.'

The words came out rather roopily, for I was feeling a bit on the stunned side. I meant to say, the room being so small and this exhibit so large, I had got that sensation of wanting air. There are some people who don't seem to be intended to be seen close to, and this aunt was one of them. Billowy curves, if you know what I mean. I should think that in her day she must have been a very handsome girl, though even then on the substantial side. By the time she came into my life, she had taken on a good deal of excess weight. She looked like a photograph of an opera singer of the 'eighties. Also the orange hair and the magenta dress.

However, she was a friendly soul. She seemed glad to see Bertram. She smiled broadly.

'So here you are at last!' she said.

I couldn't make anything of this.

'Eh?'

'But I don't think you had better see my niece just yet. She's just having a nap.'

'Oh, in that case –'

'Seems a pity to wake her, doesn't it?'

'Oh, absolutely,' I said, relieved.

'When you get the influenza, you don't sleep at night, and then if you doze off in the morning – well, it seems a pity to wake someone, doesn't it?'

'Miss Platt has influenza?'

'That's what we think it is. But, of course, you'll be able to say. But we needn't waste time. Since you're here, you can be taking a look at my knee.'

'Your knee?'

I am all for knees at their proper time and, as you might say, in their proper place, but somehow this didn't seem the moment. However, she carried on according to plan.

'What do you think of that knee?' she asked, lifting the seven veils.

Well, of course, one has to be polite.

'Terrific!' I said.

'You wouldn't believe how it hurts me sometimes.'

'Really?'

'A sort of shooting pain. It just comes and goes. And I'll tell you a funny thing.'

'What's that?' I said, feeling I could do with a good laugh.

'Lately I've been having the same pain just here, at the end of the spine.'

'You don't mean it!'

'I do. Like red-hot needles. I wish you'd have a look at it.'

'At your spine?'

'Yes.'

I shook my head. Nobody is fonder of a bit of fun than myself, and I am all for Bohemian camaraderie and making a party go, and all that. But there is a line, and we Woosters know when to draw it.

'It can't be done,' I said austerely. 'Not spines. Knees, yes. Spines, no,' I said.

She seemed surprised.

'Well,' she said, 'you're a funny sort of doctor, I must say.'

I'm pretty quick, as I said before, and I began to see that something in the nature of a misunderstanding must have arisen.

'Doctor?'

'Well, you call yourself a doctor, don't you?'

'Did you think I was a doctor?'

'Aren't you a doctor?'

'No. Not a doctor.'

We had got it straightened out. The scales had fallen from our eyes. We knew where we were.

I had suspected that she was a genial soul. She now endorsed this view. I don't think I have ever heard a woman laugh so heartily.

'Well, that's the best thing!' she said, borrowing my handkerchief to wipe her eyes. 'Did you ever! But, if you aren't the doctor, who are you?'

'Wooster's the name. I came to see Miss Platt.'

'What about?'

This was the moment, of course, when I should have come out with the cheque and sprung the big effort. But somehow I couldn't make it. You know how it is. Offering people money to release your uncle is a scaly enough job at best, and when the atmosphere's not right the shot simply isn't on the board.

'Oh, just came to see her, you know.' I had rather a bright idea. 'My uncle heard she was seedy, don't you know, and asked me to look in and make enquiries,' I said.

'Your uncle?'

'Lord Yaxley.'

'Oh! So you are Lord Yaxley's nephew?'

'That's right. I suppose he's always popping in and out here what?'

'No. I've never met him.'

'You haven't?'

'No. Rhoda talks a lot about him, of course, but for some reason she's never so much as asked him to look in for a cup of tea.'

I began to see that this Rhoda knew her business. If I'd been a girl with someone wanting to marry me and knew that there was an exhibit like this aunt hanging around the home, I, too, should have thought twice about inviting him to call until the ceremony was over and he had actually signed on the dotted line. I mean to say, a thoroughly good soul – heart of gold beyond a doubt – but not the sort of thing you wanted to spring on Romeo before the time was ripe.

'I suppose you were all very surprised when you heard about it?' she said.

'Surprised is right.'

'Of course, nothing is definitely settled yet.'

'You don't mean that? I thought –'

'Oh, no. She's thinking it over.'

'I see.'

'Of course, she feels it's a great compliment. But then sometimes she wonders if he isn't too old.'

'My Aunt Agatha has rather the same idea.'

'Of course, a title *is* a title.'

'Yes, there's that. What do you think about it yourself?'

'Oh, it doesn't matter what I think. There's no doing anything with girls these days, is there?'

'Not much.'

'What I often say is, I wonder what girls are coming to. Still, there it is.'

'Absolutely.'

There didn't seem much reason why the conversation shouldn't go on for ever. She had the air of a woman who had settled down for the day. But at this point the maid came in and said the doctor had arrived.

I got up.

'I'll be tooling off, then.'

'If you must.'

'I think I'd better.'

'Well, pip pip.'

'Toodle-oo,' I said, and out into the fresh air.

Knowing what was waiting for me at home, I would have preferred to have gone to the club and spent the rest of the day there. But the thing had to be faced.

'Well?' said Aunt Agatha, as I trickled into the sitting-room.

'Well, yes and no,' I replied.

'What do you mean? Did she refuse the money?'

'Not exactly.'

'She accepted it?'

'Well, there again, not precisely.'

I explained what had happened. I wasn't expecting her to be any too frightfully pleased, and it's as well that I wasn't, because she wasn't. In fact, as the story unfolded, her comments became fruitier and fruitier, and when I had finished she uttered an exclamation that nearly broke a window. It sounded something like "Gor!" as if she had started to say "Gorblimey!" and had remembered her ancient lineage just in time.

'I'm sorry,' I said. 'And can a man say more? I lost my nerve. The old *morale* suddenly turned blue on me. It's the sort of thing that might have happened to anyone.'

'I never heard of anything so spineless in my life.'

I shivered, like a warrior whose old wound hurts him.

'I'd be most awfully obliged, Aunt Agatha,' I said, 'if you would not use that word spine. It awakens memories.'

The door opened. Jeeves appeared.

'Sir?'

'Yes, Jeeves?'

'I thought you called, sir.'

'No, Jeeves.'

'Very good, sir.'

There are moments when, even under the eye of Aunt Agatha, I can take the firm line. And now, seeing Jeeves standing there with the light of intelligence simply fizzing in every feature, I suddenly felt how perfectly footling it was to give this pre-eminent source of balm and comfort the go-by simply because Aunt Agatha had prejudices against discussing family affairs with the staff. It might make her say "Gor!" again, but I decided to do as we ought to have done right from the start – put the case in his hands.

'Jeeves,' I said, 'this matter of Uncle George.'

'Yes, sir.'

'You know the circs?'

'Yes, sir.'

'You know what we want.'

'Yes, sir.'

'Then advise us. And make it snappy. Think on your feet.'

I heard Aunt Agatha rumble like a volcano just before it starts to set about the neighbours, but I did not wilt. I had seen the sparkle in Jeeves's eye which indicated that an idea was on the way.

'I understand that you have been visiting the young person's home, sir?'

'Just got back.'

'Then you no doubt encountered the young person's aunt?'

'Jeeves, I encountered nothing else but.'

'Then the suggestion which I am about to make will, I feel sure, appeal to you, sir. I would recommend that you confront his lordship with this woman. It has always been her intention to continue residing with her niece after the latter's marriage. Should he meet her, this reflection might give his lordship pause. As you are aware, sir, she is a kind-hearted woman, but definitely of the people.'

'Jeeves, you are right! Apart from anything else, that orange hair!'

'Exactly, sir.'

'Not to mention the magenta dress.'

'Precisely, sir.'

'I'll ask her to lunch to-morrow, to meet him. You see,' I said to Aunt Agatha, who was still fermenting in the background, 'a ripe suggestion first crack out of the box. Did I or did I not tell you –'

'That will do, Jeeves,' said Aunt Agatha.

'Very good, madam.'

For some minutes after he had gone, Aunt Agatha strayed from the point a bit, confining her remarks to what she thought of a Wooster who could lower the prestige of the clan by allowing menials to get above themselves. Then she returned to what you might call the main issue.

'Bertie,' she said, 'you will go and see this girl again to-morrow and this time you will do as I told you.'

'But, dash it! With this excellent alternative scheme, based firmly on the psychology of the individual –'

'That is quite enough, Bertie. You heard what I said. I am going. Good-bye.'

She buzzed off, little knowing of what stuff Bertram Wooster was made. The door had hardly closed before I was shouting for Jeeves.

'Jeeves,' I said, 'the recent aunt will have none of your excellent alternative schemes, but none the less I propose to go through with it unswervingly. I consider it a ball of fire. Can you get hold of this female and bring her here for lunch to-morrow?'

'Yes, sir.'

'Good. Meanwhile, I will be 'phoning Uncle George. We will do Aunt Agatha good despite herself. What is it the poet says, Jeeves?'

'The poet Burns, sir?'

'Not the poet Burns. Some other poet. About doing good by stealth.'

'"These little acts of unremembered kindness," sir?'

'That's it in a nutshell, Jeeves.'

I suppose doing good by stealth ought to give one a glow, but I can't say I found myself exactly looking forward to the binge in prospect. Uncle George by himself is a mouldy enough luncheon companion, being extremely apt to collar the conversation and confine it to a description of his symptoms, he being one of those birds who can never be brought to believe that the general public isn't agog to hear all about the lining of his stomach. Add the aunt, and you have a little gathering which might well dismay the stoutest. The moment I woke, I felt conscious of some impending doom, and the cloud, if you know what I mean, grew darker all the morning. By the time Jeeves came in with the cocktails, I was feeling pretty low.

'For two pins, Jeeves,' I said, 'I would turn the whole thing up and leg it to the Drones.'

'I can readily imagine that this will prove something of an ordeal, sir.'

'How did you get to know these people, Jeeves?'

'It was through a young fellow of my acquaintance, sir, Colonel Mainwaring-Smith's personal gentleman's gentleman. He and the young person had an understanding at the time, and he desired me to accompany him to Wistaria Lodge and meet her.'

'They were engaged?'

'Not precisely engaged, sir. An understanding.'

'What did they quarrel about?'

'They did not quarrel, sir. When his lordship began to pay his addresses, the young person, naturally flattered, began to waver between love and ambition. But even now she has not formally rescinded the understanding.'

'Then, if your scheme works and Uncle George edges out, it will do your pal a bit of good?'

'Yes, sir. Smethurst – his name is Smethurst – would consider it a consummation devoutly to be wished.'

'Rather well put, that Jeeves. Your own?'

'No, sir. The Swan of Avon, sir.'

An unseen hand without tootled on the bell, and I braced myself to play the host. The binge was on.

'Mrs Wilberforce, sir,' announced Jeeves.

'And how I'm to keep a straight face with you standing behind and saying "Madam, can I tempt you with a potato?" is more than I know,' said the aunt, sailing in, looking larger and pinker and matier than ever. 'I know him, you know,' she said, jerking a thumb after Jeeves. 'He's been round and taken tea with us.'

'So he told me.'

She gave the sitting-room the once-over.

'You've got a nice place here,' she said. 'Though I like more pink about. It's so cheerful. What's that you've got there? Cocktails?'

'Martini with a spot of absinthe,' I said, beginning to pour.

She gave a girlish squeal.

'Don't you try to make me drink that stuff! Do you know what would happen if I touched one of those things? I'd be racked with pain. What they do to the lining of your stomach!'

'Oh, I don't know.'

'I do. If you had been a barmaid as long as I was, you'd know, too.'

'Oh – er – were you a barmaid?'

'For years, when I was younger than I am. At the Criterion.'

I dropped the shaker.

'There!' she said, pointing the moral. 'That's through drinking that stuff. Makes your hand wobble. What I always used to say to the boys was, "Port, if you like. Port's wholesome. I appreciate a drop of port myself. But these new-fangled messes from America, no." But they would never listen to me.'

I was eyeing her warily. Of course, there must have been thousands of barmaids at the Criterion in its time, but still it gave one a bit of a start. It was years ago that Uncle George's dash at a *mésalliance* had occurred – long before he came into the title – but the Wooster clan still quivered at the name of the Criterion.

'Er – when you were at the Cri.,' I said, 'did you ever happen to run into a fellow of my name?'

'I've forgotten what it is. I'm always silly about names.'

'Wooster.'

'Wooster! When you were there yesterday I thought you said Foster. Wooster! Did I run into a fellow named Wooster? Well! Why, George Wooster and me – Piggy, I used to call him – were going off to the registrar's, only his family heard of it and interfered. They offered me a lot of money to give him up, and, like a silly girl, I let them persuade me. If I've wondered once what became of him, I've wondered a thousand times. Is he a relation of yours?'

'Excuse me,' I said. 'I just want a word with Jeeves.'

I legged it for the pantry.

'Jeeves!'

'Sir?'

'Do you know what's happened?'

'No, sir.'

'This female –'

'Sir?'

'She's Uncle George's barmaid!'

'Sir?'

'Oh, dash it, you must have heard of Uncle George's barmaid. You know all the family history. The barmaid he wanted to marry years ago.'

'Ah, yes, sir.'

'She's the only woman he ever loved. He's told me so a million times. Every time he gets to the fourth whisky-and-potash, he always becomes maudlin about this female. What a dashed bit of bad luck! The first thing we know, the call of the past will be echoing in his heart. I can feel it, Jeeves. She's just his sort. The first thing she did when she came in was to start talking about the lining of her stomach. You see the hideous significance of that, Jeeves? The lining of his stomach is Uncle George's favourite topic of conversation. It means that he and she are kindred souls. This woman and he will be like –'

'Deep calling to deep, sir?'

'Exactly.'

'Most disturbing, sir.'

'What's to be done?'

'I could not say, sir.'

'I'll tell you what I'm going to do – 'phone him and say the lunch is off.'

'Scarcely feasible, sir. I fancy that is his lordship at the door now.'

And so it was. Jeeves let him in, and I followed him as he navigated down the passage to the sitting-room. There was a stunned silence as he went in, and then a couple of the startled yelps you hear when old buddies get together after long separation.

'Piggy!'

'Maudie!'

'Well, I never!'

'Well, I'm dashed!'

'Did you ever!'

'Well, bless my soul!'

'Fancy you being Lord Yaxley!'

'Came into the title soon after we parted.'

'Just to think!'

'You could have knocked me down with a feather!'

I hung about in the offing, now on this leg, now on that. For all the notice they took of me, I might just have well been the late Bertram Wooster, disembodied.

'Maudie, you don't look a day older, dash it!'

'Nor do you, Piggy.'

'How have you been all these years?'

'Pretty well. The lining of my stomach isn't all it should be.'

'Good Gad! You don't say so? I have trouble with the lining of *my* stomach.'

'It's a sort of heavy feeling after meals.'

'*I* get a sort of heavy feeling after meals. What are you trying for it?'

'I've been taking Perkins' Digestine.'

'My dear girl, no use! No use at all. Tried it myself for years and got no relief. Now, if you really want something that is some good –'

I slid away. The last I saw of them, Uncle George was down beside her on the Chesterfield, buzzing hard.

'Jeeves,' I said, tottering into the pantry.

'Sir?'

'There will only be two for lunch. Count me out. If they notice I'm not there, tell them I was called away by an urgent 'phone message. The situation has got beyond Bertram, Jeeves. You will find me at the Drones.'

'Very good, sir.'

It was latish in the evening when one of the waiters came to me as I played a distrait game of snooker pool and informed me that Aunt Agatha was on the 'phone.

'Bertie!'

'Hullo?'

I was amazed to note that her voice was that of an aunt who feels that things are breaking right. It had the birdlike trill.

'Bertie, have you that cheque I gave you?'

'Yes.'

'Then tear it up. It will not be needed.'

'Eh?'

'I say it will not be needed. Your uncle has been speaking to me on the telephone. He is not going to marry that girl.'

'Not?'

'No. Apparently he has been thinking it over and sees how unsuitable it would have been. But what is astonishing is that he *is* going to be married!'

'He is?'

'Yes, to an old friend of his, a Mrs Wilberforce. A woman of a sensible age, he gave me to understand. I wonder which Wilberforces that would be. There are two main branches of the family – the Essex Wilberforces and the Cumberland Wilberforces. I believe there is also a cadet branch somewhere in Shropshire.'

'And one in East Dulwich.'

'What did you say?'

'Nothing,' I said. 'Nothing.'

I hung up. Then back to the old flat, feeling a trifle sandbagged.

'Well, Jeeves,' I said, and there was censure in the eyes. 'So I gather everything is nicely settled?'

'Yes, sir. His lordship formally announced the engagement between the sweet and cheese courses, sir.'

'He did, did he?'

'Yes, sir.'

I eyed the man sternly.

'You do not appear to be aware of it, Jeeves,' I said, in a cold, level voice, 'but this binge has depreciated your stock very considerably. I have always been accustomed to look upon you as a counsellor without equal. I have, so to speak, hung upon your lips. And now see what you have done. All this is the direct consequence of your scheme, based on the psychology of the individual. I should have thought, Jeeves, that, knowing the woman – meeting her socially, as you might say, over the afternoon cup of tea – you might have ascertained that she was Uncle George's barmaid.'

'I did, sir.'

'What!'

'I was aware of the fact, sir.'

'Then you must have known what would happen if she came to lunch and met him.'

'Yes, sir.'

'Well, I'm dashed!'

'If I might explain, sir. The young man Smethurst, who is greatly attached to the young person, is an intimate friend of mine. He applied to me some little while back in the hope that I might be able to do something to ensure that the young person followed the dictates of her heart and refrained from permitting herself to be lured by gold and the glamour of his lordship's position. There will now be no obstacle to their union.'

'I see. "Little acts of unremembered kindness," what?'

'Precisely, sir.'

'And how about Uncle George? You've landed him pretty nicely in the cart.'

'No, sir, if I may take the liberty of opposing your view. I fancy that Mrs Wilberforce should make an ideal mate for his lordship. If there was a defect in his lordship's mode of life, it was that he was a little unduly attached to the pleasures of the table –'

'Ate like a pig, you mean?'

'I would not have ventured to put it in quite that way, sir, but the expression does meet the facts of the case. He was also inclined to drink rather more than his medical adviser would have approved of. Elderly bachelors who are wealthy and without occupation tend somewhat frequently to fall into this error, sir. The future Lady Yaxley will check this. Indeed, I overheard her ladyship saying as much as I brought in the fish. She was commenting on a certain puffiness of the face which had been absent in his lordship's appearance in the earlier days of their acquaintanceship, and she observed that his lordship needed looking after. I fancy, sir, that you will find the union will turn out an extremely satisfactory one.'

It was – what's the word I want? – it was plausible, of course, but still I shook the onion.

'But, Jeeves!'

'Sir?'

'She *is* as you remarked not long ago, definitely of the people.'

He looked at me in a reproachful sort of way.

'Sturdy lower-middle-class stock, sir.'

'H'm!'

'Sir?'

'I said "H'm!" Jeeves.'

'Besides, sir, remembering what the poet Tennyson said: "Kind hearts are more than coronets".'

'And which of us is going to tell Aunt Agatha that?'

'If I might make the suggestion, sir, I would advise that we omitted to communicate with Mrs Spenser Gregson in any way. I have your suitcase practically packed. It would be a matter of but a few minutes to bring the car round from the garage –'

'And off over the horizon to where men are men?'

'Precisely, sir.'

'Jeeves,' I said. 'I'm not sure that even now I can altogether see eye to eye with you regarding your recent activities. You think you have scattered light and sweetness on every side. I am not so sure. However, with this latest suggestion you have rung the bell. I examine it narrowly and I find no flaw in it. It is the goods. I'll get the car at once.'

'Very good, sir.'

'Remember what the poet Shakespeare said, Jeeves.'

'What was that, sir?'

'"Exit hurriedly, pursued by a bear." You'll find it in one of his plays. I remember drawing a picture of it on the side of the page, when I was at school.'

Notes

p. 232 *Drones* - an invented gentleman's club – drones being a type of bee which do no work

p. 232 *topper* - top hat

p. 232 *Buffers* - an invented club modelled on one of the famous gentlemen's clubs of Mayfair such as White's

p. 232 *Harrogate/Carlsbad* - spa towns famous for their health cures

p. 233 *Burlington Arcade* - very smart shopping arcade off Piccadilly

p. 233 *scallywag* - mischief-maker

p. 234 *East Dulwich* - not a smart part of London at the time

p. 234 *noblesse* - aristocracy

p. 234 *Rummy* - odd

p. 234 *the rank is but the penny stamp . . . the poet Burns* - Bertie is trying to quote Burns's famous poem – 'A Man's a Man for A' That':
'The rank is but the guinea's stamp,

The Man's the gowd for a' that'– meaning that titles and rank are empty things beside the inner worth of the individual – the image is a gold (gowd) coin, – the 'man' is the gold, and any title is only the decoration stamped on it

p. 235   *jar* - knock

p. 236   *cognoscente* - those in the know

p. 236   *grande dame* - grand lady

p. 236   *welt* - whack, smack

p. 237   *Greta Garbo* - beautiful film star of the time

p. 238   *ptarmigan* - type of game bird

p. 238   *joie de vivre* - enjoyment of life

p. 239   *Bohemian camaraderie* - informal friendliness, not bound by social conventions.

p. 242   *little unremembered acts of kindness* - Now Bertie is quoting Wordsworth, from 'Tintern Abbey': "The best portion of a good man's life: his little, nameless unremembered acts of kindness and love."

p. 243   *'a consummation devoutly to be wished'* - Hamlet Act III scene 1

p. 243   *Swan of Avon* - Shakespeare

p. 244   *port* - type of wine

p. 244   *mésalliance* - unsuitable marriage

p. 244   *registrar's* - official, for a civil marriage

p. 246   *Chesterfield* - sofa

p. 246   *buzzing* - talking

p. 246   *distrait game* - absent-minded

p. 246   *cadet* - junior, less important

p. 248   *Kind hearts are more than coronets . . .* - '. . . and simple faith than Norman (i.e. aristocratic) blood', this quotation from the poet Tennyson has the same message as Burns's lines

25

'And Women Must Weep'

('For men must work')

(1931)

Henry Handel Richardson

The Australian writer Ethel Florence Robertson wrote under a man's name: Henry Handel Richardson. She is best known for her novel The Getting of Wisdom, *about a girl growing up in the outback of Australia. Her debut novel* Maurice Guest *was a great success in her day and is well worth reading. The title is a quotation from a poem by the Victorian poet Charles Kingsley: "But men must work and women must weep." This short story brilliantly and painfully evokes a situation many will recognise: a girl at her first dance.*

She was ready at last, the last bow tied, the last strengthening pin in place, and they said to her – Auntie Cha and Miss Bidddons – to sit down and rest while Auntie Cha 'climbed into her own togs': 'Or you'll be tired before the evening begins.' But she could not bring herself to sit, for fear of crushing her dress – it was so light, so airy. How glad she felt now that she had chosen muslin, and not silk as Auntie Cha had tried to persuade her. The gossamer-like stuff seemed to float around her as she moved, and the cut of the dress made her look so tall and so different from everyday that she hardly recognised herself in the glass; the girl reflected there – in palest blue, with a wreath of cornflowers in her hair – might have been a stranger. Never had she thought she was so pretty . . . nor had Auntie and Miss Biddons either; though all they said was: 'Well, Dolly, you'll *do*,' and: 'Yes, I think she will be a credit to you.' Something hot and stinging came up her throat at this: a kind of gratitude for her pinky-white skin, her big blue eyes and fair curly hair, and pity for those girls who hadn't got them. Or an Auntie Cha either, to dress them and see that everything was 'just so'.

Instead of sitting, she stood very stiff and straight at the window, pretending to watch for the cab, her long white gloves hanging loose over one arm so as not to soil them. But her heart was beating pit-a-pat. For this was her first real grown-up ball. It was to be held in a public hall, and Auntie Cha, where she was staying, had bought tickets and was taking her.

True, Miss Biddons rather spoilt things at the end by saying: 'Now mind you don't forget your steps in the waltz. One, two, together; four, five, six.' And in the wagonette,

250

with her dress filling one seat, Auntie Cha's the other, Auntie said: 'Now, Dolly, remember not to look too *serious*. Or you'll frighten the gentlemen off.'

She was only doing it now because of her dress: cabs were so cramped, the seats so narrow.

Alas! in getting out a little accident happened. She caught the bottom of one of her flounces – the skirt was made of nothing else – on the iron step, and ripped off the selvedge. Auntie Cha said: 'My *dear*, how clumsy!' She could have cried with vexation.

The woman who took their cloaks hunted everywhere, but could only find black cotton; so the torn selvedge – there was nearly half a yard of it – had just to be cut off. This left a raw edge, and when they went into the hall and walked across the enormous floor, with people sitting all round, staring, it seemed to Dolly as if every one had their eyes fixed on it. Auntie Cha sat down in the front row of chairs beside a lady-friend; but she slid into a chair behind.

The first dance was already over, and they were hardly seated before partners began to be taken for the second. Shyly she mustered the assembly. In the cloakroom, she had expected the woman to exclaim: 'What a sweet pretty frock!' when she handled it. (When all she did say was: 'This sort of stuff's bound to fray.') And now Dolly saw that the hall was full of *lovely* dresses, some much, much prettier than hers, which suddenly began to seem rather too plain, even a little dowdy; perhaps after all it would have been better to have chosen silk.

She wondered if Aunt Cha thought so too. For Auntie suddenly turned and looked at her, quite hard, and then said snappily: 'Come, come, child, you mustn't tuck yourself away like that, or the gentlemen will think you don't want to dance.' So she had to come out and sit in the front; and show that she had a programme, by holding it open on her lap.

When other ladies were being requested for the third time, and still nobody had asked to be introduced, Auntie began making signs and beckoning with her head to the Master of Ceremonies – a funny little fat man with a bright red beard. He waddled across the floor, and Auntie whispered to him . . . behind her fan. (But she heard. And heard him answer: 'Wants a partner? Why, certainly.') And then he went away and they could see him offering her to several gentlemen. Some pointed to the ladies they were sitting with or standing in front of; some showed their programmes were full. One or two turned their heads and looked at her. But it was no good. So he came back and said: 'Will the little lady do *me* the favour?' and she had to look glad and say: 'With pleasure,' and get up and dance with him. Perhaps she was a little slow about it . . . at any rate Auntie Cha made great round eyes at her. But she felt sure every one would know why he was asking her. It was the lancers, too, and he swung her off her feet at the corners, and was comic when he set to partners – putting one hand on his hip and the other over his head, as if he were dancing the hornpipe – and the rest of the set laughed. She was glad when it was over and she could go back to her place.

Auntie Cha's lady-friend had a son, and he was beckoned to next and there was more whispering. But he was engaged to be married, and of course preferred to dance with his fiancée. When he came and bowed – to oblige his mother – he looked quite grumpy, and didn't trouble to say all of 'May I have the pleasure?' but just 'The pleasure?' While she had to say 'Certainly,' and pretend to be very pleased, though she didn't feel it, and really didn't want much to dance with him, knowing he didn't, and that it was only out of charity. Besides, all the time they went round he was explaining things to the other girl with his eyes . . . making faces over her head. She saw him quite plainly.

After he had brought her back – and Auntie had to talk to him again – he went to a gentleman who hadn't danced at all yet, but just stood looking on. And this one needed a lot of persuasion. He was ugly, and lanky, and as soon as they stood up, said quite rudely: 'I'm no earthly good at this kind of thing, you know.' And he wasn't. He trod on her foot and put her out of step, and they got into the most dreadful muddle, right out in the middle of the floor. It was a waltz, and remembering what Miss Biddons had said, she got more and more nervous, and then went wrong herself and had to say: 'I beg your pardon,' to which he said: 'Granted.' She saw them in a mirror as they passed, and her face was red as red.

It didn't get cool again either, for she had to go on sitting out, and she felt sure he was spreading it that *she* couldn't dance. She didn't know whether Auntie Cha had seen her mistakes, but now Auntie sort of went for her. 'It's no use, Dolly, if you don't do your share. For goodness sake, try and look more agreeable!'

So after this, in the intervals between the dances, she sat with a stiff little smile gummed to her lips. And, did any likely-looking partner approach the corner where they were, this widened till she felt what it was really saying was: 'Here I am! Oh, *please* take *me*!'

She had several false hopes. Men, looking so splendid in their white shirt fronts, would walk across the floor and seem to be coming . . . and then it was always not her. Their eyes wouldn't stay on her. There she sat, with her false little smile, and her eyes fixed on them; but theirs always got away . . . flitted past . . . moved on. Once she felt quite sure. Ever such a handsome young man looked at her as if he was making straight for her. She stretched her lips, showing all her teeth (they were very good) and for an instant his eyes seemed to linger . . . really take her in, in her pretty blue dress and the cornflowers. And then at the last minute they ran away – and it wasn't her at all, but a girl sitting three seats further on; one who wasn't even pretty, or her dress either. But her own dress was beginning to get quite tashy, from the way she squeezed her hot hands down in her lap.

Quite the worst part of all was having to go on sitting in the front row, pretending you were enjoying yourself. It was so hard to know what to do with your eyes. There was nothing but the floor for them to look at – if you watched the other couples dancing they would think you were envying them. At first she made a show of studying her programme; but you couldn't go on staring at a programme for ever: and presently her shame at its emptiness grew till she could bear it no longer, and, seizing a moment when people were dancing, she slipped it down the front of her dress. Now she could say she'd lost it, if anyone asked to see it. But they didn't; they went on dancing with other girls. Oh, these men, who walked round and chose just who they fancied and left who they didn't . . . how she hated them! It wasn't fair . . . it wasn't fair. And when there was a 'leap-year dance' where the ladies invited the gentlemen, and Auntie Cha tried to push her up and make her go and said: 'Now then, Dolly, here's your chance!' she shook her head hard and dug herself deeper into her seat. She wasn't going to ask them when they never asked her.

So she said her head ached and she'd rather not. And to this she clung, sitting the while wishing with her whole heart that her dress was black and her hair grey, like Auntie Cha's. Nobody expected Auntie Cha to dance, or thought it shameful if she didn't; she could do and be just as she liked. Yes, to-night she wished she was old . . . an old, old woman. Or that she was safe at home in bed . . . this dreadful evening, to which she had once counted the days, behind her. Even, as the night wore on, that she was dead.

At supper she sat with Auntie and the other lady, and the son and girl came too. There were lovely cakes and things, but she could not eat them. Her throat was so dry that a sandwich stuck in it and nearly choked her. Perhaps the son felt a little sorry for her (or else his mother had whispered again), for afterwards he said something to the girl, and then asked her to dance. They stood up together; but it wasn't a success. Her legs seemed to have forgotten how to jump, heavy as lead they were . . . as heavy as she felt inside . . . and she couldn't think of a thing to say. So now he would put her down as stupid as well.

Her only other partner was a boy younger than she was – almost a schoolboy – who she heard them say was 'making a positive nuisance of himself.' This was to a very pretty girl called the 'belle of the ball'. And he didn't seem to mind how badly he danced (with her), for he couldn't take his eyes off this other girl; but went on staring at her all the time, and very fiercely, because she was talking and laughing with somebody else. Besides, he hopped like a grasshopper, and didn't wear gloves, and his hands were hot and sticky. She hadn't come there to dance with little boys.

They left before anybody else; there was nothing to stay for. And the drive home in the wagonette, which had to be fetched, they were so early, was dreadful; Auntie Cha just sat and pressed her lips and didn't say a word. She herself kept her face turned the other way, because her mouth was jumping in and out as if it might have to cry.

At the sound of the wheels Miss Biddons came running to the front door with questions and exclamations, dreadfully curious to know why they were back so soon. Dolly fled to her own little room and turned the key in the lock. She wanted only to be quite alone . . . where nobody could see her . . . where nobody would ever see her again. But the walls were thin, and as she tore off the wreath and ripped open her dress, now crushed to nothing from so much sitting, and threw them from her anywhere, anyhow, she could hear the two voices going on, Auntie Cha's telling and telling, and winding up at last, quite out loud with: 'Well, I don't know what it was, but the plain truth is, she didn't *take*!'

Oh, the shame of it! . . . the sting and the shame. Her first ball, and not to have 'taken', to have failed to 'attract the gentlemen' – this was a slur that would rest on her all her life. And yet . . . and yet . . . in spite of everything, a small voice that wouldn't be silenced kept on saying: 'It wasn't my fault . . . it wasn't my fault!' (Or at least not except for the one silly mistake in the steps of the waltz.) She had tried her hardest, done everything she was told to do: had dressed up to please and look pretty, sat in the front row offering her programme, smiled when she didn't feel a bit like smiling . . . and almost more than anything she thought she hated the memory of that smile (it was like trying to make people buy something they didn't think worth while.) For really, truly, right deep down in her, she hadn't wanted 'the gentlemen' any more than they'd wanted her: she had only had to pretend to. And they showed only too plainly they didn't, by choosing other girls, who were not even pretty, and dancing with them, and laughing and talking and enjoying them. And now, the many slights and humiliations of the evening crowding upon her, the long repressed tears broke through; and with the blanket pulled up over her head, her face driven deep into the pillow, she cried till she could cry no more.

Notes

p. 250   *togs* - clothes
p. 250   *muslin* - fine cotton
p. 250   *cornflowers* - deep blue flowers
p. 250   *wagonette* - a horse-drawn open carriage
p. 251   *selvedge* - ribbon or braid used to hem fabric
p. 251   *programme . . . Master of Ceremonies . . . may I have the pleasure* - in a formal dance the Master of Ceremonies, usually an older man, calls out the different dances, makes sure everyone has a partner and generally makes sure everything goes smoothly: women have programmes listing the dances, they have to wait for men to invite them to dance, on which they fill in their programme – men may 'book' dances with different women for the evening
p. 251   *lancers* - a dance for two couples
p. 251   *hornpipe* - a sailor's dance
p. 252   *leap-year dance* - referring to the old custom that in a leap year a woman 'may' propose to a man

26

The Black Ball

(1937)

Ralph Ellison

Famous for his novel The Invisible Man, *Ellison was an award-winning writer, who focused on the often harrowing African-American experience between the wars. A father – a 'janitor' in a US apartment block – and son are described in an apparently normal working day. Gradually, the story reveals the context of their oppressed situation in a segregated USA, but hope of a different future is present in the overtures of a white union man. This story is no less disturbing for keeping much of its subject under the surface.*

I had rushed through the early part of the day mopping the lobby, placing fresh sand in the tall green jars, sweeping and dusting the halls, and emptying the trash to be burned later on in the day into the incinerator. And I had stopped only once to chase out after a can of milk for Mrs. Johnson, who had a new baby and who was always nice to my boy. I had started at six o'clock, and around eight I ran out to the quarters where we lived over the garage to dress the boy and give him his fruit and cereal. He was very thoughtful sitting there in his high chair and paused several times with his spoon midway to his mouth to watch me as I chewed my toast.

"What's the matter, son?"

"Daddy, am I black?"

"Of course not, you're brown. You know you're not black."

"Well yesterday Jackie said I was so black."

"He was just kidding. You musn't let them kid you, son."

"Brown's much nicer than white, isn't it, Daddy?"

[He was four, a little brown boy in blue rompers, and when he talked and laughed with imaginary playmates, his voice was soft and round in its accents like those of most Negro Americans.]

"Some people think so. But American is better than both, son."

"Is it, Daddy?"

"Sure it is. Now forget this talk about you being black, and Daddy will be back as soon as he finishes his work."

I left him to play with his toys and a book of pictures until I returned. He was a pretty nice fellow, as he used to say after particularly quiet afternoons while I tried to study, and for which quietness he expected a treat of candy or a "picture movie," and I often let him alone while I attended to my duties in the apartments.

I had gone back and started doing the brass on the front doors when a fellow came up and stood watching from the street. He was lean and red in the face with that redness that comes from a long diet of certain foods. You see much of it in the deep South, and here in the Southwest it is not uncommon. He stood there watching, and I could feel his eyes in my back as I polished the brass.

I gave special attention to that brass because for Berry, the manager, the luster of these brass panels and door handles was the measure of all my industry. It was near time for him to arrive.

"Good morning, John," he would say, looking not at me but at the brass.

"Good morning, sir," I would say, looking not at him but at the brass. Usually his face was reflected there. For him, I *was* there. Besides that brass, his money, and the half-dozen or so plants in his office, I don't believe he had any other real interests in life.

There must be no flaws this morning. Two fellows who worked at the building across the street had already been dismissed because whites had demanded their jobs, and with the boy at that age needing special foods and me planning to enter school again next term, I couldn't afford to allow something like that out on the sidewalk to spoil my chances. Especially since Berry had told one of my friends in the building that he didn't like that "damned educated nigger."

I was so concerned with the brass that when the fellow spoke, I jumped with surprise.

"Howdy," he said. The expected drawl was there. But something was missing, something usually behind that kind of drawl.

"Good morning."

"Looks like you working purty hard over that brass."

"It gets pretty dirty overnight."

That part wasn't missing. When they did have something to say to us, they always became familiar.

"You been working here long?" he asked, leaning against the column with his elbow.

"Two months."

I turned my back to him as I worked.

"Any other colored folks working here?"

"I'm the only one," I lied. There were two others. It was none of his business anyway.

"Have much to do?"

"I have enough," I said. Why, I thought, doesn't he go on in and ask for the job? Why bother me? Why tempt me to choke him? Doesn't he know we aren't afraid to fight his kind out this way?

As I turned, picking up the bottle to pour more polish into my rag, he pulled a tobacco sack from the pocket of his old blue coat. I noticed his hands were scarred as though they had been burned.

"Ever smoke Durham?" he asked.

"No thank you," I said.

He laughed.

"Not used to anything like that, are you?"

"Not used to what?"

A little more from this guy and I would see red.

"Fellow like me offering a fellow like you something besides a rope."

I stopped to look at him. He stood there smiling with the sack in his outstretched hand. There were many wrinkles around his eyes, and I had to smile in return. In spite of myself I had to smile.

"Sure you won't smoke some Durham?"

"No thanks," I said.

He was fooled by the smile. A smile couldn't change things between my kind and his.

"I'll admit it ain't much," he said. "But it's a helluva lot different."

I stopped the polishing again to see what it was he was trying to get after.

"But," he said, "I've got something really worth a lot; that is, if you're interested."

"Let's hear it," I said.

Here, I thought, is where he tries to put one over on old "George."

"You see, I come out from the union and we intend to organize all the building-service help in this district. Maybe you been reading 'bout it in the papers?"

"I saw something about it, but what's it to do with me?"

"Well, first place we'll make 'em take some of this work off you. It'll mean shorter hours and higher wages, and better conditions in general."

"What you really mean is that you'll get in here and bounce me out. Unions don't want Negro members."

"You mean *some* unions don't. It used to be that way, but things have changed."

"Listen, fellow. You're wasting your time and mine. Your damn unions are like everything else in the country—for whites only. What ever caused *you* to give a damn about a Negro anyway? Why should *you* try to organize Negroes?"

His face had become a little white.

"See them hands?"

He stretched out his hands.

"Yes," I said, looking not at his hands but at the color draining from his face.

"Well, I got them scars in Macon County, Alabama, for saying a colored friend of mine was somewhere else on a day he was supposed to have raped a woman. He was, too, 'cause I was with him. Me and him was trying to borrow some seed fifty miles away when it happened—if it did happen. They made them scars with a gasoline torch and run me out the county 'cause they said I tried to help a nigger make a white woman out a lie. That same night they lynched him and burned down his house. They did that to him and this to me, and both of us was fifty miles away."

He was looking down at his outstretched hands as he talked.

"God," was all I could say. I felt terrible when I looked closely at his hands for the first time. It must have been hell. The skin was drawn and puckered and looked as though it had been fried. Fried hands.

"Since that time I learned a lot," he said. "I been at this kinda thing. First it was the croppers, and when they got to know me and made it too hot, I quit the country and came to town. First it was in Arkansas and now it's here. And the more I move around, the more I see, and the more I see, the more I work."

He was looking into my face now, his eyes blue in his red skin. He was looking very earnestly. I said nothing. I didn't know what to say to that. Perhaps he was telling the truth; I didn't know. He was smiling again.

"Listen," he said. "Now, don't you go trying to figger it all out right now. There's going to be a series of meetings at this number starting tonight, and I'd like mighty much to see you there. Bring any friends along you want to."

He handed me a card with a number and 8 p.m. sharp written on it. He smiled as I took the card and made as if to shake my hand but turned and walked down the steps to the street. I noticed that he limped as he moved away.

"Good morning, John," Mr. Berry said. I turned, and there he stood; derby, long black coat, stick, nose glasses, and all. He stood gazing into the brass like the wicked queen into her looking glass in the story which the boy liked so well.

"Good morning, sir," I said.

I should have finished long before.

"Did the man I saw leaving wish to see me, John?"

"Oh no, sir. He only wished to buy old clothes."

Satisfied with my work for the day, he passed inside, and I walked around to the quarters to look after the boy. It was near twelve o'clock.

I found the boy pushing a toy back and forth beneath a chair in the little room which I used for a study.

"Hi, Daddy," he called.

"Hi, son," I called. "What are you doing today?"

"Oh, I'm trucking."

"I thought you had to stand up to truck."

"Not that kind, Daddy, this kind."

He held up the toy.

"Ooh," I said. "*That* kind."

"Aw, Daddy, you're kidding. You always kid, don't you, Daddy?"

"No. When you're bad I don't kid, do I?"

"I guess not."

In fact, he wasn't—only enough to make it unnecessary for me to worry because he wasn't.

The business of trucking soon absorbed him, and I went back to the kitchen to fix his lunch and to warm up the coffee for myself.

The boy had a good appetite, so I didn't have to make him eat. I gave him his food and settled into a chair to study, but my mind wandered away, so I got up and filled a pipe hoping that would help, but it didn't, so I threw the book aside and picked up Malraux's *Man's Fate*, which Mrs. Johnson had given me, and tried to read it as I drank a cup of coffee. I had to give that up also. Those hands were on my brain, and I couldn't forget that fellow.

"Daddy," the boy called softly; it's always softly when I'm busy.

"Yes, son."

"When I grow up I think I'll drive a truck."

"You do?"

"Yes, and then I can wear a lot of buttons on my cap like the men that bring the meat to the grocery. I saw a colored man with some today, Daddy. I looked out the window and a colored man drove the truck today, and, Daddy, he had two buttons on his cap. I could see 'em plain."

He had stopped his play and was still on his knees, beside the chair in his blue overalls. I closed the book and looked at the boy a long time. I must have looked queer.

"What's the matter, Daddy?" he asked. I explained that I was thinking, and got up and walked over to stand looking out the front window. He was quiet for a while; then he started rolling his truck again.

The only nice feature about the quarters was that they were high up and offered a view in all directions. It was afternoon and the sun was brilliant. Off to the side, a boy and girl were playing tennis in a driveway. Across the street a group of little fellows in bright sunsuits were playing on a long stretch of lawn before a white stone building. Their nurse, dressed completely in white except for her dark glasses, which I saw when she raised her head, sat still as a picture, bent over a book on her knees. As the children played, the wind blew their cries over to where I stood, and as I watched, a flock of pigeons swooped down into the driveway near the stretch of green, only to take flight again wheeling in a mass as another child came skipping up the drive pulling some sort of toy. The children saw him and were running toward him in a group when the nurse looked up and called them back. She called something to the child and pointed back in the direction of the garages where he had just come from. I could see him turn slowly around and drag his toy, some kind of bird that flapped its wings like an eagle, slowly after him. He stopped and pulled a flower from one of the bushes that lined the drive, turning to look hurriedly at the nurse, and then ran back down the drive. The child had been Jackie, the little son of the white gardener who worked across the street.

As I turned away I noticed that my boy had come to stand beside me.

"What you looking at, Daddy?" he said.

"I guess Daddy was just looking out on the world."

Then he asked if he could go out and play with his ball, and since I would soon have to go down myself to water the lawn, I told him it would be all right. But he couldn't find the ball; I would have to find it for him.

"All right now," I told him. "You stay in the back out of everybody's way, and you mustn't ask anyone a lot of questions."

I always warned about the questions, even though it did little good. He ran down the stairs, and soon I could hear the *bump bump bump* of his ball bouncing against the garage doors underneath. But since it didn't make a loud noise, I didn't ask him to stop.

I picked up the book to read again, and must have fallen asleep immediately, for when I came to it was almost time to go water the lawn. When I got downstairs the boy was not there. I called, but no answer. Then I went out into the alley in back of the garages to see if he was playing there. There were three older white boys sitting talking on a pile of old packing cases. They looked uneasy when I came up. I asked if they had seen a little Negro boy, but they said they hadn't. Then I went farther down the alley behind the grocery store where the trucks drove up, and asked one of the fellows working there if he had seen my boy. He said he had been working on the platform all afternoon and that he was sure the boy had not been there. As I started away, the four o'clock whistle blew and I had to go water the lawn. I wondered where the boy could have gone. As I came back up the alley I was becoming alarmed. Then it occurred to me that he might have gone out in front in spite of my warning not to. Of course, that was where he would go, out in front to sit on the grass. I laughed at myself for becoming alarmed and decided not to punish him, even though Berry had given instructions that he was not to be seen out in the front without me. A boy that size will make you do that.

As I came around the building past the tall new evergreens, I could hear the boy crying in just that note no other child has, and when I came completely around I found him standing looking up into a window with tears on his face.

"What is it, son?" I asked. "What happened?"

"My ball, my ball, Daddy. My ball," he cried, looking up at the window.

"Yes, son. But what about the ball?"

"He threw it up in the window."

"Who did? Who threw it, son? Stop crying and tell Daddy about it."

He made an effort to stop, wiping the tears away with the back of his hand.

"A big white boy asked me to throw him my ball an', an' he took it and threw it up in that window and ran," he said, pointing.

I looked up just as Berry appeared at the window. The ball had gone into his private office.

"John, is that your boy?" he snapped.

He was red in the face.

"Yes sir, but—"

"Well, he's taken his damned ball and ruined one of my plants."

"Yes sir."

"You know he's got no business around here in front, don't you?"

"Yes!"

"Well, if I ever see him around here again, you're going to find yourself behind the black ball. Now get him on round to the back and then come up here and clean up this mess he's made."

I gave him one long hard look and then felt for the boy's hand to take him back to the quarters. I had a hard time seeing as we walked back, and scratched myself by stumbling into the evergreens as we went around the building.

The boy was not crying now, and when I looked down at him, the pain in my hand caused me to notice that it was bleeding. When we got upstairs, I sat the boy in a chair and went looking for iodine to doctor my hand.

"If anyone should ask me, young man, I'd say your face needed a good washing."

He didn't answer then, but when I came out of the bathroom, he seemed more inclined to talk.

"Daddy, what did that man mean?"

"Mean how, son?"

"About a black ball. You know, Daddy."

"Oh—that."

"You know, Daddy. What'd he mean?"

"He meant, son, that if your ball landed in his office again, Daddy would go after it behind the old black ball."

"Oh," he said, very thoughtful again. Then, after a while he told me: "Daddy, that white man can't see very good, can he, Daddy?"

"Why do you say that, son?"

"Daddy," he said impatiently. "Anybody can see my ball is white."

For the second time that day I looked at him a long time.

"Yes, son," I said. "Your ball *is* white." Mostly white, anyway, I thought.

"Will I play with the black ball, Daddy?"

"In time, son," I said. "In time."

He had already played with the ball; that he would discover later. He was learning the rules of the game already, but he didn't know it. Yes, he would play with the ball. Indeed, poor little rascal, he would play until he grew sick of playing. My, yes, the old ball game. But I'd begin telling him the rules later.

My hand was still burning from the scratch as I dragged the hose out to water the lawn, and looking down at the iodine stain, I thought of the fellow's fried hands, and felt in my pocket to make sure I still had the card he had given me. Maybe there was a color other than white on the old ball.

Notes

After the Civil War, the Southern states of America were racially segregated, with separate facilities for black and white – schools, theatres, transport, sport – segregated units in the army in both world wars, and laws forbidding inter-marriage. This began to be dismantled slowly from the end of World War I to the 1960s.

A black ball is a reference to a means of voting, for example, members of a club voting to allow someone to join, by putting white or black balls in a box – one black ball can exclude the person.

p. 256   *Howdy* - Hello
p. 256   *purty* - pretty
p. 257   *Durham* - brand of tobacco
p. 258   *croppers* - poor farmers
p. 258   *figger* - figure
p. 258   *derby* - bowler hat
p. 259   *Malraux's Man's Fate* - 1933 French novel about a failed workers' revolution

27

Lappin and Lapinova

(1938)

Virginia Woolf

One of the greatest English novelists – who explored new possibilities for the form in works such as Mrs Dalloway, To the Lighthouse *and* The Waves *– Woolf also wrote short fiction, essays and pieces of journalism. As well as unparalleled imagination and sensitivity, her work often shows a very individual sense of humour. This unusual story is like an early piece of magical realism; a fable, or a fairy tale – but with a serious underlying theme of the way in which a marriage can work through mutual suspension of disbelief and use of alter egos.*

They were married. The wedding march pealed out. The pigeons fluttered. Small boys in Eton jackets threw rice; a fox terrier sauntered across the path; and Ernest Thorburn led his bride to the car through the small inquisitive crowd of complete strangers which always collects in London to enjoy other people's happiness or unhappiness. Certainly he looked handsome and she looked shy. More rice was thrown, and the car moved off.

That was on Tuesday. Now it was Saturday. Rosalind had still to get used to the fact that she was Mrs Ernest Thorburn. Perhaps she never would get used to the fact that she was Mrs Ernest Anybody, she thought, as she sat in the bow window of the hotel looking over the lake to the mountains, and waited for her husband to come down to breakfast. Ernest was a difficult name to get used to. It was not the name she would have chosen. She would have preferred Timothy, Antony, or Peter. He did not look like Ernest either. The name suggested the Albert Memorial, mahogany sideboards, steel engravings of the Prince Consort with his family – her mother-in-law's dining-room in Porchester Terrace in short.

But here he was. Thank goodness he did not look like Ernest – no. But what did he look like? She glanced at him sideways. Well, when he was eating toast he looked like a rabbit. Not that anyone else would have seen a likeness to a creature so diminutive and timid in this spruce, muscular young man with the straight nose, the blue eyes, and the very firm mouth. But that made it all the more amusing. His nose twitched very slightly when he ate. So did her pet rabbit's. She kept watching his nose twitch; and then she had to explain, when he caught her looking at him, why she laughed.

'It's because you're like a rabbit, Ernest,' she said. 'Like a wild rabbit,' she added, looking at him. 'A hunting rabbit; a King Rabbit; a rabbit that makes laws for all the other rabbits.'

Ernest had no objection to being that kind of rabbit, and since it amused her to see him twitch his nose – he had never known that his nose twitched – he twitched it on purpose. And she laughed and laughed; and he laughed too, so that the maiden ladies and the fishing man and the Swiss waiter in his greasy black jacket all guessed right; they were very happy. But how long does such happiness last? they asked themselves; and each answered according to his own circumstances.

At lunch time, seated on a clump of heather beside the lake, 'Lettuce, rabbit?' said Rosalind, holding out the lettuce that had been provided to eat with the hard-boiled eggs. 'Come and take it out of my hand,' she added, and he stretched out and nibbled the lettuce and twitched his nose.

'Good rabbit, nice rabbit,' she said, patting him, as she used to pat her tame rabbit at home. But that was absurd. He was not a tame rabbit, whatever he was. She turned it into French. 'Lapin,' she called him. But whatever he was, he was not a French rabbit. He was simply and solely English – born at Porchester Terrace, educated at Rugby; now a clerk in His Majesty's Civil Service. So she tried 'Bunny' next; but that was worse. 'Bunny' was someone plump and soft and comic; he was thin and hard and serious. Still, his nose twitched. 'Lappin,' she exclaimed suddenly; and gave a little cry as if she had found the very word she looked for.

'Lappin, Lappin, King Lappin,' she repeated. It seemed to suit him exactly; he was not Ernest, he was King Lappin. Why? She did not know.

When there was nothing new to talk about on their long solitary walks – and it rained, as everyone had warned them that it would rain; or when they were sitting over the fire in the evening, for it was cold, and the maiden ladies had gone and the fishing man, and the waiter only came if you rang the bell for him, she let her fancy play with the story of the Lappin tribe. Under her hands – she was sewing; he was reading – they became very real, very vivid, very amusing. Ernest put down the paper and helped her. There were the black rabbits and the red; there were the enemy rabbits and the friendly. There were the wood in which they lived and the outlying prairies and the swamp. Above all there was King Lappin, who, far from having only the one trick – that he twitched his nose – became as the days passed an animal of the greatest character; Rosalind was always finding new qualities in him. But above all he was a great hunter.

'And what,' said Rosalind, on the last day of the honeymoon, 'did the King do today?'

In fact they had been climbing all day; and she had worn a blister on her heel; but she did not mean that.

Today,' said Ernest, twitching his nose as he bit the end off his cigar, 'he chased a hare.' He paused; struck a match, and twitched again.

'A woman hare,' he added.

'A white hare!' Rosalind exclaimed, as if she had been expecting this. 'Rather a small hare; silver grey; with big bright eyes?'

'Yes,' said Ernest, looking at her as she had looked at him, 'a smallish animal; with eyes popping out of her head, and two little front paws dangling.' It was exactly how she sat, with her sewing dangling in her hands; and her eyes, that were so big and bright, were certainly a little prominent.

'Ah, Lapinova,' Rosalind murmured.

'Is that what she's called?' said Ernest – 'the real Rosalind?' He looked at her. He felt very much in love with her.

'Yes; that's what she's called,' said Rosalind. 'Lapinova.' And before they went to bed that night it was all settled. He was King Lappin; she was Queen Lapinova. They were the very opposite of each other; he was bold and determined; she wary and undependable. He ruled over the busy world of rabbits; her world was a desolate, mysterious place, which she ranged mostly by moonlight. All the same, their territories touched; they were King and Queen.

Thus when they came back from their honeymoon they possessed a private world, inhabited, save for the one white hare, entirely by rabbits. No one guessed that there was such a place, and that of course made it all the more amusing. It made them feel, more even than most young married couples, in league together against the rest of the world. Often they looked slyly at each other when people talked about rabbits and woods and traps and shooting. Or they winked furtively across the table when Aunt Mary said that she could never bear to see a hare in a dish – it looked so like a baby, or when John, Ernest's sporting brother, told them what price rabbits were fetching that autumn in Wiltshire, skins and all. Sometimes when they wanted a gamekeeper, or a poacher or a Lord of the Manor, they amused themselves by distributing the parts among their friends. Ernest's mother, Mrs Reginald Thorburn, for example, fitted the part of the Squire to perfection. But it was all secret – that was the point of it; nobody save themselves knew that such a world existed.

Without that world, how, Rosalind wondered, that winter could she have lived at all? For instance, there was the golden-wedding party, when all the Thorburns assembled at Porchester Terrace to celebrate the fiftieth anniversary of that union which had been so blessed – had it not produced Ernest Thorburn? and so fruitful – had it not produced nine other sons and daughters into the bargain, many themselves married and also fruitful? She dreaded that party. But it was inevitable. As she walked upstairs she felt bitterly that she was an only child and an orphan at that; a mere drop among all those Thorburns assembled in the great drawing-room with the shiny satin wallpaper and the lustrous family portraits. The living Thorburns much resembled the painted; save that instead of painted lips they had real lips; out of which came jokes; jokes about schoolrooms, and how they had pulled the chair from under the governess; jokes about frogs and how they had put them between the virgin sheets of maiden ladies. As for herself, she had never even made an apple-pie bed. Holding her present in her hand she advanced toward her mother-in-law sumptuous in yellow satin; and toward her father-in-law decorated with a rich yellow carnation. All round them on tables and chairs there were golden tributes; some nestling in cotton wool; others branching resplendent – candlesticks; cigar boxes; chains; each stamped with the goldsmith's proof that it was solid gold, hall-marked, authentic. But her present was only a little pinchbeck box pierced with holes; an old sand caster, an eighteenth-century relic, once used to sprinkle sand over wet ink. Rather a senseless present she felt – in an age of blotting paper; and as she proffered it, she saw in front of her the stubby black handwriting in which her mother-in-law when they were engaged had expressed the hope that 'My son will make you happy'. No, she was not happy. Not at all happy. She looked at Ernest, straight as a ramrod with a nose like all the noses in the family portraits; a nose that never twitched at all.

Then they went down to dinner. She was half hidden by the great chrysanthemums that curled their red and gold petals into large tight balls. Everything was gold. A gold-edged card with gold initials intertwined recited the list of all the dishes that would be set one after another before them. She dipped her spoon in a plate of clear golden fluid. The raw white fog outside had been turned by the lamps into a golden mesh that blurred the edges of the plates and gave the pine-apples a rough golden skin. Only she herself in her white wedding dress peering ahead of her with her prominent eyes seemed insoluble as an icicle.

As the dinner wore on, however, the room grew steamy with heat. Beads of perspiration stood out on the men's foreheads. She felt that her icicle was being turned to water. She was being melted; dispersed; dissolved into nothingness; and would soon faint. Then through the surge in her head and the din in her ears she heard a woman's voice exclaim, 'But they breed so!'

The Thorburns – yes; they breed so, she echoed; looking at all the round red faces that seemed doubled in the giddiness that overcame her; and magnified in the gold mist that enhaloed them. 'They breed so.' Then John bawled:

'Little devils! . . . Shoot 'em! Jump on 'em with big boots! That's the only way to deal with 'em . . . rabbits!'

At that word, that magic word, she revived. Peeping between the chrysanthemums she saw Ernest's nose twitch. It rippled, it ran with successive twitches. And at that a mysterious catastrophe befell the Thorburns. The golden table became a moor with the gorse in full bloom; the din of voices turned to one peal of lark's laughter ringing down from the sky. It was a blue sky – clouds passed slowly. And they had all been changed – the Thorburns. She looked at her father-in-law, a furtive little man with dyed moustaches. His foible was collecting things – seals, enamel boxes, trifles from eighteenth-century dressing tables which he hid in the drawers of his study from his wife. Now she saw him as he was – a poacher, stealing off with his coat bulging with pheasants and partridges to drop them stealthily into a three-legged pot in his smoky little cottage. That was her real father-in-law – a poacher. And Celia, the unmarried daughter, who always nosed out other people's secrets, the little things they wished to hide – she was a white ferret with pink eyes, and a nose clotted with earth from her horrid underground nosings and pokings. Slung round men's shoulders, in a net, and thrust down a hole – it was a pitiable life – Celia's; it was none of her fault. So she saw Celia. And then she looked at her mother-in-law – whom they dubbed The Squire. Flushed, coarse, a bully – she was all that, as she stood returning thanks, but now that Rosalind – that is Lapinova – saw her, she saw behind her the decayed family mansion, the plaster peeling off the walls, and heard her, with a sob in her voice, giving thanks to her children (who hated her) for a world that had ceased to exist. There was a sudden silence. They all stood with their glasses raised; they all drank; then it was over.

'Oh, King Lappin!' she cried as they went home together in the fog, 'if your nose hadn't twitched just at the moment, I should have been trapped!'

'But you're safe,' said King Lappin, pressing her paw.

'Quite safe,' she answered.

And they drove back through the Park, King and Queen of the marsh, of the mist, and of the gorse-scented moor.

Thus time passed; one year; two years of time. And on a winter's night, which happened by a coincidence to be the anniversary of the golden-wedding party – but Mrs Reginald Thorburn was dead; the house was to let; and there was only a caretaker in residence – Ernest came home from the office. They had a nice little home; half a house above a saddler's shop in South Kensington, not far from the tube station. It was cold, with fog in the air, and Rosalind was sitting over the fire, sewing.

'What d'you think happened to me today?' she began as soon as he had settled himself down with his legs stretched to the blaze. 'I was crossing the stream when –'

'What stream?' Ernest interrupted her.

'The stream at the bottom, where our wood meets the black wood,' she explained.

Ernest looked completely blank for a moment.

'What the deuce are you talking about?' he asked.

'My dear Ernest!' she cried in dismay. 'King Lappin,' she added, dangling her little front paws in the firelight. But his nose did not twitch. Her hands – they turned to hands – clutched the stuff she was holding; her eyes popped half out of her head. It took him five minutes at least to change from Ernest Thorburn to King Lappin; and while she waited she felt a load on the back of her neck, as if somebody were about to wring it. At last he changed to King Lappin; his nose twitched; and they spent the evening roaming the woods much as usual.

But she slept badly. In the middle of the night she woke, feeling as if something strange had happened to her. She was stiff and cold. At last she turned on the light and looked at Ernest lying beside her. He was sound asleep. He snored. But even though he snored, his nose remained perfectly still. It looked as if it had never twitched at all. Was it possible that he was really Ernest; and that she was really married to Ernest? A vision of her mother-in-law's dining-room came before her; and there they sat, she and Ernest, grown old, under the engravings, in front of the sideboard. . . . It was their golden-wedding day. She could not bear it.

'Lappin, King Lappin!' she whispered, and for a moment his nose seemed to twitch of its own accord. But he still slept. 'Wake up, Lappin, wake up!' she cried.

Ernest woke; and seeing her sitting bolt upright beside him he asked:

'What's the matter?'

'I thought my rabbit was dead!' she whimpered. Ernest was angry.

'Don't talk such, rubbish, Rosalind,' he said. 'Lie down and go to sleep.'

He turned over. In another moment he was sound asleep and snoring.

But she could not sleep. She lay curled up on her side of the bed, like a hare in its form. She had turned out the light, but the street lamp lit the ceiling faintly, and the trees outside made a lacy network over it as if there were a shadowy grove on the ceiling in which she wandered, turning, twisting, in and out, round and round, hunting, being hunted, hearing the bay of hounds and horns; flying, escaping . . . until the maid drew the blinds and brought their early tea.

Next day she could settle to nothing. She seemed to have lost something. She felt as if her body had shrunk; it had grown small, and black and hard. Her joints seemed stiff too, and when she looked in the glass, which she did several times as she wandered about the flat, her eyes seemed to burst out of her head, like currants in a bun. The rooms also seemed to have shrunk. Large pieces of furniture jutted out at odd angles and she found herself knocking against them. At last she put on her hat and went out. She walked along the Cromwell Road; and every room she passed and peered into seemed to be a dining-room where people sat eating under steel engravings, with thick yellow lace curtains, and mahogany sideboards. At last she reached the Natural History Museum; she used to like it when she was a child. But the first thing she saw when she went in was a stuffed hare standing on sham snow with pink glass eyes. Somehow it made her shiver all over. Perhaps it would be better when dusk fell. She went home and sat over the fire, without a light, and tried to imagine that she was out alone on a moor; and there was a stream rushing; and beyond the stream a dark wood. But she could get no further than the stream. At last she squatted down on the bank on the wet grass, and sat crouched in her chair, with her hands dangling empty, and her eyes glazed, like glass eyes, in the firelight. Then there was the crack of a gun. . . . She started as if she had been shot. It was only Ernest, turning his key in the door. She waited trembling. He came in and switched on the light. There he stood tall, handsome, rubbing his hands that were red with cold.

'Sitting in the dark?' he said.

'Oh, Ernest, Ernest!' she cried, starting up in her chair.

'Well, what's up now?' he asked briskly, warming his hands at the fire.

'It's Lapinova . . .' she faltered, glancing wildly at him out of her great startled eyes. 'She's gone, Ernest. I've lost her!'

Ernest frowned. He pressed his lips tight together. 'Oh, that's what's up, is it?' he said, smiling rather grimly at his wife. For ten seconds he stood there, silent; and she waited, feeling hands tightening at the back of her neck.

'Yes,' he said at length. 'Poor Lapinova. . .' He straightened his tie at the looking-glass over the mantelpiece.

'Caught in a trap,' he said, 'killed', and sat down and read the newspaper.

So that was the end of that marriage.

Notes

p. 263   *Eton jackets* - a type of short black jacket
p. 263   *Albert Memorial* - elaborate memorial for Queen Victoria's husband Albert, located in Kensington Gardens, London
p. 263   *threw rice* - a custom at weddings, to bring good luck
p. 264   *Rugby* - famous private school
p. 266   *gorse* - scented moor

28

Stability

(1947)
Philip K. Dick

Philip K. Dick was an American pioneer of modern science fiction writing, whose vast short story output is now collected in five large volumes. This story is set in a future in which a worldwide regime rules absolutely to preserve 'stability'; the story focuses on one man discovering a mysterious device which threatens to destroy everything – is it a redemption or a disaster?

Robert Benton slowly spread his wings, flapped them several times and sailed majestically off the roof and into the darkness.

He was swallowed up by the night at once. Beneath him, hundreds of tiny dots of light betokened other roofs, from which other persons flew. A violet hue swam close to him, then vanished into the black. But Benton was in a different sort of mood, and the idea of night races did not appeal to him. The violet hue came close again and waved invitingly. Benton declined, swept upward into the higher air.

After a while he leveled off and allowed himself to coast on air currents that came up from the city beneath, the City of Lightness. A wonderful, exhilarating feeling swept through him. He pounded his huge, white wings together, flung himself in frantic joy into the small clouds that drifted past, dived at the invisible floor of the immense black bowl in which he flew, and at last descended toward the lights of the city, his leisure time approaching an end.

Somewhere far down a light more bright than the others winked at him: the Control Office. Aiming his body like an arrow, his white wings folded about him, he headed toward it. Down he went, straight and perfect. Barely a hundred feet from the light he threw his wings out, caught the firm air about him, and came gently to rest on a level roof.

Benton began to walk until a guide light came to life and he found his way to the entrance door by its beam. The door slid back at the pressure of his fingertips and he stepped past it. At once he began to descend, shooting downward at increasing speed. The small elevator suddenly stopped and he strode out into the Controller's Main Office.

"Hello," the Controller said, "take off your wings and sit down."

Benton did so, folding them neatly and hanging them from one of a row of small hooks along the wall. He selected the best chair in sight and headed toward it.

"Ah," the Controller smiled, "you value comfort."

"Well," Benton answered, "I don't want it to go to waste."

The Controller looked past his visitor and through the transparent plastic walls. Beyond were the largest single rooms in the City of Lightness. They extended as far as his eyes could see, and farther. Each was—

"What did you want to see me about?" Benton interrupted. The Controller coughed and rattled some metal paper-sheets.

"As you know," he began, "Stability is the watchword. Civilization has been climbing for centuries, especially since the twenty-fifth century. It is a law of nature, however, that civilization must either go forward or fall backward; it cannot stand still."

"I know that," Benton said, puzzled. "I also know the multiplication table. Are you going to recite that, too?"

The Controller ignored him.

"We have, however, broken that law. One hundred years ago—"

One hundred years ago! It hardly seemed as far back as that when Eric Freidenburg of the States of Free Germany stood up in the International Council Chamber and announced to the assembled delegates that man kind had at last reached its peak. Further progress forward was impossible. In the last few years, only *two* major inventions had been filed. After that, they had all watched the big graphs and charts, seen the lines going down and down, according to their squares, until they dipped into nothing. The great well of human ingenuity had run dry and then Eric had stood up and said the thing everyone knew, but was afraid to say. Naturally, since it had been made known in a formal fashion, the Council would have to begin work on the problem.

There were three ideas of solution. One of them seemed more humane than the other two. This solution was eventually adopted. It was—

Stabilization!

There was great trouble at first when the people learned about it, and mass riots took place in many leading cities. The stock market crashed, and the economy of many countries went out of control. Food prices rose, and there was mass starvation. War broke out . . . for the first time in three hundred years! But Stabilization had begun, Dissenters were destroyed, radicals were carted off. It was hard and cruel but seemed to be the only answer. At last the world settled down to a rigid state, a controlled state in which there could be no change, either backward or forward.

Each year every inhabitant took a difficult, week-long examination to test whether or not he was backsliding. All youths were given fifteen years of intensive education. Those who could not keep up with the others simply disappeared. Inventions were inspected by Control Offices to make certain that they could not upset Stability. If it seemed that they might—

"And that is why we cannot allow your invention to be put into use," the Controller explained to Benton. "I am sorry."

He watched Benton, saw him start, the blood drain from his face, his hands tremble.

"Come now," he said kindly, "don't take it so hard; there are other things to do. After all, you are not in danger of the Cart!"

But Benton only stared. At last he said,

"But you don't understand; I have no invention. I don't know what you're talking about."

"No invention!" the Controller exclaimed. "But I was here the day you entered it yourself! I saw you sign the statement of ownership! You handed *me* the model!"

He stared at Benton. Then he pressed a stud on his desk and said into a small circle of light,

"Send me up the information on number 34500-D, please."

A moment passed, and then a tube appeared in the circle of light. The Controller lifted the cylindrical object out and passed it to Benton.

"You'll find your signed statement there," he said, "and it has your fingerprints in the print squares. Only you could have made them."

Numbly, Benton opened the tube and took out the papers inside. He studied them a few moments, and then slowly put them back and handed the tube to the Controller.

"Yes," he said, "that's my writing, and those are certainly my prints. But I don't understand, I never invented a thing in my life, and I've never been here before! What is this invention?"

"What is it!" the Controller echoed, amazed. "Don't you know?"

Benton shook his head. "No, I do not," he said slowly.

"Well, if you want to find out about it, you'll have to go down to the Offices. All I can tell you is that the plans you sent us have been denied rights by the Control Board. I'm only a spokesman. You'll have to take it up with them."

Benton got up and walked to the door. As with the other, this one sprang open to his touch and he went on through into the Control Offices. As the door closed behind him the Controller called angrily,

"I don't know what you're up to, but you know the penalty for upsetting Stability!"

"I'm afraid Stability is already upset," Benton answered and went on.

The Offices were gigantic. He stared down from the catwalk on which he stood, for below him a thousand men and women worked at whizzing, efficient machines. Into the machines they were feeding reams of cards. Many of the people worked at desks, typing out sheets of information, filling charts, putting cards away, decoding messages. On the walls stupendous graphs were constantly being changed. The very air was alive with the vitalness of the work being conducted, the hum of the machines, the tap-tap of the typewriters, and the mumble of voices all merged together in a quiet, contented sound. And this vast machine, which cost countless dollars a day to keep running so smoothly, had a word: Stability!

Here, the thing that kept their world together lived. This room, these hard working people, the ruthless man who sorted cards into the pile marked "for extermination" were all functioning together like a great symphony orchestra. One person off key, one person out of time, and the entire structure would tremble. But no one faltered. No one stopped and failed at his task. Benton walked down a flight of steps to the desk of the information clerk.

"Give me the entire information on an invention entered by Robert Benton, 34500-D," he said. The clerk nodded and left the desk. In a few minutes he returned with a metal box.

"This contains the plans and a small working model of the invention," he stated. He put the box on the desk and opened it. Benton stared at the contents. A small piece of intricate machinery sat squatly in the center. Underneath was a thick pile of metal sheets with diagrams on them.

"Can I take this?" Benton asked.

"If you are the owner," the clerk replied. Benton showed his identification card, the clerk studied it and compared it with the data on the invention. At last he nodded his approval, and Benton closed the box, picked it up and quickly left the building via a side exit.

The side exit let him out on one of the larger underground streets, which was a riot of lights and passing vehicles. He located his direction, and began to search for a communications car to take him home. One came along and he boarded it. After he had been traveling for a few minutes he began to carefully lift the lid of the box and peer inside at the strange model.

"What have you got there, sir?" the robot driver asked.

"I wish I knew," Benton said ruefully. Two winged flyers swooped by and waved at him, danced in the air for a second and then vanished.

"Oh, fowl," Benton murmured, "I forgot my wings."

Well, it was too late to go back and get them, the car was just then beginning to slow down in front of his house. After paying the driver he went inside and locked the door, something seldom done. The best place to observe the contents was in his "consideration" room, where he spent his leisure time while not flying. There, among his books and magazines he could observe the invention at ease.

The set of diagrams was a complete puzzle to him, and the model itself even more so. He stared at it from all angles, from underneath, from above. He tried to interpret the technical symbols of the diagrams, but all to no avail. There was but one road now open to him. He sought out the "on" switch and clicked it.

For almost a minute nothing happened. Then the room about him began to waver and give way. For a moment it shook like a quantity of jelly. It hung steady for an instant, and then vanished.

He was falling through space like an endless tunnel, and he found himself twisting about frantically, grasping into the blackness for something to take hold of. He fell for an interminable time, helplessly, frightened. Then he had landed, completely unhurt. Although it had seemed so, the fall could not have been very long. His metallic clothes were not even ruffled. He picked himself up and looked about.

The place where he had arrived was strange to him. It was a field . . . such as he had supposed no longer to exist. Waving acres of grain waved in abundance everywhere. Yet, he was certain that in no place on earth did natural grain still grow. Yes, he was positive. He shielded his eyes and gazed at the sun, but it looked the same as it always had. He began to walk.

After an hour the wheat fields ended, but with their end came a wide forest. He knew from his studies that there were no forests left on earth. They had perished years before. Where was he, then?

He began to walk again, this time more quickly. Then he started to run. Before him a small hill rose and he raced to the top of it. Looking down the other side he stared in bewilderment. There was nothing there but a great emptiness. The ground was completely level and barren, there were no trees or any sign of life as far as his eyes could see, only the extensive bleached out land of death.

He started down the other side of the hill toward the plain. It was hot and dry under his feet, but he went forward anyway. He walked on, the ground began to hurt his feet—unaccustomed to long walking—and he grew tired. But he was determined to continue. Some small whisper within his mind compelled him to maintain his pace without slowing down.

"Don't pick it up," a voice said.

"I will," he grated, half to himself, and stooped down.

Voice! From where! He turned quickly, but there was nothing to be seen. Yet the voice had come to him and it had seemed—for a moment—as if it were perfectly natural for voices to come from the air. He examined the thing he was about to pick up. It was a glass globe about as big around as his fist.

"You will destroy your valuable Stability," the voice said.

"Nothing can destroy Stability," he answered automatically. The glass globe was cool and nice against his palm. There was something inside, but heat from the glowing orb above him made it dance before his eyes, and he could not tell exactly what it was.

"You are allowing your mind to be controlled by evil things," the voice said to him. "Put the globe down and leave."

"Evil things?" he asked, surprised. It was hot, and he was beginning to feel thirsty. He started to thrust the globe inside his tunic.

"Don't," the voice ordered, "that is what it wants you to do."

The globe was nice against his chest. It nestled there, cooling him off from the fierce heat of the sun. What was it the voice was saying?

"You were called here by it through time," the voice explained. "You obey it now without question. I am its guardian, and ever since this time-world was created I have guarded it. Go away, and leave it as you found it."

Definitely, it was too warm on the plain. He wanted to leave; the globe was now urging him to, reminding him of the heat from above, the dryness in his mouth, the tingling in his head. He started off, and as he clutched the globe to him he heard the wail of despair and fury from the phantom voice.

That was almost all he remembered. He did recall that he made his way back across the plain to the fields of grain, through them, stumbling and staggering, and at last to the spot where he had first appeared. The glass globe inside his coat urged him to pick up the small time machine from where he had left it. It whispered to him what dial to change, which button to press, which knob to set. Then he was falling again, falling back up the corridor of time, back, back to the graying mist from whence he had fallen, back to his own world.

Suddenly the globe urged him to stop. The journey through time was not yet complete: there was still something that he had to do.

"You say your name is Benton? What can I do for you?" the Controller asked. "You have never been here before, have you?"

He stared at the Controller. What did he mean? Why, he had just left the office! Or had he? What day was it? Where had he been? He rubbed his head dizzily and sat down in the big chair. The Controller watched him anxiously.

"Are you all right?" he asked. "Can I help you?"

"I'm all right," Benton said. There was something in his hands.

"I want to register this invention to be approved by the Stability Council," he said, and handed the time machine to the Controller.

"Do you have the diagrams of its construction?" the Controller asked.

Benton dug deeply into his pocket and brought out the diagrams. He tossed them on the Controller's desk and laid the model beside them.

"The Council will have no trouble determining what it is," Benton said. His head ached, and he wanted to leave. He got to his feet.

"I am going," he said, and went out the side door through which he had entered. The Controller stared after him.

"Obviously," the First Member of the Control Council said, "he had been using the thing. You say the first time he came he acted as if he had been there before, but on the second visit he had no memory of having entered an invention, or even having been there before?"

"Right," the Controller said. "I thought it was suspicious at the time of the first visit, but I did not realize until he came the second time what the meaning was. Undoubtedly, he used it."

"The Central Graph records that an unstabilizing element is about to come up," the Second Member remarked. "I would wager that Mr. Benton is it."

"A time machine!" the First Member said. "Such a thing can be dangerous. Did he have anything with him when he came the—ah—first time?"

"I saw nothing, except that he walked as if he were carrying something under his coat," the Controller replied.

"Then we must act at once. He will have been able to set up a chain of circumstance by this time that our Stabilizers will have trouble in breaking. Perhaps we should visit Mr. Benton."

Benton sat in his living room and stared. His eyes were set in a kind of glassy rigidness and he had not moved for some time. The globe had been talking to him, telling him of its plans, its hopes. Now it stopped suddenly.

"They are coming," the globe said. It was resting on the couch beside him, and its faint whisper curled to his brain like a wisp of smoke. It had not actually spoken, of course, for its language was mental. But Benton heard.

"What shall I do?" he asked.

"Do nothing," the globe said. "They will go away."

The buzzer sounded and Benton remained where he was. The buzzer sounded again, and Benton stirred restlessly. After a while the men went down the walk again and appeared to have departed.

"Now what?" Benton asked. The globe did not answer for a moment.

"I feel that the time is almost here," it said at last. "I have made no mistakes so far, and the difficult part is past. The hardest was having you come through time. It took me years—the Watcher was clever. You almost didn't answer, and it was not until I thought of the method of putting the machine in your hands that success was certain. Soon you shall release us from this globe. After such an eternity—"

There was a scraping and a murmur from the rear of the house, and Benton started up.

"They are coming in the back door!" he said. The globe rustled angrily.

The Controller and the Council Members came slowly and warily into the room. They spotted Benton and stopped.

"We didn't think that you were at home," the First Member said. Benton turned to him.

"Hello," he said. "I'm sorry that I didn't answer the bell; I had fallen asleep. What can I do for you?"

Carefully, his hand reached out toward the globe, and it seemed almost as if the globe rolled under the protection of his palm.

"What have you there?" the Controller demanded suddenly. Benton stared at him, and the globe whispered in his mind.

"Nothing but a paperweight," he smiled. "Won't you sit down?"

The men took their seats, and the First Member began to speak.

"You came to see us twice, the first time to register an invention, the second time because we had summoned you to appear, as we could not allow the invention to be issued."

"Well?" Benton demanded. "Is there something the matter with that?"

"Oh, no," the Member said, "but what was for us your first visit was for *you* your second. Several things prove this, but I will not go into them just now. The thing that is important is that you still have the machine. This is a difficult problem. Where is the machine? It should be in your possession. Although we cannot force you to give it to us, we will obtain it eventually in one way or another."

"That is true," Benton said. But where *was* the machine? He had just left it at the Controller's Office. Yet he had already picked it up and taken it into time, whereupon he had returned to the present and had returned it to the Controller's Office!

"It has ceased to exist, a non-entity in a time-spiral," the globe whispered to him, catching his thoughts. "The time-spiral reached its conclusion when you deposited the machine at the Office of Control. Now these men must leave so that we can do what must be done."

Benton rose to his feet, placing the globe behind him.

"I'm afraid that I don't have the time machine," he said. "I don't even know where it is, but you may search for it if you like."

"By breaking the laws, you have made yourself eligible for the Cart," the Controller observed. "But we feel that you have done what you did without meaning to. We do not want to punish anyone without reason, we only desire to maintain Stability. Once that is upset, nothing matters."

"You may search, but you won't find it," Benton said. The Members and the Controller began to look. They overturned chairs, searched under the carpets, behind pictures, in the walls, and they found nothing.

"You see, I was telling the truth," Benton smiled, as they returned to the living room.

"You could have hidden it outside someplace," the Member shrugged. "It doesn't matter, however."

The Controller stepped forward.

"Stability is like a gyroscope," he said. "It is difficult to turn from its course, but once started it can hardly be stopped. We do not feel that you yourself have the strength to turn that gyroscope, but there may be others who can. That remains to be seen. We are going to leave now, and you will be allowed to end your own life, or wait here for the Cart. We are giving you the choice. You will be watched, of course, and I trust that you will make no attempt to flee. If so, then it will mean your immediate destruction. Stability must be maintained, at any cost."

Benton watched them, and then laid the globe on the table. The Members looked at it with interest.

"A paperweight," Benton said. "Interesting, don't you think?"

The Members lost interest. They began to prepare to leave. But the Controller examined the globe, holding it up to the light.

"A model of a city, eh?" he said. "Such fine detail."

Benton watched him.

"Why, it seems amazing that a person could ever carve so well," the Controller continued. "What city is it? It looks like an ancient one such as Tyre or Babylon, or perhaps one far in the future. You know, it reminds me of an old legend."

He looked at Benton intently as he went on.

"The legend says that once there was a very evil city, it was so evil that God made it small and shut it up in a glass, and left a watcher of some sort to see that no one came along and released the city by smashing the glass. It is supposed to have been lying for eternity, waiting to escape.

"And this is perhaps the model of it." the Controller continued.

276

"Come on!" the First Member called at the door. "We must be going; there are lots of things left to do tonight."

The Controller turned quickly to the Members.

"Wait!" he said, "Don't leave."

He crossed the room to them, still holding the globe in his hand.

"This would be a very poor time to leave," he said, and Benton saw that while his face had lost most of its color, the mouth was set in firm lines. The Controller suddenly turned again to Benton.

"Trip through time; city in a glass globe! Does that mean anything?"

The two Council Members looked puzzled and blank.

"An ignorant man crosses time and returns with a strange glass," the Controller said. "Odd thing to bring out of time, don't you think?"

Suddenly the First Member's face blanched white.

"Good God in Heaven!" he whispered. "The accursed city! That globe?"

He stared at the round ball in disbelief. The Controller looked at Benton with an amused glance.

"Odd, how stupid we may be for a time, isn't it?" he said. "But eventually we wake up. *Don't touch it!*"

Benton slowly stepped back, his hands shaking.

"Well?" he demanded. The globe was angry at being in the Controller's hand. It began to buzz, and vibrations crept down the Controller's arm. He felt them, and took a firmer grip on the globe.

"I think it wants me to break it," he said, "it wants me to smash it on the floor so that it can get out." He watched the tiny spires and building tops in the murky mistiness of the globe, so tiny that he could cover them all with his fingers.

Benton dived. He came straight and sure, the way he had flown so many times in the air. Now every minute that he had hurtled about the warm blackness of the atmosphere of the City of Lightness came back to help him. The Controller, who had always been too busy with his work, always too piled up ahead to enjoy the airsports that the City was so proud of, went down at once. The globe bounced out of his hands and rolled across the room. Benton untangled himself and leaped up. As he raced after the small shiny sphere, he caught a glimpse of the frightened, bewildered faces of the Members, of the Controller attempting to get to his feet, face contorted with pain and horror.

The globe was calling to him, whispering to him. Benton stepped swiftly toward it, and felt a rising whisper of victory and then a scream of joy as his foot crushed the glass that imprisoned it.

The globe broke with a loud popping sound. For a time it lay there, then a mist began to rise from it. Benton returned to the couch and sat down. The mist began to fill the room. It grew and grew, it seemed almost like a living thing, so strangely did it shift and turn.

Benton began to drift into sleep. The mist crowded about him, curling over his legs, up to his chest, and finally milled about his face. He sat there, slumped over on the couch, his eyes closed, letting the strange, aged fragrance envelop him.

Then he heard the voices. Tiny and far away at first, the whisper of the globe multiplied countless times. A concert of whispering voices rose from the broken globe in a swelling crescendo of exultation. Joy of victory! He saw the tiny miniature city within the globe waver and fade, then change in size and shape. He could hear it now as well as see it. The steady throbbing of the machinery like a gigantic drum. The shaking and quivering of squat metal beings.

These beings were tended. He saw the slaves, sweating, stooped, pale men, twisting in their efforts to keep the roaring furnaces of steel and power happy. It seemed to swell before his eyes until the entire room was full of it, and the sweating workmen brushed against him and around him. He was deafened by the raging power, the grinding wheels and gears and valves. Something was pushing against him, compelling him to move forward, forward to the City, and the mist gleefully echoed the new, victorious sounds of the freed ones.

When the sun came up he was already awake. The rising bell rang, but Benton had left his sleeping-cube some time before. As he fell in with the marching ranks of his companions, he thought he recognized familiar faces for an instant—men he had known someplace before. But at once the memory passed. As they marched toward the waiting machines, chanting the tuneless sounds their ancestors had chanted for centuries, and the weight of his tools pressed against his back, he counted the time before his next rest day. It was only about three weeks to go now, and anyhow, he *might* be in line for a bonus if the Machines saw fit—

For had he not been tending *his* machine faithfully?

29

The Tower

(1955)

Marghanita Laski

Laski was an English writer in many forms and a major contributor to the development of the Oxford English Dictionary. The Tower *is a powerful and intense story set in Italy.*

The road begins to rise in a series of gentle curves, passing through pleasing groves of olives and vines, 5 km. on the left is the fork for Florence. To the right may be seen the Tower of Sacrifice (470 steps) built in 1535 by Niccolo di Ferramano; superstitious fear left the tower intact when, in 1549, the surrounding village was completely destroyed . . .

Triumphantly Caroline lifted her finger from the fine italic type. There was nothing to mar the success of this afternoon. Not only had she taken the car out alone for the first time, driving unerringly on the right-hand side of the road, but what she had achieved was not a simple drive but a cultural excursion. She had taken the Italian guide-book Neville was always urging on her, and hesitantly, haltingly, she had managed to piece out enough of the language to choose a route that took in four well-thought-of frescoes, two universally-admired campaniles, and one wooden crucifix in a village church quite a long way from the main road. It was not, after all, such a bad thing that a British Council meeting had kept Neville in Florence. True, he was certain to know all about the campaniles and the frescoes, but there was just a chance that he hadn't discovered the crucifix, and how gratifying if she could, at last, have something of her own to contribute to his constantly accumulating hoard of culture.

But could she add still more? There was at least another hour of daylight and it wouldn't take more than thirty-five minutes to get back to the flat in Florence. Perhaps there would just be time to add this tower to her dutiful collection? What was it called? She bent to the guide-book again, carefully tracing the text with her finger to be sure she was translating it correctly, word by word.

But this time her moving finger stopped abruptly at the name of Niccolo di Ferramano. There had risen in her mind a picture – no, not a picture, a portrait – of a thin white face with deep-set black eyes that stared intently into hers. Why a portrait? she asked, and then she remembered.

It had been about three months ago, just after they were married, when Neville had first brought her to Florence. He himself had already lived there for two years, and during that time had been at least as concerned to accumulate Tuscan culture for himself as to disseminate English culture to the Italians. What more natural than that he should wish to share – perhaps even to show off – his discoveries to his young wife?

Caroline had come out to Italy with the idea that when she had worked through one or two galleries and made a few trips – say to Assisi and Siena – she would have done her duty as a British Council wife, and could then settle down to examining the Florentine shops, which everyone had told her were too marvellous for words. But Neville had been contemptuous of her programme. 'You can see the stuff in the galleries at any time,' he had said, 'but I'd like you to start with the pieces that the ordinary tourist doesn't see,' and of course Caroline couldn't possibly let herself be classed as an ordinary tourist. She had been proud to accompany Neville to castles and palaces privately owned to which his work gave him entry, and there to gaze with what she hoped was pleasure on the undiscovered Raphael, the Titian that had hung on the same wall ever since it was painted, the Giotto fresco under which the family that had originally commissioned it still said their prayers.

It had been on one of these pilgrimages that she had seen the face of the young man with the black eyes. They had made a long slow drive over narrow ill-made roads and at last had come to a castle on the top of a hill. The family was, to Neville's disappointment, away, but the housekeeper remembered him and led them to a long gallery lined with five centuries of family portraits.

Though she could not have admitted it even to herself, Caroline had become almost anaesthetized to Italian art. Dutifully she had followed Neville along the gallery, listening politely while in his light well-bred voice he had told her intimate anecdotes of history, and involuntarily she had let her eyes wander round the room, glancing anywhere but at the particular portrait of Neville's immediate dissertation.

It was thus that her eye was caught by a face on the other side of the room, and forgetting what was due to politeness she caught her husband's arm and demanded, 'Neville, who's that girl over there?'

But he was pleased with her. He said, 'Ah, I'm glad you picked that one out. It's generally thought to be the best thing in the collection – a Bronzino, of course,' and they went over to look at it.

The picture was painted in rich pale colours, a green curtain, a blue dress, a young face with calm brown eyes under plaits of honey-gold hair. Caroline read out the name under the picture – *Giovanna di Ferramano, 1531–1549*. That was the year the village was destroyed, she remembered now, sitting in the car by the roadside, but then she had exclaimed, 'Neville, she was only eighteen when she died.'

'They married young in those days,' Neville commented, and Caroline said in surprise, 'Oh, was she married?' It had been the radiantly virginal character of the face that had caught at her inattention.

'Yes, she was married,' Neville answered, and added, 'Look at the portrait beside her. It's Bronzino again. What do you think of it?'

And this was when Caroline had seen the pale young man. There were no clear light colours in this picture. There was only the whiteness of the face, the blackness of the eyes, the hair, the clothes, and the glint of gold letters on the pile of books on which the young man rested his hand. Underneath this picture was written *Portrait of an Unknown Gentleman.*

'Do you mean he's her husband?' Caroline asked. 'Surely they'd know if he was, instead of calling him an Unknown Gentleman?'

'He's Niccolo di Ferramano all right,' said Neville. I've seen another portrait of him somewhere, and it's not a face one would forget, but,' he added reluctantly, because he hated to admit ignorance, 'there's apparently some queer scandal about him, and though they don't turn his picture out, they won't even mention his name. Last time I was here, the old Count himself took me through the gallery. I asked him about little Giovanna and her husband.' He laughed uneasily, 'Mind you, my Italian was far from perfect at that time, but it was horribly clear that I shouldn't have asked.' 'But what did he *say*?' Caroline demanded. 'I've tried to remember,' said Neville. 'For some reason it stuck in my mind. He said either "She was lost" or "She was damned", but which word it was I can never be sure. The portrait of Niccolo he just ignored, altogether.'

'What was wrong with Niccolo, I wonder?' mused Caroline, and Neville answered, 'I don't know but I can guess. Do you notice the lettering on those books up there, under his hand? It's all in Hebrew or Arabic. Undoubtedly the unmentionable Niccolo dabbled in Black Magic.'

Caroline shivered, 'I don't like him,' she said. 'Let's look at Giovanna again,' and they had moved back to the first portrait, and Neville had said casually, 'Do you know, she's rather like you.'

'I've just got time to look at the tower,' Caroline now said aloud, and she put the guide-book back in the pigeon-hole under the dashboard, and drove carefully along the gentle curves until she came to the fork for Florence on the left.

On the top of a little hill to the right stood a tall round tower. There was no other building in sight. In a land where every available piece of ground is cultivated, there was no cultivated ground around this tower. On the left was the fork for Florence: on the right a rough track led up to the top of the hill.

Caroline knew that she wanted to take the fork to the left, to Florence and home and Neville and – said an urgent voice inside her – for safety. This voice so much shocked her that she got out of the car and began to trudge up the dusty track towards the tower.

After all, I may not come this way again, she argued; it seems silly to miss the chance of seeing it when I've already got a reason for being interested. I'm only just going to have a quick look – and she glanced at the setting sun, telling herself that she would indeed have to be quick if she were to get back to Florence before dark.

And now she had climbed the hill and was standing in front of the tower. It was built of narrow red bricks, and only thin slits pierced its surface right up to the top where Caroline could see some kind of narrow platform encircling it. Before her was an arched doorway. I'm just going to have a quick look, she assured herself again, and then she walked in.

281

She was in an empty room with a low arched ceiling. A narrow stone staircase clung to the wall and circled round the room to disappear through a hole in the ceiling.

'There ought to be a wonderful view at the top,' said Caroline firmly to herself, and she laid her hand on the rusty rail and started to climb, and as she climbed, she counted.

'– thirty-nine, forty, forty-one,' she said, and with the forty-first step she came through the ceiling and saw over her head, far far above, the deep blue evening sky, a small circle of blue framed in a narrowing shaft round which the narrow staircase spiralled. There was no inner wall; only the rusty railing protected the climber on the inside.

'– eighty-three, eighty-four –' counted Caroline. The sky above her was losing its colour and she wondered why the narrow slit windows in the wall had all been so placed that they spiralled round the staircase too high for anyone climbing it to see through them.

'It's getting dark very quickly,' said Caroline at the hundred-and-fiftieth step. 'I know what the tower is like now. It would be much more sensible to give up and go home.'

At the two-hundred-and-sixty-ninth step, her hand, moving forward on the railing, met only empty space. For an interminable second she shivered, pressing back to the hard brick on the other side. Then hesitantly she groped forwards, upwards, and at last her fingers met the rusty rail again, and again she climbed.

But now the breaks in the rail became more and more frequent. Sometimes she had to climb several steps with her left shoulder pressed tightly to the brick wall before her searching hand could find the tenuous rusty comfort again.

At the three-hundred-and-seventy-fifth step, the rail, as her moving hand clutched it, crumpled away under her fingers, 'I'd better just go by the wall,' she told herself, and now her left hand traced the rough brick as she climbed up and up.

'Four-hundred-and-twenty-two, four-hundred-and-twenty-three,' counted Caroline with part of her brain. 'I really ought to go down now,' said another part, 'I wish – oh, I want to go down now –' but she could not. 'It would be so silly to give up,' she told herself, desperately trying to rationalize what drove her on. 'Just because one's afraid –' and then she had to stifle that thought too, and there was nothing left in her brain but the steadily mounting tally of the steps.

'– four-hundred-and-seventy!' said Caroline aloud with explosive relief, and then she stopped abruptly because the steps had stopped too. There was nothing ahead but a piece of broken railing barring her way, and the sky drained now of all its colour, was still some twenty feet above her head.

'But how idiotic,' she said to the air. 'The whole thing's absolutely pointless,' and then the fingers of her left hand, exploring the wall beside her, met not brick but wood.

She turned to see what it was, and there in the wall, level with the top step, was a small wooden door. 'So it does go somewhere after all,' she said, and she fumbled with the rusty handle. The door pushed open and she stepped through.

She was on a narrow stone platform about a yard wide. It seemed to encircle the tower. The platform sloped downwards away from the tower and its stones were smooth and very shiny – and this was all she noticed before she looked beyond the stones and down.

She was immeasurably, unbelievably high and alone and the ground below was a world away. It was not credible, not possible that she should be so far from the ground. All her being was suddenly absorbed in the single impulse to hurl herself from the sloping platform. 'I cannot go down any other way,' she said, and then she heard what she said and stepped back, frenziedly clutching the soft rotten wood of the doorway with hands sodden with sweat. There is no other way, said the voice in her brain, there is no other way.

'This is vertigo,' said Caroline. 'I've only got to close my eyes and keep still for a minute and it will pass off. It's bound to pass off. I've never had it before but I know what it is and it's vertigo.' She closed her eyes and kept very still and felt the cold sweat running down her body.

'I should be all right now,' she said at last, and carefully she stepped back through the doorway on to the four-hundred-and-seventieth step and pulled the door shut before her. She looked up at the sky, swiftly darkening with night. Then, for the first time, she looked down into the shaft of the tower, down to the narrow unprotected staircase spiralling round and round and round, and disappearing into the dark. She said – she screamed – 'I can't go down.'

She stood still on the top step, staring downwards, and slowly the last light faded from the tower. She could not move. It was not possible that she should dare to go down, step by step down the unprotected stairs into the dark below. It would be much easier to fall, said the voice in her head, to take one step to the left and fall and it would all be over. You cannot climb down.

She began to cry, shuddering with the pain of her sobs. It could not be true that she had brought herself to this peril, that there could be no safety for her unless she could climb down the menacing stairs. The reality *must* be that she was safe at home with Neville – but this was the reality and here were the stairs; at last she stopped crying and said 'Now I shall go down.'

'One!' she counted and, her right hand tearing at the brick wall, she moved first one and then the other foot down to the second step. 'Two!' she counted, and then she thought of the depth below her and stood still, stupefied with terror. The stone beneath her feet, the brick against her hand were too frail protections for her exposed body. They could not save her from the voice that repeated that it would be easier to fall. Abruptly she sat down on the step.

'Two,' she counted again, and spreading both her hands tightly against the step on each side of her, she swung her body off the second step, down on to the third. 'Three,' she counted, then 'four' then 'five', pressing closer and closer into the wall, away from the empty drop on the other side.

At the twenty-first step she said, 'I think I can do it now.' She slid her right hand up the rough wall and slowly stood upright. Then with the other hand she reached for the railing it was now too dark to see, but it was not there.

For timeless time she stood there, knowing nothing but fear, 'Twenty-one,' she said, 'twenty-one,' over and over again, but she could not step on to the twenty-second stair.

Something brushed her face. She knew it was a bat, not a hand, that touched her but still it was horror beyond conceivable horror, and it was this horror, without any sense of moving from dread to safety, that at last impelled her down the stairs.

'Twenty-three, twenty-four, twenty-five –' she counted, and around her the air was full of whispering skin-stretched wings. If one of them should touch her again, she must fall. 'Twenty-six, twenty-seven, twenty-eight –' The skin of her right hand was torn and hot with blood, for she would never lift it from the wall, only press it slowly down and force her rigid legs to move from the knowledge of each step to the peril of the next.

So Caroline came down the dark tower. She could not think. She could know nothing but fear. Only her brain remorselessly recorded the tally. 'Five hundred and one,' it counted, 'five hundred and two – and three and four –'

Notes

Florence is one of the most important art cities in Italy, full of masterpieces of the Renaissance, including the paintings of Raphael, Titian, and Giotto frescoes.

p. 279   *British Council* - cultural organisation promoting British culture internationally

30

The Gold Watch

(1959)

Mulk Raj Anand

Mulk Raj Anand was a pioneer of Indian writing in English and a chronicler of poor Indian lives. This story is set in pre-independence India, but the situation it describes is characteristic of contemporary workplaces. An Indian clerk fears he is about to be 'retired' early by his distant and indifferent white boss.

There was something about the smile of Mr. Acton, when he came over to Srijut Sudarshan Sharma's table, which betokened disaster. But as the Sahib had only said, "Mr. Sharma, I have brought something for you specially from London—you must come into my office on Monday and take it . . .", the poor old dispatch clerk could not surmise the real meaning of the General Manager's remark. The fact that Mr. Acton should come over to his table at all, fawn upon him and say what he had said was, of course, most flattering. For, very rarely did the head of the firm condescend to move down the corridor where the Indian staff of the distribution department of the great Marmalade Empire of Henry King & Co., worked. But that smile on Mr. Acton's face!—specially as Mr. Acton was not known to smile too much, being a morose, old Sahib, hard working, conscientious and a slave driver, famous as a shrewd businessman, so devoted to the job of spreading the monopoly of King's Marmalade, and sundry other products, that his wife had left him after a three month's spell of marriage and never returned to India, though no one quite knew whether she was separated or divorced from him or merely preferred to stay away. So the fact that Acton Sahib should smile was enough to give Srijut Sharma cause for thought. But then Srijut Sharma was, in spite of his nobility of soul and fundamental innocence, experienced enough in his study of the vague, detached race of the white Sahibs by now and clearly noticed the slight awkward curl of the upper lip, behind which the determined, tobacco-stained long teeth showed, for the briefest moment, a snarl suppressed by the deliberation which Acton Sahib had brought to the whole operation of coming over and pronouncing those kind words. And what could be the reason for his having being singled out, from amongst the twenty-five odd members of the distribution department? In the usual way, he, the despatch clerk, only received an occasional greeting, "Hello Sharma—how you getting on?" from the head of his own department, Mr. West; and twice or thrice a year he was called into the cubicle by West

Sahib for a reprimand, because some letters or packets had gone astray; otherwise, he himself, being the incarnation of clock-work efficiency, and well-versed in the routine of his job, there was no occasion for any break in the monotony of that anonymous, smooth working Empire, so far at least as he was concerned. To be sure, there was the continual gossip of the clerks and the accountants, the bickerings and jealousies of the people above him, for grades and promotions and pay; but he, Sharma, had been employed twenty years ago, as a special favour, was not even a matriculate, but had picked up the work somehow, and though unwanted and constantly reprimanded by West Sahib in the first few years, had been retained because of the general legend of saintliness which he had acquired . . . he had five more years of service to do, because then he would be fifty-five, and the family-raising, *grhast*, portion of his life in the fourfold scheme, prescribed by religion, finished, he hoped to retire to his home town Jullunder, where his father still ran the confectioner's shop off the Mall Road.

"And what did Acton Sahib have to say to you, Mr. Sharma?" asked Miss Violet Dixon, the plain snub-nosed Anglo Indian typist in her singsong voice.

Being an old family man of fifty, who had grayed prematurely, she considered herself safe enough with this 'gentleman' and freely conversed with him, specially during the lunch hour, while she considered almost everyone else as having only one goal in life—to sleep with her.

'Han', he said, 'he has brought something for me from England', Srijut Sharma answered.

"There are such pretty things in U.K.", she said.

'My! I wish, I could go there! My sister is there, you know! Married! . . .'

She had told Sharma all these things before. So he was not interested. Specially today, because all his thoughts were concentrated on the inner meaning of Mr. Acton's sudden visitation and the ambivalent smile.

'Well, half day today, I am off'; said Violet and moved away with the peculiar snobbish agility of the Mem Sahib she affected to be.

Srijut Sharma stared at her blankly, though taking in her regular form into his subconscious with more than the old uncle's interest he had always pretended to take in her. It was only her snub nose, like that of sarupnaka, the sister of the demon king Ravana, that stood in the way of her being married, he felt sure, for otherwise she had a tolerable figure. But he lowered his eyes as soon as the thought of Miss Dixon's body began to simmer in the cauldron of his inner life; because, as a good Hindu, every woman, apart from the wife, was to him a mother or a sister. And his obsession about the meaning of Acton Sahib's words returned, from the pent up curiosity, with greater force now that he realised the vastness of the space of time during which he would have to wait in suspense before knowing what the boss had brought for him and why.

He took up his faded sola topee, which was, apart from the bush shirt and trousers, one of the few concessions to modernity which he had made throughout his life as a good Brahmin, got up from his chair, beckoned Dugdu sepoy from the verandah on his way out and asked.

"Has Acton Sahib gone, you know?"

"Abhi Sahib in lift going down," Dugdu said.

Srijut Sharma made quickly for the stairs and, throwing all caution about slipping on the polished marble steps to the winds, hurtled down. There were three floors below him and he began to sweat, both through fear of missing the Sahib and the heat of mid-April.

As he got to the ground floor, he saw Acton Sahib already going out of the door.

It was now or never.

Srijut Sharma rushed out. But he was conscious that quite a few employees of the firm would be coming out of the two lifts and he might be seen talking to the Sahib. And that was not done — outside the office. The Sahibs belonged to their private worlds, where no intrusion was tolerated, for they refuse to listen to pleas of advancement through improper channels.

Mr. Acton's uniformed driver opened the door of the polished Buick and the Sahib sat down, spreading the shadow of grimness all around him.

Srijut Sharma hesitated, for the demeanour of the Goanese chauffeur was frightening.

By now the driver had smartly shut the back door of the car and was proceeding to his seat.

That was his only chance.

Taking off his hat, he rushed up to the window of the car, and rudely thrust his head into the presence of Mr. Acton.

Luckily for him, the Sahib did not brush him aside, but smiled a broader smile than that of a few minutes ago and said: 'You want to know, what I have brought for you — well, it is a gold watch with an inscription in it . . . See me Monday morning . . .' The Sahib's initiative in anticipating his question threw Srijut Sharma further off his balance. The sweat poured down from his forehead, even as he mumbled: 'Thank You, Sir, thank you . . .'

'Chalo, driver!' Sahib ordered.

And the chauffeur turned and looked hard at Srijut Sharma.

The despatch clerk withdrew with a sheepish, abject smile on his face and stood, hat in left hand, the right hand raised to his forehead in the attitude of a nearly military salute.

The motor car moved off.

But Srijut Sharma still stood, as though he had been struck dumb. He was neither happy nor sad at this moment. Only numbed by the shock of surprise. Why should he be singled out from the whole distribution department of Henry King & Co., for the privilege of the gift of a gold watch! He had done nothing brave that he could remember. 'A gold watch, with an inscription in it!' Oh, he knew, now: the intuitive truth rose inside him: The Sahib wanted him to retire.

The revelation rose to the surface of his awareness from the deep obsessive fear, which had possessed him for nearly half an hour, and his heart began to palpitate against his will; and the sweat sozzled his body.

He reeled a little, then adjusted himself and got on to the pavement, looking after the car, which had already turned the corner into Nicol Road.

He turned and began to walk towards Victoria Terminus station. From there he had to take his train to Thana, thirty miles out where he had resided, for cheapness, almost all the years he had been in Bombay. His steps were heavy, for he was reasonably sure now that he would get notice of retirement on Monday. He tried to think of some other possible reason why the Sahib may have decided to give him the gift of a gold watch with an inscription. There was no other explanation. His doom was sealed. What would he say to his wife? And his son had still not passed his matric. How would he support the family? The provident fund would not amount to very much specially in these days of rising prices.

He felt a pull at his heart. He paused for breath and tried to calm himself. The blood pressure! Or was it merely wind? He must not get into a panic at any cost. He steadied his gait and walked along, muttering to himself, 'Shanti! Shanti! Shanti!' as though the very incantation of the formula of peace would restore his calm and equanimity.

During the week-end, Srijut Sharma was able to conceal his panic and confusion behind the facade of an exaggerated bonhomie with the skill of an accomplished natural actor. On Saturday night he went with wife and son to see Professor Ram's Circus, which was performing opposite the Portuguese Church; and he got up later than usual on Sunday morning; spent a little longer on his prayers, but seemed normal enough on the surface.

Only, he ate very little of the gala meal of the rice-kichri put before him by his wife and seemed lost in thought for a few moments at a time. And his illiterate but shrewd wife noticed that there was something on his mind.

'Thou has not eaten at all today,' she said, as he had left the tasty papadum and the mango pickle untouched. 'Look at Hari! He has left nothing in his thali!'

'Hoon,' he answered abstractedly. And, then realising he might be found out for the worried, unhappy man he was, he tried to bluff her. 'As a matter of fact, I was thinking of some happy news that the Sahib gave me yesterday: He said, he brought a gold watch as a gift for me from Vilayat . . .'

'Then Papaji give me the silver watch, which you are using now,' said Hari his young son impetuously. 'I have no watch at all and I am always late everywhere.'

'Not so impatient, son!' counselled Hari's mother. 'Let your father get the gold watch first and then — he will surely give you his silver watch.'

In the ordinary way, Srijut Sudarshan Sharma would have endorsed his wife's sentiments. But today, he felt that, on the face of it, his son's demand was justified. How should Hari know that the silver watch, and the gold watch, and a gold ring, would be all the jewellery he, the father, would have for security against hard days if the gold watch was, as he prognosticated, only a token being offered by the firm to sugarcoat the bitter pill they would ask him to swallow — retirement five years before the appointed time. He hesitated, then lifted his head, smiled at his son and said:

'Acha, Kaka, you can have my silver watch . . .'

'Can I have it, really, Papaji-Hurray!' the boy shouted, rushing away to fetch the watch from his father's pocket. 'Give it to me now, today!'

'Vay son, you are so selfish!' his mother exclaimed. For, with the peculiar sensitiveness of the woman she had surmised from the manner in which, her husband had hung his head down and then tried to smile as he lifted his face to his son, that the father of Hari was upset inside him, or at least not in his usual mood of accepting life evenly, accompanying this acceptance with the pious invocation — 'Shanti! Shanti!'

Hari brought the silver watch, adjusted it to his left ear to see if it ticked, and, happy in the possession of it, capered a little caper.

Srijut Sharma did not say anything, but pushing his thali away, got up to wash his hands.

The next day it happened as Srijut Sharma had anticipated.

He went in to see Mr. Acton as soon as the Sahib came in, for the suspense of the week-end had mounted to a crescendo by Monday morning and he had been trembling with trepidation, pale and completely unsure of himself. The General Manager called him in immediately the peon Dugdu presented the little slip with the dispatch clerk's name on it.

'Please, sit down', said Mr. Acton, lifting his grey-haired head from the papers before him. And then, pulling his keys from his trousers' pocket by the gold chain to which they were adjusted, he opened a drawer and fetched out what Sharma thought was a beautiful red case.

'Mr. Sharma, you have been a loyal friend of this firm for many years—and-you know, your loyalty has been your greatest asset here—because . . . er . . . Otherwise, we could have got someone, with better qualifications, to do your work! . . . Now . . . we are thinking of increasing the efficiency of the business all round! . . . And, we, feel that you would also like, at your age, to retire to your native Punjab . . . So, as a token of our appreciation for your loyalty to Henry King & Co., we are presenting you this gold watch' . . . and he pushed the red case towards him.

Srijut Sharma began to speak, but though his mouth opened, he could not go on. 'I am fifty years old,' he wanted to say, 'and I still have five years to go.' His facial muscles seemed to contract, his eyes were dimmed with the fumes of frustration and bitterness, his forehead was covered with sweat. At least, they might have made a little ceremony of the presentation, he could not even utter the words: 'Thank you, Sir!'

'Of course, you will also have your provident fund and one month's leave with pay before you retire . . .'

Again, Srijut Sharma tried to voice his inner protest in words which would convey his meaning without seeming to be disloyal, for he did not want to obliterate the one concession the Sahib had made to the whole record of his service with his firm. It was just likely that Mr. Acton may remind him of his failings as a despatch clerk if he should so much as indicate that he was unamenable to the suggestion made by the Sahib on behalf of Henry King & Co.

'Look at the watch—it has an inscription in it which will please you,' said Mr. Acton, to get over the embarrassment of the tension created by the silence of the despatch clerk.

These words hypnotised Sharma and, stretching his hands across the large table, he reached out for the gift.

Mr. Acton noticed the unsureness of his hand and pushed it gently forward.

Srijut Sharma picked up the red box, but, in his eagerness to follow the Sahib's behests, dropped it, even as he had held it aloft and tried to open it.

The Sahib's face was livid as he picked up the box and hurriedly opened it. Then, lifting the watch from its socket, he wound it and applied it to his ear. It was ticking. He turned it round and showed the inscription to the despatch clerk.

Srijut Sharma put both his hands out, more steadily this time, and took the gift in the manner in which a beggar receives alms, he brought the glistening object within the orbit of his eyes, but they were too dimmed to smile, however, and, then with a great heave of his head, which rocked his body from side to side, he pronounced the words:

'Thank you, Sir . . .'

Mr. Acton got up, took the gold watch from Srijut Sharma's hands and put it back in the socket of the red case. Then he stretched his right hand towards the despatch clerk, with a brisk shake-hand gesture and offered the case to him with his left hand.

Srijut Sharma instinctively took the Sahib's right hand gratefully in his two sweating hands and opened the palms out to receive the case.

'Good luck, Sharma, ' Mr. Acton said, 'come and see me after your leave is over. And when your son matriculates let me know if I can do something for him . . .'

Dumb, and with bent head, the fumes of his violent emotions rising above the mouth which could have expressed them, he withdrew in the abject manner of his ancestors going out of the presence of feudal lords.

Mr. Acton saw the danger to the watch and went ahead to open the door, so that the clerk could go out without knocking his head against the door or fall down.

As Srijut Sharma emerged from the General Manager's office, involuntary tears flowed from his eyes and his lower lip fell in a pout that somehow controlled him from breaking down completely.

The eyes of the whole office staff were on him.

In a moment, a few of the men clustered around his person.

One of them took the case from his hands, opened it and read the inscription out aloud:

"In appreciation of the loyal service of Mr. Sharma to Henry King & co., on his retirement . . ."

The curiosity of his colleagues became a little less enthusiastic as the watch passed from hand to hand.

Unable to stand, because of the wave of dizziness that swirled in his head, Srijut Sudarshan Sharma sat down on his chair, with his head hidden in his hands and allowed the tears to roll down. One of his colleagues, Mr. Banaji, the accountant, patted his back understandingly. But the pity was too much for him.

"To be sure, Seth Makhanji, the new partner has a relation, to fill Sharma's position,' another said.

'No no,' another refuted him. 'No one is required to kill himself with work in our big concern . . . We are given the Sunday off! And a fat pension years beyond it is due. The bosses are full of love for us! . . .'

'Dam fine gold watch, but it does not go!' said Sriraman, the typist.

Mr. Banaji took the watch from Sriraman and, putting it in the case, placed it before Srijut Sharma and he signalled to the others to move away.

As Srijut Sharma realised that his colleagues had drifted away, he lifted his morose head, took the case, as well as his hat, and began to walk away.

Mr. Banaji saw him off to door, his hands on Sharma's back.

'Sahibji,' the Parsi accountant said, as the lift came up and the liftman took Srijut Sharma in.

On the way home Srijut Sharma found that the gold watch only went when it was shaken. Obviously, some delicate part had broken when he had dropped it on Mr. Acton's table. He would get it mended, but he must save all the cash he could get hold of and not go spending it on the luxury of having a watch repaired now. He shouldn't have been weak with his son and given him his old silver watch. But as there would be no office to go to any more, he would not need to look at the time very much, specially in Jullunder, where time just stood still and no one bothered about keeping appointments.

Notes

p. 285   *Sahib* - Urdu, polite title for a man
p. 285   *a matriculate* - one who has passed High School Certificate
p. 286   *Grhast* - one of the four stages of life, being a householder and raising a family
p. 286   *sarupnaka . . . avana* - figures from the ancient Indian epic, the Ramayana
p. 286   *sola topee* - lightweight helmet worn against the sun
p. 286   *Brahmin* - highest Hindu caste
p. 286   *sepoy* - doorman
p. 287   *Buick* - large American car
p. 287   *chalo* - 'Let's go'
p. 288   *rice-kichri* - dish of rice and lentils
p. 288   *papadum* - thin, crisp bread
p. 288   *Acha, Kaka* - 'All right, son'
p. 289   *Shanti! Shanti!* - peace; 'calm down'

The Reservoir

(1963)

Janet Frame

Frame was born in New Zealand, travelled widely and lived in Europe most of her life; she published many stories, novels and a memoir. 'The Reservoir' takes place in the summer holidays. Children play and experiment with danger, a place is vividly described, and the children's point of view created.

It was said to be four or five miles along the gully, past orchards and farms, paddocks filled with cattle, sheep, wheat, gorse, and the squatters of the land who were the rabbits eating like modern sculpture into the hills, though how could we know anything of modern sculpture, we knew nothing but the Warrior in the main street with his wreaths of poppies on Anzac Day, the gnomes weeping in the Gardens because the seagulls perched on their green caps and showed no respect, and how important it was for birds, animals and people, especially children, to show respect!

And that is why for so long we obeyed the command of the grownups and never walked as far as the forbidden Reservoir, but were content to return 'tired but happy' (as we wrote in our school compositions), answering the question, Where did you walk today? with a suspicion of blackmail, 'Oh, nearly, nearly to the Reservoir!'

The Reservoir was the end of the world; beyond it, you fell; beyond it were paddocks of thorns, strange cattle, strange farms, legendary people whom we would never know or recognize even if they walked among us on a Friday night downtown when we went to follow the boys and listen to the Salvation Army Band and buy a milk shake in the milk bar and then return home to find that everything was all right and safe, that our mother had not run away and caught the night train to the North Island, that our father had not shot himself with worrying over the bills, but had in fact been downtown himself and had bought the usual Friday night treat, a bag of licorice allsorts and a bag of chocolate roughs, from Woolworth's.

The Reservoir haunted our lives. We never knew one until we came to this town; we had used pump water. But here, in our new house, the water ran from the taps as soon as we turned them on, and if we were careless and left them on, our father would shout, as if the affair were his personal concern, 'Do you want the Reservoir to run dry?'

That frightened us. What should we do if the Reservoir ran dry? Would we die of thirst like Burke and Wills in the desert?

'The Reservoir,' our mother said, 'gives pure water, water safe to drink without boiling it.'

The water was in a different class, then, from the creek which flowed through the gully; yet the creek had its source in the Reservoir. Why had it not received the pampering attention of officialdom which strained weed and earth, cockabullies and trout and eels, from our tap water? Surely the Reservoir was not entirely pure?

'Oh no,' they said, when we inquired. We learned that the water from the Reservoir had been 'treated'. We supposed this to mean that during the night men in light-blue uniforms with sacks over their shoulders crept beyond the circle of pine trees which enclosed the Reservoir, and emptied the contents of the sacks into the water, to dissolve dead bodies and prevent the decay of teeth.

Then, at times, there would be news in the paper, discussed by my mother with the neighbours over the back fence. Children had been drowned in the Reservoir.

'No child,' the neighbour would say, 'ought to be allowed near the Reservoir.'

'I tell mine to keep strictly away,' my mother would reply.

And for so long we obeyed our mother's command, on our favourite walks along the gully simply following the untreated cast-off creek which we loved and which flowed day and night in our heads in all its detail—the wild sweet peas, boiled-lolly pink, and the mint growing along the banks; the exact spot in the water where the latest dead sheep could be found, and the stink of its bloated flesh and floating wool, an allowable earthy stink which we accepted with pleasant revulsion and which did not prompt the 'inky-pinky I smell Stinkie' rhyme which referred to offensive human beings only. We knew where the water was shallow and could be paddled in, where forts could be made from the rocks; we knew the frightening deep places where the eels lurked and the weeds were tangled in gruesome shapes; we knew the jumping places, the mossy stones with their dangers, limitations, and advantages; the sparkling places where the sun trickled beside the water, upon the stones; the bogs made by roaming cattle, trapping some of them to death; their gaunt telltale bones; the little valleys with their new growth of lush grass where the creek had 'changed its course', and no longer flowed.

'The creek has changed its course,' our mother would say, in a tone which implied terror and a sense of strangeness, as if a tragedy had been enacted.

We knew the moods of the creek, its levels of low-flow, half-high-flow, high-flow which all seemed to relate to interference at its source—the Reservoir. If one morning the water turned the colour of clay and crowds of bubbles were passengers on every suddenly swift wave hurrying by, we would look at one another and remark with the fatality and reverence which attends a visitation or prophecy,

'The creek's going on high-flow. They must be doing something at the Reservoir.'

By afternoon the creek would be on high-flow, turbulent, muddy, unable to be jumped across or paddled in or fished in, concealing beneath a swelling fluid darkness whatever evil which 'they', the authorities, had decided to purge so swiftly and secretly from the Reservoir.

For so long, then, we obeyed our parents, and never walked as far as the Reservoir. Other things concerned us, other curiosities, fears, challenges. The school year ended. I got a prize, a large yellow book the colour of cat's mess. Inside it were editions of newspapers, *The Worms' Weekly*, supposedly written by worms, snails, spiders. For the first part of the holidays we spent the time sitting in the long grass of our front lawn nibbling the stalks of shamrock and reading insect newspapers and relating their items to the lives of those living on our front lawn down among the summer-dry roots of the couch, tinkertailor, daisy, dandelion, shamrock, clover, and ordinary 'grass'. High summer came. The blowsy old red roses shed their petals to the regretful refrain uttered by our mother year after year at the same time, 'I should have made potpourri, I have a wonderful recipe for potpourri in Dr Chase's Book.'

Our mother never made the potpourri. She merely quarrelled with our father over how to pronounce it.

The days became unbearably long and hot. Our Christmas presents were broken or too boring to care about. Celluloid dolls had loose arms and legs and rifts in their bright pink bodies; the invisible ink had poured itself out in secret messages; diaries frustrating in their smallness (two lines to a day) had been filled in for the whole of the coming year. . . . Days at the beach were tedious, with no room in the bathing sheds so that we were forced to undress in the common room downstairs with its floor patched with wet and trailed with footmarks and sand and its tiny barred window (which made me believe that I was living in the French Revolution).

Rumours circled the burning world. The sea was drying up, soon you could paddle or walk to Australia. Sharks had been seen swimming inside the breakwater; one shark attacked a little boy and bit off his you-know-what.

We swam. We wore bathing togs all day. We gave up cowboys and ranches; and baseball and sledding; and 'those games' where we mimicked grown-up life, loving and divorcing each other, kissing and slapping, taking secret paramours when our husband was working out of town. Everything exhausted us. Cracks appeared in the earth; the grass was bled yellow, the ground was littered with beetle shells and snail shells; flies came in from the unofficial rubbish-dump at the back of the house; the twisting flypapers hung from the ceiling; a frantic buzzing filled the room as the flypapers became crowded. Even the cat put out her tiny tongue, panting in the heat.

We realized, and were glad, that school would soon reopen. What was school like? It seemed so long ago, it seemed as if we had never been to school, surely we had forgotten everything we had learned, how frightening, thrilling and strange it would all seem! Where would we go on the first day, who would teach us, what were the names of the new books?

Who would sit beside us, who would be our best friend?

The earth crackled in early-autumn haze and still the February sun dried the world; even at night the rusty sheet of roofing-iron outside by the cellar stayed warm, but with rows of sweat-marks on it; the days were still long, with night face to face with morning and almost nothing in-between but a snatch of turning sleep with the blankets on the floor and the windows wide open to moths with their bulging lamplit eyes moving through the dark and their grandfather bodies knocking, knocking upon the walls.

Day after day the sun still waited to pounce. We were tired, our skin itched, our sunburn had peeled and peeled again, the skin on our feet was hard, there was dust in our hair, our bodies clung with the salt of sea-bathing and sweat, the towels were harsh with salt.

School soon, we said again, and were glad; for lessons gave shade to rooms and corridors; cloakrooms were cold and sunless. Then, swiftly, suddenly, disease came to the town. Infantile Paralysis. Black headlines in the paper, listing the number of cases, the number of deaths. Children everywhere, out in the country, up north, down south, two streets away.

The schools did not reopen. Our lessons came by post, in smudged print on rough white paper; they seemed makeshift and false, they inspired distrust, they could not compete with the lure of the sun still shining, swelling, the world would go up in cinders, the days were too long, there was nothing to do, there was nothing to do; the lessons were dull; in the front room with the navy-blue blind half down the window and the tiny splits of light showing through, and the lesson papers sometimes covered with unexplained blots of ink as if the machine which had printed them had broken down or rebelled, the lessons were even more dull.

Ancient Egypt and the flooding of the Nile!

The Nile, when we possessed a creek of our own with individual flooding!

'Well let's go along the gully, along by the creek,' we would say, tired with all these.

Then one day when our restlessness was at its height, when the flies buzzed like bees in the flypapers, and the warped wood of the house cracked its knuckles out of boredom, the need for something to do in the heat, we found once again the only solution to our unrest.

Someone said, 'What's the creek on?'

'Half-high flow'

'Good.'

So we set out, in our bathing suits, and carrying switches of willow.

'Keep your sun hats on!' our mother called.

All right. We knew. Sunstroke when the sun clipped you over the back of the head, striking you flat on the ground. Sunstroke. Lightning. Even tidal waves were threatening us on this southern coast. The world was full of alarm.

'And don't go as far as the Reservoir!'

We dismissed the warning. There was enough to occupy us along the gully without our visiting the Reservoir. First, the couples. We liked to find a courting couple and follow them and when, as we knew they must do because they were tired or for other reasons, they found a place in the grass and lay down together, we liked to make jokes about them, amongst ourselves. 'Just wait for him to kiss her,' we would say. 'Watch. There. A beaut. Smack.'

Often we giggled and lingered even after the couple had observed us. We were waiting for them to do it. Every man and woman did it, we knew that for a fact. We speculated about technical details. Would he wear a frenchie? If he didn't wear a frenchie then she would start having a baby and be forced to get rid of it by drinking gin. Frenchies, by the way, were for sale in Woolworth's. Some said they were fingerstalls, but we knew they were frenchies and sometimes we would go downtown and into Woolworth's just to look at the frenchies for sale. We hung around the counter, sniggering. Sometimes we nearly died laughing, it was so funny.

After we tired of spying on the couples we would shout after them as we went our way.

> Pound, shillings and pence,
> a man fell over the fence,
> he fell on a lady,
> and squashed out a baby,
> pound, shillings and pence!

Sometimes a slight fear struck us—what if a man fell on us like that and squashed out a chain of babies?

Our other pastime along the gully was robbing the orchards, but this summer day the apples were small green hard and hidden by leaves. There were no couples either. We had the gully to ourselves. We followed the creek, whacking our sticks, gossiping and singing, but we stopped, immediately silent, when someone—sister or brother—said, 'Let's go to the Reservoir!'

A feeling of dread seized us. We knew, as surely as we knew our names and our address Thirty-three Stour Street Ohau Otago South Island New Zealand Southern Hemisphere The World, that we would some day visit the Reservoir, but the time seemed almost as far away as leaving school, getting a job, marrying.

And then there was the agony of deciding the right time—how did one decide these things?

'We've been told not to, you know,' one of us said timidly.

That was me. Eating bread and syrup for tea had made my hair red, my skin too, so that I blushed easily, and the grownups guessed if I told a lie.

'It's a long way,' said my little sister.

'Coward!'

But it *was* a long way, and perhaps it would take all day and night, perhaps we would have to sleep there among the pine trees with the owls hooting and the old needle-filled warrens which now reached to the centre of the earth where pools of molten lead bubbled, waiting to seize us if we tripped, and then there was the crying sound made by the trees, a sound of speech at its loneliest level where the meaning is felt but never explained, and it goes on and on in a kind of despair, trying to reach a point of understanding.

We knew that pine trees spoke in this way. We were lonely listening to them because we knew we could never help them to say it, whatever they were trying to say, for if the wind who was so close to them could not help them, how could we?

Oh no, we could not spend the night at the Reservoir among the pine trees.

'Billy Whittaker and his gang have been to the Reservoir, Billy Whittaker and the Green Feather gang, one afternoon.'

'Did he say what it was like?'

'No, he never said.'

'He's been in an iron lung.'

That was true. Only a day or two ago our mother had been reminding us in an ominous voice of the fact which roused our envy just as much as our dread, 'Billy Whittaker was in an iron lung two years ago. Infantile paralysis.'

Some people were lucky. None of us dared to hope that we would ever be surrounded by the glamour of an iron lung; we would have to be content all our lives with paltry flesh lungs.

'Well are we going to the Reservoir or not?'

That was someone trying to sound bossy like our father,—'Well am I to have salmon sandwiches or not, am I to have lunch at all today or not?'

We struck our sticks in the air. They made a whistling sound. They were supple and young. We had tried to make musical instruments out of them, time after time we hacked at the willow and the elder to make pipes to blow our music, but no sound came but our own voices. And why did two sticks rubbed together not make fire? Why couldn't we ever *make* anything out of the bits of the world lying about us?

An aeroplane passed in the sky. We craned our necks to read the writing on the underwing, for we collected aeroplane numbers.

The plane was gone, in a glint of sun.

'Are we?' someone said.

'If there's an eclipse you can't see at all. The birds stop singing and go to bed.'

'Well are we?'

Certainly we were. We had not quelled all our misgiving, but we set out to follow the creek to the Reservoir.

What is it? I wondered. They said it was a lake. I thought it was a bundle of darkness and great wheels which peeled and sliced you like an apple and drew you toward them with demonic force, in the same way that you were drawn beneath the wheels of a train if you stood too near the edge of the platform. That was the terrible danger when the Limited came rushing in and you had to approach to kiss arriving aunts.

We walked on and on, past wild sweet peas, clumps of cutty grass, horse mushrooms, ragwort, gorse, cabbage trees; and then, at the end of the gully, we came to strange territory, fences we did not know, with the barbed wire tearing at our skin and at our skirts put on over our bathing suits because we felt cold though the sun stayed in the sky.

We passed huge trees that lived with their heads in the sky, with their great arms and joints creaking with age and the burden of being trees, and their mazed and linked roots rubbed bare of earth, like bones with the flesh cleaned from them. There were strange gates to be opened or climber over, new directions to be argued and plotted, notices which said TRESPASSERS WILL BE PROSECUTED BY ORDER. And there was the remote immovable sun shedding without gentleness its influence of burning upon us and upon the town, looking down from its heavens and considering our infantile-paralysis epidemic, and the children tired of holidays and wanting to go back to school with the new stiff books with their crackling pages, the scrubbed ruler with the sun rising on one side amidst the twelfths, tenths, millimetres, the new pencils to be sharpened with the pencil shavings flying in long pickets and light-brown curls scalloped with red or blue; the brown school, the bare floors, the clump clump in the corridors on wet days!

We came to a strange paddock, a bull-paddock with its occupant planted deep in the long grass, near the gate, a jersey bull polished like a wardrobe, burnished like copper, heavy beams creaking in the wave and flow of the grass.

'Has it got a ring through its nose? Is it a real bull or a steer?'

Its nose was ringed which meant that its savagery was tamed, or so we thought; it could be tethered and led; even so, it had once been savage and it kept its pride, unlike the steers who pranced and huddled together and ran like water through the paddocks, made no impression, quarried no massive shape against the sky.

The bull stood alone.

Had not Mr Bennet been gored by a bull, his own tame bull, and been rushed to Glenham Hospital for thirty-three stitches? Remembering Mr Bennet we crept cautiously close to the paddock fence, ready to escape.

Someone said, 'Look, it's pawing the ground!'

A bull which pawed the ground was preparing for a charge. We escaped quickly through the fence. Then, plucking courage, we skirted the bushes on the far side of the paddock, climbed through the fence, and continued our walk to the Reservoir.

We had lost the creek between deep banks. We saw it now before us, and hailed it with more relief than we felt, for in its hidden course through the bull-paddock it had undergone change, it had adopted the shape, depth, mood of foreign water, foaming in a way we did not recognize as belonging to our special creek, giving no hint of its depth. It seemed to flow close to its concealed bed, not wishing any more to communicate with us. We realized with dismay that we had suddenly lost possession of our creek. Who had taken it? Why did it not belong to us any more? We hit our sticks in the air and forgot our dismay. We grew cheerful.

Till someone said that it was getting late, and we reminded one another that during the day the sun doesn't seem to move, it just remains pinned with a drawing pin against the sky, and then, while you are not looking, it suddenly slides down quick as the chopped-off head of a golden eel, into the sea, making everything in the world go dark.

'That's only in the tropics!'

We were not in the tropics. The divisions of the world in the atlas, the different coloured cubicles of latitude and longitude fascinated us.

'The sand freezes in the desert at night. Ladies wear bits of sand. . . .'

'grains . . .'

'grains or bits of sand as necklaces, and the camels . . .'

'with necks like snails . . .'

'with horns, do they have horns?'

'Minnie Stocks goes with boys. . . .'

'I know who your boy is, I know who your boy is. . . .'

> Waiting by the garden gate,

> Waiting by the garden gate . . .

'We'll never get to the Reservoir!'

'Whose idea was it?'

'I've strained my ankle!'

Someone began to cry. We stopped walking.

"I've strained my ankle."

There was an argument.

'It's not strained, it's sprained.'

'strained.'

'sprained.'

'All right sprained then. I'll have to wear a bandage, I'll have to walk on crutches. . . .'

'I had crutches once. Look. I've got a scar where I fell off my stilts. It's a white scar, like a centipede. It's on my shins.'

'Shins! Isn't it a funny word? Shins. Have you ever been kicked in the shins?'

'shins, funnybone . . .'

'It's humerus. . . .'

'knuckles . . .'

'a sprained ankle . . .'

'a strained ankle . . .'

'a whitlow, an ingrown toenail the roots of my hair warts spinal meningitis infantile paralysis . . .'

'Infantile paralysis, Infantile paralysis you have to be wheeled in a chair and wear irons on your legs and your knees knock together. . . .'

'Once you're in an iron lung you can't get out, they lock it, like a cage. . . .'

'You go in the amberlance . . .'

'*ambulance* . . .'

'amberlance . . .'

'ambulance to the hostible. . . .'

'the *hospital*, an *amberlance to the hospital* . . .'

'Infantile Paralysis . . .'

'Friar's Balsam! Friar's Balsam!'

'Baxter's Lung Preserver, Baxter's Lung Preserver!'

'Syrup of Figs, California Syrup of Figs!'

'The creek's going on high-flow!'

Yes, there were bubbles on the surface, and the water was turning muddy. Our doubts were dispelled. It was the same old creek, and there, suddenly, just ahead, was a plantation of pine trees, and already the sighing sound of it reached our ears and troubled us. We approached it, staying close to the banks of our newly claimed creek, until once again the creek deserted us, flowing its own private course where we could not follow, and we found ourselves among the pine trees, a narrow strip of them, and beyond lay a vast surface of sparkling water, dazzling our eyes, its centre chopped by tiny grey waves. Not a lake, nor a river, nor a sea.

'The Reservoir!'

The damp smell of the pine needles caught in our breath. There were no birds, only the constant sighing of the trees. We could see the water clearly now, it lay, except for the waves beyond the shore, in an almost perfect calm which we knew to be deceptive—else why were people so afraid of the Reservoir? The fringe of young pines on the edge, like toy trees, subjected to the wind, sighed and told us their sad secrets. In the Reservoir there was an appearance of neatness which concealed a disarray too frightening to be acknowledged except, without any defence, in moments of deep sleep and dreaming. The little sparkling innocent waves shone now green, now grey, petticoats, lettuce leaves; the trees sighed, and told us to be quiet, hush-sh, as if something were sleeping and should not be disturbed—perhaps that was what the trees were always telling us, to hush-sh in case we disturbed something which must never ever be awakened?

What was it? Was it sleeping in the Reservoir? Was that why people were afraid of the Reservoir?

Well we were not afraid of it, oh no, it was only the Reservoir, it was nothing to be afraid of, it was just a flat Reservoir with a fence around it, and trees, and on the far side a little house (with wheels inside?), and nothing to be afraid of.

'The Reservoir, The Reservoir!'

A noticeboard said DANGER, RESERVOIR.

Overcome with sudden glee we climbed through the fence and swung on the lower branches of the trees, shouting at intervals, gazing possessively and delightedly at the sheet of water with its wonderful calm and menace.

'The Reservoir! The Reservoir! The Reservoir!'

We quarrelled again about how to pronounce and spell the word.

Then it seemed to be getting dark—or was it that the trees were stealing the sunlight and keeping it above their heads? One of us began to run. We all ran, suddenly, wildly, not caring about our strained or sprained ankles, through the trees out into the sun where the creek, but it was our creek no longer, waited for us. We wished it were our creek, how we wished it were our creek! We had lost all account of time. Was it nearly night? Would darkness overtake us, would we have to sleep on the banks of the creek that did not belong to us any more, among the wild sweet peas and the tussocks and the dead sheep? And would the eels come up out of the creek, as people said they did, and on their travels through the paddocks would they change into people who would threaten us and bar our way, TRESPASSERS WILL BE PROSECUTED, standing arm in arm in their black glossy coats, swaying, their mouths open, ready to swallow us? Would they ever let us go home, past the orchards, along the gully? Perhaps they would give us Infantile Paralysis, perhaps we would never be able to walk home, and no one would know where we were, to bring us an iron lung with its own special key!

We arrived home, panting and scratched. How strange! The sun was still in the same place in the sky!

The question troubled us, 'Should we tell?'

The answer was decided for us. Our mother greeted us as we went in the door with, 'You haven't been long away, kiddies. Where have you been? I hope you didn't go anywhere near the Reservoir.'

Our father looked up from reading his newspapers.

'Don't let me catch you going near the Reservoir!

We said nothing. How out-of-date they were! They were actually afraid!

Notes

p. 292   *Anzac Day* - day of remembrance for those killed in war
p. 292   *Salvation Army* - Protestant religious organisation, structured in a military
          way and with brass bands who often march in the streets
p. 292   *Woolworth's* - inexpensive department store
p. 293   *Burke and Wills* - nineteenth-century European explorers who died in the
          Australian desert
p. 294   *potpourri* - dried petals used to scent a room
p. 296   *frenchie* - condom
p. 297   *iron lung* - a large cylinder in which the patient would lie – for treating patients
          whose lungs were damaged and could not breathe unaided
p. 300   *Friar's Balsam etc.* - medicines

32

Thank You M'am

(1963)

Langston Hughes

Hughes was an African-American poet, a pioneer of 'jazz poetry' and a prolific writer in every form. In Thank You M'am, *a young boy fails to snatch a bag from a woman who then turns the tables on him by treating him as the child in need of parenting that he really is.*

She was a large woman with a large purse that had everything in it but a hammer and nails. It had a long strap, and she carried it slung across her shoulder. It was about eleven o'clock at night, dark, and she was walking alone, when a boy ran up behind her and tried to snatch her purse. The strap broke with the sudden single tug the boy gave it from behind. But the boy's weight and the weight of the purse combined caused him to lose his balance. Instead of taking off full blast as he had hoped, the boy fell on his back on the sidewalk and his legs flew up. The large woman simply turned around and kicked him right square in his blue-jeaned sitter. Then she reached down, picked the boy up by his shirt front, and shook him until his teeth rattled.

After that the woman said, "Pick up my pocketbook, boy, and give it here."

She still held him tightly. But she bent down enough to permit him to stoop and pick up her purse. Then she said, "Now ain't you ashamed of yourself?"

Firmly gripped by his shirt front, the boy said, "Yes'm."

The woman said, "What did you want to do it for?"

The boy said, "I didn't aim to."

She said, "You a lie!"

By that time two or three people passed, stopped, turned to look, and some stood watching.

"If I turn you loose, will you run?" asked the woman.

"Yes'm," said the boy.

"Then I won't turn you loose," said the woman. She did not release him.

"Lady, I'm sorry," whispered the boy.

"Um-hum! Your face is dirty. I got a great mind to wash your face for you. Ain't you got nobody home to tell you to wash your face?"

"No'm," said the boy.

"Then it will get washed this evening," said the large woman, starting up the street, dragging the frightened boy behind her.

He looked as if he were fourteen or fifteen, frail and willow-wild, in tennis shoes and blue jeans.

The woman said, "You ought to be my son. I would teach you right from wrong. Least I can do right now is to wash your face. Are you hungry?"

"No'm," said the being-dragged boy. "I just want you to turn me loose."

"Was I bothering *you* when I turned that corner?" asked the woman.

"No'm."

"But you put yourself in contact with *me*," said the woman. "If you think that that contact is not going to last awhile, you got another thought coming. When I get through with you, sir, you are going to remember Mrs. Luella Bates Washington Jones."

Sweat popped out on the boy's face and he began to struggle. Mrs. Jones stopped, jerked him around in front of her, put a half nelson about his neck, and continued to drag him up the street. When she got to her door, she dragged the boy inside, down a hall, and into a large kitchenette-furnished room at the rear of the house. She switched on the light and left the door open. The boy could hear other roomers laughing and talking in the large house. Some of their doors were open, too, so he knew he and the woman were not alone. The woman still had him by the neck in the middle of her room.

She said, "What is your name?"

"Roger," answered the boy.

"Then, Roger, you go to that sink and wash your face," said the woman, whereupon she turned him loose—at last. Roger looked at the door—looked at the woman—looked at the door—*and went to the sink*.

"Let the water run until it gets warm," she said. "Here's a clean towel."

"You gonna take me to jail?" asked the boy, bending over the sink.

"Not with that face, I would not take you nowhere," said the woman.

"Here I am trying to get home to cook me a bite to eat, and you snatch my pocketbook! Maybe you ain't been to your supper either, late as it be. Have you?"

"There's nobody home at my house," said the boy.

"Then we'll eat," said the woman. "I believe you're hungry—or been hungry—to try to snatch my pocketbook!"

"I want a pair of blue suede shoes," said the boy.

"Well, you didn't have to snatch *my* pocketbook to get some suede shoes," said Mrs. Luella Bates Washington Jones. "You could of asked me."

"M'am?"

The water dripping from his face, the boy looked at her. There was a long pause. A very long pause. After he had dried his face and not knowing what else to do, dried it again, the boy turned around, wondering what next. The door was open. He could make a dash for it down the hall. He could run, run, run, *run!*

The woman was sitting on the day bed. After a while she said, "I were young once and I wanted things I could not get."

There was another long pause. The boy's mouth opened. Then he frowned, not knowing he frowned.

The woman said, "Um-hum! You thought I was going to say *but*, didn't you? You thought I was going to say, *but I didn't snatch people's pocketbooks*. Well, I wasn't going to say that." Pause. Silence. "I have done things, too, which I would not tell you, son— neither tell God, if He didn't already know. Everybody's got something in common. So you set down while I fix us something to eat. You might run that comb through your hair so you will look presentable."

In another corner of the room behind a screen was a gas plate and an icebox. Mrs. Jones got up and went behind the screen. The woman did not watch the boy to see if he was going to run now, nor did she watch her purse, which she left behind her on the day bed. But the boy took care to sit on the far side of the room, away from the purse, where he thought she could easily see him out of the corner of her eye if she wanted to. He did not trust the woman *not* to trust him. And he did not want to be mistrusted now.

"Do you need somebody to go to the store," asked the boy, "maybe to get some milk or something?"

"Don't believe I do," said the woman, "unless you just want sweet milk yourself. I was going to make cocoa out of this canned milk I got here."

"That will be fine," said the boy.

She heated some lima beans and ham she had in the icebox, made the cocoa, and set the table. The woman did not ask the boy anything about where he lived, or his folks, or anything else that would embarrass him. Instead, as they ate, she told him about her job in a hotel beauty shop that stayed open late, what the work was like, and how all kinds of women came in and out, blondes, redheads, and Spanish. Then she cut him a half of her ten-cent cake.

"Eat some more, son," she said.

When they were finished eating, she got up and said, "Now here, take this ten dollars and buy yourself some blue suede shoes. And next time, do not make the mistake of latching onto *my* pocketbook *nor nobody else's*—because shoes got by devilish ways will burn your feet. I got to get my rest now. But from here on in, son, I hope you will behave yourself."

She led him down the hall to the front door and opened it. "Good night! Behave yourself, boy!" she said, looking out into the street as he went down the steps.

The boy wanted to say something other than, "Thank you, m'am," to Mrs. Luella Bates Washington Jones, but although his lips moved, he couldn't even say that as he turned at the foot of the barren stoop and looked up at the large woman in the door. Then she shut the door.

Notes

p. 302   *purse* - handbag
p. 302   *pocketbook* - wallet
p. 303   *half nelson* - a move from wrestling: strangle-hold on the neck
p. 303   *roomers* - lodgers

33

A Visit

(1968)

Anna Kavan

Kavan, a British experimental writer, was an artist and then a writer. She travelled very widely and in this story the beautifully visualised setting could be any one of a number of countries. Her work is often on the borders of fantasy and science fiction. In this story, a leopard arrives one night – a strange magical realist story that may be read on different levels.

One hot night a leopard came into my room and lay down on the bed beside me. I was half asleep, and did not realize at first that it was a leopard. I seemed to be dreaming the sound of some large, soft-footed creature padding quietly through the house, the doors of which were wide open because of the intense heat. It was almost too dark to see the lithe, muscular shape coming into my room, treading softly on velvet paws, coming straight to the bed without hesitation, as if perfectly familiar with its position. A light spring, then warm breath on my arm, on my neck and shoulder, as the visitor sniffed me before lying down. It was not until later, when moonlight entering through the window revealed an abstract spotted design, that I recognized the form of an unusually large, handsome leopard stretched out beside me.

His breathing was deep though almost inaudible, he seemed to be sound asleep. I watched the regular contractions and expansions of the deep chest, admired the elegant relaxed body and supple limbs, and was confirmed in my conviction that the leopard is the most beautiful of all wild animals. In this particular specimen I noticed something singularly human about the formation of the skull, which was domed rather than flattened, as is generally the case with the big cats, suggesting the possibility of superior brain development inside. While I observed him, I was all the time breathing his natural odour, a wild primeval smell of sunshine, freedom, moon and crushed leaves, combined with the cool freshness of the spotted hide, still damp with the midnight moisture of jungle plants. I found this non-human scent, surrounding him like an aura of strangeness, peculiarly attractive and stimulating.

My bed, like the walls of the house, was made of palm-leaf matting stretched over stout bamboos, smooth and cool to the touch, even in the great heat. It was not so much a bed as a room within a room, an open staging about twelve feet square, so there was ample space for the leopard as well as myself. I slept better that night than I had since the hot weather started, and he too seemed to sleep peacefully at my side. The close proximity of this powerful body of another species gave me a pleasant sensation I am at a loss to name.

When I awoke in the faint light of dawn, with the parrots screeching outside, he had already got up and left the room. Looking out, I saw him standing, statuesque, in front of the house on the small strip of ground I keep cleared between it and the jungle. I thought he was contemplating departure, but I dressed and went out, and he was still there, inspecting the fringe of the dense vegetation, in which huge heavy hornbills were noisily flopping about.

I called him and fed him with some meat I had in the house. I hoped he would speak, tell me why he had come and what he wanted of me. But though he looked at me thoughtfully with his large, lustrous eyes, seeming to understand what I said, he did not answer, but remained silent all day. I must emphasize that there was no hint of obstinacy or hostility in his silence, and I did not resent it. On the contrary, I respected him for his reserve; and, as the silence continued unbroken, I gave up expecting to hear his voice. I was glad of the pretext for using mine and went on talking to him. He always appeared to listen and understand me.

The leopard was absent during much of the day. I assumed that he went hunting for his natural food; but he usually came back at intervals, and seldom seemed to be far away. It was difficult to see him among the trees, even when he was quite close, the pattern of his protective spots blended so perfectly with the pattern of sun-spots through savage branches. Only by staring with concentrated attention could I distinguish him from his background; he would be crouching there in a deep-shaded glade, or lying extended with extraordinary grace along a limb of one of the giant kowikawas, whose branch-structure supports less robust trees, as well as countless creepers and smaller growths. The odd thing was that, as soon as I'd seen him, he invariably turned his head as if conscious that I was watching. Once I saw him much further off, on the beach, which is only just visible from my house. He was standing darkly outlined against the water, gazing out to sea; but even at this distance, his head turned in my direction, though I couldn't possibly have been in his range of vision. Sometimes he would suddenly come indoors and silently go all through the house at a quick trot, unexpectedly entering one room after another, before he left again with the same mysterious abruptness. At other times he would lie just inside or outside, with his head resting on the threshold, motionless except for his watchful moving eyes, and the twitching of his sensitive nostrils in response to stimuli which my less acute senses could not perceive.

His movements were always silent, graceful, dignified, sure; and his large, dark eyes never failed to acknowledge me whenever we met in our daily comings and goings.

I was delighted with my visitor, whose silence did not conceal his awareness of me. If I walked through the jungle to visit someone, or to buy food from the neighbouring village, he would appear from nowhere and walk beside me, but always stopped before a house was in sight, never allowing himself to be seen. Every night, of course, he slept on the bed at my side. As the weeks passed he seemed to be spending more time with me during the day, sitting or lying near me while I was working, now and then coming close to gaze attentively at what I was doing.

Then, without warning, he suddenly left me. This was how it happened. The rainy season had come, bringing cooler weather; there was a chill in the early morning air, when he returned to my room as I finished dressing, and leaned against me for a moment. He had hardly ever touched me in daylight, certainly never in that deliberate fashion. I took it to mean that he wished me to do something for him, and asked what it was. Silently he led the way out of the house, pausing to look back every few steps to see whether I was coming, and into the jungle. The stormy sky was heavily clouded, it was almost dark under the trees, from which great drops of last night's rain splashed coldly on my neck and bare arms. As he evidently wanted me to accompany him further, I said I would go back for a coat.

However, he seemed to be too impatient to wait, lunging forward with long loping strides, his shoulders thrusting like steel pistons under the velvet coat, while I reluctantly followed. Torrential rain began streaming down, in five minutes the ground was a bog, into which my feet sank at each step. By now I was shivering, soaked to the skin, so I stopped and told him I couldn't go on any further. He turned his head and for a long moment his limpid eyes looked at me fixedly, with an expression I could not read. Then the beautiful head turned away, the muscles slid and bunched beneath patterned fur, as he launched himself in a tremendous leap through the shining curtain of raindrops, and was instantly hidden from sight. I walked home as fast as I could, and changed into dry clothes. I did not expect to see him again before evening, but he did not come back at all.

Nothing of any interest took place after the leopard's visit. My life resumed its former routine of work and trivial happenings. The rains came to an end, winter merged imperceptibly into spring. I took pleasure in the sun and the natural world. I felt sure the leopard meant to return, and often looked out for him, but throughout this period he never appeared. When the sky hung pure and cloudless over the jungle, many-coloured orchids began to flower on the trees. I went to see one or two people I knew; a few people visited me in my house. The leopard was never mentioned in our conversations.

The heat increased day by day, each day dawned glassily clear. The atmosphere was pervaded by the aphrodisiac perfume of wild white jasmine, which the girls wove into wreaths for their necks and hair. I painted some large new murals on the walls of my house, and started to make a terrace from a mosaic of coloured shells. For months I'd been expecting to see the leopard, but as time kept passing without a sign of him, I was gradually losing hope.

The season of oppressive heat came round in due course, and the house was left open all night. More than at any other time, it was at night, just before falling asleep, that I thought of the leopard, and, though I no longer believed it would happen, pretended that I'd wake to find him beside me again. The heat deprived me of energy, the progress of the mosaic was slow. I had never tried my hand at such work before, and being unable to calculate the total quantity of shells that would be required, I constantly ran out of supplies, and had to make tiring trips to the beach for more.

One day while I was on the shore, I saw, out to sea, a young man coming towards the land, standing upright on the crest of a huge breaker, his red cloak blowing out in the wind, and a string of pelicans solemnly flapping in line behind him. It was so odd to see this stranger, with his weird escort, approaching alone from the ocean on which no ships ever sailed, that my thoughts immediately connected him with the leopard: there must be some contact between them; perhaps he was bringing me news. As he got nearer, I shouted to him, called out greetings and questions, to which he replied. But because of the noise of the waves and the distance between us, I could not understand him. Instead of coming on to the beach to speak to me, he suddenly turned and was swept out to sea again, disappearing in clouds of spray. I was puzzled and disappointed. But I took the shells home, went on working as usual, and presently forgot the encounter.

Some time later, coming home at sunset, I was reminded of the young man of the sea by the sight of a pelican perched on the highest point of my roof. Its presence surprised me: pelicans did not leave the shore as a rule, I had never known one come as far inland as this. It suddenly struck me that the bird must be something to do with the leopard, perhaps bringing a message from him. To entice it closer, I found a small fish in the kitchen, which I put on the grass. The pelican swooped down at once, and with remarkable speed and neatness, considering its bulk, skewered the fish on its beak, and flew off with it. I called out, strained my eyes to follow its flight; but only caught a glimpse of the great wings flapping away from me over the jungle trees, before the sudden black curtain of tropical darkness came down with a rush.

Despite this inconclusive end to the episode, it revived my hope of seeing the leopard again. But there were no further developments of any description; nothing else in the least unusual occurred.

It was still the season when the earth sweltered under a simmering sky. In the afternoons the welcome trade wind blew through the rooms and cooled them, but as soon as it died down the house felt hotter than ever. Hitherto I had always derived a nostalgic pleasure from recalling my visitor; but now the memory aroused more sadness than joy, as I had finally lost all hope of his coming back.

At last the mosaic was finished and looked quite impressive, a noble animal with a fine spotted coat and a human head gazing proudly from the centre of the design. I decided it needed to be enclosed in a border of yellow shells, and made another expedition to the beach, where the sun's power was intensified by the glare off the bright green waves, sparkling as if they'd been sprinkled all over with diamonds. A hot wind whistled through my hair, blew the sand about, and lashed the sea into crashing breakers, above which flocks of sea birds flew screaming, in glistening clouds of spray. After searching for shells for a while I straightened up, feeling almost dizzy with the heat and the effort. It was at this moment, when I was dazzled by the violent colours and the terrific glare, that the young man I'd already seen reappeared like a mirage, the red of his flying cloak vibrating against the vivid emerald-green waves. This time, through a haze of shimmering brilliance, I saw that the leopard was with him, majestic and larger than life, moving as gracefully as if the waves were solid glass.

I called to him, and though he couldn't have heard me above the thundering of the surf, he turned his splendid head and gave me a long, strange, portentous look, just as he had that last time in the jungle, sparkling rainbows of spray now taking the place of rain. I hurried towards the edge of the water, then suddenly stopped, intimidated by the colossal size of the giant rollers towering over me.

I'm not a strong swimmer, it seemed insane to challenge those enormous on-coming walls of water, which would certainly hurl me back contemptuously on to the shore with all my bones broken. Their exploding roar deafened me, I was half-blinded by the salt spray, the whole beach was a swirling, glittering dazzle, in which I lost sight of the two sea-borne shapes. And when my eyes brought them back into focus, they had changed direction, turned from the land, and were already a long way off, receding fast, diminishing every second, reduced to vanishing point by the hard, blinding brilliance of sun and waves.

Long after they'd disappeared, I stood there, staring out at that turbulent sea, on which I had never once seen any kind of boat, and which now looked emptier, lonelier, and more desolate than ever before. I was paralysed by depression and disappointment, and could hardly force myself to pick up the shells I'd collected and carry them home.

That was the last time I saw the leopard. I've heard nothing of him since that day, or of the young man. For a little while I used to question the villagers who lived by the sea, some of them said they vaguely remembered a man in a red cloak riding the water. But they always ended by becoming evasive, uncertain, and making contradictory statements, so that I knew I was wasting my time.

I've never said a word about the leopard to anyone. It would be difficult to describe him to these simple people, who can never have seen a creature even remotely like him, living here in the wilds as they do, far from zoos, circuses, cinemas and television. No carnivora, no large or ferocious beasts of any sort have ever inhabited this part of the world, which is why we can leave our houses open all night without fear.

The uneventful course of my life continues, nothing happens to break the monotony of the days. Sometime, I suppose, I may forget the leopard's visit. As it is I seldom think of him, except at night when I'm waiting for sleep to come. But, very occasionally he still enters my dreams, which disturbs me and makes me feel restless and sad. Although I never remember the dreams when I wake, for days afterwards they seem to weigh me down with the obscure bitterness of a loss which should have been prevented, and for which I am myself to blame.

Notes

p. 307   *hornbills* - tropical birds
p. 307   *kowikawa* - tree

34

The Axe

(1975)

Penelope Fitzgerald

Fitzgerald was a British novelist and biographer who wrote few but brilliant short stories. Her novels – The Bookshop, The Blue Flower, Offshore *– often present ordinary life in a fantastic way. In this exquisitely ironic story, an office worker recounts an unfortunate incident in his working life with mounting horror.*

. . . You will recall that when the planned redundancies became necessary as the result of the discouraging trading figures shown by this small firm – in contrast, so I gather from the Company reports, with several of your other enterprises – you personally deputed to me the task of 'speaking' to those who were to be asked to leave. It was suggested to me that if they were asked to resign in order to avoid the unpleasantness of being given their cards, it might be unnecessary for the firm to offer any compensation. Having glanced personally through my staff sheets, you underlined the names of four people, the first being that of my clerical assistant, W. S. Singlebury. Your actual words to me were that he seemed fairly old and could probably be frightened into taking a powder. You were speaking to me in your 'democratic' style.

From this point on I feel able to write more freely, it being well understood, at office-managerial level, that you do not read more than the first two sentences of any given report. You believe that anything which cannot be put into two sentences is not worth attending to, a piece of wisdom which you usually attribute to the late Lord Beaverbrook.

As I question whether you have ever seen Singlebury, with whom this report is mainly concerned, it may be helpful to describe him. He worked for the Company for many more years than myself, and his attendance record was excellent. On Mondays, Wednesdays and Fridays, he wore a blue suit and a green knitted garment with a front zip. On Tuesdays and Thursdays he wore a pair of grey trousers of man-made material which he called 'my flannels', and a fawn cardigan. The cardigan was omitted in summer. He had, however, one distinguishing feature, very light blue eyes, with a defensive expression, as though apologizing for something which he felt guilty about but could not put right. The fact is that he was getting old. Getting old is, of course, a crime of which we grow more guilty every day.

Singlebury had no wife or dependants, and was by no means a communicative man. His room is, or was, a kind of cubby-hole adjoining mine – you have to go through it to get into my room – and it was always kept very neat. About his 'things' he did show some mild emotion. They had to be ranged in a certain pattern in respect to his in and out trays, and Singlebury stayed behind for two or three minutes every evening to do this. He also managed to retain every year the complimentary desk calendar sent to us by Dino's, the Italian café on the corner. Singlebury was in fact the only one of my personnel who was always quite certain of the date. To this too his attitude was apologetic. His phrase was, 'I'm afraid it's Tuesday.'

His work, as was freely admitted, was his life, but the nature of his duties – though they included the post-book and the addressograph – were rather hard to define, having grown round him with the years. I can only say that after he left, I was surprised myself to discover how much he had had to do.

Oddly connected in my mind with the matter of the redundancies is the irritation of the damp in the office this summer and the peculiar smell (not the ordinary smell of damp), emphasized by the sudden appearance of representatives of a firm of damp eliminators who had not been sent for by me, nor is there any record of my having done so. These people simply vanished at the end of the day and have not returned. Another firm, to whom I applied as a result of frequent complaints by the female staff, have answered my letters but have so far failed to call.

Singlebury remained unaffected by the smell. Joining, very much against his usual habit in one of the too frequent discussions of the subject, he said that he knew what it was; it was the smell of disappointment For an awkward moment I thought he must have found out by some means that he was going to be asked to go, but he went on to explain that in 1942 the whole building had been requisitioned by the Admiralty and that relatives had been allowed to wait or queue there in the hope of getting news of those missing at sea. The repeated disappointment of these women, Singlebury said, must have permeated the building like a corrosive gas. All this was very unlike him. I make it a point not to encourage anything morbid. Singlebury was quite insistent and added, as though by way of proof, that the lino in the corridors was Admiralty issue and had not been renewed since 1942 either. I was astonished to realize that he had been working in the building for so many years before the present tenancy. I realized that he must be considerably older than he had given us to understand. This, of course, will mean that there are wrong entries on his cards.

The actual notification to the redundant staff passed off rather better, in a way, than I had anticipated. By that time everyone in the office seemed inexplicably conversant with the details, and several of them in fact had gone far beyond their terms of reference, young Patel, for instance, who openly admits that he will be leaving us as soon as he can get a better job, taking me aside and telling me that to such a man as Singlebury dismissal would be like death. Dismissal is not the right word, I said. But death is, Patel replied. Singlebury himself, however, took it very quietly. Even when I raised the question of the Company's Early Retirement pension scheme, which I could not pretend was over-generous, he said very little. He was generally felt to be in a state of shock. The two girls whom you asked me to speak to were quite unaffected, having already found themselves employment as hostesses at the Dolphinarium near here. Mrs Horrocks, of Filing, on the other hand, *did* protest, and was so offensive on the question of severance pay that I was obliged to agree to refer it to a higher level. I consider this as one of the hardest day's work that I have ever done for the Company.

Just before his month's notice (if we are to call it that) was up, Singlebury, to my great surprise, asked me to come home with him one evening for a meal. In all the past years the idea of his having a home, still less asking anyone back to it, had never arisen, and I did not at all want to go there now. I felt sure, too, that he would want to reopen the matter of compensation, and only a quite unjustified feeling of guilt made me accept. We took an Underground together after work, travelling in the late rush-hour to Clapham North, and walked some distance in the rain. His place, when we eventually got to it, seemed particularly inconvenient, the entrance being through a small cleaner's shop. It consisted of one room and a shared toilet on the half-landing. The room itself was tidy, arranged, so it struck me, much on the lines of his cubby-hole, but the window was shut and it was oppressively stuffy. This is where I bury myself, said Singlebury.

There were no cooking arrangements and he left me there while he went down to fetch us something ready to eat from the Steakorama next to the cleaners. In his absence I took the opportunity to examine his room, though of course not in an inquisitive or prying manner. I was struck by the fact that none of his small store of stationery had been brought home from the office. He returned with two steaks wrapped in aluminium foil, evidently a special treat in my honour, and afterwards he went out on to the landing and made cocoa, a drink which I had not tasted for more than thirty years. The evening dragged rather. In the course of conversation it turned out that Singlebury was fond of reading. There were in fact several issues of a colour-printed encyclopaedia which he had been collecting as it came out, but unfortunately it had ceased publication after the seventh part. Reading is my hobby, he said. I pointed out that a hobby was rather something that one did with one's hands or in the open air – a relief from the work of the brain. Oh, I don't accept that distinction, Singlebury said. The mind and the body are the same. Well, one cannot deny the connection, I replied. Fear, for example, releases adrenalin, which directly affects the nerves. I don't mean connection. I mean identity, Singlebury said, the mind is the blood. Nonsense, I said, you might just as well tell me that the blood is the mind. It stands to reason that the blood can't think.

I was right, after all, in thinking that he would refer to the matter of the redundancy. This was not until he was seeing me off at the bus-stop, when for a moment he turned his grey, exposed-looking face away from me and said that he did not see how he could manage if he really had to go. He stood there like someone who has 'tried to give satisfaction' – he even used this phrase, saying that if the expression were not redolent of a bygone age, he would like to feel he had given satisfaction. Fortunately we had not long to wait for the 45 bus.

At the expiry of the month the staff gave a small tea-party for those who were leaving. I cannot describe this occasion as a success.

The following Monday I missed Singlebury as a familiar presence and also, as mentioned above, because I had never quite realized how much work he had been taking upon himself. As a direct consequence of losing him I found myself having to stay late – not altogether unwillingly, since although following general instructions I have discouraged overtime, the extra pay in my own case would be instrumental in making ends meet. Meanwhile Singlebury's desk had not been cleared – that is, of the trays, pencil-sharpener and complimentary calendar which were, of course, office property. The feeling that he would come back – not like Mrs Horrocks, who has rung up and called round incessantly – but simply come back to work out of habit and through not knowing what else to do, was very strong, without being openly mentioned. I myself half expected and dreaded it, and I had mentally prepared two or three lines of argument in order to persuade him, if he *did* come, not to try it again. Nothing happened, however, and on the Thursday I personally removed the 'things' from the cubby-hole into my own room.

Meanwhile in order to dispel certain quite unfounded rumours I thought it best to issue a notice for general circulation, pointing out that if Mr Singlebury should turn out to have taken any unwise step, and if in consequence any inquiry should be necessary, we should be the first to hear about it from the police. I dictated this to our only permanent typist, who immediately said, oh, he would never do that. He would never cause any unpleasantness like bringing police into the place, he'd do all he could to avoid that. I did not encourage any further discussion, but I asked my wife, who is very used to social work, to call round at Singlebury's place in Clapham North and find out how he was. She did not have very much luck. The people in the cleaner's shop knew, or thought they knew, that he was away, but they had not been sufficiently interested to ask where he was going.

On Friday young Patel said he would be leaving, as the damp and the smell were affecting his health. The damp is certainly not drying out in this seasonably warm weather.

I also, as you know, received another invitation on the Friday, at very short notice, in fact no notice at all; I was told to come to your house in Suffolk Park Gardens that evening for drinks. I was not unduly elated, having been asked once before after I had done rather an awkward small job for you. In our Company, justice has not only not to be done, but it must be seen not to be done. The food was quite nice; it came from your Caterers Grade 3. I spent most of the evening talking to Ted Hollow, one of the area sales-managers. I did not expect to be introduced to your wife, nor was I. Towards the end of the evening you spoke to me for three minutes in the small room with a green marble floor and matching wallpaper leading to the ground-floor toilets. You asked me if everything was all right, to which I replied, all right for whom? You said that nobody's fault was nobody's funeral. I said that I had tried to give satisfaction. Passing on towards the washbasins, you told me with seeming cordiality to be careful and watch it when I had mixed drinks.

I would describe my feeling at this point as resentment, and I cannot identify exactly the moment when it passed into unease. I do know that I was acutely uneasy as I crossed the hall and saw two of your domestic staff, a man and a woman, holding my coat, which I had left in the lobby, and apparently trying to brush it. Your domestic staff all appear to be of foreign extraction and I personally feel sorry for them and do not grudge them a smile at the oddly assorted guests. Then I saw they were not smiling at my coat but that they seemed to be examining their fingers and looking at me earnestly and silently, and the collar or shoulders of my coat was covered with blood. As I came up to them, although they were still both absolutely silent, the illusion or impression passed, and I put on my coat and left the house in what I hope was a normal manner.

I now come to the present time. The feeling of uneasiness which I have described as making itself felt in your house has not diminished during this past weekend, and partly to take my mind off it and partly for the reasons I have given, I decided to work overtime again tonight, Monday the 23rd. This was in spite of the fact that the damp smell had become almost a stench, as of something putrid, which must have affected my nerves to some extent, because when I went out to get something to eat at Dino's I left the lights on, both in my own office, and in the entrance hall. I mean that for the first time since I began to work for the Company I left them on deliberately. As I walked to the corner I looked back and saw the two solitary lights looking somewhat forlorn in contrast to the glitter of the Arab-American Mutual Loan Corporation opposite. After my meal I felt absolutely reluctant to go back to the building, and wished then that I had not given way to the impulse to leave the lights on, but since I had done so and they must be turned off, I had no choice.

As I stood in the empty hallway I could hear the numerous creakings, settlings and faint tickings of an old building, possibly associated with the plumbing system. The lifts for reasons of economy do not operate after 6.30 p.m., so I began to walk up the stairs. After one flight I felt a strong creeping tension in the nerves of the back such as any of us feel when there is danger from behind; one might say that the body was thinking for itself on these occasions. I did not look round, but simply continued upwards as rapidly as I could. At the third floor I paused, and could hear footsteps coming patiently up behind me. This was not a surprise; I had been expecting them all evening.

Just at the door of my own office, or rather of the cubby-hole, for I have to pass through that, I turned, and saw at the end of the dim corridor what I had also expected, Singlebury, advancing towards me with his unmistakable shuffling step. My first reaction was a kind of bewilderment as to why he, who had been such an excellent timekeeper, so regular day by day, should become a creature of the night. He was wearing the blue suit. This I could make out by its familiar outline, but it was not till he came halfway down the corridor towards me, and reached the patch of light falling through the window from the street, that I saw that he was not himself – I mean that his head was nodding or rather swivelling irregularly from side to side. It crossed my mind that Singlebury was drunk. I had never known him drunk or indeed seen him take anything to drink, even at the office Christmas party, but one cannot estimate the effect that trouble will have upon a man. I began to think what steps I should take in this situation. I turned on the light in his cubby-hole as I went through and waited at the entrance of my own office. As he appeared in the outer doorway I saw that I had not been correct about the reason for the odd movement of the head. The throat was cut from ear to ear so that the head was nearly severed from the shoulders. It was this which had given the impression of nodding, or rather, lolling. As he walked into his cubbyhole Singlebury raised both hands and tried to steady the head as though conscious that something was wrong. The eyes were thickly filmed over, as one sees in the carcasses in a butcher's shop.

I shut and locked my door, and not wishing to give way to nausea, or to lose all control of myself, I sat down at my desk. My work was waiting for me as I had left it – it was the file on the matter of the damp elimination – and, there not being anything else to do, I tried to look through it. On the other side of the door I could hear Singlebury sit down also, and then try the drawers of the table, evidently looking for the 'things' without which he could not start work. After the drawers had been tried, one after another, several times, there was almost total silence.

The present position is that I am locked in my office and would not, no matter what you offered me, indeed I could not, go out through the cubbyhole and pass what is sitting at the desk. The early cleaners will not be here for seven hours and forty-five minutes. I have passed the time so far as best I could in writing this report. One consideration strikes me. If what I have next door is a visitant which should not be walking but buried in the earth, then its wound cannot bleed, and there will be no stream of blood moving slowly under the whole width of the communicating door. However I am sitting at the moment with my back to the door, so that, without turning round, I have no means of telling whether it has done so or not.

Notes

p. 311   *taking a powder* - depart quickly to avoid a difficult situation
p. 311   *my flannels* - a flannel suit would be a smart, very conventional suit for work
p. 313   *Clapham North* - a London suburb

35

When It Happens

(1977)

Margaret Atwood

Atwood is a Canadian novelist, short story writer, poet and environmental activist. She is well known for many novels including The Handmaid's Tale *and* Cat's Eye. *In* When It Happens, *a middle-aged woman goes about her daily routine of household chores and looking after her family, but gradually a frightening reality seems to dawn that a disaster has taken place and she must ultimately fend for herself.*

Mrs. Burridge is putting up green tomato pickles. There are twelve quarts in each lot with a bit left over, and that is the end of the jars. At the store they tell her there's a strike on at the factory where they get made. She doesn't know anything about that but you can't buy them anywhere, and even before this they were double what they were last year; she considers herself lucky she had those in the cellar. She has a lot of green tomatoes because she heard on the weather last night there was going to be a killer frost, so she put on her parka and her work gloves and took the lantern out to the garden in the pitch-dark and picked off all the ones she could see, over three bushels. She can lift the full baskets herself but she asked Frank to carry them in for her; he grumbles, but he likes it when she asks. In the morning the news said the growers had been hit and that would shoot the price up, not that the growers would get any of it themselves, everyone knows it's the stores that make the money.

She feels richer than she did yesterday, but on the other hand there isn't that much you can do with green tomatoes. The pickles hardly made a dint in them, and Frank has said, as he does every year, that they will never eat twenty-four quarts of green tomato pickle with just the two of them and the children gone. Except when they come to visit and eat me out of house and home, Mrs. Burridge adds silently. The truth is she has always made two batches and the children never liked it anyway, it was Frank ate them all and she knows perfectly well he'll do it again, without even noticing. He likes it on bread and cheese when he's watching the hockey games, during every commercial he goes out to the kitchen and makes himself another slice, even if he's just had a big meal, leaving a trail of crumbs and bits of pickle from the counter across the floor and over the front-room rug to his big chair. It used to annoy Mrs. Burridge, especially the crumbs, but now she watches him with a kind of sadness; she once thought their life together would go on forever but she has come to realize this is not the case.

She doesn't even feel like teasing him about his spare tire any more, though she does it all the same because he would miss it if she stopped. "There you go," she says, in the angular, prodding, metallic voice she cannot change because everyone expects it from her, if she spoke any other way they would think she was ill, "you keep on munching away like that and it'll be easy for me to get you out of bed in the mornings, I'll just give you a push and you'll roll all the way down the stairs like a barrel." And he answers in his methodical voice, pretending to be lazy even though he isn't, "You need a little fun in life," as though his pickles and cheese are slightly disreputable, almost like an orgy. Every year he tells her she's made too much but there would be a fuss all right if he went down to the cellar one day and there wasn't any left.

Mrs. Burridge has made her own pickles since 1952, which was the first year she had the garden. She remembers it especially because her daughter Sarah was on the way and she had trouble bending down to do the weeding. When she herself was growing up everyone did their own pickles, and their own canning and preserving too. But after the war most women gave it up, there was more money then and it was easier to buy things at the store. Mrs. Burridge never gave it up, though most of her friends thought she was wasting her time, and now she is glad she didn't, it kept her in practice while the others were having to learn all over again. Though with the sugar going up the way it is, she can't understand how long anyone is going to be able to afford even the homemade things.

On paper Frank is making more money than he ever has; yet they seem to have less to spend. They could always sell the farm, she supposes, to people from the city who would use it as a weekend place; they could get what seems like a very high price, several of the farms south of them have gone that way. But Mrs. Burridge does not have much faith in money; also it is a waste of the land, and this is her home, she has it arranged the way she wants it.

When the second batch is on and simmering she goes to the back door, opens it and stands with her arms folded across her stomach, looking out. She catches herself doing this four or five times a day now and she doesn't quite know why. There isn't much to see, just the barn and the back field with the row of dead elms Frank keeps saying he's going to cut down, and the top of Clarke's place sticking over the hill. She isn't sure what she is looking for but she has the odd idea she may see something burning, smoke coming up from the horizon, a column of it or perhaps more than one column, off to the south. This is such a peculiar thought for her to have that she hasn't told it to anyone else. Yesterday Frank saw her standing at the back door and asked her about it at dinner; anything he wants to talk to her about he saves up till dinner, even if he thinks about it in the morning. He wondered why she was at the back door, doing nothing at all for over ten minutes, and Mrs. Burridge told him a lie, which made her very uneasy. She said she heard a strange dog barking, which wasn't a good story because their own dogs were right there and they didn't notice a thing. But Frank let it pass; perhaps he thinks she is getting funny in her old age and doesn't want to call attention to it, which would be like him. He'll track mud all over her nice shiny kitchen floor but he'd hate to hurt anyone's feelings. Mrs. Burridge decides, a little wistfully, that despite his pig-headedness he is a kind and likeable man, and for her this is like renouncing a cherished and unquestionable belief, such as the flatness of the earth. He has made her angry so many times.

When the pickles are cool she labels them as she always does with the name and the date and carries them down the cellar stairs. The cellar is the old kind, with stone walls and a dirt floor. Mrs. Burridge likes to have everything neat—she still irons her sheets—so she had Frank build her some shelves right after they were married. The pickles go on one side, jams and jellies on the other, and the quarts of preserves along the bottom. It used to make her feel safe to have all that food in the cellar; she would think to herself, Well, if there's a snowstorm or anything and we're cut off, it won't be so bad. It doesn't make her feel safe any more. Instead she thinks that if she has to leave suddenly she won't be able to take any of the jars with her, they'd be too heavy to carry.

She comes back up the stairs after the last trip. It's not as easy as it used to be, her knee still bothers her as it has ever since she fell six years ago, she tripped on the second-last step. She's asked Frank a million times to fix the stairs but he hasn't done it, that's what she means by pig-headed. If she asks him more than twice to do something he calls it nagging, and maybe it is, but who's going to do it if he won't? The cold vacant hole at the back of this question is too much for her.

She has to stop herself from going to the back door again. Instead she goes to the back window and looks out, she can see almost the same things anyway. Frank is going towards the barn, carrying something, it looks like a wrench. The way he walks, slower than he used to, bent forward a little—from the back he's like an old man, how many years has he been walking that way?—makes her think, He can't protect me. She doesn't think this on purpose, it simply occurs to her, and it isn't only him, it's all of them, they've lost the power, you can tell by the way they walk. They are all waiting, just as Mrs. Burridge is, for whatever it is to happen. Whether they realize it or not. Lately when she's gone to the Dominion Store in town she has seen a look on the faces of the women there, she knows most of them, she wouldn't be mistaken—an anxious, closed look, as if they are frightened of something but won't talk about it. They're wondering what they will do, perhaps they think there's nothing they can do. This air of helplessness exasperates Mrs. Burridge, who has always been practical.

For weeks she has wanted to go to Frank and ask him to teach her how to use the gun. In fact he has two guns, a shotgun and a twenty-two rifle; he used to like going after a few ducks in the fall, and of course there are the groundhogs, they have to be shot because of the holes they make in the fields. Frank drives over on the tractor five or six times a year. A lot of men get injured by overturning tractors. But she can't ask him because she can't explain to him why she needs to know, and if she doesn't explain he will only tease. "Anyone can shoot a gun," he'll say, "all you have to do is pull the trigger . . . oh, you mean you want to hit something, well now, that's different, who you planning to kill?" Perhaps he won't say that; perhaps this is only the way he talked twenty years ago, before she stopped taking an interest in things outside the house. But Mrs. Burridge will never know because she will never ask. She doesn't have the heart to say to him, *Maybe you'll be dead. Maybe you'll go off somewhere when it happens, maybe there will be a war.* She can remember the last war.

Nothing has changed outside the window, so she turns away and sits down at the kitchen table to make out her shopping list Tomorrow is their day for going into town. She tries to plan the day so she can sit down at intervals; otherwise her feet start swelling up. That began with Sarah and got worse with the other two children and it's never really gone away. All her life, ever since she got married, she has made lists of things that have to be bought, sewed, planted, cooked, stored; she already has her list made for next Christmas, all the names and the gift she will buy for each, and the list of what she needs for Christmas dinner. But she can't seem to get interested in it, it's too far away. She can't believe in a distant future that is orderly like the past, she no longer seems to have the energy; it's as if she is saving it up for when she will have to use it.

She is even having trouble with the shopping list. Instead of concentrating on the paper—she writes on the backs of the used-up days off the page-a-day calendar Frank gives her every New Year's—she is gazing around the kitchen, looking at all the things she will have to leave behind when she goes. That will be the hardest part. Her mother's china, her silver, even though it is an old-fashioned pattern and the silver is wearing off, the egg timer in the shape of a chicken Sarah gave her when she was twelve, the ceramic salt and pepper shakers, green horses with perforated heads, that one of the other children brought back from the Ex. She thinks of walking up the stairs, the sheets folded in the chest, the towels stacked neatly on the shelves, the beds made, the quilt that was her grandmother's, it makes her want to cry. On her bureau, the wedding picture, herself in a shiny satin gown (the satin was a mistake, it emphasized her hips), Frank in the suit he has not worn since except to funerals, his hair cut too short on the sides and a surprising tuft at the top, like a woodpecker's. The children when they were babies. She thinks of her girls now and hopes they will not have babies; it is no longer the right time for it.

Mrs. Burridge wishes someone would be more precise, so she could make better plans. Everyone knows something is going to happen, you can tell by reading the newspapers and watching the television, but nobody is sure what it will be, nobody can be exact. She has her own ideas about it though. At first it will simply become quieter. She will have an odd feeling that something is wrong but it will be a few days before she is able to pin it down. Then she will notice that the planes are no longer flying over on their way to the Malton Airport, and that the noise from the highway two miles away, which is quite distinct when the leaves are off the trees, has almost disappeared. The television will be non-committal about it; in fact, the television, which right now is filled with bad news, of strikes, shortages, famines, layoffs and price increases, will become sweet-tempered and placating, and long intervals of classical music will appear on the radio. About this time Mrs. Burridge will realize that the news is being censored as it was during the war.

Mrs. Burridge is not positive about what will happen next; that is, she knows what will happen but she is not positive about the order. She expects it will be the gas and oil: the oil delivery man will simply not turn up at his usual time, and one morning the corner filling station will be closed. Just that, no explanations, because of course they— she does not know who "they" are, but she has always believed in their existence—they do not want people to panic. They are trying to keep things looking normal, possibly they have already started on this program and that is in fact why things still do look normal. Luckily she and Frank have the diesel fuel tank in the shed, it is three-quarters full, and they don't use the filling station anyway, they have their own gas pump. She has Frank bring in the old wood stove, the one they stored under the barn when they had the furnace and the electricity put in, and for once she blesses Frank's habit of putting things off. She was after him for years to take that stove to the dump. He cuts down the dead elms, finally, and they burn them in the stove.

The telephone wires are blown down in a storm and no one comes to fix them; or this is what Mrs. Burridge deduces. At any rate, the phone goes dead. Mrs. Burridge doesn't particularly mind, she never liked using the phone much anyway, but it does make her feel cut off.

About now men begin to appear on the back road, the gravel road that goes past the gate, walking usually by themselves, sometimes in pairs. They seem to be heading north. Most of them are young, in their twenties, Mrs. Burridge would guess. They are not dressed like the men around here. It's been so long since she has seen anyone *walking* along this road that she becomes alarmed. She begins leaving the dogs off their chains, she has kept them chained at night ever since one of them bit a Jehovah's Witness early one Sunday morning. Mrs. Burridge doesn't hold with the Witnesses—she is United— but she respects their perseverance, at least they have the courage of their convictions which is more than you can say for some members of her own church, and she always buys a *Watchtower*. Maybe they have been right all along.

It is about this time too that she takes one of the guns, she thinks it will be the shotgun as she will have a better chance of hitting something, and hides it, along with the shells, under a piece of roofing behind the barn. She does not tell Frank; he will have the twenty-two. She has already picked out the spot.

They do not want to waste the little gasoline they still have left in the pump so they do not make unnecessary trips. They begin to eat the chickens, which Mrs. Burridge does not look forward to. She hates cleaning and plucking them, and the angriest she ever got at Frank was the time he and Henry Clarke decided to go into turkey farming. They did it too, despite all she had to say against it, and she had to cope with the turkeys escaping and scratching in the garden and impossible to catch, in her opinion they were the stupidest birds in God's creation, and she had to clean and pluck a turkey a week until luckily the blackhead wiped out a third of the flock, which was enough to discourage them, they sold off the rest at a loss. It was the only time she was actually glad to see Frank lose money on one of his ventures.

Mrs. Burridge will feel things are getting serious on the day the electricity goes off and does not come back on. She knows, with a kind of fatalism, that this will happen in November, when the freezer is full of the vegetables but before it is cold enough to keep the packages frozen outside. She stands and looks at the Pliofilm bags of beans and corn and spinach and carrots, melting and sodden, and thinks, Why couldn't they have waited till spring? It is the waste, of food and also of her hard work, that aggravates her the most. She salvages what she can. During the Depression, she remembers, they used to say those on farms were better off than those in the city, because at least they had food; if you could keep the farm, that is; but she is no longer sure this is true. She feels beleaguered, isolated, like someone shut up inside a fortress, though no one has bothered them, in fact no one has passed their way for days, not even the solitary walking men.

With the electricity off they can no longer get the television. The radio stations, when they broadcast at all, give out nothing but soothing music, which Mrs. Burridge does not find soothing in the least.

One morning she goes to the back door and looks out and there are the columns of smoke, right where she's been expecting to see them, off to the south. She calls Frank and they stand watching. The smoke is thick and black, oily, as though something has exploded. She does not know what Frank is thinking; she herself is wondering about the children. She has had no news of them in weeks, but how could she? They stopped delivering mail some time now.

Fifteen minutes later, Henry Clarke drives into the yard in his half-ton truck. This is very unusual as no one has been driving anywhere lately. There is another man with him, and Mrs. Burridge identifies him as the man three farms up who moved in four or five years ago. Frank goes out and talks with them, and they drive over to the gas pump and start pumping the rest of the precious gas into the truck. Frank comes back to the house. He tells her there's a little trouble down the road, they are going along to see about it and she isn't to worry. He goes into the back room, comes out with the twenty-two, asks her where the shotgun is. She says she doesn't know. He searches for it, fruitlessly—she can hear him swearing, he does not swear in her presence—until he gives up. He comes out, kisses her goodbye, which is unusual too, and says he'll be back in a couple of hours. She watches the three of them drive off in Henry Clarke's truck, towards the smoke, she knows he will not come back. She supposes she ought to feel more emotional about it, but she is well prepared, she has been saying goodbye to him silently for years.

She re-enters the house and closes the door. She is fifty-one, her feet hurt, and she does not know where she can go, but she realizes she cannot stay here. There will now be a lot of hungry people, those that can make it this far out of the cities will be young and tough, her house is a beacon, signalling warmth and food. It will be fought over, but not by her.

She goes upstairs, searches in the cupboard, and puts on her heavy slacks and her two thickest sweaters. Downstairs she gathers up all the food that will be light enough for her to carry: raisins, cooking chocolate, dried prunes and apricots, half a loaf of bread, some milk powder which she puts into a quart freezer bag, a piece of cheese. Then she unearths the shotgun from behind the barn. She thinks briefly of killing the livestock, the chickens, the heifers and the pig, so no one will do it who does not know the right way; but she herself does not know the right way, she has never killed anything in her life, Frank always did it, so she contents herself with opening the henhouse door and the gate into the back field. She hopes the animals will run away but she knows they probably will not.

She takes one last look around the house. As an afterthought, she adds her toothbrush to the bundle: she does not like the feel of unbrushed teeth. She does not go down into the cellar but she has an image of her carefully sealed bottles and jars, red and yellow and purple, shattered on the floor, in a sticky puddle that looks like blood. Those who come will be wasteful, what they cannot eat themselves they will destroy. She thinks about setting fire to the house herself, before anyone else can do it.

Mrs. Burridge sits at her kitchen table. On the back of her calendar page, it's for a Monday, she has written *Oatmeal*, in her evenly spaced public-school handwriting that always got a star and has not changed very much since then. The dogs are a problem. After some thought she unchains them, but she does not let them past the gate: at a crucial moment they might give her away. She walks north in her heavy boots, carrying her parka because it is not yet cold enough to put it on, and her package of food and the shotgun which she has taken care to load. She passes the cemetery where her father and mother and her grandmother and grandfather are buried; the church used to be there but it burned down sixteen years ago and was rebuilt closer to the highway. Frank's people are in the other cemetery, his go back to the great-grandfather but they are Anglican, not that he kept it up. There is no one else on the road; she feels a little foolish. What if she is wrong and Frank comes back after all, what if nothing, really, is the matter? *Shortening*, she writes. She intends to make a lemon meringue pie for Sunday, when two of the children are coming up from the city for dinner.

It is almost evening and Mrs. Burridge is tired. She is in a part of the country she cannot remember, though she has stayed on the same road and it is a road she knows well; she has driven along it many times with Frank. But walking is not the same as driving. On one side there is a field, no buildings, on the other a woodlot; a stream flows through a culvert under the road. Mrs. Burridge kneels down to drink: the water is ice-cold and tastes of iron. Later there will be a frost, she can feel it. She puts on her parka and her gloves, and turns into the forest where she will not be seen. There she will eat some raisins and cheese and try to rest, waiting for the moon to rise so she can continue walking. It is now quite dark. She smells earth, wood, rotting leaves.

Suddenly her eye is caught by a flicker of red, and before she can turn back—how can this happen so quickly?—it takes shape, it is a small fire, off to the right, and two men are crouching near it. They have seen her, too: one of them rises and comes towards her. His teeth bare, he is smiling; he thinks she will be easy, an old woman. He says something but she cannot imagine what it is, she does not know how people dressed like that would talk.

They have spotted her gun, their eyes have fastened on it, they want it. Mrs. Burridge knows what she must do. She must wait until they are close enough and then she must raise the gun and shoot them, using one barrel for each, aiming at the faces. Otherwise they will kill her, she has no doubt about that. She will have to be fast, which is too bad because her hands feel thick and wooden; she is afraid, she does not want the loud noise or the burst of red that will follow, she has never killed anything in her life. She has no pictures beyond this point. You never know how you will act in a thing like that until it actually happens.

Mrs. Burridge looks at the kitchen clock. On her list she writes *Cheese*, they are eating more cheese now than they used to because of the price of meat. She gets up and goes to the kitchen door.

Notes

p. 317   *bushels* - a measure = 8 gallons
p. 321   *Pliofilm* - plastic used for wrapping fruit

36

Words

(1985)

Carol Shields

Shields was born in the USA but spent most of her life in Canada. A short story writer and novelist, best known perhaps for Larry's Party, The Stone Diaries *and* Unless, *she also wrote essays and biographies.* Words *is an intriguing story that works on two levels: is it about global warming or is it about language? Shields' expert control of structure and language gives us insights into both, while playing with our sense of perspective in this story.*

When the world first started heating up, an international conference was held in Rome to discuss ways of dealing with the situation.

Ian's small northern country—small in terms of population, that is, not in size—sent him to the meetings as a junior observer, and it was there he met Isobel, who was representing her country as a full-fledged delegate. She wore a terrible green dress the first time he saw her, and rather clumsy shoes, but he could see that her neck was slender, her waist narrow and her legs long and brown. For so young a woman, she was astonishingly articulate; in fact, it was her voice more than anything else that he fell in love with—its hills and valleys and its pliant, easy-sided wit. It was a voice that could be distinguished in any gathering, being both sweet and husky and having an edging of contralto merriment that seemed to Ian as rare and fine as a border of gold leaf.

They played truant, missing half the study sessions, the two of them lingering instead over tall, cool drinks in the café they found on the Via Traflori. There, under a cheerful striped canopy, Isobel leaned across a little table and placed long, ribbony Spanish phrases into Ian's mouth, encouraging and praising him when he got them right. And he, in his somewhat stiff northern voice, gave back the English equivalents: table, chair, glass, cold, hot, money, street, people, mouth. In the evenings, walking in the gardens in front of the institute where the conference was being held, they turned to each other and promised with their eyes, and in two languages as well, to love each other for ever.

The second International Conference was held ten years later. The situation had become grave. One could use the word *crisis* and not be embarrassed. Ian—by then married to Isobel, who was at home with the children—attended every session, and he listened attentively to the position papers of various physicists, engineers, geographers and linguists from all parts of the world. It was a solemn but distinguished assembly; many eminent men and women took their places at the lectern, including the spidery old Scottish demographer who years earlier had made the first correlation between substrata temperatures and highly verbalized societies. In every case, these speakers presented their concerns with admirable brevity, each word weighted and frugally chosen, and not one of them exceeded the two-minute time limitation. For by now no one really doubted that it was the extravagance and proliferation of language that had caused the temperature of the earth's crust to rise, and in places— California, Japan, London—to crack open and form long ragged lakes of fire. The evidence was everywhere and it was incontrovertible; thermal maps and measurements, sonar readings, caloric separations, a network of subterranean monitoring systems—all these had reinforced the integrity of the original Scottish theories.

But the delegates, sitting in the plenary session of the second International Conference, were still reluctant to take regulatory action. It was partly a case of heads-in-the-sand; it was—human nature being what it is—partly a matter of political advantage or commercial gain. There lingered, too, a somewhat surprising nostalgia for traditional liberties and for the old verbal order of the world. Discussion at the conference had gone around and around all week, pointless and wasteful, and it looked very much as though the final meeting would end in yet another welter of indecision and deferral. It was at that point that Ian, seated in the front row, rose and requested permission to speak.

He was granted a one-minute slot on the agenda. In fact, he spoke for several minutes, but his eloquence, his sincerity (and no doubt his strong, boyish appearance, his shaggy hair and his blue eyes) seemed to merit an exception. Certainly not one person sitting in that gathering had any wish to stop him.

It was unfortunate, tragic some thought, that a freak failure in the electronic system— only a plug accidentally pulled from its socket—prevented his exact words from being recorded, but those who were present remembered afterward how passionately he pleaded his love for the planet. (In truth—though who could know this?—he was thinking chiefly of his love for Isobel and his two children.)

We are living in a fool's dream, he told his fellow delegates, and the time has come for us to wake. Voluntary restraints were no longer adequate to preserve the little earth, which was the only home we know. Halfway measures like the old three-hour *temps tranquilles* were next to useless since they were never, or almost never, enforced. The evening curfew-lingua was ridiculously lenient. Abuses of every sort abounded, particularly the use of highly percussive words or words that were redolent with emotional potency, even though it had been established that these two classes of words were particularly damaging to bedrock and shales. Multilingualism continued to flourish. Wasteful antiphonic structures were actually on the increase in the more heavily populated regions, as was the use of elaborate ceremonial metaphor. It was as though, by refusing to make linguistic sacrifices, the human race had willed its own destruction.

When he finished speaking, the applause was prolonged and powerful. It perhaps held an element of shame, too; this young man had found the courage to say at last what should have been said long before. One after another the delegates rose to their feet, and soon their clapping fell into a steady rhythmic beat that had the effect of holding Ian hostage on the platform. The chairman whispered into his ear, begging him for a few additional words.

He assented. He could not say no. And, in a fever that was remarkably similar to the fever he had suffered as a child during a severe case of measles, or like the fever of love he had succumbed to ten years earlier in Rome, he announced to the audience, holding up a hand for attention, that he would be the first to take a vow of complete silence for the sake of the planet that had fathered him.

Almost at once he regretted his words, but hubris kept him from recanting for the first twenty-four hours and, after that, a kind of stubbornness took over. Isobel met him at the airport with the words, "You went too far." Later, after a miserable, silent attempt at lovemaking, she said, "I'll never forgive you." His children, clamoring to hear about his moment of heroism, poked at him, at his face and chest and arms, as though he were inert. He tried to tell them with his eyes that he was still their father, that he still loved them.

"Leave him alone," Isobel said sharply. "He might as well be a stranger now. He's no different than anyone else."

She became loud and shrewish. When his silent followers arrived at their door—and in time there were thousands of them, each with the same blank face and gold armband— she admitted them with bad grace. She grew garrulous. She rambled on and on, bitter and blaming, sometimes incoherent, sometimes obscene, sometimes reverting to a coarse, primitive schoolyard Spanish, sometimes shouting to herself or cursing into the mirror or chanting oaths—anything to furnish the emptiness of the house with words. She became disoriented. The solid plaster of the walls fell away from her, melting into a drift of vapor. There seemed to be no shadows, no sense of dimension, no delicate separation between one object and another. Privately, she pleaded with her husband for an act of apostasy. Later she taunted him. "Show me you're still human," she would say. "Give me just one word." The word *betrayal* came frequently out of her wide mobile mouth, and so did the scornful epithet *martyr*.

But time passes and people forget. She forgot, finally, what it was that had betrayed her. Next she forgot her husband's name. Sometimes she forgot that she had a husband at all, for how could anything be said to exist, she asked herself loudly, hoarsely—even a husband, even one's self—if it didn't also exist in the shape of a word.

He worried that she might be arrested, but for some reason—his position probably— she was always let off with a warning. In their own house she ignored him, passing him on the stairs without a look, or crossing in front of him as though he were a stuffed chair. Often she disappeared for hours, venturing out alone into the heat of the night, and he began to suspect she had taken a lover.

The thought preyed on him, though in fact he had long since forgotten the word for *wife* and also the word for *fidelity*. One night, when she left the house, he attempted to follow her, but clearly she was suspicious because she walked very quickly, looking back over her shoulder, making a series of unnecessary turns and choosing narrow old streets whose curbs were blackened by fire. Within minutes he lost sight of her; soon after that he was driven back by the heat.

The next night he tried again, and this time he saw her disappear into an ancient, dilapidated building, the sort of enclosure, he remembered, where children had once gone to learn to read and write. Unexpectedly, he felt a flash of pity; what a sad place for a tryst. He waited briefly, then entered the building and went up a flight of smoldering stairs that seemed on the point of collapse. There he found a dim corridor, thick with smoke, and a single room at one end.

Through the door he heard a waterfall of voices. There must have been a dozen people inside, all of them talking. The talk seemed to be about poetry. Someone—a woman—was giving a lecture. There were interruptions, a discussion, some laughter. He heard his wife's voice, her old gilt-edged contralto, asking a question, and the sound of it made him draw in his breath so sharply that something hard, like a cinder or a particle of gravel, formed in his throat.

It stayed stubbornly lodged there all night. He found it painful to breathe, and even Isobel noticed how he thrashed about in bed, gasping wildly for air. In the morning she called a doctor, who could find nothing wrong, but she remained uneasy, and that evening she stayed home and made him cups of iced honey-and-lemon tea to ease his throat. He took her hand at one point and held it to his lips as though it might be possible to find the air he needed inside the crevices of her skin. By now the scraping in his throat had become terrible, a raw agonizing rasp like a dull knife sawing through limestone. She looked at his face, from which the healthy, blood-filled elasticity had gone and felt herself brushed by a current of air, or what might have been the memory of a name.

He began to choke violently, and she heard something grotesque come out of his mouth, a sound that was only half-human, but that rode on a curious rhythmic wave that for some reason stirred her deeply. She imagined it to be the word *Isobel*. "Isobel?" she asked, trying to remember its meaning. He said it a second time, and this time the syllables were more clearly formed.

The light of terror came into his eyes, or perhaps the beginning of a new fever; she managed to calm him by stroking his arm. Then she called the children inside the house, locked the doors and windows against the unbearable heat, and they began, slowly, patiently, hands linked, at the beginning where they had begun before—with table, chair, bed, cool, else, other, sleep, face, mouth, breath, tongue.

Notes

p. 324   *contralto* - deep female voice
p. 325   *demographer* - one who studies statistics about human behaviour
p. 325   *temps tranquille* - quiet time
p. 325   *antiphonic* - from music, where two voices sing alternately
p. 326   *apostasy* - renunciation of belief

The Man Who Walked on the Moon

(1985)

J.G. Ballard

Ballard, a British novelist and short story writer who wrote The Drowned World *and* Empire of the Sun, *is well known especially for his fantasy and innovative science fiction writing. However, his work often focuses on real places and the ways in which place affects character. This story, set in Brazil, focuses on a man who claims to have been a famous astronaut and now scrapes a living selling photos of himself with tourists while living in a sordid hovel.*

I, too, was once an astronaut. As you see me sitting here, in this modest café with its distant glimpse of Copacabana Beach, you probably assume that I am a man of few achievements. The shabby briefcase between my worn heels, the stained suit with its frayed cuffs, the unsavoury hands ready to seize the first offer of a free drink, the whole air of failure . . . no doubt you think that I am a minor clerk who has missed promotion once too often, and that I amount to nothing, a person of no past and less future.

For many years I believed this myself. I had been abandoned by the authorities, who were glad to see me exiled to another continent, reduced to begging from the American tourists. I suffered from acute amnesia, and certain domestic problems with my wife and my mother. They now share my small apartment at Ipanema, while I am forced to live in a room above the projection booth of the Luxor Cinema, my thoughts drowned by the sound-tracks of science-fiction films.

So many tragic events leave me unsure of myself. Nonetheless, my confidence is returning, and a sense of my true history and worth. Chapters of my life are still hidden from me, and seem as jumbled as the film extracts which the projectionists screen each morning as they focus their cameras. I have still forgotten my years of training, and my mind bars from me any memory of the actual space-flights. But I am certain that I was once an astronaut.

Years ago, before I went into space, I followed many professions – freelance journalist, translator, on one occasion even a war correspondent sent to a small war, which unfortunately was never declared. I was in and out of newspaper offices all day, hoping for that one assignment that would match my talents.

Sadly, all this effort failed to get me to the top, and after ten years I found myself displaced by a younger generation. A certain reticence in my character, a sharpness of manner, set me off from my fellow journalists. Even the editors would laugh at me behind my back. I was given trivial assignments – film reviewing, or writing reports on office-equipment fairs. When the circulation wars began, in a doomed response to the onward sweep of television, the editors openly took exception to my waspish style. I became a part-time translator, and taught for an hour each day at a language school, but my income plummeted. My mother, whom I had supported for many years, was forced to leave her home and join my wife and myself in our apartment at Ipanema.

At first my wife resented this, but soon she and my mother teamed up against me. They became impatient with the hours I spent delaying my unhappy visits to the single newspaper office that still held out hope – my journey to work was a transit between one door slammed on my heels and another slammed in my face.

My last friend at the newspaper commiserated with me, as I stood forlornly in the lobby. 'For heaven's sake, find a human-interest story! Something tender and affecting, that's what they want upstairs – life isn't an avant-garde movie!'

Pondering this sensible advice, I wandered into the crowded streets. I dreaded the thought of returning home without an assignment. The two women had taken to opening the apartment door together. They would stare at me accusingly, almost barring me from my own home.

Around me were the million faces of the city. People strode past, so occupied with their own lives that they almost pushed me from the pavement. A million human interest stories, of a banal and pointless kind, an encyclopaedia of mediocrity . . . Giving up, I left Copacabana Avenue and took refuge among the tables of a small café in a side-street.

It was there that I met the American astronaut, and began my own career in space.

The café terrace was almost deserted, as the office workers returned to their desks after lunch. Behind me, in the shade of the canvas awning, a fair-haired man in a threadbare tropical suit sat beside an empty glass. Guarding my coffee from the flies, I gazed at the small segment of sea visible beyond Copacabana Beach. Slowed by their mid-day meals, groups of American and European tourists strolled down from the hotels, waving away the jewellery salesmen and lottery touts. Perhaps I would visit Paris or New York, make a new life for myself as a literary critic . . .

A tartan shirt blocked my view of the sea and its narrow dream of escape. An elderly American, camera slung from his heavy neck, leaned across the table, his grey-haired wife in a loose floral dress beside him.

'Are you the astronaut?' the woman asked in a friendly but sly way, as if about to broach an indiscretion. 'The hotel said you would be at this café . . .'

'An astronaut?'

'Yes, the astronaut Commander Scranton . . .?'

'No, I regret that I'm not an astronaut.' Then it occurred to me that this provincial couple, probably a dentist and his wife from the corn-belt, might benefit from a well-informed courier. Perhaps they imagined that their cruise ship had berthed at Miami? I stood up, managing a gallant smile. 'Of course, I'm a qualified translator. If you –'

'No, no . . .' Dismissing me with a wave, they moved through the empty tables. 'We came to see Mr Scranton.'

Baffled by this bizarre exchange, I watched them approach the man in the tropical suit. A nondescript fellow in his late forties, he had thinning blond hair and a strong-jawed American face from which all confidence had long been drained. He stared in a resigned way at his hands, which waited beside his empty glass, as if unable to explain to them that little refreshment would reach them that day. He was clearly undernourished, perhaps an ex-seaman who had jumped ship, one of thousands of down-and-outs trying to live by their wits on some of the hardest pavements in the world.

However, he looked up sharply enough as the elderly couple approached him. When they repeated their question about the astronaut he beckoned them to a seat. To my surprise, the waiter was summoned, and drinks were brought to the table. The husband unpacked his camera, while a relaxed conversation took place between his wife and this seedy figure.

'Dear, don't forget Mr Scranton . . .'

'Oh, please forgive me.'

The husband removed several bank-notes from his wallet. His wife passed them across the table to Scranton, who then stood up. Photographs were taken, first of Scranton standing next to the smiling wife, then of the husband grinning broadly beside the gaunt American. The source of all this good humour eluded me, as it did Scranton, whose eyes stared gravely at the street with a degree of respect due to the surface of the moon. But already a second group of tourists had walked down from Copacabana Beach, and I heard more laughter when one called out: 'There's the astronaut . . . !'

Quite mystified, I watched a further round of photographs being taken. The couples stood on either side of the American, grinning away as if he were a camel driver posing for pennies against a backdrop of the pyramids.

I ordered a small brandy from the waiter. He had ignored all this, pocketing his tips with a straight face.

'This fellow . . . ?' I asked. 'Who is he? An astronaut?'

'Of course . . .' The waiter flicked a bottle-top into the air and treated the sky to a knowing sneer. 'Who else but the man in the moon?'

The tourists had gone, strolling past the leatherware and jewellery stores. Alone now after his brief fame, the American sat among the empty glasses, counting the money he had collected.

The man in the moon?

Then I remembered the newspaper headline, and the exposé I had read two years earlier of this impoverished American who claimed to have been an astronaut, and told his story to the tourists for the price of a drink. At first almost everyone believed him, and he had become a popular figure in the hotel lobbies along Copacabana Beach.

Apparently he had flown on one of the Apollo missions from Cape Kennedy in the 1970s, and his long-jawed face and stoical pilot's eyes seemed vaguely familiar from the magazine photographs. He was properly reticent, but if pressed with a tourist dollar could talk convincingly about the early lunar flights. In its way it was deeply moving to sit at a café table with a man who had walked on the moon . . .

Then an over-curious reporter exploded the whole pretence. No man named Scranton had ever flown in space, and the American authorities confirmed that his photograph was not that of any past or present astronaut. In fact he was a failed crop-duster from Florida who had lost his pilot's licence and whose knowledge of the Apollo flights had been mugged up from newspapers and television programmes.

Surprisingly, Scranton's career had not ended there and then, but moved on to a second tragi-comical phase. Far from consigning him to oblivion, the exposure brought him a genuine small celebrity. Banished from the grand hotels of Copacabana, he hung about the cheaper cafés in the side-streets, still claiming to have been an astronaut, ignoring those who derided him from their car windows. The dignified way in which he maintained his fraud tapped a certain good-humoured tolerance, much like the affection felt in the United States for those eccentric old men who falsely claimed to their deaths that they were veterans of the American Civil War.

So Scranton stayed on, willing to talk for a few dollars about his journey to the moon, quoting the same tired phrases that failed to convince the youngest schoolboy. Soon no one bothered to question him closely, and his chief function was to be photographed beside parties of visitors, an amusing oddity of the tourist trail.

But perhaps the American was more devious than he appeared, with his shabby suit and hangdog gaze? As I sat there, guarding the brandy I could barely afford, I resented Scranton's bogus celebrity, and the tourist revenue it brought him. For years I, too, had maintained a charade – the mask of good humour that I presented to my colleagues in the newspaper world – but it had brought me nothing. Scranton at least was left alone for most of his time, something I craved more than any celebrity. Comparing our situations, there was plainly a strong element of injustice – the notorious British criminal who made a comfortable living being photographed by the tourists in the more expensive Copacabana restaurants had at least robbed one of Her Majesty's mail-trains.

At the same time, was this the human-interest story that would help me to remake my career? Could I provide a final ironic twist by revealing that, thanks to his exposure, the bogus astronaut was now doubly successful?

During the next days I visited the café promptly at noon. Note book at the ready, I kept a careful watch for Scranton. He usually appeared in the early afternoon, as soon as the clerks and secretaries had finished their coffee. In that brief lull, when the shadows crossed from one side of the street to the other, Scranton would materialise, as if from a trapdoor in the pavement. He was always alone, walking straight-backed in his faded suit, but with the uncertainty of someone who suspects that he is keeping an appointment on the wrong day. He would slip into his place under the café awning, order a glass of beer from the sceptical waiter and then gaze across the street at the vistas of an invisible space.

It soon became clear that Scranton's celebrity was as threadbare as his shirt cuffs. Few tourists visited him, and often a whole afternoon passed without a single customer. Then the waiter would scrape the chairs around Scranton's table, trying to distract him from his reveries of an imaginary moon. Indeed, on the fourth day, within a few minutes of Scranton's arrival, the waiter slapped the table-top with his towel, already cancelling the afternoon's performance.

'Away, away . . . it's impossible!' He seized the newspaper that Scranton had found on a nearby chair. 'No more stories about the moon . . .'

Scranton stood up, head bowed beneath the awning. He seemed resigned to this abuse. 'All right . . . I can take my trade down the street.'

To forestall this, I left my seat and moved through the empty tables.

'Mr Scranton? Perhaps we can speak? I'd like to buy you a drink.'

'By all means.' Scranton beckoned me to a chair. Ready for business, he sat upright, and with a conscious effort managed to bring the focus of his gaze from infinity to a distance of fifty feet away. He was poorly nourished, and his perfunctory shave revealed an almost tubercular pallor. Yet there was a certain resolute quality about this vagrant figure that I had not expected. Sitting beside him, I was aware of an intense and almost wilful isolation, not just in this foreign city, but in the world at large.

I showed him my card. 'I'm writing a book of criticism on the science-fiction cinema. It would be interesting to hear your opinions. You are Commander Scranton, the Apollo astronaut?'

'That is correct.'

'Good. I wondered how you viewed the science-fiction film . . . how convincing you found the presentation of outer space, the lunar surface and so on . . .'

Scranton stared bleakly at the table-top. A faint smile exposed his yellowing teeth, and I assumed that he had seen through my little ruse.

'I'll be happy to set you straight,' he told me. 'But I make a small charge.'

'Of course,' I searched in my pockets. 'Your professional expertise, naturally . . .'

I placed some coins on the table, intending to hunt for a modest bank-note. Scranton selected three of the coins, enough to pay for a loaf of bread, and pushed the rest towards me.

'Science-fiction films–? They're good. Very accurate. On the whole I'd say they do an excellent job.'

'That's encouraging to hear. These Hollywood epics are not usually noted for their realism.'

'Well . . . you have to understand that the Apollo teams brought back a lot of film footage.'

'I'm sure.' I tried to keep the amusement out of my voice. 'The studios must have been grateful to you. After all, you could describe the actual moon-walks.'

Scranton nodded sagely. 'I acted as consultant to one of the Hollywood majors. All in all, you can take it from me that those pictures are pretty realistic.'

'Fascinating . . . coming from you that has authority. As a matter of interest, what was being on the moon literally like?'

For the first time Scranton seemed to notice me. Had he glimpsed some shared strain in our characters? This care-worn American had all the refinement of an unemployed car mechanic, and yet he seemed almost tempted to befriend me.

'Being on the moon?' His tired gaze inspected the narrow street of cheap jewellery stores, with its office messengers and lottery touts, the off-duty taxi-drivers leaning against their cars. 'It was just like being here.'

'So . . .' I put away my notebook. Any further subterfuge was unnecessary. I had treated our meeting as a joke, but Scranton was sincere, and anyway utterly indifferent to my opinion of him. The tourists and passing policemen, the middle-aged women sitting at a nearby table, together barely existed for him. They were no more than shadows on the screen of his mind, through which he could see the horizons of an almost planetary emptiness.

For the first time I was in the presence of someone who had nothing – even less than the beggars of Rio, for they at least were linked to the material world by their longings for it. Scranton embodied the absolute loneliness of the human being in space and time, a situation which in many ways I shared. Even the act of convincing himself that he was a former astronaut only emphasised his isolation.

'A remarkable story,' I commented. 'One can't help wondering if we were right to leave this planet. I'm reminded of the question posed by the Chilean painter Matta – "Why must we fear a disaster in space in order to understand our own times?" It's a pity you didn't bring back any mementoes of your moon-walks.'

Scranton's shoulders straightened. I could see him counting the coins on the table. 'I do have certain materials . . .'

I nearly laughed. 'What? A piece of lunar rock? Some moon dust?'

'Various photographic materials.'

'Photographs?' Was it possible that Scranton had told the truth, and that he had indeed been an astronaut? If I could prove that the whole notion of his imposture was an error, an oversight by the journalist who had investigated the case, I would have the makings of a front-page scoop . . . 'Could I see them? – perhaps I could use them in my book . . . ?'

'Well . . .' Scranton felt for the coins in his pocket. He looked hungry, and obviously thought only of spending them on a loaf of bread.

'Of course,' I added, I'll provide an extra fee. As for my book, the publishers might well pay many hundreds of dollars.'

'Hundreds . . .' Scranton seemed impressed. He shook his head, as if amused by the ways of the world. I expected him to be shy of revealing where he lived, but he stood up and gestured me to finish my drink. 'I'm staying a few minutes' walk from here.'

He waited among the tables, staring across the street. Seeing the passers-by through his eyes, I was aware that they had begun to seem almost transparent, shadow players created by a frolic of the sun.

We soon arrived at Scranton's modest room behind the Luxor Cinema, a small theatre off Copacabana Avenue that had seen better days. Two former storerooms and an office above the projection booth had been let as apartments, which we reached after climbing a dank emergency stairway.

Exhausted by the effort, Scranton swayed against the door. He wiped the spit from his mouth onto the lapel of his jacket, and ushered me into the room. 'Make yourself comfortable . . .'

A dusty light fell across the narrow bed, reflected in the cold-water tap of a greasy handbasin supported from the wall by its waste-pipe. Sheets of newspaper were wrapped around a pillow, stained with sweat and some unsavoury mucus, perhaps after an attack of malarial or tubercular fever.

Eager to leave this infectious den, I drew out my wallet. 'The photographs . . . ?'

Scranton sat on the bed, staring at the yellowing wall behind me as if he had forgotten that I was there. Once again I was aware of his ability to isolate himself from the surrounding world, a talent I envied him, if little else.

'Sure . . . they're over here.' He stood up and went to the suitcase that lay on a card table behind the door. Taking the money from me, he opened the lid and lifted out a bundle of magazines. Among them were loose pages torn from *Life* and *Newsweek*, and special supplements of the Rio newspapers devoted to the Apollo space-flights and the moon landings. The familiar images of Armstrong and the lunar module, the space-walks and splashdowns had been endlessly thumbed. The captions were marked with coloured pencil, as if Scranton had spent hours memorising these photographs brought back from the tideways of space.

I moved the magazines to one side, hoping to find some documentary evidence of Scranton's own involvement in the space-flights, perhaps a close-up photograph taken by a fellow astronaut.

'Is this it? There's nothing else?'

'That's it.' Scranton gestured encouragingly. 'They're good pictures. Pretty well what it was like.'

'I suppose that's true. I had hoped . . .'

I peered at Scranton, expecting some small show of embarrassment. These faded pages, far from being the mementoes of a real astronaut, were obviously the prompt cards of an impostor. However, there was not the slightest doubt that Scranton was sincere.

I stood in the street below the portico of the Luxor Cinema, whose garish posters, advertising some science-fiction spectacular, seemed as inflamed as the mind of the American. Despite all that I had suspected, I felt an intense disappointment. I had deluded myself, thinking that Scranton would rescue my career. Now I was left with nothing but an empty notebook and the tram journey back to the crowded apartment in Ipanema. I dreaded the prospect of seeing my wife and my mother at the door, their eyes screwed to the same accusing focus.

Nonetheless, as I walked down Copacabana Avenue to the tram-stop, I felt a curious sense of release. The noisy pavements, the arrogant pickpockets plucking at my clothes, the traffic that aggravated the slightest tendency to migraines, all seemed to have receded, as if a small distance had opened between myself and the congested world. My meeting with Scranton, my brief involvement with this marooned man, allowed me to see everything in a more detached way. The businessmen with their briefcases, the afternoon tarts swinging their shiny handbags, the salesmen with their sheets of lottery tickets, almost deferred to me. Time and space had altered their perspectives, and the city was yielding to me. As I crossed the road to the tram-stop several minutes seemed to pass. But I was not run over.

This sense of a loosening air persisted as I rode back to Ipanema. My fellow passengers, who would usually have irritated me with their cheap scent and vulgar clothes, their look of bored animals in a menagerie, now scarcely intruded into my vision. I gazed down corridors of light that ran between them like the aisles of an open-air cathedral.

'You've found a story,' my wife announced within a second of opening the door.

'They've commissioned an article,' my mother confirmed. 'I knew they would.'

They stepped back and watched me as I made a leisurely tour of the cramped apartment. My changed demeanour clearly impressed them. They pestered me with questions, but even their presence was less bothersome. The universe, thanks to Scranton's example, had loosened its grip. Sitting at the dinner table, I silenced them with a raised finger.

'I am about to embark on a new career . . .'

From then on I became ever more involved with Scranton. I had not intended to see the American again, but the germ of his loneliness had entered my blood. Within two days I returned to the café in the side-street, but the tables were deserted. I watched as two parties of tourists stopped to ask for 'the astronaut'. I then questioned the waiter, suspecting that he had banished the poor man. But, no, the American would be back the next day, he had been ill, or perhaps had secretly gone to the moon on business.

In fact, it was three days before Scranton at last appeared. Materialising from the afternoon heat, he entered the café and sat under the awning. At first he failed to notice that I was there, but Scranton's mere presence was enough to satisfy me. The crowds and traffic, which had begun once again to close around me, halted their clamour and withdrew. On the noisy street were imposed the silences of a lunar landscape.

However, it was all too clear that Scranton had been ill. His face was sallow with fever, and the effort of sitting in his chair soon tired him. When the first American tourists stopped at his table he barely rose from his seat, and while the photographs were taken he held tightly to the awning above his head.

By the next afternoon his fever had subsided, but he was so strained and ill-kempt that the waiter at first refused to admit him to the café. A trio of Californian spinsters who approached his table were clearly unsure that this decaying figure was indeed the bogus astronaut, and would have left had I not ushered them back to Scranton.

'Yes, this is Commander Scranton, the famous astronaut. I am his associate – do let me hold your camera . . .'

I waited impatiently for them to leave, and sat down at Scranton's table. Ill the American might be, but I needed him. After ordering a brandy, I helped Scranton to hold the glass. As I pressed the spinsters' bank-note into his pocket I could feel that his suit was soaked with sweat.

'I'll walk you back to your room. Don't thank me, it's in my direction.'

'Well, I could use an arm.' Scranton stared at the street, as if its few yards encompassed a Grand Canyon of space. 'It's getting to be a long way.'

'A long way! Scranton, I understand that . . .'

It took us half an hour to cover the few hundred yards to the Luxor Cinema. But already time was becoming an elastic dimension, and from then on most of my waking hours were spent with Scranton. Each morning I would visit the shabby room behind the cinema, bringing a paper bag of sweet-cakes and a flask of tea I had prepared in the apartment under my wife's suspicious gaze. Often the American had little idea who I was, but this no longer worried me. He lay in his narrow bed, letting me raise his head as I changed the sheets of newspaper that covered his pillow. When he spoke, his voice was too weak to be heard above the sound-tracks of the science-fiction films that boomed through the crumbling walls.

Even in this moribund state, Scranton's example was a powerful tonic, and when I left him in the evening I would walk the crowded streets without any fear. Sometimes my former colleagues called to me from the steps of the newspaper office, but I was barely aware of them, as if they were planetary visitors hailing me from the edge of a remote crater.

Looking back on these exhilarating days, I regret only that I never called a doctor to see Scranton. Frequently, though, the American would recover his strength, and after I had shaved him we would go down into the street. I relished these outings with Scranton. Arm in arm, we moved through the afternoon crowds, which seemed to part around us. Our fellow-pedestrians had become remote and fleeting figures, little more than tricks of the sun. Sometimes, I could no longer see their faces. It was then that I observed the world through Scranton's eyes, and knew what it was to be an astronaut.

Needless to say, the rest of my life had collapsed at my feet. Having given up my work as a translator, I soon ran out of money, and was forced to borrow from my mother. At my wife's instigation, the features editor of the newspaper called me to his office, and made it plain that as an immense concession (in fact he had always been intrigued by my wife) he would let me review a science-fiction film at the Luxor. Before walking out, I told him that I was already too familiar with the film, and my one hope was to see it banned from the city forever.

So ended my connection with the newspaper. Soon after, the two women evicted me from my apartment. I was happy to leave them, taking with me only the reclining sun-chair on which my wife passed most of her days in preparation for her new career as a model. The sun-chair became my bed when I moved into Scranton's room.

By then the decline in Scranton's health forced me to be with him constantly. Far from being an object of charity, Scranton was now my only source of income. Our needs for several days could be met by a single session with the American tourists. I did my best to care for Scranton, but during his final illness I was too immersed in that sense of an emptying world even to notice the young doctor whose alarmed presence filled the tiny room. By a last irony, towards the end even Scranton himself seemed barely visible to me. As he died I was reading the mucus-stained headlines on his pillow.

After Scranton's death I remained in his room at the Luxor. Despite the fame he had once enjoyed, his burial at the Protestant cemetery was attended only by myself, but in a sense this was just, as he and I were the only real inhabitants of the city. Later I went through the few possessions in his suitcase, and found a faded pilot's log-book. Its pages confirmed that Scranton had worked as a pilot for a crop-spraying company in Florida throughout the years of the Apollo programme.

Nonetheless, Scranton had travelled in space. He had known the loneliness of separation from all other human beings, he had gazed at the empty perspectives that I myself had seen. Curiously, the pages torn from the news magazines seemed more real than the pilot's log-book. The photographs of Armstrong and his fellow astronauts were really of Scranton and myself as we walked together on the moon of this world.

I reflected on this as I sat at the small café in the side-street. As a gesture to Scranton's memory, I had chosen his chair below the awning. I thought of the planetary landscapes that Scranton had taught me to see, those empty vistas devoid of human beings. Already I was aware of a previous career, which my wife and the pressures of everyday life had hidden from me. There were the years of training for a great voyage, and a coastline similar to that of Cape Kennedy receding below me . . .

My reverie was interrupted by a pair of American tourists. A middle-aged man and his daughter, who held the family camera to her chin, approached the table.

'Excuse me,' the man asked with an over-ready smile. 'Are you the . . . the astronaut? We were –told by the hotel that you might be here . . .'

I stared at them without rancour, treating them to a glimpse of those eyes that had seen the void. I, too, had walked on the moon.

'Please sit down,' I told them casually. 'Yes, I am the astronaut.'

Notes

p. 328   *Copacabana* - main beach in Rio de Janeiro, Brazil
p. 328   *Ipanema* - suburb of Rio
p. 329   *corn-belt* - region in Midwest USA
p. 331   *crop-duster* - person who sprays crops with pesticide from a plane

38

A Walk to the Jetty

(1985)

Jamaica Kincaid

Kincaid is an Antiguan now living in the USA. She started as a journalist and worked for The New Yorker, *writing stories and also non-fiction. In this story, a girl leaves home for the first time, also for good. As well as the family drama of the situation, it is positioned in a colonial context as she leaves a colony to seek work in England.*

"My name is Annie John." These were the first words that came into my mind as I woke up on the morning of the last day I spent in Antigua, and they stayed there, lined up one behind the other, marching up and down, for I don't know how long. At noon on that day, a ship on which I was to be a passenger would sail to Barbados, and there I would board another ship, which would sail to England, where I would study to become a nurse. My name was the last thing I saw the night before, just as I was falling asleep; it was written in big, black letters all over my trunk, sometimes followed by my address in Antigua, sometimes followed by my address as it would be in England. I did not want to go to England, I did not want to be a nurse, but I would have chosen going off to live in a cavern and keeping house for seven unruly men rather than go on with my life as it stood. I never wanted to lie in this bed again, my legs hanging out way past the foot of it, tossing and turning on my mattress, with its cotton stuffing all lumped just where it wasn't a good place to be lumped. I never wanted to lie in my bed again and hear Mr. Ephraim driving his sheep to pasture—a signal to my mother that she should get up to prepare my father's and my bath and breakfast. I never wanted to lie in my bed and hear her get dressed, washing her face, brushing her teeth, and gargling. I especially never wanted to lie in my bed and hear my mother gargling again.

Lying there in the half-dark of my room, I could see my shelf, with my books—some of them prizes I had won in school, some of them gifts from my mother—and with photographs of people I was supposed to love forever no matter what, and with my old thermos, which was given to me for my eighth birthday, and some shells I had gathered at different times I spent at the sea. In one corner stood my washstand and its beautiful basin of white enamel with blooming red hibiscus painted at the bottom and an urn that matched. In another corner were my old school shoes and my Sunday shoes. In still another corner, a bureau held my old clothes. I knew everything in this room, inside out and outside in. I had lived in this room for thirteen of my seventeen years. I could see in my mind's eye even the day my father was adding it onto the rest of the house. Everywhere I looked stood something that had meant a lot to me, that had given me pleasure at some point, or could remind me of a time that was a happy time. But as I was lying there my heart could have burst open with joy at the thought of never having to see any of it again.

If someone had asked me for a little summing up of my life at that moment as I lay in bed, I would have said, "My name is Annie John. I was born on the fifteenth of September, seventeen years ago, at Holberton Hospital, at five o'clock in the morning. At the time I was born, the moon was going down at one end of the sky and the sun was coming up at the other. My mother's name is Annie also. My father's name is Alexander, and he is thirty-five years older than my mother. Two of his children are four and six years older than she is. Looking at how sickly he has become and looking at the way my mother now has to run up and down for him, gathering the herbs and barks that he boils in water, which he drinks instead of the medicine the doctor has ordered for him, I plan not only never to marry an old man but certainly never to marry at all. The house we live in my father built with his own hands. The bed I am lying in my father built with his own hands. If I get up and sit on a chair, it is a chair my father built with his own hands. When my mother uses a large wooden spoon to stir the porridge we sometimes eat as part of our breakfast, it will be a spoon that my father has carved with his own hands. The sheets on my bed my mother made with her own hands. The curtains hanging at my window my mother made with her own hands. The nightie I am wearing, with scalloped neck and hem and sleeves, my mother made with her own hands. When I look at things in a certain way, I suppose I should say that the two of them made me with their own hands. For most of my life, when the three of us went anywhere together I stood between the two of them or sat between the two of them. But then I got too big, and there I was, shoulder to shoulder with them more or less, and it became not very comfortable to walk down the street together. And so now there they are together and here I am apart. I don't see them now the way I used to, and I don't love them now the way I used to. The bitter thing about it is that they are just the same and it is I who have changed, so all the things I used to be and all the things I used to feel are as false as the teeth in my father's head. Why, I wonder, didn't I see the hypocrite in my mother when, over the years, she said that she loved me and could hardly live without me, while at the same time proposing and arranging separation after separation, including this one, which, unbeknownst to her, *I* have arranged to be permanent? So now I, too, have hypocrisy, and breasts (small ones), and hair growing in the appropriate places, and sharp eyes, and I have made a vow never to be fooled again."

Lying in my bed for the last time, I thought, This is what I add up to. At that, I felt as if someone had placed me in a hole and was forcing me first down and then up against the pressure of gravity. I shook myself and prepared to get up. I said to myself, "I am getting up out of this bed for the last time." Everything I would do that morning until I got on the ship that would take me to England I would be doing for the last time, for I had made up my mind that, come what may, the road for me now went only in one direction: away from my home, away from my mother, away from my father, away from the everlasting blue sky, away from the everlasting hot sun, away from people who said to me, "This happened during the time your mother was carrying you." If I had been asked to put into words why I felt this way, if I had been given years to reflect and come up with the words of why I felt this way, I would not have been able to come up with so much as the letter "A." I only knew that I felt the way I did, and that this feeling was the strongest thing in my life.

The Anglican church bell struck seven. My father had already bathed and dressed and was in his workshop puttering around. As if the day of my leaving were something to celebrate, they were treating it as a holiday, and nothing in the usual way would take place. My father would not go to work at all. When I got up, my mother greeted me with a big, bright "Good morning"—so big and bright that I shrank before it. I bathed quickly in some warm bark water that my mother had prepared for me. I put on my underclothes—all of them white and all of them smelling funny. Along with my earrings, my neck chain, and my bracelets, all made of gold from British Guiana, my underclothes had been sent to my mother's obeah woman, and whatever she had done to my jewelry and underclothes would help protect me from evil spirits and every kind of misfortune. The things I never wanted to see or hear or do again now made up at least three weeks' worth of grocery lists. I placed a mark against obeah women, jewelry, and white underclothes. Over my underclothes, I put on an around-the-yard dress of my mother's. The clothes I would wear for my voyage were a dark-blue pleated skirt and a blue-and-white checked blouse (the blue in the blouse matched exactly the blue of my skirt) with a large sailor collar and with a tie made from the same material as the skirt—a blouse that came down a long way past my waist, over my skirt. They were lying on a chair, freshly ironed by my mother. Putting on my clothes was the last thing I would do just before leaving the house. Miss Cornelia came and pressed my hair and then shaped it into what felt like a hundred corkscrews, all lying flat against my head so that my hat would fit properly.

At breakfast, I was seated in my usual spot, with my mother at one end of the table, my father at the other, and me in the middle, so that as they talked to me or to each other I would shift my head to the left or to the right and get a good look at them. We were having a Sunday breakfast, a breakfast as if we had just come back from Sunday-morning services: salt fish and antroba and souse and hard-boiled eggs, and even special Sunday bread from Mr. Daniel, our baker. On Sundays, we ate this big breakfast at eleven o'clock and then we didn't eat again until four o'clock, when we had our big Sunday dinner. It was the best breakfast we ate, and the only breakfast better than that was the one we ate on Christmas morning. My parents were in a festive mood, saying what a wonderful time I would have in my new life, what a wonderful opportunity this was for me, and what a lucky person I was. They were eating away as they talked, my father's false teeth making that clop-clop sound like a horse on a walk as he talked, my mother's mouth going up and down like a donkey's as she chewed each mouthful thirty-two times. (I had long ago counted, because it was something she made me do also, and I was trying to see if this was just one of her rules that applied only to me.) I was looking at them with a smile on my face but disgust in my heart when my mother said, "Of course, you are a young lady now, and we won't be surprised if in due time you write to say that one day soon you are to be married."

Without thinking, I said, with bad feeling that I didn't hide very well, "How absurd!"

My parents immediately stopped eating and looked at me as if they had not seen me before. My father was the first to go back to his food. My mother continued to look. I don't know what went through her mind, but I could see her using her tongue to dislodge food stuck in the far corners of her mouth.

Many of my mother's friends now came to say goodbye to me, and to wish me God's blessings. I thanked them and showed the proper amount of joy at the glorious things they pointed out to me that my future held and showed the proper amount of sorrow at how much my parents and everyone else who loved me would miss me. My body ached a little at all this false going back and forth, at all this taking in of people gazing at me with heads tilted, love and pity on their smiling faces. I could have left without saying any goodbyes to them and I wouldn't have missed it. There was only one person I felt I should say goodbye to, and that was my former friend Gwen. We had long ago drifted apart, and when I saw her now my heart nearly split in two with embarrassment at the feelings I used to have for her and things I had shared with her. She had now degenerated into complete silliness, hardly able to complete a sentence without putting in a few giggles. Along with the giggles, she had developed some other schoolgirl traits that she did not have when she was actually a schoolgirl, so beneath her were such things then. When we were saying our goodbyes, it was all I could do not to say cruelly, "Why are you behaving like such a monkey?" Instead, I put everything on a friendly plain, wishing her well and the best in the future. It was then that she told me that she was more or less engaged to a boy she had known while growing up early on in Nevis, and that soon, in a year or so, they would be married. My reply to her was "Good luck," and she thought I meant her well, so she grabbed me and said, "Thank you. I knew you would be happy about it." But to me it was as if she had shown me a high point from which she was going to jump and hoped to land in one piece on her feet. We parted, and when I turned away I didn't look back.

My mother had arranged with a stevedore to take my trunk to the jetty ahead of me. At ten o'clock on the dot, I was dressed, and we set off for the jetty. An hour after that, I would board a launch that would take me out to sea, where I then would board the ship. Starting out, as if for old time's sake and without giving it a thought, we lined up in the old way: I walking between my mother and my father. I loomed way above my father and could see the top of his head. We must have made a strange sight: a grown girl all dressed up in the middle of a morning, in the middle of the week, walking in step in the middle between her two parents, for people we didn't know stared at us. It was all of half an hour's walk from our house to the jetty, but I was passing through most of the years of my life. We passed by the house where Miss Dulcie, the seamstress that I had been apprenticed to for a time, lived, and just as I was passing by, a wave of bad feeling for her came over me, because I suddenly remembered that the months I spent with her all she had me do was sweep the floor, which was always full of threads and pins and needles, and I never seemed to sweep it clean enough to please her. Then she would send me to the store to buy buttons or thread, though I was only allowed to do this if I was given a sample of the button or thread, and then she would find fault even though they were an exact match of the samples she had given me. And all the while she said to me,

"A girl like you will never learn to sew properly, you know." At the time, I don't suppose I minded it, because it was customary to treat the first-year apprentice with such scorn, but now I placed on the dustheap of my life Miss Dulcie and everything that I had had to do with her.

We were soon on the road that I had taken to school, to church, to Sunday school, to choir practice, to Brownie meetings, to Girl Guide meetings, to meet a friend. I was five years old when I first walked on this road unaccompanied by someone to hold my hand. My mother had placed three pennies in my little basket, which was a duplicate of her bigger basket, and sent me to the chemist's shop to buy a pennyworth of senna leaves, a pennyworth of eucalyptus leaves, and a penny-worth of camphor. She then instructed me on what side of the road to walk, where to make a turn, where to cross, how to look carefully before I crossed, and if I met anyone that I knew to politely pass greetings and keep on my way. I was wearing a freshly ironed yellow dress that had printed on it scenes of acrobats flying through the air and swinging on a trapeze. I had just had a bath, and after it, instead of powdering me with my baby-smelling talcum powder, my mother had, as a special favor, let me use her own talcum powder, which smelled quite perfumy and came in a can that had painted on it people going out to dinner in nineteenth-century London and was called Mazie. How it pleased me to walk out the door and bend my head down to sniff at myself and see that I smelled just like my mother. I went to the chemist's shop, and he had to come from behind the counter and bend down to hear what it was that I wanted to buy, my voice was so little and timid then. I went back just the way I had come, and when I walked into the yard and presented my basket with its three packages to my mother, her eyes filled with tears and she swooped me up and held me high in the air and said that I was wonderful and good and that there would never be anybody better. If I had just conquered Persia, she couldn't have been more proud of me.

We passed by our church—the church in which I had been christened and received and had sung in the junior choir. We passed by a house in which a girl I used to like and was sure I couldn't live without had lived. Once, when she had mumps, I went to visit her against my mother's wishes, and we sat on her bed and ate the cure of roasted, buttered sweet potatoes that had been placed on her swollen jaws, held there by a piece of white cloth. I don't know how, but my mother found out about it, and I don't know how, but she put an end to our friendship. Shortly after, the girl moved with her family across the sea to somewhere else. We passed the doll store, where I would go with my mother when I was little and point out the doll I wanted that year for Christmas. We passed the store where I bought the much-fought-over shoes I wore to church to be received in. We passed the bank. On my sixth birthday, I was given, among other things, the present of a sixpence. My mother and I then went to this bank, and with the sixpence I opened my own savings account. I was given a little gray book with my name in big letters on it, and in the balance column it said "6d." Every Saturday morning after that, I was given a sixpence—later a shilling, and later a two-and-sixpence piece—and I would take it to the bank for deposit. I had never been allowed to withdraw even a farthing from my bank account until just a few weeks before I was to leave; then the whole account was closed out, and I received from the bank the sum of six pounds ten shillings and two and a half pence.

We passed the office of the doctor who told my mother three times that I did not need glasses, that if my eyes were feeling weak a glass of carrot juice a day would make them strong again. This happened when I was eight. And so every day at recess I would run to my school gate and meet my mother, who was waiting for me with a glass of juice from carrots she had just grated and then squeezed, and I would drink it and then run back to meet my chums. I knew there was nothing at all wrong with my eyes, but I had recently read a story in *The Schoolgirl's Own Annual* in which the heroine, a girl a few years older than I was then, cut such a figure to my mind with the way she was always adjusting her small, round, horn-rimmed glasses that I felt I must have a pair exactly like them. When it became clear that I didn't need glasses, I began to complain about the glare of the sun being too much for my eyes, and I walked around with my hands shielding them—especially in my mother's presence. My mother then bought for me a pair of sunglasses with the exact horn-rimmed frames I wanted, and how I enjoyed the gestures of blowing on the lenses, wiping them with the hem of my uniform, adjusting the glasses when they slipped down my nose, and just removing them from their case and putting them on. In three weeks, I grew tired of them and they found a nice resting place in a drawer, along with some other things that at one time or another I couldn't live without.

We passed the store that sold only grooming aids, all imported from England. This store had in it a large porcelain dog—white, with black spots all over and a red ribbon of satin tied around its neck. The dog sat in front of a white porcelain bowl that was always filled with fresh water, and it sat in such a way that it looked as if it had just taken a long drink. When I was a small child, I would ask my mother, if ever we were near this store, to please take me to see the dog, and I would stand in front of it, bent over slightly, my hands resting on my knees, and stare at it and stare at it. I thought this dog more beautiful and more real than any actual dog I had ever seen or any actual dog I would ever see. I must have outgrown my interest in the dog, for when it disappeared I never asked what became of it. We passed the library, and if there was anything on this walk that I might have wept over leaving, this most surely would have been the thing. My mother had been a member of the library long before I was born. And since she took me everywhere with her when I was quite little, when she went to the library she took me along there, too. I would sit in her lap very quietly as she read books that she did not want to take home with her. I could not read the words yet, but just the way they looked on the page was interesting to me. Once, a book she was reading had a large picture of a man in it, and when I asked her who he was she told me that he was Louis Pasteur and that the book was about his life. It stuck in my mind, because she said it was because of him that she boiled my milk to purify it before I was allowed to drink it, that it was his idea, and that that was why the process was called pasteurization. One of the things I had put away in my mother's old trunk in which she kept all my childhood things was my library card. At that moment, I owed sevenpence in overdue fees.

As I passed by all these places, it was as if I were in a dream, for I didn't notice the people coming and going in and out of them, I didn't feel my feet touch ground, I didn't even feel my own body—I just saw these places as if they were hanging in the air, not having top or bottom, and as if I had gone in and out of them all in the same moment. The sun was bright; the sky was blue and just above my head. We then arrived at the jetty.

My heart now beat fast, and no matter how hard I tried, I couldn't keep my mouth from falling open and my nostrils from spreading to the ends of my face. My old fear of slipping between the boards of the jetty and falling into the dark-green water where the dark-green eels lived came over me. When my father's stomach started to go bad, the doctor had recommended a walk every evening right after he ate his dinner. Sometimes he would take me with him. When he took me with him, we usually went to the jetty, and there he would sit and talk to the night watchman about cricket or some other thing that didn't interest me, because it was not personal; they didn't talk about their wives, or their children, or their parents, or about any of their likes and dislikes. They talked about things in such a strange way, and I didn't see what they found funny, but sometimes they made each other laugh so much that their guffaws would bound out to sea and send back an echo. I was always sorry when we got to the jetty and saw that the night watchman on duty was the one he enjoyed speaking to; it was like being locked up in a book filled with numbers and diagrams and what-ifs. For the thing about not being able to understand and enjoy what they were saying was I had nothing to take my mind off my fear of slipping in between the boards of the jetty.

Now, too, I had nothing to take my mind off what was happening to me. My mother and my father—I was leaving them forever. My home on an island—I was leaving it forever. What to make of everything? I felt a familiar hollow space inside. I felt I was being held down against my will. I felt I was burning up from head to toe. I felt that someone was tearing me up into little pieces and soon I would be able to see all the little pieces as they floated out into nothing in the deep blue sea. I didn't know whether to laugh or cry. I could see that it would be better not to think too clearly about any one thing. The launch was being made ready to take me, along with some other passengers, out to the ship that was anchored in the sea. My father paid our fares, and we joined a line of people waiting to board. My mother checked my bag to make sure that I had my passport, the money she had given me, and a sheet of paper placed between some pages in my Bible on which were written the names of the relatives—people I had not known existed—with whom I would live in England. Across from the jetty was a wharf, and some stevedores were loading and unloading barges. I don't know why seeing that struck me so, but suddenly a wave of strong feeling came over me, and my heart swelled with a great gladness as the words "I shall never see this again" spilled out inside me. But then, just as quickly, my heart shriveled up and the words "I shall never see this again" stabbed at me. I don't know what stopped me from falling in a heap at my parents' feet.

When we were all on board, the launch headed out to sea. Away from the jetty, the water became the customary blue, and the launch left a wide path in it that looked like a road. I passed by sounds and smells that were so familiar that I had long ago stopped paying any attention to them. But now here they were, and the ever-present "I shall never see this again" bobbed up and down inside me. There was the sound of the seagull diving down into the water and coming up with something silverish in its mouth. There was the smell of the sea and the sight of small pieces of rubbish floating around in it. There were boats filled with fishermen coming in early. There was the sound of their voices as they shouted greetings to each other. There was the hot sun, there was the blue sea, there was the blue sky. Not very far away, there was the white sand of the shore, with the run-down houses all crowded in next to each other, for in some places only poor people lived near the shore. I was seated in the launch between my parents, and when I realized that I was gripping their hands tightly I glanced quickly to see if they were looking at me with scorn, for I felt sure that they must have known of my never-see-this-again feelings. But instead my father kissed me on the forehead and my mother kissed me on the mouth, and they both gave over their hands to me, so that I could grip them as much as I wanted. I was on the verge of feeling that it had all been a mistake, but I remembered that I wasn't a child anymore, and that now when I made up my mind about something I had to see it through. At that moment, we came to the ship, and that was that.

The goodbyes had to be quick, the captain said. My mother introduced herself to him and then introduced me. She told him to keep an eye on me, for I had never gone this far away from home on my own. She gave him a letter to pass on to the captain of the next ship that I would board in Barbados. They walked me to my cabin, a small space that I would share with someone else—a woman I did not know. I had never before slept in a room with someone I did not know. My father kissed me goodbye and told me to be good and to write home often. After he said this, he looked at me, then looked at the floor and swung his left foot, then looked at me again. I could see that he wanted to say something else, something that he had never said to me before, but then he just turned and walked away. My mother said, "Well," and then she threw her arms around me. Big tears streamed down her face, and it must have been that for I could not bear to see my mother cry—which started me crying, too. She then tightened her arms around me and held me to her close, so that I felt that I couldn't breathe. With that, my tears dried up and I was suddenly on my guard. "What does she want now?" I said to myself. Still holding me close to her, she said, in a voice that raked across my skin, "It doesn't matter what you do or where you go, I'll always be your mother and this will always be your home."

I dragged myself away from her and backed off a little, and then I shook myself, as if to wake myself out of a stupor. We looked at each other for a long time with smiles on our faces, but I know the opposite of that was in my heart. As if responding to some invisible cue, we both said, at the very same moment, "Well." Then my mother turned around and walked out the cabin door. I stood there for I don't know how long, and then I remembered that it was customary to stand on deck and wave to your relatives who were returning to shore. From the deck, I could not see my father, but I could see my mother facing the ship, her eyes searching to pick me out. I removed from my bag a red cotton handkerchief that she had earlier given me for this purpose, and I waved it wildly in the air. Recognizing me immediately, she waved back just as wildly, and we continued to do this until she became just a dot in the matchbox-size launch swallowed up in the big blue sea.

I went back to my cabin and lay down on my berth. Everything trembled as if it had a spring at its very center. I could hear the small waves lap-lapping around the ship. They made an unexpected sound, as if a vessel filled with liquid had been placed on its side and now was slowly emptying out.

Notes

p. 338 *thermos* - insulated flask for carrying hot drinks
p. 340 *Anglican* - part of the Church of England
p. 340 *British Guiana* - or Guyana, former British colony in South America
p. 340 *obeah* - fortune-teller
p. 340 *antroba and souse* - aubergine in spicy sauce
p. 341 *stevedore* - porter at the dock who loads/unloads ships

39

In the Mountains

(1987)

Ruth Prawer Jhabvala

A British/German American writer living in India, Prawer Jhabvala was best known for her film scripts for the Merchant Ivory films, particularly those based on E. M. Forster's novels. She also wrote many novels and stories about India such as Heat and Dust. In the Mountains *two people, who are both escaping former lives, live in the mountains and befriend one another: a family visit highlights their relationship.*

When one lives alone for most of the time and meets almost nobody, then care for one's outward appearance tends to drop away. That was what happened to Pritam. As the years went by and she continued living by herself, her appearance became rougher and shabbier, and though she was still in her thirties, she completely forgot to care for herself or think about herself as a physical person.

Her mother was just the opposite. She was plump and pampered, loved pastries and silk saris, and always smelled of lavender. Pritam smelled of – what was it? Her mother, enfolded in Pritam's embrace after a separation of many months, found herself sniffing in an attempt to identify the odour emanating from her. Perhaps it was from Pritam's clothes, which she probably did not change as frequently as was desirable. Tears came to the mother's eyes. They were partly for what her daughter had become and partly for the happiness of being with her again.

Pritam thumped her on the back. Her mother always cried at their meetings and at their partings. Pritam usually could not help being touched by these tears, even though she was aware of the mixed causes that evoked them. Now, to hide her own feelings, she became gruffer and more manly, and even gave the old lady a push toward a chair. 'Go on, sit down,' she said. 'I suppose you are dying for your cup of tea.' She had it all ready, and the mother took it gratefully, for she loved and needed tea, and the journey up from the plains had greatly tired her.

But she could not drink with enjoyment. Pritam's tea was always too strong for her – a black country brew such as peasants drink, and the milk was also that of peasants, too newly rich and warm from the buffalo. And they were in this rough and barely furnished room in the rough stone house perched on the mountainside. And there was Pritam herself. The mother had to concentrate all her energies on struggling against more tears.

347

'I suppose you don't like the tea,' Pritam said challengingly. She watched severely while the mother proved herself by drinking it up to the last drop, and Pritam refilled the cup. She asked, 'How is everybody? Same as usual? Eating, making money?'

'No, no,' said the mother, not so much denying the fact that this was what the family was doing as protesting against Pritam's saying so.

'Aren't they going up to Simla this year?'

'On Thursday,' the mother said, and shifted uncomfortably.

'And stopping here?'

'Yes. For lunch.'

The mother kept her eyes lowered. She said nothing more, though there was more to say. It would have to wait till a better hour. Let Pritam first get over the prospect of entertaining members of her family for a few hours on Thursday. It was nothing new or unexpected, for some of them stopped by every year on their way farther up the mountains. However much they may have desired to do so, they couldn't just drive past; it wouldn't be decent. But the prospect of meeting held no pleasure for anyone. Quite often there was a quarrel, and then Pritam cursed them as they drove away, and they sighed at the necessity of keeping up family relationships, instead of having their lunch comfortably in the hotel a few miles farther on.

Pritam said, 'I suppose you will be going with them,' and went on at once, 'Naturally, why should you stay? What is there for you here?'

'I want to stay.'

'No, you love to be in Simla. It's so nice and jolly, and meeting everyone walking on the Mall, and tea in Davico's. Nothing like that here. You even hate my tea.'

'I want to stay with you.'

'But I don't want you!' Pritam was laughing, not angry. 'You will be in my way, and then how will I carry on all my big love affairs?'

'What, what?'

Pritam clapped her hands in delight. 'Oh no. I'm telling you nothing, because then you will want to stay and you will scare everyone away.' She gave her mother a sly look and added, 'You will scare poor Doctor Sahib away.'

'Oh, Doctor Sahib,' said the old lady, relieved to find it had all been a joke. But she continued with disapproval, 'Does he still come here?'

'Well, what do you think?' Pritam stopped laughing now and became offended. 'If he doesn't come, then who will come? Except some goats and monkeys, perhaps. I know he is not good enough for you. You don't like him to come here. You would prefer me to know only goats and monkeys. And the family, of course.'

'When did I say I don't like him?' the mother said.

'People don't have to say. And other people are quite capable of feeling without anyone saying. Here.' Pritam snatched up her mother's cup and filled it, with rather a vengeful air, for the third time.

Actually, it wasn't true that the mother disliked Doctor Sahib. He came to visit the next morning, and as soon as she saw him she had her usual sentiment about him – not dislike but disapproval. He certainly did not look like a person fit to be on terms of social intercourse with any member of her family. He was a tiny man, shabby and even dirty. He wore a kind of suit, but it was in a terrible condition and so were his shoes. One eye of his spectacles, for some reason, was blacked out with a piece of cardboard.

'Ah!' he exclaimed when he saw her. 'Mother has come!' And he was so genuinely happy that her disapproval could not stand up to him – at least, not entirely.

'Mother brings us tidings and good cheer from the great world outside,' Doctor Sahib went on. 'What are we but two mountain hermits? Or I could even say two mountain bears.'

He sat at a respectful distance away from the mother, who was ensconced in a basket chair. She had come to sit in the garden. There was a magnificent view from here of the plains below and the mountains above; however, she had not come out to enjoy the scenery but to get the benefit of the morning sun. Although it was the height of summer, she always felt freezing cold inside the house, which seemed like a stone tomb.

'Has Madam told you about our winter?' Doctor Sahib said. 'Oh, what these two bears have gone through! Ask her.'

'His roof fell in,' Pritam said.

'One night I was sleeping in my bed. Suddenly – what shall I tell you – crash, bang! Boom and bang! To me it seemed that all the mountains were falling and, let alone the mountains, heaven itself was coming down into my poor house. I said, "Doctor Sahib, your hour has come."'

'I told him, I told him all summer, "The first snowfall and your roof will fall in." And when it happened all he could do was stand there and wring his hands. What an idiot!'

'If it hadn't been for Madam, God knows what would have become of me. But she took me in and all winter she allowed me to have my corner by her own fireside.'

The mother looked at them with startled eyes.

'Oh yes, all winter,' Pritam said, mocking her. 'And all alone, just the two of us. Why did you have to tell her?' she reproached Doctor Sahib. 'Now she is shocked. Just look at her face. She is thinking we are two guilty lovers.'

The mother flushed, and so did Doctor Sahib. An expression of bashfulness came into his face, mixed with regret, with melancholy. He was silent for some time, his head lowered. Then he said to the mother, 'Look, can you see it?' He pointed at his house, which nestled farther down the mountainside, some way below Pritam's. It was a tiny house, not much more than a hut. 'All hale and hearty again. Madam had the roof fixed, and now I am snug and safe once more in my own little kingdom.'

Pritam said, 'One day the whole place is going to come down, not just the roof, and then what will you do?'

He spread his arms in acceptance and resignation. He had no choice as to place of residence. His family had brought him here and installed him in the house; they gave him a tiny allowance but only on condition that he wouldn't return to Delhi. As was evident from his fluent English, Doctor Sahib was an educated man, though it was not quite clear whether he really had qualified as a doctor. If he had, he may have done something disreputable and been struck off the register. Some such air hung about him. He was a great embarrassment to his family. Unable to make a living, he had gone around scrounging from family friends, and at one point had sat on the pavement in New Delhi's most fashionable shopping district and attempted to sell cigarettes and matches.

Later, when he had gone, Pritam said, 'Don't you think I've got a dashing lover?'

'I know it's not true,' the mother said, defending herself. 'But other people, what will they think – alone with him in the house all winter? You know how people are.'

'What people?'

It was true. There weren't any. To the mother, this was a cause for regret. She looked at the mountains stretching away into the distance – a scene of desolation. But Pritam's eyes were half-shut with satisfaction as she gazed across the empty spaces and saw birds cleaving through the mist, afloat in the pure mountain sky.

'I was waiting for you all winter,' the mother said. 'I had your room ready, and every day we went in there to dust and change the flowers.' She broke out, 'Why didn't you come? Why stay in this place when you can be at home and lead a proper life like everybody else?'

Pritam laughed. 'Oh but I'm not like everybody else! That's the last thing!'

The mother was silent. She could not deny that Pritam was different. When she was a girl, they had worried about her and yet they had also been proud of her. She had been a big, handsome girl with independent views. People admired her and thought it a fine thing that a girl could be so emancipated in India and lead a free life, just as in other places.

Now the mother decided to break the news. She said, 'He is coming with them on Thursday.'

'Who is coming with them?'

'Sarla's husband.' She did not look at Pritam after saying this.

After a moment's silence Pritam cried, 'So let him come! They can all come – everyone welcome. My goodness, what's so special about him that you should make such a face? What's so special about any of them? They may come, they may eat, they may go away again, and good-bye. Why should I care for anyone? I don't care. And also you! You also may go – right now, this minute, if you like – and I will stand here and wave to you and laugh!'

In an attempt to stop her, the mother asked, 'What will you cook for them on Thursday?'

That did bring her up short. For a moment she gazed at her mother wildly, as if she were mad herself or thought her mother mad. Then she said, 'My God, do you ever think of anything except food?'

'I eat too much,' the old lady gladly admitted. 'Dr Puri says I must reduce.'

Pritam didn't sleep well that night. She felt hot, and tossed about heavily, and finally got up and turned on the light and wandered around the house in her nightclothes. Then she unlatched the door and let herself out. The night air was crisp, and it refreshed her at once. She loved being out in all this immense silence. Moonlight lay on top of the mountains, so that even those that were green looked as if they were covered in snow.

There was only one light – a very human little speck – in all that darkness. It came from Doctor Sahib's house, some way below hers. She wondered if he had fallen asleep with the light on. It happened sometimes that he dozed off where he was sitting and when he woke up again it was morning. But other times he really did stay awake all night, too excited by his reading and thinking to be able to sleep. Pritam decided to go down and investigate. The path was very steep, but she picked her way down, as sure and steady as a mountain goat. She peered in at his window. He was awake, sitting at his table with his head supported on his hand, and reading by the light of a kerosene lamp. His house had once had electricity, but after the disaster last winter it could not be got to work again. Pritam was quite glad about that, for the wiring had always been uncertain, and he had been in constant danger of being electrocuted.

She rapped on the glass to rouse him, then went around to let herself in by the door. At the sound of her knock, he had jumped to his feet; he was startled, and no less so when he discovered who his visitor was. He stared at her through his one glass lens, and his lower lip trembled in agitation.

She was irritated. 'If you're so frightened, why don't you lock your door? You should lock it. Any kind of person can come in and do anything he wants.' It struck her how much like a murder victim he looked. He was so small and weak – one blow on the head would do it. Some morning she would come down and find him lying huddled on the floor.

But there he was, alive, and, now that he had got over the shock, laughing and flustered and happy to see her. He fussed around and invited her to sit on his only chair, dusting the seat with his hand and drawing it out for her in so courtly a manner that she became instinctively graceful as she settled herself on it and pulled her nightdress over her knees.

'Look at me, in my nightie,' she said, laughing. 'I suppose you're shocked. If Mother knew. If she could see me! But of course she is fast asleep and snoring in her bed. Why are you awake? Reading one of your stupid books – what stuff you cram into your head day and night. Anyone would go crazy.'

Doctor Sahib was very fond of reading. He read mostly historical romances and was influenced and even inspired by them. He believed very strongly in past births, and these books helped him to learn about the historical eras through which he might have passed.

'A fascinating story,' he said. 'There is a married lady – a queen, as a matter of fact – who falls hopelessly in love with a monk.'

'Goodness! Hopelessly?'

'You see, these monks – naturally – they were under a vow of chastity and that means – well – you know . . .'

'Of course I know.'

351

'So there was great anguish on both sides. Because he also felt burning love for the lady and endured horrible penances in order to subdue himself. Would you like me to read to you? There are some sublime passages.'

'What is the use? These are not things to read in books but to experience in life. Have you ever been hopelessly in love?'

He turned away his face, so that now only his cardboard lens was looking at her. However, it seemed not blank but full of expression.

She said, 'There are people in the world whose feelings are much stronger than other people's. Of course they must suffer. If you are not satisfied only with eating and drinking but want something else . . . You should see my family. They care for nothing – only physical things, only enjoyment.'

'Mine exactly the same.'

'There is one cousin, Sarla – I have nothing against her, she is not a bad person. But I tell you it would be just as well to be born an animal. Perhaps I shouldn't talk like this, but it's true.'

'It is true. And in previous births these people really were animals.'

'Do you think so?'

'Or some very low form of human being. But the queens and the really great people, they become – well, they become like you. Please don't laugh! I have told you before what you were in your last birth.'

She went on laughing. 'You've told me so many things,' she said.

'All true. Because you have passed through many incarnations. And in each one you were a very outstanding personality, a highly developed soul, but each time you also had a difficult life, marked by sorrow and suffering.'

Pritam had stopped laughing. She gazed sadly at the blank wall over his head.

'It is the fate of all highly developed souls,' he said. 'It is the price to be paid.'

'I know.' She fetched a sigh from her innermost being.

'I think a lot about this problem. Just tonight, before you came, I sat here reading my book. I'm not ashamed to admit that tears came streaming from my eyes, so that I couldn't go on reading, on account of not being able to see the print. Then I looked up and I asked, "Oh, Lord, why must these good and noble souls endure such torment, while others, less good and noble, can enjoy themselves freely?"'

'Yes, why?' Pritam asked.

'I shall tell you. I shall explain.' He was excited, inspired now. He looked at her fully, and even his cardboard lens seemed radiant. 'Now, as I was reading about this monk – a saint, by the way – and how he struggled and battled against nature, then I could not but think of my own self. Yes, I too, though not a saint, struggle and battle here alone in my small hut. I cry out in anguish, and the suffering endured is terrible but also – oh, Madam – glorious! A privilege.'

Pritam looked at a crack that ran right across the wall and seemed to be splitting it apart. One more heavy snowfall, she thought, and the whole hut would come down. Meanwhile he sat here and talked nonsense and she listened to him. She got up abruptly.

He cried, 'I have talked too much! You are bored!'

'Look at the time,' she said. The window was milk-white with dawn. She turned down the kerosene lamp and opened the door. Trees and mountains were floating in a pale mist, attempting to surface like swimmers through water. 'Oh my God,' she said, 'it's time to get up. And I'm going to have such a day today, with all of them coming.'

'They are coming today?'

'Yes, and you needn't bother to visit. They are not your type at all. Not one bit.'

He laughed. 'All right.'

'Not mine, either,' she said, beginning the upward climb back to her house.

Pritam loved to cook and was very good at it. Her kitchen was a primitive little outbuilding in which she bustled about. Her hair fell into her face and stuck to her forehead; several times she tried to push it back with her elbow but only succeeded in leaving a black soot mark. When her mother pointed this out to her, she laughed and smeared at it and made it worse.

Her good humour carried her successfully over the arrival of the relatives. They came in three carloads, and suddenly the house was full of fashionably dressed people with loud voices. Pritam came dashing out of the kitchen just as she was and embraced everyone indiscriminately, including Sarla and her husband, Bobby. In the bustle of arrival and the excitement of many people, the meeting went off easily. The mother was relieved. Pritam and Bobby hadn't met for eight years – in fact, not since Bobby had been married to Sarla.

Soon Pritam was serving a vast, superbly cooked meal. She went around piling their plates, urging them to take, take more, glad at seeing them enjoy her food. She still hadn't changed her clothes, and the smear of soot was still on her face. The mother – whose main fear had been that Pritam would be surly and difficult – was not relieved but upset by Pritam's good mood. She thought to herself, why should she be like that with them – what have they ever done for her that she should show them such affection and be like a servant to them? She even looked like their servant. The old lady's temper mounted, and when she saw Pritam piling rice on to Bobby's plate – when she saw her serving *him* like a servant, and the way he turned around to compliment her about the food, making Pritam proud and shy and pleased – then the mother could not bear any more. She went into the bedroom and lay down on the bed. She felt ill; her blood pressure had risen and all her pulses throbbed. She shut her eyes and tried to shut out the merry, sociable sounds coming from the next room.

After a while Pritam came in and said, 'Why aren't you eating?'

The old lady didn't answer.

'What's the matter?'

'Go. Go away. Go to your guests.'

'Oh my God, she is sulking!' Pritam said, and laughed out loud – not to annoy her mother but to rally her, the way she would a child. But the mother continued to lie there with her eyes shut.

Pritam said, 'Should I get you some food?'

'I don't want it,' the mother said. But suddenly she opened her eyes and sat up. She said, 'You should give food to him. He also should be invited. Or perhaps you think he is not good enough for your guests?'

'Who?'

'Who. You know very well. You should know. You were with him the whole night.'

Pritam gave a quick glance over her shoulder at the open door, then advanced toward her mother. 'So you have been spying on me,' she said. The mother shrank back. 'You pretended to be asleep, and all the time you were spying on me.'

'Not like that, Daughter –'

'And now you are having filthy thoughts about me.'

'Not like that!'

'Yes, like that!'

Both were shouting. The conversation in the next room had died down. The mother whispered, 'Shut the door,' and Pritam did so.

Then the mother said in a gentle, loving voice, 'I'm glad he is here with you. He is a good friend to you.' She looked into Pritam's face, but it did not lighten, and she went on, 'That is why I said he should be invited. When other friends come, we should not neglect our old friends who have stood by us in our hour of need.'

Pritam snorted scornfully.

'And he would have enjoyed the food so much,' the mother said. 'I think he doesn't often eat well.'

Pritam laughed. 'You should see what he eats!' she said. 'But he is lucky to get even that. At least his family send him money now. Before he came here, do you want to hear what he did? He has told me himself. He used to go to the kitchens of the restaurants and beg for food. And they gave him scraps and he ate them – he has told me himself. He ate leftover scraps from other people's plates like a sweeper or a dog. And you want such a person to be my friend.'

She turned away from her mother's startled, suffering face. She ran out of the room and out through the next room, past all the guests. She climbed up a path that ran from the back of her house to a little cleared plateau. She lay down in the grass, which was alive with insects; she was level with the tops of trees and with the birds that pecked and called from inside them. She often came here. She looked down at the view but didn't see it, it was so familiar to her. The only unusual sight was the three cars parked outside her house. A chauffeur was wiping a windshield. Then someone came out of the house and, reaching inside a car door, emerged with a bottle. It was Bobby.

Pritam watched him, and when he was about to go back into the house, she aimed a pebble that fell at his feet. He looked up. He smiled. 'Hi, there!' he called.

She beckoned him to climb up to her. He hesitated for a moment, looking at the bottle and towards the house, but then gave the toss of his head that she knew well, and began to pick his way along the path. She put her hand over her mouth to cover a laugh as she watched him crawl up towards her on all fours. When finally he arrived, he was out of breath and dishevelled, and there was a little blood on his hand where he had grazed it. He flung himself on the grass beside her and gave a great 'Whoof!' of relief.

She hadn't seen him for eight years, and her whole life had changed in the meantime, but it didn't seem to her that he had changed all that much. Perhaps he was a little heavier, but it suited him, made him look more manly than ever. He was lying face down on the grass, and she watched his shoulder blades twitch inside his finely striped shirt as he breathed in exhaustion.

'You are in very poor condition,' she said.

'Isn't it terrible?'

'Don't you play tennis any more?'

'Mostly golf now.'

He sat up and put the bottle to his mouth and tilted back his head. She watched his throat moving as the liquid glided down. He finished with a sound of satisfaction and passed the bottle to her, and without wiping it she put her lips where his had been and drank. The whisky leaped up in her like fire. They had often sat like this together, passing a bottle of Scotch between them.

He seemed to be perfectly content to be there with her. He sat with his knees drawn up and let his eyes linger appreciatively over the view. It was the way she had often seen him look at attractive girls. 'Nice,' he said, as he had said on those occasions. She laughed, and then she too looked and tried to imagine how he was seeing it.

'A nice place,' he said. 'I like it. I wish I could live here.'

'You!' She laughed again.

He made a serious face. 'I love peace and solitude. You don't know me. I've changed a lot.' He turned right around towards her, still very solemn, and for the first time she felt him gazing full into her face. She put up her hand and said quickly, 'I've been cooking all day.'

He looked away, as if wanting to spare her, and this delicacy hurt her more than anything. She said heavily, 'I've changed.'

'Oh no!' he said in haste. 'You are just the same. As soon as I saw you, I thought: Look at Priti, she is just the same.' And again he turned towards her to allow her to see his eyes, stretching them wide open for her benefit. It was a habit of his she knew well; he would always challenge the person to whom he was lying to read anything but complete honesty in his eyes.

She said, 'You had better go. Everyone will wonder where you are.'

'Let them.' And when she shook her head, he said, in his wheedling voice, 'Let me stay with you. It has been such a long time. Shall I tell you something? I was so excited yesterday thinking: Tomorrow I shall see her again. I couldn't sleep all night. No, really – it's true.'

Of course she knew it wasn't. He slept like a bear; nothing could disturb that. The thought amused her, and her mouth corners twitched. Encouraged, he moved in closer. 'I think about you very often,' he said. 'I remember so many things – you have no idea. All the discussions we had about our terrible social system. It was great.'

Once they had had a very fine talk about free love. They had gone to a place they knew about, by a lake. At first they were quite frivolous, sitting on a ledge overlooking the lake, but as they got deeper into their conversation about free love (they both, it turned out, believed in it) they became more and more serious and, after that, very quiet, until in the end they had nothing more to say. Then they only sat there, and though it was very still and the water had nothing but tiny ripples on it, like wrinkles in silk, they felt as if they were in a storm. But of course it was their hearts beating and their blood rushing. It was the most marvellous experience they had ever had in their whole lives. After that, they often returned there or went to other similar places that they found, and as soon as they were alone together that same storm broke out.

Now Bobby heaved a sigh. To make himself feel better, he took another drink from his bottle and then passed it to her. 'It's funny,' he said. 'I have this fantastic social life. I meet such a lot of people, but there isn't one person I can talk with the way I talk with you. I mean, about serious subjects.'

'And with Sarla?'

'Sarla is all right, but she isn't really interested in serious subjects. I don't think she ever thinks about them. But I do.'

To prove it, he again assumed a very solemn expression and turned his face toward her, so that she could study it. How little he had changed!

'Give me another drink,' she said, needing it.

He passed her the bottle. 'People think I'm an extrovert type, and of course I do have to lead a very extrovert sort of life,' he said. 'And there is the business too – ever since Daddy had his stroke, I have to spend a lot of time in the office. But very often, you know what I like to do? Just lie on my bed and listen to nice tunes on my cassette. And then I have a lot of thoughts.'

'What about?'

'Oh, all sorts of things. You would be surprised.'

She was filled with sensations she had thought she would never have again. No doubt they were partly due to the whisky; she hadn't drunk in a long time. She thought he must be feeling the way she did; in the past they had always felt the same. She put out her hand to touch him – first his cheek, which was rough and manly, and then his neck, which was soft and smooth. He had been talking, but when she touched him he fell silent. She left her hand lying on his neck, loving to touch it. He remained silent, and there was something strange. For a moment, she didn't remove her hand – she was embarrassed to do so – and when at last she did, she noticed that he looked at it. She looked at it too. The skin was rough and not too clean, and neither were her nails, and one of them was broken. She hid her hands behind her back.

Now he was talking again, and talking quite fast. 'Honestly, Priti, I think you're really lucky to be living here,' he said. 'No one to bother you, no worries, and all this fantastic scenery.' He turned his head again to admire it and made his eyes sparkle with appreciation. He also took a deep breath.

'And such marvellous air,' he said. 'No wonder you keep fit and healthy. Who lives there?' He pointed at Doctor Sahib's house below.

Pritam answered eagerly. 'Oh, I'm very lucky – he is such an interesting personality. If only you could meet him.'

'What a pity,' Bobby said politely. Down below, there was a lot of activity around the three cars. Things were being rolled up and stowed away in preparation for departure.

'Yes, you don't meet such people every day. He is a doctor, not only of medicine but all sorts of other things too. He does a lot of research and thinking, and that is why he lives up here. Because it is so quiet.'

Now people could be seen coming out of Pritam's house. They turned this way and that, looking up and calling Pritam's name.

'They are looking for you,' Bobby said. He replaced the cap of his whisky bottle and got up and waited for her to get up too. But she took her time.

'You see, for serious thinking you have to have absolute peace and quiet,' she said. 'I mean, if you are a real thinker, a sort of philosopher type.'

She got up. She stood and looked down at the people searching and calling for her. 'Whenever I wake up at night, I can see his light on. He is always with some book, studying, studying.'

'Fantastic,' Bobby said, though his attention was distracted by the people below.

'He knows all about past lives. He can tell you exactly what you were in all your previous births.'

'Really?' Bobby said, turning towards her again.

'He has told me all about my incarnations.'

'Really? Would he know about me too?'

'Perhaps. If you were an interesting personality. Yes all right, coming!' she called down at last.

She began the steep climb down, but it was so easy for her that she could look back at him over her shoulder and continue talking. 'He is only interested in studying highly developed souls, so unless you were someone really quite special in a previous birth he wouldn't be able to tell you anything.'

'What were you?' Bobby said. He had begun to follow her. Although the conversation was interesting to him, he could not concentrate on it, because he had to keep looking down at the path and place his feet with caution.

'I don't think I can tell you,' she said, walking on ahead. 'It is something you are supposed to know only in your innermost self.'

'What?' he said, but just then he slipped, and it was all he could do to save himself from falling.

'In your innermost self!' she repeated in a louder voice, though without looking back. Nimbly, she ran down the remainder of the path and was soon among the people who had been calling her.

They were relieved to see her. It seemed the old lady was being very troublesome. She refused to have her bag packed, refused to get into the car and be driven up to Simla. She said she wanted to stay with Pritam.

'So let her,' Pritam said.

Her relatives exchanged exasperated glances. Some of the ladies were so tired of the whole thing that they had given up and sat on the steps of the veranda, fanning themselves. Others, more patient, explained to Pritam that it was all very well for her to say let her stay, but how was she going to look after her? The old lady needed so many things – a masseuse in the morning, a cup of Horlicks at eleven and another at three, and one never knew when the doctor would have to be called for her blood pressure. None of these facilities was available in Pritam's house, and they knew exactly what would happen – after a day, or at the most two, Pritam would send them an SOS, and they would have to come back all the way from Simla to fetch her away.

Pritam went into the bedroom, shutting the door behind her. The mother was lying on her bed, with her face to the wall. She didn't move or turn around or give any sign of life until Pritam said, 'It's me.' Then her mother said, 'I'm not going with them.'

Pritam said, 'You will have to have a cold bath every day, because I'm not going to keep lighting the boiler for you. Do you know who has to chop the wood? Me, Pritam.'

'I don't need hot water. If you don't need it, I don't.'

'And there is no Horlicks.'

'Tcha!' said her mother. She was still lying on the bed, though she had turned around now and was facing Pritam. She did not look very well. Her face seemed puffed and flushed.

'And your blood pressure?' Pritam asked.

'It is quite all right.'

'Yes, and what if it isn't? There is no Dr Puri here, or anyone like that.'

The mother shut her eyes, as if it were a great effort. After a time, she found the strength to say, 'There is a doctor.'

'God help us!' Pritam said, and laughed out loud.

'He *is* a doctor.' The mother compressed her little mouth stubbornly over her dentures. Pritam did not contradict her, though she was still laughing to herself. They were silent together but not in disagreement. Pritam opened the door to leave.

'Did you keep any food for him?' the mother said.

'There is enough to last him a week.'

She went out and told the others that her mother was staying. She wouldn't listen to any arguments, and after a while they gave up. All they wanted was to get away as quickly as possible. They piled into their cars and waved at her from the windows. She waved back. When she was out of sight, they sank back against the upholstery with sighs of relief. They felt it had gone off quite well this time. At least there had been no quarrel. They discussed her for a while and felt that she was improving; perhaps she was quietening down with middle age.

Pritam waited for the cars to reach the bend below and then – quite without malice but with excellent aim – she threw three stones. Each one squarely hit the roof of a different car as they passed, one after the other. She could hear the sound faintly from up here. She thought how amazed they would be inside their cars, wondering what had hit them, and how they would crane out of the windows but not be able to see anything. They would decide that it was just some stones crumbling off the hillside – perhaps the beginning of a landslide; you never could tell in the mountains.

She picked up another stone and flung it all the way down at Doctor Sahib's corrugated tin roof. It landed with a terrific clatter, and he came running out. He looked straight up to where she was standing, and his one lens glittered at her in the sun.

She put her hands to her mouth and called, 'Food!' He gave a sign of joyful assent and straightaway, as nimble as herself, began the familiar climb up.

Notes

p. 348   *Simla* - capital of Himachal Pradesh in Northern India – it is in a mountainous region, where those who can afford it traditionally go to escape the greatest heat of the cities. In this story, the family are on their way to a holiday from work in Delhi

p. 348   *Mall; Davico's* - main street and restaurant in Simla

p. 358   *masseuse* - woman who gives massages

p. 358   *Horlicks* - powdered milk drink

40

Showing the Flag

(1989)
Jane Gardam

Gardam is a British writer of many novels, short stories and children's books. In Showing the Flag, *a boy is en route to France on his own for the first time, nervous about being met – but he discovers inner resources and ultimately realises he has not been abandoned.*

The boy with big ears, whose father was dead, kissed his mother with a sliding away of the eyes, heaved up his two immense suitcases and loped up the gang-plank. At the top he dropped the cases briefly to give a quick sideways wave, keeping his face forward. He jerked the cases up again, grimaced, tramped on and his mother far below, weeping but laughing, said, 'Oh, Pym! It's the size of the cases. They're nearly as big as he is. Oh, I can't bear it.'

'He is going for a sensible time,' said her elderly woman friend. 'Three months is a good long time. The cases must necessarily be heavy.'

'I can't bear it,' wept the other, dabbing her streaming cheeks, laughing at her weakness.

'Of course you can. You must. It's not as if he's never been away before.'

'Since six. He's been away since he was six. Oh, boarding-schools. Oh, children – why does one have them? Children – it's all renunciation. Having them is just learning to give them up.'

'It is the custom of the country,' said the elderly friend – unmarried. She was a Miss Pym. 'It is in the culture of the English middle class. We teach our children how to endure.'

'He has endured. He has learned.'

'Oh, he scarcely knew his father, Gwen. Don't be silly. His father was hardly ever at home.'

"He missed him. Not of course as I—"

'You scarcely saw him either,' said sane Miss Pym. She was a plain-spoken woman.

'I loved him,' said Gwen, impressive in her heavy hanging musquash coat and flat velvet bandeau (it was the nineteen-twenties). 'And now I have lost Philip. Oh, can we find tea?' She held her tightly-squeezed handkerchief in her fist, out in front of her like a blind woman, and her friend led her away through the crowds, among the crates and high-piled luggage and the other fluttering handkerchiefs. Arm in arm the two women disappeared, slowly, floppily in their expensive boat-shaped shoes, and Philip who had found a good position for the suitcases beside a long slatted seat, hung over the rail and waved to them in vain.

When the last flicker of them had gone he blew through his teeth a bit until a whistle came and swung his feet at the bottom rail along the deck, scuffing his shoes like a two-year-old, though he was nearly thirteen. As the ship got away towards France he hung further over the rail and called down at the seagulls who were wheeling and screeching round the open port-hole of the galley. A bucket of scraps was flung out. The seagulls screamed at it and caught most of it before it hit the foam. They plunged. 'Hungry,' thought Philip. 'I'm hungry. I hope the food's going to be good. Messy French stuff. They all say it's going to be good, but it'll be no better than school. It's just disguised school.'

'The seagulls eat like school.' He watched enviously the birds tearing horrors from each other's beaks, flying free. Were they French or English seagulls? Where did they nest? They spoke a universal language, seagulls. And all birds. All animals. Presumably. Didn't need to learn French. 'They're ahead of people,' thought Philip, covering his great red ears.

It was bitterly cold. Maybe it would be warmer in Paris.

He was to get to Paris on the boat-train by himself and would there be met by a Major Foster. They would know one another by a small paper Union Jack pinned to a lapel on each of them. Philip was keeping his Union Jack in his coat pocket at present, in a small brass tin. Every few minutes he felt the tin to make sure that it was still there.

He left the rail and sat on the long seat beside the suitcases. He could not remember actually having seen the flag in the tin, only hearing about it there. He had seen it when it was part of a small packet of Union Jacks, tied in a bundle. He had heard nothing else but Union Jacks it seemed for weeks: his mother's search for just the right one, the dispatch of the Major's identical one to Paris with the instructions to him about the lapel. The (rather long) wait for the letter of confirmation from the Major that the Union Jack had been safely received. Then a further letter about the positioning of the Union Jack on the *right* lapel, in the centre and with a gold safety-pin.

Philip however could not remember the act of placing the Union Jack inside the tin. After all, she might just have forgotten. Not that it was the sort of thing she ever did do – forget. But during the last few months – after the funeral which he hadn't gone to, and which she hadn't gone to, being too ill in bed and her friend Miss Pym paddling about nursing her and bossing her in a darkened room – after the funeral there had been some sort of break. Only a short break of course. His mother wasn't one to break. She was terrific, his mother. Everyone knew she was terrific. She kept everything right. Never made a mistake. Ace organiser. He'd heard them saying in the kitchen that it was her being so perfect had killed his father, though goodness knows, thought Philip, what that meant.

Oh, his mother was a whizz. Organising, packing, making decisions. 'These are your gifts. These are your life-blood,' had said Miss Pym. 'You are by nature an administrator – quite wasted now as a mere mother.' His school matron always sighed over his trunk at the end of term. 'However did your mother get so much in?' she said. There was not a shoe not filled with socks, not a sock that did not hide a card of special darning-wool or extra buttons. Bundles of Cash's name-tapes would be folded into a face flannel. Soap in a little soap-shaped celluloid box would rest inside a cocoa mug, and the cocoa mug would rest inside a cricket cap and the cricket cap would be slid into a Wellington boot.

No. She'd never have forgotten the Union Jack.

'I think it's rather a lot to expect of a Frenchman,' had said Miss Pym. 'To wear the English flag.'

'The Fosters are French-Canadian,' had said his mother. 'They're very English. Very patriotic, although they live in the Avenue Longchamps.'

'I hope their French is not patriotic. If so there's very little point in Philip going.'

'They are patriotic to France as well.'

'How odd,' said Pym. 'That is unusual.'

Philip took the tin out of his pocket and shook it and there seemed to be no rattle from inside. But then when he opened the lid, there lay the little paper flag quite safe beside its pin and the wind at once scooped it up and blew it away among the seagulls.

Philip ran to the rail and watched it plucked outwards and upwards, up and up, then round and down. Down it went, a little bright speck until it became invisible in the churning sea.

'*Calais*,' said the fat French lady along the seat beside him. 'You see? Here is France.' Philip immediately got up and walked away. He looked at the scummy waves slopping at the green jetty, the tall leaning houses. There was a different smell. This was abroad. Foreign soil. In a moment he was going to set foot upon it.

And he was lost and would never be found.

'*Le petit*,' said the French lady coming up alongside him at the rail and stroking his hair. He wagged his head furiously and moved further away. '*Tout seul*,' and she burst into a spate of French at her husband. Philip knew that the French meant that the barbaric English had abandoned this child. Not able to consider this concept he shouldered the suitcases and made for the quay, and there was approached by a ruffian who tried to take them both from him. He hung on to them tight, even when the man began to scream and shout. He aimed a kick at the man and tramped away, the cases grazing the ground. Not one person on the crowded quay paid attention to the attempted theft.

Philip showed his passport and was swirled into the crowd. '*Paris*,' cried the fat lady, swinging into view, '*Paris – ah, le petit!*' and she held her rounded arm out boldly but shelteringly in his direction, leaning towards him. Her husband who had a sharp nose and black beret and teeth began to talk fast and furiously into the nearest of Philip's vulnerable ears.

But Philip behaved as though he were quite alone. He climbed into the train, found his seat, took off his gaberdine rain-coat, folded it onto a little rack and looked at the huge suitcases and the higher luggage-rack with nonchalance. The rest of the carriage regarded them with amazement and several people passionately urged that the racks were unequal to the challenge ahead of them. Another ruffian came in and seemed to want to remove the cases altogether but Philip with a vehemence that astonished him and the ruffian and the whole carriage and a stretch of the corridor, flung himself in the man's path and across his property. He turned bright red and his ears redder and cried out, 'No, no, no.'

This caused more discussion and the ruffian, lifting his gaze to the ceiling and his hands near it, went shouting away. The suitcases were then successfully stowed on the racks, two of the Frenchmen shook hands with Philip and an old woman wearing a long black dress and a lace head-dress like some sort of queen, offered him a sweet which he refused. Huddled in his corner seat he looked out of the window and wondered what to do.

Rattling tracks, bleak cement, scruffy houses all tipping about and needing a coat of paint. Shutters. Railway lines insolently slung across streets, all in among fruit-stalls, all muddly. Rain.

No Union Jack.

Rain. Fields. Grey. Everything measured out by rulers. Small towns, now villages. Gardens. Allotments. No Union Jack.

Men in blue overalls. More berets. Black suits. Stout women with fierce brows. Men standing looking at their allotments, very still and concentrated like saying their prayers. Vegetables in very straight rows. Men carefully bending down and plucking out minute, invisible weeds. Mix-up of muddle and order. Like Mother. No Union Jack.

What should he do? Major Foster would be wearing his Union Jack and Philip would go up to him and say— But in all the hundreds of people getting off the train at Paris there might be a dozen boys of twelve. Perhaps a hundred. The Major would go sweeping by. 'Oh no. I'm sorry. They were very particular. The boy I am to meet will be wearing—'

And he'd be speaking in French of course. Probably French-Canadians spoke no English. It hadn't been clear. Miss Pym had written all the letters to the Foster family because she could write French, and the replies had been in French. Miss Pym had taken them away to translate with the dictionary under her arm. No Union Jack.

How stupid. How stupid of his mother. Why hadn't she sewed the Union Jack on his raincoat in the first place? She loved sewing. She was always mending and sewing, not even listening to his father and Miss Pym scrapping away about politics, just looking across at them now and then, or looking over, smiling, at him. His socks were more darns than socks because she so loved darning. Loved making things perfect. Loved making everything seem all right.

So then she sends him away with a rotten little Woolworth's Union Jack out of a cheap packet of them, loose in a tin. And not waving either when she'd said goodbye. Not crying at all. He knew about that crying-and-laughing-together she did. He'd never thought anything of it. He wondered if it had been the laughing-and-crying and all the darning and soupy Miss Pym and her French that had killed his father.

After all, she hadn't really seemed to mind his father dying. Gone off to bed for the funeral. Perhaps she'd really wanted him to die. Wanted to be free of him so that she could have long, cosy chats with Miss Pym. Horrible Miss Pym speaking her mind all the time. Not liking his father and showing it. Not liking boys. Not liking him. Goopy-goo about his mother. Organising these Fosters. Very glad he was going away. Making no secret of that.

Perhaps his mother also was glad that he was going away.

Philip when this thought arrived concentrated upon the colourless, hedgeless, straight-edged French fields. Rattle-crash the train went over the level-crossings that sliced the roads in half. Long poles hung with metal aprons. Funny people. Lots of them on bicycles, clustered round, waiting to cross. Very dangerous. Very daring. People full of – what? Different from home. Full of energy. No, not energy – what? Fireworks. Explosives. Confidence. That was it. Not as if they needed to keep private their secret thoughts.

If they suddenly discovered for instance that their mothers did not love them they would not sit dumb and numb in a corner.

People in the carriage were now getting out packets of food. One of the hand-shaking men offered Philip a slanted slice of bread, orange and white. Somebody else offered him wine. He shook his head at all of it and looked out of the window. When the talk in the carriage began to get lively he got up and took down the raincoat and took from the pocket the packet of lunch his mother had made up for him herself, with her own fair hands, ha-ha. He sat with it on his knee. He was too sad, too shy to open it.

Also he didn't really want it. His mother had packed it up so carefully. Like a work of art. Greaseproof corners turned into triangles, like a beautifully-made bed. The package was fastened with two elastic bands, criss-cross, making four neat squares. And even his name on it in clear black pencil, PHILIP. How silly could you get? Who else would it be for? *Madly* careful, that's what she was. And then she goes and leaves the Union Jack loose in the box.

And she knew how flimsy it was. She must have expected it to blow away. She expected everything. She'd expected a wind. She'd gone on at breakfast-time about him getting seasick. And she knew he'd be more than likely to open the box.

Oh, she'd known what would happen all right. She'd gone off without even waving, her yellow fur arm on the yellow fur arm of Pym. She did not love him, want him, know him and she never had. It was all just darning and being perfect.

She wanted him lost.

All that about flags was just a blind. She *wanted* him to miss the Major. Wanted rid of the bother of him. Wanted him to disappear. She was a wicked woman who had killed her husband. All that laughing as she cried.

One night when he was young Philip had come downstairs after being put to bed, to get a book from the morning room and through the dining room door had heard his father singing at table:

> Oh me and oh my
> Oh dear and oh dear
> I ain't gonna drink
> No more damned beer

and Miss Pym had come sailing out of the room with her lips pressed together. 'Coarse,' he had heard her say. 'Coarse,' and then, seeing him standing in his pyjamas at the foot of the stairs in the summer evening light, 'Go to bed, Philip. Don't look so stricken. There is a point when every child sees through his parents.'

But his father's singing hadn't made Philip think any less of him. He'd always rather liked his father, or what he saw of him. He'd not been able to talk to children, just looked awkward and done card-tricks. Once in the town, seeing his son walking on the other side of the road, his father had raised his hat to him. What did she mean 'see through'?

But now he was seeing through his mother. He was seeing through her all right. He knew her now. The stupid woman. All that fuss trailing about for flags in Canterbury and then she gets one that blows away. Accidentally-on-purpose-ha-ha. She'd be free now. Free for life. Free to be with Stinkerpym. They'd got rid of him together, making sure the flag was really flimsy. Brilliantly they had evaded the law and there would be no evidence of their plot. Philip the only son would simply disappear.

Well, he wouldn't. At least he would, because he'd never go back. Not to Canterbury, never. Thirteen was all right. He'd manage. Look at *Kidnapped*. Look at *Treasure Island*. You can get on without your mother. When he'd got to Paris he'd— He had some money. He'd just put up in a hotel for a few nights. Get work. He could probably get work somewhere as a kitchen boy or – well, somewhere where there was food.

He was very hungry now. Probably Major Foster and his sisters would have got a good dinner ready for him. This dinner he would never eat, never see, as he would never see the beautiful house they all said would be like a little palace near the Bois de Boulogne. Too bad. He'd go to the Paris stews. At least they sounded as if you didn't go hungry.

And since he was so hungry at the moment he would eat his mother's sandwiches. She could hardly have poisoned them.

Could she?

As he opened the greaseproof paper he considered the enigma of his mother, how she flitted in and out of his life, always waving him away on trains. Sending him to boarding school at six.

'And even now I could fox her,' he thought. 'Even now I could tear a bit off this greaseproof and draw a union-jack on it and pin it on the lapel with the pin in the box. I could write my name on it too. I could borrow a pencil.'

He looked round the carriage wondering which of them he might ask. It would be an easy sentence to say. He'd even done it at school. And he had begun to like the look of the French faces.

But no. He'd go to the stews.

He opened the sandwiches and there was an envelope on top and inside it a piece of paper and his mother's huge handwriting saying 'Oh Philip, my darling, don't hate me for fussing, but I do so love you.'

Pinned to the paper was a spare Union Jack.

Notes

p. 360   *showing the flag* - a naval term: a boat displays its nationality by its flag
p. 360   *gang-plank* - movable walkway between boat and land
p. 361   *boat-train* - the train that meets the boat
p. 362   *Le petit . . . tout seul* - 'Little boy . . . all alone'

41

Sharmaji

(1991)

Anjana Appachana

Appachana is an Indian writer now living in the USA. This is a funny and very recognisable story of office life in Delhi and the character of a skiver and chancer who will not toe the line.

Sharma was late for work. When he signed his name in the attendance register, the clerk in the personnel department shook his head disapprovingly.

'Very bad, very bad, Sharmaji,' he said, clicking his tongue. 'This is the fourteenth time you are late this month.'

Sharma's brow darkened. 'You keep quiet, Mahesh,' he replied. 'Who are you to tell me I'm late? You are a clerk, I am a clerk. You don't have the authority to tell me anything. Understood?'

Mahesh retreated behind his desk. He said, 'What I am telling you, I am telling you for your own good. Why you must take it in the wrong spirit I do not understand.'

'You don't tell me what is good for me,' Sharma said. He raised his voice. 'I am twenty-five years older than you.'

He had an audience by now. The other latecomers and those working in the personnel department were watching with intense interest.

Sharma continued, 'I have been in this company for twenty-five years. At that time you were in your mother's womb.' He surveyed his delighted audience. 'He thinks that after reading our personal files he has power over us.' He snapped his fingers in front of Mahesh's face. 'I can show you how much power you have! What can a pipsqueak like you teach me! It is for *me* to teach *you*!'

'Sharmaji,' said Mahesh, folding his hands, 'I take back my words. Now please leave me alone. And I beg of you, do not shout in the personnel department. It sounds very bad.'

Sharma chuckled. He raised his voice. 'Shouting? I am not shouting. I am talking to you. Is it forbidden to talk in the personnel department? Is this an office or a school?' He smiled again at his audience. Everyone was spellbound. He said, 'So Mahesh, you now think you can tell me how to behave. Very good. What else can you teach me?'

367

'Yes, Mahesh, tell him,' urged Gupta, the clerk from the accounts department. He was also late, but only for the ninth time in the month.

Mahesh looked harassed. 'You keep out of this, Gupta. This is not your business.'

'Mahesh,' said Gupta. 'You are in the wrong profession. You should have been a teacher, a professor. Join Delhi University. We will all give you recommendations!'

Everyone roared with laughter. Mohan, the peon, was the loudest. 'Today we are having fun,' he said between guffaws. 'Oh, this is wonderful!'

'What is wonderful, Mohan?'

It was the personnel officer, Miss Das. A sudden silence fell in the room. Everyone looked away. She glanced at her watch and then at the silent group. 'What is happening?' she asked. 'Why is there this *mela* here?'

'Madam, we came to sign the attendance register,' Sharma said.

Gupta slid out of the room.

She looked pointedly at her watch. 'The register, should have been signed forty-five minutes ago.'

Sharma looked her straight in the eyes. 'Madam,' he said, 'what to do, my daughter has a temperature. I had to take her to the clinic so I got a little late.'

'Did you inform your manager that you would be late?'

'I don't have a phone at home, madam.'

'Why didn't you inform him yesterday?'

'Madam, I did not know yesterday. My daughter fell ill this morning.'

She looked at the register. 'Has your daughter been ill fourteen days of the month?'

Mahesh smirked.

'Oh, madam,' said Sharma, 'that was my other daughter. You know this virus, madam. All my daughters have been falling ill, one after the other. I have three.'

'Fourteen days,' she repeated, shaking her head.

'Yes madam, three daughters with this virus. Well, madam, I should be getting along.' He sauntered out of the room.

In the corridor he bumped into Gupta smoking a cigarette. 'What Gupta,' he said, 'you left me alone to face her.'

'What to do?' said Gupta. 'She has already told me off twice. She thinks it is still Indiraji's raj. Cigarette?'

'Might as well,' said Sharma, and took one. 'So, how are things with you?'

Gupta lit his cigarette. 'All right, so so.' He gave a bashful smile. 'My parents are searching for a girl for me. I have to get married before December. The astrologer has said that the two years after December will be very inauspicious for marriage.'

'Are you looking for a working girl, or what?'

'Yes. We think that might be preferable. How can we manage on my salary? But they bring less dowry. And my sister has to be married off next month. It is very difficult.'

'So, anything fixed up yet?'

'No, I have seen four girls so far. All dark.'

'Do not worry, Gupta. You will surely find a fair bride. Now, how about some chai?'

'Good idea.'

They strolled to the canteen and ordered tea. It arrived, steaming hot, and they drank it with satisfaction. 'Terrible tea,' said Sharma. 'This company has no care for its employees. They are stingy even in the tea they give us – no milk, or sugar. This tea is worth ten paisa. They charge us fifty paisa. Then they say it is subsidised. Ha! Subsidised!'

'Why should they care?' said Gupta. 'They only want to make money. Profit, profit, profit. That is all they care about. We are the ones who do all the work and they are the ones who benefit. This is life.'

Sharma sighed. 'Yes, this is life,' he echoed. 'Give me another cigarette, Gupta. After tea a cigarette is a must.'

They both had another.

'How is your Mrs?' asked Gupta.

Sharma grinned self-consciously. 'She is going to become a mother.'

'Arre!' exclaimed Gupta. 'What are you doing, Sharmaji? You already have three and the Government says one or two, bas.'

'They are all girls, Gupta. Who will look after us in our old age?'

'Forgive me, Sharmaji,' Gupta said, clicking his tongue, 'but I am talking to you as old friend. You already have three daughters. You will have to spend all your money marrying them off. And now one more is coming. Suppose that too is a girl?'

Sharma sighed heavily. 'That is in God's hands. After all, it is fate. I have to suffer in this life for the sins I have committed in my previous life.' He sighed again. 'Gupta, yar, it is so difficult to manage these days. Since my daughters were born I have been putting aside fifty rupees every month for their marriages. Even then it will not be enough to marry them off.'

Gupta patted Sharma. 'Why worry about the future? Deal with things as they come. Think yourself fortunate that at least you are in the purchase department.'

'That is true, that is true,' agreed Sharma. 'Where would a mere clerk's salary take me?'

They ordered some more tea and smoked another cigarette. For some time there was an amiable silence. Then Gupta leaned towards Sharma confidentially. 'Have you heard the latest?'

'What?'

'You don't know?'

'No – what?'

'You won't believe it.'

'Arre, tell me Gupta.'

'Miss Das smokes.'

'Impossible!'

'Yes, yes, she smokes. Rahul saw her smoking.'

'Where?'

'In a restaurant in Connaught Place.'

'Alone?'

'No, not alone. She was sitting with a man and smoking. And when she saw Rahul, she stubbed it out.'

'I cannot believe it.'

'Even I find it difficult to believe.'

'She has a boyfriend?'

'Must be having a boyfriend.'

'Is she engaged?'

'Don't know. She's a quiet one.'

Sharma considered the news. 'Rahul is a great gossip. He talks too much. One never knows how much truth there is in what he says. He does no work, have you noticed? All he does is gossip.'

'Then you think it is not true?'

'I did not say that. It could be true. It could be untrue. Myself, I feel it is not true. Miss Das does not look the smoking kind. She appears to be a good girl.'

'But why should Rahul make it up? What does he have against her?'

'Yes, yes, you have a point. Truly, this is disturbing. But she must be engaged. She does not seem to be the kind to go around with men.'

'Maybe. Maybe not.'

Sharma chewed his lips. He shook his head. 'I will find out.'

Gupta looked at his watch. He got up. 'Sharmaji, it is already 11.30. We had better go to our departments.'

Sharma pulled him down. 'Stop acting so conscientious. No one will miss us. Lunchtime is at 12.30. We might as well stay here till lunch is over.'

Gupta looked worried. 'I am not conscientious,' he disclaimed. 'It is just that my boss has been after my life these days. If he knows I'm here he'll again say that I don't work.'

'Oh, *sit* down,' said Sharma. 'Even my boss is after my life. They are all like that, these managers. They think that only they work. Just because they stay here after office hours they expect people to believe that they work. Ha! All that is to impress the general manager. How else can they get their promotions? All maska.'

Gupta sat down.

'Jagdish,' called Sharma. 'More chai.'

The third round of tea arrived.

The electricity went off.

'Bas,' said Sharma. 'Now who can work? These power cuts will kill us all.' He sat back in his chair.

'My boss says that it is no excuse,' said Gupta gloomily. 'He says that if a power cut lasts three hours it doesn't mean that we don't work for three hours. He says that we are here to work.'

'He can keep saying that,' said Sharma contemptuously. 'Does he think we're animals? They all think that we have no feelings. Work all day, work when the electricity goes off, work without increments, work without promotions, work, work, work. That is all they care about. No concern for us as human beings.'

'Hai Ram,' Gupta whispered. 'Don't look behind you. She's here.'

'Who?'

'Miss Das. She's seen us.'

'So what if she's seen us?'

'She'll tell our managers.'

'Let her tell them.'

'Sharmaji, I have already been warned.'

'Nothing to worry about. What can he do to you? The union will support you.'

'Sharmaji, it will be in my records if they give me a warning letter.'

'So let it be in your records, Gupta. Anyway you are in their bad books.'

'Suppose they give me a charge-sheet?'

'Now you are panicking. Relax. Nothing can happen. Now we have a union.'

'She's gone. Sharmaji, I'm going back to the department.'

'Arre, Gupta, sit down. Just half an hour for the lunch break. We will both go back to our departments after lunch.'

'No, no, I am going now. Excuse me, Sharmaji, see you later.' He rushed out.

Sharma shook his head. Everyone was scared. That was the problem. He opened the newspaper lying on the table and read for some time. The same news. Nothing changed. He yawned.

'There you are, Sharmaji.' It was Harish, the peon from the purchase department. 'Borwankar Sahib is calling you to his office.' He chuckled. 'He is in a bad temper. There will be fireworks today!'

Sharma looked at him unsmilingly. 'It is lunchtime. Tell him I will come after lunch.'

'Sharmaji, you had better go now. He is in a very bad temper.'

'You don't tell me what to do. You have given me the message. Now go.'

Harish smacked his forehead in despair. 'All right, all right, I will go. Don't tell me later that I did not warn you.' He left.

Sharma curled his lips contemptuously. He leaned further against his chair. He scratched an unshaven cheek. From his pocket he took out a paan wrapped in a piece of paper and put it in his mouth. Contemplatively, he chewed.

'Should we eat, Sharmaji?' It was Gupta.

'Back so soon?' asked Sharma, surprised.

'Yes, it is 12.30 – lunchtime,' Gupta said happily.

'I haven't got my lunch,' said Sharma sadly. 'Last week my wife left for her mother's with the girls for a month. I have no time to cook.'

'Why didn't you tell me earlier, Sharmaji?' exclaimed Gupta. 'You mustn't keep such problems from old friends. From tomorrow, till your wife comes home, I will ask my mother to pack extra lunch. It will be enough for both of us.'

'Gupta,' said Sharma emotionally, 'you are a true friend.'

'It is nothing.'

They shared Gupta's lunch. Then they went down to the dhaba opposite the building. There they ordered puri-aloo. It was a wonderful meal. Then they each had a large glass of lassi. After it was over they sat back, replete, content, drowsy.

'Gupta,' said Sharma, rubbing his stomach, 'I am falling asleep.'

'Me too,' groaned Gupta. 'I cannot keep my eyes open. Hai Ram.'

The heat, their meal and the lassi were having their effect. They could barely keep awake. Sleep . . . wonderful sleep.

'They should have a rest room in the office where we could take a short nap after lunch,' said Gupta. 'Then we would be ready to work, refreshed.'

'Yes,' sighed Sharma. 'In the summer especially, one cannot keep awake after lunch.'

'Sharmaji, it is already half an hour past lunchtime. Let us go back.'

Reluctantly, Sharma rose. He blinked his eyes against the afternoon sun. This was torture. Slowly, they began walking back to the building.

Suddenly Sharma stopped. 'Paan,' he said. 'I must have a paan. Let us go to the paan shop.'

Gupta hesitated. 'All right,' he said, 'but let us hurry.'

At the paan shop they bought four paans, ate one each and had the other two wrapped up. When they reached the office building they found that the electricity had not returned. They could not take the lift.

'I will die,' said Sharma. I cannot climb up four floors after a meal like that.' He sat down on the steps.

Mohan passed him on the way upstairs. He hooted with laughter. 'Sharmaji, everyone does it, why can't you? Kaamchor!' He bounded up the stairs before Sharma could respond.

'Haramzada,' muttered Sharma. 'Even the peons in the personnel department are getting too big for their boots.' He got up and slowly began climbing up the stairs with Gupta. 'And they expect us to work in these conditions,' he said. 'They think we are animals.'

Gupta clicked his tongue in sympathy.

On the third floor Sharma said, 'If I don't have some tea I will collapse.'

'In this heat, Sharmaji?'

'I am tired, I am sleepy. Only tea will do the job. Chalo, let us go to the canteen.'

'Sharmaji, you go. My boss has been taking rounds of our office.'

'Sharma, could you please come to my office?' It was Mr Borwankar, Sharma's boss. Gupta slid away to his department.

Sharma sighed. 'Yes, Borwankar Sahib. I will come.'

He followed his manager to his office.

'Sit down.'

Sharma sighed and sat.

'I had called you to my office more than an hour ago.'

'It was lunchtime, sir.'

'Indeed.'

'Yes, sir.'

'What happened after lunch?'

'I am here sir, after lunch.'

'It is forty-five minutes past lunchtime.'

'I went to the dhaba to eat, sir. There was a long queue there, so I was delayed, sir. All this was because my daughters have been getting the virus, sir, and my wife has no time to pack lunch for me, sir. I am sure you understand, sir. After all, how can I work on an empty stomach? I feel so weak these days sir, so tired. I think I am also getting the virus.'

'Where have you been all morning?'

'Here, sir.'

'Here – where?'

'In the department, sir.'

'You were not at your desk all morning.'

'Sir, what are you saying? I must have gone down to the personnel department or the accounts department for some work.'

'What work?'

Sharma was silent. He shook his head. He looked sadly at Mr Borwankar. He said, 'Borwankar sahib, why are you taking this tone with me? You ask me questions as though you have no faith in me. This is not a detective agency. Why must you interrogate me in this manner? All right, I was not in my department, but that was because I had work in other departments. Still, if it is your wish, I will not go to other departments even if I have work there. I will sit at my desk and work only at my desk. Yes, yes, I will do that. The company does not want me to consult other departments. All right, I will not consult other departments. You will see, work will suffer, but why should I care when you do not? I have been in this company for twenty-five years, but no one cares. For twenty-five years the company has bled me, sucked me dry. What do you know? You have been here only two years. You know nothing. Twenty-five years ago I joined as a clerk. Today I am still a clerk. Why should I work?'

His outburst had touched something raw in him. Overwhelmed and defiant, he glared at Mr Borwankar.

'Sharma, you still haven't answered my question.'

Sharma shrugged his shoulders. 'Borwankar sahib, what is the point of answering? Even if I answer, you will not believe me.' He reflected and said sadly, 'No, there is no point telling you anything. What can you understand?'

Mr Borwankar said dryly, 'I understand that you haven't been at your desk all morning. You were seen loitering in the corridor and drinking tea in the canteen. Presumably that is what you did all morning. And that is what you have been doing virtually every day. In addition, you never come to work on time. Today you were half-an-hour late. This is your fourteenth late arrival this month. Last month you were late twenty days and the previous month, fifteen days. What do you have to say for yourself?'

'What can I say? This is the only work the personnel department has. Every day they sit and count how many late arrivals there are. For that they get paid. Even I can count.'

'Sharma, you are evading all my questions. I have already warned you three times. Each time you gave me to understand that things would change. Nothing has changed. Your work output is zero. Your attitude leaves much to be desired.'

There was a knock at the door and the personnel officer entered. She sat next to Sharma. Mr Borwankar said, 'Under the circumstances I have no alternative but to give you this.' He gave Sharma a typed sheet of paper.

Sharma read it slowly. It was a charge-sheet accusing him of being absent from his workplace all morning and of coming late to work on specified days. If he did not answer in twenty-four hours it would be presumed that he had accepted the charges.

His hands trembled. So. After twenty-five years – this.

He tossed the paper back to Mr Borwankar and got up. He said, 'You can keep your piece of paper.'

'Sharmaji,' said Miss Das, 'please accept it. Not accepting a charge-sheet is a very serious offence.'

Sharma replied, 'I will do nothing without consulting the general secretary of the workers' union.'

He walked out of the room.

Sharma found Adesh Singh, general secretary of the workers' union, on the production floor, listlessly assembling some components. He walked up to him and said, 'I want to talk to you, come to the canteen.'

Adesh's supervisor looked up from the end of the table. Adesh went up to her. 'Madam,' he said, 'please excuse me for ten minutes. Something serious has come up.'

She replied, 'Adesh, you know I cannot permit time for union activities during office hours. Go in the tea break.'

Adesh continued standing before her. After some time he said, 'Madam, may I go to the canteen to drink some water?'

'You are not thirsty.'

He looked at her in amazement. He said, 'Who are you to say that I am not thirsty? Madam, you surprise me. You permit everyone to go the bathroom or to the canteen for a drink of water. In fact, they do not even ask your permission to go. Why do you make an exception in my case? Is it because I am the general secretary of the union? Does the general secretary have no right to be thirsty? Have things come to such a pass that a worker is denied *water*? Is this the management's new rule?'

'Go, please go.'

'Yes, madam, I will go. I do not need permission from you to quench my thirst. There has been no electricity most of this morning. And yet you deny me water.'

The other workers listened, rapt.

With his hand on his chest, Adesh said, 'Madam, what you have said has hurt me here . . . right here.' He drew a shuddering breath. 'You think we have no feelings, no hearts. You think that only officers have feelings. But madam, believe me, our hearts are more vulnerable than yours. We feel . . . we feel. Sharmaji, chalo.'

With dignity, he walked out of the production floor, Sharma trailing behind him. In the canteen, Adesh wiped his brow. 'Yes, Sharmaji. Now what has happened?'

'What can I tell you? They have given me a charge-sheet.'

'What does it say?'

'That I haven't been in my office all morning and that I don't come to work on time.'

'Is that true?'

'What does that matter? What truth is there in this world?'

Adesh picked his teeth reflectively. 'So, what do you want me to do?'

'You tell me.'

'Accept the charge-sheet. Deny the charges. What else?'

'Then they'll institute an inquiry.'

'Let them. They need witnesses for that. No worker will be a witness.'

'The officers will. Mr Borwankar will. Miss Das will. And those latecomings are on record.'

'Then accept the charges. They'll let you off with a warning letter.'

'How can you say that?'

'I'll see to that.'

'All right. But you come with me to Borwankar sahib.'

They both meditated for some time.

'Some chai?' asked Adesh.

'Yes, of course.'

They ordered tea. Sharma lit a cigarette and smoked sadly.

'Sharmaji,' said Adesh deliberately, 'you had better mend your ways. I can't help you out next time.'

The tea arrived.

'What do you mean, mend my ways?' asked Sharma sulkily.

'You know what I mean. You don't seem to know your limits.'

'Don't lecture me. You are the general secretary of the union. Your duty is to get me out of this, not give me speeches.'

'You keep quiet. If you want me to help you, hold your tongue.'

Sharma simmered. Again, insults from someone so much younger. They finished their tea. 'Chalo,' said Adesh. They went to Mr Borwankar's office and knocked on the door.

'Come in.' They entered. He was talking to the personnel officer. 'Please sit down.' They sat.

'Please show me the charge-sheet,' said Adesh.

'Why are you here, Adesh?' asked Mr Borwankar.

'Why not? You have the personnel officer as your witness. Sharmaji has me as his. Who knows what false accusations the management is making against the poor man.'

Mr Borwankar handed the charge-sheet to Sharma. Adesh took it from Sharma and read it. He looked up, shock registering on his face. 'What is all this, Borwankar sahib? Madam, what does this mean?'

'Isn't that evident?' replied Mr Borwankar.

'No, it isn't. Sharmaji was at his desk all morning. I saw him there.'

'And what, pray, were you doing in the purchase department all morning?'

'Borwankar sahib, you cannot intimidate me. I do not work under you. If anyone can question me, it is my supervisor. She had sent me there on some work. I had to check up on some material. You are not the only person who has work outside your room. We all do. There are other workers who saw Sharmaji at his desk. You will get proof. I can get any number of workers to give it in writing that Sharmaji was at his desk all morning.'

'Indeed. Go ahead. All that can be investigated when there is an inquiry. Sharma, will you please sign the copy and accept the charge-sheet? Enough time has been wasted.'

Sharma and Adesh exchanged glances.

'Sign it,' said Adesh.

Sharma took the letter and signed the copy. He got up. He said, 'Madam, advise the company to change its attitude to workers. Giving charge-sheets left and right is not the answer.' He left.

Adesh looked accusingly at Mr Borwankar. 'Sir,' he said. 'Do you know what you are doing to that man? You have broken him. You have betrayed him.'

'Adesh,' said Mr Borwankar wearily. 'Please spare me the dramatics.'

'Ask him to speak to me,' said Miss Das.

Adesh nodded. 'All right, I'll do that. Tell me, do you intend to hold an inquiry?'

'That depends on whether he accepts the charges, doesn't it?'

'Sir, I request you to let him off with a warning letter this time. I will talk to him. I will din some sense into his thick head. I will see to it that he changes his ways. His wife and children are away these days. He is lonely. He is unwell.'

Miss Das said, 'I thought his daughter was ill and that was why he was late today?'

'That is true. His family left this afternoon. From today he is all alone. He is lost. Madam, why are you asking questions? You as a personnel officer should understand.'

She smiled faintly. 'I do,' she said. 'Ask him to speak to me.'

Adesh said, 'So there will be no inquiry?'

There was a pause. Miss Das said, 'He must accept the charges and apologise in writing.'

Adesh shook his head. 'Yes, yes, you must have your pound of flesh. Yes, I will tell him.' He rose wearily.

Miss Das was in her office when Sharma entered.

'Come in, Sharmaji, please sit down.'

Sharma sighed and sat. He passed his hand over his brow. 'It is so hot,' he said. 'How do you expect us to work with these power cuts, Miss Das?'

'What to do, Sharmaji? That is how life is in Delhi. Would you like a glass of cold water?'

'Certainly.' He gulped down the water. 'What advantages there are to being an officer! You have flasks of cold water in your room. We poor workers have to go to the canteen to drink water. And when we go there and someone sees that we are not at our workplace, we are accused of shirking work.' He returned the glass. 'Thank you, madam.'

'You're welcome.'

There was a short silence and then she said, 'Sharmaji, it seems that you are greatly distressed. What is the matter?'

Sharma gave a short laugh. 'What a question to ask! You give me a charge-sheet and then you ask me why I am distressed. What, madam, does the personnel department not know even this much?'

'I'm sorry, that's not what I meant. I meant that you have been looking run down and depressed for the last few days.'

Sharma looked at her in wonder. 'So,' he said, '*someone* has noticed. Yes, madam, I have been run down and depressed the last few days. I have been run down and depressed the last few months, the last several years. I do not remember what happiness is, madam . . . I cannot remember. And if I do remember, it is so distant a fragment of the past that I feel . . . maybe it never was. The future stretches before me like the night. Ah, madam, what can I tell you? What do you know of life? You are still young, you are not even married. Make the most of this time, madam, it will never return. With marriage, children and careers – much is lost madam, much is lost. You know nothing yet, nothing. When you were sitting there with Borwankar sahib, I thought, poor Miss Das, already she is so involved in office politics. Soon even she will be corrupted. She sees that I, an employee twenty-five years in the company, is given a charge-sheet. I, who have given my best years to the company. She sees. Does she feel anything? Does she care? If she feels, she cannot show it. But maybe she does feel. Maybe her heart goes out to this man. She has to do her duty. She has to be there. But maybe she asks herself, what is happening? Should this be happening? And maybe, something deep within her answers, no it should not. Maybe her heart beats in silent sympathy for this man so completely broken by the company's cruel policies. But she can say nothing. She is after all, in the personnel department. And the personnel department has to be diplomatic. It sees and hears all, it can say nothing. I understand. I do not blame you. But madam, beware. You know nothing of the evils surrounding you. You are too innocent. You do not know what people say, the rumours they spread. Look at me. You must have heard how people talk about me. They make me out to be sometimes a rakshash, sometimes a Harijan. They say I am a bad influence on people. They say I do not work. They say people should not mix with me. I, who was one of the first people to join the company twenty-five years ago. If I did not work, why did the company give me a special award for excellent work twenty years ago? You look surprised. You do not know. Of course, they will not tell you. They know you are intelligent. They know you will ask, what has happened to this man? You wish to know madam, yes?

'Madam, what can I tell you? Where can I begin? What was I then? What am I now! That Mahesh in your department, I was his age when I joined this company. Look at him. He is too big for his boots. He tells me I'm late. He flaunts his power just because he is in the personnel department. Madam, keep an eye on him. He is dangerous. He will alienate everyone from the personnel department if he continues this way. Let me tell you something. He does no work. He sits with his register and pretends he is filling it in. Actually he is doing nothing of the sort. He is planning wicked schemes. He is counting how many times Gupta and I are late. Madam, do you know how often other people are late? No you do not. That is because Mahesh does not give you their names. He gives names of only some people. I happen to be one of those unfortunate few. Madam, keep an eye on him. He is crooked. He will only give you the information that suits him. He will let you down, madam. You are too trusting. That is good. That is also bad. People will take advantage of you. Like they took advantage of me. Once, many years ago, even I was like you; trusting and innocent. I believed everything I was told. I worked hard. Not once was I late. And people said, look at Sharma, he is our best worker. I got an award. And after that – nothing. Other people rose. Other people got increments. Other people got promotions. Poor Sharma got left behind. Other people buttered their bosses. And I, fool that I was, I believed that only hard work succeeds. Did Srivastava become purchase officer through hard work? Was Tiwari promoted from peon to clerk because he worked hard? No, they all did maska. They accompanied their managers to their homes. They ran personal errands for them. They did jobs for their bosses' wives. Hah! I know how they got their promotions. I refused. I was idealistic. I had principles. And here I am, still a clerk. Now *those* men order me around, tell me, Sharma do this, Sharma do that. And

Sharma does it, even though inside, his heart is breaking. Madam, some more water, if I may.'

She gave him another glass of water. She said, 'Sharmaji, I did not know all this.'

He drank the water and wiped his mouth. 'Madam, you know nothing. Even now, you know nothing. You don't know what goes on in this place.'

'What?'

He looked behind him at the door. He got up and opened it. No one. He sat at his chair and leaned forward. In hushed tones, he said, 'Dhanda of girls.'

'I don't understand.'

'Madam, forgive me, you are too innocent. I will keep quiet. I should not have mentioned it.' He looked behind him again. He paused. He whispered. 'When girls are recruited in this company, they have to perform certain favours for certain men for having got in.'

'Oh.'

'I have shocked you, madam. Forgive me. But it is true.' He leaned closer to the desk. He said, 'These men are still working here. These girls are still working here. So much dirt, madam. What can you understand of these things?'

'Who are these men?'

He leaned back. 'I cannot reveal their names, madam.'

'Why not? You can help me remove this dirt.'

'Oh no, madam, no, no.'

'Why not, Sharmaji?'

'No, madam, no. Do not ask me why.'

'But if you don't tell me, Sharmaji, it will continue.'

Sharma smiled gently. 'But you see, it is not happening now. It is a thing of the past. Since you joined the company such things have stopped. People are scared. They say that a woman has come to the personnel department and that this woman is honest. She will protect our girls. Now there is nothing to worry about. Rest assured, madam. All is well, now that you are here.'

'All is not well, Sharmaji. How can all be well when you continue coming late to work every other day and are never at your workplace?'

'Madam, madam, madam.' Sharma wagged an admonishing finger at her. 'You are very persistent. That is your job. You are personnel officer. That is your duty. Good. That is good.'

'So, Sharmaji, what happened today?'

'What can I say, madam? Sometimes I curse fate for bringing me into this world, for flinging me amid such people. Often I ask myself – what sins did I commit in my last birth to suffer so in this one? There is no answer. God has his own ways, madam, who knows why, who knows how?

'I see you are smiling, madam? I know what you are thinking. You are thinking – this Sharma talks too much. Why is Sharma saying all this? Sharma has not answered my question. But I have, madam, I have. Reflect carefully over all that I have told you. You will find the answers. There are no simple answers to simple questions. I read a poem once, an English poem that was translated into Hindi. Somewhere it said:

There are no small questions for small men

All men are Hamlet on an empty street

Or a windy quay

All men are Lear in the market

When the tradesmen have gone.

'Madam, if he had not written the poem, I would have written it. Even here someone has done it before me. Can you understand what he is saying, madam? You nod your head. Then you understand me. Your questions are answered, madam. Madam, some more water, please.'

She poured out another glass of water. He drank it thirstily. 'Sharmaji, may I make a request?'

'Madam, any request.'

'From tomorrow you will make an effort to come to work on time?'

'Of course, madam, of course.'

'And I don't want to see you in the canteen or corridors during office hours.'

'Whatever you say, madam, whatever you say.'

'Thank you.'

Sharma gazed at her fondly. 'Do not thank me, madam. Why are you thanking me?' He paused. He said, 'Madam, you have made a request. I agreed. Now may I make one?'

'Certainly.'

'Put in a word for me to Borwankar sahib, madam. In his mind it is set that Sharma is bad. Once such an impression is made, it does not change. In this company especially. Tell Borwankar sahib, Sharma once got a special award. Tell him, his promotion is long overdue. Tell him, is it fair that Sharma remains a clerk for twenty-five years? You have influence, madam. You are personnel officer. If you tell Borwankar sahib, Borwankar sahib will listen.'

'Sharmaji, now everything depends on you. I can do nothing.'

Sharma sighed. 'Yes, that is what they all say. Well, you have been kind, madam. You have patiently listened to me. Madam, do you like cosmetics . . . lipsticks?'

'Like what, Sharmaji?'

'I can get these things very cheap, madam, even free. After all I am in the purchase department. I can get you imported scents and lipsticks, electronic items, cassettes.'

'How?'

'Oh, come, come, madam. What can I get you?'

'Nothing, thank you, Sharmaji.'

Sharma nodded his head seriously. 'You are absolutely right in refusing. Even I refuse. They keep telling me, Sharmaji, please take this, Sharmaji, please take that. They say, you place such large orders for your company; let us give you some gifts to show you our appreciation. But I say, no. No. I am not like the rest. I will not give to anyone, I will not take from anyone. For that they respect me. After all, if there is no self-respect, then what is there?'

'Well, madam, I must leave. Here is my answer to the charge-sheet.' He handed the paper to Miss Das.

She read it. She said, 'So, you have denied being absent from the workplace, saying that your manager is victimising you. You have accepted coming late to work, saying that your children have been ill. And you have apologised if this has caused any misunderstanding, Sharmaji!'

'Madam, madam, let us not argue any more. You asked me to apologise. I have apologised. Now let bygones be bygones. Let a new chapter begin.'

Miss Das put the paper away. 'Some more water, Sharmaji?'

'No, madam, thank you.' He rose from his chair. 'I must be leaving.'

'Don't hesitate to come to me if you have any problems.'

'Madam, I do not have any problems. Borwankar sahib has problems. Mahesh has problems. Even your peon Mohan has problems. Yes, if they continue to have problems, I will come to you.'

He got up and was about to leave the room when a thought seemed to strike him. He appeared to hesitate, and then spoke. 'Madam, before I leave, I must ask you a question of a rather personal nature. As a brother, I would like to ask you. Please do not mind.'

'Yes?'

'Madam, you have a good job, you are young. Like an elder brother, let me give you some advice. You must not postpone marriage, no woman should be alone in this world. I am speaking out of concern for you. Maybe, you are already engaged?'

'I am married.'

Sharma reeled. 'Madam!'

She began to laugh.

'But madam, you are *Miss* Das.'

'Yes, I've retained my maiden name.'

'Why?'

'Why not?'

Sharma considered. 'A woman goes into another family. She must take the name of the family.'

'I have not gone into any family. My husband and I are both working.'

Sharma stared at her. 'You are very modern.'

'And that is bad?'

He reflected. 'Maybe not. I cannot say. When did this take place, madam?'

'Two months ago.'

'Madam, forgive me for saying this, but this is very bad, very very bad. You did not tell any of us. You did not distribute any sweets. I am greatly offended. This is a cause for celebration, not secrecy.'

'It was no secret, Sharmaji.'

'Oh well.' He surveyed her. 'You don't even look married. No sindoor, no mangalsutra, no jewellery. What is this, madam?'

'No need for all that, Sharmaji.'

Sharma shook his head in despair. 'What can I say? I suppose things are changing. I would like to meet your husband, madam. Is he also good and kind like you?'

She looked confused. 'You will certainly meet him one day.'

'Good. Very good. Well, madam, I will go. From my side, please say namaste to your husband.'

'Certainly.'

With great dignity he sailed out of the room. A minute later he returned. 'Madam,' he said with a slight shrug, 'I was wondering, you wouldn't be interested in reading some of my poetry would you?'

'I would very much like to.'

Sharma smiled. He nodded. 'I will get them tomorrow. Madam, I wrote these poems many, many years ago. Since then I have written nothing, nothing at all. Still . . . they are very philosophical, very deep, very complex. Tomorrow, at 9 a.m. I will share them with you.'

She replied, 'In the lunch break.'

He frowned. 'There will be another power cut in the afternoon. How can I read my poetry to you, drenched in sweat?' He considered.

She smiled.

He capitulated. 'If you insist, then, the lunch break.'

Outside the office, Sharma looked at his watch. It was already 5 p.m., just half an hour left for office to get over. Slowly he walked down the corridor, softly humming an old love song to himself. Suddenly he was flooded with memories. Once . . . years ago, he had loved, loved madly, crazily. Her large kajal-filled eyes had haunted him, bewitched him. Those eyes . . . those eyes. He would have gladly died for her. Shy, smitten, he had said nothing. She had never known. Sharma stopped and swallowed. He felt his heart would burst. Twenty-five years.

'Sharmaji, coming to the canteen?' It was Gupta, bounding down the stairs, two at a time.

Sharma smiled indulgently. 'Not scared of your boss now?'

'He has gone out of the office on some work. Chalo, let us have some chai, Sharmaji.'

Gently, Sharma shook his head. 'I have some work.' He patted Gupta. 'You go.'

Gupta stared at him, open-mouthed.

'Gupta,' said Sharma, 'Miss Das does not have a boyfriend. She is married. People in this office are always spreading dirty rumours. Do not listen to them.'

He gave Gupta a final pat and walked to his department, still humming. When he entered the room his fellow clerks grinned.

'You are an elusive man, Sharmaji,' said Rahul. 'Everyone has been looking for you today. Where were you?'

Sharma shrugged his shoulders modestly. 'There were things to do, many things to do. And there is still so much to be done. Rahul, life is very brief, very fleeting.'

Rahul chuckled. 'All right, Sharmaji, I will leave you to your considerations.' He went back to his typing.

Sharma sat on his desk. He took the paan out of his pocket and carefully removed its wrapping. He put it in his mouth. Chewing, he opened his drawer and took out a sheet of paper. Lovingly, he placed it on his desk, licked his pencil and began a new poem.

Notes

p. 380   *poem* - from Edward Bond, *Theatre Poems* 1964
p. 370   *maska* - flattery, buttering up, putting on an act to impress
p. 367   *pipsqueak* - young upstart
p. 368   *mela* - gathering/party
p. 368   *Indiraji's raj* - reference to the only female Prime Minister of India, Indira Gandhi
p. 369   *chai* - tea
p. 369   *bas* - enough
p. 369   *peon* - office boy
p. 372   *dhaba* - road-side food stall
p. 372   *puri-aloo* - potato dish
p. 372   *paan* - betel leaf for chewing
p. 372   *Haramzada* - 'the bastard'
p. 378   *rakshash* - demon
p. 378   *Harijan* - term used by Gandhi for the 'Untouchable' caste, it means 'children of God'
p. 382   *sindoor* - red mark on forehead worn by married Hindu women
p. 382   *mangalsutra* - necklace worn by married Hindu women
p. 382   *namaste* - respectful greeting – 'I salute the God within you'

42

Mrs. Sen's

(1999)

Jhumpa Lahiri

Lahiri is an Indian American writer of a novel – The Namesake *– and two very fine collections of short stories, which often focus on the tensions between cultures;* The Third and Final Continent *appeared in* Stories of Ourselves, *volume 1. In this story, a boy goes to a 'baby sitter' who is gradually revealed to us through his eyes as she mourns her life in India and tries to adapt to the USA.*

Eliot had been going to Mrs. Sen's for nearly a month, ever since school started in September. The year before he was looked after by a university student named Abby, a slim, freckled girl who read books without pictures on their covers, and refused to prepare any food for Eliot containing meat. Before that an older woman, Mrs. Linden, greeted him when he came home each afternoon, sipping coffee from a thermos and working on crossword puzzles while Eliot played on his own. Abby received her degree and moved off to another university, while Mrs. Linden was, in the end, fired when Eliot's mother discovered that Mrs. Linden's thermos contained more whiskey than coffee. Mrs. Sen came to them in tidy ballpoint script, posted on an index card outside the supermarket: "Professor's wife, responsible and kind, I will care for your child in my home." On the telephone Eliot's mother told Mrs. Sen that the previous baby-sitters had come to their house. "Eliot is eleven. He can feed and entertain himself; I just want an adult in the house, in case of an emergency." But Mrs. Sen did not know how to drive.

* * *

'As you can see, our home is quite clean, quite safe for a child," Mrs. Sen had said at their first meeting. It was a university apartment located on the fringes of the campus. The lobby was tiled in unattractive squares of tan, with a row of mailboxes marked with masking tape or white labels. Inside, intersecting shadows left by a vacuum cleaner were frozen on the surface of a plush pear-colored carpet. Mismatched remnants of other carpets were positioned in front of the sofa and chairs, like individual welcome mats anticipating where a person's feet would contact the floor. White drum-shaped lampshades flanking the sofa were still wrapped in the manufacturer's plastic. The TV and the telephone were covered by pieces of yellow fabric with scalloped edges. There was tea in a tall gray pot, along with mugs, and butter biscuits on a tray. Mr. Sen, a short, stocky man with slightly protuberant eyes and glasses with black rectangular frames, had been there, too. He crossed his legs with some effort, and held his mug with both hands very close to his mouth, even when he wasn't drinking. Neither Mr. nor Mrs. Sen wore shoes; Eliot noticed several pairs lined on the shelves of a small bookcase by the front door. They wore flip-flops. "Mr. Sen teaches mathematics at the university," Mrs. Sen had said by way of introduction, as if they were only distantly acquainted.

She was about thirty. She had a small gap between her teeth and faded pockmarks on her chin, yet her eyes were beautiful, with thick, flaring brows and liquid flourishes that extended beyond the natural width of the lids. She wore a shimmering white sari patterned with orange paisleys, more suitable for an evening affair than for that quiet, faintly drizzling August afternoon. Her lips were coated in a complementary coral gloss, and a bit of the color had strayed beyond the borders.

Yet it was his mother, Eliot had thought, in her cuffed, beige shorts and her rope-soled shoes, who looked odd. Her cropped hair, a shade similar to her shorts, seemed too lank and sensible, and in that room where all things were so carefully covered, her shaved knees and thighs too exposed. She refused a biscuit each time Mrs. Sen extended the plate in her direction, and asked a long series of questions, the answers to which she recorded on a steno pad. Would there be other children in the apartment? Had Mrs. Sen cared for children before? How long had she lived in this country? Most of all she was concerned that Mrs. Sen did not know how to drive. Eliot's mother worked in an office fifty miles north, and his father, the last she had heard, lived two thousand miles west.

"I have been giving her lessons, actually," Mr. Sen said, setting his mug on the coffee table. It was the first time he had spoken. "By my estimate Mrs. Sen should have her driver's license by December."

"Is that so?" Eliot's mother noted the information on her pad.

"Yes, I am learning," Mrs. Sen said. "But I am a slow student. At home, you know, we have a driver."

"You mean a chauffeur?"

Mrs. Sen glanced at Mr. Sen, who nodded.

Eliot's mother nodded, too, looking around the room. 'And that's all . . . in India?"

"Yes," Mrs. Sen replied. The mention of the word seemed to release something in her. She neatened the border of her sari where it rose diagonally across her chest. She, too, looked around the room, as if she noticed in the lampshades, in the teapot, in the shadows frozen on the carpet, something the rest of them could not. "Everything is there."

Eliot didn't mind going to Mrs. Sen's after school. By September the tiny beach house where he and his mother lived year-round was already cold; Eliot and his mother had to bring a portable heater along whenever they moved from one room to another, and to seal the windows with plastic sheets and a hair drier. The beach was barren and dull to play on alone; the only neighbors who stayed on past Labor Day, a young married couple, had no children, and Eliot no longer found it interesting to gather broken mussel shells in his bucket, or to stroke the seaweed, strewn like strips of emerald lasagna on the sand. Mrs. Sen's apartment was warm, sometimes too warm; the radiators continuously hissed like a pressure cooker. Eliot learned to remove his sneakers first thing in Mrs. Sen's doorway, and to place them on the bookcase next to a row of Mrs. Sen's slippers, each a different color, with soles as flat as cardboard and a ring of leather to hold her big toe.

He especially enjoyed watching Mrs. Sen as she chopped things, seated on newspapers on the living room floor. Instead of a knife she used a blade that curved like the prow of a Viking ship, sailing to battle in distant seas. The blade was hinged at one end to a narrow wooden base. The steel, more black than silver, lacked a uniform polish, and had a serrated crest, she told Eliot, for grating. Each afternoon Mrs. Sen lifted the blade and locked it into place, so that it met the base at an angle. Facing the sharp edge without ever touching it, she took whole vegetables between her hands and hacked them apart: cauliflower, cabbage, butternut squash. She split things in half, then quarters, speedily producing florets, cubes, slices, and shreds. She could peel a potato in seconds. At times she sat cross-legged, at times with legs splayed, surrounded by an array of colanders and shallow bowls of water in which she immersed her chopped ingredients.

While she worked she kept an eye on the television and an eye on Eliot, but she never seemed to keep an eye on the blade. Nevertheless she refused to let Eliot walk around when she was chopping. "Just sit, sit please, it will take just two more minutes," she said, pointing to the sofa, which was draped at all times with a green and black bedcover printed with rows of elephants bearing palanquins on their backs. The daily procedure took about an hour. In order to occupy Eliot she supplied him with the comics section of the newspaper, and crackers spread with peanut butter, and sometimes a Popsicle, or carrot sticks sculpted with her blade. She would have roped off the area if she could. Once, though, she broke her own rule; in need of additional supplies, and reluctant to rise from the catastrophic mess that barricaded her, she asked Eliot to fetch something from the kitchen. "If you don't mind, there is a plastic bowl, large enough to hold this spinach, in the cabinet next to the fridge. Careful, oh dear, be careful," she cautioned as he approached. "Just leave it, thank you, on the coffee table, I can reach."

She had brought the blade from India, where apparently there was at least one in every household. "Whenever there is a wedding in the family," she told Eliot one day, "or a large celebration of any kind, my mother sends out word in the evening for all the neighborhood women to bring blades just like this one, and then they sit in an enormous circle on the roof of our building, laughing and gossiping and slicing fifty kilos of vegetables through the night." Her profile hovered protectively over her work, a confetti of cucumber, eggplant, and onion skins heaped around her. "It is impossible to fall asleep those nights, listening to their chatter." She paused to look at a pine tree framed by the living room window. "Here, in this place where Mr. Sen has brought me, I cannot sometimes sleep in so much silence."

Another day she sat prying the pimpled yellow fat off chicken parts, then dividing them between thigh and leg. As the bones cracked apart over the blade her golden bangles jostled, her forearms glowed, and she exhaled audibly through her nose. At one point she paused, gripping the chicken with both hands, and stared out the window. Fat and sinew clung to her fingers.

"Eliot, if I began to scream right now at the top of my lungs, would someone come?"

"Mrs. Sen, what's wrong?"

"Nothing. I am only asking if someone would come."

Eliot shrugged. "Maybe."

'At home that is all you have to do. Not everybody has a telephone. But just raise your voice a bit, or express grief or joy of any kind, and one whole neighborhood and half of another has come to share the news, to help with arrangements."

By then Eliot understood that when Mrs. Sen said home, she meant India, not the apartment where she sat chopping vegetables. He thought of his own home, just five miles away, and the young married couple who waved from time to time as they jogged at sunset along the shore. On Labor Day they'd had a party. People were piled on the deck, eating, drinking, the sound of their laughter rising above the weary sigh of the waves. Eliot and his mother weren't invited. It was one of the rare days his mother had off, but they didn't go anywhere. She did the laundry, and balanced the checkbook, and, with Eliot's help, vacuumed the inside of the car. Eliot had suggested that they go through the car wash a few miles down the road as they did every now and then, so that they could sit inside, safe and dry, as soap and water and a circle of giant canvas ribbons slapped the windshield, but his mother said she was too tired, and sprayed the car with a hose. When, by evening, the crowd on the neighbors' deck began dancing, she looked up their number in the phone book and asked them to keep it down.

"They might call you," Eliot said eventually to Mrs. Sen. "But they might complain that you were making too much noise."

From where Eliot sat on the sofa he could detect her curious scent of mothballs and cumin, and he could see the perfectly centered part in her braided hair, which was shaded with crushed vermilion and therefore appeared to be blushing. At first Eliot had wondered if she had cut her scalp, or if something had bitten her there. But then one day he saw her standing before the bathroom mirror, solemnly applying, with the head of a thumbtack, a fresh stroke of scarlet powder, which she stored in a small jam jar. A few grains of the powder fell onto the bridge of her nose as she used the thumbtack to stamp a dot above her eyebrows. "I must wear the powder every day," she explained when Eliot asked her what it was for, "for the rest of the days that I am married."

"Like a wedding ring, you mean?"

"Exactly, Eliot, exactly like a wedding ring. Only with no fear of losing it in the dishwater."

By the time Eliot's mother arrived at twenty past six, Mrs. Sen always made sure all evidence of her chopping was disposed of. The blade was scrubbed, rinsed, dried, folded, and stowed away in a cupboard with the aid of a stepladder. With Eliot's help the newspapers were crushed with all the peels and seeds and skins inside them. Brimming bowls and colanders lined the countertop, spices and pastes were measured and blended, and eventually a collection of broths simmered over periwinkle flames on the stove. It was never a special occasion, nor was she ever expecting company. It was merely dinner for herself and Mr. Sen, as indicated by the two plates and two glasses she set, without napkins or silverware, on the square Formica table at one end of the living room.

As he pressed the newspapers deeper into the garbage pail, Eliot felt that he and Mrs. Sen were disobeying some unspoken rule. Perhaps it was because of the urgency with which Mrs. Sen accomplished everything, pinching salt and sugar between her fingernails, running water through lentils, sponging all imaginable surfaces, shutting cupboard doors with a series of successive clicks. It gave him a little shock to see his mother all of a sudden, in the transparent stockings and shoulder-padded suits she wore to her job, peering into the corners of Mrs. Sen's apartment. She tended to hover on the far side of the door frame, calling to Eliot to put on his sneakers and gather his things, but Mrs. Sen would not allow it. Each evening she insisted that his mother sit on the sofa, where she was served something to eat: a glass of bright pink yogurt with rose syrup, breaded mincemeat with raisins, a bowl of semolina halvah.

"Really, Mrs. Sen. I take a late lunch. You shouldn't go to so much trouble."

"It is no trouble. Just like Eliot. No trouble at all."

His mother nibbled Mrs. Sen's concoctions with eyes cast upward, in search of an opinion. She kept her knees pressed together, the high heels she never removed pressed into the pear-colored carpet. "It's delicious," she would conclude, setting down the plate after a bite or two. Eliot knew she didn't like the tastes; she'd told him so once in the car. He also knew she didn't eat lunch at work, because the first thing she did when they were back at the beach house was pour herself a glass of wine and eat bread and cheese, sometimes so much of it that she wasn't hungry for the pizza they normally ordered for dinner. She sat at the table as he ate, drinking more wine and asking how his day was, but eventually she went to the deck to smoke a cigarette, leaving Eliot to wrap up the leftovers.

* * *

Each afternoon Mrs. Sen stood in a grove of pine trees by the main road where the school bus dropped off Eliot along with two or three other children who lived nearby. Eliot always sensed that Mrs. Sen had been waiting for some time, as if eager to greet a person she hadn't seen in years. The hair at her temples blew about in the breeze, the column of vermilion fresh in her part. She wore navy blue sunglasses a little too big for her face. Her sari, a different pattern each day, fluttered below the hem of a checkered all-weather coat. Acorns and caterpillars dotted the asphalt loop that framed the complex of about a dozen brick buildings, all identical, embedded in a communal expanse of log chips. As they walked back from the bus stop she produced a sandwich bag from her pocket, and offered Eliot the peeled wedges of an orange, or lightly salted peanuts, which she had already shelled.

They proceeded directly to the car, and for twenty minutes Mrs. Sen practiced driving. It was a toffee-colored sedan with vinyl seats. There was an AM radio with chrome buttons, and on the ledge over the back seat, a box of Kleenex and an ice scraper. Mrs. Sen told Eliot she didn't feel right leaving him alone in the apartment, but Eliot knew she wanted him sitting beside her because she was afraid. She dreaded the roar of the ignition, and placed her hands over her ears to block out the sound as she pressed her slippered feet to the gas, revving the engine.

"Mr. Sen says that once I receive my license, everything will improve. What do you think, Eliot? Will things improve?"

"You could go places," Eliot suggested. "You could go anywhere."

"Could I drive all the way to Calcutta? How long would that take, Eliot? Ten thousand miles, at fifty miles per hour?"

Eliot could not do the math in his head. He watched Mrs. Sen adjust the driver's seat, the rearview mirror, the sunglasses on top of her head. She tuned the radio to a station that played symphonies. "Is it Beethoven?" she asked once, pronouncing the first part of the composer's name not "bay," but "bee," like the insect. She rolled down the window on her side, and asked Eliot to do the same. Eventually she pressed her foot to the brake pedal, manipulated the automatic gear shift as if it were an enormous, leaky pen, and backed inch by inch out of the parking space. She circled the apartment complex once, then once again.

"How am I doing, Eliot? Am I going to pass?"

She was continuously distracted. She stopped the car without warning to listen to something on the radio, or to stare at something, anything, in the road. If she passed a person, she waved. If she saw a bird twenty feet in front of her, she beeped the horn with her index finger and waited for it to fly away. In India, she said, the driver sat on the right side, not the left. Slowly they crept past the swing set, the laundry building, the dark green trash bins, the rows of parked cars. Each time they approached the grove of pine trees where the asphalt loop met the main road, she leaned forward, pinning all her weight against the brake as cars hurtled past. It was a narrow road painted with a solid yellow stripe, with one lane of traffic in either direction.

"Impossible, Eliot. How can I go there?"

"You need to wait until no one's coming."

"Why will not anybody slow down?"

"No one's coming now."

"But what about the car from the right, do you see? And look, a truck is behind it. Anyway, I am not allowed on the main road without Mr. Sen."

"You have to turn and speed up fast," Eliot said. That was the way his mother did it, as if without thinking. It seemed so simple when he sat beside his mother, gliding in the evenings back to the beach house. Then the road was just a road, the other cars merely part of the scenery. But when he sat with Mrs. Sen, under an autumn sun that glowed without warmth through the trees, he saw how that same stream of cars made her knuckles pale, her wrists tremble, and her English falter.

"Everyone, this people, too much in their world."

Two things, Eliot learned, made Mrs. Sen happy. One was the arrival of a letter from her family. It was her custom to check the mailbox after driving practice. She would unlock the box, but she would ask Eliot to reach inside, telling him what to look for, and then she would shut her eyes and shield them with her hands while he shuffled through the bills and magazines that came in Mr. Sen's name. At first Eliot found Mrs. Sen's anxiety incomprehensible; his mother had a p.o. box in town, and she collected mail so infrequently that once their electricity was cut off for three days. Weeks passed at Mrs. Sen's before he found a blue aerogram, grainy to the touch, crammed with stamps showing a bald man at a spinning wheel, and blackened by postmarks.

"Is this it, Mrs. Sen?"

For the first time she embraced him, clasping his face to her sari, surrounding him with her odor of mothballs and cumin. She seized the letter from his hands.

As soon as they were inside the apartment she kicked off her slippers this way and that, drew a wire pin from her hair, and slit the top and sides of the aerogram in three strokes. Her eyes darted back and forth as she read. As soon as she was finished, she cast aside the embroidery that covered the telephone, dialed, and asked, "Yes, is Mr. Sen there, please? It is Mrs. Sen and it is very important."

Subsequently she spoke in her own language, rapid and riotous to Eliot's ears; it was dear that she was reading the contents of the letter, word by word. As she read her voice was louder and seemed to shift in key. Though she stood plainly before him, Eliot had the sensation that Mrs. Sen was no longer present in the room with the pear-colored carpet.

Afterward the apartment was suddenly too small to contain her. They crossed the main road and walked a short distance to the university quadrangle, where bells in a stone tower chimed on the hour. They wandered through the student union, and dragged a tray together along the cafeteria ledge, and ate french fries heaped in a cardboard boat among students chatting at circular tables. Eliot drank soda from a paper cup, Mrs. Sen steeped a tea bag with sugar and cream. After eating they explored the art building, looking at sculptures and silk screens in cool corridors thick with the fragrance of wet paint and clay. They walked past the mathematics building, where Mr. Sen taught his classes.

They ended up in the noisy, chlorine-scented wing of the athletic building where, through a wide window on the fourth floor, they watched swimmers crossing from end to end in glaring turquoise pools. Mrs. Sen took the aerogram from India out of her purse and studied the front and back. She unfolded it and reread to herself, sighing every now and then. When she had finished she gazed for some time at the swimmers.

"My sister has had a baby girl. By the time I see her, depending if Mr. Sen gets his tenure, she will be three years old. Her own aunt will be a stranger. If we sit side by side on a train she will not know my face." She put away the letter, then placed a hand on Eliot's head. "Do you miss your mother, Eliot, these afternoons with me?"

The thought had never occurred to him.

"You must miss her. When I think of you, only a boy, separated from your mother for so much of the day, I am ashamed."

"I see her at night."

"When I was your age I was without knowing that one day I would be so far. You are wiser than that, Eliot. You already taste the way things must be."

The other thing that made Mrs. Sen happy was fish from the seaside. It was always a whole fish she desired, not shellfish, or the fillets Eliot's mother had broiled one night a few months ago when she'd invited a man from her office to dinner — a man who'd spent the night in his mother's bedroom, but whom Eliot never saw again. One evening when Eliot's mother came to pick him up, Mrs. Sen served her a tuna croquette, explaining that it was really supposed to be made with a fish called bhetki. "It is very frustrating," Mrs. Sen apologized, with an emphasis on the second syllable of the word. "To live so close to the ocean and not to have so much fish." In the summer, she said, she liked to go to a market by the beach. She added that while the fish there tasted nothing like the fish in India, at least it was fresh. Now that it was getting colder, the boats were no longer going out regularly, and sometimes there was no whole fish available for weeks at a time.

"Try the supermarket," his mother suggested.

Mrs. Sen shook her head. "In the supermarket I can feed a cat thirty-two dinners from one of thirty-two tins, but I can never find a single fish I like, never a single." Mrs. Sen said she had grown up eating fish twice a day. She added that in Calcutta people ate fish first thing in the morning, last thing before bed, as a snack after school if they were lucky. They ate the tail, the eggs, even the head. It was available in any market, at any hour, from dawn until midnight. "All you have to do is leave the house and walk a bit, and there you are."

Every few days Mrs. Sen would open up the yellow pages, dial a number that she had ticked in the margin, and ask if there was any whole fish available. If so, she would ask the market to hold it. "Under Sen, yes, S as in Sam, N as in New York. Mr. Sen will be there to pick it up." Then she would call Mr. Sen at the university. A few minutes later Mr. Sen would arrive, patting Eliot on the head but not kissing Mrs. Sen. He read his mail at the Formica table and drank a cup of tea before heading out; half an hour later he would return, carrying a paper bag with a smiling lobster drawn on the front of it, and hand it to Mrs. Sen, and head back to the university to teach his evening class. One day, when he handed Mrs. Sen the paper bag, he said, "No more fish for a while. Cook the chicken in the freezer. I need to start holding office hours."

For the next few days, instead of calling the fish market, Mrs. Sen thawed chicken legs in the kitchen sink and chopped them with her blade. One day she made a stew with green beans and tinned sardines. But the following week the man who ran the fish market called Mrs. Sen; he assumed she wanted the fish, and said he would hold it until the end of the day under her name. She was flattered. "Isn't that nice of him, Eliot? The man said he looked up my name in the telephone book. He said there is only one Sen. Do you know how many Sens are in the Calcutta telephone book?"

She told Eliot to put on his shoes and his jacket, and then she called Mr. Sen at the university. Eliot tied his sneakers by the bookcase and waited for her to join him, to choose from her row of slippers. After a few minutes he called out her name. When Mrs. Sen did not reply, he untied his sneakers and returned to the living room, where he found her on the sofa, weeping. Her face was in her hands and tears dripped through her fingers. Through them she murmured something about a meeting Mr. Sen was required to attend. Slowly she stood up and rearranged the cloth over the telephone. Eliot followed her, walking for the first time in his sneakers across the pear-colored carpet. She stared at him. Her lower eyelids were swollen into thin pink crests. "Tell me, Eliot. Is it too much to ask?"

Before he could answer, she took him by the hand and led him to the bedroom, whose door was normally kept shut. Apart from the bed, which lacked a headboard, the only other things in the room were a side table with a telephone on it, an ironing board, and a bureau. She flung open the drawers of the bureau and the door of the closet, filled with saris of every imaginable texture and shade, brocaded with gold and silver threads. Some were transparent, tissue thin, others as thick as drapes, with tassels knotted along the edges. In the closet they were on hangers; in the drawers they were folded flat, or wound tightly like thick scrolls. She sifted through the drawers, letting saris spill over the edges. "When have I ever worn this one? And this? And this?" She tossed the saris one by one from the drawers, then pried several from their hangers. They landed like a pile of tangled sheets on the bed. The room was filled with an intense smell of mothballs.

"'Send pictures,' they write. 'Send pictures of your new life.' What picture can I send?" She sat, exhausted, on the edge of the bed, where there was now barely room for her. "They think I live the life of a queen, Eliot." She looked around the blank walls of the room. "They think I press buttons and the house is clean. They think I live in a palace."

The phone rang. Mrs. Sen let it ring several times before picking up the extension by the bed. During the conversation she seemed only to be replying to things, and wiping her face with the ends of one of the saris. When she got off the phone she stuffed the saris without folding them back into the drawers, and then she and Eliot put on their shoes and went to the car, where they waited for Mr. Sen to meet them.

"Why don't you drive today?" Mr. Sen asked when he appeared, rapping on the hood of the car with his knuckles. They always spoke to each other in English when Eliot was present.

"Not today. Another day."

"How do you expect to pass the test if you refuse to drive on a road with other cars?"

"Eliot is here today."

"He is here every day. It's for your own good. Eliot, tell Mrs. Sen it's for her own good."

She refused.

They drove in silence, along the same roads that Eliot and his mother took back to the beach house each evening. But in the back seat of Mr. and Mrs. Sen's car the ride seemed unfamiliar, and took longer than usual. The gulls whose tedious cries woke him each morning now thrilled him as they dipped and flapped across the sky. They passed one beach after another, and the shacks, now locked up, that sold frozen lemonade and quahogs in summer. Only one of the shacks was open. It was the fish market.

Mrs. Sen unlocked her door and turned toward Mr. Sen, who had not yet unfastened his seat belt. 'Are you coming?"

Mr. Sen handed her some bills from his wallet. "I have a meeting in twenty minutes," he said, staring at the dashboard as he spoke. "Please don't waste time."

Eliot accompanied her into the dank little shop, whose walls were festooned with nets and starfish and buoys. A group of tourists with cameras around their necks huddled by the counter, some sampling stuffed clams, others pointing to a large chart illustrating fifty different varieties of North Atlantic fish. Mrs. Sen took a ticket from the machine at the counter and waited in line. Eliot stood by the lobsters, which stirred one on top of another in their murky tank, their claws bound by yellow rubber bands. He watched as Mrs. Sen laughed and chatted, when it was her turn in line, with a man with a bright red face and yellow teeth, dressed in a black rubber apron. In either hand he held a mackerel by the tail.

"You are sure what you sell me is very fresh?"

'Any fresher and they'd answer that question themselves."

The dial shivered toward its verdict on the scale.

"You want this cleaned, Mrs. Sen?"

She nodded. "Leave the heads on, please."

"You got cats at home?"

"No cats. Only a husband."

Later, in the apartment, she pulled the blade out of the cupboard, spread newspapers across the carpet, and inspected her treasures. One by one she drew them from the paper wrapping, wrinkled and tinged with blood. She stroked the tails, prodded the bellies, pried apart the gutted flesh. With a pair of scissors she clipped the fins. She tucked a finger under the gills, a red so bright they made her vermilion seem pale. She grasped the body, lined with inky streaks, at either end, and notched it at intervals against the blade.

"Why do you do that?" Eliot asked.

"To see how many pieces. If I cut properly, from this fish I will get three meals." She sawed off the head and set it on a pie plate.

In November came a series of days when Mrs. Sen refused to practice driving. The blade never emerged from the cupboard, newspapers were not spread on the floor. She did not call the fish store, nor did she thaw chicken. In silence she prepared crackers with peanut butter for Eliot, then sat reading old aerograms from a shoebox. When it was time for Eliot to leave she gathered together his things without inviting his mother to sit on the sofa and eat something first. When, eventually, his mother asked him in the car if he'd noticed a change in Mrs. Sen's behavior, he said he hadn't. He didn't tell her that Mrs. Sen paced the apartment, staring at the plastic-covered lampshades as if noticing them for the first time. He didn't tell her she switched on the television but never watched it, or that she made herself tea but let it grow cold on the coffee table. One day she played a tape of something she called a raga; it sounded a little bit like someone plucking very slowly and then very quickly on a violin, and Mrs. Sen said it was supposed to be heard only in the late afternoon, as the sun was setting. As the music played, for nearly an hour, she sat on the sofa with her eyes closed. Afterward she said, "It is more sad even than your Beethoven, isn't it?" Another day she played a cassette of people talking in her language — a farewell present, she told Eliot, that her family had made for her. As the succession of voices laughed and said their bit, Mrs. Sen identified each speaker. "My third uncle, my cousin, my father, my grandfather." One speaker sang a song. Another recited a poem. The final voice on the tape belonged to Mrs. Sen's mother. It was quieter and sounded more serious than the others. There was a pause between each sentence, and during this pause Mrs. Sen translated for Eliot: "The price of goat rose two rupees. The mangoes at the market are not very sweet. College Street is flooded." She turned off the tape. "These are things that happened the day I left India." The next day she played the same cassette all over again. This time, when her grandfather was speaking, she stopped the tape. She told Eliot she'd received a letter over the weekend. Her grandfather was dead.

A week later Mrs. Sen began cooking again. One day as she sat slicing cabbage on the living room floor, Mr. Sen called. He wanted to take Eliot and Mrs. Sen to the seaside. For the occasion Mrs. Sen put on a red sari and red lipstick; she freshened the vermilion in her part and rebraided her hair. She knotted a scarf under her chin, arranged her sunglasses on top of her head, and put a pocket camera in her purse. As Mr. Sen backed out of the parking lot, he put his arm across the top of the front seat, so that it looked as if he had his arm around Mrs. Sen. "It's getting too cold for that top coat," he said to her at one point. "We should get you something warmer." At the shop they bought mackerel, and butterfish, and sea bass. This time Mr. Sen came into the shop with them. It was Mr. Sen who asked whether the fish was fresh and to cut it this way or that way. They bought so much fish that Eliot had to hold one of the bags. After they put the bags in the trunk, Mr. Sen announced that he was hungry, and Mrs. Sen agreed, so they crossed the street to a restaurant where the take-out window was still open. They sat at a picnic table and ate two baskets of clam cakes. Mrs. Sen put a good deal of Tabasco sauce and black pepper on hers. "Like pakoras, no?" Her face was flushed, her lipstick faded, and she laughed at everything Mr. Sen said.

Behind the restaurant was a small beach, and when they were done eating they walked for a while along the shore, into a wind so strong that they had to walk backward. Mrs. Sen pointed to the water, and said that at a certain moment, each wave resembled a sari drying on a clothesline. "Impossible!" she shouted eventually, laughing as she turned back, her eyes teary. "I cannot move." Instead she took a picture of Eliot and Mr. Sen standing on the sand. "Now one of us," she said, pressing Eliot against her checkered coat and giving the camera to Mr. Sen. Finally the camera was given to Eliot. "Hold it steady," said Mr. Sen. Eliot looked through the tiny window in the camera and waited for Mr. and Mrs. Sen to move closer together, but they didn't. They didn't hold hands or put their arms around each other's waists. Both smiled with their mouths closed, squinting into the wind, Mrs. Sen's red sari leaping like flames under her coat.

In the car, warm at last and exhausted from the wind and the clam cakes, they admired the dunes, the ships they could see in the distance, the view of the lighthouse, the peach and purple sky. After a while Mr. Sen slowed down and stopped by the side of the road.

"What's wrong?" Mrs. Sen asked.

"You are going to drive home today."

"Not today."

"Yes, today." Mr. Sen stepped out of the car and opened the door on Mrs. Sen's side. A fierce wind blew into the car, accompanied by the sound of waves crashing on the shore. Finally she slid over to the driver's side, but spent a long time adjusting her sari and her sunglasses. Eliot turned and looked through the back window. The road was empty. Mrs. Sen turned on the radio, filling up the car with violin music.

"There's no need," Mr. Sen said, clicking it off.

"It helps me to concentrate," Mrs. Sen said, and turned the radio on again.

"Put on your signal," Mr. Sen directed.

"I know what to do."

For about a mile she was fine, though far slower than the other cars that passed her. But when the town approached, and traffic fights loomed on wires in the distance, she went even slower.

"Switch lanes," Mr. Sen said. "You will have to bear left at the rotary."

Mrs. Sen did not.

"Switch lanes, I tell you." He shut off the radio. 'Are you listening to me?"

A car beeped its horn, then another. She beeped defiantly in response, stopped, then pulled without signaling to the side of the road. "No more," she said, her forehead resting against the top of the steering wheel. "I hate it. I hate driving. I won't go on."

She stopped driving after that. The next time the fish store called she did not call Mr. Sen at his office. She had decided to try something new. There was a town bus that ran on an hourly schedule between the university and the seaside. After the university it made two stops, first at a nursing home, then at a shopping plaza without a name, which consisted of a bookstore, a shoe store, a drugstore, a pet store, and a record store. On benches under the portico, elderly women from the nursing home sat in pairs, in knee-length overcoats with oversized buttons, eating lozenges.

"Eliot," Mrs. Sen asked him while they were sitting on the bus, "will you put your mother in a nursing home when she is old?"

"Maybe," he said. "But I would visit every day."

"You say that now, but you will see, when you are a man your life will be in places you cannot know now." She counted on her fingers: "You will have a wife, and children of your own, and they will want to be driven to different places at the same time. No matter how kind they are, one day they will complain about visiting your mother, and you will get tired of it too, Eliot. You will miss one day, and another, and then she will have to drag herself onto a bus just to get herself a bag of lozenges."

At the fish shop the ice beds were nearly empty, as were the lobster tanks, where rust-colored stains were visible through the water. A sign said the shop would be closing for winter at the end of the month. There was only one person working behind the counter, a young boy who did not recognize Mrs. Sen as he handed her a bag reserved under her name.

"Has it been cleaned and scaled?" Mrs. Sen asked.

The boy shrugged. "My boss left early. He just said to give you this bag."

In the parking lot Mrs. Sen consulted the bus schedule. They would have to wait forty-five minutes for the next one, and so they crossed the street and bought clam cakes at the take-out window they had been to before. There was no place to sit. The picnic tables were no longer in use, their benches chained upside down on top of them.

On the way home an old woman on the bus kept watching them, her eyes shifting from Mrs. Sen to Eliot to the blood-lined bag between their feet. She wore a black overcoat, and in her lap she held, with gnarled, colorless hands, a crisp white bag from the drugstore. The only other passengers were two college students, boyfriend and girlfriend, wearing matching sweatshirts, their fingers linked, slouched in the back seat. In silence Eliot and Mrs. Sen ate the last few clam cakes in the bag. Mrs. Sen had forgotten napkins, and traces of fried batter dotted the corners of her mouth. When they reached the nursing home the woman in the overcoat stood up, said something to the driver, then stepped off the bus. The driver turned his head and glanced back at Mrs. Sen. "What's in the bag?"

Mrs. Sen looked up, startled.

"Speak English?" The bus began to move again, causing the driver to look at Mrs. Sen and Eliot in his enormous rearview mirror.

"Yes, I can speak."

"Then what's in the bag?"

"A fish," Mrs. Sen replied.

"The smell seems to be bothering the other passengers. Kid, maybe you should open her window or something."

One afternoon a few days later the phone rang. Some very tasty halibut had arrived on the boats. Would Mrs. Sen like to pick one up? She called Mr. Sen, but he was not at his desk. A second time she tried calling, then a third. Eventually she went to the kitchen and returned to the living room with the blade, an eggplant, and some newspapers. Without having to be told Eliot took his place on the sofa and watched as she sliced the stems off the eggplant. She divided it into long, slender strips, then into small squares, smaller and smaller, as small as sugar cubes.

"I am going to put these in a very tasty stew with fish and green bananas," she announced. "Only I will have to do without the green bananas."

'Are we going to get the fish?"

"We are going to get the fish."

"Is Mr. Sen going to take us?"

"Put on your shoes."

They left the apartment without cleaning up. Outside it was so cold that Eliot could feel the chill on his teeth. They got in the car, and Mrs. Sen drove around the asphalt loop several times. Each time she paused by the grove of pine trees to observe the traffic on the main road. Eliot thought she was just practicing while they waited for Mr. Sen. But then she gave a signal and turned.

The accident occurred quickly. After about a mile Mrs. Sen took a left before she should have, and though the oncoming car managed to swerve out of her way, she was so startled by the horn that she lost control of the wheel and hit a telephone pole on the opposite corner. A policeman arrived and asked to see her license, but she did not have one to show him. "Mr. Sen teaches mathematics at the university" was all she said by way of explanation.

The damage was slight. Mrs. Sen cut her lip, Eliot complained briefly of a pain in his ribs, and the car's fender would have to be straightened. The policeman thought Mrs. Sen had also cut her scalp, but it was only the vermilion. When Mr. Sen arrived, driven by one of his colleagues, he spoke at length with the policeman as he filled out some forms, but he said nothing to Mrs. Sen as he drove them back to the apartment. When they got out of the car, Mr. Sen patted Eliot's head. "The policeman said you were lucky. Very lucky to come out without a scratch."

After taking off her slippers and putting them on the bookcase, Mrs. Sen put away the blade that was still on the living room floor and threw the eggplant pieces and the newspapers into the garbage pail. She prepared a plate of crackers with peanut butter, placed them on the coffee table, and turned on the television for Eliot's benefit. "If he is still hungry give him a Popsicle from the box in the freezer," she said to Mr. Sen, who sat at the Formica table sorting through the mail. Then she went into her bedroom and shut the door. When Eliot's mother arrived at quarter to six, Mr. Sen told her the details of the accident and offered a check reimbursing November's payment. As he wrote out the check he apologized on behalf of Mrs. Sen. He said she was resting, though when Eliot had gone to the bathroom he'd heard her crying. His mother was satisfied with the arrangement, and in a sense, she confessed to Eliot as they drove home, she was relieved. It was the last afternoon Eliot spent with Mrs. Sen, or with any baby-sitter. From then on his mother gave him a key, which he wore on a string around his neck. He was to call the neighbors in case of an emergency, and to let himself into the beach house after school. The first day, just as he was taking off his coat, the phone rang. It was his mother calling from her office. "You're a big boy now, Eliot," she told him. 'You okay?" Eliot looked out the kitchen window, at gray waves receding from the shore, and said that he was fine.

Notes

p. 385   *steno pad* - stenography pad: shorthand notebook
p. 385   *Labor day* - September public holiday in the USA
p. 386   *Popsicle* - ice lolly

p. 387   *periwinkle* - i.e. blue-coloured
p. 390   *aerogram* - lightweight paper and envelope combined for international post
p. 390   *tenure* - permanent university post
p. 392   *quahogs* - type of clam
p. 393   *raga* - piece of classical Indian music
p. 394   *pakora* - fried snack
p. 396   *eggplant* - aubergine

43

A Thousand Years of Good Prayers

(2006)
Yiyun Li

Li Yiyun, who publishes as Yiyun Li, grew up in Beijing and moved to the USA where she is now an academic in California; she has published two award-winning collections of short stories. This story focuses on a father/ daughter relationship and the different ways in which the generations adjust to a new culture.

A rocket scientist, Mr. Shi tells people when they ask about his profession in China. Retired, he then adds, out of modesty, when people marvel. Mr. Shi learned the phrase from a woman during a layover at Detroit, when he tried to explain to her his work, drawing pictures when his English failed to help. "A rocket scientist!" the woman exclaimed, laughing out loud.

People he meets in America, already friendly, seem more so when they learn his profession, so he likes to repeat the words whenever possible. Five days into his visit at his daughter's place, in this Midwest town, Mr. Shi has made quite a few acquaintances. Mothers with babies in strollers wave at him. An old couple, the husband in suit and the wife in skirt, show up in the park every morning at nine o'clock, her hand on his arm; they stop and greet him, the husband always the one speaking, the wife smiling. A woman living in the retirement home a block away comes to talk to him. She is seventy-seven, two years his senior, and was originally from Iran. Despite the fact they both speak little English, they have no problem understanding each other, and in no time they become friends.

"America good country," she says often. "Sons make rich money."

America is indeed a good country. Mr. Shi's daughter works as a librarian in the East Asian department in the college library and earns more in a year than he made in twenty.

"My daughter, she make lots of money, too."

"I love America. Good country for everybody."

"Yes, yes. A rocket scientist I am in China. But very poor. Rocket scientist, you know?" Mr. Shi says, his hands making a peak.

"I love China. China a good country, very old," the woman says.

"America is young country, like young people."

"America a happy country."

'Young people are more happy than old people," Mr. Shi says, and then realizes that it is too abrupt a conclusion. He himself feels happier at this moment than he remembers he ever did in his life. The woman in front of him, who loves everything with or without a good reason, seems happy, too.

Sometimes they run out of English. She switches to Persian, mixed with a few English words. Mr. Shi finds it hard to speak Chinese to her. It is she who carries the conversation alone then, for ten or twenty minutes. He nods and smiles effusively. He does not understand much of what she is saying, but he feels her joy in talking to him, the same joy he feels listening to her.

Mr. Shi starts to look forward to the mornings when he sits in the park and waits for her. "Madam" is what he uses to address her, as he has never asked her name. Madam wears colors that he does not imagine a woman of her age, or where she came from, would wear, red and orange and purple and yellow. She has a pair of metal barrettes, a white elephant and a blue-and-green peacock. They clasp on her thin hair in a wobbly way that reminds him of his daughter when she was a small child—before her hair was fully grown, with a plastic butterfly hanging loose on her forehead. Mr. Shi, for a brief moment, wants to tell Madam how much he misses the days when his daughter was small and life was hopeful. But he is sure, even before he starts, that his English would fail him. Besides, it is never his habit to talk about the past.

In the evenings, when his daughter comes home, Mr. Shi has the supper ready. He took a cooking class after his wife died, a few years ago, and ever since has studied the culinary art with the same fervor with which he studied mathematics and physics when he was a college student. "Every man is born with more talents than he knows how to use," he says at dinner. "I would've never imagined taking up cooking, but here I am, better than I imagined."

"Yes, very impressive," his daughter says.

"And likewise"—Mr. Shi takes a quick glance at his daughter—"life provides more happiness than we ever know. We have to train ourselves to look for it."

His daughter does not reply. Despite the pride he takes in his cooking and her praises for it, she eats little and eats out of duty. It worries him that she is not putting enough enthusiasm into life as she should be. Of course, she has her reasons, newly divorced after seven years of marriage. His ex-son-in-law went back to Beijing permanently after the divorce. Mr. Shi does not know what led the boat of their marriage to run into a hidden rock, but whatever the reason is, it must not be her fault. She is made for a good wife, soft-voiced and kindhearted, dutiful and beautiful, a younger version of her mother. When his daughter called to inform him of the divorce, Mr. Shi imagined her in inconsolable pain, and asked to come to America, to help her recover. She refused, and he started calling daily and pleading, spending a good solid month of his pension on the long-distance bill. She finally agreed when he announced that his wish for his seventy-fifth birthday was to take a look at America. A lie it was, but the lie turned out to be a good reason. America is worth taking a look at; more than that, America makes him a new person, a rocket scientist, a good conversationalist, a loving father, a happy man.

After dinner, Mr. Shi's daughter either retreats to her bedroom to read or drives away and comes home at late hours. Mr. Shi asks to go out with her, to accompany her to the movies he imagines that she watches alone, but she refuses in a polite but firm manner. It is certainly not healthy for a woman, especially a contemplative woman like his daughter, to spend too much time alone. He starts to talk more to tackle her solitude, asking questions about the part of her life he is not witnessing. How was her work of the day? he asks. Fine, she says tiredly. Not discouraged, he asks about her colleagues, whether there are more females than males, how old they are, and, if they are married, whether they have children. He asks what she eats for lunch and whether she eats alone, what kind of computer she uses, and what books she reads. He asks about her old school friends, people he believes she is out of contact with because of the shame of the divorce. He asks about her plan for the future, hoping she understands the urgency of her situation. Women in their marriageable twenties and early thirties are like lychees that have been picked from the tree; each passing day makes them less fresh and less desirable, and only too soon will they lose their value, and have to be gotten rid of at a sale price.

Mr. Shi knows enough not to mention the sale price. Still, he cannot help but lecture on the fruitfulness of life. The more he talks, the more he is moved by his own patience. His daughter, however, does not improve. She eats less and becomes quieter each day. When he finally points out that she is not enjoying her life as she should, she says, "How do you get this conclusion? I'm enjoying my life all right."

"But that's a lie. A happy person will never be so quiet!"

She looks up from the bowl of rice. "Baba, you used to be very quiet, remember? Were you unhappy then?"

Mr. Shi, not prepared for such directness from his daughter, is unable to reply. He waits for her to apologize and change the topic, as people with good manners do when they realize they are embarrassing others with their questions, but she does not let him go. Her eyes behind her glasses, wide open and unrelenting, remind him of her in her younger years. When she was four or five, she went after him every possible moment, asking questions and demanding answers. The eyes remind him of her mother too; at one time in their marriage, she gazed at him with this questioning look, waiting for an answer he did not have for her.

He sighs. "Of course I've always been happy."

"There you go, Baba. We can be quiet *and* happy, can't we?"

"Why not talk about your happiness with me?" Mr. Shi says. "Tell me more about your work."

"You didn't talk much about your work either, remember? Even when I asked."

"A rocket scientist, you know how it was. My work was confidential."

"You didn't talk much about anything," his daughter says.

Mr. Shi opens his mouth but finds no words coming. After a long moment, he says, "I talk more now. I'm improving, no?"

"Sure," his daughter says.

"That's what you need to do. Talk more," Mr. Shi says. "And start now."

His daughter, however, is less enthusiastic. She finishes her meal quickly in her usual silence and leaves the apartment before he finishes his.

The next morning, Mr. Shi confesses to Madam, "The daughter, she's not happy."

"Daughter a happy thing to have," Madam says.

"She's divorced."

Madam nods, and starts to talk in Persian. Mr. Shi is not sure if Madam knows what divorce means. A woman so boldly in love with the world like her must have been shielded from life's unpleasantness, by her husband, or her sons maybe. Mr. Shi looks at Madam, her face brightened by her talking and laughing, and almost envies her for the energy that his daughter, forty years younger, does not possess. For the day Madam wears a bright orange blouse with prints of purple monkeys, all tumbling and grinning; on her head she wears a scarf with the same pattern. A displaced woman she is, but no doubt happily displaced. Mr. Shi tries to recall what he knows about Iran and the country's recent history; with his limited knowledge, all he can conclude is that Madam must be a lucky woman. A lucky man he is, too, despite all the big and small imperfections. How extraordinary, Mr. Shi thinks, that Madam and he, from different worlds and with different languages, have this opportunity to sit and talk in the autumn sunshine.

"In China we say, *Xiu bai shi ke tong zhou*," Mr. Shi says when Madam stops. It takes three hundred years of prayers to have the chance to cross a river with someone in the same boat, he thinks of explaining to Madam in English, but then, what's the difference between the languages? Madam would understand him, with or without the translation. *"That we get to meet and talk to each other—it must have taken a long time of good prayers to get us here,"* he says in Chinese to Madam.

Madam smiles in agreement.

"There's a reason for every relationship, that's what the saying means. Husband and wife, parents and children, friends and enemies, strangers you bump into in the street. It takes three thousand years of prayers to place your head side by side with your loved one's on the pillow. For father and daughter? A thousand years, maybe. People don't end up randomly as father and daughter, that's for sure. But the daughter, she doesn't understand this. She must be thinking I'm a nuisance. She prefers I shut up because that's how she's known me always. She doesn't understand that I didn't talk much with her mother and her because I was a rocket scientist back then. Everything was confidential. We worked all day and when evening came, the security guards came to collect all our notebooks and scratch papers. We signed our names on the archive folders, and that was a day's work. Never allowed to tell our family what we were doing. We were trained not to talk."

Madam listens, both hands folding on her heart. Mr. Shi hasn't been sitting so close to a woman his age since his wife died; even when she was alive, he had never talked this much to her. His eyes feel heavy. Imagine he's traveled half a world to his daughter, to make up for all the talks he denied her when she was younger, but only to find her uninterested in his words. Imagine Madam, a stranger who does not even know his language, listens to him with more understanding. Mr. Shi massages his eyes with his two thumbs. A man his age shouldn't indulge himself in unhealthy emotions; he takes long breaths, and laughs slightly. "*Of course, there's a reason for a bad relationship, too—I must be praying halfheartedly for a thousand years for the daughter.*"

Madam nods solemnly. She understands him, he knows, but he does not want to burden her with his petty unhappiness. He rubs his hands as if to get rid of the dust of memory. "Old stories," he says in his best English. "Old stories are not exciting."

"I love stories," Madam says, and starts to talk. Mr. Shi listens, and she smiles all the time. He looks at the grinning monkeys on her head, bobbing up and down when she breaks out laughing.

"Lucky people we are," he says after she finishes talking. "In America, we can talk anything."

"America good country." Madam nods. "I love America."

That evening, Mr. Shi says to his daughter, "I met this Iranian lady in the park. Have you met her?"

"No."

"You should meet her sometime. She's so very optimistic. You may find her illuminating for your situation."

"What's my situation?" his daughter asks without looking up from her food.

"You tell me," Mr. Shi says. When his daughter makes no move to help the conversation, he says, "You're experiencing a dark time."

"How do you know she would shed light on my life?"

Mr. Shi opens his mouth, but cannot find an answer. He is afraid that if he explains he and Madam talk in different languages, his daughter will think of him as a crazy old man. Things that make sense at one time suddenly seem absurd in a different light. He feels disappointed in his daughter, someone he shares a language with but with whom he can no longer share a dear moment. After a long pause, he says, "You know, a woman shouldn't ask such direct questions. A good woman is deferential and knows how to make people talk."

"I'm divorced, so certainly I'm not a good woman according to your standard."

Mr. Shi, thinking his daughter is unfairly sarcastic, ignores her. "Your mother was an example of a good woman."

"Did she succeed in making you talk?" his daughter asks, and her eyes, looking directly into his, are fiercer than he knows.

"Your mother wouldn't be so confrontational."

"Baba, first you accused me of being too quiet. I start to talk, and you are saying I'm talking in a wrong way."

"Talking is not only asking questions. Talking is you telling people how you feel about them, and inviting them to tell you how they feel about you."

"Baba, since when did you become a therapist?"

"I'm here to help you, and I'm trying my best," Mr. Shi says. "I need to know why you ended up in a divorce. I need to know what went wrong and help you to find the right person the next time. You're my daughter and I want you to be happy. I don't want you to fall twice."

"Baba, I didn't ask you before, but how long do you plan to stay in America?" his daughter says.

"Until you recover."

His daughter stands up, the legs of the chair scraping the floor.

"We're the only family for each other now," Mr. Shi says, almost pleading, but his daughter closes her bedroom door before he says more. Mr. Shi looks at the dishes that are barely touched by his daughter, the fried tofu cubes stuffed with chopped mushrooms, shrimps, and ginger, the collage of bamboo shoots, red peppers, and snow peas. Even though his daughter admires his cooking every evening, he senses the half-heartedness in her praise; she does not know the cooking has become his praying, and she leaves the prayers unanswered.

"The wife would've done a better job of cheering the daughter up," Mr. Shi says to Madam the next morning. He feels more at ease speaking to her in Chinese now. *"They were closer to each other. Wasn't that I was not close to them. I loved them dearly. It's what happened when you were a rocket scientist. I worked hard during the day, and at night I couldn't stop thinking about my work. Everything was confidential so I couldn't talk to my family about what I was thinking about. But the wife, she was the most understanding woman in the world. She knew I was so occupied with my work, and she wouldn't interrupt my thoughts, and wouldn't let the daughter, either. I know now that it was not healthy for the daughter. I should've left my working self in the office. I was too young to understand that. Now the daughter, she doesn't have anything to say to me."*

Truly it was his mistake, never establishing a habit of talking to his daughter. But then, he argues for himself—in his time, a man like him, among the few chosen to work for a grand cause, he had to bear more duties toward his work than his family. Honorable and sad, but honorable more than sad.

At the dinner table that evening, Mr. Shi's daughter informs him that she's found a Chinese-speaking travel agency that runs tours both on the East Coast and the West. "You're here to take a look at America. I think it's best you take a couple of tours before winter comes."

"Are they expensive?"

"I'll pay, Baba. It's what you wanted for your birthday, no?"

She is his daughter after all; she remembers his wish and she honors it. But what she does not understand is that the America he wants to see is the country where she is happily married. He scoops vegetables and fish into her bowl. "You should eat more," he says in a gentle voice.

"So, I'm going to call them tomorrow and book the tours," his daughter says.

"You know, staying here probably does more good for me. I'm an old man now, not very good for traveling."

"But there's not much to see here."

"Why not? This is the America I wanted to see. Don't worry. I have my friends here. I won't be too much of an annoyance to you."

The phone rings before his daughter replies. She picks up the phone and automatically goes into her bedroom. He waits for the bang of the door. She never takes a call in front of him, even with strangers trying to sell her something on the phone. A few evenings when she talked longer and talked in a hushed voice, he had to struggle not to put his ear on the door and listen. This evening, however, she seems to have a second thought, and leaves the bedroom door open.

He listens to her speak English on the phone, her voice shriller than he has ever known it to be. She speaks fast and laughs often. He does not understand her words, but even more, he does not understand her manner. Her voice, too sharp, too loud, too immodest, is so unpleasant to his ears that for a moment he feels as if he had accidentally caught a glimpse of her naked body, a total stranger, not the daughter he knows.

He stares at her when she comes out of the room. She puts the receiver back, and sits down at the table without saying anything. He watches her face for a moment, and asks, "Who was it on the phone?"

"A friend."

"A male friend, or a female?"

"A male."

He waits for her to give further explanation, but she seems to have no such intention. After a while, he says, "Is this man—is he a special friend?"

"Special? Sure."

"How special is he?"

"Baba, maybe this'll make you worry less about me—yes, he is a very special one. More than a friend," his daughter says. "A lover. Do you feel better now that you know my life isn't as miserable as you thought?"

"Is he American?"

"An American now, yes, but he came from Romania."

At least the man grew up in a communist country, Mr. Shi thinks, trying to be positive. "Do you know him well? Does he understand you—where you were from, and your culture—well? Remember, you can't make the same mistakes twice. You have to be really careful."

"We've known each other for a long time."

"A long time? A month is not a long time!"

"Longer than that, Baba."

"One and half months at most, right? Listen, I know you are in pain, but a woman shouldn't rush, especially in your situation. Abandoned women—they make mistakes in loneliness!"

His daughter looks up. "Baba, my marriage wasn't what you thought. I wasn't abandoned."

Mr. Shi looks at his daughter, her eyes candid with resolve and relief. For a moment he almost wants her to spare him any further detail, but like all people, once she starts talking, he cannot stop her. "Baba, we were divorced because of this man. I was the abandoner, if you want to use the term."

"But why?"

"Things go wrong in a marriage, Baba."

"One night of being husband and wife in bed makes them in love for a hundred days. You were married for seven years! How could you do this to your husband? What was the problem, anyway, besides your little extramarital affair?" Mr. Shi says. A disloyal woman is the last thing he raised his daughter to be.

"There's no point talking about it now."

"I'm your father. I have a right to know," Mr. Shi says, banging on the table with a hand.

"Our problem was I never talked enough for my husband. He always suspected that I was hiding something from him because I was quiet."

'You were hiding a lover from him."

Mr. Shi's daughter ignores his words. "The more he asked me to talk, the more I wanted to be quiet and alone. I'm not good at talking, as you've pointed out."

"But that's a lie. You just talked over the phone with such immodesty! You talked, you laughed, like a prostitute!"

Mr. Shi's daughter, startled by the vehemence of his words, looks at him for a long moment before she replies in a softer voice. "It's different, Baba. We talk in English, and it's easier. I don't talk well in Chinese."

"That's a ridiculous excuse!"

"Baba, if you grew up in a language that you never used to express your feelings, it would be easier to take up another language and talk more in the new language. It makes you a new person."

"Are you blaming your mother and me for your adultery?"

"That's not what I'm saying, Baba!"

"But isn't it what you meant? We didn't do a good job bringing you up in Chinese so you decided to find a new language and a new lover when you couldn't talk to your husband honestly about your marriage."

'You never talked, and Mama never talked, when you both knew there was a problem in your marriage. I learned not to talk."

"Your mother and I never had a problem. We were just quiet people."

"But it's a lie!"

"No, it's not. I know I made the mistake of being too preoccupied with my work, but you have to understand I was quiet because of my profession."

"Baba," Mr. Shi's daughter said, pity in her eyes. "You know it's a lie, too. You were never a rocket scientist. Mama knew. I knew. Everybody knew."

Mr. Shi stares at his daughter for a long time. "I don't understand what you mean."

"But you know, Baba. You never talked about what you did at work, true, but other people—they talked about you."

Mr. Shi tries to find some words to defend himself, but his lips quiver without making a sound.

His daughter says, "I'm sorry, Baba. I didn't mean to hurt you."

Mr. Shi takes long breaths and tries to maintain his dignity. It is not hard to do so, after all, as he has, for all his life, remained calm about disasters. "You didn't hurt me. Like you said, you were only talking about truth," he says, and stands up. Before he retreats to the guest bedroom, she says quietly behind him, "Baba, I'll book the tours for you tomorrow."

Mr. Shi sits in the park and waits to say his farewell to Madam. He has asked his daughter to arrange for him to leave from San Francisco after his tour of America. There'll still be a week before he leaves, but he has only the courage to talk to Madam one last time, to clarify all the lies he has told about himself. He was not a rocket scientist. He had had the training, and had been one for three years out of the thirty-eight years he worked for the Institute. *Hard for a young man to remain quiet about his work,* Mr. Shi rehearses in his mind. *A young rocket scientist, such pride and glory. You just wanted to share the excitement with someone.*

That someone—twenty-five years old, forty-two years ago—was the girl working on the card-punching machine for Mr. Shi. Punchers they were called back then, a profession that has long been replaced by more advanced computers, but of all the things that have disappeared from his life, a card puncher is what he misses most. *His* card puncher. *"Name is Yilan,"* Mr. Shi says aloud to the air, and someone greets the name with a happy hello. Madam is walking toward him with basket of autumn leaves. She picks up one and hands it to Mr. Shi. "Beautiful," she says.

Mr. Shi studies the leaf, its veins to the tiniest branches, the different shades of yellow and orange. Never before has he seen the world in such detail; He tries to remember the softened edges and dulled colors he was more used to, but like a patient with his cataracts taken away, he finds everything sharp and bright, appalling yet attractive. "I want to tell something to you," Mr. Shi says, and Madam flashes an eager smile. Mr. Shi shifts on the bench, and says in English, "I was not a rocket scientist."

Madam nods hard. Mr. Shi looks at her, and then looks away. *"I was not a rocket scientist because of a woman. The only thing we did was talk. Nothing wrong with talking, you would imagine, but no, talking between a married man and an unmarried girl was not accepted. That's how sad our time was back then."* Yes, sad is the word, not crazy as young people use to talk about that period. *"One would always want to talk, even when not talking was part of our training."* And talking, such a commonplace thing, but how people got addicted to it! Their talking started from five minutes of break in the office, and later they sat in the cafeteria and talked the whole lunch break. They talked about their hope and excitement in the grand history they were taking part in, of building the first rocket for their young communist mother.

"Once you started talking, you talked more, and more. It was different than going home and talking to your wife because you didn't have to hide anything. We talked about our own lives, of course. Talking is like riding with an unreined horse, you don't know where you end up and you don't have to think about it. That's what our talking was like, but we weren't having an affair as they said. We were never in love," Mr. Shi says, and then, for a short moment, is confused by his own words. What kind of love is he talking about? Surely they were in love, not the love they were suspected of having—he always kept a respectful distance, their hands never touched. But a love in which they talked freely, a love in which their minds touched—wasn't it love, too? Wasn't it how his daughter ended her marriage, because of all the talking with another man? Mr. Shi shifts on the bench, and starts to sweat despite the cool breeze of October. He insisted they were innocent when they were accused of having an affair; he appealed for her when she was sent down to a provincial town. She was a good puncher, but a puncher was always easier to train. He was, however, promised to remain in the position on the condition that he publicly admitted his love affair and gave a self-criticism. He refused because he believed he was wronged. *"I stopped being a rocket scientist at thirty-two. Never was I involved in any research after that, but everything at work was confidential so the wife didn't know."* At least that was what he thought until the previous night. He was assigned to the lowest position that could happen to someone with his training—he decorated offices for the birthdays of Chairman Mao and the Party; he wheeled the notebooks and paperwork from one research group to the other; in the evening he collected his colleagues' notebooks and paperwork, logged them in, and locked them in the file cabinet in the presence of two security guards. He maintained his dignity at work, and went home to his wife as a preoccupied and silent rocket scientist. He looked away from the questions in his wife's eyes until the questions disappeared one day; he watched his daughter grow up, quiet and understanding as his wife was, a good girl, a good woman. Thirty-two guards he worked with during his career, young men in uniforms and carrying empty holsters on their belts, but the bayonets on their rifles were real.

But then, there was no other choice for him. The decision he made—wasn't it out of loyalty to the wife, and to the other woman? How could he have admitted the love affair, hurt his good wife, and remained a selfish rocket scientist—or, even more impossible, given up a career, a wife, and a two-year-old daughter for the not so glorious desire to spend a lifetime with another woman? *"It is what we sacrifice that makes life meaningful"*— Mr. Shi says the line that was often repeated in their training. He shakes his head hard. A foreign country gives one foreign thoughts, he thinks. For an old man like him, it is not healthy to ponder too much over memory. A good man should live in the present moment, with Madam, a dear friend sitting next to him, holding up a perfect golden ginkgo leaf to the sunshine for him to see.

Notes

p. 399   *layover* - rest during a journey
p. 399   *stroller* - push-chair for baby
p. 400   *barrettes* - hair slides
p. 401   *lychees* - tropical fruit

44

Mrs Mahmood

(2007)

Segun Afolabi

Afolabi is a Nigerian writer who has travelled and lived in the USA, Asia and Europe, as well as Africa. In Mrs Mahmood, *a shop assistant in a sports shop in London foils a burglar but is then foiled. This story has a clever use of first-person narrative and a strong sense of place.*

Isobel and I live above the route of an underground line. We hadn't been told this before we moved in so it came as a shock the first time the 6.25 rumbled beneath our heads. Isobel thought it might be an earthquake. I knew exactly what it was. My heart sank. Now, sometimes I lie awake at night waiting for another train to pass so that I can fall asleep; I find it comforting somehow. The regularity, the mild vibrations, the dim, distant thrum of carriages carrying other people elsewhere. I couldn't live in a quiet place now. My tolerance for tranquillity has gone.

In the sports shop where I work it's noisy too; it can quite often seem overwhelming. We are not large area-wise but we have a high concentration of stock. Also, being near the university is a boon during term time. It gets busy, and I prefer that to sparse custom.

What happened the other week should not have come as a surprise. Deidra was serving on the cash till. I was balanced on a ladder, rehanging the tracksuit bottoms, smoothing them down where people had thrown them back haphazardly. Cedric was serving a boy of about thirteen, helping him choose a pair of running shoes. Nike. Size nine.

I shifted the ladder to another section of the shop. I think a clean, immaculate appearance is the essence of a caring, responsible enterprise. It sends out a message beyond the doors: Experience and Understanding you will find here. That's what I believe in. Understanding. It's what I strive for.

They do not like me doing this, the other staff, the rinse and interference of it. I think they would prefer me out the back taking care of the accounts, harrying suppliers, rushing in new stock. I don't know this for certain. I am the manager, I should have mentioned. Perhaps it puts them on edge, as if I am constantly watching, scrutinising. But that isn't my priority. I'm just particular about order, things running in straight lines. Dust doing a disappearing act. Perhaps I get this from my wife.

I wasn't paying particular attention to what was happening in the shop. I tend to run on automatic pilot when I'm doing the mundane tasks. That way I can free my mind to concentrate on improvements, long-term plans. The boy with the trainers was wandering around the shop floor, testing out the shoes. He walked a few metres, stopped, then reached up on his toes. Sometimes I'll look at the young, wonder whether they are headed for great things. This one seemed to soar like a gazelle, he did not waver on his feet. Then he crouched down low, stood up again and made his way back to the chair. I like that in a customer, someone who really knows what he wants. Someone who can pick out strengths and weaknesses and isn't afraid to do so in the setting of the shop. A lot of people are quite shy. They'll wear a pair of shoes, stand up, sit down, then immediately say, Yes, I'll take these. They might look flushed, a little sheepish, as if they have caused an inconvenience, put out a member of staff. Often I will want to say something to them. Ask them to walk around a bit, deliberate. But I don't say anything of course; it's money in the till after all.

Cedric asked the boy some questions, went through the usual routine about the feel of them, what they might be used for. The boy looked down at the shoes and scrunched his feet around. He wore a slight grimace as if he couldn't quite make up his mind. There was another boy then. I don't know where he appeared from, but he had been inside the shop all along. He called for assistance and Cedric moved to help him. It occurred to me to step down from the ladder, to assist, but then I did not.

Without a moment's hesitation, the boy in the trainers walked out of the shop. He did not run or look behind himself or suddenly tear off down the street. He walked away as if he had been wearing his own shoes, walking out of his own house. I watched impassively. By the time I had reached the door, he was some way down Tottenham Court Road. I started to run. He glanced around, noticed me, and then he began to sprint. There were pedestrians about, tackling their Christmas shopping. I like this time of day because people seem less brusque; they are more relaxed. The hard, brittle city edge that coats the beginning of the day has worn down.

Perhaps it is odd to see an older man puffing down a street. The clumsy sweep and sway of it, the heavy body bounding along. All I know is that very few people were looking at the boy, but all eyes managed to fix on me. Paths cleared. People stood back. It may have been an alarming sight.

When I was seventeen, I took a coach to Hastings. There were thirty of us on board. There was an athletics meeting between four or five schools and we all knew this occasion was important. Gold medals in any event might lead to county representation. Our athletics instructor, Mr Mayers, paced the coach, dispensing pep talks, trying to steel our morale.

The track at the school in Hastings was new, better than anything we had previously used. This was a school where no one thought anything of flying abroad for the half-term. Most of the other competitors had arrived before us. They looked polished, almost professional, as we straggled off the coach. My stomach yapped a little, then growled and I could feel my lunch lurch.

As the start drew near we poured onto the field, talking, stretching, warming up. A group from another school turned to look at us, then folded in among themselves like bats. It was no secret I had broken a string of county records for my age group the previous year. My picture had appeared in the local newspaper. And then there were some sentences in the gazette. I hung medals and certificates on the walls at school. I talked incessantly of my own prowess. I make no apology for this, either now or then: I used to think it was an essential ingredient of success. I could envisage my life stretching out ahead of me, consisting of adulation and accomplishment in equal measure.

Thirty minutes into the games and it was clear we had serious competition. People were not even qualifying in the heats. Suddenly it seemed to me that the bar on the high jump was insurmountable, distances on the field too arduous. I felt tired in a way I had never experienced before. Not from fatigue or from running too hard. It was simply exhausting to watch success slip so quickly away.

There comes a time when you realise all the effort you've put in – all those early mornings, the rigorous diet, the training, pushing yourself to the limit – amounts to nothing. I told friends I would return the next year, invigorated. I convinced myself of that at the time. But I never picked up another pair of running shoes, never stepped onto another track.

I don't think the boy ever guessed I would catch up with him. He probably thought he could shake me, an old dog giving up the chase. But I caught him all right. I could tell he was shocked; he didn't say a word. He did not struggle. Halfway back to the shop we met Cedric. There was a queue of traffic alongside us. The air was beginning to thin in the onslaught of winter darkness.

I caught a glimpse of the other boy lurking behind a pillar. I realised then he had been a decoy. I cannot describe how I felt then. Cheated? Flummoxed? Enraged? All three?

Cedric told him to take off the shoes. They were unsaleable now. The boy slipped them off nonchalantly, kicked them to one side. Then he began to put on his own worn-out trainers. I should have noted that from the beginning; no one enters a shoe shop wearing decrepit shoes. I've noticed that. The boy sat there, saturnine, bored, as if this happened every other day. When I said I would call the police, his expression did not change. I don't know what I was expecting. Remorse? Something, anything to let me know he had registered regret. But that did not happen. Not after my threat to resort to the law or my rising tone of voice or Cedric's more temperate approach. The boy's face just expressed contempt.

You could say I lost my temper. I could feel suppressed rage seeping from my chest, like a disturbed wound. I raised my hand, then slowly brought it down again and scratched the back of my neck. I was ready to strike out. The boy didn't even cringe. He showed no emotion whatsoever. I don't like to see that in children, coldness, valves already shut off. Perhaps that's exactly what he expected. Quite possibly he had been struck before.

It's a good thing we haven't any children, Isobel and I. I can't abide surly behaviour. I am just the sort of person who could so easily lose control.

Cedric told me to cool off. Deidra led me back to the office, like an invalid. When I sat down my hands were trembling, the knuckles doing some kind of dance. In the end the boy's mother was contacted. She apologised, even paid for the shoes, and thanked

411

the staff for not alerting the police. That's what Cedric told me the next day. I left early. That's not something I often do.

I drove to the supermarket, bought sea bass, mineral water and a bottle of white wine. For once I had arrived home before Isobel and I wanted to surprise her. Also, I needed something to do with my hands, to keep myself occupied. I turned the music up loud, opened the wine and started on that. Isobel doesn't drink during the week. She says it impairs her judgement, her reasoning, and she likes to keep her mind clear. She is an orthoptist at a children's hospital, not that it would make any difference to her work.

I heard the door shut. Then the music was turned down so that it was almost inaudible.

'Turn it back up!' I shouted from the kitchen. I was still simmering. I walked into the living room, a glass of wine in one hand, a bowl of steaming white rice in the other.

She was lingering by the stereo, wearing her long beige coat, her bag limp over her shoulder. I waved the bowl about so that steam plumed into the air. It was supposed to be a jovial gesture. She took one good look at me. 'What's wrong?' she said.

I shrugged and sauntered back into the kitchen. 'Time to eat!' I called.

In Isobel's work with the children she often gets to see a side to life I am unaware of. Sometimes she strikes a tone with me that isn't appropriate. 'Now then,' she might say quietly, 'tell me all about it.' Her hands held gently together, her voice smooth, modulated. I know she would like children of our own, but me, I'm not so sure.

I explained what had happened during the day. The shoes marching out defiantly, the high-street chase, how I'd wanted to lash out. I have always thought of myself as a particular kind of man, the kind that could never strike a child. No matter what. But that's all over now.

Isobel made a few cooing noises. I didn't know what she meant. She gathered up the dishes and walked into the kitchen. She was wearing a batik wraparound the colour of blueberries swirled in yoghurt, a white T-shirt and an oversized tan cardigan. You could say that Isobel is stunning and you would not be exaggerating. I could hear the hot tap gushing, the basin filling up with suds. When she returned, I was in the middle of pouring the last of the wine.

'Well, Mr Mahmood,' she shrugged, but she didn't sound upset. 'Theft is something you just have to get used to. I thought you'd be used to it by now?'

'Theft?' I repeated. 'I'm not worried about that,' even though I always have been. I explained again about the insolent boy. I thought she might be shocked.

'Oh that! That's nothing new,' she said. 'I've sometimes wanted to hit out, you know. You can't help that.'

I nibbled the edge of my glass.

'It's only natural to feel anger at that kind of behaviour,' she continued. 'They're doing it for a reason, though. You have to remember that.'

I wasn't quite sure how to take this, the ease with which she'd said it. I stood up and the table swam before me. I was a bit drunk – I am not often that way – I simply couldn't settle down. I placed the rest of the crockery into Isobel's foamy sink. My muscles were aching already from the mid-afternoon sprint.

I picked up the car keys and announced I was going for a drive. She immediately grabbed them off me and said, 'Let's go,' as I knew she would.

We decided to visit the hill in order to walk off the alcohol. The evening was slick with fresh-fallen drizzle and as soon as we reached Elsworthy Road neither of us was in the mood to leave the warmth of the car. Instead we carried on, through Camden and then to the centre of town to look at the lights along Bond Street. Isobel was driving slowly. She didn't want to miss a thing.

'I simply *have* to go there.' She kept pointing to shops. Expensive shops.

'Yes,' I said, agreeing too quickly. I felt nauseous. I opened the window a crack and leaned up against the door. Isobel looked across at me. 'Eyes on the road, please,' I snapped. By the time we reached Piccadilly, I felt calmer, more refreshed.

Isobel, I think, was led to expect an undemanding life. To have things easily provided, frequent trips around the world. I don't think she ever envisaged being with someone like me. It must have come as a surprise, gone against everything her parents had encouraged her towards, to suddenly find on her wedding day, me and not some high-flown tycoon exchanging the marital vows. I know her mother was crestfallen. It wasn't difficult to notice that. Mr Hamilton put on a brave face, but in the beginning none of that mattered to us. Young love, as they often say, is blind. Life in a warm milky sea.

Perhaps it was the mother, her insistence. Dreams she had always aspired to, and been let down, so she turned to Isobel. I am only speculating. Perhaps I'm way off the mark. My mother used to say, when she was living, that it did not matter who you loved, what you did in this world as long as there was a little happiness in it.

I used to get annoyed with Isobel because sometimes she would remind me of her mother. Her distrusts, her exactitude, the way she held herself so stiffly when I wanted her simply to let go. The way she turned from certain things – music, say or people, raised voices – because they seemed to crowd the light. Who and what she thought she ought to be.

There was a time fraught with difficulties when I wasn't sure what we were doing. But that's passed. I fought for Isobel the way I've fought for most things in my life. I know she did not want me in the beginning. Not for a long time after that.

We'll catch a bus sometimes, a train, discover a part of town or the country we have never been to before. Occasionally we have caught the wrong train, a bus going in the opposite direction. But there won't be any panic, a rushing towards the exit. Quite often we'll remain seated and let the vehicle lead the way. Isobel doesn't mind this, although I know she would never allow such a thing to happen on her own.

Like me, she has lived in other places – Guadeloupe, Martinique, New York City after that – so she doesn't mind the travelling. Perhaps it comes from living a fractured existence. All that broken geography. Learning to live a different life.

Isobel once said I was abrupt with people, I cut them off, that underneath a warm exterior I harboured a cold nature.

'When?' I demanded. 'When am I like this? Examples please.'

'Oh, I don't know,' she laughed. 'All the time, really. In a way.'

At the back of my mind I feared she was thinking about having children again, but she did not mention it. I think a part of what she was saying has something to do with living in the city. I often strike a particular note with people and I can't say why. The sales representatives, for example, who come into the shop. Sometimes I make them feel as if they are the most important encounter of my day. That what they are saying bears close attention. What they are doing is admirable. At the end of it all – the bright photographs illustrating technicoloured shoes, leotards, samples of baseball caps, something that has happened in their day, their lives – there comes a point when they realise they have done most of the talking. They're talked out. And all I have given of myself is the minimum, the bare bones, while I know everything that has happened to them, the dry reality of their day. Sometimes there will be a moment when they realise this. It is awkward because it's a signal to me that they might want something in exchange – muscle, blood, a heart, something more vibrant. And I know that there isn't any of that, only bones. Does that make me cold?

My customers, on the other hand, I treat as if we'll meet again. That's a favourite part of my job, the interaction, so I try to get it right. People don't like to admit they don't know, that they might need some help. I have learned that over time, so I ask the staff to approach them in a particular manner – not invasive or aggressive – so they are put at ease. People don't like to feel crowded. There is a kind of satisfaction in watching them select an item, try something on. I love it when they walk out with bags of shopping in their hands, contented. Or the ones who ask demurely if they can wear the shoes out of the shop.

That happened today, this afternoon. Someone came into the shop. Someone famous. I'd seen him during the summer on my television screen. He wasn't shopping for himself; he had a young boy with him, most probably his son.

I let Deidra do the talking, make the sale, do all of that. He bought a pair of football boots. Not the best, I noted. It was the boy's choice.

They were warm people, relaxed. I watched them from where I stood, half-heartedly checking the stock. They smiled along with Deidra. The boy kept giggling. His father laughed out loud. A few customers sidled up for autographs. He was in the last Olympics, that one. An Olympian. He had a winner's smile.

At one stage he caught me looking and I turned away. I think I lost my nerve then. I don't remember, I just felt weak. I fled into the office and sat staring at the paperwork. Half an hour may have passed. I thought I should telephone Isobel at the hospital. 'Who?' she would say. 'Which Olympics?'

Instead I slipped out of the building. It was wrong of me; I wouldn't tolerate that kind of behaviour in anyone else.

It was cold outside, but bright and still. People moved less briskly in the streets, the reality of the new year setting in. I walked to Charing Cross with the intention of turning back. But then I just kept moving.

Along Whitehall a bus waited patiently for its passengers to alight. It was stationary when I caught up with it and so, without hesitating, I stepped on. I didn't check where it was going. I just wanted to go and go and go, be carried somewhere far away.

It is a helpless feeling to know that no matter how hard you run, however much you exert yourself, you are never going to move faster than this, overtake the man in front. Perhaps I understood that then, when I was seventeen. I could, in a minor way, have grasped something early on: that there is a moment or a series of moments in life when you must wear a different pair of shoes, walk in another direction from the one you had planned, and however well you succeed in your pursuits, there will always be an element of regret.

The bus shuddered across the river. A refuse container made its sluggish progress beneath the bridge. I got off at the next stop and crossed the road into the park. It surprised me to see people there in the middle of the week, in the cold. I left the path after a while and slipped onto the field. There were some children at one end playing at the long jump. I walked around the perimeter slowly and I could hear their laughter. The track seemed warm and buoyant beneath me. There were signs – paint peeling off wooden benches, sections of the track torn out – of decay and neglect. The trees in the distance rustled slightly, but I did not feel the breeze.

I don't know why I behaved the way I did, that day in the shop with the thief. He had looked so angry with me. As if *I* had been in the wrong. What if Cedric had not been there? Would I have struck out? I would like to think not, but I'm not so certain now. Sometimes I think I would take better care of my shop – the expensive shoes, the labelled clothing, the sports equipment – than I would my own child. And I am blind with fear.

I took off my jacket, laid it down to one side of the field. I stretched my limbs slowly, deliberately, the way I had been taught, because at my age things can so easily go wrong. I took up position and cast my eye to the end of the track. The children had stopped what they were doing. They were quiet now. Watching. And then I was sailing, the wind unfurling round my ears, the soft rubber track making me feel supple. As I neared the end of the straight I didn't stop as I had intended, but instead, rounded the bend and ran at a slower pace back to the start. When I finished there was a faint applause and when I looked up, there were the children in the distance who must have been cheering me on. I hadn't heard them. I had heard nothing except the wind and my quick heartbeat, my laboured breath.

Perhaps I have failed in my life, in my endeavours. Perhaps the meaning of it all has passed me by. I cannot say for certain that it has. I just don't know. I cannot say that in a year from now I will be lulled to sleep by underground trains. I could be someplace very far from here. Sometimes I long for heat.

If it came right down to it, if I thought about it clean out, pared back the skin, the tired flesh and arrived at the bones, I realise the one certainty in my life is Isobel.

Notes

p. 409   *rinse* - slang meaning to do something many times to the point of boredom
p. 409   *underground line* - the London underground train – tube system
p. 411   *saturnine* - gloomy
p. 412   *batik* - type of colourful fabric dyeing
p. 412   *orthoptist* - kind of eye doctor

45

Promenade

(2009)

Henrietta Rose-Innes

Rose-Innes is a South African writer from Cape Town. In this story, a jogger, past his best and trying to stave off old age, starts meeting a slightly menacing figure on his daily route in this contemplation of ageing within a very vivid depiction of daily life.

I haven't changed much, over the years. When I look in the mirror, the experience is much the same as it was when I was a younger man. My teeth have not yellowed and my eyesight is remarkably good. Even my finger- and toenails, I suspect, do not edge out from my extremities as rapidly as other people's do. Everyone assumes that I'm in my early forties, when in fact I'm fifty-four – a long way from retirement, but still significantly older than my colleagues at the ad agency. Of course I'm balding now, but even this has helped to freeze me in time. I used to style my hair differently, part it this way and that, grow it and trim it; but I am stuck now with this look, this length: a conservative short cut around the bald spot at the crown. Anything else looks foolish.

It is partially the adipose layer beneath the skin, I believe, that helps to preserve my looks. Slightly plump people, I've often noticed, seem to age better than the bony ones: the skin stays taut for longer, the skeleton submerged. Yes, I am a little overweight, as I have been since my early thirties. I've tried to lose the excess, but my body remains impervious. A few years back I put myself through a stern fitness regime – low-fat foods, the gym. There was no observable impact on my weight or muscle tone. I have a metabolism in perfect equilibrium, it seems. Still, I exercise, frequently if moderately. Because what would happen if I stopped?

So it is that every evening after work, at six sharp, I take my promenade along the sea wall near my flat. I clip along at a steady pace: a little more than a walk, a little less than a jog. My fists are bunched before my chest; I thrust them forward and back, kicking my feet one-two, one-two, my elbows winging to the sides. Yes, I am one of those speed-walkers. I know it's undignified, but it's the only way to get up any kind of sweat without actually running. I have the gear: special lightweight jogging shorts, athletic socks, sweat-wicking tops in the latest high-tech fabrics. (No vests; I really am too old for that.) Once a year I buy a new pair of Nikes or New Balances, a virtuous treat.

On my outward journey, the sea lies to my left, grey or blue or silver. Fifteen minutes at a swift stride from my flat down the steep street, to the sea wall and along the path to the traffic lights opposite the garage and café. Here I pause to stretch on the strip of lawn, before continuing for another fifteen minutes along the promenade as far as the public telephones. Then I wheel round and go back in the other direction, one-two, one-two, with the sea on my right, half an hour, pausing only to cross at the lights to the café for the day's *Argus*. I roll the newspaper tightly and hold it baton-like in one hand for the rest of the route home (only unsatisfactory on the weekends, when the editions are too fat for comfort). I always take with me just enough change in the special zip-up pocket in my top – plus twenty cents, because sometimes they put up the price without warning – and my house key. No wallet or mobile phone; although the promenade is busy and safe at that time, you can never be too careful. And I like to stay light.

The thing about walking along a sea wall is that your options are limited: you can only go forward or back. You can't head off to the side without falling into the sea, or ploughing across the lawn through the children's swings and roundabouts and into the traffic. The lack of choice is soothing, and I'm quite content to follow my established route, each time the same. It is a beautiful walk, especially on still evenings when the sea is flat and the sky clear, or lightly flecked with peachy clouds. The water glows and swirls like cognac. Everyone I meet, coming or going, is gilded on either the left or right sides of their faces with pink or saffron, and they all seem serene and calm and somehow meditative in the generous light. I know I do.

People comment on that: my serenity. But often I am not calm inside, not at all, especially not in the boiling light of those late evenings. It is a dramatic coastline, and there are often grand effects: towering clouds, beating waves, gleams on the rocks where Darwin, they say, once stood and pondered geological time and the ancient congress of molten stone.

But it is not these that affect me so. It is purely the light coming over the sea, a brilliant luminosity not encountered from any other vantage point in the city. It cuts me with a kind of ecstasy – as if I'm on the verge of revelation, one I'm powerless to halt. I have been brought almost to tears, some evenings on the promenade.

There is a particular moment, when the sky goes coral pink and the breaking surf is chalk-blue, almost fluorescent in the fading light. And then each incoming swell feels as if it is rolling through my body, just under the skin, from the soles of my feet all the way to my fingernails, rolling out over the quick, making me want to reach out my fingers and touch. Although I am a controlled man, I am not immune to these things.

Controlled, that's another word I've heard people – my workmates – use to describe me. I'm a senior copywriter, moderately good at my job; good at controlling words, certainly. Words for pictures of sunsets, often with cars or couples in front of them. But I grope after language to describe the feelings I experience on my evening walks, the light in the air and on the sea. This pleases me: that some things remain beyond my grasp. That they cannot be rendered down.

Perhaps this is why I have no ambition. I've held the same position at the same agency for fifteen years and have no desire for anything greater, for a managerial position, even as the new hires are promoted around me. Such things, I know, could never fulfil my more obscure longings. I'm happy to run in place.

There are always a lot of people moving up and down the promenade: smooth-skinned models looping along in Rollerblades too heavy for their frail ankles; the old woman who sits on the same bench every evening to feed the pigeons; cheerful ladies in tracksuits, trying to shift a kilogramme or two; resolute athletes with corded thighs. Dog walkers and drug dealers and beggars, and lovers in each other's arms as they watch the sun go down. Some of them I have seen every other evening for the past three years, which is how long I've been taking my promenade now. Others are new. Recently I've started to feel I recognize individual seagulls along the route, although this is surely my imagination.

One evening a young man comes past me, sweating and steaming in a cloud of musk. Although covered up in a tracksuit, his body is obviously muscular; not the smooth, inflated-looking muscles that you see on some of the gym boys, not well-fed recreational beef, but the hard, functional build of someone who works with his body for a living. Shorter than me, but strong. He jogs fast and purposefully.

I notice him again a few days later, and from then on he intersects regularly with my evening promenade, three times a week: Mondays, Wednesdays, Saturdays. I see him going only the one way. He must loop back, as I do; but his circuit is clearly far more expansive and demanding than my own. Time-wise, he is rigid. I always pass him on my outbound trip, and always, it seems, at exactly the same place: just opposite the traffic lights where I pause to do my stretches. He waits to cross the road there, bouncing on his toes, swivelling his torso aggressively left and right. Perhaps he's heading for the gym.

Always dressed in bright, deep colours, I notice; he must have half a dozen different tracksuits, in pillar-box red, racing green, midnight blue. (These phrases come to me involuntarily.) He always wears the complete assemblage, matched top and bottom, which is quite formal – never casual in a T-shirt. A white towel is looped round his neck and sometimes he grasps its ends as he waits at the traffic lights, pulling it against the back of his dark neck. A strong, almost cuboidal block of a jaw. I think he must be a boxer. Something in the way he moves, in the build. Or maybe it's just the way he holds his fists, loosely clenched, that gives me this idea.

My certainty about his occupation grows. Who but a professional athlete would need to train so often and so hard, swathed in towel and sweat-dark tracksuit? His arms are bulkier than a long-distance runner's would need to be, he is light on his feet with a dancing stride, and there's a kind of sprightly aggression in his movements. Enormous hands, for his height. They make me self-conscious about my own flushed fists.

Two men, changeless, beating the same if opposite route; it is comforting. I've read about boxers' battles to keep their weight at certain limits, and I imagine that we are caught in a similar stasis. Like me, he is fighting to keep his body where it is.

After a while we start to nod to each other, cautiously. To test my boxing theory, one day I put up my fists – not sure, really, what I intend. He balls his and twitches them towards his chin. No smile, though. It feels tenuous, the moment: me with fists raised, unsure if this is a playful act.

418

Up close, I see the imperfections – the damaged skin of his brows, the way the scarring seems to have resulted in the loss of eyebrows. I notice that his nose looks broken, his earlobes thick. (Are those cauliflower ears?) Despite this coarsening of the features, he has an appealing face, set in an expression of youthful resolution, lit on one side by the setting sun.

It becomes a jokey ritual, a greeting every time we pass. The lifted hands in imaginary gloves. At least, I think it's a joke. It grows from there.

One evening, when we come face to face, he and I do that little step-step dance that happens when two people are walking straight into each other: both to the same side and then both back again.

I smile. His fists come up and this time he pauses to spar with me. Now, flinching, I know I'm right: only a pro could direct such a sparkling combination of quick almost-touches to my ribs, my jaw, my nose. The huge fists lunge at me, snap back; so close, I feel a tickle of warm air on my face and smell his sweat. I raise my hands to parry.

And after that it happens every time: each evening we do the two-step dance and spend a few moments trading phantom blows. A smile never crosses his face, as if the scars prevent it. But at the end, just before he skips to the side and jogs on, he'll give me a look and tip up his chin in brief and surely humorous acknowledgement.

A month passes, two. The woman who feeds the birds looks increasingly fragile, until I start to worry that she'll be overpowered by the sturdy pigeons bickering around her; then one day she is gone. Shortly thereafter I see the pigeons have constructed another old woman in their midst. The couples part and reconfigure, but the boxer and I remain the same, locked in our pattern, running and standing still.

Other people loop in other cycles round us, stitching up their days with a quick up-and-down along the water's edge. I think of ants, crawling in opposing circles. Clockwise ants every now and then touching mouth parts with their anticlockwise comrades, passing cryptic messages. Some promenaders I will doubtless never meet, caught as we are in orbits that never intersect; but the boxer and I are in sync.

My days pass mildly; I have other routines. The promenade is not my only circular occupation. I sit on Sunday afternoons in the flat and read the newspaper. I go out to buy myself coffee and croissants. I go to work, where I produce copy about faster, stronger, younger. When I hear my own words on TV, I don't remember ever writing them.

Sitting in my padded swivel chair before my computer station, hands poised to tap the keys, I am trapped in stillness. There is a strong desire to jump up and swing my arms, to dispel this immobility, but I stay where I am and the spasm passes. My colleagues at the other workstations do not notice this fleeting turmoil, do not see that I have paused in my typing to contemplate for a moment some grand gesture. I flex my hands, let them drop mildly back to the keyboard. My fingers renew their automatic labour.

Mondays, Wednesdays, Saturdays. We never speak, but our greetings are progressively more familiar. In our small, intense interactions I notice things in great detail: the fact that his irises are black, fading to amber rims. A chipped tooth in his slightly open mouth.

Our sparring becomes elaborate. I think he might be teaching me to box. It's all very controlled, but of course there is also a tremor of fear. Huge fists in your face, what can you do but imagine those hands rubbing out your features, smearing your nose, forcing your teeth into your mouth? That's never happened to me, of course, but I can imagine the very specific sensations: nose-break pain, tooth-shatter pain, taste of blood. I do not know exactly what the mock-blows signify – violence or camaraderie. Each thrust has the potential to explode, is centimetres from rocketing into my face, from crushing my chest. I can far more easily imagine receiving such blows than delivering them. I try to picture pushing my hand all the way, sticking it between the big fists to press against that jaw. Impossible.

Sometimes, trotting on after our shadow-play I am trembling slightly, feeling the sting of invisible gloves on my body, the smack of fists. I think of the phrase 'glass jaw'. Compared to his stony features, I am all crystal.

One Wednesday afternoon, I stay home from work with a cold. I switch on the TV at some unusual hour to catch the afternoon news: SABC2 or 3, which I would not normally watch. And I see him, I'm sure it's him, in red shorts shiny under the bright lights of the ring, his knuckles encased in bulbous mitts like cartoon hands. His lips are distended by a gum guard and he looks smaller with his top off, but I know him by his movements: the sideways skip and jump, fists flung out in that dancing rhythm. He and his opponent in blue are both compact men – is it featherweight? – but their bodies are pure wire-hard muscle, shiny brown with sweat. I don't catch his name over the dinging bell, the shouts of the crowd; and anyway, the commentary is in another language.

I lean forward, face close to the screen. It only lasts a couple of rounds. The one small, hard man drills the other to the floor with sweat-spraying strokes. I feel each blow as a twitch in my upper arms. And then it is over: blue lies flat on his back, toes up and out. My boxer's hands are raised above his head in victory, blood streaming from his brow.

Only after the ads come on do I relax my hands and let myself lean back on the couch.

He is absent from the promenade for a week. When he reappears, I am warier of him, almost ducking away from his shadow-strokes, but he is too skilful to touch me. Often I think about speaking to him, but my mouth is dry, and he is exercising so hard, so earnestly. I don't want to break his concentration.

I am not eloquent here, in this conversation of bodies. Still, I have come to depend on these playful altercations, these little knockabouts in which neither one of us falls to the ground.

Today, for the first time in months, my routine is broken. What is it that delays me? A foolish thing. A flutter of wings in my chest as I'm putting on my shoes, a kind of rushing. Something to startle a man of my age. I have to sit for a few moments, gathering myself. Only fifty-four. I have had no trouble before now. I eat well; my life does not have unusual stresses. I exercise.

As a result, I am ten minutes late in getting away. Maybe twelve. I don't check the exact time of my leaving, nor do I feel the need to hurry especially, to catch up. I am rigid in my habits, but not to that degree. The heart flutter has upset me and I'm not thinking of anything else. I set out cautiously.

I do not think of the boxer, of how I have disrupted the pattern of our meetings. I do not consider that my delay will in turn mean that he is not delayed. His circuit from unknown origin to unknown destination will not, now, be paused for our customary sparring. He will not lose that five or ten seconds, and thus will cross the road five or ten seconds sooner. I do not think of these things, and if I did, I would not see the significance.

I feel old and tired and a little sick; for once I am not in the mood for the bracing sea air, the spray, the demanding sunset light. I do not feel like meeting the radiant, youthful figure of the boxer, holding up his hands.

Ten minutes, maybe twelve. Long enough for it all to be over by the time I reach the stretch beyond the children's swings, coming up to the traffic lights. I see the small crowd ahead. A car is slewed at a shocked angle in the road, windscreen spiderwebbed. People stand with their heads down, rapt, staring at something at their centre. An ambulance pulls up. I lengthen my stride.

As I come alongside I see only people's backs. I push my way through joggers and walkers. Cooling flesh slicked with sunscreen and sweat. A couple of dogs twisting their leads round their owners' legs, weaving a mesh between me and what lies on the pavement. I step over crossed leads, squeeze between shoulders.

The boxer is lying on his back, hands at his sides, legs spread, toes pointed up and away from each other. A dachshund sniffs at his bright white trainers. There is blood. My hands, the backs of my hands, tingle as if they have just been slapped. My knuckles tingle. My face aches. I back away.

I walk on. The ambulance drives past me, but it goes slowly with no siren or lights flashing. I walk and walk. Something has reset my clock and I no longer know when to turn round. On beyond the café, on along the sea wall, beyond the phones, on until the path ends at the wall of the marina and I can go no more; otherwise I might walk for ever. Stepping up to the wall that blocks my path, I punch it with my left hand. Not hard, only enough to hurt my knuckles, not to bloody them. I wouldn't know how to hit that hard. I do it just once, then stand staring at the concrete for a moment before turning away.

I don't go back along the promenade. Instead I cross the road to the other side, towards the shops and hotels and away from the sea. The ocean is gentle and tired this evening. The incoming and outgoing waves seem to be confirming something, some truth about tides turning, time passing. Such flat phrases for that eternal suffering rhythm, but this is the best I can do.

I walk home a different way, through backstreets. It takes me a long time. I stop halfway at a random bistro and order coffee, decaf for the heart, and pick up the newspaper I failed to buy earlier. I don't know where I am in the day. I read the newspaper front to back, the sports pages and the classifieds and the obituaries. Then at last I continue home along an unfamiliar route. Down the steep roads, I can't avoid glimpsing the band of soft radiance generated by the sea. I can feel that brightness in the corner of my eye, but here where I am walking the world is darker. I'm cold in my T-shirt.

As I pass the window of the Woolworths on the corner, it is old, vain habit that makes me glance into the silvered glass. And I see clearly that age has come to me at last:

decades, it seems, since this morning. The expensive walking clothes hang loose. And I know that from now on the years, which never burdened me before, will gather on my body, heavier and heavier in the life that remains. Time has started up again, speeding me down.

I step away from the glass and close my eyes. I raise up the boxer in my mind. Lifting my hands to my chest, I pick up the pace, one-two, one-two, elbows out. Through the evening streets I complete my promenade.

Notes

p. 417   *Argus* - newspaper
p. 419   *cauliflower ear* - term for ears damaged and mis-shaped from a blow, found in rugby players and boxers

46

The Plantation

(2010)

Ovo Adagha

Adagha is a Nigerian writer and editor of international short story anthologies. In this story set in a small village in Nigeria, a leak in an oil-pipe is discovered in the forest – what effect will it have on the villagers? This is a richly descriptive story.

1

The plantation grew from the moist underbelly of the Jesse swamps. That place where a luxuriant mesh of greenery blocked away the sun and surrounded everything in sight; just as it surrounded Namidi that morning as he moved about to inspect his trees and traps. He walked across the winding tract of grassy soil – beaten out of the forest at the onset of planting seasons by the young men of the village, with hoes and machetes, spurred on by the bullish power of the native beer. It was the *harmattan* season; the parching land breeze charged at him from the rubber trees and made the hairs on his skin bristle.

This place was an emblem of life to him – the high-pitched whistle of the birds; the cold drizzle of early morning dew; the soft, earthy, muskiness of the air; the endless reams of foliage and the rubber trees that glistened with sap. The plantation seemed to glow with a curious mysteriousness which followed him about as he moved abstractedly, slashing at the banners of plant-leaves that heaved across his path, his face a picture of dark brooding.

There followed a small moment of prickling silence, when it seemed as if the murmur of the plantation was suspended in a state of waiting; as though giving audience to some novelty event. Namidi's nostrils picked up an odd, sickly smell that set his stomach on edge as he moved about; and with it floated an alien, trickling sound. He paused in mid-stride and cocked his ears at the trees. He stood still for a long time, listening, watching and sniffing, until, perhaps touched by an uncertain impulse, he looked behind a thicket a few feet away.

If the trees had started talking to him he would not have been more surprised. A stream of fluid burst forth from the ground and splashed all around in a wayward arc. It flowed across the adjoining greenery, which seemed to shrink away from the onslaught. He watched as a puddle of fluid gathered around him and washed across the plantation. With his senses invaded by the strong stench, he realized it was petrol.

Once, many years ago, some men from the city in khaki uniforms had come to the village with long pipes and heavy trucks. Their spectacle had held the attention of the village people for many days. They had dug across the village grounds, through the plantation and the nearby forests; buried the pipes and then left. A pipe must have broken, was the first thought that came to Namidi; he must ask the village head to do something about it.

But such noble thoughts soon evaporated as he turned the matter over in his mind. Yes, it was surely petrol, but of what benefit would this be to him? There was an opportunity here, if only the meddling of the villagers would let him. Then a small grin lit up his face. Yes, he knew what to do.

He filled the rubber gourd with some petrol and then started towards the village. When he emerged from the plantation the early morning sun was rising confidently in the skies. He walked on, scarcely responding to the greetings of the village women going to their farms. He, who usually lingered over greetings, now wished the women would all disappear and leave him alone.

'Greetings, Sir,' a group of women rallied at him.

'Greetings, good women,' he replied and hurried on without a glance in their direction.

'What is wrong with him?' one of them asked as they appraised the retreating figure. Namidi was moving briskly on the narrow path, his head thrust forward, like it was going to fall away from his neck.

'He looks like he has seen a ghost,' another said, clapping her hands excitedly.

'And he has this smell around him,' another one added.

'It smells like something they use with their rubber,' said another one. They stared at the departing figure and shook their heads in puzzlement.

Namidi moved as quickly as he could, his heart full of intent. Some riches are too hard won, he thought to himself, too long waited for to be shared, especially in this village where no man lacked the capacity for greed and treachery. Of what use is it to come upon a herd of bush meat, if it will only serve the main course of a public feast? For long he had wandered and waited in the plantation for a chance to redeem himself from the poverty that had beset his adult life. Now it was within his grasp to settle it. He would not share his discovery with anyone, he decided.

To avoid detection, he left the road and started walking off into the bush track: a steep, snaking slope of dense foliage and caked mud. He laboured up the path until he reached the village clearing; all the while nodding his head and whispering to himself.

The village itself was a cluster of thatched roofs, no more than a clearing in the jungle. Namidi had lived there all his life and knew all about it: the small huts that were eked out of red clay, with their shaggy cabbage of palm-frond roofs that seemed to recede as one approached – stretched on a paltry piece of land with minuscule space between them; the rainfall and gossip that ploughed on endlessly without season; and how the very ground on which the village stood seemed eternally swathed in a blanket of rust. Ah, he knew all about it – the indescribable weariness and dreariness of it all.

'Ochuko! Ochuko! Where in God's name is this boy?' Namidi called out when he got to his house.

Papa! a small, breathless voice rang out from behind the hut.

Namidi turned and regarded his six-year-old son as he came bouncing towards him from the backyard with the reckless abandon of a child, his over-sized knickers flapping against his thighs as he ran. Two years ago some missionaries had built a new school on the outskirts of the village. But the fees were expensive and he could not afford to send any of his three children there with the meagre earnings from his rubber farm. Namidi felt diminished each time he saw his boy playing in the sand while the school bells rang in the distance. It seemed as if the bells in his mind started clanging loudly at this thought, willing him to return to the plantation with the utmost haste.

'Go and call your mother for me,' he said.

The boy set off again, humping and jumping towards his mother's kitchen.

'What is it?' his wife, Mama Efe, enquired as she emerged from the hut. She was a thin, shrivelled woman with a hardened look about her. Years and years of toiling in the sun had drawn the skin taut over her cheek-bones so that time and suffering seemed etched on her features.

'What's that smell you brought home today?' she asked, with a wary, suspicious frown on her face.

Namidi was gazing at his hut; at the lines of rotten bamboo that stuck out of its window panes. It seemed like the thatched roof and clay-red walls were cowering before him and the smell of new money. He turned around with a perspiring face and told her about his findings.

'We must go there now before the busybodies get wind of it,' he added, trying to infect her with a sense of urgency.

'What if a fire starts, eh?' she queried, worriedly. In her mind, there appeared a flash of blurred images writhing inside a great flame; of grotesque-looking figures being planted in the ground; and of grey-clothed people standing around the fresh mounds of soil, with a charged, funereal quality.

Looking at her, at the doubt and anxiety that suddenly clouded her face, Namidi experienced a brief pang of fear; but he tossed the thought away quickly from his mind, without repining, and said:

'It won't, I am the only one who knows.' His eyebrows arched menacingly, admonishing her to say no more.

She asked no further questions, but she thought within herself: this thing is a ghoulish business and will come to no good.

Namidi, his wife and three children carved an odd, almost patriarchal procession as they left the house with huge, empty cans. Namidi led the line, towering and frowning, as

425

he strode determinedly down the bush path; his children followed, awe-struck and excited by the scent of adventure, picking their way bare-footed over the rough path; his wife completed the moving line of ancient slave-rite figures, tagging along on hardened feet, her face brooding and disturbed. Their advance took them to where they were greeted by an ensemble of close-knit trees that stretched and heaved into the track, forming an intimidating profusion of branches, fronds and creepers. The air was stale and thick with damp sweat. Yet Namidi retained all the doggedness that was upon him since the time he made the discovery. It was the road that would lead them to riches, he thought cheekily to himself. And as his wife and children trudged mechanically behind him, his mind was closed to all else except his destination.

In the stroking brightness of the sun, an owl in full glide flapped its brown-streaked wings, turned its head and then sounded a doleful note as it flew past the trudging party below.

2

The narrow path they followed was surrounded on both sides by a flagging ledge of greenery. Mama Efe cast a pallid shadow on the ground as they worked their way back and forth from the plantation to the house, with large hauls of petrol. She followed him, without a word, saying nothing of the storm that was gathering in her heart.

Trouble lay in wait in for them, she knew. She felt herself sapped of all will, and of any sort of resistance. Her heart throbbed with anxiety; yet not a word of complaint came from her. There was a time when she could have derided or opposed him in some way, but years of waging lost battles in her marriage had doused her spirits with meekness and tiredness. Why, she knew how stubborn her husband could be; how he would never change his mind once it was made up. She used to think it was his strength. But she knew all about it now – all the ruin his rigidness had cast upon them.

On the third trip to the plantation they were accosted by Jackson – a greasy-looking youth from the village with a Boy Scout scarf tied around his neck. He was always up to no good and spent his days chasing birds and grasshoppers in the plantation. The lad took one sniff at Namidi and his eyebrows stretched wide.

'Why, are you working in Shell now?' he said, and grinned knowingly at Namidi.

Mama Efe was watching her husband as he eyed the youth with a look of baleful hatred.

'What business of yours is it?' he countered in a cold voice, and surveyed the youth disdainfully, like some errant, wayward fly.

'You should know, anything that happens in this village I make it my business'; Jackson said, and rubbed his hands.

Namidi looked annoyed, like he had been insulted. He advanced towards the youth, eyes blazing, but held himself together with some effort when his wife placed a restraining arm on him. He turned away and continued walking, stiff-necked, down the narrow track. The youth followed at some distance, his eyes darting at about, searching for clues. Mama Efe, a few steps behind her husband, was trembling with dread. He said not a word but she knew that darkness was brewing within him – the way he flicked his head with irritation, and slashed his cutlass at the swaying creepers. It made her all the more nervous, the entire business. And she wished she could depart from it.

Already, the smell of the petrol had reached them; so too had the hissing sound from the plantation. Jackson uttered a cry behind them and then ran off in the opposite direction towards the village.

3

Not long after, the local people from the village and nearby fishing villages converged at the spill site to fetch petrol. The day had progressed to a burning noon, with the sun gliding overhead like a circle of fire. The market, the school and the farms were all deserted. Fishermen, artisans, farmers and women abandoned their wares and swarmed to the plantation, which seemed to glitter with a wave of sweat-drenched, dark bodies. Away to the right, to the left, and all around, the plantation sparked with keen contests as the people jostled and fought each other for space around the site. Metal pans and buckets clashed and flashed in the sweltering heat like weapons of survival.

The petrol was gradually swallowed by huge cans, pans and any element of storage the villagers could muster. But it flowed on still, steadily giving in to the ceaseless mania of sucking, the avid thirst of animals long deprived of nurturing milk. The plantation reeled from the endless trampling of feet, but took it all in; except for the petrol, foreign to its depths, which was resisted and only allowed to brim over the soil surface; enough for the villagers to swim or sink in.

Namidi, his clothes dripping with perspiration and petrol, stationed Ochuko at an embankment, some distance away from the bustle. He was to watch over the family possessions while his parents and siblings did their best at the pits.

But the boy wandered about intermittently and played with his friend, Onome. It was in their manner to climb a tree wherever they could find one. They could not resist the lure of the plantation and the rubber trees. Up they climbed, laughing and swinging playfully from branch to branch, while the villagers below bubbled and brawled.

To the children, the fortune-hunters presented hearty entertainment. They giggled with glee at the sound of high-pitched voices drawn tight with tension; as grown men charged and shoved riotously at each other; as here and there a woman lost her footing, and rolled in a heap in the slimy soil. Onome taunted Ochuko with mimicries of his father's belligerent displays in the heat of battle. 'Hey you, get away from there. Is this your plantation?' Namidi barked at anyone that came close to him. 'Hey you, get away from that tree. Is this your plantation?' Onome screamed at Ochuko in parody.

They lost interest in the brawling at the site and kept themselves busy with all manner of play. Soon they were playing soldiers, launching between branches and taking mock shots at each other – their fingers serving as makeshift guns. Onome took aim at Ochuko and fired. And as Ochuko swerved to duck behind a branch, there was a flash of light from inside the spill site and a deafening explosion that shook the tree he was hanging on. His young adversary fell headlong from the tree, screamed and lay still.

Ochuko froze. There followed a brief moment when the world seemed engulfed in a blanket of yellow light. And then it broke loose with a gut-wrenching choir of yelling that rang out all at once. The boy stared at the growing roost of figures that broke out frenziedly from the smoky interior, running and swaying in scattered directions. He watched it all with a childish fascination.

But it was the heat that finally got to him – the hot, stifling sensation that suddenly seized him in a tight, airless embrace and threw him from the tree. In a flash, he was up on his feet and running off towards the village clearing. He ran, followed by the acrid smell of burnt chicken feathers; by the long grasses and the screaming demons that leaped up and down behind him. The sky had turned grey and cast over him like imminent nightfall; but instead of easing down stealthily, the demons picked up pace, screaming and gathering behind him in a swift veil of smoke and blackness. It made him run faster and faster towards the village and the familiar outlines of his father's hut.

Huge billows of smoke rose from the heart of the plantation as the dust-laden boy – his eyes itching with soot and tears – emerged from it. He ran into the hut and hid himself under his mother's bed.

4

Ochuko and his twin, elder siblings, Emi and Efe, were like young musketeers. On many occasions, they would scamper home from an adventure gone awry. Once, during a village ritual festival, they had lit a masquerade from behind, and then wheeled away in different directions, as the violated masquerade fought with the flames and roared its indignation to the world around and beyond. Usually they would arrive one after the other at their mother's bed, breathing heavily and shaking with mirth. It was there, under the bed, that Ochuko waited for them. He was breathless, but elated by his escape from the smoking demons. A little while later, after the sweat had dried from his body, he began to feel cold. He ventured to go outside, but then it was already dark. He heard the sound of running feet. Terrified, he whirled around and dived under the bed once again.

His were the pair of eyes that blinked and shone all night in the darkness. He tensed for a long time, listening for the fleeting, brush-like sound of his mother's footsteps and the grating, angry thuds that were his father's. Mother will be home soon to bathe him, he thought with some conviction. He waited and listened to the silence, occasionally broken by the distant wail of a woman crying, and the sound of feet running past the hut.

At the corner of the cooking sill, a small hurricane lamp – which his mother always kept alive – waned and flickered gallantly for long periods. But the dim, smoky light petered out as the night wore on. Soon, a gang of rats, unbridled by their invisibility, celebrated by squealing and rustling up and down the earthenware. The boy lay paralysed by terror, every fibre of him trembling at the scrambling noises they made. Still, he lay in a stiff and innocent concealment. From the holes in the earth floor of the hut sprang a line of ants. It was their time of the night and, roused by the fresh smell of dried, oily sweat, they poured forth from an underground hub. He shivered in helpless immobility as their scrawny legs climbed and formed a defiant trail across his back;

as their droppings stoked and moistened the thin hairs on his skin. He lay very still as they walked over him.

It was pitch dark for a long time. And even in the treacherous silence that followed, the boy waited and listened; but all he heard was the faraway bird-call of the coming dawn.

Notes

Nigeria is the biggest oil producer in Africa – in this story a major oil pipe, running through an area of small rubber plantations and farms, springs a leak.

p. 423   *machete* - a broad bladed knife that can be used as an axe
p. 423   *harmattan* - dry wind which blows over west Africa from the desert
p. 424   *rubber gourd* - a kind of pot used to collect rubber from the rubber trees
p. 424   *bush meat* - wild animals that could be hunted for food
p. 426   *Shell* - the oil company
p. 427   *cutlass* - short sword
p. 428   *masquerade* - mask used in festival processions, masked figure

47

Haywards Heath

(2010)

Aminatta Forna

A Scottish writer, Forna's work is heavily influenced by her Sierra Leonean heritage. In Haywards Heath, *an ageing academic returns from his own unspecified country to re-visit England where he studied, and meet once again the woman he once loved, now in a retirement home. A subtle exploration of the workings of time.*

The car radio issued a blast of sound so sudden and brutish that Attila nearly came to an emergency stop. It took a moment to gather himself. In his chest his heart beat wildly, and his scalp had shrunk against his skull, hair follicles tightened in alarm, altogether a sign he was more nervous than he let himself believe, though in every other way he was feeling pretty good about things. The weather, for one: a cool, clear spring day. The prospect of the drive on clean-surfaced, empty roads. An escape from the city, time to himself.

The youth at the car-hire desk must have turned on the radio when he brought the car round. The new generation could not tolerate the sound of silence. This was the second car, there having been little possibility of Attila's bulk being contained by the first. The desk clerk had failed to see what a fool could not have missed. Still, had it been otherwise, he wouldn't be driving a Jaguar XJ from the Prestige range for the same price. Attila fiddled with the radio until he found something pleasing. Gradually he felt his scalp withdraw its grip on his cranium.

At Crawley he left the M23. He thought he should eat and turned off the main road towards Haywards Heath. Haywards Heath. It had been a joke between himself and Rosie for a long time. The overseas students all had a hard time pronouncing it. *Ay-wads 'eat.* A sly tease, she would ask each new acquaintance to repeat the name of her hometown. After his turn she'd glanced at him over her sherry glass and he'd held her gaze until she'd turned away. He knew, from the way she stood, the way she walked, mostly from the way she refused to turn back in his direction, that she felt the mark of his gaze on her skin, like a touch on the back of her neck. Afterwards and perversely, many months into their affair, she denied she'd noticed him that evening. He wore a Malcolm X goatee and a suit to attend lectures. This made her feel sorry for him, she said. They were in their third year

430

when they met, together for three more. By the time of their graduation ceremony he was already 6,000 miles away.

At the London hospital where he worked as a visiting consultant – visits that had occurred twice yearly for the last five years, because of his expertise in displaced populations, in trauma – he had exhaled all the breath in his lungs at the sound of her name. 'Early retirement,' his colleague replied in answer to Attila's careful enquiries. The idea for the trip came to him in a moment and had taken over. He had been consumed by the details: renting the car, planning the route, driving on the left-hand side of the road.

He thought again about food. At a pub he pulled over and parked. Inside he found a booth and ordered duck à l'orange, which arrived garnished with a rose of tomato peel, which he also consumed. He drew no stares. He opened the atlas out on the table. He reckoned he was less than five miles away. After he had eaten, he carried the map to the publican, who jerked his head at the Jaguar and said, 'What, no satnav? Where you headed?'

'Haywards Heath,' pronounced Attila, perfectly.

Next to Attila in the passenger seat, the publican pushed the buttons of the device and rubbed the tips of his fingers along the wood of the dashboard. Then, guided by the patient, electronic voice, Attila passed through one village after another. When he missed a turning, the voice redirected him in the same even tone. Attila found himself unaccountably irked by the smoothness of her voice. He took another wrong turn, quite deliberately. She proved unflappable.

Now he knew how his patients felt. He analysed his own behaviour. Prevarication. He drove steadily for ten minutes following the voice's orders.

'You have arrived at your destination.'

What had he imagined? A bungalow. Shelves of books and papers. A quiet, ordered existence writing for professional journals. Some vanity constrained his imagination before it could reach the point of giving her a husband.

Rosie hadn't published in years.

At the desk he asked for her by her maiden name.

'Are you a relative?' asked the woman, unblinkingly.

Attila hesitated. The woman was black herself. A young African man in a white nurse's uniform moved noiselessly across the hall carpet. 'A friend,' Attila said finally.

'In the day room,'

The air was overheated, filled with static and the smells of cooked food and talcum powder. Nobody minded him as he moved heavily through the building. In the day room residents slept in the pale sunlight. Others were gathered in a semicircle round a radio. He found her by the window, a newspaper on her lap. She hadn't noticed him. In that moment he was aware of the possibility of turning back, and also of all he had to say, all that had happened, the foreseen and the unforeseen. He wished now he had brought, something, flowers or chocolates.

'Hello, Rosie.' When she didn't respond, he moved into the line of her vision.

Now she looked directly at him, 'Hello,' she said, and smiled.

'Hello, Rosie,' he repeated. He stood, his hands by his side. He smiled, too, and shook his head. 'How are you?'

'I'm very well,' she nodded.

'Your former colleagues helped me find you.' He moved to sit next to her.

'Did they?' She didn't turn to him and so he examined her offered profile for a few moments. How much beauty there was still. Spontaneously he took her hand. His greatest fear had been that an excess of courtesy would surround their meeting. The last time they saw each other she had not wanted him to leave. He told her it was a condition of his scholarship. They'd argued for weeks, months. 'What about us?' she'd pleaded. But he went back to his country anyway, full of ideas of himself, of the future. Which one of them had been naïve?

They sat in silence and the silence felt comfortable already.

'Are you married?'

'I was,' replied Attila. 'She died.'

'Ah, I'm sorry.' She tutted and shook her head. 'That must have been difficult for you.'

He said nothing. The events had unfolded on news programmes around the world; he'd wondered then why she never made contact.

Outside, an elderly resident on a bench threw crumbs for a lone blackbird. Next to her a young woman turned away to speak into a mobile phone, her free hand thrust deep into the pocket of her coat. Where to begin?

In the end he said simply, 'I'm sorry. I'm sorry I didn't stay, *that* I didn't stay.' He waited for her response in silence. She must know exactly what he meant. It's what he came here to say, though he had not, until this moment, admitted it to himself.

She patted him on the arm with her free hand and the action brought him comfort. 'It's all right.' They sat once more in silence. When she spoke, she said, 'I'm afraid you'll have to tell me your name again, dear.'

He closed his eyes and breathed deeply. 'Attila.'

She smiled. 'I have a friend with the same name. What a coincidence! He's coming to see me anytime soon. I'm waiting for him. Maybe you two will meet.'

'Excuse me.' He rose and went in search of the men's room. Inside he leaned his back against the cubicle door until he gained some control of his breathing. The temperature in the place had brought him out in a sweat. He washed his hands and loosened the collar of his shirt. After he left the lavatory he didn't return immediately to the day room, but roamed the ground floor of the building. Through a porthole in a door he saw the young African helper spooning food into the mouth of an elderly woman. Something about the scene stopped Attila: the hand at her back, which prevented her from slumping, the infinite care in the way the young man wiped her slackened mouth with a napkin. At one point the careworker looked up, straight at Attila, Their eyes met. The young man said nothing but bent once more to his task. Attila turned away.

To Rosie he suggested a walk in the grounds and was relieved when she accepted.

'How long have you lived here?'

She misunderstood and replied, 'Since I was a girl. In Haywards Heath. What about you?'

'I went to university near here. It was a long time ago.'

But she was already distracted: 'People say you can't have two robins in the same garden, but there's no truth in it. Look!' And then, 'A wren. I do believe there are more of them than there were twenty years ago.'

She held on to his arm, seemingly awash with the wonder of it all. She reached out to touch the drops of rain on the leaves, tilted her head, gazed at the sky and closed her eyes. He waited and watched her. She stretched out her arms. He had a memory of a photograph of her in the exact same pose. Where was it now? She let her arms drop back to her sides. They completed a first tour of the garden.

Rosie said, 'Shall we do another turn, Attila? Another turn?' It was a phrase she had used often in the past: at the funfair, boating on a lake, on a dance floor. She teased him for being too serious.

Attila felt light-headed and – somewhat bizarrely – youthful. It was the effect of Rosie's mood, her enthusiasm for this unremarkable, chrysanthemum-bordered square of lawn, also the fact of being the youngest in the place by twenty years, excepting the staff. Fewer silver strands in Rosie's dark hair than in his own. He remembered she had no brothers or sisters.

They passed for the second time the woman on the bench, her daughter still speaking on the telephone. Rosie bent forward, plucked a sweet from the box on the old woman's lap and popped it into her mouth. Rosie gave an impish giggle. The sweet bulged in her cheek. 'She won't miss one. They're my favourite.' She gripped his arm and leaned her head against his shoulder. He inclined his head to hers and smelled the faint brackish odour of her hair, resisted the urge to kiss it. Behind them the old woman sat staring into the middle distance, her hands curled limply around the box of sweets. Attila could hear the daughter finish her call.

'Promise you'll come and visit me again, won't you?' Rosie said suddenly, raising her head. 'It's deathly dull in here.'

He gave his promise and meant it. Perhaps if he kept coming, she would eventually remember him, as she almost had today. On this slender hope he hung his heart.

Two months later he returned carrying a box of Newbury Fruits. The sweets had not been especially easy to find, and the packaging had changed, as might be expected after forty years. Along the way he had stopped at the same pub, where the publican remembered him, or, more accurately, the Jaguar, which had been replaced by a Vauxhall for this trip.

Rosie wasn't in the day room, or in the garden, though the weather was fine enough to permit it. Attila retraced his steps back towards reception. The woman, a different one to before, angled her head in the direction of a corridor. Attila advanced down it, bearing the box of sweets clamped in his huge hand.

In the dining room he found an afternoon dance underway; a dozen people moved slowly to the sound of 'The Blue Danube'. Mostly residents danced with members of staff. Around the room elders dozed and snored, made soporific as flies by music and heat.

There, in the centre, Rosie, cradled in the arms of the young African worker Attila had noticed during his last visit. Her forehead was pressed against his chest, her hand in his, eyes closed. The careworker had his head bent towards her. He had young, smooth skin and, Attila noticed for the first time, a small beard.

For some minutes Attila stood and watched. Then he placed the box of sweets down on a table and reached for a chair. As he did so, the music ground to a halt; people began to shuffle from the floor. He bent to pick up the box of sweets, heard Rosie say his name and looked up. The smile was already on his face.

But she was not looking his way, seemed not to be aware of his presence in the room. Rather she was looking up at the young careworker, who still held her in his arms. 'Shall we do another turn, Attila? Another turn. What do you say?'

And the young man replied, 'Whatever makes you happy, Rosie.'

Rosie nodded. The music began again. Attila replaced the box of Newbury Fruits on the table. He sat down and watched.

Notes

p. 430   *Malcolm X goatee* - African American political leader in the USA in the 1960s wore this distinctive kind of long thin beard
p. 432   *porthole* - round window
p. 434   *The Blue Danube* - a waltz tune by Johann Strauss

48

The Paper Menagerie

(2011)

Ken Liu

Liu is a Chinese American writer of short stories, and a translator from Chinese to English. In this story, a boy grows up torn between two cultures but learns to value his Chinese heritage after his mother dies.

One of my earliest memories starts with me sobbing. I refused to be soothed no matter what Mom and Dad tried.

Dad gave up and left the bedroom, but Mom took me into the kitchen and sat me down at the breakfast table.

"*Kan, kan,*" she said, as she pulled a sheet of wrapping paper from on top of the fridge. For years, Mom carefully sliced open the wrappings around Christmas gifts and saved them on top of the fridge in a thick stack.

She set the paper down, plain side facing up, and began to fold it. I stopped crying and watched her, curious.

She turned the paper over and folded it again. She pleated, packed, tucked, rolled, and twisted until the paper disappeared between her cupped hands. Then she lifted the folded-up paper packet to her mouth and blew into it, like a balloon.

"*Kan,*" she said, "*laohu.*" She put her hands down on the table and let go.

A little paper tiger stood on the table, the size of two fists placed together. The skin of the tiger was the pattern on the wrapping paper, white background with red candy canes and green Christmas trees.

I reached out to Mom's creation. Its tail twitched, and it pounced playfully at my finger. "*Rawrr-sa,*" it growled, the sound somewhere between a cat and rustling newspapers.

I laughed, startled, and stroked its back with an index finger. The paper tiger vibrated under my finger, purring.

"*Zhe jiao zhezhi,*" Mom said. *This is called origami.*

I didn't know this at the time, but Mom's kind was special. She breathed into them so that they shared her breath, and thus moved with her life. This was her magic.

Dad had picked Mom out of a catalog.

One time, when I was in high school, I asked Dad about the details. He was trying to get me to speak to Mom again.

He had signed up for the introduction service back in the spring of 1973. Flipping through the pages steadily, he had spent no more than a few seconds on each page until he saw the picture of Mom.

I've never seen this picture. Dad described it: Mom was sitting in a chair, her side to the camera, wearing a tight green silk cheongsam. Her head was turned to the camera so that her long black hair was draped artfully over her chest and shoulder. She looked out at him with the eyes of a calm child.

"That was the last page of the catalog I saw," he said.

The catalog said she was eighteen, loved to dance, and spoke good English because she was from Hong Kong. None of these facts turned out to be true.

He wrote to her, and the company passed their messages back and forth. Finally, he flew to Hong Kong to meet her.

"The people at the company had been writing her responses. She didn't know any English other than 'hello' and 'good-bye.'"

What kind of woman puts herself into a catalog so that she can be bought? The high-school-me thought I knew so much about everything. Contempt felt good, like wine.

Instead of storming into the office to demand his money back, he paid a waitress at the hotel restaurant to translate for them.

"She would look at me, her eyes halfway between scared and hopeful, while I spoke. And when the girl began translating what I said, she'd start to smile slowly."

He flew back to Connecticut and began to apply for the papers for her to come to him. I was born a year later, in the Year of the Tiger.

At my request, Mom also made a goat, a deer, and a water buffalo out of wrapping paper. They would run around the living room while Laohu chased after them, growling. When he caught them he would press down until the air went out of them and they became just flat, folded-up pieces of paper. I would then have to blow into them to reinflate them so they could run around some more.

Sometimes, the animals got into trouble. Once, the water buffalo jumped into a dish of soy sauce on the table at dinner. (He wanted to wallow, like a real water buffalo.) I picked him out quickly but the capillary action had already pulled the dark liquid high up into his legs. The sauce-softened legs would not hold him up, and he collapsed onto the table. I dried him out in the sun, but his legs became crooked after that, and he ran around with a limp. Mom eventually wrapped his legs in Saran wrap so that he could wallow to his heart's content (just not in soy sauce).

Also, Laohu liked to pounce at sparrows when he and I played in the backyard. But one time, a cornered bird struck back in desperation and tore his ear. He whimpered and winced as I held him and Mom patched his ear together with tape. He avoided birds after that.

And then one day, I saw a TV documentary about sharks and asked Mom for one of my own. She made the shark, but he flapped about on the table unhappily. I filled the sink with water and put him in. He swam around and around happily. However, after a while he became soggy and translucent, and slowly sank to the bottom, the folds coming undone. I reached in to rescue him, and all I ended up with was a wet piece of paper.

Laohu put his front paws together at the edge of the sink and rested his head on them. Ears drooping, he made a low growl in his throat that made me feel guilty.

Mom made a new shark for me, this time out of tinfoil. The shark lived happily in a large goldfish bowl. Laohu and I liked to sit next to the bowl to watch the tinfoil shark chasing the goldfish, Laohu sticking his face up against the bowl on the other side so that I saw his eyes, magnified to the size of coffee cups, staring at me from across the bowl.

When I was ten, we moved to a new house across town. Two of the women neighbors came by to welcome us. Dad served them drinks and then apologized for having to run off to the utility company to straighten out the prior owner's bills. "Make yourselves at home. My wife doesn't speak much English, so don't think she's being rude for not talking to you."

While I read in the dining room, Mom unpacked in the kitchen. The neighbors conversed in the living room, not trying to be particularly quiet.

"He seems like a normal enough man. Why did he do that?"

"Something about the mixing never seems right. The child looks unfinished. Slanty eyes, white face. A little monster."

"Do you think *he* can speak English?"

The women hushed. After a while they came into the dining room.

"Hello there! What's your name?"

"Jack," I said.

"That doesn't sound very Chinesey."

Mom came into the dining room then. She smiled at the women. The three of them stood in a triangle around me, smiling and nodding at each other, with nothing to say, until Dad came back.

Mark, one of the neighborhood boys, came over with his Star Wars action figures. Obi-Wan Kenobi's lightsaber lit up and he could swing his arms and say, in a tinny voice, "Use the Force!" I didn't think the figure looked much like the real Obi-Wan at all.

Together, we watched him repeat this performance five times on the coffee table. "Can he do anything else?" I asked.

Mark was annoyed by my question. "Look at all the details," he said.

I looked at the details. I wasn't sure what I was supposed to say.

Mark was disappointed by my response. "Show me your toys."

I didn't have any toys except my paper menagerie. I brought Laohu out from my bedroom. By then he was very worn, patched all over with tape and glue, evidence of the years of repairs Mom and I had done on him. He was no longer as nimble and surefooted as before. I sat him down on the coffee table. I could hear the skittering steps of the other animals behind in the hallway, timidly peeking into the living room.

"*Xiao laohu*," I said, and stopped. I switched to English. "This is Tiger." Cautiously, Laohu strode up and purred at Mark, sniffing his hands.

Mark examined the Christmas-wrap pattern of Laohu's skin. "That doesn't look like a tiger at all. Your mom makes toys for you from trash?"

I had never thought of Laohu as *trash*. But looking at him now, he was really just a piece of wrapping paper.

Mark pushed Obi-Wan's head again. The lightsaber flashed; he moved his arms up and down. "Use the Force!"

Laohu turned and pounced, knocking the plastic figure off the table. It hit the floor and broke, and Obi-Wan's head rolled under the couch. "*Rawwww*," Laohu laughed. I joined him.

Mark punched me, hard. "This was very expensive! You can't even find it in the stores now. It probably cost more than what your dad paid for your mom!"

I stumbled and fell to the floor. Laohu growled and leapt at Mark's face.

Mark screamed, more out of fear and surprise than pain. Laohu was only made of paper, after all.

Mark grabbed Laohu and his snarl was choked off as Mark crumpled him in his hand and tore him in half. He balled up the two pieces of paper and threw them at me. "Here's your stupid cheap Chinese garbage."

After Mark left, I spent a long time trying, without success, to tape together the pieces, smooth out the paper, and follow the creases to refold Laohu. Slowly, the other animals came into the living room and gathered around us, me and the torn wrapping paper that used to be Laohu.

My fight with Mark didn't end there. Mark was popular at school. I never want to think again about the two weeks that followed.

I came home that Friday at the end of the two weeks. "*Xuexiao hao ma?*" Mom asked. I said nothing and went to the bathroom. I looked into the mirror. *I look nothing like her, nothing.*

At dinner I asked Dad, "Do I have a chink face?"

Dad put down his chopsticks. Even though I had never told him what happened in school, he seemed to understand. He closed his eyes and rubbed the bridge of his nose. "No, you don't."

Mom looked at Dad, not understanding. She looked back at me. "*Sha jiao* chink?"

"English," I said. "Speak English."

She tried. "What happen?"

I pushed the chopsticks and the bowl before me away: stir-fried green peppers with five-spice beef. "We should eat American food."

Dad tried to reason. "A lot of families cook Chinese sometimes."

"We are not other families." I looked at him. *Other families don't have moms who don't belong.*

He looked away. And then he put a hand on Mom's shoulder. "I'll get you a cookbook."

Mom turned to me. "*Bu haochi?*"

"English," I said, raising my voice. "Speak English."

Mom reached out to touch my forehead, feeling for my temperature. "*Fashao la?*"

I brushed her hand away. "I'm fine. Speak English!" I was shouting.

"Speak English to him," Dad said to Mom. "You knew this was going to happen someday. What did you expect?"

Mom dropped her hands to her side. She sat, looking from Dad to me, and back to Dad again. She tried to speak, stopped, and tried again, and stopped again.

"You have to," Dad said. "I've been too easy on you. Jack needs to fit in."

Mom looked at him. "If I say 'love,' I feel here." She pointed to her lips. "If I say '*ai*,' I feel here." She put her hand over her heart.

Dad shook his head. "You are in America."

Mom hunched down in her seat, looking like the water buffalo when Laohu used to pounce on him and squeeze the air of life out of him.

"And I want some real toys."

Dad bought me a full set of Star Wars action figures. I gave the Obi-Wan Kenobi to Mark.

I packed the paper menagerie in a large shoe box and put it under the bed.

The next morning, the animals had escaped and took over their old favorite spots in my room. I caught them all and put them back into the shoe box, taping the lid shut. But the animals made so much noise in the box that I finally shoved it into the corner of the attic as far away from my room as possible.

If Mom spoke to me in Chinese, I refused to answer her. After a while, she tried to use more English. But her accent and broken sentences embarrassed me. I tried to correct her. Eventually, she stopped speaking altogether if I was around.

Mom began to mime things if she needed to let me know something. She tried to hug me the way she saw American mothers did on TV. I thought her movements exaggerated, uncertain, ridiculous, graceless. She saw that I was annoyed, and stopped.

"You shouldn't treat your mother that way," Dad said. But he couldn't look me in the eyes as he said it. Deep in his heart, he must have realized that it was a mistake to have tried to take a Chinese peasant girl and expect her to fit in the suburbs of Connecticut.

Mom learned to cook American style. I played video games and studied French.

Every once in a while, I would see her at the kitchen table studying the plain side of a sheet of wrapping paper. Later a new paper animal would appear on my nightstand and try to cuddle up to me. I caught them, squeezed them until the air went out of them, and then stuffed them away in the box in the attic.

Mom finally stopped making the animals when I was in high school. By then her English was much better, but I was already at that age when I wasn't interested in what she had to say whatever language she used.

Sometimes, when I came home and saw her tiny body busily moving about in the kitchen, singing a song in Chinese to herself, it was hard for me to believe that she gave birth to me. We had nothing in common. She might as well be from the moon. I would hurry on to my room, where I could continue my all-American pursuit of happiness.

Dad and I stood, one on each side of Mom lying in her hospital bed. She was not yet even forty, but she looked much older.

For years she had refused to go to the doctor for the pain inside her that she said was no big deal. By the time an ambulance finally carried her in, the cancer had spread far beyond the limits of surgery.

My mind was not in the room. It was the middle of the on-campus recruiting season, and I was focused on résumés, transcripts, and strategically constructed interview schedules. I schemed about how to lie to the corporate recruiters most effectively so that they'd offer to buy me. I understood intellectually that it was terrible to think about this while your mother lay dying. But that understanding didn't mean I could change how I felt.

She was conscious. Dad held her left hand with both of his own. He leaned down to kiss her forehead. He seemed weak and old in a way that startled me. I realized that I knew almost as little about Dad as I did about Mom.

Mom smiled at him. "I'm fine."

She turned to me, still smiling. "I know you have to go back to school." Her voice was very weak, and it was difficult to hear her over the hum of the machines hooked up to her. "Go. Don't worry about me. This is not a big deal. Just do well in school."

I reached out to touch her hand, because I thought that was what I was supposed to do. I was relieved. I was already thinking about the flight back, and the bright California sunshine.

She whispered something to Dad. He nodded and left the room.

"Jack, if—" She was caught up in a fit of coughing, and could not speak for some time. "If I don't make it, don't be too sad and hurt your health. Focus on your life. Just keep that box you have in the attic with you, and every year, at *Qingming*, just take it out and think about me. I'll be with you always."

Qingming was the Chinese Festival for the Dead. When I was very young, Mom used to write a letter on *Qingming* to her dead parents back in China, telling them the good news about the past year of her life in America. She would read the letter out loud to me, and if I made a comment about something, she would write it down in the letter too. Then she would fold the letter into a paper crane and release it, facing west. We would then watch as the crane flapped its crisp wings on its long journey west, toward the Pacific, toward China, toward the graves of Mom's family.

It had been many years since I last did that with her.

"I don't know anything about the Chinese calendar," I said. "Just rest, Mom."

"Just keep the box with you and open it once in a while. Just open—" She began to cough again.

"It's okay, Mom." I stroked her arm awkwardly.

"*Haizi, mama ai ni—*" Her cough took over again. An image from years ago flashed into my memory: Mom saying and then putting her hand over her heart.

"All right, Mom. Stop talking."

Dad came back, and I said that I needed to get to the airport early because I didn't want to miss my flight.

She died when my plane was somewhere over Nevada.

Dad aged rapidly after Mom died. The house was too big for him and had to be sold. My girlfriend, Susan, and I went to help him pack and clean the place.

Susan found the shoe box in the attic. The paper menagerie, hidden in the uninsulated darkness of the attic for so long, had become brittle, and the bright wrapping paper patterns had faded.

"I've never seen origami like this," Susan said. "Your mom was an amazing artist."

The paper animals did not move. Perhaps whatever magic had animated them stopped when Mom died. Or perhaps I had only imagined that these paper constructions were once alive. The memory of children could not be trusted.

It was the first weekend in April, two years after Mom's death. Susan was out of town on one of her endless trips as a management consultant, and I was home, lazily flipping through the TV channels.

I paused at a documentary about sharks. Suddenly I saw, in my mind, Mom's hands, as they folded and refolded tinfoil to make a shark for me while Laohu and I watched.

A rustle. I looked up and saw that a ball of wrapping paper and torn tape was on the floor next to the bookshelf. I walked over to pick it up for the trash.

The ball of paper shifted, unfurled itself, and I saw that it was Laohu, who I hadn't thought about in a very long time. "*Rawrr-sa.*" Mom must have put him back together after I had given up.

He was smaller than I remembered. Or maybe it was just that back then my fists were smaller.

Susan had put the paper animals around our apartment as decoration. She probably left Laohu in a pretty hidden corner because he looked so shabby.

I sat down on the floor and reached out a finger. Laohu's tail twitched, and he pounced playfully. I laughed, stroking his back. Laohu purred under my hand.

"How've you been, old buddy?"

Laohu stopped playing. He got up, jumped with feline grace into my lap, and proceeded to unfold himself.

In my lap was a square of creased wrapping paper, the plain side up. It was filled with dense Chinese characters. I had never learned to read Chinese, but I knew the characters for "son," and they were at the top, where you'd expect them in a letter addressed to you, written in Mom's awkward, childish handwriting.

I went to the computer to check the Internet. Today was *Qingming*.

I took the letter with me downtown, where I knew the Chinese tour buses stopped. I stopped every tourist, asking, "*Nin hui du zhongwen ma?*" *Can you read Chinese?* I hadn't spoken Chinese in so long that I wasn't sure if they understood.

A young woman agreed to help. We sat down on a bench together, and she read the letter to me aloud. The language that I had tried to forget for years came back, and I felt the words sinking into me, through my skin, through my bones, until they squeezed tight around my heart.

Son,

We haven't talked in a long time. You are so angry when I try to touch you that I'm afraid. And I think maybe this pain I feel all the time now is something serious.

So I decided to write to you. I'm going to write in the paper animals I made for you that you used to like so much.

The animals will stop moving when I stop breathing. But if I write to you with all my heart, I'll leave a little of myself behind on this paper, in these words. Then, if you think of me on Qingming, *when the spirits of the departed are allowed to visit their families, you'll make the parts of myself I leave behind come alive too. The creatures I made for you will again leap and run and pounce, and maybe you'll get to see these words then.*

Because I have to write with all my heart, I need to write to you in Chinese.

All this time I still haven't told you the story of my life. When you were little, I always thought I'd tell you the story when you were older, so you could understand. But somehow that chance never came up.

I was born in 1957, in Sigulu Village, Hebei Province. Your grandparents were both from very poor peasant families with few relatives. Only a few years after I was born, the Great Famines struck China, during which thirty million people died. The first memory I have was waking up to see my mother eating dirt so that she could fill her belly and leave the last bit of flour for me.

Things got better after that. Sigulu is famous for its zhezhi *papercraft, and my mother taught me how to make paper animals and give them life. This was practical magic in the life of the village. We made paper birds to chase grasshoppers away from the fields, and paper tigers to keep away the mice. For Chinese New Year my friends and I made red paper dragons. I'll never forget the sight of all those little dragons zooming across the sky overhead, holding up strings of exploding firecrackers to scare away all the bad memories of the past year. You would have loved it.*

Then came the Cultural Revolution in 1966. Neighbor turned on neighbor, and brother against brother. Someone remembered that my mother's brother, my uncle, had left for Hong Kong back in 1946 and became a merchant there. Having a relative in Hong Kong meant we were spies and enemies of the people, and we had to be struggled against in every way. Your poor grandmother—she couldn't take the abuse and threw herself down a well. Then some

442

boys with hunting muskets dragged your grandfather away one day into the woods, and he never came back.

There I was, a ten-year-old orphan. The only relative I had in the world was my uncle in Hong Kong. I snuck away one night and climbed onto a freight train going south.

Down in Guangdong Province a few days later, some men caught me stealing food from a field. When they heard that I was trying to get to Hong Kong, they laughed. "It's your lucky day. Our trade is to bring girls to Hong Kong."

They hid me in the bottom of a truck along with other girls and smuggled us across the border.

We were taken to a basement and told to stand up and look healthy and intelligent for the buyers. Families paid the warehouse a fee and came by to look us over and select one of us to "adopt."

The Chin family picked me to take care of their two boys. I got up every morning at four to prepare breakfast. I fed and bathed the boys. I shopped for food. I did the laundry and swept the floors. I followed the boys around and did their bidding. At night I was locked into a cupboard in the kitchen to sleep. If I was slow or did anything wrong I was beaten. If the boys did anything wrong I was beaten. If I was caught trying to learn English I was beaten.

"Why do you want to learn English?" Mr. Chin asked. "You want to go to the police? We'll tell the police that you are a mainlander illegally in Hong Kong. They'd love to have you in their prison."

Six years I lived like this. One day, an old woman who sold fish to me in the morning market pulled me aside.

"I know girls like you. How old are you now, sixteen? One day, the man who owns you will get drunk, and he'll look at you and pull you to him and you can't stop him. The wife will find out, and then you will think you really have gone to hell. You have to get out of this life. I know someone who can help."

She told me about American men who wanted Asian wives. If I can cook, clean, and take care of my American husband, he'll give me a good life. It was the only hope I had. And that was how I got into the catalog with all those lies and met your father. It is not a very romantic story, but it is my story.

In the suburbs of Connecticut, I was lonely. Your father was kind and gentle with me, and I was very grateful to him. But no one understood me, and I understood nothing.

But then you were born! I was so happy when I looked into your face and saw shades of my mother, my father, and myself. I had lost my entire family, all of Sigulu, everything I ever knew and loved. But there you were, and your face was proof that they were real. I hadn't made them up.

Now I had someone to talk to. I would teach you my language, and we could together remake a small piece of everything that I loved and lost. When you said your first words to me, in Chinese that had the same accent as my mother and me, I cried for hours. When I made the first zhezhi *animals for you, and you laughed, I felt there were no worries in the world.*

You grew up a little, and now you could even help your father and I talk to each other. I was really at home now. I finally found a good life. I wished my parents could be here, so that I could cook for them and give them a good life too. But my parents were no longer around. You know what the Chinese think is the saddest feeling in the world? It's for a child to finally grow the desire to take care of his parents, only to realize that they were long gone.

Son, I know that you do not like your Chinese eyes, which are my eyes. I know that you do not like your Chinese hair, which is my hair. But can you understand how much joy your very existence brought to me? And can you understand how it felt when you stopped talking to me and won't let me talk to you in Chinese? I felt I was losing everything all over again.

Why won't you talk to me, son? The pain makes it hard to write.

The young woman handed the paper back to me. I could not bear to look into her face.

Without looking up, I asked for her help in tracing out the character for *ai* on the paper below Mom's letter. I wrote the character again and again on the paper, intertwining my pen strokes with her words.

The young woman reached out and put a hand on my shoulder. Then she got up and left, leaving me alone with my mother.

Following the creases, I refolded the paper back into Laohu. I cradled him in the crook of my arm, and as he purred, we began the walk home.

Notes

p. 435   *Kan* - Chinese – watch
p. 435   *laohu* - tiger
p. 436   *cheongsam* - dress
p. 436   *Saran wrap* - plastic clingfilm
p. 438   *Xuexiao hao ma?* - how was school?
p. 438   *Sha jiao?* - having a tantrum?
p. 439   *Bu haochi?* - does it taste bad?
p. 439   *Fashao la?* - do you have a temperature?
p. 441   *ai* - love
p. 441   *Haizi, mama ai ni* - I love you, my child

49

Fluke

(2014)

Romesh Gunesekera

Born in Sri Lanka and now living in London, Gunesekera chairs the Commonwealth Short Story Prize. In this ironic, descriptive story, a courier wryly observes the new businessmen at work.

Mr Weerakoon is a smart man with an eye for design. His blue suit is tight so that he looks like he is bursting with energy, which I imagine impresses his clients who are in need of gurus with vitality. His briefcase, which doubles as a computer case, is also blue. Pale blue. To my mind that is less impressive, but it does give him a very modern look like his wedge of shaped black hair. The case is made of pretend leather and has a neoprene sleeve. I know because he told me so.

'Neoprene sleeve inside,' he spluttered, jabbing at the bag. 'Flexible, lightweight, ultra-protection. From Singapore. Good, no?'

He got into the back seat, even though he was my only passenger, saying loudly that he had some preparation to do before the meeting. He opened the case and pulled out a smart silvery laptop before I had closed the door.

I loaded the two cardboard boxes in the back and got behind the wheel. 'AC, sir?' I know now not to take the climate for granted. Sometimes, heading south, passengers can completely surprise you with their eco-preferences and worries about melting ice caps.

'Put it full. Very sticky day.' He checked his watch. 'We have to be there by ten o'clock. You can make it?'

'No problem, sir. Once we pass Moratuwa, traffic will clear.'

'Ten-thirty I do the first session: setting goals, objectives, priorities. After lunch, we do the Plan.' He caught my eyes in the rear-view mirror and grinned. 'Yesterday Kurunegala, today Kalutara, tomorrow Kirulapone. Boom time, no? Kuala Lumpur is my ultimate goal.'

By the time I got on to Galle Road, he was deep in his screen of bullet points and exploding pie charts. Although I could hear the odd mumbling and the occasional click of a tongue or keyboard, he didn't say anything more to me until we reached the Blue Water turn-off.

He checked his watch again. 'Good timing, Vasantha. Very good.'

I turned in through the massive gates and drove right up to a porch big enough for an aircraft.

When we stopped, Mr Weerakoon zipped up the laptop and patted the bag as if it were a pet. He got out and asked me to bring the boxes I had packed in the back to the meeting room after I had parked the van. 'There will be a big sign: Marketing: The Secret of Success.'

He checked his pockets, patted his blue case again, and waddled down the long straight walkway towards the reception desk in the wide pavilion. He was a man of the modern world. The brand-new face of our remodelled country open at last for full-on business.

*

The meeting room was large and spacious with a view of the pool and the coconut trees around it. You could just about glimpse the sea beyond the steep beach. There were two secretive women and about a dozen shy men milling about near the entrance to the room, several half-throttled by their plump polyester ties. A dumbstruck Buddhist monk—a bhikkhu—in freshly laundered robes stood by a pillar with his tightly furled umbrella, equally speechless.

Mr Weerakoon was inside fiddling with some cables, looking flustered.

I put the boxes on a table by the side. 'Any problem, sir?' I asked.

'Bloody projector doesn't work. I have it all on the computer but there is no connection.'

'Shall I call the technician?'

'He was here, but didn't know what the heck was wrong. Bugger has gone now to look for some jack.'

I am not a computer man, but I do have a knack with machines. Someone once told me that the human body has magnetism in it, and with some people the flow is such that machines respond to their touch, and immediately straighten out the kinks in their system. I took the cables from Mr Weerakoon and jiggled them about. The plugs all fitted their sockets, so I rocked the projector, tipping it one way and then the other. I pressed in the cross-head screws at the back and gave the plastic Ouija board underneath a couple of firm taps. 'Try now, sir,' I said.

He switched it on again and the screen behind him lit up with a picture of a purple bud bursting into flower. He looked back over his shoulder and grinned. 'Bravo! How did you do that?'

'Chinese say you need good chi.' I was pleased to have been able to help.

'You better stay in the room then. Keep that Gucci flowing. Good for you anyway. You might get a tip or two about marketing. You are a small-size entrepreneur, no?'

I reckon neither he nor I could spell the word, never mind pronounce it, but I thanked him nevertheless and asked what I should do with his boxes. He told me to lay out the brochures and the handouts on the side table, next to the coconut cookies. 'My own marketing,' he winked.

A few minutes later the delegates sidled in, shuffling papers and cell phones nervously and choosing their seats around the conference doughnut. Numbers had swelled to more than twenty, but there were still some empty chairs. I perched on a stool at the far end by the boxes where I had a fine view of the pool outside. There was a painted stork standing by it. I couldn't tell if the bird was real. These days it is so hard to spot a fake.

Mr Weerakoon greeted his delegates, bouncing on his toes with the vroom of an enthusiast and then launched into his presentation. The computer worked perfectly and the screenshots faded in and out of flashy diagrams and big bold spinning statements, like paper aeroplanes. Although he said it was about marketing principles applicable to any size of business, it seemed miles too complicated for a one-man/one-van business like mine. The few bits that I could follow seemed to me to be plain common sense: figure out what you want, what your customers want and when they want it. The other stuff about bell curves and market segmentation and www dot shots seemed so much hot air. When I started my business, the whole thing was very simple. I got my pension from the old corporation at fifty-five and decided to do only what I love—drive. I could have got another office job in some private company but who would want to work in Colombo if they didn't have to? That was the time when you had to go through security even for a pee and the building might explode any day with some suicide bomber in a pink sari. No one believed the war would ever really end. So, when Ismail told me that Lionel wanted to get rid of his van—the minibus run had become too competitive for him—and suggested I buy it, I did. I only had to change the colour to blue (because white worries too many people, given all our white van disappearances) and paint a big silver V in English on the side. Then I put the word out at a couple of hotels, the golf club and the offices of my former bosses that I was a man with a van for hire. My marketing was executed in about half the time Mr. W took to get his notes in order. Plus a drive around town with a carton of cupcakes for the secretaries, PAs and fixers-at-large. After that, pure patience.

At twelve-thirty exactly, Mr Weerakoon shut the lid of his computer. 'Lunch break,' he announced. 'In the afternoon, we plunge into planning.'

The monk in front of me muttered something about his stomach. The two young women touched each other's wrists and smiled.

Mr Weerakoon beckoned me. 'You wait here until they are all out and then lock the door. My computer we'll keep in here. Safe, no?'

'Yes, sir.' I do whatever my customer wants me to do. That's the key. It is no big secret.

*

On the terrace, by the pool, a special buffet lunch had been laid out especially for the marketing seminar. There was a board on the grass declaring it in big red letters and an exclamation mark.

Mr Weerakoon saw me. 'Locked up?'

'Yes, sir.'

He held out his hand for the key. 'Come then, you can have your lunch with us. We have some no-shows, so there is plenty of food.'

'Thank you, sir,' I said. Nice-looking spread. Rice and curry as well as a creamy stroganoff and something inevitably Chinese with spring onions and black bean sauce.

I helped myself to a spoonful from every dish and sat at a table by the water's edge. The other delegates seemed to break into age groups. The younger men laughed and circled the two women with newfound jargon while the older ones ogled weakly from the coconut bar. One beefish man with a sharp nose and large startled eyes hurried over late from the washroom, shaking water off his hands. He looked hardier than the others and smiled at no one. He helped himself to a heap of rice and stroganoff and came to my table.

'So, how?' he asked.

'Nice and cool,' I said. 'By the water.'

'Yes. Without water we are nothing.'

I tried to fathom it. 'What? Nothing?'

'Sri Lanka is an island. Without water we would just be part of India.'

He had a point. 'But what about Africa?'

His lips tightened. 'Valleys, rifts. No chance. Not Africa. But anyway, we are fortunate to have the sea.' He put his plate down and studied the topography of his food. Then he looked at me. 'Lucky'

'I suppose so.'

'Lucky,' he said again and stuck out his hand. 'My name is Lucky.'

I stood up and shook his hand, reckoning it was OK. His hands had been thoroughly wet. Washed, I had no doubt, with soap and water. I could smell the sissy lemongrass from the pretty ceramic dispensers in the washrooms. 'I see. I am Vasantha.'

'What's your business?'

'Transport,' I said.

'Mine too, now.' He smirked as though it was a very shady business. 'Water transport.'

He sprinkled salt all over his plate and sat down.

'You mean bowsers or boats?'

He laughed, tipping his head back. 'Very good. Very good.' When his head was level again, his eyes had hardened. 'Navy. We have a fleet parked down the coast.'

'Why marketing, then?' I asked puzzled. 'Is the navy selling stock?' He might have been a naval commander but rank does not bother me. I've had former ministers and high-rolling hoodlums in my van. They are all just punters and in the van they are putty in my hands. I don't give a toss about their social standing or net worth, only their willingness to talk to me. And, very importantly, their personal hygiene. You have to keep the van clean and fresh, otherwise your clients will get put off. No customers, no business. No business, no life. Lemongrass is just the ticket, as far as I am concerned.

'The war is over.' He spoke in a mix of Sinhala and English. 'We have ships doing nothing. So now they have started whale-watching cruises for tourists. Brilliant idea, no? Mirissa is fantastic for it. My concept is to go more comprehensive. They say we have five hundred million bucks in the bank.' He held his fists up in the air as though the money was in them. 'My plan is to persuade the big boys to go into the hotel business as well. Offshore, onshore.' He banged his fists together. 'Connect cruise to hotel and pull the Japanese. Put a casino as well. The rest of the world will follow.'

'The Japanese certainly have a thing about whales, according to an article I read in the newspaper.'

'Exactly. You have to think strategically. If you don't start the fight, you don't get to throw the first punch. Every navy in the world learnt the lesson of Pearl Harbour.'

I hummed my assent, swallowing a mouthful. It made sense. 'You did battles in the navy?'

'Mannar.' His scalp inched back as if at some private marketing folly. 'Very tough.'

'So, you must be happy now. Chasing whales must be better than chasing Sea Tigers.'

He smiled again. 'That's a good one. We should put it on a banner. You are a real marketing guru, no? Yes, whales are much, much better. Everything is good now, except for this stupid WC business.'

I glanced at his hands again. They still looked damp. 'No towels in the washroom?'

'You know, those bloody buggers in Europe and America want to stick their noses into every little nook and cranny. It is very unsettling.' He swatted a fly that had landed on the edge of the table. He got it. Back-of-the-hand Obama shot. But his face seemed to grow more troubled with every thought. 'Uncertainty is not good, no? Not good for tourism, not good for me, not good for you. We all make mistakes, it is not always a war crime. We have to learn not to scratch at the scabs, no?'

I felt I was getting out of my depth. I finished the last of my stir-fry dollop, Chinafying the stroganoff. 'I think I'll go get some pudding,' I said. 'Nice wattalappam on the side there.'

'You know, we used to have a round bomb that looked just like that. We called it *what'll-happ'n.*' His mouth twitched, signalling another upheaval. 'So, be very careful.'

On my way to the dessert table, Mr Weerakoon caught up with me. 'My phone is gone,' he squealed, all panicky. 'It must have slipped out of my pocket in the van. Can you see if it is there? Brand-new Nokia. It'll be a disaster if it is gone. Big, big disaster.'

I told him not to worry. Cell phones are forever sliding out of pockets in my van. I find them lodged between seats, silted up under the springs, scuttled in the back by the spare tyre. All over the place. Nursing secrets, aching to spill the beans.

Forgoing my pudding, I went to the van and sure enough, it was there nestling at the back with a bottle of mineral water and a packet of cream puffs. The screen was locked but his pin was still the usual four zeros.

By the time I got back, the navy's latest secret weapon for commercial supremacy had settled on a lounger for a snooze. The puddings had been cleared. I managed to grab a plantain off the fruit bowl before that too disappeared, and went to find Mr Weerakoon and give him his phone.

*

I didn't go back into the afternoon session. I wanted to close my eyes out in the open. The others, including the refreshed torpedo and the sated monk, had wandered back into the room to map their future strategies of success in our brave new world of infinite opportunities. There was a soothing sea breeze making music with the trees, the sound of the sea keeping the same soft time it has done since the world began. I wondered what the whales out there in their sea lanes knew of us and our schemes. Even if they had any inkling, would they care?

In the sea air, we can all sleep like old people whose memories have finally receded and left them in peace. That afternoon, under the trees, it seemed as though everything could be forgotten: the trouble brewing under my van, the perforations on the exhaust pipe, the worn treads of the offside rear tyre, the unpaid electricity bill at home waiting for some extra cash flow, that last argument I had with my father, twenty years ago and still knotting my stomach, Mrs Subramaniam's letter I steamed open and decided not to post for her husband's sake. And then, there is everything else that has happened. With luck, one can forget it all, scabs or no scabs. Just float on our unexpected good fortune and snore with the whales—head down in our great comfortable sea of amnesia.

The trick is to learn how to be lulled into sleep. I thought I should tell Mr Weerakoon that, on our way back. Marketing is a doddle. Dealing with a cock-up is the real problem. Small mistakes that grow into bigger ones. God knows we have had plenty of those. A tip from me to him: find out from the sailor how to sleep easy. Whatever your foibles, your wanton misdeeds, you can dream of new ventures and be a success if you can sleep easy. It can't be that difficult. People do it all over the place. A secure pin number is a good start.

Notes

p. 445   *gurus* - teachers, here used ironically
p. 445   *AC* - air conditioning
p. 445   *Kurunegala . . . Kalutara . . . Kirulapone* - major cities in Sri Lanka
p. 446   *bhikkhu* - ordained Buddhist monk
p. 446   *Ouija board* - a metaphorical usage – a Ouija board is used in séances allegedly
             to contact spirits, so the computer mysteriously links to other worlds
p. 446   *good chi* - positive energy; 'good vibes'
p. 449   *Mirissa* - beach resort

p. 449   *Mannar* - town and fort in the Northern province of Sri Lanka

p. 449   *Pearl Harbor* - Japan bombed this US naval base in 1941, bringing the USA
         into the Second World War

p. 449   *Chinafying the stroganoff* - that is, putting soy sauce on a European dish

p. 449   *wattalappam* - coconut custard pudding

Acknowledgements

The authors and publishers acknowledge the following sources of copyright material and are grateful for the permissions granted. While every effort has been made, it has not always been possible to identify the sources of all the material used, or to trace all copyright holders. If any omissions are brought to our notice, we will be happy to include the appropriate acknowledgements on reprinting.

'Indian Summer of an Uncle', *Carry On, Jeeves* by P.G. Wodehouse. Published by Herbert Jenkins, 1925. Copyright © P.G. Wodehouse. Reproduced by permission of the author's estate c/o Rogers, Coleridge & White Ltd., 20 Powis Mews, London W11 1JN

The short story 'The Black Ball' in its entirety from *FLYING HOME AND OTHER STORIES* by Ralph Ellison (Penguin Books, 2016), copyright © Fanny Ellison, 1996, introduction copyright © John F. Callahan, 1996, reproduced by permission of Penguin Books Ltd.

'Stability' from *COLLECTED SHORT STORIES*, by Philip K. Dick, copyright © Philip K. Dick, 1987, used by permission of The Wylie Agency (UK) Limited

'The Tower' by Marghanita Laski in *The Penguin Book of Ghost Stories*, used with permission from David Higham Associates Ltd.

'The Gold Watch' by Mulk Raj Anand, used by kind permission of the Literary Estate of the author, © Mulk Raj Anand

'The Reservoir' from *YOU ARE NOW ENTERING THE HUMAN HEART* by Janet Frame, copyright © Janet Frame, 1983, used by permission of The Wylie Agency (UK) Limited

'Thank You, M'am' from *SHORT STORIES* by Langston Hughes, copyright © 1996 by Ramona Bass and Arnold Rampersad, reprinted by permission of Hill and Wang, a division of Farrar, Straus and Giroux, and by permission of David Higham Associates Ltd.

'A Visit' by Anna Kavan from *Julian and the Bazooka* (Peter Owen Ltd 1970), used with permission from David Higham Associates Ltd.

'The Axe' by Penelope Fitzgerald, reprinted by permission of HarperCollins Publishers Ltd © 2000 Penelope Fitzgerald

'When It Happens' from *Dancing Girls and Other Stories* by Margaret Atwood, published by Jonathan Cape, reprinted by permission of The Random House Group Limited, © O.W. Toad Limited 1977, 1982, and reprinted by permission of Emblem/McClelland & Stewart, a division of Penguin Random House Limited

'Words' from *Collected Stories of Carol Shields* (Harper Perennial 2005), used by kind permission of the Carol Shields Literary Trust

'The Man Who Walked on The Moon' by J.G.Ballard, copyright © J.G. Ballard 2001, used by permission of The Wylie Agency (UK) Limited

'A Walk to the Jetty', from *ANNIE JOHN* by Jamaica Kincaid, Copyright © Jamaica Kincaid, 1983, 1984, 1985, used by permission of The Wylie Agency (UK) Limited

'In the Mountains' by Ruth Prawer Jhabvala (Copyright © Ruth Prawer Jhabvala), reprinted by permission of A.M. Heath & Co Ltd., and reprinted by permission of Counterpoint, copyright © 1957, 1963, 1966, 1968, 1971, 1975, 1986, 2000 by Ruth Prawer Jhabcala, from *Out of India, the Vintage Book of Indian Writing*

'Showing the Flag' by Jane Gardam from *The Stories*, in *Showing the Flag and Other Stories*, Granta, 2014, with permission from David Higham Associates Ltd.

'Sharmaji' from *Incantations and Other Stories* by Anjana Appachana, New Brunswick: Rutgers University Press, 1992, copyright © 1992 by Anjana Appachana, used by kind permission of the author, and reprinted by permission of Rutgers University Press

'Mrs Sen's' by Jhumpa Lahiri in *Interpreter of Maladies*, reprinted by permission of HarperCollins Publishers Ltd © 2000 Jhumpa Lahiri

'A Thousand Years of Good Prayers' from *A THOUSAND YEARS OF GOOD PRAYERS: STORIES* by Yiyun Li, reprinted by permission of HarperCollins Publishers Ltd © 2005 Yiyun Li and used by permission of Random House, an imprint and division of Penguin Random House LLC. All rights reserved. Any third party use of this material, outside of this publication, is prohibited. Interested parties must apply firectly to Penguin Random House LLC for permission

'Mrs Mahood' from *A Life Elsewhere* by Segun Afolabi, published by Jonathan Cape, reprinted by permission of The Random House Group Limited © Segun Afolabi 2006

'Promenade' by Henrietta Rose-Innes from *The Granta Book of the African Short Story* (Granta, 2011), copyright © 2011 Henrietta Rose-Innes, reprinted by permission of the author

'The Plantation' by Ovo Adagha is used by kind permission of the author

'Haywards Heath' by Aminatta Forna in *The Granta Book of the African Short Story*, (Granta 2011), copyright © Aminatta Forna, used with permission from David Godwin Associates

'The Paper Menagerie' by Ken Liu in *The Paper Menagerie and Other Stories* (Head of Zeus, 2016), used with permission from Scovil Chichak Galen Literary Agency

'Fluke' from *Noontide Toll* by Romesh Gunesekera, copyright © 2014 by Romesh Gunesekera, reprinted with permission from Granta Books, and permission of The New Press www.thenewpress.com, and with permission from Penguin Random House India